Phaethon's Children:
The Este Court and Its Culture in Early Modern Ferrara

Medieval and Renaissance Texts and Studies

Volume 286

Phaethon's Children: The Este Court and Its Culture in Early Modern Ferrara

edited by
Dennis Looney and Deanna Shemek

Arizona Center for Medieval and Renaissance Studies
Tempe, Arizona
2005

Library of Congress Cataloging-in-Publication Data

Phaethon's children : the Este court and its culture in early modern Ferrara / edited by Dennis Looney and Deanna Shemek.
p. cm. — (Medieval Renassance texts and studies ; v. 286)
Includes bibliographical references and index.
ISBN 0-86698-329-5 (alk. paper)
1. Este family. 2. Ferrara (Italy)— Civilization. 3. Ferrara (Italy)— Intellectual life. 4. Ferrara (Italy)— Politics and government. 5. Renaissance — Italy — Ferrara. I. Looney, Dennis. II. Shemek, Deanna. III. Series: Medieval & Renaissance Texts & Studies (Series) ; v. 286.

DG975.F42P43 2005
945'.4505 — dc22

2005004731

This book is made to last.
It is set in Elegant Garamond
smyth-sewn and printed on acid-free paper
to library specifications

Printed in the United States of America

Cover image:
Le Dignita dei Consoli, pg. 3 Detail, letter F.

Contents

Acknowledgements

As co-editors of *Phaethon's Children*, we heartily thank all the contributors for the patience and diligence that have made it possible. We also record here our gratitude to each other for a shared commitment that required coordinating our activities not only over several years, but also across every continent and ocean of the earth. For though we began with a conversation in Eugene, then returned to our homes in Santa Cruz and Pittsburgh, as might be expected, our lives — and the vicissitudes of publishing a multi-authored collection — eventually required our working as far apart as two co-editors could be. From the coast of California to a gas station in Kenya, from Pittsburgh's libraries to Settignano's Villa I Tatti, from Brazil to Malaysia, from Hungary to Pennsylvania, we exchanged the thoughts and labors the project required, often marveling at our ability to bridge such distances. We hope and believe that the book is better for having seasoned thus over space and time.

We thank Zoe Sodja, whose technical expertise and good humor were crucial in unifying these essays for submission, and the University of California, Santa Cruz, for funding Ms. Sodja's work. An editorial meeting was facilitated with funding from the Department of Literature at the University of California, Santa Cruz. The Richard D. and Mary Jane Edwards Fund at the University of Pittsburgh supported preparation of the manuscript. The Department of French and Italian at the University of Pittsburgh provided funding for two undergraduate student assistants, Carmelo Galati and Valeria Fabbro, who helped to prepare the manuscript for submission. Mr. Galati did the lion's share of the work in preparing the Estense genealogical table. Special thanks to Rosamund Looney who compiled the index. To Robert E. Bjork, director of MRTS, to Roy Rukkila, managing director, and his predecessor, David Kent, and to Leslie MacCoull for expert and informed copyediting, we express our thanks on behalf of the volume's contributors. We also thank the anonymous readers for the press and the following friends and colleagues with whom we discussed the project at various times: Albert Russell Ascoli, Daniel Javitch, Thomas F. Mayer, Tyrus Miller, William Mullen, Mark Possanza, Charles M. Rosenberg, Guido Ruggiero, Francesca Savòia, Joanna Thornton, and Elissa B. Weaver. Special thanks to Professors Ascoli and Weaver who organized the conference, "Ferrara: Cultural

Change from Boiardo to Tasso," at the Center for Renaissance Studies, Newberry Library, 1995, where papers underlying several of these essays were first presented. Their initial insights and continued enthusiasm have contributed greatly to this book.

We dedicate *Phaethon's Children* to Werner Gundersheimer, whose scholarly dedication to Ferrarese studies has inspired us all.

D.L. and D.S.
October 2004

About the Editors

Dennis Looney teaches in the Department of French and Italian at the University of Pittsburgh, where he also currently serves as Assistant Dean in the Humanities and has a secondary appointment in the Department of Classics. He teaches courses on the classical tradition in European literary culture, with a focus on the relationship between Italian vernacular culture and classical culture as articulated through Renaissance Humanism. He has published articles on Dante, Petrarch, Boiardo, Ariosto, Tasso, Herodotus, and Ovid, among others. His book, *Compromising the Classics: Romance Epic Narrative in the Italian Renaissance* (Wayne State UP, 1996) was Finalist for the MLA's Marraro-Scaglione Prize for Italian Literary Studies, 1996–1997.

Deanna Shemek teaches Italian literature at the University of California, Santa Cruz, where she also currently serves as a Provost of Cowell College. Her previous publications include *Ladies Errant: Wayward Women and Social Order in Early Modern Italy* (Duke University Press, 1998) and essays on Ariosto, Aretino, Domenichi, G. C. Croce, Isabella d'Este and others. She is editor and co-translator of Adriana Cavarero's *Stately Bodies: Literature, Philosophy, and the Question of Gender* (University of Michigan Press, 2002). She is currently preparing an edition of the selected letters of Isabella d'Este.

Illustrations and Examples

Ferrarese Studies: Tracking the Rise and Fall of an Urban Lordship in the Renaissance

Dennis Looney

Ludovico Ariosto crafts a series of allusions in *Orlando Furioso* (1532) to suggest an oblique connection between his sometime patrons the Este family and a legendary figure from the earliest mists of time along the Po River valley, Phaethon. The classical story, most familiar from Ovid's *Metamorphoses* (1.750–2.339), has it that Phaethon, unconvinced that he was the child of a god, tricked his father, Apollo, into letting him drive the chariot of the sun as a test of Apollo's paternity. Unable to control the horses, Phaethon rode too close to the earth and scorched the planet before Jupiter knocked him out of the chariot with a deadly lightning bolt. He came crashing down to earth into the Po River near the future site of Estense Ferrara. In Ovid's version, Phaethon's sisters metamorphose into poplars as they mourn his death, their tears hardening into jewel-like drops of amber (2.340–366). His friend and cousin, Cycnus, while mourning is transformed into the first swan and thus assumes the archetypal role of the plaintive poet who laments the loss of one beloved (2.370–380). It is to this myth of Phaethon that Ariosto alludes in his genealogical review of the lords of Ferrara, the long-ruling House of Este (*OF* 3.34). But the Phaethon story affords the poet far more than the opportunity to connect the city of his patrons to divine and ancient events. With it Ariosto illuminates the darker side of poetic inspiration, a condition the poet himself assumes at certain moments in the poem.[1] The myth of Phaethon allows the poet moreover to draw attention to the political and moral problem of overreaching one's station, and thus it enables him to allude to the Este family's difficulty in maintaining its precarious position in the shifting

[1] Albert Russell Ascoli makes this argument in *Ariosto's Bitter Harmony: Crisis and Evasion in the Italian Renaissance* (Princeton: Princeton University Press, 1987), 341, 373, 388.

political realities of early modernity.[2] Medieval and Renaissance allegorists tended to interpret the myth along such lines, emphasizing the danger of foolhardy pride like Phaethon's in a ruler.[3] Ariosto's allusions to the myth may even reflect a local concern of the Ferrarese court with the issues of paternity and the legitimacy of succession among members of the ruling family, for the myth heightens awareness of the potential problems of generational conflict in a dynastic family.

Ariosto was not the first or the last to use this "mythology of the Po valley as a cradle of poetry."[4] In fact, the story of Phaethon is something of a commonplace in Ferrarese verse, prose, and art, from the arrival of humanistic learning in Ferrara in the first half of the 1400s to the devolution at the end of the 1500s.[5] The person most responsible for the introduction of humanism into the intellectual milieu of Ferrara was Guarino da Verona, who, at the invitation of Niccolò III d'Este in the late 1420s, founded his famous school where he began to produce many of the scholars who would contribute to humanism's reassessment of the classical past in the decades to follow. Appropriately the classical myth of Phaethon was used to mark Guarino's death in 1460, a pivotal moment in Ferrarese cultural history. The humanist Ludovico Carbone, devoted alumnus of the school, delivered the public funeral oration for the deceased master. By a rhetorical sleight of hand Carbone conjures up the ghost of his former teacher in his eulogy: "But what is this? . . . I recognize him. It is the shade of Guarino whose authority commands me to be silent" (*Oratio* 410). The spirit then begins to speak with satisfaction of the success of his many pupils, singling out Carbone for special praise. But one admonitory sentence near the end of the piece casts a shadow over the oration's positive tone: *Recordare Phaethontis incendium!* "Remember Phaethon's fire and the fall of Icarus! Because

---

[2] Ariosto concludes the Phaethon stanza with a couplet that ominously looks forward to the devolution of 1598: "And this the Apostolic seat will give him [Azzo VII] in payment for a thousand debts," Ludovico Ariosto, *Orlando Furioso*, trans. Allan Gilbert (New York: Vanni, 1954), 3.34.7–8. The papacy's threats to seize Ferrara, frequent in Ariosto's day, were finally realized at the end of the century despite the Estes' repeated claims, to which the poet refers here, that the Church was actually in debt to the city! Unless stated otherwise, translations are my own.

[3] See H. David Brumble, *Classical Myths and Legends in the Middle Ages and Renaissance* (London: Fitzroy Dearborn, 1998), 267–70.

[4] The phrase is from Ronald L. Martinez, "Two Odysseys: Rinaldo's Po Journey and the Poet's Homecoming in Orlando Furioso," in *Renaissance Transactions: Ariosto and Tasso*, ed. Valeria Finucci (Durham, NC: Duke University Press, 1999), 17–55, here 40.

[5] The myth is also claimed, with interesting local adaptations, by early historiographers of Turin. See, for example, Emanuele Tesauro, *Historia dell'augusta città di Torino*, 2 vols. (Turin: Zappata, 1679; reprint, Bologna: Forni, 1988), 1–3; 60–61.

they longed for things beyond measure and out of reach, their end was worthy of their desire" (*Oratio* 414).[6] Carbone's Guarino, speaking as a ghostly font of classical wisdom, evokes the myth to warn his Ferrarese listeners to practice prudent moderation, lest they suffer a fate similar to Phaethon's. The warning quickly dissipates into more glowing praise of Carbone himself and of Borso d'Este, the ruling Estense leader in 1460, with the funeral oration coming to its conclusion on an unexpectedly upbeat note.

In the decade following Guarino's death, the painter known as the "maestro ferrarese" adorns a tarot card with Phaethon's image, indicating the myth's penetration of popular as well as humanistic culture.[7] In these same years, Matteo Maria Boiardo was coming into his own as a poet and courtier in the Estense circle. Boiardo's pastoral verse wears easily its allusions to the myth of Phaethon, which is a prominent feature of the poet's elegiac vocabulary. Galatea laments in *Egloga II*: "Ove son le sorelle di Fetonte / che solìano ombreggiar di tal verdura / questo bel fiume . . . ?" (Where are Phaethon's sisters who usually cast such a shade over this beautiful river?) Boiardo's modern elaborations of the pastoral tradition seem relatively untroubled, as if the poet were the inheritor of a bucolic world in which grieving women really could metamorphose into trees that cry amber and, transformed, cast their strange and suggestive shadow over the landscape. The Ferrara of Borso and Ercole, in the decades of the 1460s, 1470s, and 1480s, appears to be a magical world of pleasures and delights epitomized by the magnificent ducal refuge, Palazzo Schifanoia, a setting whose very name reminds guests that it is a place from which all worry is banished.[8] There is little

[6] For a general reading of the use of the Phaethon myth and its links to the story of Icarus in European culture, with a focus on French and Italian examples, see Robert Vivier, *Frères du ciel. Quelques aventures poétiques d'Icare et de Phaéton* (Paris: Nizet, 1962).

[7] See the card "Sol XXXXIIII" in the Tarocchi del Mantegna. This is a collection of fifty cards divided into five series of ten images each. There are two redactions of the cards, completed in approximately 1460–1465, by an artist (not Mantegna) in the circle of Francesco del Cossa. The series on the planets and stars contains a card of the Sun on which Phaethon appears (71). For a discussion of the cards, see Claudia Cerri Via, "I Tarocchi cosidetti del 'Mantegna': Origine, significato, e fortuna di un ciclo di immagini," in *Le carte di corte. I Tarocchi. Gioco e magia alla corte degli Estensi*, ed. Giordano Berti and Andrea Vitali (Bologna: Nuova Alfa, 1987), 49–77. The cards, according to Via, were not intended as playing cards; rather their primary function was didactic, something like contemporary flash cards (49–50). See also the full discussion in Arthur M. Hind, *Early Italian Engravings . . .* vol. 2 (London: Quaritch, 1938), 221–40.The image of the card "Sol" appears in vol. 4, plate 363.

[8] The compound noun "schifanoia" derives from "schifare," to shun or dislike, and "noia," annoyance or boredom. It is believed that the Marquis Alberto d'Este, grandfather of Ercole I's generation, gave the palace its name sometime in the second half of the fourteenth century.

pressing concern to heed the ominous warning of the ghost of Guarino in Carbone's work of 1460. At least not yet.

Ariosto, for his part, also calls on the myth in his elegiac verse transforming the never-never land of literary pastoral into his own country and translating the grief over Phaethon into the public Ferrarese despair over the death of the duchess, Leonora d'Este, in 1493. Here, Ferrara and its surrounding territories metamorphose into a landscape of suffering: "The sun . . . saw Ferrara sad and bereft and recognized the sorrowful river. . . . The grievous people so ready to weep — you could almost see the Heliades at riverside calling after Phaethon" (*Capitolo* 1:40–48). Composed when he was only nineteen, Ariosto's poetic dirge on Leonora's death presaged a period of genuine fear and uncertainty for the Ferrarese as the French prepared to invade northern Italy on the eve of the new century, thus setting in motion a chain of events that contributed to the Italian political crisis of the early Cinquecento. The moment of the French descent is registered dramatically in the famous final stanza of Boiardo's *Orlando Innamorato* in which the poet breaks off his narrative amidst the chaotic arrival of the French armies from the north, hoping to resume it at a later date. But that was not meant to be, for Boiardo died a year after Leonora in 1494.

Boiardo does not allude to the Phaethon story in his vast narrative, *Orlando Innamorato*, for the world of his poem is simply too bright to allow such darkness into it.[9] But writing post-1494, Ariosto incorporates the myth into his *Orlando Furioso* through a careful network of associations that illuminate, among other things, the potential danger of poetic inspiration. Apollo's reluctant decision to allow his son to assume the reins of the chariot is a paradigm that Ariosto uses to suggest different ways of interpreting the behavior of the Este rulers. On the one hand, his patrons, Cardinal Ippolito d'Este and, after the cardinal's death, Alfonso I, appear to be bearers of Apollonian rationality and light; on the other hand, the two brothers are at times portrayed and described as challengers of established authority, imitators of Phaethon himself.[10] While the Phaethon myth can figure such contradictory tension, it does not suggest ways to resolve it, as if Ariosto were implying that the Ferrarese should remember Phaethon's fate because they are destined inevitably to reenact it.

---

[9] Nor does Boiardo refer to the myth in his translation of Herodotus. In failing to translate approximately the latter two-thirds of Book III, Boiardo omitted a section (115) in which Herodotus refers to the Eridanus or Po, "where they say our amber comes from," only to question its possible existence and to suggest that its name had been invented by a poet! One can easily imagine how Boiardo would have played with that passage. See Herodotus, *Histories*, (Cambridge, MA: Harvard University Press, 1981).

[10] Ascoli, *Ariosto's Bitter Harmony*, 341.

One of Ariosto's contemporaries, Lilio Gregorio Giraldi (1479–1552), was a Ferrarese humanist who was born during the reign of Ercole I, lived through that of Alfonso I, and died under Ercole II. Widely acclaimed in his day as an important man of letters, he enjoyed fame which nonetheless did not prevent him from "encountering many setbacks of fortune" over the course of a long and productive life.[11] As he drew near to his end, he returned to Ferrara a broken man to die among close friends. Of him, Montaigne writes: "I regard it as a disgrace to our century that we have, as I understand, allowed [a man] of the highest learning to die in extreme want. . . ."[12] Perhaps it is predictable, then, that Giraldi refers to the fate of Phaethon at several points in his interpretative narrative of classical mythology, not in overtly mythographical discourse that links the story to his hometown's origins, but in the moralistic tones of an allegorist for whom Phaethon exemplifies the dangers of daring too much.[13]

If the myth illustrates the dangers of youthful ambition, it is no surprise to encounter it repeatedly in Torquato Tasso's poetry, but one cringes to find the poet calling himself a new Phaethon (*Rime d'occasione* 559 + 738) and alluding to the mythological figure as his protector (*Rime d'occasione* 630).[14] If mythology had anything to do with it, Tasso's fate was sealed by the comparison. One wonders what Tasso thought when he was welcomed to the Palazzo del Te in 1587 by Francesco III, the Gonzaga duke of Mantua, grandson of Isabella d'Este and by extension one of Phaethon's grandchildren through the network of Ferrara-Mantua connections. What went through Tasso's mind when he saw Giulio Romano's striking fresco of Phaethon's fall that decorates the octagonal-vaulted ceiling in the "Camera di Fetonte"? This was just after he had been allowed to leave the Sant'Anna hospital in Ferrara where Duke Alfonso II had had him confined for seven long years. Tasso had indeed become a new Phaethon

---

[11] Jean Seznec, *The Survival of the Pagan Gods: The Mythological Tradition and Its Place in Renaissance Humanism and Art*, trans. Barbara F. Sessions (Princeton: Princeton University Press, 1972), 230. Giraldi refers to his fate in the preface to the fourth section of *De deis gentium*: Lilio Gregorio Giraldi, *De deis gentium* (New York: Garland, 1976 [1548]), 179–80. Giraldi's prefaces to the sections of his mythography, composed as letters to old friends, provide a fascinating, albeit somewhat nostalgic, glimpse into the world of Ferrarese humanism in the late 1540s.

[12] Cited in Seznec, *The Survival of the Pagan Gods*, 231.

[13] Giraldi, *De deis gentium*, 239, 329.

[14] Tasso refers to Phaethon in his *Rime d'amore* at: 149.13–14; 160.14; 460.2–3; and in his *Rime d'occasione* at: 532.51–56; 559; 630.11; 738; 794.1–6; 917.1–4; 949; 1150; 1163.1–3; 1164.5–6; 1311.4–11. References are to Torquato Tasso, *Rime*, ed. Angelo Solerti (Bologna: Romagnoli-dall'Acqua, 1898–1902).

who was in a slow-motion free fall from the time he left his Ferrarese imprisonment till his death in 1595.

Giovan Battista Aleotti, the ducal architect for Alfonso II from 1575 until the duke's death in 1597 and subsequently consultant to Pope Clement VIII, labored over fifty years on a massive volume on Ferrarese waterworks and land reclamation projects, *Della scienza et dell'arte del ben regolare le acque di Gio. Battista Aleotti detto l'Argenta architetto del Papa, et del pubblico ne la città di Ferrara* (1632).[15] Aleotti was a faithful servant of the Estense, and one senses in the many tributes to Alfonso he inserts throughout the work a personal mourning for the man as well as sadness for Ferrara itself in the post-Estense years. After the devolution Aleotti was appointed the public architect for papal Ferrara, but he played second fiddle to the many Jesuits (whom he believed were incompetent) brought in to direct and redesign projects along the Po. Aleotti remained loyal to the Estense in Modena, becoming an informant on water and land projects for the court, often communicating by secret letters to members of the powerful Bentivoglio family about upcoming plans involving waterworks. Although his clandestine reporting changed nothing, he was eventually repaid with a house in Ferrara. Twice Aleotti refers to the story of Phaethon in the opening literary-historical section of his technical treatise, qualifying the first reference with a nice turn of phrase, "o vero o favola che sia," "whether it be true or a tale" (*Della scienza*, 225). He then adduces several sources (Claudian, Cato), which provide rational accounts for Phaethon's presence in Ferrarese legend (e.g., perhaps he was a leader of Greek colonizers to the area). Aleotti did not use the myth to adumbrate his foreboding sense that Ferrara's waterworks had fallen into bad hands, as he might have. Nevertheless, this practical engineer could not resist at least a couple of passing references to the legendary precursor of the Ferrarese.

And finally we come to the devolution of 1598, the event that marks the official end of Estense government in Ferrara. When Pope Clement VIII made his triumphal entry into the city — the pageantry is carefully described in the festival *livrets* published in honor of the occasion — "le sorelle di Fetonte" appeared again, this time as part of the decorations in a painted tableau by one of the town gates.[16]

---

[15] Available in a superb edition by Massimo Rossi (Modena: Panini, 2000).

[16] See the last page of the *Livret* for the entry of Pope Clement: Bonner Mitchell, *1598: A Year of Pageantry in Renaissance Ferrara* (Binghamton, NY: Medieval and Renaissance Texts and Studies, 1990). Angelo Rocca, a cleric who traveled in the entourage of Clement, has left a full account of the trip from Rome to Ferrara, with a detailed description of the festival decorations in the city, including the tableau with the Heliades. See Angelo Rocca, *De sacrosancto Christi corpore romanis pontificibus iter conficientibus praeferendo*

The need for the Church to recuperate the city (the phrase *Ferraria recuperata* recurs throughout the official documents on the devolution) arose in part because Ferrara had languished under a succession of bad governors or, at least, ultimately an unproductive one: Alfonso II had failed to produce an heir. Alfonso, then, is the final example of a Phaethon who, taking over the reins of government from his father, fails to control the chariot of state, as it were, and thus enables the Church to reassert its long-standing claim to the city. Direct allusion to Alfonso as Phaethon during the papal party's procession into the city would have been indecorous. But can we read in the painted representation of the Heliades one last reference to the legendary episode in Ferrara's past? Phaethon's sisters line the banks of the Po mourning the loss of their foolhardy brother over his watery grave much as the citizens of Ferrara lament the loss of the House of Este. While retellings of the myth often focus on how the tears of the Heliades swell the Po,[17] the decorations for Clement's procession depict the Po as having run dry suggesting that there was no longer even a river for the Ferrarese to cry over.[18] In Clementine propaganda recuperating the city and restoring its fecundity meant saving the Po, whose course needed to be dredged and reinvigorated in order to irrigate the barren lands of the river valley.[19] By 1598, the tears of the Heliades, like the story of Phaethon, were no longer needed in Ferrarese mythology. The departure of the Este for Modena altered irrevocably the circumstances that made meaningful the context for such legendary mythology.[20]

Phaethon's Children: The Este Court and its Culture in Early Modern Ferrara returns to the purported scene of this legend with a collection of essays ranging

---

commentarii antiquissimi ritus causam, et originem . . . Clemente VIII. Pont. Max. Ferrariem proficiscente (Rome: Guillelmum Facciottum, 1599), Tableau at 86–87.

[17] For a thorough discussion of the myth in Greek, Alexandrian, and Roman poetry, see G. Knaack, "Phaëthon," in *Ausführliches Lexikon der griechischen und römischen Mythologie*, ed. W. W. Roscher (Leipzig: Teubner, 1902–1909), 2175–2202; and the editor's introduction (3–32) to J. Diggle, ed., *Euripides' Phaethon* (Cambridge: Cambridge University Press, 1970).

[18] Angelo Rocca's description of the same tableau prompts a digression on the myth and the river itself, focusing on its current sorry state in 1598. See *De sacrosancti Christi corpore*, 86.

[19] Cardinal Aldobrandini, who arrived in Ferrara on 29 January 1598 to prepare for the triumphal entry of Clement later in May, advised the pope on the politics of water management in the city and its surrounding territories in a letter of 9 February1598, housed in the Archivio Segreto Vaticano, Armadio 46, 1, fols. 142v–144r.

[20] Nevertheless, the myth's local resonance is still being felt as late as 1879. Ettore Novelli dedicates a poem, *Fetonte*, to the Ferrarese Countess Alma Avogli Trotti when she marries that year. See Ettore Novelli, *Fetonte* (Imola: Galeati, 1879).

across numerous disciplines in Ferrarese studies. Unlike virtually any other Italian state, Ferrara bears the mark of a single family of rulers that held the government tightly within its grip for over three centuries. This continuity of the Este family's rule provided Ferrara with a tight coherence of cultural and political programs.[21] Estense patronage, while not always as magnificent as the ruling family wanted the citizens of Ferrara to believe, fostered a courtly setting in which, and sometimes for which, recognizably Ferrarese cultural products were created and made public.[22] In this volume we look at the similarities among the different forms of that cultural production and ask how that production is specifically Ferrarese. Estense rule and its cultural and political continuity may also account for the odd lack of interest in Ferrara by historians of early modernity in Italy. Ferrara was not, as were Florence, Venice, and even Milan, the stage for experimentation with new governmental forms, or a major passageway for trade from other continents; nor was it the seat of a world religion as was Rome. Set within a cluster of inland northern courts removed from international borders, it carried on intense political and cultural relations with the states that contended for the Italian peninsula while remaining an extremely stable and conservative state across which the winds of major Western power struggles gusted in intermittent storms. As early as the mid-sixteenth century the Florentine historiographer Gabriele Simeoni (c. 1507–1570) could suggest that Ferrara was "a model of stability" in comparison with the governments of several other northern Italian states.[23] Though small and forced to survive on limited resources, Ferrara maintained a degree of political and

---

[21] M. A. Mastronardi, "L'immagine di Ferrara nella letteratura estense," in *Acta Conventus Neo-Latini Abulensis: Proceedings of the Tenth International Congress of Neo-Latin Studies, Avila, 4–9 August 1997*, ed. Roger Green et al., MRTS 207 (Tempe, AZ: Medieval and Renaissance Texts and Studies, 2000), 423–30.

[22] In "The Courts," in *The Origins of the State in Italy, 1300–1600*, ed. Julius Kirschner (Chicago: University of Chicago Press, 1991), 136–51, Trevor Dean has argued that the "creation of a specific courtly culture is . . . debatable" in fifteenth- and sixteenth-century Italy (146), and he points out that much more preliminary research needs to be completed before we can resolve questions about the courts, patrons, producers, cultural forms, and courtly culture. While respectful of Dean's precautions, I do think we can venture certain generalizations about the similarity of the various cultural forms produced in the orbit of the Este family between around 1450 and 1598, if not about the congruity of court and state in Ferrara during those years.

[23] Eric W. Cochrane mentions Simeoni's *Commentarii alla tetrarchia di Vinegia, di Milano, di Mantova et di Ferrara* in Eric W. Cochrane, *Historians and Historiography in the Italian Renaissance* (Chicago: University of Chicago Press, 1981), 350. See Gabriele Simeoni, *Commentarii di Gabriello Symeoni Fiorentino sopra alla tetrarchia di Vinegia, di Milano, di Mantova, et di Ferrara* (Venice: Comino da Trino di Monferrato, 1546), 94.

cultural independence from other states, including, surprisingly, the Church to which it was tied due to the Estes' role as papal vicars. Ferrara cultivated this separateness through the internecine struggles of the mid-1400s, through the various political crises of the early Cinquecento and the Counter-Reformation of the late sixteenth century, before finally devolving to papal rule in 1598. Over these two centuries, the Estense city developed cultural practices, visual arts, music, and literature that bear a distinct Ferrarese imprint and that demand study within the specific context of Ferrarese history. One of the purposes of the present volume is to suggest the range of materials that beckons researchers to Ferrara in the fields of literary studies, history, the history of visual arts and culture, musicology, anthropology, women's studies, ethnic and religious studies, theater and performance history, and other specializations, materials that have played a primary role in the cultural and political history of Italy as well as Ferrara but which are often not remarked in their regional specificity.

Where and when does the study of Ferrara and the Este acquire consistency as a research area in its own right? The scholarly attention devoted to Florence and Tuscany over the years has relegated Ferrara to the background or, still worse, obscured it by taking Florentine history as a general paradigm for the rest of the peninsula. As Riccardo Bruscagli observes in the volume's opening essay, already in the sixteenth century Machiavelli and Guicciardini, perhaps understandably, registered their prejudice for Florence over Ferrara in various of their works. Given that these two Florentines established the scientific discourse of early modern political culture, it is no wonder that Ferrara subsequently received short shrift in the scholarly tradition. Much as the members of the Medici ducal entourage positioned themselves to take diplomatic precedence over the declining Este family in the latter half of the sixteenth century, Florence continued to be the primary focus of attention among scholars well beyond the lifetimes of Machiavelli and Guicciardini. Florentine centrality and Ferrarese marginality became norms of cultural historical inquiry for centuries to come.

But Florentine priority was of little import to the legions of local historians in Ferrara and Modena who began to amass and sift through great quantities of archival material in the years following the devolution of 1598, in those subsequent centuries when Ferrara, as Werner Gundersheimer surveys in the volume's concluding essay, for all practical purposes went to sleep. A strong secretarial and archival tradition had been an integral part of the courtly culture of Ferrara before its eventual demise, with a significant accumulation of documents in the period leading up to 1598. Men like Pellegrino Prisciani ("most accurate investigator" according to Muratori),[24] Giovambattista Giraldi Cinzio,

---

[24] L. A. Muratori, *Antichità Estensi* (Modena: Stamperia ducale, 1717–1740), 37.

and Giambattista Pigna left detailed documents of Ferrarese culture prior to 1598, not to mention the men and women who wrote the many thousands of epistles, briefs, and letters from the pre-devolution period that fill the Este archives. Post-1598, there followed an extraordinary sequence of official historians who worked for the Estense family out of the ducal library and archives in Modena, doing their utmost to preserve and analyze Ferrarese history, big and small, for future study. The first and arguably greatest of these scholars devoted to the preservation of Ferrarese culture was Ludovico Muratori (1672–1750), who collected much material on Ferrara in his monumental *Antichità Estensi* (cited above) and *Rerum Italicarum Scriptores* (1723–1738).[25] Girolamo Tiraboschi (1731–1794) picked up where Muratori left off, utilizing and synthesizing the research of his predecessor at the Estense library in his *Storia della letteratura italiana* and his *Dizionario topografico-storico degli stati estensi*.[26] Ferrara may have grown dormant after 1598, but Estense culture endured from the seventeenth century onward as a focal point of scholarly research, due in large part to the successful efforts of scholars like Muratori and Tiraboschi.[27] The transfer of the Este family and the establishment of its archives in Modena meant that one had to go there (one still does to some extent) to encounter Estense Ferrara. This spatial paradox further complicates the issues of centrality and marginality as they relate to Ferrara's history in general and Ferrarese studies in particular. For Ferrara is divided from itself, split off geographically from the records of much of its history.

Ferrara's centrality in the Renaissance as an innovative urban setting came clearly into focus in the mid-nineteenth century through the research of Jacob Burckhardt, who called it "the first really modern city in Europe" in his com-

---

[25] L. A. Muratori, *Rerum Italicarum Scriptores* (Milan: Typographia Societatis Palatinae, 1723–1738).

[26] Girolamo Tiraboschi, *Dizionario topografico-storico degli stati estensi* (Modena, 1824–1825), *Storia della letteratura italiana* (Modena, 1771–1782).

[27] A second tier of historians after Muratori and Tiraboschi includes men like Gasparo Sardi, Girolamo Baruffaldi, and Antonio Frizzi, all of whom also comment interestingly on the place of the Phaethon myth at the origins of Ferrarese history. Gasparo Sardi, *Libro delle historie ferraresi del Sig. Gasparo Sardi . . . Aggiuntivi di più quattro libri del Sig. Dottor Faustini sino alla devolutione del ducato di Ferrara alla Santa Sede* (Ferrara: Giuseppe Gironi, 1646) links Phaethon to Egyptian culture; Girolamo Baruffaldi, *Dell'Istoria di Ferrara scritta dal dottor D. Girolamo Baruffaldi Ferrarese . . .* (Ferrara: Bernardino Pomatelli, 1700) mentions the myth as he discusses the Po; on the verge of positivism and in a catastrophist mode, Frizzi proposes that Phaethon was actually a meteor: Antonio Frizzi, *Memorie per la storia di Ferrara*, 5 vols. (Ferrara: F. Pomatelli, 1846–1888), 1:15–16.

mentary on the state as a work of art.[28] Burckhardt's focus on Duke Ercole I's creation of this modern state — he comments that the city's modern street plan was constructed "at the bidding of the ruler" — would prepare the way for subsequent analyses of the patronage system of the Este family, to which scholars have returned with particular interest recently. For their part, Burckhardt and other nineteenth-century scholars undertook the task of interpreting the extensive archival materials on Ferrarese culture that the antiquarians of previous generations had collected. Many of these historians, Antonio Frizzi for example, sought to rationalize the study of Ferrara, separating the history of the city from the genealogy of the Estense family.

Much of this work was carried out in the chauvinistic spirit that burgeoned, somewhat paradoxically, as the different localities across the Italian peninsula were organized into the unified nation of Italy. In the aftermath of the tumultuous 1860s, political leaders began to press for a system of higher education that would contribute to the country's newfound unity. The national educational system, established as scientific positivism came into its own in nineteenth-century Europe, programmatically fostered institutions of higher learning that placed high value on the physical sciences — an emphasis that affected the faculties of humanities as well. During the 1870s and 1880s, for example, many humanistic journals of a scientific cast published their first issues, often under the auspices of the national universities. One of these journals, *Giornale storico della letteratura italiana* (1883), was sponsored by the University of Turin, an institution founded in 1400 but revitalized by new programs in the sciences in the nineteenth century.[29] In the initial number of the *Giornale storico*, which came to symbolize the scientific scholarship that still engages many literary critics in Italy, its editorial board outlined the kind of scholarly projects it would promote: biographical studies of authors, bibliographical research, editions of texts, collections of documents, and archival work on literary sources. The journal's editorial policy featured a thinly veiled criticism of the critical principles of the Neapolitan professor and savant, Francesco De Sanctis (1817–1883). De Sanctis and his many followers had been promoting an interpretation of the Italian classics that was, at its worst, devoid of any understanding of the cultural setting in which those works were created. The *Giornale storico* came into being to confront this sort of ahistorical aesthetic response to literature associated with

---

[28] Jacob Burckhardt, *The Civilization of the Renaissance in Italy* (Oxford: Phaidon, 1944), 31.

[29] The university's "Facoltà di Lettere" (its combined departments of humanities) sponsored the publication of the journal.

Italian Romanticism.[30] This confrontational setting, then, produced the first positivistic studies of many Ferrarese authors, most notably Ariosto and Tasso, and it affected the development of Ferrarese studies in general.

Positivist scholarship culminated in two masterpieces that focus primarily on Ariosto but also deal extensively with Ferrarese culture in his lifetime from 1474–1533: Michele Catalano's *Vita di Ludovico Ariosto*, published in Geneva in 1930–1931, and the bibliographical reference manual, *Annali delle edizioni ariostee*, by Giuseppe Agnelli and Giuseppe Ravegnani published in Bologna in 1933. These works are monuments to a kind of academic scholarship that was about to undergo a transformation, as radical political change swept through the provinces of Emilia-Romagna and eventually made its way to Rome in the person of Benito Mussolini. Ferrara, noted throughout its history for its social tolerance, suddenly became "one of the principal strongholds of the Italian fascist movement,"[31] such that a new brand of criticism openly vied with positivism in the reception of Ariosto and Ferrarese culture under the Estensi. Alongside academics in the field, popularizing historians like Rodolfo Renier, Alessandro Luzio, Titina Strano, and Guido Angelo Facchini staked their reputations on reassessments of Ferrarese Renaissance culture from a fascist slant. Throughout the nineteenth and into the early twentieth centuries Ferrara had become a subject of interest to popular historians, journalists, and travel writers, including many Anglo-American authors, for example, Ella Noyes and Edmund Gardner. But the new brand of com-mentator in the 1920s and 1930s took Ferrara to the people with a vengeance. Facchini's name reappears as secretary of the Comitato Ariostesco that prepared for the celebrations in honor of the Ferrarese poet in the late 1920s and early '30s. Facchini helped to organize an extensive series of lectures and presentations in Ferrara, thirty-nine of which were published in a volume, *L'Ottava d'oro: La vita e l'opera di Ludovico Ariosto*, to mark the fourth centenary of the poet's death in 1933. The volume was meant to bring together not only the best scholars currently working on Ariosto but also journalists, novelists, poets — men and one woman ("per non far torto alla parola iniziale del Furioso") of letters.[32]

---

[30] Cultural, or at least regional, politics contributed to the attack on the aesthetic tendencies of De Sanctis and his school. Critics from northern Italy were prejudiced against the Neapolitan and his followers.

[31] Paul Corner, *Fascism in Ferrara: 1915–1925* (Oxford: Oxford University Press, 1975), x.

[32] "To keep from discrediting the *Furioso*'s opening word," xvi. The reference here is to the first lines of Ariosto's poem, "Le donne . . . io canto": "Of women I sing." Not to pick a bone with the editor, Baldini's organizational prowess, or his reading skills, but Ariosto states that he sings of women *in the plural*. The reference to the text ironically

In the preface Antonio Baldini recycles an earlier description of Ariosto as a writer who plays a "fascio" of different musical instruments, which produce a symphony never heard before despite their "babelic" diversity. The use of the term "fascio" (bundle or group) to describe an ensemble of instruments calls attention to itself and highlights the volume's historical moment on the eve of rampant fascism. Baldini concludes his preface with an even more striking image that underscores the growing militant nationalism of the day. Apparently taking *Orlando Furioso* as a paranoid metonymy for Italy itself, Baldini declares: "One thing is certain: Ariosto's work has never been so completely attacked from so many different sides with weapons of such diversity over a sixteen-month period. And his work has emerged from this final assault more beautiful and glittering than ever."[33] Gabriele D'Annunzio, Ferrarese by birth and fascist intellectual by habit, leads the charge against Ariosto's poem with two messages that serve as epigraphs to the volume. And then the ultimate confirmation that this book is about much more than literary criticism: Italo Balbo, a major exponent of violent fascist brigades (Corner, *Fascism in Ferrara*, 251) and president of the Comitato Ariostesco, delivered the inaugural lecture on 6 May 1928, "Il volo di Astolfo," which is the first essay in the volume. In 1926 Mussolini had promoted Balbo from his position as head of the Ferrarese fascists to the command of the Italian air force, and in 1933 Balbo was shifted to the governorship of Libya — a very powerful political figure, at times rumored to rival even Mussolini himself, and a man with a vocation for flying if not for literary criticism. In his telling period piece Balbo often waxes eloquent: "Our people cannot live without poetry. Nor can Italian Fascism live, that is, grow, develop, expand, spiritually and morally, without poetry."[34]

While *L'Ottava d'oro* had no lasting impact on the interpretation of Ariosto's major work or on the analysis of the cultural context that produced it, the book represents an important moment in the development of Ferrarese studies. It could not have been produced without the scholarship of positivism and it would not have assumed its final form without the fascist move to popularize classical Italian culture, the program to take Ariosto and Ferrara to the people, whether through

---

and unintentionally emphasizes the isolation of the lone token female among the fascist Ariostisti.

[33] *L'Ottava d'oro*, xvii.

[34] *L'Ottava d'oro*, 6. In World War II, Balbo would crash to his death like a latter-day Phaethon under suspicious circumstances, "shot down in error by Italian anti-aircraft emplacements" (Corner, *Fascism in Ferrara*, 282). Of interest is the fascist memorializing of Balbo's role in the creation of *Ottava d'oro* in Mario Calura, "Italo Balbo. Per la storia e per l'arte ferrarese," in *Atti e memorie della Deputazione di storia patria per l'Emilia e la Romagna* (Ferrara: Premiata Tipografia Sociale, 1942), 1–14.

new editions of his works or the reinstauration of public festivals like the Palio di San Giorgio. But World War II disrupted the scholarly community that produced the volume, and post-war Italy would have a very different conception of the relations between popular culture and official power.

It is no accident that the first audible voice after the war to speak up on early modern Ferrara is that of a historical materialist, Antonio Piromalli, whose *La cultura a Ferrara al tempo di Ariosto* (Florence: La Nuova Italia, 1953) adapted the political perspective of Antonio Gramsci to focus on Ferrara as the creation of despotic tyrants rather than enlightened princes. Piromalli argued that there was a hidden but ever-present level of popular resistance to the Este regime, which had much in common with the local fight against the fascists in the 1940s. Piromalli's anachronistic but not totally wrong-headed work elicited major responses in the following decades. Varese Chiappini's *Gli Estensi* (Luciano: Dall'Oglio, 1967) and Werner Gundersheimer's *Ferrara: The Style of a Renaissance Despotism* (Princeton: Princeton University Press, 1973) both make the case for a more comprehensive and nuanced understanding of the Ferrarese urban lordship that developed under the Este family in the Renaissance. Chiappini and Gundersheimer argue that Estense despotism, if not always benign, was generally achieved with the consent of at least some of the people and was directly responsible for much of the cultural well-being of Ferrara in the fifteenth and sixteenth centuries.

During the late 1970s a group of Italian scholars from different disciplines coalesced into a loosely-formed association whose purpose was to promote the study of the phenomenon of the court in early modern Italy. The group, "Centro Studi Europa delle Corti," published an important, if controversial, series of interdisciplinary studies on topics connected with Ferrarese studies over the 1980s and 1990s.[35] Many of these same scholars have also been associated with the Istituto di Studi Rinascimentali in Ferrara, another institution newly formed in the 1980s, which has been an important venue and catalyst for research on Ferrara. The Istituto assists in the organization of conferences on Ferrarese culture and regularly produces records of them, for example, *La corte e lo spazio: Ferrara estense* (Rome: Bulzoni, 1982) and *La corte di Ferrara e il suo mecenatismo 1441–1598 / The Court of Ferrara and its Patronage* (Modena: Panini, 1990). The Istituto's most visible contribution to Ferrarese studies, however, is un-

---

[35] The conceptual framework underlying the Centro's project, that of a unifying and regularized European court culture, has not been without its critics. See Kristen Lippincott, "The Neo-Latin Historical Epics of the North Italian Courts: An Examination of 'Courtly Culture' in the Fifteenth Century," *Renaissance Studies* 3 (1989): 415–28. And see also Trevor Dean, "The Courts," especially 138–39.

questionably the journal *Schifanoia*, published annually since 1980. *Schifanoia*, like the scholarship of the "Europa delle Corti" group, is marked by its interdisciplinary research on the complex cultural phenomenon of the court-centered early modern city.

The interdisciplinary studies of Ferrarese culture that characterize *Schifanoia* are also found in the volume produced jointly by the Universities of Ferrara and Wales, *The Renaissance in Ferrara and its European Horizons* (1984). There has followed a succession of noteworthy monographs on specific topics connected with Ferrara and its culture. Several of the contributors to *Phaethon's Children* figure prominently in a small boom of Ferrarese studies in the Anglo-American world: Werner Gundersheimer's book on Ferrara mentioned above; Lewis Lockwood on *Music in Renaissance Ferrara, 1400–1505* (Cambridge, MA: Harvard University Press, 1984); and Trevor Dean on a slightly earlier period in Ferrarese history in *Land and Power in Late Medieval Ferrara* (Cambridge: Cambridge University Press, 1988). Other more recent monographs include: Charles Rosenberg, *The Este Monuments and Urban Development in Renaissance Ferrara* (Cambridge: Cambridge University Press, 1997); and Thomas Tuohy, *Herculean Ferrara* (Cambridge: Cambridge University Press, 1996).

The 1990s was a decade of Ferrarese centenaries documented in an assortment of volumes that focus variously on Boiardo, Ariosto, Tasso, and the different Estense cultures which produced them and which they in turn helped to foster. An international conference held in 1992 to celebrate the six-hundredth anniversary of the founding of the Università degli Studi di Ferrara led to the publication of *Alla Corte degli Estensi. Filosofia, arte e cultura a Ferrara nei secoli XV e XVI*, edited by M. Bertozzi (Ferrara: Università degli studi, 1994). The collection of twenty-five essays ranges widely from the impact of humanism on teaching at the university to art, literature, philosophy, and religious reform in Ferrara during the Renaissance. The university's impact on the cultural life of Ferrara is a theme throughout the volume. An international conference on Boiardo at Scandiano in 1994 was crowned with the publication of a two-volume collection, *Il Boiardo e il mondo estense nel Quattrocento* (Padua: Antenore, 1998). The organizers also produced an impressive newsletter, "effimero ma non da buttare," in preparation for the conference, *Il Boiardo*, which came out in four issues in 1993–1994. A selection of papers presented at a conference at Columbia University in 1994 was organized into a volume on Boiardo and Ferrarese culture in the fifteenth century.[36] The following year, in 1995, the Istituto di Studi Rinascimentali di Ferrara organized an international conference on Torquato

[36] Jo Ann Cavallo and Charles S. Ross, eds., *Fortune and Romance: Boiardo in America*, MRTS 183 (Tempe, AZ: Medieval and Renaissance Texts and Studies, 1998).

Tasso, which culminated in the publication of a massive three-volume work, *Torquato Tasso e la cultura estense*.[37] A 1995 conference held at the Newberry Library in Chicago dealt more generally with Ferrara: "Ferrara: Cultural Change from Boiardo to Tasso" and is the original source for many of the essays in *Phaethon's Children*. In 1996 and 1997, two conferences in the USA and Italy on Dosso Dossi, the Ferrarese painter, resulted in the publication of a collection of eighteen essays, *Dosso's Fate: Painting and Court Culture in Renaissance Italy*.[38] And in 1999, the University of Milan sponsored a conference on Ariosto's minor works, the proceedings of which have been published in *Fra satira e rime ariostesche*.[39] In 2000, Adriano Prosperi edited a volume with 17 major essays on early modern Ferrara, *Il Rinascimento. Situazioni e personaggi,* in the *Storia di Ferrara* series, which includes essays by contributors to *Phaethon's Children* that complement their work in this volume.[40] Finally, Jadranka Bentini has recently edited an exhibition catalogue on Estense culture, *Gli Este a Ferrara: una corte nel Rinascimento*, based on an exhibit mounted in the Castello di Ferrara in 2004.

Phaethon's Children: The Este Court and its Culture in Early Modern Ferrara opens with a survey of Ferrarese culture from the 1400s to 1598 by Riccardo Bruscagli, whose essay, "Ferrara: Arts and Ideologies in a Renaissance State," anticipates in various ways the rest of the volume. Bruscagli explores the particularities of this small urban lordship, which produced a radically innovative culture within the boundaries of its conservative and stable political setting. While Florence experienced one political "mutazione" after another, as documented by Guicciardini and Machiavelli, Ferrara maintained its identity as an independent feudal state. In that stable setting it produced an art and a literature of a visionary and fantastic nature, which deeply marked future production of Renaissance epic, comedy, tragedy, and pastoral drama. Ferrara's literary art was at the avant-garde of vernacular classicism in the sixteenth century. Bruscagli weighs the paradox of these experimental arts within a political culture that hardly changed at all. And he considers how the failure of the state to change brought about its literal undoing, an undoing that left its traces on Ferrarese artistic production.

---

37 G. Venturi, ed., *Torquato Tasso e la cultura estense*, 3 vols. (Florence: Olschki, 1999).

38 Luisa Ciammitti, Steven F. Ostrow, and Salvatore Settis, eds., *Dosso's Fate: Painting and Court Culture in Renaissance Italy* (Los Angeles: Getty Research Institute for the History of Art and the Humanities, 1998).

39 Claudia Berra, ed., *Fra satire e rime ariostesche* (Milan: Cisalpino, 2000).

40 Jane Fair Bestor, "Gli illegittimi e beneficiati della casa estense," in *Il Rinascimento. Situazioni e personaggi*, ed. Adriano Prosperi (Ferrara: Corbo, 2000), 77–102; Lewis Lockwood, "Musica a corte e in chiesa nel XV secolo," in *Il Rinascimento*, ed. Prosperi, 313–31.

Este rule depended on dynastic continuity, an obvious statement the simplicity of which turns derisive at the end of the family's long reign, when Alfonso II dies without an heir and the city devolves to the papacy in 1598. But at other moments in the long history of the House of Este, at crucial junctures in its development as a ruling entity when there were no legitimate rulers, or at least none powerful enough to take control, the solution was to promote an illegitimate member of the family to be ruler. Niccolò III, who ruled Ferrara from 1393 to 1441, began the process of modifying the medieval structures of the Este feudal aristocracy into what would become a Renaissance principality. His shrewd diplomacy enabled three of his sons, Leonello, Borso, and Ercole, to rule in more or less peaceful succession until 1505. The two elder sons, Leonello and Borso, were born illegitimate, with only Leonello legitimated. The Este family was deft at handling the laws of marriage and the rules governing legitimacy and illegitimacy to its dynastic and political advantage. If the situation required it, the family's lineage could be recast so that an illegitimate member would appear to have legitimate status. Jane Fair Bestor discusses in "Marriage and Succession in the House of Este: A Literary Perspective" the way the Estensi manipulated literary texts as media in which to elaborate legitimate political identities for themselves, and thus to fend off questions of their rightful rule. Considering Tito Strozzi's *Borsiad*, Boiardo's *Orlando Innamorato*, and a letter by Pietro Aretino, Bestor shows the integral role played by writers in the anchoring of Estensi political legitimacy. The use of bastards as political pawns served the House of Este well until it became a liability, which happened when the family, in its conflicts with other ruling families and with the papacy, became obsessed with emphasizing its nobility. At the beginning of the sixteenth century the Este had embraced the laws of primogeniture that necessitated a different code of behavior in those who subsequently became rulers. The change in behavior anticipates certain attitudes that will be registered elsewhere and later in Ferrarese society.

Diane Ghirardo turns to lowlier residents of Ferrara and to the physical and social topography of the city with an essay on one of its marginal groups, the prostitutes who worked in Ferrara's state-run brothels. "Marginal Spaces of Prostitution in Renaissance Ferrara" offers a panoramic view of the policing of women's spaces by Ferrarese authorities, as they carved the urban landscape into areas designated for chaste and unchaste women. Moreover, as she shows, these two categories of women were each subject to more specific spatial regulation: chaste women were confined to convents and homes where they were instructed to remain inside the monastic or domestic threshold, and prostitutes were subject to severe punishments for venturing beyond designated areas of the city, in some cases even for leaving their cramped quarters within the brothel. Ghirardo's essay discovers a relatively hidden community within traditional

Italian historiography and highlights the "gendered geography" of Renaissance Italian cities. It furthermore suggests ways in which architectural and legal history may open new vistas on the social and cultural past.

Richard M. Tristano's essay, "The *Istoria Imperiale* of Matteo Maria Boiardo and Fifteenth-Century Ferrarese Courtly Culture," makes a case for the importance of Boiardo as more than merely a court poet of the Este. He argues outright for a rehabilitation of Boiardo's reputation as a historian. After first examining the work and responding to claims that it should be considered merely some kind of translation of Riccobaldo's medieval history, Tristano asks why Boiardo composed it at all, and he situates his interpretation in the context of readings of other historians and literary critics who have considered the piece primarily in relation to the poet's *Orlando Innamorato.* Tristano investigates what the *Istoria* tells us about Ferrarese courtly culture and Estense patronage at the time of Ercole I. His focus on the depiction of Charlemagne and what he describes as the Estense interlace in the *Istoria* recognizes important similarities between the historical work and the discourse of Boiardo's poem, especially as regards the understanding of narrative at play in each work. But ultimately Tristano concludes that the *Istoria* deserves to be read as a hybrid example of medievalizing humanist history.

In "Ferrarese Chroniclers and the Este State, 1490–1505," Trevor Dean examines a narrow but important slice of time during the Estense rule, the concluding years of Ercole I's reign, from 1490 to 1505, when Ercole puts his imprint on the Ferrara we now recognize. Dean finds that what interests the city's diarists at the end of Ercole's rule is not art, but crime; not the fees of patronage, but the cost of grain; not Boiardo and other court poets, not state theater, but Ercole as ruler. Three of the four diaries he considers express concern over the contested legitimacy of the duke's authority, and of those three, two raise serious questions about Ercole's efficacy as ruler. We sense in various passages of the diaries a growing rift between the ducal court and the people of Ferrara. Beyond 1505 (and the scope of Dean's essay), we can begin to measure the size of the rift by calculating Ariosto's more distant relationship with his Este patrons as compared to what had been Boiardo's closer proximity to the center of courtly power in the generation of Ercole.

Albert Russell Ascoli's work on Ariosto has defined that poet for recent readers as an author who responds to a series of crises during the Italian Renaissance, approximately from the descent of Charles VIII into Italy in 1494 to the sack of Rome in 1527. His reading of Ariosto's *Furioso* is consistently nuanced with a keen sense of the cultural history that informs the poem. In his essay for this volume, "Ariosto's 'Fier Pastor': Structure and Historical Meaning in *Orlando Furioso*," Ascoli addresses the issue of how Ariosto's awareness of his historical context affected his reworking of the poem over the course of its three editions, from 1516 to 1532. Posing the question of the role of history in each version of the poem, Ascoli concludes that Ariosto confronts the historical crises of his day directly in the first edition of the *Furioso*, but is much more evasive in the third and final one in which the episode of Ruggiero-Bradamante-Leone "sets the myth of Estense genealogy in sharp relief, but also tends . . . to make it part and parcel of the *Furioso*'s chivalric fictions," (222). In addition to this new reading of the poem's definitive shaping by the cultural politics underlying its interlaced narrative, Ascoli provides a focused reading of *Furioso* 17 that throws into relief the poem's parallel between the man-eating monster known as the Orco and Pope Leo X, both of whom belong in the reference field of the term "Fier Pastor."

In "Tears of Amber: Titian's *Andrians,* the River Po and the Iconology of Difference," Anthony Colantuono examines the impact of humanism on the last of a series of paintings commissioned for Duke Alfonso I's personal study. Colantuono's research in this essay and elsewhere focuses on the dynamic interaction among artists, patrons, and intellectuals in the Estense court. As we see from the essays by Bestor, Tristano, and Lockwood in this volume, the apparent escapism of the popular romance and even of Ferrara's pleasure palace, Schifanoia, belie a serious commitment to the arts as an arena for political propaganda and personal self-promotion from the earlier Este reigns. Alfonso I's court (1505–1534) continued this tradition by fostering the creation of highly serious, erudite, humanistically-inspired artistic endeavors that glorified the city of Ferrara and its surrounding territories. Colantuono shows how Titian's painting, ostensibly a glimpse of a bacchic revelry on the island of Andros, is in fact a careful and detailed pictorial argument on the importance of the River Po and the fecundity of its watershed around Ferrara. Titian's praise of the Po in the 1520s marks a highpoint in rhetoric, both pictorial and literary, about this important economic and cultural resource. Two generations later as the papacy moved in to take control of Ferrara, the condition of the Po had degenerated radically as it began to silt up, reducing the productivity of the Ferrarese lands around the river. By 1598 the mighty Po and the hearty vintages produced along its banks were a distant memory.

Lewis Lockwood looks at issues of patronage that distinguish Ferrara from its major (and much larger) rivals in "From Josquin Desprez to Cipriano de Rore: Tradition and Transformation in Sixteenth-Century Ferrarese Musical Culture." The continuity of the Este family enabled a given ruler in the role of patron to allude to art commissioned by a predecessor. While there are interesting tensions between Ferrara and its rival cities in patronizing the arts (the contest between Florence and Ferrara underlies David Quint's reading of Tasso to follow), the internal dynamics of patronage within the Este family itself are also noteworthy, as one member vies with the reputation of a previous one. Or — the case that Lockwood explores so provocatively — a descendant may take advantage of the reputation and good name of a forefather, as when Ercole II recycles music composed for Ercole I to proclaim his own devout religiosity and to make a name for himself as a defender of the faith. That Trevor Dean finds in Ugo Caleffini's diary a quiet criticism of Ercole I's religiosity shows how well the earlier duke had learned to marshal his artists to the advantage of his public image. Lockwood's essay raises issues of art and politics at the heart of the enterprise behind *Phaethon's Children*, as he focuses on Josquin Desprez's *Missa Hercules Dux Ferrariae* at a nexus of Estense self-representation in music, painting, and religious controversy.

Deanna Shemek turns to the Estes' most famous daughter, who emigrated as a young bride to the neighboring court at Mantua. "In Continuous Expectation: Isabella d'Este's Epistolary Desire" considers the hardships for women imposed by the dynastic marriage network that held together the Italian courts. Removed from her home surroundings at the age of fifteen to become the marchesa of Mantua, Isabella d'Este was to become one of the most celebrated women of her time. Shemek shows how social, artistic, and political life for Isabella depended on her highly developed practice of letter writing, and she focuses in particular on Isabella's early struggles to establish regular patterns of correspondence with the Ferrarese court and with her often absent husband, Francesco Gonzaga II. Isabella's deft use of the letter as a means of constructing and maintaining her sphere of political influence is located by Shemek within a theoretical context for the examination of letters in general as they figure in the history of women's writing.

A noticeable feature of Ferrara's culture, from pre-modernity to the time of Giorgio Bassani's post-war *Cinque Storie Ferraresi*, has been the enormous contribution made to the city's life by its resident Jewish population. Robert Bonfil explores the Ferrarese reception of Jews and Jewish culture in the sixteenth century. The Este family had a utilitarian motive for allowing Jews, who filled the important socio-economic niche of moneylenders to the poor, to settle in Ferrara when they were exiled from other cities. But the Jewish community developed into more than merely a group of moneylenders. The city was reputed to be a haven for Jewish immigrants, especially Portuguese New Christians, the *conversos*, for whom it became an important printing center that disseminated the transplanted culture. It was, one said, "Italy's safest port, where God's mercy had ordained" that the new immigrants "might rest from their distressing journeys," (316). Bonfil's examination of several documents, including Ercole II's charter to establish a *yeshivah* in 1556, leads him to conclude that the Este fostered a cultural exchange between Christians and Jews that was noteworthy for its lack of religious polemics. But the incorporation of the Jews into the Ferrarese body politic was a slow and at times tortured process. While Ercole's policy encouraged a greater openness toward Jewish intellectuals, Bonfil reads in it much ambiguity as well.

Indeed, as the city of not only many Jews, but also the militant Christian burner of vanities, Girolamo Savonarola, Ferrara has a long history of religious conflict and turmoil. During the convulsive decades of the first half of the Cinquecento Ferrara was home to a number of Protestant reformers. Janet Levarie Smarr traces the brilliant and in many ways tragic career of Olympia Morata in her piece, "Olympia Morata: From Classicist to Reformer." Morata's short life takes her away from the court of Renata with its Protestant leanings to self-imposed exile in Germany, distant from what she came to call "the idolatry of Italy." Morata grew up amid the humanists of the ducal court, her father a university professor who was the private tutor of the duke's sons in the 1530s. The young girl's philological prowess impressed her father and his scholarly friends, and before long she was translating into and out of Latin and Greek, her projects including an early version in Latin of the *Decameron* 1.2, with its attack on the papal court. Shortly after Paul III's visit to Ferrara in 1543, the members of Olympia's immediate circle began to leave the city for fear of condemnation and punishment for heresy. Morata marries a German student, a radical Protestant himself, moves to the north and dies soon thereafter, but not before she develops from a budding classical scholar into a Protestant reformer. Smarr considers this personal transformation in the context of the tumultuous moment in which Morata lived, considering as well the complicated relation of Ferrara to Europe in the 1540s and 1550s.

Louise George Clubb examines the interstices between art and political power in her essay on the ducal theater: "Staging Ferrara: State Theater from Borso to Alfonso II." While Clubb's sweeping survey touches on many of the ways theater interacts with politics in Ferrara from Borso's day onward, she considers in particular three plays — an anonymous Florentine *Griselda*, Sforza Oddi's *Prigione d'amore*, and Giambattista Della Porta's *Georgio* — that set their action in Ferrara, and in so doing provide a glimpse of the changing view of the city "that had become a theatrical landscape in the minds of contemporaries," (350). Torquato Tasso, as Bruscagli shows in the volume's opening essay, interpreted the city and its courtly culture as one large theatrical space. The perspectives of the anonymous Florentine (perhaps of Lorenzo the Magnificent's circle), the Perugian jurist Oddi, and the Neapolitan dramatist Della Porta provide readers with a unique glimpse of the culture of Ferrara. The unexpected point of view is perhaps most useful at the end of the sixteenth century and in the post-devolution world of the seventeenth alluded to in Della Porta's Christian tragedy on St. George. Clubb's analysis of the play in the context of Clement VIII's theatrics during the 1590s as he prepared for his entrance onto the stage of Ferrarese politics sheds light simultaneously on the dramatic text and on the troubled final years of Este rule in the city.

David Quint's contribution to our understanding of these poets has focused on the relation of genre and ideology, examining in particular the historical development of the interrelations between romance and epic. From antiquity through Ariosto to Tasso and beyond, Quint has studied the impact of a given cultural paradigm on a poet's work within these two genres. His earlier research on Tasso's *Gerusalemme Liberata* shows how the poet's preoccupation with religious politics in post-Tridentine Italy affects his poetic choices, narrative and otherwise. In his essay for this volume, "The Debate between Arms and Letters in the *Gerusalemme Liberata*," he examines in detail Tasso's participation in a sixteenth-century cultural debate over appropriate forms of heroism, intellectual vs. military, a debate at least as old as the literary West. Quint's starting point is Tasso's imitation of the contest for the arms of Achilles between Ulysses and Ajax as retold by Ovid in *Metamorphoses* 13. But he moves far beyond that literary model to consider how Tasso's recasting of the debate, "a debate that had newly become topical in Tasso's Ferrara as the Estense Duchy sought to assert its precedence over Medicean Florence" (364), is affected by his own historical moment. This leads Quint to consider ultimately the growing conflict between social classes, the landed aristocratic gentry, on the one hand, and the new clerisy of the court, on the other. Tasso's anxiety over this opposition reflects his culture's own uneasiness. That concern addresses nothing less than the future of Ferrara on the eve of its demise.

Clement VIII's triumphal entry into Ferrara in the year of its devolution to the papacy, 1598, was arguably the last great moment in the history of that once illustrious city. Papal Ferrara lost its imagination, then its lifeblood, slowly but surely, such that Charles Dickens on a stopover along the Grand Tour could refer to it as "a city of the dead." More than one visitor was struck by the paradox of the wide streets of Europe's first modern city now abandoned, empty, depopulated. Under papal supervision Ferrara eventually closed down, becoming only a sleepy regulation district whose former glories grew dimmer with time. Werner Gundersheimer, in the volume's concluding essay, "The Experience of Ferrara: English and American Travelers and the Failure of Understanding," examines the condition of the city after 1598, as described in the writings and journals of Anglo-American travelers. The first point to note is that relatively few visitors even went to Ferrara and of those who did, few stayed very long, for the city had become nothing more than a stopover en route between Bologna and Venice. Gundersheimer considers the myriad reasons for the typical traveler's inability to appreciate Ferrara for what it was or for what it had been in its glory days, as he notes that it has taken "nearly four centuries to begin to arrive at a more balanced and comprehensive understanding of the Ferrarese contribution to Italian civilization" (395).

The aim of *Phaethon's Children: The Este Court and its Culture in Early Modern Ferra ra* is to build on early and recent scholarship toward a deeper appreciation of Ferrara's place in early modern Italy. To that end, we not only hope that this volume will argue Ferrarese culture as a field of inquiry within Italian and European studies; we also intend it as a provisional introduction to that field for researchers unfamiliar with its background and breadth. There is, we hasten to add, much more to Estense Ferrara than can be treated in one collection of essays. Thus while each study included here gestures toward wider and interconnected areas of research, we have been unable to include separate considerations of medicine, the history of science, printing, and architecture in Ferrara. In the wake of earlier, discrete studies of Ferrara and of recent work such as we have collected here, we may now be, as Gundersheimer writes, arriving at a better comprehension of this city, beginning to overcome a failure of understanding that has kept Ferrara marginalized over centuries of Renaissance historiography. A feature of that arrival, we argue, is Ferrara's recognition as a geographic, political, and cultural case meriting scholarly dialogues and collaborations analogous to those that thrive around Florence, Venice, Rome, and other important Renaissance states. Phaethon's crash may have founded a mythical Ferrara, and his rise and fall may prefigure the fortunes of the rulers who made the city famous. Our concern as contributors to this volume, however, has been to turn from the demigod to his human offspring and from myth to history, to argue collectively that a vital culture calls for continued investigation on the Ferrarese banks of the Po.

Ferrara: Arts and Ideologies in a Renaissance State

Riccardo Bruscagli

After the 1527 sack of Rome, the subsequent flight of the Medici from Florence, and the return of popular government to that city, Francesco Guicciardini sought peace and safety in his suburban villa of Finocchieto. Accused of embezzling the salaries of Florentine soldiers during the war against Charles V, Guicciardini had fallen from grace and been stripped of all honors. In those very depressing months the Florentine historian wrote, among other things, two orations: the *Accusatoria* and the *Defensoria*.[1] In these works he projected his personal and judicial predicament from two different perspectives: that of a fictional prosecutor and that of a no-less-fictional defender. In both, he scrutinized his own responsibilities, behavior, and attitudes during the years of his government in the papal states of Romagna, or, as they were then called, Lombardia. Guicciardini was, of course, no Machiavelli, and irony was not his *forte*. In the *Accusatoria*, however, he managed to create a rather savory character, a lawyer who pronounces an oration before the court recently re-appointed in Florence and known as the Quaranta. Guicciardini's creation is very much a man of the people, a figure of righteous anger (an "arrabbiato") deeply imbued with class hatred, who sincerely despises Guicciardini for his role as papal minister. From this lawyer's point of view, the states of Lombardy appear to be realms of radical inequality and arbitrary privilege. His indignation is that of a staunch supporter of Florentine "libertà" who confronts the antidemocratic habits of northern cities:

---

[1] Francesco Guicciardini, *Opere*, ed. E. Scarano (Turin: UTET, 1970), 1:485–604.

> So bene come si vive in coteste città, so che quegli uomini non ebbono mai né libertà né imperio, conoscono solo lo interesse loro, e di fare piacere a più potenti di loro; non hanno nelle cose loro gravità, non vergogna, non conscienza; sono non manco servili con l'animo che con la necessità; una raccomandazione in Lombardia di uno conte, uno priego in Romagna di uno governatore, uno cenno di uno vescovo non che di uno cardinale, gli farebbe ogni dì fare mille sagramenti falsi.[2]
>
> ["I am well aware of how one lives in those cities, I know that those men have never had either freedom or government; they know only their own interests and how to please those more powerful than themselves. They have no gravity in their own affairs, no shame, no conscience. They are no less servile in spirit than they are by necessity. A recommendation from a count in Lombardy, a plea from a governor in Romagna, a nod from a bishop (much less from a cardinal) would move them any day to a thousand sacrileges."]

Both Reggio and Modena, where Guicciardini had been the papal governor, had been part of the Este state since the fifteenth century but had been lost to the papacy under the belligerent pontificate of Julius II. The *Accusatoria* raises Florentine political disgust — whether republican, democratic, egalitarian, or libertarian — to the level of caricature. Represented in his artful prose but also deeply felt by Guicciardini himself is the *Accusatoria*'s outrage at what seems to be merely a system of private privileges and tyrannical lordship in Ferrara. Guicciardini had already addressed a very bitter note to Ferrara and its duke in his *Ricordo* 93, accusing Ercole d'Este at that time of *crimen laesi populi,* "faccendo quello che appartiene a fare al popolo e a' privati" ["doing things which are appropriate for the people and for private persons to do"]. He goes on to say: "Merita grandissima riprensione el duca di Ferrara faccendo mercatantie, monopoli, e altre cose meccaniche che aspettano fare a' privati" ["The duke of Ferrara deserves the severest criticism for engaging in trade, monopolies, and other practices that pertain to private individuals"]. We might conclude that, viewed from Florence, the northern state of the Estensi was, on the one hand, a regime of social and political inequality. On the other hand, Ferrara was not even a true monarchy since all the "cose meccaniche" — all the commercial and financial activities — were governed and personally handled by the lord and his family.

---

[2] Guicciardini, *Opere*, ed. Scarano, 1.6: 528–29.

The state as a private enterprise: how distasteful for the Florentine cult of "libertà." It is not for me here to adjudicate between these contradictory views of government and power. But one must note that if the image of Ferrara in the Renaissance is highly problematic, this is in part because it has been damaged and compromised by the prestige of Florence's very different culture. It is true that we owe to Florence a celebrated tradition of Renaissance historiography and political thought. It is also the case, however, that Florence's splendid heritage can be a very misleading one, for the difficulties we still face in constructing an image of Ferrara in the Renaissance arise also from the fact that Ferrara was unable to craft its own historiography, its own political thought. It is thus possible that our perspective on the matter is *de facto* that of the Florentines, that of Guicciardini, or even worse, that of his fictional prosecutor in the *Accusatoria*. Our view of the city may even be that of Machiavelli, who dismissed the example of Ferrara as uninteresting for his purposes in the *Prince*. Notably, the *Prince* is not a treatise on principalities in general. It dwells on the "new principalities" and on the *new prince*, on the act of founding a new regime. In this regard Ferrara makes for dull political science: the duke of Ferrara is already well rooted in his reign, and he requires no Machiavellian *virtù* in order to maintain power. According to Machiavelli's second chapter, on hereditary principalities, the lord of Ferrara resisted the Venetians in 1484 and Pope Julius II in 1510 because he was "antiquato in quello dominio" ["long established in that dominion"]: "Perché el principe naturale ha minori cagioni e minore necessità di offendere e se estraordinari vizii non lo fanno odiare, è ragionevole che naturalmente sia benvoluto da' sua" ["Because the long-reigning prince has fewer causes and less need to offend; and if extraordinary vices don't make him the object of hatred, it is reasonable to assume that he will be naturally loved by his people"]. Hated or simply ignored by the triumphant political tradition of Renaissance culture, Ferrara responded with awkward, blunt instruments like Giovambattista Pigna's *Historia de' principi d'Este*, a long and unbearable encomium on the ruling family that could hardly compete with the works of Machiavelli or Guicciardini.

Comparison between Ferrara and Florence is not only unfair, however, it is also incongruous. Florence developed its complex political and historical thought not only in the openness and vitality of its republican tradition, but also amid the frustrating if exceptionally sophisticated institutional debates that originated between 1492 and 1530. This period was marked by the convulsive transition from the republican to the monarchic regime, with all its "variazioni" or "mutazioni," to cite two key terms from both Machiavelli and Guicciardini. How could we expect anything of the kind from Ferrara? After all, there were no "mutazioni" or "variazioni," no institutional experiments in Ferrara: its political nervousness, its institutional fragility, its instability were of another sort altogether. Ferrara did not elaborate its own image in terms of direct political debate or historical speculation, nor was the city able to produce anything similar to the impressive, excruciatingly lucid anatomy of its own public body that made Florence the homeland of the modern science of the state. Ferrara's strategy was completely different, and it must be investigated on its own terms.

Ferrara produced over the years not a culture of self-consciousness, but an art and a literature of a visionary and fantastic nature. Ferrarese culture is a construction of images: stages, backdrops, marvelous fictions, literary dreams. The weaker and more threatened its own political existence became — by Venice, by the Pope, by capricious games of war and peace, especially during the years of the Italian wars — the more extroverted, spectacular, and magnificent became Ferrara's poetic self-representation and its luxurious theater. So much of this imagery is now forever lost. Some of it was ephemeral by nature: the theater, the music, the "spectacula" (to recall the title of Pellegrino Prisciani's book); the banquets, the dancing, the feasts, the charm and the beauty of the dames and the cavaliers were produced as experiences, to be known only by those in attendance. Another portion of this heritage was pillaged to a degree unequalled in any other center of Italian Renaissance civilization. Sabadino degli Arienti's *De Triumphis religionis* details the nature of that loss.[3] His careful description of the "delizia" of Belriguardo, with its gardens, its gaudy decorations, its cycle of frescoes representing the fable of Cupid and Psyche (far anticipating the Palazzo Te in Mantua) is heartbreaking in its evocation of vanished treasures. And what of the urban ducal residence known as the "prisco palacio," the "delizie" of Belfiore, and the little paradise of Belvedere Island where Tasso staged his *Aminta* in 1573? Also of stunning richness were the ducal collections, the "quadreria" [painting collection] and the famous Estense library.

Only the inventories now remain from this collection of books that were periodically checked out but always remained, it seems, scattered about the rooms of the palazzo and castello. The surviving inventories are not library catalogues but rather lists of objects kept in the various rooms: *Lancelot* and *Guiron le courtois* claim their place in one list next to cauldrons, pans, lamps, and fabrics. We know little about how this incredible patrimony disappeared. The last will and testament of Alfonso II, Ferrara's last duke, registers various

[3] See Giovanni Sabadino degli Arienti, *De triumphis religionis: Art and Life and the Court of Ercole I d'Este*, ed. Werner L. Gundersheimer (Geneva: Droz, 1972).

caches of books but avoids listing them in detail.[4] Very little of the collection remains in Ferrara itself: the *Spagna* copied and illuminated for Borso and the beautiful *Tolomeo*, for example, are there. A bit more remains in Modena: Borso's famous, splendidly illuminated Bible; and the less famous but very important *Attila,* one of the more significant poems written in Francoveneto and a true relic from among the ducal family's oldest possessions.[5] What of the rest? In recent years the Estense Library in Modena has been trying to pull together what we know about volumes from the ducal library that have been identified in collections across Europe. The results have been encouraging and critically enlightening. What we had (perhaps romantically) considered to be the material destruction of the original library, its fading away along the obscure paths of history, now stands in need of correction. What actually happened is apparently much simpler. The fact is that the Este, once they were settled in Modena, probably sold the library piece by piece, just as they sold the *quadreria*, but in a much less obvious, less spectacular manner.

Once again, the contrast with Florence is striking. While the Biblioteca Laurenziana was being built in Florence, Ferrara was treating its main library with daring nonchalance, regarding its books not as intellectual tools but as objets d'art, decorative embellishments, or "supellectili" ["furnishings"] in the term of the period inventories. A malicious Florentine might say that such was Ferrara's punishment for mistreating its heritage. A benevolent Florentine will say instead that such a difference in cultures requires that we look into Ferrara's civilization without prejudice, without insisting on a parallel history. We should instead attend to the style of the city by looking at some of its cultural images and allowing ourselves to be captured by their charm. In their own way those images may speak to us of the culture that produced them.

In 1437, a peculiar character who used to show up periodically at various courts of the north was received and initially welcomed into the inner circle of Leonello d'Este's court.[6] Ugolino Pisani, who was something between a literary

---

[4] The testament of Alfonso II is published in P. Sella, "Inventario testamentario dei beni della Biblioteca di Alfonso II d'Este," *Atti e memorie della Deputazione ferrarese di storia patria* 28 (1931): 131–395.

[5] A general as well as accurate account of the Este library through the various phases of the dynasty is provided by A. Tissoni Benvenuti, "Il mondo cavalleresco e la corte estense," in *I libri di Orlando innamorato*, ed. R. Bruscagli (Modena: Panini, 1987), 13–33. This whole volume is useful as a reference book on early Renaissance Ferrara. See also Riccardo Bruscagli, *Stagioni della civiltà estense* (Pisa: Nistri-Lischi, 1983).

[6] This episode is well described in M. Villoresi, *Da Guarino a Boiardo: La cultura teatrale a Ferrara nel Quattrocento* (Rome: Bulzoni, 1994).

figure, a poet, and a jester, this time brought a gift for the marquis and his friends: a book entitled *Repetitio Zanini coqui [The Private Lessons of Johnny the Cook]*. A parody of a dissertation defense, here presented not by a student or a scholar but by a cook, the book was deeply rooted in the linguistic and literary traditions of the universities of the Padania, which we know were strong points of resistance against the mounting tide of the modern *humanae litterae*. The *Repetitio* belonged to a goliardic genre, heavy with thick humor and full of stylistic and linguistic impertinence. Leonello, Guarino Veronese, and the other intellectuals of the court rejected this book on various grounds. The prince maintained his usual benevolent attitude and, in a very understated way, handed the booklet to Guarino without a word. Guarino could not help giggling and smiling with an air of superiority as he began to read. He then passed the book to Tomaso of Rieti and finally to Tito Vespasiano Strozzi, who openly uttered the common disgust of the Ferrarese court — or more precisely, of Leonellos's inner, classicist circle — at such a literary product, with its prehumanist, medieval comic style. To be precise, it was not that Plautus or Terence were unknown to Pisani. But they were not yet recognized as appropriate models; they were merely two among many possible sources for comic material.

This little scene is carefully described in Angelo Decembrio's *Politia letteraria*, a monumental dialogue written by one of the most influential literati of Leonello d'Este's time, but published much later in the Cinquecento; it still awaits a modern critical edition and a decent commentary.[7] As raw and spare as it comes down to us, however, Decembrio's book is without doubt our most precious and eloquent testament to Ferrarese taste in Leonello's years. The scene in which the *Repetitio Zanini coqui* is rejected as a "librum unctuosa fuligine, sartaginibus et coquinariis ollis redolentem" ["a book blackened with greasy grime, reeking of frying pans and kitchen pots"] represents an epitome of the cultural attitude the *Politia* tries to capture. Perhaps we need not fantasize that in presenting his book Ugolino Pisani intended to tease Leonello and his touchy humanistic friends. Their reaction shows to what degree we must take seriously the title of Decembrio's dialogue, *Politia letteraria*: "purity and elegance in literature." Far more than the endless and often exasperating discussions among the interlocutors about ancient authors and texts, more than the flattering passages where the prince himself appears as a philologist and an antiquarian capable of emending a text or discussing a variant under the very

---

[7] The *Politia letteraria* was first published in 1540 (in Augsburg, by Heinrich Staynet); a second, better edition followed in 1562 (in Basel, by Johann Hervagen). A modern critical edition based on the manuscript Vat. Lat. 1794 has long been desired.

pleased eyes of his mentor Guarino — more, in other words, than the *pars construens* of the *Politia* — the novella about Ugolino Pisani, with its sharply sarcastic rejection of traditional Lombard culture, indicates the climate that Guarino's humanist hegemony aimed to establish in Ferrara. For Guarino not only founded and developed a premier humanistic tradition in the city, he also tried to disconnect Ferrara from traditional northern culture by rejecting as obsolete and unacceptable — even unpresentable and embarrassing — cultural products such as the *Repetitio*, which up to that time had been considered perfectly in tune with the intellectual traditions of the *Padania.*

Historians have traditionally contrasted the superior refinement of Ferrarese culture during the years of Leonello with the rougher, crasser atmosphere of the city's subsequent rule by the marquis Borso, Leonello's step-brother and — like Leonello — an illegitimate son of the prolific Niccolò III. The contrast between Leonello and Borso is obvious, but it cannot be reduced to a *chiaroscuro* effect of culture and ignorance, refinement and grossness, a passion for art and books, on the one hand, and an exclusive love of feasts and banquets on the other. It is true that the realm of Leonello and Guarino comes to an end with Borso. We have more than one bit of evidence that Guarino, in fact, contemplated leaving Ferrara after Leonello's death; and many episodes show quite clearly that a transition took place at that point in Ferrarese culture.[8] But as it turns out Guarino never did abandon the Estense capital. His salary was reduced by Borso, and his favorite disciple, Ludovico Carbone, quickly lost his job as instructor of the princes Rinaldo and Gurone. But after Guarino died, his chair was immediately granted to his son, and Ferrara cultivated a dynasty of humanists assured by an uninterrupted professorship of classics at its university.

It is also true that Borso did not know any Latin. On the other hand, there is abundant documentation of his passionate involvement with vernacular literature, especially with chivalric romances in French and Italian. Court poets continued to dedicate works of exquisite humanistic taste to Borso, works he apparently was not even able to read, let alone appreciate. Tribraco dedicated to him the *Divi Borsi Estensis Triumphus*, Biondo Flavio the *De laudibus militiae*, and above all Tito Vespasiano Strozzi, Boiardo's uncle, named the *Borsias* for him. This was a dynastic poem in a pure classical style; it represented an alternative to the courtly encomium that was also distinct from the chivalric one that attracted the young Ariosto when, before beginning his *Furioso*, he experimented with his *Obizzeide.* It would therefore be unfair to say

---

[8] This phase of Ferrarese culture is examined in detail in the above-mentioned Villoresi, *Da Guarino a Boiardo*, 111–15.

that the flow of humanistic culture was stopped or discouraged in Ferrara by Borso d'Este. My impression, rather, is that Borso managed to include the cultural legacy of his stepbrother in a much broader and articulated strategy, in which the vernacular and especially the chivalric tradition again found a place and was liberated from any inferiority complex. Borso's cultural programs elaborated a new, richer image of Ferrara, no longer circumscribed by the snobbish atmosphere of the *Politia letteraria*, but rather presented in a much more open, more varied and multi-layered context. Borso may not have been a humanist prince, but he certainly knew how to operate among the people. He was famous for his cordiality and gregariousness (which contrasted with Leonello's dry sophistication), and he used this warmth to his advantage in politicizing the arts and culture of Ferrara. Borso conveyed an image of the court much closer to the people, much more involved with the life of the commoners, much more exposed and dramatic. He used religion, for example, as a powerful bridge between the feudal lord and his subjects and as a prime factor of popular identification with the ruling family.

The characteristic extroversion of Borso's monarchic style is confirmed by the kind of art he promoted and patronized, from his famous Bible to the frescoes of Palazzo Schifanoia, which were begun during his reign and represent his court's role in the life of Ferrara. In these celebrated frescoes, we see Borso hunting, riding horses, giving money to the *buffoni*, enjoying himself. As we know, the iconology of Schifanoia very probably depends on the erudition of Ferrara's most prominent humanist, Pellegrino Prisciani. In the top zone appear the Olympian deities, while in the middle zone are depicted the demons of the decades of each month. Both reflect the memory of an esoteric knowledge which, beyond Rome and Greece, retraced lost and rare traditions of Indian astrology and astronomy. This is all very well known, thanks to the work of Aby Warburg.[9] I would like to suggest, however, that it seems questionable to separate the third zone, in which the actions of Borso's court are realistically illustrated, from the mythological and esoteric zones above. If the extravagant doctrine of Pellegrino Prisciani lies behind the two superior zones, we should not assume that a simple, photographic narrative animates the lower courtly zone of the frescoes. Life at court is solemnly scanned, instead, by the seasonal rhythms of time, according to a calendar void of any religious and liturgical reference, totally and disarmingly pagan. One might say that the image represents a secular reversal of the showy piousness

---

[9] A useful, updated account of Warburg's (and post-Warburgian) studies on Schifanoia's iconology appears in M. Bertocchi, *La tirannia degli astri: Aby Warburg e l'astrologia di Palazzo Schifanoia* (Bologna: Cappelli, 1985).

of the marquis. In the art of Schifanoia, Borso's court legitimates itself not through God, like the First Family of a civic Christian community. Rather, Borso's court appears in all its earthiness, present and inevitable as the weather and the seasons, as the crops and the harvest.

At the same time that Prisciani was working for Borso, the young Boiardo commenced his career under him and for him. One should resist the stereotype of a Matteo Maria Boiardo totally identified with Ercole d'Este and almost passionately in love with the "signor gentile" who appears as the unparalleled protagonist of the encomiastic genealogies of the *Orlando innamorato*. That Boiardo evolved later in the 1480s, when Ercole was already the duke of Ferrara. Things work differently in Boiardo's poetic exordium of 1463–1464, the *Laudes Estensium* and the *Pastoralia*. Boiardo was then twenty-three; and he composed these *carmina* in the very year when Ercole and his brother Sigismondo returned to Ferrara after long years spent in Naples, where they had been more or less exiled by the suspicious Leonello.[10] Unmarried and childless, Borso called back his stepbrothers to prepare a smooth succession, immediately entrusting the government of Modena to Ercole and Reggio to Sigismondo. These are the "Estensi" celebrated in the *Laudes* of the young Boiardo, who presents them in that work according to a careful scale of importance and reverence.

The lowest place belongs to Sigismondo, who peeks out here and there as a charming, good-looking young man with blond hair, but nothing more. The highest place is reserved for Borso, not only as the present ruler, but also as the artifex of a new harmony among the members of the ruling family and the person most responsible for the re-establishment of dynastic legitimacy in the city: "genus Aestense et maiorum ingentia facta / Et tantum veteres exuperavit avos, / quantum sideribus praefulget lucida Phoebe, / et quantum colles despicit altus Athos" (*Laudes* IV). ["The Este family line has exceeded the great deeds of its greatest and most venerable ancestors by as much as the splendid moon outshines the stars and as much as Mount Athos looks down on the hills."] To put it more simply, Borso is openly recognized for having done more for the family and the monarchy in Ferrara than all his ancestors put together. In the middle, the *Laudes* focus on Ercole, who enjoys the unfair advantage of a name that begs obviously for panegyric. Indeed, Boiardo cannot resist the inevitable comparison between this contemporary Hercules and the ancient one, especially in *Laus* VI, which he devotes to the "simillima gesta"

---

[10] For this early period of Boiardo's poetic production as well as for a complete profile of the poet, see Riccardo Bruscagli, "Matteo Maria Boiardo," in *Storia della Letteratura Italiana*, ed. E. Malato (Rome: Salerno, 1996), 635–708.

["very same feats"] of the ancient and the modern heroes. But modern and fitting praise outshines mythological homage. The modern Ercole glitters with typical courtly virtues, which already show him to be a magnanimous, liberal, courteous prince: "Non illum fulvi torquet mala cura metalli, / et stimulos dirae spernit avaritiae" (XII). ["Evil anxiety over golden metal does not pervert him; and he rejects the temptations of cruel greed."] It seems very important to emphasize this "Borsean" beginning for Boiardo, the writer to whom Ferrara most owed its powerful impulse toward a high-profile intellectual and cultural image. And we must also recall that Boiardo's *Orlando innamorato*, which was first published in 1482 and dedicated to Ercole, had naturally taken off much earlier, and at least could have been conceived in the years of Borso's rule. Therefore, the fact that Borso was able to acquire for himself and his successors the title of duke seems at this point to be simply the formal recognition of the central role he played in defining and enhancing the image of Ferrara as one of the capitals of Renaissance Italy.

Poised between the age of Borso and the age of Ercole, the *Orlando innamorato* did much more, of course, for Ferrarese identity than merely update the encomiastic machinery of the Este dynasty.[11] The *Innamorato* is also an encomiastic romance, and with the introduction of the Este ancestor, Ruggiero, in the second and especially the third book of his poem, Boiardo intended to shape a new image of the ruling family. Not in the sense, though, as we have traditionally believed, that he wanted to deny the descent of the Este from Gano of Maganza, the traitor of Roncevaux, and thus to wash an odious stain from the face of the dynasty. As Antonia Benvenuti has pointed out, the family's descent from Gano was not unacceptable in and of itself, and this particular genealogy was not an invention of the adversaries of the Este alone.[12] Boiardo, in fact, chose to pursue an ancestry for his lords that was not merely more respectable, but also more daring.

It was a question of birds. The supporters of the descent from Gano identified the white eagle in the Este coat of arms as derived from the falcon of the Maganza house. Boiardo instead maintains that the Este eagle had always been an *eagle*, and that it must be identified with nothing less than the Trojan eagle, reminiscent of the one that Jupiter sent down to kidnap

---

[11] For a general introduction to the *Orlando innamorato*, see the *Introduzione* to the most recent edition of the poem: Matteo Maria Boiardo, *Orlando innamorato*, ed. Riccardo Bruscagli (Turin: Einaudi, 1995), V–XXXIII.

[12] See A. Tissoni Benvenuti, "Note preliminari al commento dell' 'Innamoramento d'Orlando'," in *Il commento ai testi*, ed. O. Besomi and C. Caruso (Basel-Boston-Berlin: Birkhauser Verlag, 1992), 305–6.

Ganymede and transport him to Olympus. More precisely, the white eagle was supposed to have been primordial, for legend held that the Trojans turned the bird black after the death of Hector. In Boiardo's fantasy, this glorious mascot actually passed from Hector to his son Astyanax who, in the account of *Orlando innamorato,* did not die on Troy's final night (as related, by contrast, in the most common version of the Trojan legend). Astyanax survived and became the ancestor of Ruggiero, and therefore of the House of Este, as the hero proudly reports to an already adoring Bradamante in the *Innamorato* (Canto III v). Troy? Hector? A family, a *gens*, descended from the defeated heroes of the Trojan war? This brings to mind an obvious comparison. While Vergil had cast Caesar and Augustus as descendents of Aeneas, Boiardo has his lords derive from Hector himself, a much more illustrious hero, even, than the one who served the political ends of the *Aeneid*. The challenge is obvious: Hector *versus* Aeneas, the house of Este *versus* the *gens Julia*, the *Orlando innamorato versus* the *Aeneid*, Boiardo, finally, *versus* Vergil.

Yet the encomiastic machine, though original, complex, and still today not thoroughly understood, is only the most explicit device in Boiardo's Ferrarese cultural strategy. We find Boiardo's major device in the exquisitely literary operation of his delivery in 1482 to Ferrara and to Italian literature of a peculiar narrative concoction we can call *romance* in English with some approximation, but which I would insist on calling by the more specific and appropriate Italian name of the period, *romanzo*.

Romanzo for Boiardo meant a macro-plot constructed of many subplots, of the sort he had encountered in the great French romances of the 1100s and 1200s and their Italian derivations. It meant a narrative woven of many threads and further complicated by *novelle* Boiardo inserted as set-piece episodes within the ever-incomplete corpus of the poem. Above all, it meant a constant textual simulation of orality, such that the narration pretends to be delivered by an actor-poet to an audience, both of whom are present and acknowledged within the text, as in the indigenous, extremely popular *cantari*. This last feature of the *romanzo* shaped by Boiardo — its representation of the act of its enunciation by a singing poet — will become the focus of the hottest literary polemics of the following century, those which debate the relative merits of epics and *romanzi*. In 1482 the *romanzo* was still a fresh invention for Italians. Boiardo's poem encapsulated the characteristic frenzy of the *romanzo* as a text not simply told, but recited and acted out to some extent and thus possessed of a peculiar excitement and directness. But it also served fundamentally to promote Ferrara and its culture. In fact, the poem's recitation is set from the very beginning in a very peculiar ambiance, to which increasing precision and detail are added as the text unfolds. From the first verse, the audience is one of "signori e cavallier." At 1.19, the poet notes the "cortese damiselle e graziose" in the audience, and at the very end, in the proem to the last canto, it is clear that "questa corte" to which the poet has been addressing his song is not a generic social milieu. The *Orlando innamorato*'s ambience is the very court of Ferrara, which is both the recipient of the "bella istoria" and more and more explicitly a source of inspiration for the narrator himself. The poem's reminiscence of the ancient dames and cavaliers is no mere act of fascinated nostalgia, but the celebration of the return of gaiety and Courtesy ("allegrezza e cortesia") which have been long banned but are now re-flourishing "among us," that is, at the modern court of Boiardo's Este:

> Così nel tempo che virtù fioria
> ne li antiqui segnori e cavallieri,
> con noi stava allegrezza e cortesia,
> e poi fuggirno per strani sentieri,
> sì che un gran tempo smarirno la via,
> né del più ritornar ferno pensieri;
> ora è il mal vento e quel verno compito,
> e torna il mondo di virtù fiorito. (2.2.2)

> [So, in the time when virtue bloomed
> In lords and cavaliers of old,
> We lived with joy and courtesy,
> But then they fled down distant roads
> And for a long time lost the way
> And nevermore returned; but now
> The winter and sharp winds are gone,
> And virtue blossoms as before.][13]

The return of ancient chivalry to the court of Ferrara in the peculiar, complex, and rich ideology that enfolds the *Innamorato* and transforms it into a sort of manifesto for a new era and a new, triumphant Ferrara enjoyed a very short life. The *Innamorato*'s originality appears most dramatically when we see that ideology shatter to pieces in the *Orlando furioso* (not to mention in Boiardo's other sequel-writing imitators, but this was perhaps predictable). Only a few years separate the final, posthumous edition of Boiardo's poem

---

[13] Translations of the *Innamorato* refer to Matteo Maria Boiardo, *Orlando Innamorato*, trans. Charles Stanley Ross (Berkeley: University of California Press, 1989), here 382–83.

(1495) and the beginning of the *Furioso,* which Ariosto was working on at least as early as 1509.[14] Those few years sufficed to erase completely the renaissance of ancient chivalry that the *Innamorato* had offered to Ferrara as a dream and a national myth. This myth of chivalry becomes more and more distant, in fact, as we move from the first edition of *Orlando furioso* (1516) to the definitive one (1532). Is it not ominous that in 1516 the first verse of Ariosto's poem read "Di donne e cavalier gli antiqui amori" ["Of ladies and knights the ancient loves"], whereas in the last version the adjective "antiqui" [ancient], so characteristic of Boiardo's poetry and ideology, is eliminated in a substitute verse — "Le donne, i cavalier, l'armi, gli amori" ["of ladies, knights, arms, and love"] ? This is a splendid verse, of course, but also ideologically more anodyne, less compromising than the "return of the ancient knights." That return, which was central to Boiardo's myth of origins, was obliterated by Ariosto's simply renouncing mention of the "antiqui amori." But this is just a detail, however symptomatic it may be.

What can we note about the self-representation of the narrator and his audience within Ariosto's text? What about the portrait of the court in its narrative? The prologue of the *Furioso* is already quite eloquent. No "signori e cavallieri" ["lords and knights"], no courtly audience called upon to listen, but a Vergilian opening ("io canto"; "I sing") and a classic dedication offered by the poet to his lord: "Piacciavi, generosa Erculea prole, / ornamento e splendor del secol nostro, / Ippolito, aggradir questo che vuole / e darvi sol può l'umil servo vostro" ["Seed of Ercole, adornment and splendor of our age, Hippolytus, great of heart, may it please you to accept this which your lowly servant would, and alone is able to, give you"]. [15] Sperone Speroni may have been overly critical, yet he was quite right when he later chastised Ariosto for the inconsistency of such a prologue with the unpredictable resurfacing in the rest of the narration of a courtly audience similar to the one that Boiardo had summoned: "'l Boiardo fu 'l primo che ciò fece; perché anche nel principio del libro parlò alli auditori; onde fece bene a far così di canto in canto, e di libro in libro. Ma l'Ariosto, che non comincia così, non fa bene a dar licenzia nel fin de' canti alli auditori, che non avea prima invitati . . . ." [Boiardo was the first to do this. Since even at the opening of his book he addressed his audience, he did well to continue doing so from one canto to the next and from one book to the

[14] An account of Ariosto's literary career (and mainly of his masterpiece) appears together with an updated essential bibliography in Giulio Ferroni, "Ludovico Ariosto," in *Storia della Letteratura Italiana*, ed. Malato, 353–455.

[15] Ludovico Ariosto, *Orlando Furioso*, trans. Guido Waldman (Oxford and New York: Oxford University Press, 1974).

next. But Ariosto, who did not begin in that manner, did not do well to take leave of his listeners at the end of his cantos, since he hadn't invited them in the first place].[16] The fact is that the *Orlando furioso* plays down the simulation of orality as it had been elaborated in the *Innamorato*. Ariosto overlaps the Boiardesque oral device with a different mode, already an epic one, in which the public is more vaguely defined — is it an audience of readers or listeners? — and the main addressee is not, or is not always, the courtly audience (the "brigata"), but also the lord for whom the work has been written and from whom the poet expects his own reward.

There is another intriguing detail that suggests much: the ambiguous term "signor." No one could swear that Ariosto played with this particular word on purpose, but so many times the reader doesn't know if the vocative "signor" is a plural — the "signori" of the court, the listeners of the narration — or if it is singular — the "signore" par excellence, Ippolito. After all, the "public" — and not the audience of the *Furioso* strictly speaking — appears in the prologue of the last canto as an ideal assembly of the gentlemen, ladies, writers, poets, and artists of his time. Thus the poet breaks the bounds of the courtly scene and addresses a more vast, inclusive world. And what chivalric pedagogy could Ariosto impart to his public? The collapse of Boiardesque narrative devices coincides, in fact, with the fall of Boiardo's ideology: the myth of courtesy's revival is simply ignored in the *Furioso*, and the "bontà dei cavalieri antiqui (I.22)" ["goodness of the ancient knights"] is quoted in a context which, if not sarcastic or even ironic, is nevertheless a far cry from exemplarity. All values have become contradictory, ambiguous, untrustworthy in Ariosto's poem, where even the most positive behavior (in characters such as Zerbino or Isabella) is depicted as self-destructive and where the chivalric code works like an uncoordinated machine. The *Furioso* celebrates nothing less than the asymmetry of the world. Ferrara is far away. Or better yet: far away is the ancient Ferrara of Borso and Ercole, with its presumption of a municipal identity.

If Ariosto publishes his poem three times, it is because he is writing *in* Ferrara but not *for* Ferrara. He is writing the new Italian literature, and he wants to enter the mainstream of a new national classicism — a Tuscan classicism, of course. Abandoning the ancient myths of Boiardo and reflecting instead a perplexed and disenchanted vision of reality, Ariosto succeeds in a unique enterprise. He brings into the very heart of this new Italian literature an endangered genre, which could easily have been identified as a local specialty and ignored as such by the sophisticated new classicism. This

---

[16] See Sperone Speroni, *Opere* (Venice: Domenico Occhi, 1740), 5: 521.

operation was extremely successful but also very contradictory. How many times in the Cinquecento were readers and critics — ready to erase the *romanzo* from the list of the officially accepted genres of the new vernacular literature — forced to stop in front of the *Furioso* and recognize, often halfheartedly, that however questionable the poem's content, its linguistic and stylistic beauty were such that it could not easily be dismissed? This was the real contribution that Ariosto made to Ferrara with his *Orlando furioso*. He was able to bridge the most glorious innovation of Ferrarese poetry into a new, national literary system, thereby placing his city front and center within the avant-garde literature of his time: certainly a move up from the back seat where a provincial affection for the old "volgar uso tetro" ["popular, gloomy style"][17] would have left Ferrara's culture splendidly obsolete.

By this point Ferrara was not just a prominent protagonist of Renaissance classicism; Ferrara was home to *the* avant-garde of the new vernacular classicism. One wonders what Renaissance literature would have been without Ferrara, the city where a new theater of comedy and tragedy was born; where pastoral drama thrived; where the epic dream of the century came true. In the central decades of the Cinquecento, the post-Ariostesque phase of Ferrarese civilization once again changed dramatically and underwent a deep process of intellectual restructuring. Ferrara's traditional propensity for literary fictions, its peculiar capacity for expressing itself through figments of its culture's imagination, remained intact; but this fictionality was increasingly packaged in sophisticated theoretical and poetic envelopes. In 1963 Carlo Dionisotti, reviewing a book by P. R. Horne on Giambattista Giraldi, noticed that one of the merits of this Ferrarese professor, writer, and intellectual was to have initiated a hot debate on modern tragedy. This was the first *querelle* on literary genres in the sixteenth century, coming much earlier than the more famous one on the *romanzo* and the epic that started (or at least had its heyday) after the publication of Tasso's *Jerusalem Delivered*.[18] I would dare say not only that the *querelle* on modern tragedy was Giraldi's precocious initiative, but that he also initiated the *querelle* over the *romanzo* and the epic poem. It is quite misleading indeed to characterize that debate as one about Ariosto *versus*

---

[17] This is the expression used by Ariosto, (Ludovico Ariosto, *Orlando furioso*, ed. Santorre Debenedetti and Cesare Segre [Bologna: Commissione per i testi di lingua, 1960], 46.15) to indicate the poetic flavor of Quattrocento vernacular lyric poetry, prior to Bembo's imposition of Petrarchist orthodoxy.

[18] See the review by Carlo Dionisotti of P. R. Horne, *The Tragedies of G. B. Giraldi* (Oxford: Oxford University Press, 1962) in *Giornale storico della letteratura italiana* 140 (1963): 114–21.

Tasso, and to assume that only the epiphanic appearance of the *Jerusalem Delivered* opened a critically worthy and intellectually noteworthy discussion. That happened very late in the century, in 1584, while Tasso was imprisoned in Sant'Anna. The fire actually ignited among the Neapolitans (or more precisely the Capuan entourage) upon the publication of Camillo Pellegrino's *Carafa*, which was followed by the Florentine response from Salviati and the Crusca Academy. Naples and Florence: note this geography. Ferrara was cut off from the debate and the two big writers, Ariosto and Tasso, were discussed as Italian poets, in total disregard for their relationship with Ferrara and the Este court. The fact that the *Furioso* and the *Liberata* belong to the same cultural world is almost obliterated in these polemics.

But let us restrict ourselves, for the moment, to the age of Giraldi. What is important to emphasize is that the notoriety of the late and conclusive *querelle* over epic and romanzo, Ariosto and Tasso, has overshadowed the first and possibly more genuine phase of the debate that took place in the 1550s and not in the 1580s. The earlier phase was obviously unaware of the future splendor of the *Jerusalem Delivered* and focused, instead, on Giraldi's own *Ercole* (1557) and on other contemporary *romanzi* (the *Amadigi* by Bernardo Tasso, the *Costante* of Bolognetti, the *Avarchide* and *Girone il cortese* of Alamanni).[19] Unreadable texts indeed! But the literary *atelier* that they defined, the complexity and richness of the discussions that flourished around them and — if not the perfume of the Graces, at least the brilliance of scholarly intelligence that accompanied them — are among the most captivating features of our Renaissance literature. Characteristically, Ferrara's intellectual community does not indulge in systematic commentaries but produces theories in the form of debates directly related to the creative activity of the writers, to their *poiesis*. Even the *Discorso intorno al comporre de' romanzi* (1554), which might appear to be the most "professorial" writing of Giambattista Giraldi, is more an implicit and preemptive defense of the author's own *Ercole* than it is a theory of the *romanzo* at large; and it dwells on a narrative model that is a faithful portrait of Giraldi's own heroic poem. This poem retains and vigorously defends the basic narrative device of the modern Ferrarese *romanzo*, that is, its simulated orality. At the same time, it is very distant from the full-scale *entrelacement* of Boiardo and Ariosto, with its plurality of adventures and heroes. It focuses on many exploits of just one, unique heroic character's life story and thus observes perfectly Giraldi's prescriptions that, "avendo a scrivere in forma di romanzi . . . , è meglio appigliarsi a molte azioni d'un uomo, che

---

[19] For an account of this phase of the debate, see R. Bruscagli, "Vita d'eroe: L'*Ercole*," *Schifanoia* 12 (1991): 9–19.

ad una sola" [" if one wishes to take up the writing of *romanzi*, it is better to concentrate on a man's many actions than on only one"]; and that is better to write about a single "argomento che sia intorno a tutta la vita d'un uomo" ["story that revolves around the whole life of one man"].

A myopic reading of such debates has often presented them as a sort of quibbling between supporters of different species of plots: one action, more than one action, one protagonist, more than one protagonist. But in Giraldi's treatise — not to mention in his beautiful correspondence on this subject with Bernardo Tasso, who in the same years (1556–1557) was working on his *Amadigi* — we find much more than academic, rhetorical fencing. Clearly Ferrara's problem, given the precedent of Ariosto's *Furioso*, was not merely one of upgrading the degree of classicism in the local, traditional chivalric genre. The problem was narratological as much as ideological, and it involved serious thinking about the moral engineering of a hero, about building up the model of a modern, perfect cavalier. *This* was the subject of debate in Ferrara in the mid-1550s. Obviously, the terms of such debate had little to do with those of the subsequent, more famous Ariosto-Tasso *querelle* at the end of the century. This difference is even more poignant if we put together other pieces of the Ferrarese and Giraldian puzzles. While shaping the figure of a modern epic hero and perfect knight — that is, of a totally positive protagonist — Giraldi appeared obsessed also with the other side, the dark side, of the matter: with the problems of modeling a negative hero, a defective protagonist, or a suitable tragic persona. Torquato Tasso himself, in his *Discorsi*, will later compare the positive hero of the epic poem with the negative or defective hero of tragedy.[20] He will observe, citing the case of Hercules, that it is possible for an epic poem and a tragedy to have the same character as protagonist, provided that the character is handled differently in each genre: "E se alcuna volta il tragico e l'epico prendono per soggetto la persona medesima, è da loro considerata diversamente e con vari rispetti. Considera l'epico in Ercole, in Teseo, in Agamennone, in Aiace, in Pirro il valore e l'eccellenza dell'armi; gli risguarda

---

[20] Tasso dwells on the relationship between the epic and the tragic hero in many *loci* of his works, especially in his *Discorsi dell'arte poetica e in particolare sopra il poema eroico* (1564) and in the later *Discorsi del poema eroico* (1587). Both are published in Torquato Tasso, *Opere*, ed. Bruno Maier (Milan: Rizzoli, 1965). See for example the debate over tragic and epic "materia" (*Arte poetica*, 4–5; *Poema eroico*, 173); the comparison between the effects of "orrore e compassione" in tragedy, and that of "meraviglia" in the epic poem (*Poema eroico*, 159–62); the contrast between the style of epic — "magnifico" — and that of tragedy — "semplice" (*Arte poetica*, 48–49; *Poema eroico*, 312).

il tragico come caduti per qualche errore ne l'infelicità" [And if the tragic and epic poets sometimes choose the same person as subject, they regard him differently and in different aspects. In Hercules, Theseus, Agamemnon, Ajax, Pyrrhus, the epic poet considers their valor and excellence in arms; the tragic poet sees them as fallen through some error into unhappiness.][21] In general, this complementary duplicity of Giraldi's research escapes his critics, who typically dissect his writings into many pieces that correspond to various aspects of his literary interests. One sometimes has the impression of dealing not with a single Giraldi, but with many: the theorist, the epic poet, the dramatist, the novelist.[22] But his establishment of the opposition between the perfection of the epic hero and the imperfection of the tragic hero, the latter stained by his (or her) "colpa tragica" ["tragic guilt"], turned out to be ominous indeed for the development not only of Italian, but also of European literature. Without Giraldi's stubborn defense of the tragic hero as a "persona mezzana" ["average person"] — not completely virtuous but not totally evil, and sharply distinguished from the moral perfection of the epic personae — the course of European tragedy, with its tormented, mixed-up, contradictory characters, would have been quite different.

Torquato Tasso himself, in a passage of his dialogue *Il Gianluca ovvero de le maschere* [Gianluca, or: On Masks], recalled his first impression of Ferrara, upon arriving in the city during the festivities for the wedding of Duke Alfonso II with Barbara of Austria:

> Quando prima vidi Ferrara . . . mi parve che tutta la città fosse una maravigliosa e non più veduta scena dipinta e luminosa, piena di mille forme e di mille apparenze; e l'azioni di quel tempo, simili a quelle che son rappresentate ne' teatri con varie lingue, e vari interlocutori. E non bastandomi d'essere divenuto spettatore, volli divenire un di

---

[21] See Torquato Tasso, *Discorsi dell'arte poetica e in particolare sopra il poema eroico* (1564), in *Opere*, ed. E. Mazzali (Milan-Naples: Ricciardi, 1959), 1: 14–15, and Torquato Tasso, *Discourses on the Heroic Poem*, trans. M. Cavalchini and I. Samuel (Oxford: Clarendon Press, 1973), 44.

[22] A modern attempt to consider Giraldi in the complexity of his literary and critical achievements (after the erudite compilations of the "scuola storica") are the proceedings of the "Giornate di Studio" organized in 1989 (27–29 April) by the Istituto di Studi Rinascimentali di Ferrara and the Centro di Studi su Matteo Bandello e la Cultura Rinascimentale: see *Schifanoia* 12 (1991), cited in note 19 above.

> quelli ch'eran parte de la comedia, e mescolarmi con gli altri.[23]

> [When I first saw Ferrara . . . it seemed to me that the whole city was a marvelous, painted, shining stage never seen before, full of thousands of shapes and apparitions. And the goings-on of that time seemed similar to those performed in theaters in different languages by various players. And not being satisfied with being a spectator, I wanted to become one of those who had a part in the play, to mingle among the others.]

The distance between fiction and reality is annulled: the whole city is transformed into a splendid theatrical stage. Daily life metamorphoses into a performance, where everyone acts and enjoys the overexcited, vicarious experience of a performer. Such an image represents all too well the last phase of the Este civilization. On the one hand, the city's pervasive masquerade seems to illustrate not only its grandeur but also its fragility: the young Tasso may have been totally overwhelmed and seduced by the lights, the colors, the luxuriant refinement of the performance, but a modern observer, aware that the Este court was bound to disappear from the Ferrarese stage in so few years, is inevitably tempted to read all this splendor as mere show, like a thin layer of scarcely reassuring make-up — as the typical case of a society, or at least an elite, dancing on the edge of an abyss. This picture is all too fitting, on the other hand, in relation to Tasso himself and to the personal mythology he began to cultivate very early about his life and his literary destiny. The city as a theater, a stage under spotlights: the young poet as actor, a performer surrounded by the audience of his dreams. The spectacular, hallucinatory quality of courtly life was personally lived, suffered, and mythologized by no one in the Renaissance better than by Torquato Tasso in Ferrara. The stress, the competitiveness, the frenzy and narcissism of the courtly stage had no better, subtler, or more enthusiastic performer than Tasso from the early 1570s until 1586.

Tasso's image of the city in his *Aminta* is, significantly, a very ambiguous one. Ferrara is described here in the words of Tirsi (a double for Tasso himself), who recalls his own first experience of the city. Mopso, the envious, unreliable shepherd under whose guise Tasso introduced his by-then hated Paduan mentor Sperone Speroni, had warned Tirsi against the dangers of the

---

[23] See *Gianluca overo delle maschere*, in Torquato Tasso, *Dialoghi*, ed. E. Raimondi (Florence: Sansoni, 1958), 675.

"gran cittade in riva al fiume" ["great city on the river's shores"] inhabited by "astuti e scaltri cittadini" ["astute and clever citizens"] e "cortigian malvagi" ["wicked courtiers"] and had especially badmouthed the court, "magazzino delle ciance" ["a warehouse of chatter"], "incantato alloggiamento" ["bewitched dwelling place"], the house of sorceresses and the theater of frightful metamorphoses. But his direct experience had been totally different. Tirsi had encountered a "felice albergo" ["happy lodging"] guarded by a man "d'aspetto magnanimo e robusto" ["of magnanimous and sturdy mien"] (that is, Duke Alfonso II), and filled with "celesti dee, ninfe leggiadre e belle" ["heavenly goddesses, lovely and graceful nymphs"] and endowed with "novi Lini ed Orfei" ["modern Linuses and Orpheuses"]. Among them was Elpino, the most prestigious of those poets — that is, Giambattista Pigna, the ducal secretary, who was then at the peak of his success. The happy ending of this experience is much more than an obligatory homage to the city and its lord. Tasso actually invested all his poetic resources in Ferrara, the duke, and the Este dynasty. Nevertheless, in the *Aminta* he seems worried about the unpredictable, treacherous, untrustworthy side of the court and is unable to suppress the anxiety that the place arouses in him beneath the glittering surface of his courtly encomium. Tasso is in fact a true product of the culture and life of the courts: he could breathe nowhere else; and yet he had to recognize that the air there was heavily polluted. Dependence on the courts, after all, ran in Tasso's family.

Tasso often seems haunted by the presence, or the memory, of his father Bernardo, an accomplished but less successful courtier and a skilled but not irresistible writer, who had sought both social and literary recognition all his life, carrying with him everywhere and working day and night on his cultivated, intelligent, polished — and ultimately disappointing — *Amadigi*.[24] One has the impression that Torquato wanted to be anyone other than Bernardo. In Venice in 1562, two years after his father had finally published in that same city his *Amadigi*, Torquato defiantly debuted with his first literary work, the *Rinaldo*. In these same years he attended classes taught by Sigonio in Padua and listened carefully to the lucubrations of the Aristotelians. But to seek his fortune, to write the poem that he hoped would supplant the *Orlando furioso* in the hearts of the public, he went to Ferrara. Stubbornly and with immense courage and ambition, he presented himself to the Este court as the new incarnation of the local tradition of chivalric literature. This link between the court and Tasso's literary ambition is essential for understanding not only

---

[24] A detailed reconstruction of Bernardo Tasso's life and literary career can be found in E. Williamson, *Bernardo Tasso* (Rome: Edizioni di Storia e Letteratura, 1951).

the *Jerusalem Delivered,* but also the trajectory of the *romanzo* in the sixteenth century in general. Tasso, of course, had also read his father's *Amadigi* in this light, and he knew firsthand of Bernardo's tormented elaboration of the poem, which had been shaped in its first version as a single-action, Homeric, epic narrative, but was later restructured as an interlaced *romanzo.* According to Torquato, there were good reasons for these revisions:

> Leggeva alcuni suoi canti al principe suo padrone; e quando eli commence a leggere, erano le camere piene di gentiluomini ascoltatori; ma nel fine, tutti erano spartiti: da la qual cosa egli prese argumento che l'unità dell'azione fosse poco dilettevole per sua natura, non per difetto d'arte che egli avesse . . . [P]er non perder il nome di buon cortigiano, non si curò di ritener a forza quello d'ottimo poeta.[25]
>
> ["He was reading some of his cantos to his lord the prince; and when he began reading, the rooms were full of listening gentlemen. But at the end, they had all disappeared. From this experience he took the lesson not that there was some defect in his own skill as a writer but that the unity of action gives little delight by its nature . . . [I]n order to preserve his reputation as a good courtier, however, he did not insist on keeping that of an excellent poet."]

Note the opposition between "cortigiano" and "poeta," and Torquato's approval of Bernardo's decision: artistic motives must recede if they are negatively received by the audience. In so many ways, when defending his *Liberata* Tasso always refers to the taste, approval, or agreement of the "common people," but he distinguishes this desired audience from both the masses and the specialists:

> Io non mi proposi mai di piacere al volgo stupido; ma non vorrei però solamente soddisfare ai maestri dell'arte. Anzi sono ambiziosissimo de l'applauso de gli uomini mediocri; e quasiché altrettanto affetto la buona opinione di questi tali quanto quella de' più intendenti. Prego dunque Vostra Signoria [Scipione Gonzaga] che me ne scriva quel tanto c'avrà potuto sottrarre dal parere de' cortigiani galanti e de gli uomini mezzani.[26]

---

[25] See the *Apologia della* Gerusalemme liberata in Torquato Tasso, *Prose*, ed. E. Mazzali (Milan-Naples: Ricciardi, 1959), 417.

[26] Torquato Tasso, *Lettere poetiche*, ed. C. Molinari (Parma: Guanda, 1995).

["I never set out to please the ignorant masses, and yet I want to satisfy more than just the artistic experts. Indeed, I am terribly interested in the applause of average men. I seek the good opinion of such men almost as much as that of more knowledgeable ones. And so I pray Your Lordship [Scipione Gonzaga] to write me whatever you may have gathered about the opinions of the gallant courtiers and the average men"].

One notes that for Tasso the taste of average men, as opposed to the abstractness of the Aristotelians or the pure theorists, is not "popular." It was the taste of the courts, "de' cortigiani galanti" — which he saw as a representative sample of the public — that Tasso sought, focused upon, and pursued in Ferrara. And yet the *Jerusalem Delivered* is hardly a dynastic poem. Yes, Rinaldo is another ancestor of the ruling family to whom the chivalric tradition of Ferrarese literature pays homage, but this theme remains very marginal to the poem. The collapse of the simulation of orality, here substituted by the rigorous impersonality of the epic mode, cuts off from the *Jerusalem Delivered* not only the presence of the court, but also every allusion to a courtly audience. Tasso carefully eliminates the performative code of the *romanzo* from his poem, so that his narrative stands in the void of epic solemnity and has nothing more to do with the cordial, interlocutory style of the *romanzo* and its capacity to include in the narrative a specific social ambiance. Ferrara has no place in the final product of its own chivalric literature. Thus while the *Liberata* could only have been born in Ferrara, and while it was intentionally engendered, conceived, and produced precisely there, Tasso used the city, its court, and its tradition as an ideal stage. Ferrara was a testing ground or a laboratory for previewing the reception of his poem and improving the design of his literary strategy. All this happened through a poet's cynical calculation, his obsessive investment of energies, his inflated expectations, which certainly surpassed anything the place could offer him and which probably caused his final, dramatic rejection. Tasso was thrown off the only stage he judged worthy of his performance.

Many times the melancholy of the late Tasso, with his madness, his imprisonment, and the turbulent circumstances of the *Liberata*'s publication, have been employed as a dramatic, emotional, and convincing ending for the history of Ferrara itself. The sorry fate of this poet has seemed a perfect analogue of the melancholic destiny of the Estense city. But this idea is more a rhetorical special effect than an historic truth. In Tasso's late years, after his release from Sant'Anna, he was able to rebuild his literary career, rewriting the *Liberata* into the *Conquistata* and the *Galealto* into the *Torrismondo*. He planned the editorial project of his *Rime* and converted himself to the vogue of the new religious poetry (writing the *Mondo creato*, *Lacrime della Vergine Maria*, and so on). These facts still await full scholarly recognition, and more work in this area could dramatically change our ideas about the late, sorry fate of this poet. In any case the end of Ferrara, with its devolution to the Holy See in 1598, could hardly be associated with the heroic dream of the Tassian epics or even with the noble ambitions of his last literary undertakings. Few endings were indeed less heroic than Ferrara's. Lucrezia d'Este sold out the city to her beloved cardinal, Cinzio Aldobrandini. Cesare d'Este grasped that further resistance would be noble but useless, so he packed up and left. And four days later Aldobrandini entered the city to a very warm welcome.

It is astonishing how easily the Ferrara of the Este disappeared. Perhaps the ease of the change tells us how fragile that power had been, how vulnerable it really was under the impressive surface of courtly masquerade. Nobody tried to stop or to limit Cesare's pillaging. He moved out of town taking with him as much as he could carry, as if the art and the treasures of the city were so many of his own personal belongings. Beyond that hurried vacating of the premises, a future of deprivation, loss, and effacement opened out for Ferrara. Paradoxically, that future created images of Ferrara that still endure: Ferrara as the "city of silence" in Gabriele D'Annunzio's decadent poetry; Ferrara as the empty, infinitely melancholic space of twentieth-century metaphysical painting; Ferrara as the concrete and yet intensely spiritual setting of Michelangelo Antonioni's cinematic imagination. This late Ferrara's void and its sense of absence seem so contemporary, so close to us. But the desolation is of old; it recalls to us the city's ancient vulnerability and its still-unresolved trauma.

Marriage and Succession in the House of Este: A Literary Perspective[1]

Jane Fair Bestor

The House of Este stands out among the ruling dynasties of Italy on account of its unique succession. For almost one hundred fifty years, illegitimates ruled its dominions. The first member of the house to be elected lord of Ferrara, Obizzo II (r. 1264–1293), was illegitimately born. From 1352 until 1471, not a single legitimately born Este held office. Then, in 1471, Borso d'Este, first duke of Ferrara, Modena, and Reggio, died and was succeeded by his legitimate brother Ercole. This event ended what had become virtually a custom of illegitimate succession.[2]

At the same time that the Este were consolidating their dominions, governments throughout Italy and Western Europe were becoming increasingly active in regulating family life through statutory and other initia-

---

[1] I thank the Lila AchesonWallace Reader's Digest Endowment Fund at Villa I Tatti, The Harvard University Center for Italian Renaissance Studies, for its support, and Patricia Emison for inviting me to present a talk on this material at the University of New Hampshire. Her thoughtful comments and the hospitality of her family made the occasion a memorable one. I am also grateful to David Quint for his close reading of two drafts of this essay as my ideas evolved. He has helped me to clarify my arguments and saved me from numerous mistakes; any that remain are my responsibility. The final version reflects the meticulous editing of Leslie MacCoull.

[2] For the legal, moral, and political dimensions of the Estense succession, see Jane Fair Bestor, "Bastardy and Legitimacy in the Formation of a Regional State in Italy: The Estense Succession," *Comparative Studies in Society and History* 38 (1996): 549–85; eadem, "Gli illegittimi e beneficiati della casa estense," in *Il Rinascimento. Situazioni e personaggi*, ed. Adriano Prosperi (Ferrara: Corbo, 2000), 77–102.

tives.[3] They showed a special concern for marriage, the basic institution of lay society, which sanctified the family and its property arrangements, made procreation licit, and supported the rearing of children for citizenship.[4] The Este were no exception; the statutes of Ferrara promulgated by Borso d'Este in 1456 included a provision regulating the succession of illegitimates in order to encourage procreation in marriage.[5] The Church also participated in this

---

[3] See, for example, James A. Brundage, *Law, Sex, and Christian Society in Medieval Europe* (Chicago: University of Chicago Press, 1987). Representative of the general trend are statutory initiatives respecting illegitimates in Florence, for which see Thomas Kuehn, *Illegitimacy in Renaissance Florence* (Ann Arbor: University of Michigan Press, 2002), chap. 2.

[4] Guido Ruggiero, "Marriage, Love, Sex, and Renaissance Civic Morality," in *Sexuality and Gender in Early Modern Europe*, ed. James Grantham Turner (Cambridge: Cambridge University Press, 1993), 10–30. Ruggiero argues that marriage was central to a moral discourse that "served both to legitimate and define the city-state" and that was distinct from another separate and coherent discourse bound up with an illicit world of love and sex outside of marriage (11). This emphasis on separate discourses reflects his heavy reliance on ideal portrayals of marriage and family by Republican humanists such as Leon Battista Alberti and Francesco Barbaro.

[5] "Since by the Mosaic or old law it is ordained thus, that the son of a handmaid will not be heir with a free son, and in order that everyone will strive more readily and ardently to procreate legitimate offspring, we decree that no one not born from a lawful marriage, though legitimized with whatsoever phrase or form or privilege, can or should succeed to his father or other agnate on intestacy, unless he was legitimized by the express will or consent of the father or agnate whose heredity is at stake before or after the death, as the case may be, if legitimate and natural children or other agnates are alive who could and ought by law to succeed to the person of the deceased. We do not aim on this account to apply ourselves to legitimation, but only to the goods of citizens and subjects for public advantage [Cum ex lege mosaica vel veteri sancitum sic non erit filius ancille heres cum filio libero [a paraphrase of the Vulgate Bible, Genesis 21:10 and Galatians 4:30]: et ut facilius et ardentius studeant omnes ad procreandam sobolem legittimam: statuimus nullum non natum ex legittimo matrimonio, etiam legittimatum cum quacumque clausula vel forma aut privilegio, posse aut debere succedere patri ab intestato vel alteri agnato, nisi legittimatus fuerit de voluntate aut consensu expresso patris vel agnati de cuius hereditate agitur ante mortem vel post mortem, singula singulis congrue referendis, extantibus filiis vel aliis agnatis legittimis et naturalibus qui de iure succedere possent et deberent persone defuncte. Non intendentes propterea ad legittimationem manum porrigere, sed solum de bonis civium et subditorum pro utilitate publica]": *Statuta civitatis Ferrariae* ([1476], Book 2, rubrica cxlii, *Quod legitimati non succedant*. Kuehn, *Illegitimacy in Renaissance Florence*, 75, views this as a tough law. But as the consent at issue was a requirement of the *ius commune*, it seems to me to speak more to Borso's need to portray himself as a guardian of public morality than anything else.

disciplining of family life. Although canonists had long condemned concubinage among the laity as well as clergy, the "multitude of sinners" had discouraged efforts to enforce the law. The gap between law and practice became a matter of increasing concern, until finally in 1514 the Fifth Lateran Council ordered the enforcement of punitive measures to ensure universal compliance.[6]

This essay examines literary treatments of the Estense succession between the reigns of Borso and Ercole II (d.1559) in light of the widespread and growing concern to promote marriage and lawful procreation. In part one I consider two epic poems from the fifteenth century: Tito Strozzi's neo-Latin *Borsiad* and the *Orlando Innamorato* of Matteo Maria Boiardo. Written in the vernacular and already in print during Boiardo's life, *Orlando innamorato* has captivated readers over the centuries. The *Borsiad*, in contrast, remained in manuscript and was almost unknown until Walther Ludwig's painstaking edition appeared in 1977.[7] There he discusses the literary sources of Strozzi's treatment of the succession and places it in social context. No one has looked systematically at the themes of illegitimacy and succession in *Orlando innamorato*. Yet illegitimacy figures importantly in the Carolingian and Arthurian traditions on which Boiardo drew, and the Estense succession invited attention to this theme. Certain twelfth-and thirteenth-century poems represent both Carlemagne and Arthur as bastards, and in a distinctive Franco-Italian tradition, Orlando himself, rather than his uncle Charlemagne, is a bastard.[8]

I show here that the two poems are in conversation on the recent history of the House of Este. From their authors' shared knowledge of Ferrarese

---

[6] J. Alberigo et al., eds., *Conciliorum oecumenicorum decreta*, 3rd ed. (Bologna: Istituto per le scienze religiose, 1972), 623, my translation: "Whether they are laity or clergy, men who keep concubines should be punished by the penalties of the same canons, and the tolerance, or bad custom, which should rather be called a corruption, of those in the past on account of the multitude of sinners or any other excuse of any sort, should not favor them, but they should be severely punished according to the judgement of law [Concubinarii autem, sive laici sive clerici fuerint, eorundem canonum poenis multentur: neque superiorum tolerantia seu prava consuetudo, quae potius curruptela dicenda est, a multitudine peccantium, aliave quaelibet excusatio eis aliquo modo suffragetur, sed iuxta iuris censuram severe puniantur]." See also Brundage, *Law, Sex, and Christian Society*, 514–15.

[7] Walther Ludwig, ed., *Die Borsias des Tito Strozzi: Ein lateinisches Epos der Renaissance* (Munich: Wilhelm Fink Verlag, 1977).

[8] Dominique Boutet, "Bâtardise et sexualité dans l'image littéraire de la royauté (XIIe–XIIIe siècles)," in *Femmes: Mariages-lignages, XIIe–XIVe siècles* (Brussels: De Boeck University, 1992), 55–68 and sources cited. See also note 45 below.

history and mores and from their intertwined life histories, one would expect them to offer a similar perspective on events. Both men came from noble families. Boiardo's mother was Strozzi's sister Lucia. Although Strozzi, born in 1425, was of an older generation, he outlived his nephew (c.1440–1494), dying only months after Duke Ercole I d'Este in 1505.[9] Both men received a humanist education and served as courtiers and administrators for the Este. But they began their poems under different lords, a circumstance that stamped their approaches to the succession.

In part two I turn to the succession in the sixteenth century and to the use of literary texts to try to shape events. By the early 1500s, the social and political climate was changing. Ercole I had justified his accession to office in 1471 on the grounds that he was Niccolò III's oldest legitimate son. Papal and imperial law also required legitimacy for the succession to duchies held in fief, although history showed that this requirement might be subject to negotiation. After the death of Ercole's oldest legitimate son and successor, Alfonso I, in 1534, a conflict within the House of Este turned on whether Alfonso had married his mistress, Laura Eustochia. On this question hinged their sons' ability to claim legitimation by subsequent marriage, the strongest possible form of legitimation. I show that a letter from the writer Pietro Aretino to Laura served as a catalyst to generate public belief that the couple had married, making their sons legitimate and eligible to rule.

The way the European dynasties reproduced themselves had legal and ethical significance. The task before us is to understand how our texts exploit these legal and ethical meanings of action in their language and structure. The question is how to proceed. Historians may be integrating literature increasingly into their "documentary field," but there is no consensus among them or between them and literary critics on how to go about it.[10]

---

[9] For Strozzi's life, see Walther Ludwig, "Einleitung," in *Die Borsias des Tito Strozzi*, 11–59; for Boiardo's, F. Forti, "Matteo Maria Boiardo," in *Dizionario Biografico degli Italiani*, ed. Alberto M. Ghisalberti. 59+ vols. (Rome: Istituto della Enciclopedia italiana, 1960–), 11: 211–23.

[10] Jacques Le Goff, "Preface," to Dominique Boutet and Armand Strubel, *Littérature, Politique, et Société dans la France du Moyen Âge* (Paris: Presses Universitaires de France, 1979), 9–18, here 18, notes historians' increasing use of literary texts with optimism about their capacity to respect both the specificity of a work and its character as a "document of total history" involving complex relations among society, literature, and the structure of powers. François Rigolot is less sanguine in underscoring the differences in approach between social and political historians, on the one hand, and literary scholars on the other: François Rigolot, "A Literary Critic's Response to a Social Historian: The Gifts of Montaigne," *Journal of Medieval and Renaissance Studies* 17 (1987): 111–28.

In *Epic and Empire*, David Quint observes that epic poetry from the time of Virgil on was an "overtly political" genre. But the narrative creates its own world, and the political content of epic is accordingly expressed through topical and poetic allusions. Tracing these allusions, Quint argues, provides the best hope for grasping the way a work is connected to its historical occasion and to the epic tradition.[11]

An allusion "usually presupposes a close relation between poet and audience, a social emphasis, a community of knowledge, and a prizing of tradition. . . ."[12] Many kinds of knowledge may be implicated in the structure of meaning of a literary text. In the case of the poems, the historian's archives can contribute to their recovery. The historian may also contribute a sense of problem based on knowledge of the situation in which a text was produced.

Aretino's letter provokes puzzlement. Ostensibly a letter of condolence on the death of Laura's father, it is also the first written testimony of her purported marriage to Alfonso. The social roles of the writer and addressee and the very clarity of reference raise questions about intended audience and aim. I argue that Aretino manipulates the classical letter of condolence in anticipation of the rules of evidence in marriage cases. If this suggestion is correct, the success of the letter depended on disguising its goal. In cases such as this, the historian's archive can help to discover the hidden by providing information about a text's effects and the circumstances, legal and political, that made them desirable.

Before we turn to the texts themselves, a brief review of the succession is in order. It is a striking fact, given the centrality of marriage in Catholic theology and in canon law, that the illegitimately born Este who ruled Ferrara held office with papal support. In the early fourteenth century, a series of popes

---

[11] David Quint, *Epic and Empire: Politics and Generic Form From Virgil to Milton* (Princeton: Princeton University Press, 1993), 8, 14. For the most part, students of *Orlando Innamorato* have not identified any political agenda in it beyond the encomiastic: Jo Ann Cavallo, "L'*Orlando Innamorato* come *speculum principis*," in *Il Boiardo e il mondo estense nel Quattrocento*, ed. Giuseppe Anceschi and Tina Matarrese, 2 vols. (Padua: Editrice Antenore, 1998), 1: 297–321, here 297. Yet both the epic and romance traditions on which Boiardo draws show a concern for issues of rulership, even if the epics are more obviously and consistently "public minded": W. T .H. Jackson, *The Anatomy of Love* (New York: Columbia University Press, 1971), 15; Elspeth Kennedy, *Lancelot and the Grail* (Oxford: Clarendon Press, 1986), 311.

[12] Earl Miner, "Allusion," in *The New Princeton Encyclopedia of Poetry and Poetics*, ed. A. Preminger and T. V. F. Brogan (Princeton: Princeton University Press, 1993), 38–40, here 39. He defines allusion as "a poet's deliberate incorporation of identifiable elements from other sources, preceding or contemporaneous, textual or extratextual" (38–39).

tried to bring Ferrara under direct ecclesiastical rule, even attempting to discredit the marquises by bringing them to trial for heresy on the grounds that they (among other misdeeds) "seized and took the wives and daughters of men, knowing them carnally, saying that it was not a sin."[13] The failure of this effort led to the establishment of an apostolic vicariate over Ferrara that confirmed the Este as temporal rulers, though now on behalf of the Church.

Under the mantle of papal legitimacy, the marquises continued to pursue erotic pleasures outside of marriage. In the 1340s, Pope Clement VI ordered Obizzo III (d. 1352) to marry his mistress, Lippa Ariosto, as a condition for endorsing his plan of succession. The marquis complied — but only as Lippa was dying, in order to ensure that all of his children were born illegitimate.[14] The relative weakness of successive popes and marquises suggested the wisdom of mutual support, a course which ensured that the negotiations concerning legitimation entered into the mutual constitution of the papal and Estense states within the factional framework of peninsular politics. Reasons of state prevailed over theological considerations. In a signal instance they also prevailed over the law of succession. Niccolò III (d. 1441) lacked legitimate sons but had numerous illegitimately born offspring of both sexes. In 1425, he beheaded his second wife and his oldest illegitimate son for having an affair. He then married a third time and produced two legitimate sons, Ercole and Sigismondo, only to appoint the illegitimately born Leonello as his universal heir. Given the existence of the legitimates, Leonello's succession to all of Niccolò III's dominions violated the rules of the European common law, or *ius commune*.[15]

In his last testament, Niccolò declared that primogeniture should be the rule of succession.[16] By making Leonello his heir, he made clear that legitimacy was not a requirement but only a preference contingent on other factors, such as age and ability. On Leonello's death in 1450, his illegitimate brother Borso, who followed him in birth order, succeeded to office instead of either his legitimate son Niccolò or his much younger legitimate brother, Ercole. Borso justified his elevation by election. His success demonstrated the continuing importance of relations of power within the house and the strength of the pattern of fraternal succession that had prevailed in the fourteenth century. Despite previous commitments to Niccolò di Leonello, Pope Nicholas V

---

[13] Friedrich Bock, "Der Este-Prozess von 1321," *Archivum fratrum praedicatorum* 7 (1937): 31–111, esp. 45, 71.

[14] See text below at notes 76–77 for further discussion.

[15] Bestor, "Bastardy and Legitimacy," 570–72.

[16] Archivio di Stato di Modena (hereafter ASMo), A.S.E., Casa e Stato, b.324, fasc.10, 26 December 1442 (1441). See also Bestor, "Bastardy and Legitimacy," 571–72.

quickly confirmed Borso as papal vicar over Ferrara. The deals the Este worked out with their papal overlords in the fourteenth and fifteenth centuries reflected their concern first, to preserve concord among brothers and later, to maintain the unity of the patrimony. They considered these factors key to maintaining political stability. By comparison, illegitimacy was a lesser problem.

I. Epic Poetry and the Succession in the Fifteenth Century

Tito Strozzi's *Borsiad*

Tito Strozzi planned his neo-Latin epic, the *Borsiad*, as a celebration of the life and deeds of Borso d'Este. After Borso's death in 1471, he expanded its scope to include the contemporary history and genealogy of the House of Este, hoping, without success, to win Ercole's support for the project.[17] To justify the illegitimate Borso's assumption of office, Strozzi fused motifs from classical mythology and Christian salvation history. The narrative begins with an assembly of the gods, who seek a cure for humans' persistently quarrelsome and evil ways. Jupiter, who as omnipotent creator is an allegory of God the Father, decides to create a man from the House of Este who "will excel the great minds and acts of his ancestors, give new temples to the gods, and keep his peoples in peace in the midst of the tumult of arms."[18] This ideal ruler, Jupiter decrees, is "to be born the way that deities are born, owing nothing to any bonds or laws of human marriage, from which our power now derogates by the considered reason of things."[19]

---

[17] For a discussion of the genesis and transmission of the work, see Ludwig, "Einleitung," and, in the context of a polemic against the concept of courtly culture, Kristen Lippincott, "The Neo-Latin Historical Epics of the North Italian Courts: An Examination of 'Courtly Culture' in the Fifteenth Century," *Renaissance Studies* 3 (1989): 415–28, here 422–25, 427. Strozzi had completed the first three books, including an account of the coupling of Borso's parents, and was working on the fourth book at the time of Borso's death: Ludwig, "Einleitung," 38–39.

[18] "Ipse virum magna virtute . . . / . . . creabo. / . . . Ille patrum ingentes animos superabit et acta, / caelitibus nova templa dabit medioque tumultu /armorum populos tranquilla in pace tenebit": *Borsias*, ed. Ludwig, 1.360–361, 366–368 (86). For Jupiter's attributes, see *Borsias* 1.56–59 (78, also 234).

[19] "Illum etenim nasci volumus, quo numina ritu / nascuntur, nullis vinclis nec legibus ullis / mortalis thalami debentem, nostra quibus nunc / derogat expensa rerum ratione potestas": *Borsias* 1.362–365 (86).

In changing the law for Borso's parents, Jupiter places his act in implicit relation to the dispensing power of the prince in civil and canon law. Acting by his authority and "from certain knowledge and from a lawful cause," the pope or other prince could dispense a bastard to hold a high temporal or spiritual dignity, notwithstanding any defect of birth, or any laws, constitutions, or customs to the contrary, even derogating from his own laws if necessary.[20] According to medieval legal-political theory, the pope, acting with absolute power (*potestas absoluta*) conceived by analogy with God's power, could even dispense from divine laws — if he did not thereby induce people to sin. But he could dispense from the law only for good cause. One such cause was expediency, understood as the primacy of public over private welfare.[21] Furthermore, dispensation could apply only to *past* actions, in order to reconcile cause with the need to discourage unlawful behavior.

In decreeing the mode of Borso's birth, Jupiter exercises his absolute power to free Borso's parents *in advance* from the requirement of marriage for sexual intercourse. This event in epic time thus anticipates and cancels the opprobrium of their extramarital liaison, which was, in fact, adulterous (a point that is omitted). Jupiter's cause, or reason, is expediency. Putting an end to human woes through Borso's birth is more important than his parents' marital status. Expediency, by implication, must govern the conduct of princes, freeing it from the rules that apply to ordinary mortals. Born in the way that deities are born, Borso is, in effect, a god.[22]

---

[20] See, for example, Pope Martin V's bull ratifying the vicariate of Ferrara for Niccolò III, with Leonello to succeed him after his death: ASMo, A.S.E., Casa e Stato, Membranacei, cass.24, no.4, 12 December 1430.

[21] For the concept of absolute power in theology and its appropriation by the canonists, and for the doctrine of *causa* with respect to dispensation and the dispensing power generally, see Kenneth Pennington, *The Prince and the Law, 1200–1600* (Berkeley: University of California Press, 1993), 54–65.

[22] The epithet *divus*, meaning "godlike, divine," first came into prominent use in Estense circles with reference to Borso: Werner L. Gundersheimer, *Ferrara: The Style of a Renaissance Despotism* (Princeton: Princeton University Press, 1973), 127–28. Literary, artistic, and personal factors all played a role in this development. On a visit to Ferrara during Leonello's reign, Aeneas Silvius Piccolomini (later Pope Pius II) observed that the marquis had "a very handsome brother . . . whom the Ferrarese worship almost as a god. He is more handsome than can be described, pleasant and forbearing, outstanding in liberality, robust of body, without fault [In sero venit frater eius admodum pulcer, Borsius nomine, quem Ferrarienses quasi deum colunt. Hic forma plusquam dici potest pulcra est, facetus et modestus, liberalitate insignis, robustus corpore, nulla in eo menda est]": Aeneas Silvius Piccolomini (Pope Pius II), *De viris illustribus*, ed. Adrianus Van Heck (Vatican City: Biblioteca Apostolica Vaticana, 1991), 23.

By observing the law in derogating from the law of marriage, Jupiter creates the fiction of a lawful union. To sustain it Borso's parents must couple according to basic principles of law and morality. If his father, Niccolò III d'Este, were to take his mother, Stella Tolomei, by force, he would commit the crime of *stuprum*, or rape, against a high-born virgin. But if Stella were to allow herself to be seduced, she would defame herself and thereby irrevocably compromise Leonello's and Borso's probity.[23] Jupiter's will is accordingly easier to decree than to realize. Stella flees Niccolò's advances. She retreats to the dominion of the Bentivoglio and seeks "to follow the laws and life of the unmarried [goddess] Diana."[24] It takes more than the rest of book one and half of book two to achieve their coupling in an expenditure of poetic and divine labor that testifies to the importance of the issues at stake: the moral integrity of the parents and thus the honor of their sons.

At Jupiter's behest, Mercury appears to Stella and tells the "pure virgin" not to disdain Niccolò's prayers. She is destined to produce outstanding offspring who will come from a priestly race (the Tolomei were related to the Piccolomini of Siena, the family of Pope Pius II [r. 1458–1464]).[25] Stella is not sure, however, whether she has had a true vision of the god or just a vain dream. She finally confers with her old nurse, a substitute for her dead mother, who counsels her to preserve the fame of her virginal modesty — unless Niccolò joins himself to her in lawful marriage.[26] Stella remains committed to chastity, though Cupid, at Jupiter's behest, has shot her with his arrows and she now begins to feel the effects. Once she is ready to love, the impatient Jupiter orders Juno and Venus to remove Stella from her abode in Bologna and bring her to Niccolò in Ferrara, where the goddesses are to "join her to him in the covenant of the conjugal bed."[27] Niccolò thus triumphs over his beloved's scruples without committing a crime, while Stella retains her integrity in not yielding to his advances of her own free will. Yet her favorable response to Niccolò makes the union consensual, thus affirming a basic principle of Christian marriage.

---

[23] In voluntary sex crimes, women were commonly considered to be the more serious offenders: see Brundage, *Law, Sex and Christian Society*, 305–7, 396.

[24] *Borsias,* 1.395–396 (87).

[25] *Borsias*, 2.52–75 (93–94).

[26] *Borsias,* 2.163–165 (96).

[27] "Huic illam socialis foedere lecti / iungite!": *Borsias*, 2.342–343 (100). A play on words here assimilates the couple's irregular union to marriage: according to Charlton T. Lewis and Charles Short, eds., *A Latin Dictionary* (Oxford: Clarendon, 1975), s.v., "socialis" is used "in Ovid several times like conjugialis, *of marriage, conjugal, nuptial*... "

Allusions to the Annunciation add a religious sanction to the emphasis on legality, enriching the narrative pattern of fall and salvation. Mercury, Jupiter's messenger, recalls the Angel Gabriel in Luke 1:26–38, while the "pure virgin" Stella exemplifies the Virgin Mary.[28] She ensures that Borso, like Jesus, will be born of a priestly as well as a princely line. This casting of the Christian narrative in classical form sets the scene for the appearance of Borso, the "Christlike priest," as Ludwig aptly describes him.[29] In blurring the boundary between divine birth in classical mythology and in Christian theology, the *Borsiad* hints at a further parallel between Borso and Jesus. Drawing on St. Jerome, the canon lawyer Gratian affirmed that Christ "is the true high-priest born of adulterous minglings."[30]

After describing the coupling of Niccolò and Stella and the birth of Leonello and Borso, the *Borsiad* shifts to Leonello's death, which raises the problem of the succession. Jupiter again intervenes, sending Juno to ensure the virtuous Borso's election and thereby stave off chaos, since Niccolò di Leonello is too young to rule and Ercole and Sigismondo are absent in Naples. Meliaduse, whom Niccolò III had passed over in favor of Leonello, wishes to give up his chance at office in recognition of his younger brother's outstanding qualities.[31] In contrast to other accounts of Borso's elevation, then, Strozzi stresses not the will of the people but divine choice.[32]

Among the three early Renaissance neo-Latin epics that centered on the lives of illegitimately born lords — Francesco Sforza, Sigismondo Malatesta, and Borso d'Este — the *Borsiad* stands out for its concern with the hero's

---

[28] *Borsias*, 251.

[29] *Borsias*, 255. See Boutet, "Bâtardise et sexualité," 65–68, for a medieval variant of this salvation scheme in the story of King Arthur. Boutet explains the figure of the bastard savior king in structural terms: "The king, maintainer of the order of the world, is at the same time the living expression of the fundamental disorder that marks the terrestial . . ." (68).

[30] Gratian, "Decretum," in *Corpus iuris canonici*, ed. E. Friedberg (Leipzig: Officina Bernhardi Tauchnitz, 1879) vol.1, 222, D.56 c.8: "Et sicut ille [Iesus Christus] verus est pontifex ex adulterinis natus coniunctionibus. . . ." Gratian takes Jerome's text to affirm that only faith and adherence to Christ's example, and not the circumstances of one's birth, are necessary qualifications for the priesthood (cf. Matthew 1:1–16, Jerome, "Commentaria in Evangelium S. Matthaei," in *PL* 26:22). Following Gratian's interpretation of the whole canonic tradition, the Church taught otherwise, but the text was enshrined in the canonic corpus and thus became readily accessible for other interpretations and applications.

[31] *Borsias*, 2.413–549 (102–6).

[32] *Borsias*, 258–59.

illegitimacy: why?[33] One reason is that Borso took office despite the claims of two legitimate candidates, whereas Sforza and Malatesta had no competition from their immediate families. His position thus needed defense, and Strozzi gives a bold one: Jupiter/God himself has set aside the rules of marriage for Borso's parents. Another reason for the focus on Borso's birth has to do with his mother. As a kinswoman of Pius II, Stella offered an opportunity for politically resonant poetic invention.[34] As a mistress, however, she also created a problem, one that was exacerbated by her connection to Pius both as pope and in his earlier life as Aeneas Silvius Piccolomini, secretary to Emperor Frederick III.

In his biography of Frederick, Piccolomini asserts that Frederick considered Borso to be unworthy (*indignum*) of becoming duke of Modena and Reggio, a title that Borso coveted, on account of his illegitimate birth. But Borso's money and lavish hospitality during the emperor's trip to Italy in 1452 went far to assuage this concern, as did the praises of Borso by his envoys and the envoys of his cities. Furthermore, Piccolomini tells us, "it was agreed" that even if Borso's mother "was not Niccolò's lawful wife, she was nonetheless a noblewoman from the ancient house of the Sienese Tolomei, a wise and honorable woman, and many people related that she was corrupted not by money or pleading but by princely force and power, and that Niccolò also promised to marry her."[35]

---

[33] The first was Francesco Filelfo's (unfinished) *Sforziad*, begun by June of 1451; the second was Basinio Basini's epic poem, the *Hesperis*, celebrating the martial exploits of Sigismondo Malatesta: Lippincott, "Neo-Latin Historical Epics," 418–20. The *Hesperis* is available in L. Drudi, ed., *Basini Parmensis poetae opera praestantiora nunc primum edita et opportunis commentariis illustrata*, 2 vols. in 3 (Rimini: Typo Albertiniana, 1794), 1:1–288. The *Sforziad* exists only in manuscript form, and I rely here on the summary in Carlo de' Rosmini, *Vita di Francesco Filelfo da Tolentino*, 3 vols. (Milan: Musi, 1808), 2:158–74.

[34] Strozzi calls attention twice to Stella's connection to Pius, at *Borsiad* 1.409–413 (87) and 2.70–73 (93). He also gives the origin of her family as Siena and frequently refers to her by the family name of Tolomei, including several references to the "Tolomeia virgo," whereas her family in Ferrara went by the name of dell'Assassino: *Borsias*, 1.390, 2.50, 2.181, 2.205, 2.239, 2.333, (86, 93, 96–98, 100). The issue of maternal rank raised in this paper invites comparison with the discussion in Boutet, "Bâtardise et sexualité," 60–64, and is dealt with extensively in my book manuscript, for which see note 70.

[35] "Matrem eius etsi legitima Nicolai coniunx non fuerat, nobilem tamen ex vetusta Ptolomaeorum Senensium domo natam constabat, honestam et sapientem foeminam, neque pretio neque precibus sed vi corruptam, et potentia principia, cui etiam promissum fuisse matrimonium quamplurimi tradiderunt": Aeneas Silvius Piccolomini (Pope Pius II), *Historia rerum Friderici Tertii Imperatoris* (Strasbourg: J. Staedelli et J. F. Spoor, 1685), 94–95; see also *Borsias*, 253. Documentary sources suggest that Niccolò made a deal with

Because of the kinship between his family and the Tolomei, Piccolomini had an interest in how Stella was portrayed. Piccolomini also represents Frederick as being deeply concerned with the rank and morals of Borso's mother. Stella came from a respectable family, and her honor could be plausibly defended in terms of a narrative of female frailty defenseless before princely aggression. We have no independent evidence confirming Piccolomini's report of the deliberations or any reason to think that the biography, written between 1452 and 1458, circulated very widely or had any impact during Borso's reign.[36] But allegations of sexual aggression on Niccolò's part would have undermined Estense claims to rule by virtue: assault on a high-born virgin was a crime and a tyrannous act.[37] It was wholly inconsistent with Borso's emphasis on his own adherence to justice and his theme of justice as a virtue inhering in his family's blood.[38]

Stella's family and that the bride and her family did well by the arrangement: For an impressive list of donations made by Niccolò to Stella in April of 1402, around the beginning of their liaison, see ASMo, Camera, Notai camerali ferraresi, Jacobus Delaito, XXIII, fols.182r–186r. Bestor, "Gli illegitimi e beneficiati," 97, n.23 mentions some of the positions held by members of Stella's family at the Estense court during and after Niccolò's lifetime.

[36] It appears not to have been published until the seventeenth century, in the edition cited in the preceding note.

[37] Machiavelli asserts that what makes a prince hated above all is being a usurper of the property and women of his subjects: Niccolò Machiavelli, *Opere*, ed. Rinaldo Rinaldi, gen. ed. Alessandro Montevecchi, 4 vols. (Turin: UTET, 1971–), 1:305. Ludwig notes the parallels between Piccolomini's account and the depiction of Stella's character in the *Borsiad*, but the account is too generic to allow us to conclude that Strozzi had the history in mind in developing the narrative: *Borsias*, 253.

[38] For Borso's celebration of justice and Tito Strozzi's praise of him as "most just" on the inscription of his monument, see Charles M. Rosenberg, *The Este Monuments and Urban Redevelopment in Renaissance Ferrara* (Cambridge: Cambridge University Press, 1997), chap. 6. In response to an accusation of fraud against his nephew, Niccolò di Leonello, Borso responded: "We thank the most high God that in his mercy he has endowed our natural instinct in such a form that not only we, but all those of our house have placed this virtue [justice] as the principal and outstanding item before all the others, seeming to us as is the truth that this is the one that makes man eternal, and that it makes him illustrious with every perfection of virtue, when he is adorned with some spark of this justice [Regratiamo l'altissimo dio che ni ha per sua clementia dotati il nostro instincto naturale in forma che nonche nui, ma tuti quelli de casa nostra habiamo preposta questa virtu come capo principale et singulare a tute le altre, parendoni come è il vero che questa sia quella che facia l'homo eterno, et che'l renda illustre de ogni perfectione de virtù, quando l'è ornato di qualche sintilla de epsa justitia]": Letter (2 March 1471) from Borso d'Este to Hieronymus de' Alegri da Verona, ASMo, A.S.E., Casa e Stato, Cancelleria C–2, c.32.

Piccolomini's elevation to pope as Pius II (r.1458–1464) raised anew the issue of his relationship to Stella Tolomei. To complicate matters, he also became hostile to Borso for not supporting his plan for a crusade. Pius took revenge in his memoirs for this failure to remember his advocacy of Borso's imperial investiture, attacking the duke's character and calling attention to the long history of illegitimate succession in his house:

> It is an extraordinary thing about that family that within our fathers' memory no legitimate heir has ever inherited the principate; the sons of their mistresses have been so much more fortunate than those of their wives. It is a circumstance contrary not only to Christian custom but to the law of almost all nations. Niccolò, a bastard of our time, was a man of great abilities but given over to pleasure. . . . Niccolò had several sons, both legitimate and illegitimate. His legitimate children were prevented from succeeding him by their father's own decision. He designated as his successor his bastard son by a Sienese concubine, Leonello. . . . Leonello was succeeded by Borso, his brother by the same mother. Leonello's son was passed over either because he was legitimate or because he was absent and a minor.[39]

In evoking the concept of the law of nations (*ius gentium*) from Justinian's *Digest*, the phrase "contrary . . . to the law of almost all nations (*omnium fere gentium legibus adversa*)" suggests that the comportment of the Este not only violated Christian law, but was also unnatural. Pius uses irony to underscore the point. The accession of illegitimates was not a last resort, a solution dictated by the lack of legitimate sons, but the product of a deliberate choice.

Pius's *Commentaries* illustrate the use of defamatory tactics as a means of social control.[40] Honor was a good and a form of social capital. It was therefore

---

[39] Aeneas Silvius Piccolomini (Pope Pius II), *The Commentaries of Pius II*, ed. F. Gragg, 5 vols., Smith College Studies in History (Northampton, MA: Smith College, 1937–1957), vol. 25, Bk. 2 (1939–1940), 181–82. The *Commentaries* were not published until the late sixteenth century, nor did they circulate widely in manuscript, yet there is some evidence to suggest that copies did circulate: see Gary Ianziti, *Humanistic Historiography under the Sforzas* (Oxford: Clarendon Press, 1988), 165–67. The pope probably also conveyed his views orally.

[40] These tactics included paintings, displayed on the walls of public buildings, that showed their victims hung in effigy or in other poses surrounded by devils and symbols of the vices: Samuel Y. Edgerton, *Pictures and Punishment: Art and Criminal Prosecution during the Florentine Renaissance* (Ithaca: Cornell University Press, 1985), chaps. 2 and 3. Pius II had his archenemy Sigismondo Malatesta, lord of Rimini, burned in effigy

a fit object of revenge upon those who failed to live up to their commitments or to an approved standard of behavior. Defamation or the risk of defamation was matched by heroic image making such as we find in Strozzi's poem.

The factional character of political life in Italy encouraged the production of messages concerning reputation, or *fama*. The strength of factions depended on the unity of their members, who were open to attack if they displayed insufficient zeal or switched allegiance. But if a preoccupation with *fama* — one's own and everybody else's — was daily business in the Renaissance, what, if anything, was special about the situation that faced illegitimately born rulers? The answer is that illegitimates were thought to be predisposed to vice because of their defective origin. The jurists considered honor a necessary qualification for those who exercised great legal power, in order to ensure their proper use of discretion. The exercise of *imperium*, the power of command, was a noble office, though not one that necessarily required nobility of birth.[41] In legal theory illegitimates were defective; as a class they were considered incapable of exercising the self-restraint essential to honor.[42] At the same time, it was recognized that some illegitimately born persons were potentially great leaders and that necessity might require their elevation to positions of power. Pius's treatment of Borso shows that once in power they became effectively legitimates — until their conduct suggested otherwise.

The *Borsiad* presents us with an elaborate "nuptial" drama that transforms the criminal and sinful character of Borso's adulterous conception and birth into a cosmic scheme of salvation. This scheme was connected to the historical and literary circumstances in which it was produced: the recent history of the succession and the contemporary vogue for neo-Latin epic. It was also informed by a legal doctrine and associated moral discourse that made that history and constructions of Borso's birth damaging for justifications of Estense

in front of St. Peter's and described his actions in his *Commentaries*, thereby spreading Malatesta's notoriety further: Edgerton, *Pictures and Punishment*, 70, n. 41.

[41] See, for example, Bartolus de Saxoferrato, *Commentaria in primam Digesti veteris partem* (Rome: Il Cigno Galileo Galilei, 1996; reprint, anastatic copy of 1526 Venetian edition by Baptista de Tortis), D.2. l.3, fol. 50v. Myron Gilmore suggests that in distinguishing between the "officium nobile iudicis" and the "officium mercenarium," Bartolus seems to apprehend "the distinction in the Roman constitution between that part of the magistrate's power in which he had discretion and that in which he was bound by the law": Myron Piper Gilmore, *Argument from Roman Law in Political Thought 1200–1600* (Cambridge, MA: Harvard University Press, 1941), 38.

[42] See most recently Kuehn, *Illegitimacy in Renaissance Florence*, chap.1. Kuehn notes the exclusion of illegitimates in Florence from the Arte dei Giudici e Notai, which effectively excluded them from practicing as notaries or lawyers (80).

rule and that, in any case, controlled the terms of the strategy available to the epic's mythological protagonists for bringing Niccolò and Stella together.[43]

Illegitimacy in the *Orlando Innamorato*

In the *Borsiad*, illegitimacy is transformed from an obstacle to rule into a manifestation of Providence. In the *Orlando Innamorato*, in contrast, illegitimacy is associated with a moral flaw, the subordination of reason to passion, that undermines the capacity for leadership. Through the figure of Orlando, illegitimacy links the narrative frame to the problematic history of the Estense succession, which is a sub-text of the Estense genealogies in the poem. Boiardo presupposes a considerable knowledge of epic and romance on the part of his readers, and nowhere more so than in his treatment of Orlando. He assumes Orlando's illegitimacy, which comes to the forefront of action in the form of insult only at moments of great dramatic tension.

In the first canto of the poem, Boiardo introduces Orlando as a paragon of knightly prowess and pride, and thus as a fitting subject to illustrate love's power to conquer even the most apparently resilient of men. He is soon put to the test when the fair Angelica arrives at Charlemagne's court. She and her brother have been sent by their father, King Galafrone of Cathay, in a plot to destroy the Christians. Her beauty is supposed to incite knights to fight her brother for her hand, but magic makes him invincible, and he can claim their persons as the price of his victory.

Infatuated with Angelica, Orlando deserts the court in quest of her. The emperor's forces then begin to lose to the attacking Saracens. Enraged at the absence of leading warriors from his entourage, Charlemagne cries: "Where are those men who owe me fealty; / Have they abandoned me today? / Ranaldo? Gano of Pontieri? / And where's Orlando? — bastard traitor! / You renegade son-of-a-whore! / May I fall dead if you come back / And I don't hang you with my hands!"[44]

---

[43] We do not know how much law Tito Strozzi knew or how he acquired his knowledge, but the prominence of the law faculty at the University of Ferrara and the importance of lawyers among the prince's advisors would have made it relatively easy to pick up the basic information discussed here. In addition, the distinguished Florentine jurist Antonio di Vanni Strozzi maintained close relations with his relatives from Ferrara and may have discussed the Estense succession with them (Lorenzo Fabbri, personal communication).

[44] "Ove son quei che me dièn fare omaggio, / Che m'hanno abandonato in questo giorno? / Ov'è Gan da Pontieri? Ove è Ranaldo? / Ove ene Orlando, traitor bastardo? / Figliol de una puttana, rinegato! / Che, stu ritorni a me, poss'io morire, / Se con le

Boiardo could expect his readers to know that the "whore" in question was the emperor's own sister, Berta. According to a long-standing tradition in Italy, she had conceived Orlando out of wedlock through her passion for Milone d'Anglante, son of the baron Bernardo de Chiaramonte and thus a man of social standing considerably inferior to her own. In the widely known version of the story by Andrea da Barberino in the *Reali di Francia*, which Boiardo drew on to construct a Trojan and Frankish ancestry for the House of Este, Berta is found out six months into her pregnancy. She and Milone are imprisoned, but Duke Namo of Bavaria brings them together and they secretly marry. In other versions of the story also known to Boiardo they do not marry before the baby's birth, and in a few French versions Orlando is the product of incest between Berta and Charlemagne himself.[45] What matters in the *Innamorato* is not whether Orlando is really a bastard, but that both Charlemagne and Rinaldo call him one, and that the only other prominent figure in the poem to be so identified is Ferraguto, an equally hot-headed lover. Orlando himself charges the importunate Ferraguto, who refuses for love of Angelica even to abide by Charlemagne's pact with her brother, with being a "low-born rascal, son of a whore."[46] The insult is ironic, since Orlando thereby identifies Ferraguto with himself. He underscores this identification by his eagerness to fight the adversary whom in defaming he claims has no honor to defend.[47]

---

proprie man non t'ho impiccato!": Matteo Maria Boiardo, *Orlando Innamorato*, trans. and ed. Charles Stanley Ross (Berkeley: University of California Press, 1989), 1.2.64–65 (58–59). I have taken all references to the epic from Ross's edition, modifying his translation where indicated.

[45] Pio Rajna, *I Reali di Francia, Vol. I: Ricerche intorno ai reali di Francia* (Bologna: Gaetano Romagnoli, 1872), 253–64; Andrea da Barberino, *Li reali di Francia* (Venice: Tipografia di Alvisopoli, 1821), 456–59. The *Aspramonte* picks up the story after the couple's exile; in it they marry only after Charlemagne finds Berta and Orlando on his trip to Rome and recalls Milon from banishment: Andrea da Barberino, *L'Aspramonte*, ed. Marco Boni (Bologna: Per i Tipi dell'Antiquaria Palmaverde, 1951), 7. Since *Aspramonte* appears in an inventory of the Estense Library from 1474, Boiardo could well have drawn on it: 174, 195. The story of Orlando was a primarily Franco-Italian innovation based on Carolingian narratives and more recent French material, including possibly the *Lai de Milun* of Marie de France: Rajna, *I Reali di Francia*, 253–55. See also Gaston Paris, *Histoire poétique de Charlemagne* (Paris: Librairie A. Franck, 1865), 170–71.

[46] "Vil ribaldello, figlio de puttana!": *Orlando Innamorato*, 1.3.76, (72), my translation.

[47] Boiardo uses the rules of chivalry to reinforce or undermine the claims to honor of his characters. For a report that bastardy disqualified Antonio della Scala from engaging in personal combat to decide the outcome of the war between Padua and Verona in 1385–1386, see Galeazzo Gatari and Bartolomeo Gatari, "Cronaca carrarese," in *Rerum*

The attributes associated with illegitimacy in the Middle Ages and early modern period are consistent with the irrational love that Boiardo explores in the poem through these two male characters. It was a topos of theological, moral, and legal writings that children born out of wedlock were "imitators of the paternal vice," that is, incontinence.[48] The theme of illegitimacy thus supports the pattern of meaning concerning different kinds of love that is integral to the *Innamorato*.[49] This pattern intersects with the theme of rulership and communal destiny through Orlando's position in the imperial family.

In the *Reali di Francia*, Milone and Berta are excommunicated and forced to flee after Charlemagne threatens Berta with death.[50] In all versions they end up in Sutri, in southern Italy, where they live in poverty. There, many years later, they (or in some versions Berta and Orlando) meet up with Charlemagne, who finally forgives his sister and adopts Orlando, now a young man of great valor, as his son.[51] The adoption explains the special wrath that Charlemagne directs toward him in the *Innamorato*. Orlando is not only a vassal who owes fealty by virtue of a feudal contract; he is also a nephew and son, statuses that oblige him to show steadfast loyalty.

Despite Orlando's illegitimacy, Charlemagne does not question his worth until he fails to fulfill his social obligations, which form a key dimension of personal honor. But once Orlando fails, the emperor invokes his bastardy to explain his conduct. He is morally flawed by the circumstances of his begetting as the son of a "whore" — a charge from which the *Borsiad* frees Borso. Although Charlemagne is ignorant of Orlando's whereabouts, readers of the poem have been following his amorous adventures and can link them to the inherited susceptibility of bastards to the sin of luxury, that is, an inability to submit eros to reason.

---

italicarum scriptores, ed. A. Medin and G. Tolomei (Bologna: Zanichelli, 1909–1932), 245, quoted in Benjamin G. Kohl, *Padua under the Carrara, 1318–1405* (Baltimore, MD: Johns Hopkins University Press, 1998), 235.

[48] See, for example, Klaus Schreiner, "'Defectus natalium' — Geburt aus einem unrechtmäßigen Schoß als Problem klösterlicher Gemeinschaftsbildung," in *Illegitimität im Spätmittelalter*, ed. Ludwig Schmugge (Munich: R. Oldenbourg Verlag, 1994), 85–114, esp. 98–99.

[49] On the theme of love in the *Innamorato*, see especially Jo Ann Cavallo, *Boiardo's Orlando Innamorato: An Ethics of Desire* (London: Associated University Presses, 1993) and sources cited.

[50] Andrea da Barberino, *Reali di Francia*, 458–59.

[51] Rajna, *Reali di Francia*, 253–64; also Andrea da Barberino, *L'Aspramonte*, 3, 6–7; Andrea da Barberino, *Reali di Francia*, 456–79.

In the opening cantos of the *Innamorato*, then, Orlando's behavior, which is linked to his illegitimacy, disrupts the well-being of the ruling house of the Franks and jeopardizes the safety of Christendom. Fortunately for Charlemagne, Orlando's cousin Ranaldo reappears to aid the Christian cause, though he, too, soon proves unreliable. Charlemagne replaces Orlando with Ranaldo, calling him son and placing the kingdom in his hands.[52] Constantly compared for their valor, the cousins are frequently at odds. When Orlando provokes him to uncontrollable rage, Ranaldo repeats Charlemagne's charge of bastardy, thereby suggesting once again Orlando's predisposition to be ruled by passion: "Tell me, you big bastard, what's your boast? / . . . You are the true son of a whore, / Who after losing her honor, esteems it no longer / And is more brazen after her sin than before."[53]

Ranaldo himself resists eros after an initial infatuation with Angelica. But neither he nor Orlando can provide a foundation for an ideal Christian realm.[54] Instead the lovers Ruggiero and Bradamante, founders of the House of Este, carry the promise of the future. Their relationship exemplifies "the proper earthly love which is, according to the poem, eros in union with agape and under the control of reason."[55] The appropriate expression of this love is marriage, which unites the couples who exemplify it in the poem and provides a fruitful basis for familial growth. Jo Ann Cavallo speaks accordingly of a "marriage ethic" in the *Innamorato*.[56] Two genealogies of the descendants of

---

[52] "Lo imperator strettamente lo abbraccia, / E dice: — Figlio, io ti vo'racordare / Ch'io pono il regno mio nelle tue braccia, / Il quale è in tutto per pericolare. / Via se ne è gito, e non so dove, Orlando: / Il stato mio a te lo racomando": *Orlando Innamorato* 1.4.18 (76–77).

[53] "Di che hai superbia, dimme, bastardone? / . . . Ben sei proprio figliol d'una puttana, / Qual, perso che ha l'onor, più non lo stima / E più sfacciata è dopo il fal che in prima": *Orlando Innamorato* 1.27.17 (352, my translation). Ranaldo has previously refused to fight Orlando on the grounds that they are cousins — in this case, refusal to fight is a sign of amity — but when Orlando persists in challenging him and starts slinging insults, Ranaldo is stung into responding with both words and deeds: *Orlando Innamorato*, 1.26.60–64. In a case of mistaken identity in *Innamorato* 2.12, Astolfo thinks that Orlando has insulted him (the culprit is really Brandimarte) and calls him a "whoreson (*figlio de putana*)," and a "cross-eyed bastard (*bastardo stralunato*)": *Orlando innamorato* 2.12.44 and 2.12.49 (524–27).

[54] Indeed, Ranaldo's chastity is coupled with an inability to reciprocate and, even with the opposite of reciprocity, theft. In 1.27.19, Orlando responds to the charge of bastardy by calling Ranaldo a thief, and in 2.9.33 he charges Ranaldo with being base for wanting to take plunder.

[55] Cavallo, *Ethics of Desire*, 159.

[56] Cavallo, *Ethics of Desire*, 159.

Ruggiero and Bradamante are presented in book two, and in the third, unfinished book, where their marriage was to occur, Ruggiero recites his ancestry — "the other lineage, still finer" than the royal stem of France going back to Astyanax and the House of Troy, which provided the Este with a Trojan pedigree and a French connection.[57]

The genealogical material on the Este in the *Innamorato* has been seen primarily as an encomium of Ercole I and his ancestors. Because of the competition between Ercole and Niccolò di Leonello, however, praise of Ercole implied an argument concerning marriage and family consistent with the themes of the epic. Already in his early Latin epic, the *Carmina de laudibus Estensium*, Boiardo had taken a stand on the conflict over the succession created by Niccolò III, who willed that it pass through Leonello and Leonello's son Niccolò, rather than through his own firstborn legitimate son, Ercole. The *Carmina*, written between 1462 and 1464, proclaim Ercole, rather than Niccolò di Leonello, to be "the worthy heir and continuator of the glorious traditions of the Estense dynasty" and praise Borso for calling his half-brother back from exile.[58]

We can find more than panegyric in the Estense material in the *Innamorato* by exploring Charles Ross's observation that repetition plays an integral role in Boiardo's technique.[59] The poem contains two Estense genealogies, a doubling that has yet to be accounted for. The first is in the form of the astrologer and seer Atlante's prophecy concerning the future of Ruggiero, ancestor of the House of Este, and his descendants, who "will attend to all that's worthy, / All that is good — all courtesy, / All that brings joy, and love, and grace — / And they will flourish on this earth."[60] Here Boiardo foregrounds the epic dimension of his poem, making named Estense lords key to the political salvation of Italy and thus comparing them favorably to the heroes of Charlemagne's court.[61]

The second, much more elaborate, genealogy appears four cantos later as a sequence of four narratives painted on the walls of the loggia in the fairy Febosilla's palace. Although this genealogy does not identify its subjects by name, they are easily recognized from Atlante's prophecy, from readers' inde-

---

[57] *Orlando Innamorato*, 3.5.29 (804–5).

[58] Emilio Bigi, "La poesia latina del Boiardo," in *Il Boiardo e la critica contemporanea*, ed. Giuseppe Anceschi (Florence: L. S. Olschki, 1970), 83–84; see also Boiardo's epigrams in Bertoni, *Nuovi studi*, 83–89.

[59] See "Introduction," to *Orlando Innamorato*, ed. Ross, 1–29, here 19–20.

[60] *Orlando Innamorato*, 2.21.55 (632–33).

[61] See Raffaele Donnarumma, *Storia dell'* Orlando Innamorato (Lucca: Maria Pacini Fazzi Editore), 172–75, for the Virgilian dimension of this epic theme.

pendent knowledge of the events depicted, and from a reference to the Estense insignia of a white eagle on a blue field. Instead of a true prophecy that will happen just as predicted — the claim Atlante makes for his speech — the genealogy here is a visual narrative that has to be interpreted like other illustrations, writings, and oral tales that are found throughout the epic. The first two sides of the loggia, described in *Innamorato* 2.25.43–49, elaborate on the theme of the Este as defenders of Holy Church against the emperors and their local allies in 2.21.56–57. Stanzas 2.25.50–56 expand on the treatment of Niccolò III and Ercole in 2.21.58–59. In striking contrast to the *Borsiad*, neither Leonello nor Borso appears. Despite Leonello's renown as a student of humanistic studies and Borso's ducal title, they usurped the place of their legitimate younger brother and are therefore unworthy to be included.

Boiardo sets up a parallel between father and son. They both face difficult situations as children, only to assert their virtue — the military strength of their ancestors — in overcoming their adversaries. But this similarity underscores a key difference. Whereas Niccolò stands alone during his childhood for lack of close relatives or allies, Ercole's kinsmen are the source of his problems. They have seized his patrimony and denied him his rightful position. The different destinies of father and son unfold as different patterns of movement. After vanquishing his enemies — including a rival branch of his own house — Niccolò vaunts his hard-won freedom in travels to Spain and France, whose king exalts him as a kinsman, and in making a pilgrimage to the Holy Land. Ercole, in contrast, is hounded by fortune far from home and makes a name for himself abroad through his feats of valor. Boiardo leaves him on this grand stage, but readers know that after demonstrating his possession of ancestral virtù, Ercole returns home to claim his rightful heritage.[62]

The fortune that hounds Ercole and drives him away in *Innamorato* 2.25.54 has been set in motion by his father and his father's loves, which produced Leonello and led to Niccolò's unlawful decision to make Leonello, rather than Ercole, his oldest legitimate son, his universal heir. In *Innamorato* 2.25.53, the narrator slyly alludes to Niccolò III's prodigious love life: "The master made a mistake and did badly — / Because he did not paint how he was human, / How he was liberal and full of love / It did not fit; there was no space."[63] The "mistake" is actually a just assessment of the difficulty of

---

[62] "Ma lui sol a virtute diè di piglio, / E quella ne portò fuor di sua casa; / Ogni altra cosa in preda era rimasa (Virtuous strength was his concern, / And he maintained it far from home; / His other property was seized)": *Orlando Innamorato*, 2.25.54 (682–83).

[63] "Error prese il maestro, e fece male, / Ché non dipense come egli era umano, / Come era liberale e d'amor pieno; / Non vi capia, ché'l campo venne meno": *Orlando Innamorato*, 2.25.53, (682) my translation. The expression "donna piena" means pregnant

rendering either the scope of largesse or the fullness of love of the ruler celebrated for his sexual prowess in the popular jingle, "On this side and on the other side of the Po / All are children of Niccolò."[64]

The narrator's assessment of Niccolò turns on the contrast between his "humanity" and the "god-like person (*persona sopranaturale*)" evidenced in his military prowess.[65] Like Orlando, he is internally divided between a heroic aspect and his all too human nature, a division that Ercole overcomes through a synthesis of valor and correct love. The painter highlights the difference between father and son by acknowledging his failure to do Ercole justice. This time, his failure arises not from error but from the intellect's inability to depict the virtue of Ercole's heart — "la virtù del core" — precisely the quality that Niccolò, who is "full of love," lacks. The virtuous heart is one that disciplines love with reason, an attribute that sets the legitimate Ercole apart from his illegitimately born father and brothers.

Venus *in malo* — lasciviousness and lust — lay at the root of a conflict over succession that had jeopardized the existence of the House of Este and the independence of Ferrara. Not only did Niccolò III's scheme for his house give

---

woman: Salvatore Battaglia, ed., *Grande dizionario della lingua italiana*, 20+ vols. (Turin: UTET, 1961–), 13: 408, 'pieno', sense 2. The description of a man, in this case Niccolò, as being "d'amor pieno" would suggest that he is full of libido. The variant of paralipsis in these lines draws on the reader's knowledge and humorous response to Niccolò's excesses to build a critical contrast with Ercole.

[64] The coupling of love and liberality underscores the concreteness of the reference to Niccolò's sexual exploits, which have an ambiguous significance here as both a sign of virility and a source of dynastic problems. Trevor Dean notes that gifts of land and the conversion of fiefs to allods or leases by the Este as a form of benefice became common only in the early fifteenth century, during Niccolò's reign; in other words, the marquis broadened the scope of largesse during a period of considerable weakness. Like his ancestors, he used such gifts — which often comprised land taken from the Church or from enemies of the Este — along with tax immunities, gifts of money, assignments of revenue, and loans as a means of establishing and maintaining political relations: Trevor Dean, *Land and Power in Late Medieval Ferrara*, Cambridge Studies in Medieval Life and Thought (Cambridge: Cambridge University Press, 1988), 59–63. Kinsmen of the marquis's mistresses numbered among the many beneficiaries, but the link between love and liberality in the context of Boiardo's epic treatment of Niccolò — besides the sheer scope of the marquis's activities in these areas — may be the absence of virtue in both types of act arising from their self-directed character. For the egotism of lust, see Cavallo, *Ethics of Desire,* 8, 36–49; for the topos of liberality as a virtue when giving is made "for the sake of the noble" and without expectation of a return, see James Gordley, *The Philosophical Origins of Modern Contract Doctrine* (Oxford: Oxford University Press, 1991), 10–15.

[65] *Orlando Innamorato*, 2.25.50, 53 (682–83).

Borso a dubious claim to office, it also placed the legitimately born Ercole in a shaky position. Niccolò threatened the stability of social categories by transforming Ercole into a functional illegitimate. Disabilities with respect to succession were the most evident legal consequence of illegitimate birth.[66] Niccolò even gave Ercole a name associated with bastardy. Boiardo alludes to the mythical hero Hercules's birth from an adulterous union in calling Ercole "the other son of Amphitryon."[67]

At the time of Borso's death, Ercole depended on arms to prevail over Niccolò di Leonello, thus becoming open to the charge of winning the duchy through force rather than right. After his elevation to duke, he remained vulnerable to the threat of rebellion. This fear ended only in September of 1476, after Niccolò di Leonello staged a rebellion against his uncle and was captured and beheaded — around or shortly before the time that Boiardo began writing the *Innamorato*. The poem appears to call on the Este to order their house on the foundation of benevolent love and marriage. Only thus, Boiardo seems to suggest, can they and their subjects achieve peace and stability.[68]

Boiardo's ideal of love rests on the premise of free choice, a principle that, although upheld in Christian theology and law, was frequently ignored in practice, perhaps especially among ruling elites. Princely marriages were made not for love but for advantage. Duty yielded no room for desire. By the social standards of his day, Boiardo's moral truths are fictions. Those who agreed that

---

[66] See, for example, Michael M. Sheehan, "Illegitimacy in Late Medieval England: Laws, Dispensation and Practice," in *Illegitimität im Spätmittelalter*, ed. Schmugge, 115–21, here 119; Kuehn, *Illegitimacy in Renaissance Florence*, 74.

[67] *Orlando Innamorato*, 2.21.59.1 (634–35). Here Ross's translation, "the other Hercules," misses the point. The allusion is to the Plautine/Boccaccian version of Hercules's birth and thus to his bastardy: see Giovanni Boccaccio, *Genealogia deorum* (Venice: Augustinus de Zannis de Portesio, 1511), bk. 12, cap. 28–31, fol. 89v. According to this story, Hercules and his brother Iphicles shared Alcmena's womb, but Iphicles was the son of Alcmena's husband, the Theban warrior Amphitryon, while Hercules was engendered by Alcmena from Jove disguised as Amphitryon. Hercules was thus the son of the "other" Amphitryon, but Boiardo transfers the modifier "l'altro" from father to son, playfully suppressing the import of the allusion by identifying Hercules with Iphicles as sons of the same father.

[68] The view presented here is at odds with Antonia Tissoni Benvenuti's argument for dating the drafting of book one of the *Innamorato* to Borso's reign: Antonia Tissoni Benvenuti, "Sul testo dell' Inamoramento de Orlando," in *Il Boiardo e il mondo estense nel quattrocento*, 2: 923–42, here 932–33, and eadem, "Introduzione," in Matteo Maria Boiardo, *Opere*, ed. Antonia Tissoni Benvenuti and Cristina Montagnani, 2 vols. (Milan: Riccardo Ricciardi Editore, 1999), 1: xi–xxxiii, here xiv–xvi.

love should be expressed in marriage but who insisted on the presence of love often found themselves outcasts, as the "foolish woman" Polissena d'Este discovered when she defied her uncle Ercole I's wishes and, "in love with Scaramuza Visconti, placing her appetites above every other thing, made a marriage with him by words of the present."[69] But with or without love, marriage provided the reference point for evaluating sexual behavior outside of marriage. This explains why Strozzi draws on the Christian rules of marriage in making the case that Borso's parents were exempt from them.

II. Pietro Aretino and the Estense Succession in the Sixteenth Century

Considered from the standpoint of their own time, the epics of Strozzi and Boiardo present conflicting but equally possible views on the importance of marriage in schemes of princely succession. Over the long term, however, Boiardo's claims on behalf of marriage as the foundation of dynastic succession were increasingly realized in practice. As their temporal power increased, the popes were able to insist on legitimacy as a requirement in the terms of investiture for apostolic vicariates and fiefs. This context provided scope for *literati* to play a subversive role in alliance with those, such as Alfonso I's mistress, Laura Eustochia, who resisted the change. Laura looked back to the fourteenth century and the history of another Estense mistress, Lippa degli Ariosti, in devising a scheme to protect her illegitimate sons' interests. This scheme required publicity, and the last text I consider here is a letter from the publicist Pietro Aretino that suggests that he answered this need.[70]

---

[69] "... questa femina bestiale ... inamorata de Scaramuza Vesconte, proponendo li soi appetiti ad ogni altra cossa, ha contracto matrimonio cum lui per parola de presente": Letter of Eleonora d'Aragona to Francesco Gonzaga, 4 November 1484, ASMo, AG b.1183. The adjective "bestiale," coupled with the reference to "appetites," evokes the animality of irrational behavior dominated by bodily drives.

[70] What follows is a compressed version of chapter 7 of my book manuscript, *Succession and Statecraft in Renaissance Italy: The Este of Ferrara, 1264–1598.* See also Jane Fair Bestor, "Titian's Portrait of Laura Eustochia: the Decorum of Female Beauty and the Motif of the Black Page," *Renaissance Studies* 17 (2003): 628–73. The surname "Dianti" that historians use today was a late attempt to provide Laura with a respectable family origin and is attested neither during the duke's lifetime, nor even, apparently, during her own. The name "Eustochia," which Alfonso must have given her at the inception of their relationship, is relevant to understanding both his symbolic construction of her situation and Titian's use of this symbolism in his official portrait. I therefore think it advisable to restore the name to her.

Alfonso had three legitimate sons — Ercole II, Ippolito II and Francesco — and a daughter, Leonora, by his second wife, Lucrezia Borgia. Then, after Lucrezia's death, he had two more sons — named Alfonso and Alfonsino after himself — by Laura, the beautiful daughter of a Ferrarese artisan whom he established as his mistress in 1526. Although Alfonso could have given the boys the strongest possible legitimacy, short of birth in wedlock, by subsequently marrying their mother and thereby transforming them into "lawful and true offspring (*iusti et veri filii*)," he chose not to do this up to the time of his death. Instead he had Cardinal Innocenzo Cibo legitimize the boys by rescript, or decree.[71] In his will Alfonso ordered that primogeniture be observed in the succession to his dominions, stipulating that if all three of his legitimately born sons and their legitimate male descendants died out, then the illegitimately born Alfonso was to succeed on the same terms, and after him Alfonsino.[72]

After the duke's death, his successor, Ercole II, sought to win recognition of his position from Pope Paul III by obtaining renewal of the papal investiture for Ferrara. The negotiations were painfully slow, and at some point it became clear that legitimacy would be a requirement for succession, though how it would be defined was not clear.[73] As a result, sons who were legitimated by decree, a form of legitimation not involving marriage, would be disqualified from the succession.[74] In the future, succession would depend on the marriage of one's parents. But if the criterion was legitimacy alone, the marriage could take place before or after the children's birth, provided that the parents were eligible to marry when the child was born. Legitimation by a subsequent marriage was based on the power of marriage to wash away the filth of sin. Nonetheless, there was a subtle but important distinction between children who were born in marriage and who were thus legitimate and natural (*legitimi*

---

[71] ASMo, A.S.E., Casa e Stato b.355, Act of legitimation of Alfonso and Alfonsino by Cardinal Deacon Innocenzo Cibo, 17 April 1532. Although the cardinal was authorized to legitimize "ad feuda, emphitiosis, et alia bona ecclesiastica," the act had no weight with respect to succession to the duchies and was probably a measure of last resort on Alfonso's part in view of papal hostility.

[72] ASMo, A.S.E., Casa e Stato, b.325, Alfonso I, testament of 8 April 1532, (25) and testament of 28 August 1533, (27).

[73] ASMo, A.S.E., Cancelleria, Carteggio di Principi Esteri, Roma b. 1299/14.

[74] Though Pope Paul III read legitimacy of birth back into the investiture of Ercole I with Ferrara from his predecessor Pope Alexander VI, the act had not said anything about legitimacy as a qualification but only specified primogeniture, a point that explains the terms of Alfonso's wills: Augustin Theiner, *Codex diplomaticus dominii temporalis Sanctae Sedis*, 3 vols. (Rome: Imprimerie du Vatican, 1861–1862), 3:536.

et naturales), and those who were legitimate by a subsequent marriage, or *iusti et veri filii*. The latter were considered to be fully legitimate from the time of their parents' marriage, but in the view of most jurists, they were legitimate only by a fiction of law prior to that point.[75] In Roman and canon law they were included among the legitimately born for the purposes of any legitimacy requirement, but the situation was far from clear with respect to feudal contracts and customary rules of succession. Thus there was considerable tension between canonic ideas concerning legitimation by subsequent marriage and the rules that might govern the succession to papal fiefs.

Laura Eustochia first began to use the Estense cognomen in sign of her marriage to Alfonso about four years after his death, in the summer of 1538. This timing suggests that she was aware of the trend of the negotiations and sought to protect her sons' place in the succession by affirming their legitimacy. Her appropriation of the name constituted a presumptive sign of her transformation from mistress into wife. But she needed a story to validate the claim of marriage. The basis for such a narrative existed in the marriage of Obizzo III d'Este to his mistress Lippa degli Ariosti, "la bella Lippa da Bologna," just before her death in 1347. Lippa had been Obizzo's mistress prior to their marriage. She, like Laura, had borne her lover children, some of whom were legitimated by the couple's subsequent marriage. Laura could claim to have married Alfonso during the last year of his life, even at the time of his death. None of the references to her marriage refer to it explicitly as a marriage on the point of death. But the figure of *matrimonium in articulo mortis* had achieved an established place in the doctrine of legitimacy by the end of the fourteenth century and must have been familiar to Ferrarese.

Obizzo's marriage had taken place under very different circumstances from those faced by Laura.[76] His oldest children were born in adultery while he was married to Jacoba de' Pepoli. If he had married Lippa immediately after Jacoba's death in 1341, his younger children would have been legitimately born and therefore of superior rank to their elder siblings. In order to avoid a destructive conflict within the House of Este based on the competing claims

---

[75] Antonio Roselli, "Tractatus legitimationum," in *Tractatus universi iuris*, 22 vols. in 28 (Venice: Societas Aquilae Renovantis, 1584), 8.2, fols. 79vb–80ra qualifies in this way the view of the canonist Antonio da Butrio that children legitimated by subsequent marriage were legitimate "according to a fiction (*secundam fictionem*)"; see also Ludovico Sardi, *Tractatus de naturalibus liberis, legitimatione, atque successione eorum*, in *Tractatus universi iuris* (1584), 8.2, fol. 35va. For a general discussion of legal fictions with respect to legitimation, see Kuehn, *Illegitimacy in Renaissance Florence*, 62–64.

[76] For a full account, see Bestor, "Bastardy and Legitimacy," 562–66.

of seniority and legitimacy of birth, Obizzo delayed marriage to Lippa in order to make all of the children illegitimate. But Pope Clement VI had made marriage a condition for legitimating the older children by decree, which alone would make them eligible to succeed their father. Obizzo therefore wed Lippa in a very public ceremony complete with dowry — but as she was dying, so that no children would be born in marriage, a situation that would also have made the pope's legitimation of the children born in adultery unlawful. The younger children became "lawful and true offspring" by virtue of the marriage, but the performative character of this act did not jeopardize the achievement of Obizzo's main goal: to restore full legal capacity to his *adulterini* so that all the children could be placed on the same legal footing. Only thus could he make all of the sons joint heirs and institute a system of succession that would give each one a chance to rule.[77] In contrast, marriage and not legitimation by rescript was Laura's central concern. By the later 1530s, illegitimates had a chance to succeed only on the showing that they were, after all, legitimate by the power of marriage to legitimize fully.

Lippa's story was known in Ferrara. The primary source used by ducal officials and others for the history of the Este and Ferrara in the fourteenth century, the *Cronica vetus*, was readily available in the ducal library and recorded under the date of 27 November 1347, the death of

> the noble lady Lippa degli Ariosti of Bologna, wife of the magnificent and illustrious lord, lord Marquis Obizzo, etc. whom he married at the end of her life at the admonition of the lord Pope Clement VI, from which lady the lord marquis had procreated eleven children, namely, seven boys and four girls, etc. and she was honorably buried in the place of the Brothers Minor of Ferrara as was fitting, etc.[78]

The text of the ecclesiastical inquiry into the marriage of Obizza and Lippa was preserved in the Estense archives, and the case was alluded to in the *Tractatus legitimationum* of canon lawyer Antonio Roselli.[79] Furthermore, the Ariosti remained prominent in Ferrarese affairs and had every interest in keeping alive public knowledge of their kinship to the Estense through Lippa — as Ludovico's allusion to the "bella Lippa" in his *Orlando Furioso* attests.

---

[77] Bestor, "Bastardy and Legitimacy," 566.

[78] The *Cronica vetus* was edited and published by L. A. Muratori as the *Chronicon estense*: see L. A. Muratori, *Chronicon Estense*, *Rerum Italicarum Scriptores* 15 (Milan: Ex Typographia Societatis Palatinae, 1729), 443–44.

[79] Roselli, *Tractatus legitimationum*, fol. 77va.

Laura and her intimates may not have been reading histories of Ferrara or legal treatises, but they had connections to others who were. Many of the acts from the late 1530s and '40s in which Laura signs her name as Laura Eustochia Estense, or in which she is referred to by this name, are subscribed by the notary Battista Saracchi. Saracchi was a trusted servant of Alfonso I and had redacted both of his extant wills. He was clearly aware of Alfonso's affection for Laura and of her sons' place in his scheme for the succession. Saracchi, in turn, was friendly with Gaspare Sardi, a Ferrarese humanist with a passion for the history of his native city and its ruling family. Sardi not only was a man of letters but also had some training in law at the University of Ferrara.[80] If Saracchi was not already familiar with the story of Lippa degli Ariosti's deathbed marriage, he could well have learned it from Sardi, as well as its practical value as a model for preserving the intentions toward Laura's sons expressed in Alfonso's will.[81]

Within less than a year after the Estense name began to appear in Laura's registers, the negotiations between Pope Paul III and Ercole II finally reached a successful conclusion. By the terms of the investiture that was formally ratified in February of 1539, legitimacy of birth, the most stringent definition of legitimacy, became a criterion of succession to the duchy of Ferrara.[82] Laura's sons were therefore effectively disqualified. Nonetheless, she continued to use the Estense name and sought ways to give the marriage publicity, as a letter from Pietro Aretino to her, dated October of 1542, attests. The reason for this persistence can perhaps be explained by the internal crisis within the House of Este at this time. Ercole's wife, Princess Renée of France, had strong Protestant sympathies and defended persecuted Protestants.[83] In 1541 the

---

[80] ASMo, Archivio per materie, Letterati, b.60, letter of Gaspare Sardi to Alessandro Marocello, Ferrara, 28 October 1553.

[81] Under cover of copying another text, Fra Paolo da Legnago's Estense genealogy, composed sometime around 1559, Gaspare Sardi asserts that Alfonso had three wives: Anna Sforza, Lucrezia Borgia, and "the lady Laura, virtuous and good but not of noble blood": "Genealogia delli Estensi accopiata per mi Guasparo di Sardi dal libro di Fra Paolo da Legnago," Miscellanea, Biblioteca Estense Universitaria Modena (BEUM), F.3.3 (Ital. 410), c.8v. This seems to have been the first testimony to Laura's marriage by a local historian. Sardi's caution in stating his views may be ascribed to his status as official historian of the House of Este; his magnum opus, the *Historie Ferraresi*, which stopped before Alfonso's reign, was published only in 1556 in Ferrara.

[82] Theiner, *Codex diplomaticus*, 3:536.

[83] For an excellent discussion of Renée/Renata and her position in Ferrara, see Chiara Franceschini, "La corte di Renata di Francia (1528–1560)," in *Il Rinascimento. Situazioni e personaggi*, ed. Adriano Prosperi, *Storia di Ferrara* 6 (Ferrara: Corbo, 2000), 185–214.

repression of Protestants began to intensify in Italy, culminating in the bull *Licet ab initio* of 21 July 1542, in which Pope Paul created the "Holy Office" of the general Roman Inquisition to coordinate local efforts to repress heretics and preserve the faith. Laura may have gambled that if Renée and her children became discredited on account of their Protestant connections, her own sons, if they could claim legitimacy, would be positioned to win public support for office. It is thus possible that Aretino's letter was timed to exploit the political problems arising for Ercole II from his wife's conduct.

Aretino's letter to Laura is an artful play on the humanist letter of condolence. In the opening line, the author indicates that he has received news from Laura of her father's death. But instead of following the conventions of the genre and praising his virtues and the benefits that he conferred upon his daughter, Aretino turns the tables and extols her benefits, hitherto unknown, to her father.[84] Laura's communication, Aretino writes, has made him realize "the ignorance of all the present age; and I say it in reference to you, who for being one of its most notable marvels, merit that it bow down to you, as you are bowed down to by me."[85] His letter aims to make others realize the "maraviglia" that is Laura.

What, the writer asks, is the source of greater obligation, the flesh and bones with which Laura's father clothed her, or her enrichment of him in the form of honors and joy derived from being the father-in-law of a sublime prince? After this allusion to Laura's low birth (*istato ignoto*), Aretino builds an account of Laura's father's good fortune from which to move into the consolation proper. He urges Laura to exult instead of grieve; after achieving the pinnacle of earthly happiness, her parent is now in heaven, contemplating how the stars honor her, promoted by the will of God as a reward for virtue. At this high point, Aretino proclaims the opinion of those in the know that Laura and Alfonso were married:

---

[84] On letters of consolation in Greco-Roman antiquity, see Stanley K. Stowers, *Letter Writing in Greco-Roman Antiquity*, Library of Early Christianity (Philadelphia: Westminster Press, 1986), esp. 142, and George W. McClure, *Sorrow and Consolation in Italian Humanism* (Princeton: Princeton University Press, 1991), 32, for the influence of ancient models on Petrarch, who played a major role in revitalizing the classical tradition.

[85] "La fama nuntia de la perdita del vostro bon Genitore mi ha fatto accorgere de la ignoranza di tutto il presente secolo; e lo dico in proposito di voi, che per essere una de le sue piu notabili maraviglie, meritate ch'egli v'inchini, come sete inclinata da me": Pietro Aretino, *Il terzo libro de le lettere di Messer Pietro Aretino* (Venice: Appresso Gabriel Giolito de Ferrari, 1546), fol. 13v.

> the general opinion of the most famous people bears witness that only the greatness of soul of the catholic Duke Alfonso was sufficient to perform a duty of such boundless goodness, which made him condescend to marry the inviolable Signora Laura, and that excepting the excellence of quality of the inviolable Signora Laura, no one was sufficient to obtain a gift of such holy value, which destined her to win the catholic Duke Alfonso as her husband.[86]

This carefully wrought chiasmus underscores the difference in status between the parties through verbal mimesis, representing Alfonso as stooping in Christian humility to marry Laura while she, in turn, is exalted by winning a princely husband.

Laura could not fashion herself as a lawful wife on her own. She needed the affirmation of an authoritative third party, some person or persons strategically placed to give out 'information' that would be picked up and gain credence through repeated utterance. That a letter from Pietro Aretino to "Signora Laura Estense" is the earliest evidence of a marriage between Laura and Alfonso is immensely suggestive. Through the effective use of praise and blame, Aretino had made himself both feared and sought after by every ruler with a stake in the affairs of Italy.[87] Settling in the relative freedom of Venice, with its lively publishing industry, he began to collect and publish his letters in 1537 — the first person, or so he claimed, to do so in the vernacular. By vastly increasing the circulation of the letters, a venture that proved wildly successful, he sought to make himself a creator of public opinion and thereby force princes "to fear his sarcasms more and to solicit his praises with greater generosity."[88] The "scourge of princes" had thus constructed the public that Laura needed. His audience of readers must have overlapped considerably with the addressees of the letters, including not only temporal and ecclesiastical

---

[86] "In tanto il grido de le piu chiare genti fa fede, come solo la grandezza de l'animo del catholico Duca Alfonso era bastante ad eseguire uno ufficio di si smisurata bontade, che lo facesse condescendere a torre in mogliera la inviolabile Signora Laura: e che da la eccellenza de la qualità da la inviolabile Signora Laura infuora niuna era sofficiente ad ottenere un dono di si santo pregio; che la destinasse a conseguire in marito il catholico Duca Alfonso": Aretino, *Terzo libro di lettere*, fol. 14v.

[87] For Aretino's life see Christopher Cairns, *Pietro Aretino and the Republic of Venice* (Florence: L. S. Olschki, 1985); Paul Larivaille, *Pietro Aretino* (Rome: Salerno Editrice, 1997); Patricia Labalme, "Personality and Politics in Venice: Pietro Aretino," in *Titian: His World and his Legacy*, ed. David Rosand, Bampton Lectures in America 21 (New York: Columbia University Press, 1982), 119–32.

[88] Larivaille, *Pietro Aretino*, 223.

princes who could intercede with the pope and emperor to recognize the claims of Laura's children, but also influential members of their entourages, as well as other writers who could spread the message in their own work.[89]

The 'news' of the marriage was soon picked up by Ludovico Domenichi in his book *La nobilta delle donne*, published in Venice in 1549 and reprinted in a corrected edition in 1551.[90] In 1546, Aretino had charged Domenichi with presenting the newly published volume in which the letter appeared to Cosimo de' Medici, to whom he dedicated the work. By this means the knowledge spread to the Medici and their court, including Giorgio Vasari, another friend and correspondent of Aretino and a fellow Aretine. Vasari mentions the marriage in his chapter on Titian in the second edition of *The Lives*, published in 1568.[91] The Dominican Fra Leandro Alberti affirms Laura's married status in his *Descrittione di tutta Italia*, published in 1550. He probably learned about the marriage from Gaspare Sardi, whom he praises in the work and who assisted with its publication.[92] Alberti, in turn, was the likely source of Marco Guazzo's knowledge, published in his *Cronaca* in Venice in 1553.[93] Paolo Giovio, who had to reckon with both his patron, Cardinal Ippolito II d'Este, and Aretino, a potentially dangerous enemy, opted for a studied opacity on the subject of the marriage in his *Liber de vita et rebus gestis Alphonsi Atestini*, published in 1551. He states that Laura underwent a change in status from being a concubine to holding "the place of a wife," an equivocation that allowed readers to reach their own conclusions.[94]

---

89 Larivaille, *Pietro Aretino*, 146–48 discusses the social composition of Aretino's correspondence. For the role of the press in amplifying and reinforcing messages, see Elizabeth L. Eisenstein, *The Printing Press as an Agent of Change: Communications and Cultural Transformations in Early Modern Europe* (Cambridge: Cambridge University Press, 1979), 1:149–50.

90 Ludovico Domenichi, *La nobiltà delle donne* (Venice, 1549), fol. 260v; idem, *La nobiltà delle donne corretta, & di nuovo ristampata* (Venice, 1551), fol. 260v.

91 Giorgio Vasari, *Le vite de' piu eccellenti pittori, scultori e architettori, nelle redazioni del 1550 e 1568*, ed. Rosanna Bettarini and Paola Barocchi, 6 vols. (Florence: Sansoni, 1966–1987), 6:159. Patricia Lee Rubin, *Giorgio Vasari: Art and History* (New Haven: Yale University Press, 1995), 117 notes that Aretino's letters were a source for *The Lives*.

92 Leandro Alberti, *Descrittione di tutta Italia* (Bologna: Anselmo Giaccarelli, 1550), fol. 312v. For Alberti's praise of Sardi, see fol. 313v. For their friendship and Sardi's efforts to ensure the publication of the *Descrittione*, see Giuseppe Campori, "Sei lettere inedite di Fra Leandro Alberti a Gaspare Sardi ed una del Sardi a Iacopo Tebaldi," *Atti e memorie delle RR. Deputazioni di storia patria per le provincie modenesi e parmensi* 1 (1863): 413–20.

93 Marco Guazzo, *Cronaca* (Venice: Francesco Bidoni, 1553), fol. 345r.

94 Paolo Giovio, *Liber de vita et rebus gestis Alphonsi Atestini* (Florence, 1551), 57–58. T. C. Price Zimmermann describes the difficult but gradually improving relationship between Giovio and Aretino in *Paolo Giovio: The Historian and the Crisis of Sixteenth-*

Thanks to these and other writers, by the end of the sixteenth century Laura had made her marriage to Alfonso I common knowledge, or *publica vox et fama*. The evidence of a *publica vox* could be used to support the legitimacy of her sons in a court of law. Even if the marriage could be proved, her claim was relatively weak; after all, Paul III's act of investiture for Ercole II had qualified only legitimate and natural sons for the succession. But the canonists had argued vigorously for a different standard of legitimacy with respect to feudal succession. What mattered was the ability to construct plausible arguments in a case that would be determined primarily on political grounds. The practical legal significance of *publica vox et fama* was based on the need of legal authorities to take into account the power of opinion in order to construct lasting legal judgements.

In the end, however, despite the success of her publicity campaign, Laura's strategy failed. It was doomed by the refusal of Ercole II and his successor, Alfonso II, to recognize her marriage. The reason for their conduct probably lies in her ignoble birth. Maternal rank had always mattered, as Frederick III's reputed concern over Borso's mother reveals. In placing Ercole's first son and successor, Alfonso, in the genealogy of his mother's house rather than in that of the lower-ranking Este, Boiardo celebrated the elevation in prestige that Ercole and his descendants gained through his alliance with the royal house of Aragon.[95] From then on, marriage alliances with ruling houses throughout Europe became a means of preserving Ferrarese independence, and the maternal rank of the Este became a major political asset. This situation is reflected in Ariosto's catalogue of illustrious wives in *Orlando Furioso*.[96] The struggle for precedence between the Este and the Medici in the second half of the sixteenth century only heightened the concern with rank. In this context, Laura must have seemed especially unworthy to be called the wife and mother of future dukes.

The dukes' refusal to recognize Laura's marriage became significant when Alfonso proved to be sterile. Unless he could somehow produce a legitimate heir descending from Alfonso I, Ferrara would devolve to the papacy. Although by this time Laura and both her sons were dead, Alfonso might have promoted her grandson Cesare as the legitimate successor to the patrimony. But instead of backing Cesare as the rightful candidate, he kept postponing the issue and then sought permission to name his successor. By evidencing his continuing reluctance to accept Laura's sons as legitimate, Alfonso gave successive popes

---

Century Italy (Princeton: Princeton University Press, 1995), 115, 158, 169, 336 n. 106.

[95] *Orlando Innamorato*, 2.27.58–59 (704–7).

[96] *Orlando Furioso*, 13.66–73.

a reason to invalidate Cesare's candidacy. They were able to represent the prospective devolution of Ferrara as the result of a straightforward application of legal rules to a natural fact. Nature and not the papacy did in the Este. But the subversion wrought by nature was not completed before Alfonso made Cesare his universal heir. Although Cesare was forced to withdraw to Modena, he and his descendants continued to press their claims over the former duchy. The artefacts produced in Laura's campaign to establish herself as Alfonso's wife took on a new significance as counters in the legal contest over arcane points of feudal and ecclesiastical law between the Este and the papacy.

The dukes' refusal to recognize Laura's marriage to Alfonso is ironic. From Obizzo III to Niccolò III, Estense lords had placed the transmission of their patrimony intact above considerations of rank in deciding the succession, an ordering of priorities that helped to ensure the continuity of their rule over Ferrara from 1264 to 1598. At the same time, Alfonso II's situation suggests the difficulty inherent in framing the political question of succession in legal terms. Whatever the reasons for his continuing hesitation over recognizing Laura's marriage, he could not be sure that the best legal argument would prevail before a collective judge — the pope together with the college of cardinals — who was also party to the suit. Identifying two possible candidates in his house, Cesare and the marquis Filippo d'Este di San Martino (of an illegitimate line from Sigismondo di Niccolò III), Alfonso temporized to see which one might gain sufficient backing from a European power, or even one of the popes, to force a change in papal policy.[97] In pursuing a purely political solution, he further undermined the credibility of Cesare's legal position.

In a final irony, at least one observer of the conflict between the Este and the papacy adduced the history of bastard rule — the fact the Este had an interest in hiding — as an argument for Cesare's right to keep Ferrara. In his *Historie Venitiane*, the Venetian nobleman Nicolò Contarini asserted that this history evidenced the autonomy of the House of Este from the papacy. Not papal policy, therefore, but the principles of election and testamentary discretion should have governed the succession of Alfonso II.[98]

---

[97] Luciano Chiappini, *Gli Estensi*, 2nd ed. (Varese: Dall'Oglio, 1967), 307–15.

[98] J. Salmons, "An Unpublished Account of the End of Este Rule in Ferrara: Niccolò Contarini's *Istorie Veneziane* and Events in Ferrara 1597–98," in *The Renaissance in Ferrara and its European Horizons*, ed. idem and Walter Moretti (Cardiff: University of Wales Press, 1984), 123–44, here 127–30.

Conclusion

In this essay, we have seen how three literary texts defend, criticize, or provide grounds for contesting the Estense succession. Together they illustrate a shift over time in attitudes toward the relationship of the succession to the legal doctrine of marriage. The *Borsiad* presupposes the rule scheme but exempts Borso's parents from its dictates. The *Orlando Innamorato* presupposes the rules and makes a case for the obligation of the Este to comply. Aretino's letter presupposes the rules and aids Laura in changing her status to fit them.

Our texts highlight a number of moral tensions in the politics of succession. One dimension of this tension, the conflict between equity and ideas about pollution (derived in ecclesiastical circles from the Old Testament and based on taboo), is found already in the discordant canons that Gratian assembled in his *Decretum* on whether priests' sons should be admitted to holy offices. The analogy that Strozzi draws between the births of Borso and Jesus affirms a basic principle of St. Jerome and other Church Fathers, namely that the sins of the parents cannot be visited on their children; what matters is the quality of their own life and faith. Borso's virtues qualify him to serve as a redeemer irrespective of his parents' union out of wedlock.[99] In his portrayal of Orlando, in contrast, Boiardo draws on the contrary view that imputed the defect of the origin (concupiscence) to the seed.[100] This symbolism also makes sense of his exclusion of Leonello and Borso from the Estense genealogies.

Yet questions remain about the place of the moral scheme of illegitimacy in the *Innamorato*. After all, the rivalry between Orlando and Ranaldo foregrounds their relative equality. Bastards may be inclined to a certain type of sin, but they do not have a monopoly on sinning. Ranaldo, no less than Orlando, falls short of chivalric ideals. His relative poverty makes him avaricious, paralleling his tendency to withhold love. In a telling episode, he tries to steal a gold chair, which is protected by a magic spell, from the fairy Morgana. Ranaldo's desperate — and ultimately unsuccessful — efforts to prevail against the spell show him to be as irrational in greed as Orlando is in love. At the same time, he also exposes Orlando's criticism of his greedy behavior as relative to his social position (Orlando is fat with temporal and ecclesiastical benefices), indicts the clergy for hypocrisy on the same grounds, and suggests the existence of a vicious cycle within the chivalric enterprise between a lust for property and the need to pay off knights.[101] This episode

---

[99] Gratian, *Decretum,* D.56, c.5, c.8; see also c.4, c.6, c.7, c.9, in *CJC*, 1: 220–22.

[100] Gratian, *Decretum*, D.56, c.13, also c.10 in *CJC*, 1: 222–23.

[101] *Orlando Innamorato*, 2.9.32–40 (488–91).

highlights the *Innamorato*'s concern with the social-political and moral bases of chivalry and not just with the gap between chivalric ideals and actual conduct. The issues extend to a consideration of the social grounds and contexts of moral judgement.

In this regard, it is striking that "bastard" occurs as an epithet in moments of tension. The effect is to highlight relationships and role expectations rather than, again, to insist on the uniquely flawed personhood of illegitimates. Yet the poem exploits the moral meanings attached to illegitimacy in a fashion that seems to support Cavallo's thesis concerning the existence of a hierarchy of different kinds of love. Such a hierarchy, culminating in marital love, makes sense in the poem in relation to the strong associations between marriage, peace, and the extension of amity.

The illegitimacy motif highlights a practical problem of governance arising from the structure of authority in the Christian empire. The tyranny of King Agramante, who leads the African forces against the Christians, is matched by Charlemagne's weakness. On top of a foreign invasion that he cannot withstand, the emperor faces an internal conflict between his two greatest knights that he cannot resolve. Promising to terminate their quarrel with a just solution, all he can offer is a contest of feats of arms.[102] Internal weakness feeds into defeat against the pagan onslaught. This situation recalls the dynastic conflicts over office that threatened the independence of states like Ferrara; indeed, Orlando's assertion that "neither rulers nor lovers want to share the object of their desire" highlights the parallels between romantic and political competition in the poem.[103] The *Innamorato* appears to offer a solution, suggesting that adherence to the laws of marriage and to the rule of legitimate succession are vital to achieving the goods of peace and stability.

In seeming to advocate for a solution to a real political problem, *Orlando Innamorato* may have more in common with the *Borsiad* than appears on the surface. Both poems can be seen to rely on arguments from necessity and to share a concern for relations of power. Strozzi uses the argument of necessity to free the prince even from the divinely instituted law of marriage. Boiardo, in contrast, can be seen to argue that necessity requires the prince to obey the law of marriage.

Aretino's letter inserts itself into the moral and political space between Alfonso I's testamentary disposition of the Estense patrimony and the contractual relations between Pope Paul III and Ercole II. Alfonso's will could not bind his successor, but it could show him what he ought to do, both as lord

---

[102] *Orlando Innamorato,* 2.21.21. and 2.23.15–16 (626, 650).

[103] "Ché compagnia non vôle amor né stato": *Orlando Innamorato,* 1.25.56 (334).

and as a son bound by the obligation of filial *pietas*. Once it became clear that the terms of the will regarding succession would be disregarded, Laura and her advisers found a means to comply with the thrust of papal policy while subverting its aim of limiting the candidates for lordship to the legitimate descendants of Lucrezia Borgia. In attempting to give force to Alfonso's intentions, they could see themselves as carrying on his opposition to papal demands that threatened the welfare of his house and state.

Of our three texts, only the letter supported a legal requirement for a change of status. The poems provide literary legitimations of Borso and Ercole by changing the terms of discourse surrounding their succession. Divine will and Borso's superhuman attributes justify his rule in the *Borsiad*. Ercole's virtuous heart and exemplary conduct rather than military superiority explain his elevation as duke in *Orlando Innamorato*. The attributes of both men show their fidelity to the model of their ancestors, who can be traced back to the heroes of Troy.

Neither lord needed an epic poem, nor can a desire to counter detractors at home or abroad explain the poets' decision to write. Strozzi's dedication to his project highlights his belief in its intrinsic value. He continued to work on the *Borsiad* long after Borso's death, even though it conflicted with the revisionist perspective of Ercole's supporters. The choice of a demanding literary form suggests Strozzi's desire to appeal to the ages. In the absence of descendants to venerate Borso's name, the epic could justify the recent history of the House of Este and immortalize him, together with the poet who preserved his memory.

Succession to the Lordship of Ferrara from 1240 to 1598

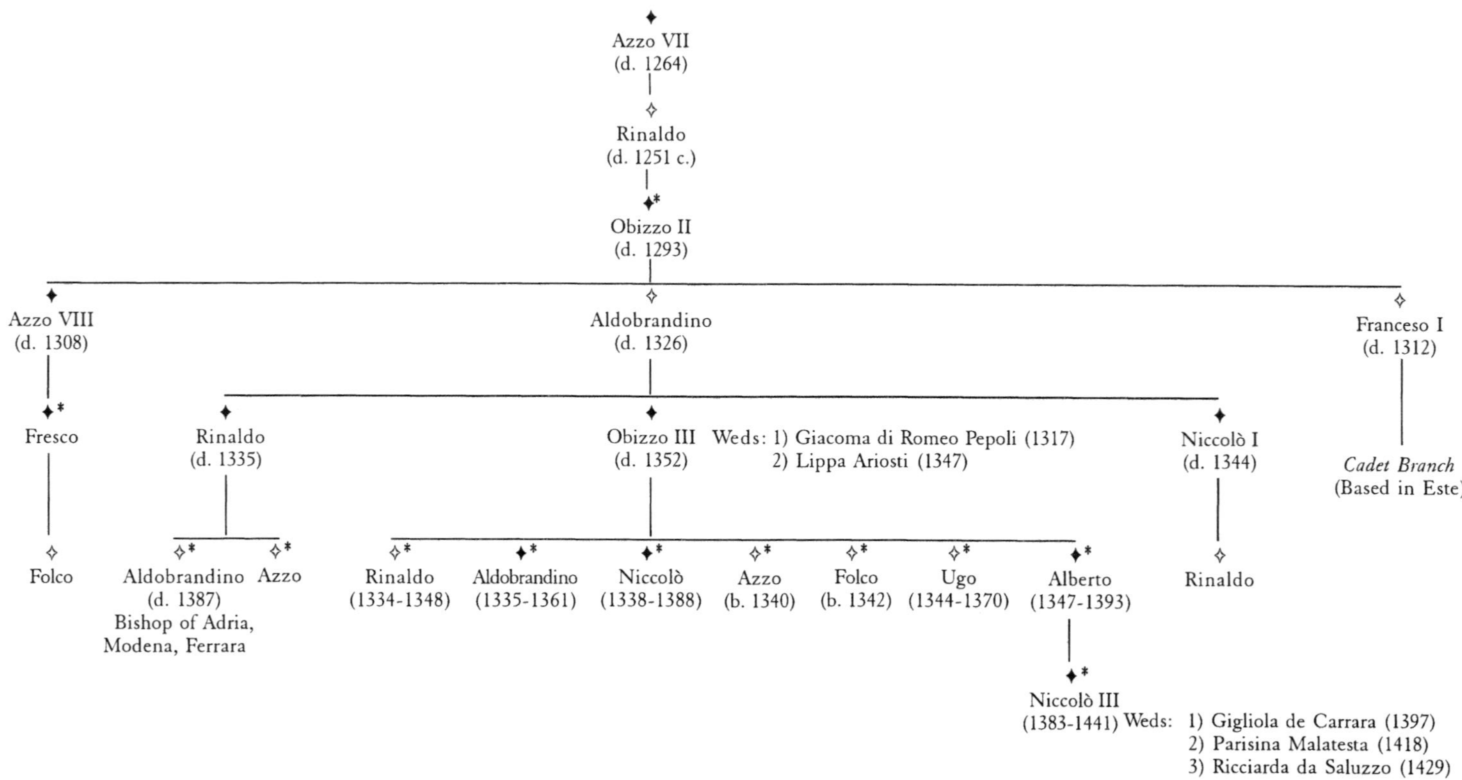

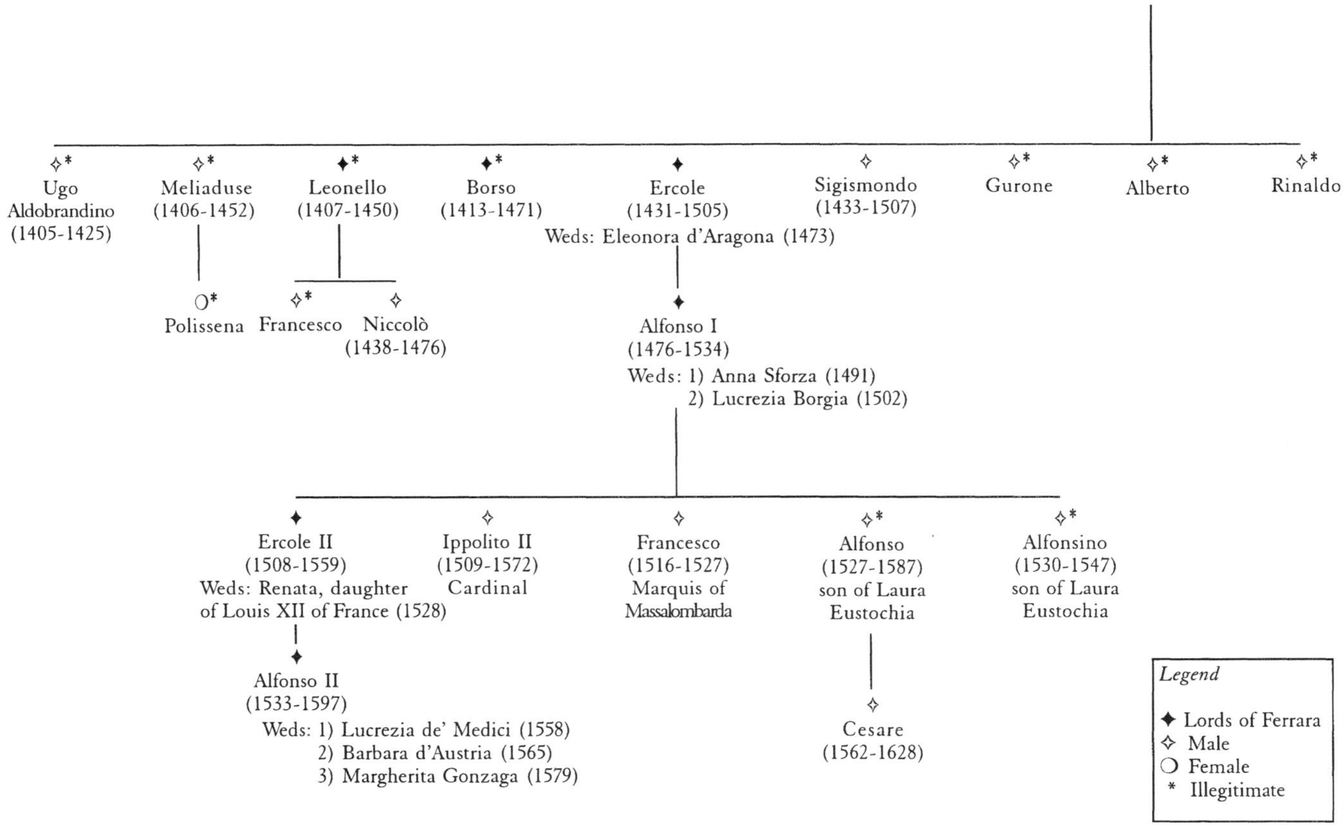
✧* Ugo Aldobrandino (1405-1425)
✧* Meliaduse (1406-1452)
✦* Leonello (1407-1450)
✦* Borso (1413-1471)
✦ Ercole (1431-1505)
Weds: Eleonora d'Aragona (1473)
✧ Sigismondo (1433-1507)
✧* Gurone
✧* Alberto
✧* Rinaldo
○* Polissena
✧* Francesco
✧ Niccolò (1438-1476)
✦ Alfonso I (1476-1534)
Weds: 1) Anna Sforza (1491)
2) Lucrezia Borgia (1502)
✦ Ercole II (1508-1559)
Weds: Renata, daughter of Louis XII of France (1528)
✧ Ippolito II (1509-1572) Cardinal
✧ Francesco (1516-1527) Marquis of Massalombarda
✧* Alfonso (1527-1587) son of Laura Eustochia
✧* Alfonsino (1530-1547) son of Laura Eustochia
✦ Alfonso II (1533-1597)
Weds: 1) Lucrezia de' Medici (1558)
2) Barbara d'Austria (1565)
3) Margherita Gonzaga (1579)
✧ Cesare (1562-1628)
Legend
✦ Lords of Ferrara
✧ Male
○ Female
* Illegitimate

Marginal Spaces of Prostitution in Renaissance Ferrara[1]

Diane Yvonne Ghirardo

On any given morning in 1471, the prostitute Giovanna of Venice, then resident of a Ferrarese brothel on via Malborghetto, might have contemplated with resignation the options open to her for a day on the town.[2] Unless it was Saturday and she planned to go to the public market near the cathedral, legally she could

[1] A version of this article appeared as "The Topography of Prostitution in Renaissance Ferrara," in *Journal of the Society of Architectural Historians* 60 (2001): 402–31. I am grateful to the Graham Foundation for providing funds in the early phases of this project. Thanks also to Tito Manlio Cerioli; Adriano Franceschini; Loretta Vancini, Liliana Visser, and Luisa Spensieri at the Archivio di Stato, Ferrara; Don Enrico Peverada of the Archivio Storico Diocesano, Ferrara; Laura Bigoni at the Fototeca, Civic Museums of Ancient Art; Professor John Pollini; Professor Karen Kensek; Anupama Mann; Professor Gwen Wright; Professor Jon Snyder; Professor Margaret Crawford; Paolo Malacarne and his staff, Federico and Marco, at Hotel San Paolo. The staff of the Biblioteca Comunale Ariostea was most helpful in locating images, manuscripts, and maps, as were the staffs of the Archivio di Stato, Modena, and the Archivio Storico Comunale in Ferrara. Luca Gavagna of Le Immagini precisely and promptly photographed maps and documents. Elizabeth Moll and Priscilla Duville helped enormously with preparation of images, including the new maps drawn by Elizabeth Moll. Colleagues at the University of Technology, Sydney; University College, London; and the University of Cape Town, South Africa, especially Associate Dean Stephen Harfield, Dr. Iain Borden, Dr. Jane Rendell, Associate Dean Derek Japha, and Chair Jo Noero, offered spirited and provocative comments and warm hospitality. Dr. Ferruccio Trabalzi, UCLA, helped throughout years of research in a variety of ways. Finally, the women of the Feminist Studies community and the Feminist Reading Group were of far greater support and sustenance than they know in offering a much-needed refuge at the University of Southern California.

[2] Archivio di Stato, Ferrara (ASFe), Archivio Notarile Antico (ANA), Notaio (Not.) Lodovico Portelli, Matr. 217, busta (b) 1, 10v–11r, 6 August 1476, "Promisio facta per Joanna de Venezia meretricem et eius lenonem Johanni Cazano."

not leave her *chiuso* (single-room or small residence) at all.[3] She was also prohibited from frequenting any of the city's other inns or hostelries on pain of immediate expulsion.[4] Nor could she or the women living in the other twenty-two *chiusi* elect to rent a room elsewhere, even at another inn, because Ferrara's laws flatly forbade private citizens to rent rooms or apartments to prostitutes.[5] Even if Giovanna chose to ignore the laws and stroll through the city's streets, statutes obliged her to don a yellow mantle so as to render her immediately recognizable as a woman living dishonorably (*disonesta*), hence less likely to be confused with an honorable woman (*donna onesta*).[6] In the event that Giovanna flouted these regulations and was unlucky enough to be apprehended, Ferrara's statutes, ducal proclamations, and the statutes of the office of *bollette* confronted Giovanna with punishments as diverse as a fine, a public whipping, torture, being paraded partially nude through the streets and having people hit her while hurling insults and rotten food (*la scopa*), or being banished from the city.

Even in the unlikely circumstance that she scrupulously obeyed the rules, she might nonetheless be expelled without warning: whenever a spasm of moralizing seized city leaders, or when a newly appointed official zealously performed his duty, or when authorities sought to engage divine intervention to prevent the spread of the plague or to prevail in war, sinners of all sorts were summarily banished. Such scapegoating accelerated at the end of the fifteenth century, when Duke Ercole I came under the influence of the fiery reformer Fra Girolamo Savonarola.[7] Giovanna's legal tenure as a prostitute in Ferrara was always under threat, then, her situation always precarious and vulnerable. The issue was not her immoral activities, which, after all, the city supervised and taxed: space rather than sex preoccupied civic authorities.

---

[3] ASFe, ASC/SF, Busta 9 (b), fascicolo (f) 17, *Statuti dell'Ufficio delle Bollette (Bollette)*, article 68, 23 April 1450, "Contra meretrices et hospites." A rental contract of 1469 locates the Montealbano brothel on via Malborghetto: ASFe, ANA, Not. Giovanni Castelli, Matr. 128, b. 3, 12v–14v, "Affictus Santini de Mediolano et fratris a Simone et fratre de Mediolano," 25 November 1469, now in Angelica Gamba, "La prostituzione a Ferrara nel tardo medioevo," diss., University of Ferrara, 1997.

[4] ASFe, ASC/SF, *Bollette*, article 68, followed by article 80, 28 December 1461, "Proclama contra publicas meretrices euntes hospitiis et tabernis," and article 90, 23 August 1464, "Quod non liceat alicui tabernario prestare domicilium alicui mulieri inhoneste viventi."

[5] ASFe, ASC/SF, *Bollette*, article 50, 5 October 1486, "Proclama contra lenones ferrarienses et meretrices et contra illos quoscumque sibi domos locantes."

[6] ASFe, ASC/SF, *Bollette*, article 3, 1438, "De meretricum banda."

[7] Luciano Chiappini, "Girolamo Savonarola ed Ercole I d'Este," *Atti e memorie della Deputazione ferrarese di storia patria* 7 (1952): 32–45.

Giovanna's situation differed in key respects from that of her pimp, Giovanni Cazano. Prostitution in itself was not illegal; a prostitute violated the law only if she evaded spatial controls or engaged in unruly behavior. On the other hand, pimping (*lenocinio*) was illegal for Ferrarese citizens, although not for foreigners, and here too spatial issues figured prominently. Space, time, and money were the standards by which city officials gauged which Ferrarese citizens were pimps: if a man slept in the room of a prostitute more than twice in one week, if he lived or talked with her for at least an hour more than three times a week, or if he lived off her earnings, then he could be declared a pimp.[8] Eligible for two months in prison, a fine, and torture, a *lenone* might also be freely beaten by Ferrarese citizens if his occupation were detected. If he continued to pimp after a conviction, he risked having his nose, foot, or hand cut off. In any event, other than the ritual declarations in the statutes and occasional ducal proclamations, a foreign pimp such as Giovanni suffered no such assaults on his purse or dignity. As a man, even one living dishonorably by fifteenth-century standards, Giovanni could move throughout the city at will, unfettered by the dense network of spatial limitations and dress requirements that encumbered Giovanna.

The contrast between the possibilities available to women and men were familiar to other prostitutes in Ferrara, and indeed, to all women in Renaissance cities, who, depending on class and social condition, labored under various types of spatial controls.[9] Although governed by strict social and political hierarchies, men enacted and policed spatial policies, while women were expected to submit to their dictates in everything from property rights to access to the city's streets. Giovanni could represent himself in the rental of a *chiuso*, for example, while Giovanna could not. Formal policies governed the enclosure of women and girls in convents, while informal policies and social mores forbade respectable women, particularly young unmarried women, from wandering about the city unchaperoned.[10] Family honor depended upon the virginity of its female members until they married; if they did not marry, the same codes of family honor required that they retire to a convent, that is, out of sight to a place where their chastity, at least theoretically, was not at risk.[11]

---

[8] ASFe, ASC/SF, *Bollette,* article 83, 29 April 1462, "Proclama contra lenones ferrarienses et eos qui habitassent in civitate ferrariae per spatium decem annorum."

[9] At the most basic level, spatial controls included participation in communal deliberations and political life in general, but also participation in ecclesiastic and civic rituals.

[10] Robert C. Davis, "The Geography of Gender in the Renaissance," in *Gender and Society in Renaissance Italy*, ed. Judith C. Brown and Robert C. Davis (London and New York: Longman, 1998), 19–38.

[11] Although the bibliography on this subject is large, a good recent summary is Michael Rocke, "Gender and Sexual Culture in Renaissance Italy," in *Gender and Society in Renaissance Italy*, ed. Brown and Davis, 50–70.

In the gendered geographies of Renaissance Italian cities, the female figure perhaps most discussed, most visible in the public domain, and most vexing for authorities was the public prostitute (*meretrice*).[12] Although preachers and writers exhorted women to conform to a wide range of behavioral practices, civic statutes and laws specified spatial controls only for prostitutes.[13] Custom or statutory provision regulated a wide range of activities and professions in Ferrara, from the sale of firewood or fish to the fabrication of gold or shoes, and in many cases the activities tended to cluster near one another. In the late fifteenth century, for example, fishermen and farmers marketed their wares in the piazza of Castelnuovo near the Porta S. Agnese, while animals were sold in the piazza of Castelvecchio, and clothing in the shops which lined the southern flank of the cathedral.[14] Prostitution, however, was not simply one among many professions. Unlike goldsmiths, armament manufacturers, fishermen, notaries, and doctors, prostitutes could not organize into guilds, and only they labored under statutory requirements to live in a particular building. Specifically, of all professions, only prostitutes confronted legal constraints on their movement through and presence in city streets. It was no accident that the spaces and spatial practices associated with a second marginal group in Renaissance Ferrara, the Jews, in many respects intersected with those concerning prostitutes.

By definition, a prostitute was neither a virgin nor under the direct supervision and control of a man. What troubled citizens and officials was less the moral issue of her concupiscence than her visibility in the public realm, her presence and activities within the city's public spaces. In Ferrara alone, nearly two dozen proclamations from the Ufficio delle Bollette in the fifteenth century defined the city spatially and temporally for *meretrici*, even if the ritual recurrence of the pronouncements suggests a wide gap between the ideal and the real. Given the evident preoccupation with prostitutes in the public realm, it is surprising

---

[12] The most extensive recent study of prostitution in Renaissance Italy is Maria Serena Mazzi, *Prostitute e lenoni nella Firenze del Quattrocento* (Milan: Il Saggiatore, 1991). An excellent and early study of women and space is Dennis Romano, "Gender and the Urban Geography of Renaissance Venice," *Journal of Social History* 23 (1989): 339–53. For an account of the property inventory and life of a sixteenth-century courtesan of considerably higher status than the women discussed here, see Cathy Santore, "Julia Lombardo, 'Somtuosa Meretrize': A Portrait by Property," *Renaissance Quarterly* 41 (1988): 44–83.

[13] See for example Francesco da Barberino, *Reggimento e costumi di donna*, ed. Giuseppe Sansone (Turin: Loescher-Chiantore, 1957); Cherubino da Spoleto, *Regole della vita matrimoniale*, ed. Francesco Zambini (Bologna: Commissione per i testi di lingua, 1888). Statutes also outlined certain spatial controls on Jews.

[14] Filippo Rodi, *Annali di Ferrara a l'anno 1598*, BL., Additional MS. It. 16,521. Vol. I, Book 1, 77v.

that other than a few references to prostitutes and public brothels in the major fifteenth- and sixteenth-century diaries by Ferrarese citizens, so little is known about precise locations of brothels or their daily operation. In fact, the published diaries of Ugo Caleffini, Bernardino Zambotti, Giovanni Maria Zerbinati and other authors identify only one brothel by name and location: El Gambaro (or Gambero), near the church of S. Cristoforo.[15] Nor, with the exception of Angelica Gamba's recent unpublished thesis, has scholarly attention been directed to the city's prostitutes and brothels more generally.[16] The situation differs little in scholarship on other Italian Renaissance cities.

Axes of accident and bias coincide in the recording of Ferrara's history, guaranteeing that scant scholarly attention has been dedicated to the city's non-patrician women, especially prostitutes. Historians consistently attended to the lives, dynastic policies, and glittering courts of the city's ruling family, the Este, rather than to the city's decidedly less glamorous and marginalized female population. To be sure, records that might reveal more about the lives of residents other than members of the upper classes are extremely limited.[17] Two major fires, in 1385 and again in 1945, destroyed enormous caches of irreplaceable documents, many of which might have facilitated fuller accounts of the social and spatial construction of prostitution. In Renaissance architectural history, these factors intersect with an emphatic bias for buildings designed in the neo-antique or classical style, usually by architects patronized by powerful Renaissance courts and whose names have been handed down reverently to successive generations of architects. Contemporary conventions precluded the possibility of women

---

[15] Giuseppe Pardi, ed., *Diario ferrarese dall'anno 1409 sino al 1502 di autori incerti,* Rerum Italicarum Scriptores, 24 (Bologna: Zanichelli, 1928–1938); idem, ed., *Diario di Ugo Caleffini (1471–1494)*, 2 vols. (Ferrara: R. Deputazione di Storia Patria per l'Emilia e la Romagna, 1938); Bernardino Zambotti, *Diario ferrarese dall'anno 1476 sino al 1504*, ed. Giuseppe Pardi, Rerum Italicarum Scriptores 24.7 (Bologna: Zanichelli, 1934), vii, II; Giovanni Maria Zerbinati, *Croniche di Ferrara: quali comenzano del anno 1500 sino al 1527*, ed. Maria Giuseppina Muzzarelli (Ferrara: Deputazione provinciale ferrarese di storia patria, 1989), Ser. Monumenti, Vol. 13.

[16] I am indebted to Dott.ssa Angelica Gamba for providing a copy of her important thesis, "La prostituzione a Ferrara nel tardo medioevo," which treats fourteenth- and fifteenth-century prostitution. Included as appendices are transcriptions of several notarial documents and letters regarding prostitutes and prostitution. Her analysis of the economic operation of Ferrara's brothels is especially careful, but citations are not always accurate.

[17] As Napoleon's armies advanced on Ferrara in 1796, church officials destroyed records that could be considered incriminating, including those of the Inquisition; copies of the Inquisition records at the Sant'Ufficio in Rome were shipped to Paris, and even though many records were returned to the church, those of Ferrara's Inquisition were apparently lost.

engaging in such activities, and since prominent architects rarely designed structures specifically associated with women, historians could easily ignore them. A long bibliography documents the work of Ferrara's most famous late fifteenth-century architect, Biagio Rossetti, for example, but virtually nothing has been written about the construction and architectural history of the city's many female monasteries.[18] Exclusive focus on palaces, military fortifications, public buildings, and cathedrals means that buildings or facilities associated with women, such as brothels, laundries, convents, housing for widows, and kitchens, garner little more than passing mention precisely because they provided settings for activities not valued in male-dominated Renaissance cities.[19] At best, historians divulge novelty items such as the underground passage that Alfonso I d'Este constructed between Castello Estense and the house of his *inamorata* Laura Dianti.[20]

In this paper, I propose to initiate an alternative understanding of the Renaissance city as comprised of gendered spaces and spatial practices, with one of the chief imperatives being the spatial control of women. In structuring urban

---

[18] The most well-known modern study of Rossetti is Bernardo Zevi, *Sapere vedere la città: Ferrara di Biagio Rossetti, "la prima città moderna europea"* (Turin: Einaudi, 1997). More recently, see Luciana Finelli, *Il Duca Ercole I e il suo architetto Biagio Rossetti. Architettura e città nella Padania tra Quattro e Cinquecento* (Rome: Edizioni Kappa, 1995); and Ada Francesca Marcianò, *L'età di Biagio Rossetti. Rinascimenti di Casa d'Este* (Ferrara: Corbo, 1991).

[19] The chief undergraduate textbooks where this preference is evident are Spiro Kostof, *A History of Architecture: Settings and Rituals* (New York: Oxford University Press, 1985); Marvin Trachtenberg and Isabelle Hyman, *Architecture: From Prehistory to Post-Modernism* (Englewood Cliffs, NJ: Prentice Hall, 1986); L. H. Heydenreich and W. Lotz, *Architecture in Italy 1400–1600* (Harmondsworth: Penguin, 1974); and Peter Murray, *The Architecture of the Renaissance* (New York: Schocken Books, 1966). Although other merits of these texts are significant, they ignore women and women's spaces. My purpose is not to castigate them, but to encourage different approaches. These books provide the introduction to Renaissance architectural history for most students; the more specialized literature offers little more. Recently, new Ph.D.s have demonstrated growing interest in matters such as women's convents; see, for example, Laura Jane McGough, "'Raised from the Devil's Jaws': A Convent for Repentant Prostitutes in Venice, 1530–1670" (Ph.D. diss., Northwestern University, 1997); Barbara J. Sabatine, "The Church of Santa Caterina dei Funari and the Vergini Miserabili of Rome" (Ph.D. diss., University of California, Los Angeles, 1992); Saundra L. Weddle, "Enclosing Le Murate: The Ideology of Enclosure and the Architecture of a Florentine Convent" (Ph.D. diss., Cornell University, 1997). See also Barbara Giordano, "Il monastero agostiniano di Santa Maria delle Grazie detto Mortara" (Bachelor's thesis, University of Ferrara, 1998). I have written a brief description of some of the architectural features of convents in Diane Ghirardo, "Virtually Visible," *Thresholds* 19 (1999): 41–47.

[20] Cittadella, *Notizie*, 329.

and architectural programs, secular and civic leaders enacted social and spatial practices regarding women's access to avowedly male domains. By location, construction, official and unofficial regulations, the buildings they erected and the cities they designed, enlarged, or revamped embodied distinctly patriarchal views about how women were to be restricted spatially, socially, and economically. Whatever the other merits of their scholarship, subsequent architectural and urban historians consistently ignored the gendering of Renaissance Italian cities and spaces, instead treating urban buildings and spaces as embodying values that were gender-neutral and universal.[21]

A well-documented set of beliefs about female inferiority, weakness, and irrationality underlay these spatial practices. An extensive and rich body of scholarship on this subject allows me to leave that discussion to specialists in the field.[22] My interest is in the spatial practices themselves, how they were enacted in cities such as Ferrara, how they influenced the city's architecture and urbanism, and how those practices have affected our understanding of Italian Renaissance building. The larger study of which this essay is but a chapter examines the ways in which many types of buildings and spaces in Renaissance Ferrara were gendered, while here I will examine the practices as they affected prostitutes, Ferrara's brothels, and the spaces of prostitution during the fifteenth and sixteenth centuries.[23]

---

[21] Zevi's study of Rossetti's Ferrara is exemplary: the female convents in the Herculean addition and brothels are not even mentioned. A singular exception to this rule is T. Tuohy, *Herculean Ferrara: Ercole d'Este (1471–1505) and the Invention of a Ducal Capital* (Cambridge: Cambridge University Press, 1996), which includes discussions of ducal constructions of various types, including the city's convents. Charles M. Rosenberg's study of Ferrarese urbanism and monuments also includes discussion of some of the city's convents: *The Este Monuments and Urban Redevelopment in Renaissance Ferrara* (Cambridge: Cambridge University Press, 1997), 145–48.

[22] The bibliography on these issues is now quite large; I want to mention only a few recent studies that also bear on women in Ferrara and neighboring cities: Deanna Shemek, *Ladies Errant: Wayward Women and Social Order in Early Modern Italy* (Durham, NC: Duke University Press, 1998); Margaret F. Rosenthal, *The Honest Courtesan* (Chicago: University of Chicago Press, 1992); Veronica Franco, *Poems and Selected Letters*, trans. and ed. Ann Rosalind Jones and Margaret F. Rosenthal (Chicago: University of Chicago Press, 1998).

[23] A preliminary article written in 1996 in which I discuss the gendered spaces of Ferrara appeared in 2000: Diane Ghirardo, "Women and Space: How Architectural History Erases Women," in *Intersections: Architectural History and Critical Theory*, ed. I. Borden and J. Rendell (London: Routledge, 2000), 170–200.

Prostitutes in the public sphere: spatial controls

Mazzi's pathbreaking study of Quattrocento prostitution in Florence demonstrates that, overwhelmingly, the city's prostitutes emigrated from elsewhere in Italy or Europe.[24] What little surfaces in fragmentary court documents suggests that the same was true of Ferrara. Like Giovanna from Venice, prostitutes moved to Ferrara from elsewhere in Italy or Europe: Ursola daughter of the German dye maker Zeno, Ursolina of Udine, Lucia of Bologna, Ambrosina from Como.[25] From at least the fourteenth through the seventeenth centuries, prostitutes commonly moved from their home towns to practice their trade: a prominent sixteenth-century courtesan in Rome was Camilla the Sienese, and in 1624 a list of prostitutes living on the Strada della Campana in Rome included Antonia Fiorentina, Francesca Ferarese, Narda Napoletana.[26] The first evidence of a spatial consequence of prostitution, then, was often departure from home, presumably to a place where families would not be shamed by the woman's profession and where she could be anonymous.

The paucity of records makes it impossible to determine which young women were driven by any or all of several possibilities: poverty, widowhood, rape, or, as contemporary records quaintly phrased it, "deflowering." A young woman who succumbed — with or without force — to a man who promised marriage often found herself abandoned. She thus forfeited her honor, the one asset that could enable her to contract a respectable marriage. Whatever the cause, relocation to foreign cities appears to have been a common practice.

The second consequence concerned limitations on movement and spatial location, not only where her business was conducted, but quite literally whether she could walk on city streets at all. The thirteenth-century statutes of Ferrara forbade all public prostitutes (*ganea* or *galnea*) from living or loitering in the city, specifically between the Po River and the central via Sabbioni, from Porta Agnese to Porta Leone, near the church of San Francesco and in via S. Paolo. The statutes also insisted that, in the interests of public decency, they were forbidden

---

[24] Mazzi, *Prostitute e lenoni,* 293; see also Richard C. Trexler, *Public Life in Renaissance Florence* (Ithaca: Cornell University Press, 1980).

[25] ASFe, ANA, Not. V. Lucenti, matr. 201, b. 2, "Obligatio Ursoline et Lucie Meretrices Facta Magistro Jannino Franzexeno," 13 January 1473.

[26] Archivio di Stato, Roma (ASR), Tribunale Criminale del Governatore (Trib Crim Gov), Atti di Cancelleria, Miscellenea, b. 105; Trib Crim Gov, Processi, Sec. XVI, 1557, b. 33, process 19. The women's names were Camilla the Sienese, Antonia the Florentine, Francesca the Ferrarese, Narda the Neapolitan.

to frequent Borgo S. Leonardo and Borgo S. Guglielmo, two settlements clustered just outside the northern walls.[27]

In a pattern common to most European cities, by the fourteenth and fifteenth centuries these prohibitions disappeared from the city's statutes, and prostitution shifted close to or inside Ferrara's city walls with the establishment of public brothels (*postriboli*) and the enactment of a system of taxation on the spirits consumed in the taverns connected to prostitution.[28] Insufficient evidence exists to document the precise modalities by which this took place in Ferrara, but by the late fourteenth century, notarial records document the presence of public brothels.[29] By bringing the brothels into the city, authorities expected to be able to exert greater control over where and how prostitutes lived, and to profit from associated taxes. Not surprisingly, the rules regarding confinement to brothels in Ferrara appear to have been officially ignored. Letters in the Este archives document that Ercole I knew of prostitution flourishing in city taverns other than the public brothels, for example, but that he was quite willing to tolerate this because of the tax revenues generated.[30]

Periodically, official *gride* also exhorted concubines to enter the public brothel, highlighting an option for unmarried women to engage in illicit sexual relations.[31]

---

[27] William Montorsi, *Statuta Ferrariae anno MCCLXXXVII* (Ferrara: Cassa di risparmio di Ferrara, 1955), articles LXXI, LXXII, LXXIII, LXXIIII, 275–76. Article LXXI, "Statuimus quod nulla galnea publica moretur supra ripam Ferrarie neque in civitate a via Sablonum usque ad Padum." Article LXXII, ". . . quod nulla galnea publica et famosa moretur in burgo Sancti Leonardi et Sancti Guilielmi, incipiendo a porta Sancte Agnetis eundo per viam Novam, qua itur ad Lungolam per viam Magnam usque ad trivium Caldiroli; et si aliqua reperta fuerit fustigetur per civitatem." Article LXXIII, ". . . quod nulla publica galnea morari debeat in aliqua domo sive domibus positis supra viam terralii Sancti Pauli usque ad locum fratrum Predicatorum." Article LXXIIII, "Statuimus quod nulla ganea moretur a porta Beate Agnetis Virginis usque ad portam Leonis, et a loco Beati Francisci usque cantonem domini episcopi, nec in via Sancti Pauli, nec in aliqua contrata posita infra hos confines. Et potestas teneatur precise facere procurari semel in mense per familiam suam." The only other spatial limitation concerned Jews, who were obligated to remain indoors in the days preceding Easter, evidently for their own safety.

[28] Jacques Roussiaud, *La prostitutione nel Medioevo* (Rome-Bari: Laterza, 1995).

[29] ASFe, ANA, Matr. 7, Pietro Pincerna, b. 1, f. 4, cc. 8rv, 8 April 1379, "Affictus Baldino di Simone de Bergamo e Bono dei Danieli."

[30] ASMo, Camera Ducale (CD), Leggi e decreti, C, V, 200, 26 October 1478, Ercole d'Este to Eleonora d'Aragona; now Appendix 8 in Gamba, "La prostituzione."

[31] ASFe, *Bollette*, 25 April 1496, article 131, "Ad dei Omnipotentis Laudem et Gloriam Contra Blasfemates, Sodomites, Baratarios Ludos, Concubinarios, Meretrices, Lenones, Datiarios, et Officiales Passium Ac Beccarios Vendentes Tempore Festivitatum," 45v–46r.

Concubines were supported by a single man for anywhere from a few months to years, relationships which the women often hoped would be regularized by marriage. Modenese *meretrice* Moranda Magnanini of Fanano had a stable relationship with Bernardino da Carpi, she informed the officials of the Inquisition, and he had promised to "pigliar[la] per moglie."[32] Despite the erstwhile efforts of Ferrarese officials to classify and isolate promiscuous women in brothels, concubinage blurred the lines between prostitutes who lived in brothels and married women, and indeed, some women at different times in their lives may have been all three. The existence of concubinage rendered the task of identifying prostitutes with special garments and locations all the more vexing. When Giovanni Castelli served as chief of the *Ufficio delle Bollette* (taxes and licenses office), he attempted to define prostitutes in a proclamation issued in 1476, first in terms of location and then in terms of behavior and reputation:

> ". . . a cadauna putana et meretrice publica, cussi habitante in lo postribulo de San Biasio et del Gambaro de la cita de Ferrara [. . .] che carnalmente si facia conoscere, mo' da questo mo' da quello altro, o che habia nome et fama di femine impudice et inhonesta vita. . . ."[33]

Gride concerning the spatial limitations of *meretrici* cited among their objectives the protection of respectable women's honor and sense of public decency.[34] The risks associated with the promiscuous mixing of respectable and dishonorable women were high: a woman assaulted by a man in a street known to be frequented by prostitutes had no legal recourse for avenging her honor, for in theory she should not have been there in the first place.[35] Then there were married women, for whom prostitution was an occasional although at times risky activity, undertaken in order to supplement family income. In 1482, Margherita, a "prostitute housewife" (*meretrice casalenga*), alias *la fachina*, was killed by the

---

[32] ". . . pigliar[la] per moglie": ASMo, Fondo Inquisitione, b. 9, case 3, "Contra Moranda Magnanini da Fanano, meretricem," 22 August 1596, 5v.

[33] ASFe, ASC, *Bollette*, article 114, 17 May 1476, Commissio ducalis contra meretrices publicas facientes et committentes insultum contra aliquem: ". . . to any whore or public prostitute, either living in the brothel of S. Biagio or El Gambaro in the city of Ferrara [. . .] who allows first this one then that one to know her carnally, or who is known by public reputation as a shameful woman of dishonorable life . . ."

[34] ". . . Anchora per levare ogni occasione de infectione, et perché né li ochii né le orechie ne la fama de le done che vivono bene sino offese . . ." ASFe, *Bollette,* 25 April 1496, article 131.

[35] Luciano Maragna, ed., *Gli statuti del Polesine di Rovigo durante il dominio estense* (Ferrara: Copy Express, 1996), 82.

son of her lover, Francesco D'Ortona, whose family crumbled when he became involved with her.[36] Had she lived, she ran the risk of being denounced as a prostitute by her neighbors or her husband and forced to enter a brothel. In a shaming ritual that lives on in contemporary Italy as the insult gesture of *le corne* (the cuckold's horns), a husband who allowed himself to be cuckolded suffered the embarrassment of being forced to tour the city's taverns and inns to the sound of tambourines with a pair of horns on his head, to be belittled by his compatriots as a cuckold.[37] Antonio dei Paxi forestalled such a fate in 1451 by reporting that his wife, Luciana Bianca, had left him and committed adultery *cum pluribus*. Just to make his own role clear, he added that all of this happened against his will.[38]

The persistence of proclamations demanding that any women having sexual contact with more than one man enter the brothel suggests that women shifted into and out of different types of sexual relations during their lives depending upon financial need and family circumstances. The likelihood of a woman creating scandal in her neighborhood because of an illicit relationship was even greater when the line separating honorable women from dishonorable ones was elusive — hence the repeated efforts to fix it precisely once and for all by confining dishonorable women to brothels. Although no records from the fifteenth and sixteenth centuries remain that would help us determine how well this rule was enforced, trial records from late sixteenth-century Modena and early seventeenth-century Ferrara indicate significant non-compliance.[39]

Prostitutes in the public sphere: behavior codes and enforcement

Civic authorities regulated more than just the visibility of prostitutes in city streets; they also maintained surveillance over the women's comportment. The injunction in the 1287 statutes against *galnea* and *ribaldi* gambling or engaging

---

[36] *Diario di Ugo Caleffini*, 10 Feb. 1482, 272. A *fachino* is a porter, but what the alias meant for Margarita is not clear.

[37] ASFe, ASC, *Bollette,* article 40.

[38] ASMo, CD, *Libri dei Malefici*, Reg. 2 (1451), 22 September, c. 111r.

[39] Many of the relevant records for fifteenth- through seventeenth-century Ferrara are at the Archivio Storico Diocesano, and in Modena at the Archivio di Stato, Modena, in particular the records of the Inquisition. Modena offers a useful comparison because it was under direct Este dominion throughout the fifteenth and sixteenth centuries, and the official in charge of prostitutes in Ferrara during the fifteenth century performed the same duties in Modena. The historical links suggest that policies and enforcement were likely to have been quite similar.

in rowdy behavior in the cathedral or its portico gives some idea of the raucous character of public life in late medieval Ferrara.[40] Giovanni Castello, notary for the *Ufficio delle Bollette,* in May of 1476 issued a bulletin enjoining prostitutes from committing various sorts of offenses against citizens. He specified that these acts included stealing money, or other things in large or small quantities, or committing any type of insult or dishonor against another, or stealing someone's hat, or dragging an unwilling man into their room " . . . como hano alcuno de epse meretrice usato de fare per lo passato." Punishment would be swift and merciless: a public and brutal whipping in Ferrara's piazze followed by eight days in jail until the women made restitution.[41] A mere six months later, a second proclamation denounced such thefts again, noting that the prostitutes were stealing from farmers and foreigners; this time, however, prostitutes were forbidden to commit violence against any person of any social level. The fine leveled was double the normal one. Repeated denunciations of prostitutes' actions to civic officials " . . . de che ogni qual di ni e facto querele et lamentele al officio da le bollette," prompted these pronouncements.[42]

Whether this behavior was commonplace or related to specific events is not clear. Given the proximity of dates, for example, the rowdiness that triggered official response might be linked with the public festivals on the feast of St. George on 24 April 1476, particularly given the participation of prostitutes in the running of the Palio for women, as depicted in the fresco for the month of April in the Palazzo Schifanoia.[43] General economic conditions might also be a factor; when the second proclamation was issued in November 1476, Ferrara was blanketed with snow, and high prices for grain led to economic hardships for many, including prostitutes.[44]

---

[40] Montorsi, *Statuta*, article LXVI, 274: " . . . quod nullus ribaldus nec aliqua ganea debeat morari ad ludendum nec ad standum in episcopatu Ferrarie nec sub porticibus ipsius episcopatus."

[41] " . . . as some of these prostitutes have been accustomed to doing in the past": ASFe, ASC, *Bollette*, article 114, 17 May 1476, now in Gamba, "La prostituzione," appendix 13. Most punishments took place in public, but in Ferrara, most crimes could be resolved primarily by the payment of a fine in order to avoid a public whipping or other type of torture.

[42] " . . . de che ogni qual dì ni è facto querele et lamentele al officio da le bollette" [" . . . about which charges and compaints arrive in the Uffio delle Bollette every day"]: ASFe, ASC. *Bollette,* article 116, 29 November 1476, now in Gamba, "La prostituzione," appendix 14.

[43] Zambotti, *Diario ferrarese*, 6–7; Shemek, *Ladies Errant*, chap. 1, 17–44.

[44] *Diario di Ugo Caleffini*, 175.

Whether these or other proclamations were efficacious is doubtful; so often were they repeated — two variations of the same sets of regulations re-issued in just a few months in 1462 and again in 1476 — that they must not have accomplished their objectives.[45] A certain inconsistency attends to city officials as well. In his diary, Zambotti records measures he took against prostitutes on 21 July 1489, while he was serving as head of the *Ufficio delle Bollette*:

> Fu facta la crida che niuna meretrice possa stare in questa nostra citade, e che niuno Ferrarexe possa essere roffiano, e che tuti quelli ge darano caxe, cadino a la pena de lire 50, e che ciaschaduno scià dove le siano, le dibiano dare, fra il termene de tri zorni, in nota a li officiali da le bolete.[46]

Just one month later, Zambotti proudly announced the punishments he inflicted on two prostitutes, at once demonstrating his firmness in handling the offense, and at the same time revealing that the officials of the Bollette had not enforced the earlier injunction:

> A doe meretrice del loco pubblico io, come suo superiore a le bolete, feci dare dui squassi de corda a ciaschuna, a uno travo messo fora in Piaza a le fenestre del podestà, perchè le haveano ferite uno contadino e toltege per forza uno paro de scarpe e una bretta, e a tal spectaculo ge feci venire presente tute le altre meretrice.[47]

In the insult codes of Renaissance Italy, knocking off a man's hat profoundly insulted his manhood, and the theft of his hat or other clothes constituted an even greater offense against his male dignity.[48]

---

[45] ASFe, ASC, *Bollette,* article 83, 29 April 1462, and 22 September 1462.

[46] Zambotti, *Diario*, 209: "21 July. A proclamation was issued that no prostitute could remain in this our city, and that no Ferrarese citizen could be a procurer, and that anyone who has given them housing is subject to a penalty of 50 lire, and that anyone who knows where they are living must notify the officials of the Bollette within three days."

[47] Zambotti, *Diario*, 209: "21 August. I, as chief of the [office of] the Bollette, had two turns of the cord inflicted on two prostitutes from the public brothel on a scaffolding in the public square in front of the podesta's windows, because they wounded a farmer and took a pair of shoes and a cap from him by force, and I made all the other prostitutes come to see the spectacle."

[48] Sharon Strocchia, "Gender and the Rites of Honour in Italian Renaissance Cities," in *Gender and Society*, ed. Brown and Davis, 39–60, esp. 57–58.

In his account of the life of Ludovico Ariosto, Michele Catalano recounted that in 1496 the wife of a police officer was punished with the *scopa* for having affairs: she traversed the main city streets on foot, following which she was pelted with rotten fruit and sticks.[49] Such public punishments reinforced the "public" character of the prostitute or the woman guilty of illicit sex in the public domain, where *fama pubblica* (reputation) remained the most certain measure of a woman's honor.

Prostitutes often came to know well the jail cells in the Palazzo della Ragione. They appeared before the courts for a diverse array of offenses, including debts to owners of inns and brothels, fisticuffs with other prostitutes, sometimes on the streets, stealing from clients, and violence against clients who tried to escape without paying.[50] Though fragmentary, the remaining judicial records also indicate that the spatial and clothing requirements outlined above were enforced. Caterina the Venetian was found guilty of failing to wear the yellow cloth as required of prostitutes in 1458, and another Caterina, "Schiava" (the Slav), was punished for the same offense in 1461.[51] In 1471, documents that record names of prisoners in Ferrara's jail included the following three women, all identified as *meretrix*: Agata of Florence, Giovanna of Piacenza, and Romanella, but with no indication of the offenses they committed.[52] Patchy as the records are, a certain recidivism is apparent: Romanella ended up in prison again in 1472.[53] Prostitutes were required to register at the Ufficio delle Bollette upon moving to Ferrara, and to purchase a pass whenever they wanted to leave the city temporarily or permanently, all of which entailed paying fees. Although such fees extended

---

[49] Michele Catalano, *Vita di Ludovico Ariosto, ricostruita su nuovi documenti*, 2 vols. (Geneva: Olschki, 1931), 1: 106, cited in Gamba, "La prostituzione," 233; see Shemek's translation, *Ladies Errant*, 36–37.

[50] Ursolina and Lucia contracted a debt with the owner of El Gambero brothel. ASFe, ANA, Vitale Lucenti, Matr. 201, b. 1, 24r, 19 January 1473, "Obligatio Ursoline et Lucie meretricum facta Magistro Joannino franxoso," cited in Gamba, "La prostituzione," 259. Another Caterina, this time a "*polacca*," beat one of her colleagues in the brothel with a club in 1458; ASMo., Memoriale 11, c. 131v, 8 June 1458; Anna, alias "Rebatino," clubbed Franchino of Reggio for attempting to get away without paying: ASMo, *Maleficio*, 2, 3 December 1459.

[51] ASMo, Memoriale 11, December 1458; ASMo, Memoriale 14, 15 September 1461, cited in Gamba, "La prostituzione," 271. Given the large numbers of Slavs in Venice, it is not unlikely that Caterina the Venetian and Caterina the Slav referred to the same woman.

[52] ASFe, ASC, Ser. Pat. *Libro Commissioni,* B 7, f. 10, 8 November 1471, c. 101r. Cittadella records the same three prostitutes, but gives the incorrect date of 1470; Cittadella, *Notizie amministrative,* 112.

[53] Ibid., c. 116.

to everyone, the charges for pimps and prostitutes were double the normal sum, a burden which they and their pimps regularly sought to evade.[54] Elisabetta "Schiava" was fined for leaving the city without permission in 1459, and Bartolomea was also fined 75 lire for the same offense. [55]

The elaborate system of spatial controls and injunctions against bad behavior by prostitutes often came down to money: access to money gave the *meretrice* the opportunity to pay a fine to evade corporal punishment. But prostitution was not always a lucrative full-time occupation, particularly in Ferrara, where the tax burden was onerous for most of the population. Gamba documented a significant number of prostitutes indebted to the operators of the brothels, which turned them into what amounted to indentured servants, but with no fixed date on which the obligation ended.[56] Wealthy Ferrarese were obviously aware of this practice, for some left bequests to allow a prostitute to pay off her debt and leave the brothel; even Marchese Nicolò III and Duke Borso granted prostitutes money to clear up their debts to brothel owners.[57]

Ferrara's public documents assert that *meretrici* were expected to maintain a distance from *donne oneste*. Evidence from the archives of the Inquisition in Modena in the sixteenth century and Ferrara in the early seventeenth century indicates that the lines were more fluid than other judicial records would suggest. Modena was part of the Este territory, and indeed, in the fifteenth century, the same officers at times supervised the *Uffici del Malefizio* and the taxes on prostitution in both cities.[58] In the late sixteenth century, a significant number of investigations by the Inquisition involved Modenese prostitutes. The accusation against them was not public or clandestine prostitution, but rather casting spells and incantations, especially to help women regain or acquire a man's affections. Their expertise in such matters apparently rested on the notion that as prostitutes, they had special understandings of matters of love and sex. Ippolita de Bennis of Ferrara recounted in 1596 how she saw Moranda Magnanini of Fanano, a prostitute, determine through incantations whether lovers really loved and cared

---

[54] *Diario ferrarese di autori incerti*, 202–3.

[55] ASMo, *Maleficio*, 1459–1460, 35v, 23 July 1459; Bartolomea Fiorata, 25r, 20 April 1459.

[56] Gamba, "La prostituzione," 164–69.

[57] ASMo, CD, Libri Camerali Diversi, "Entrata e spesa," 4; Memoriale n. 20 (1468–71), 271, both cited in Gamba, "La prostituzione," 253.

[58] Giovanni Greco of Constantinople is listed as being in charge of collecting the taxes on the brothels in Ferrara from 1434 through the 1440s: ASMo, Camera Ducale, Libri camerali diversi, Entrata et Spesa anno 1434, reg. 4, c. 2r.; his sons continued to run Ferrara's brothel or sublet it to others until the 1480s (see below, note 68).

for her or her clients.[59] In her case as in those of other prostitutes examined by the Inquisition, married female neighbors appear to have frequented the houses of prostitutes with relative ease and to have sought their help for prayers and incantations, with no particular concern for the fact that they were prostitutes or concubines. Married men and priests found this mixing of *donne oneste* with dishonorable ones troubling; complaints about women of ill-repute living throughout Ferrara rather than only in the brothels were directed to Duke Ercole by some of his officials in the 1490s.[60] Comparable complaints from ordinary citizens in Rome reveal that they were outraged that these women

> pubbli[cavano] di giorno per strada li fatti suoi dishonesti, toccando l'huomini per le loro vergogne e facendo altri ati dishonestissimi avanti donne maritate e zittelle con grandissimo scandalo. . . . [61]

Although they asserted that these activities shamed their wives and daughters, the risk of confusing their daughters with the prostitutes was equally compelling, because the men who signed similar petitions asserted that they needed to keep their women in the house, or to move away, "per non star mescolati in detta infamia."[62]

The rituals Moranda and other prostitutes practiced attached special importance to the thresholds of houses or rooms. Women repeatedly testified in Inquisition hearings about depositing items on the doorway or conducting special activities in the liminal zone between the street and the house. The portal or threshold has historically acted in Italy as a sacred barrier between private and public space. In Roman antiquity, figures such as the phallus posted at

---

[59] ASMo, Fondo Inquisizione, b. 9, Processo 3, "Contra Moranda Magnanini di Fanano," 2 August 1596, c. 2v.

[60] ASMo, Cancelleria Ducale, Carteggio Fattorale (CD/CF), b. 22/1, f. 25, 16 September 1490, to Duchess Eleonora; f. 8, from Giacomo Prisciani to Duchess Eleonora, 27 February 1490; f. 26, from Leonello Sogari to Duke Ercole, 29 April 1491; f. 25, Giacomo Prisciani to Duke Ercole, 4 May 1491, now transcribed as appendices 15–18 in Gamba,"La prostituzione."

[61] ". . . publicly displayed their dishonorable behavior during the day, touching men's privates and doing other dishonorable acts in front of married and single women giving rise to great scandal." ASR, Trib Crim, Atti di Cancelleria Miscellanea, b. 105, foglio 34, 1624.

[62] ". . . so as not to be mixed up in that infamy." ASR, Trib Crim, Atti di Cancelleria Miscellanea, b. 105, foglio 36, 1624.

doorways guarded against evil spirits entering the home.[63] One of the distinguishing features of prostitutes and other women of ill repute in Renaissance Italy was that they apparently breached this zone with impunity, leaning out of windows and loitering at open doorways. In this way they evaded the ban on movement in public streets while drumming up business without actually breaking the law. Indeed, illustrations of prostitutes frequently depict them as lingering in doorways or leaning out of windows soliciting business, behavior frowned upon for respectable women by writers of the time precisely because it reflected the behavior of a *meretrice.*

Comportment that might be acceptable, or at least tolerable, inside, could well be a crime outside. A telling contrast is the case of the Roman prostitute Maddalena Prosperi, who tried to defend herself against a charge of wearing men's clothes in public by claiming that while wearing her lover's clothes she only leaned out the doorway, but never actually crossed the threshold into the street.[64] The danger of a woman dressing as a man was particularly acute because in doing so she could embrace male spatial prerogatives and move freely through the streets to taverns and inns.[65]

One of the typical insult gestures in sixteenth-century Rome among prostitutes involved setting fire to another prostitute's door, as Camilla Senese was accused of doing in 1557 to the door of Lucrezia Greca.[66] As spatial markers, doors and thresholds became the locus of public insults, and also marked the point at which a prostitute passed into the city's public space and fell under the

---

[63] Numerous books about housing in Roman Italy document the importance of the threshold; among recent texts see John R. Clarke, *The Houses of Roman Italy 100 B.C.–A.D. 250. Ritual Space and Decoration* (Berkeley: University of California Press, 1991), 4–10; Andrew Wallace-Hadrill, *House and Society in Pompeii and Herculaneum* (Princeton: Princeton University Press, 1994), esp. 3–61.

[64] ASR, Trib Crim Gov, Processi, Sec. XVII, b. 534, case 5, 28 June 1660, "Contra Maddalena Prosperi et altri."

[65] Cesare Vecellio, *Habiti antichi et moderni di tutto il mondo* (Venice: Appresso i Sessa, 1598), noted that many prostitutes dressed in a masculine fashion; Valerie Hotchkiss examined some of the implications of cross-dressing during the Renaissance in *Clothes Make the Man* (New York: Garland, 1996).

[66] ASR, Trib Crim Gov, Processi, Sec. XVI, b. 2, case 19, 23 October 1557, "Contra Camillam Senens. curalem." In addition to burning the door, the two women traded insults from the windows of their houses, calling one another *sfondata puttana, poltrona*, and *porcha vacca.* Camilla either instigated or performed the same insult to another prostitute two years later. For a transcription of that trial, see Thomas V. Cohen and Elizabeth S. Cohen, *Words and Deeds in Renaissance Rome: Trials before the Papal Magistrates* (Toronto: University of Toronto Press, 1993), esp. 92–100.

supervision of civic authorities, just as entering the city gates did for foreigners. The practice, or at least the threat, persists in Rome among the working class, as evidenced by insults I have heard women hurl at one another.

Brothels: Character and Location

Although Ferrara's public brothels date at least to the late fourteenth century, little has been known about their exact locations or physical characteristics.[67] Like other structures associated with women, little effort has been expended on understanding ownership and operation. An investigation of diaries and public records in Modena and Ferrara now allows us to flesh out some of this information.

In the fifteenth century, the public brothels were located in the San Romano district east of the Cathedral, in the *contrada* of Santa Croce, and near the *contrada* of San Biagio — near the city's northern, western, and southern boundaries. The church of San Biagio was situated on today's Corso Isonzo, just south of viale Cavour, in the westernmost extension of the city. Given the earlier statutory prohibitions against prostitutes living within the city, it is no surprise that the two for which we have detailed information in the fifteenth century were located adjacent to the fifteenth-century walls. According to a rental contract of 1469, the S. Biagio brothel was part of the Montealbano tavern located west of the castle, near the old city walls approximately on via Boccacanale di S. Stefano between viale Cavour and via Ripagrande.[68] Twenty-three *chiusi* and a tavern were located between the *contrade* Rotta and Mutina near the gardens of the hospital of S. Giustina. Bordered on three sides by via Malborghetto, the new ducal stables

---

[67] For example, in his transcription of the chronicles of Ferrara in the fifteenth century by unknown author(s), Giuseppe Pardi identifies the location of the new brothel of 1501 as being near the gate of S. Agnese al Terraglio, northwest of the old walls. But the text reads, "che le putane publice dovessero stare de dreto da l'hospetale de Sancta Agnexe . . ." (*Diario*, 268, n. 3), and the hospital of S. Agnese (or conservatory) is near via delle Volte in the Borgo Superiore, as in Fig. 13b.

[68] ASFe, ANA, Giovanni Castelli, Matr. 128, b. 3, 12v–14v, 25 November 1469, "Affictus Santini de Mediolano et Fratris a Simone et Fratre de Mediolano"; transcribed as Appendix 21 in Gamba, "La prostituzione." Further description of the site of this tavern and brothel is in ASFe, ANA, Mat. 165, Baldessare Canani, b. 2, fasc. 4, 11 ottobre 1488, Memorial to Eleanora d'Este, indicating that the property had been in the hands of Zoane Grego de Constantinopoli [Giovanni Greco of Constantinople] and his wife Isabetta since 1426, and that it was now in the hands of their son Matio da Millano [Matteo of Milan]. Greco was the city official who supervised brothels in Ferrara and Modena in the early fifteenth century.

and two *chiusi* belonging to Antonio de Fabro, the rear of the complex faced the old earthen walls west of the canal of S. Stefano.

The name Montealbano also designated the plot of land on which the brothel and tavern sat; owned by the Poveri di Christo, a religious organization, the property had been invested in Giovanni Greco and his wife Isabetta in 1426.[69] The sale contract and subsequent documentation of the construction of a vast new stable complex for the Duke's horses in 1488 help pin down the precise location. In a transaction witnessed by architect Biagio Rossetti in April 1488, Matteo da Milano sold the Montealbano osteria and *chiusi* to Ercole I.[70] Within two weeks, payments for the demolition of the osteria and the *chiusi* began to be recorded, and construction initiated on the new stables designed by Biagio Rossetti, always referring to expenses for the construction located "dove era il bordello zoe a San Biaxi," between the contrà della Rotta and via Malborghetto.[71] The brothel, then, was situated in the upper third of the block bordered by today's via Cavour, via Garibaldi, Corso Isonzo, and via Aldigheri. Aleotti's 1605 plan of Ferrara illustrates the site of the stables, which is also where the brothel had been. The church and gardens of Santa Giustina occupied the southern part of the block, so the Jewish cemetery was located in the middle of the block.

Brothel operators either paid for licenses or rented the spaces directly from the ducal chamber.[72] Inconsistent terminology in Ferrarese documents makes ownership difficult to determine, because the available records did not distinguish among different types of ownership or operation. A proclamation of 1476 referred to the complexes at S. Biagio, El Gambaro, and Santa Croce collectively as *postriboli,* while only El Gambaro was referred to by name and as a *loco pubblico* (public brothel).[73] Although at times quite lucrative, revenues from prostitution could vary considerably, and not necessarily because of a decline in clientele. Orlando da Ferrara, who conducted the city's brothels and jail until 1426, complained that he was still in debt after six years because so many prostitutes had fled the city in 1417–1418 to avoid the plague.[74]

---

[69] ASFe, ANA, Matr. 165, Canani, b. 2, f. 4, Memorial to Eleanora d'Este, 11 October 1488.

[70] ASFe, ANA, Mat. 231, Gentile Sardi, b. 2, f. 2, 23 April 1488.

[71] ASMo, CD, Munizioni e fabbriche, Reg. 21 (1488), cc. 5, 10, 35.

[72] Several memoranda from Canani to the Duke or Duchess outline terms of rental contracts and fees paid to the Duke for brothels and taverns; ASFe, ANA, Mat. 165, Baldessare Canani, b. 2, fasc. 4, Memorandum to Eleanora d'Este, 17 October 1488; Memorandum to Ercole d'Este, 20 June 1488.

[73] ASFe, ASC, *Bollette*, 18 May 1476.

[74] ASMo, CD, Libri Camerali Diversi, n. 2, 24 December 1426, c. 1.

The brothel and inn on via del Gambaro appears to have been owned by the Este, with the operation transferred from time to time to new overseers upon payment of rents and taxes.[75] Perhaps dating back to the late fourteenth century, El Gambaro gave its name to the street where it sat, roughly on the northern edge of today's via Bersaglieri del Po.[76] In the fifteenth century, it appears to have been located just outside of the city walls between a fourteenth-century gate visible only in Fra Paolino Minorita's plan of 1322–1325, the Porta di Santa Croce, and the ditch that became via Giovecca after Ercole's enlargement of the city.[77] It was much smaller than the brothel at San Biagio, consisting only of four bedrooms, one of which also had facilities for serving wine and food. The rental contract lists the contents of the rooms: bedcovers, benches, small tables, trunks, and kitchen utensils in one room.

That El Gambaro and the brothel in Santa Croce were too small to contain the prostitute population emerges from a series of letters from Giacomo Prisciani, Chief of the *Ufficio delle Bollette,* and Leonello Sogari, Chief of the *Ufficio del dazio del vino* [Office of Wine Taxes].[78] The two officials lamented that "... epse meretrize son sparse per la cità in diversi logi, ..." and that Ferrara was "la più copiosa et bene fornita de publiche meretrice che disonestamente vivono," but they appeared most alarmed by the fact that prostitutes and pimps not living in the public brothel no longer paid the appropriate fees and taxes, and indeed, that the tax on wine which formerly brought in between eight and twelve hundred lire was now yielding less than one hundred lire annually.[79] Their concerns might also indicate a higher level of concubinage and home-based prostitution by housewives. Ultimately both officials proposed that the Duke construct a much larger brothel in the *contrà* of Santa Croce, with twenty-five rooms for the

---

[75] ASFe, ANA, Lodovico Portelli, matr. 217, b. 1, 6 August 1476, 37r–38v, "Affictus Federici de Flandria et Petri de Salandria magistro Zanini de Picardia."

[76] Gamba indentifies a fourteenth-century brothel in Sesto San Romano, an old, populous district just behind the cathedral, also the site of El Gambaro, which suggests that they may be the same brothel: "La prostituzione," 217.

[77] BAV Vat. Lat. 1960, Fra Paolino Minorita, "Plan of the territory and city of Ferrara, 1322–25," 267r.

[78] ASMo, Cancelleria Ducale, Carteggio Fattorale (CD/CF), b. 22/1, f. 25, 16 September 1490, to Duchess Eleonora; f. 8, from Giacomo Prisciani to Duchess Eleonora, 27 February 1490; f. 26, from Leonello Sogari to Duke Ercole, 29 April 1491; f. 25, Giacomo Prisciani to Duke Ercole, 4 May 1491, now transcribed as appendices 15–18 in Gamba, "La prostituzione."

[79] "... those prostitutes are scattered about the city in diverse places," and that Ferrara was "... the [city] most copiously and well supplied with public prostitutes who live dishonorably." ASMo, CD/CF, b. 22/1, f. 25, 16 September 1490; f. 8, 27 February 1491.

prostitutes and an honorable and commodious inn *(ostaria)* in the middle.[80] Prisciani pointed out that Ferrara once had a comparably sized brothel, much as other cities did, a size that he believed was optimum.[81] While such an argument might have appealed to Ercole, it would have been less attractive to Eleonora d'Aragona, his wife. In an earlier dispute between the proprietor of the Hostaria de la Nave in 1478 and the priests at the church of San Francesco, the Duchess allowed the priests to appropriate a house that Giangiorgio da Milano had rented across from the Oratory of S. Sebastiano on the grounds that he might allow prostitutes to occupy it, just as he allowed them to work out of his *ostaria*.[82] Though notoriously uninvolved in the day-to-day governance of the city, Ercole sprang into action in response to his wife's decision. He reproached her and ordered the house returned to Giangiorgio, observing that the priests had never complained about the prostitutes before, and noted that they had turned down an offer to rent the house themselves before it was offered to Giangiorgio. Most importantly, when Giangiorgio appealed to the Duke to overturn the Duchess's ruling he also offered to double his annual tax.[83]

The brothel proposed by Prisciani appears not to have been built, nor would the idea to build a significantly larger public brothel in the 1490s have earned Ercole's support, as he fell increasingly under the reforming influence of Girolamo Savonarola. When the construction of Ercole's addition to Ferrara got underway, in fact, one of the structures slated for demolition was El Gambaro:

> Septembre, a dì 3 de luni [1498]. El Gambaro, che hera logo publico per le meretrice e taverna, fu levato hozi e comenzato a desfare le caxe e cazate le femene ge herano, per fare la via dritta a traverso la fossa per andare in Terra nova a la piaza de verso la Certoxa.[84]

For at least two and one-half years El Gambaro was not replaced, but finally in 1501 an anonymous diarist reported that

---

[80] ASMo, CD/CF, b. 22/1, f. 25, Prisciani to Duke Ercole, 4 May 1491.

[81] ASMo, CD/CF, b. 22/1, f. 8, Prisciani to Duchess Eleonora, 27 February 1491.

[82] ASMo, CD, Leggi e decreti, C, V, p. 200, 26 October 1478, Ercole to Eleonora; now appendix 8 in Gamba, "La prostituzione."

[83] ASMo, CD, Leggi e decreti, C, V, P. 211, 12 November 1478, Ercole to Eleonora; now appendix 9 in Gamba, "La prostituzione."

[84] "September 3, Monday [1498]. El Gambaro, which was a public brothel for prostitutes and a tavern, was removed today, and the houses began to be torn down and the women who were there were thrown out, [in order] to make the straight road across the ditch to the new addition at the piazza toward the Certosa [monastery] . . .": Zambotti, *Diario ferrarese*, 283.

> Et sino a principio de Aprille fu dato principio che le putane publice dovessero stare de dreto da l'hospetale de Sancta Agnexe in Ferrara, et che de di chi sono le case le possino afitare a le putane, ma che altrove che lì le non posano stare, soto pena de essere fruste per Ferrara.[85]

No further indication appeared in the diaries or in other public records as to exactly where the new brothel was located other than "behind the hospital of Sant'Agnese." This structure is but two short blocks north of via delle Volte, historically a street with several osterie, taverns, and brothels (continuously as such well into the post-World War II period). In the fourteenth century, a brothel was located on the contrada of S. Paolo, a main cross street of via delle Volte; therefore it seems logical to assume that the brothel was located close to or on via delle Volte, or perhaps on via Romiti, where a brothel had been located on the corner of via Romiti and via delle Scienze (formerly via di S. Agnese) at least since the end of the sixteenth century. However, the chronicle of Giulio and Giacomo di Antiginni, an otherwise short and relatively modest document, at once gave more detailed information and opened up further questions.[86] In a chronicle mainly dedicated to notices of births, deaths, and marriages, along with occasional lapidary information about wars and aristocratic events, Giulio's proud announcement in 1501 is remarkable. The sole entry recounts that the *postribolo* had been established that year in the *contrada* of S. Agnese by closing off a small street between Giulio's house and that of a neighbor, Antonio Grifuni. By order of the *Giudice dei dodici Savi* Tito Strozzi and of the chief of the *Ufficio delle Bollette*, two walls were erected to block off the *contradella*, and the two men each received half of the street, Antonio receiving the part toward Palazzo del Paradiso, and Giulio the other half.[87]

---

[85] "From the beginning of April it became the principle that public whores must stay [in the area] behind the Hospital of Sant'Agnese in Ferrara, and those who own the houses can rent them to whores, but they cannot live elsewhere, on penalty of being whipped through [the streets of] Ferrara. . . .": *Diario ferrarese di autori incerti*, 268.

[86] BCA, Ms. Cl. 1, 757, Giulio and Giacomo di Antiginni, *Annali di Ferrara dal 1384 al 1514*, 43.

[87] The text of the entry reads as follows: "El Postribolo fo fato q[ues]to a[n]no in la contrata de S. Agnexe in ferara. Per quela Chaxone fo aserata e murata la contradela che è tra la chaxa de Ant.o grifuni e Zulio di Antigin[n]i. Cioé fo fato dui muri, uno de co dela dita contradela presso el [palazzo del] paradixo e laltro muro da laltro co al chantun de dre da laltro co dela dita chaxa de Zulio per [com]issione de Messer Tito de Strozi zudixe de li xii savii: et deli sopori de le bolet fo concesso e dato al dicto Ant.o grifu[ni] et Zulio di Antigin[n]i la dita contradela c[i]oe la meta di per omo et cosi dito

Although the author was at pains to explain exactly where the new brothel was located, his indications are nonetheless confusing. Via di S. Agnese corresponds to today's via delle Scienze. The word *contrata* used in the text, however, can signify one street as well as include smaller, adjacent streets, as it appears to in this case, where he refers specifically to the street blocked off as the *contradella* between the two houses. The hospital, later conservatory, of S. Agnese sits directly across from the church, just one half block south of Palazzo del Paradiso. The brothel (behind the hospital of S. Agnese) to which the anonymous chronicler refers in the passage above surely was in this immediate area. But precisely which building is it? Without archaeological explorations or additional documentary evidence a definitive determination is impossible; but there are at least two, and probably more, plausible prospects. One straddles via Ragno, formerly via delle Androne. On Andrea Bolzoni's map of 1782, this structure appears to be just like all of the other vaulted covered passageways on via delle Volte, but in actuality, the pre-existing street has been blocked off.[88] A second is a narrow addition between two structures also on via Ragno, at the terminus of vicolo (also via) della Lupa.

Additional evidence supports these possibilities. Two streets lead from S. Agnese to via Ragno (delle Androne); vicolo della Lupa breaks off from via delle Scienze and descends directly to the eastern segment of via Ragno, while via del Carbone cuts in front of the church of S. Agnese and then veers sharply to the left, ending up on the other side of via Ragno. Both streets were once called

---

Zulia fè fare la meta delo primo muro a tutte soe spexe et lo muro de dreto lo fe fe (sic) fare ol co[m]mu[ne] de ferara et cosi dito Ant.o grifu[ni] et dito Zulio partino la dita contradela. Al dito ant.o tocho la mura del co presso el paradixo et al dito Zulio tocho laltra meta de dal co de dre. La confine zie drito uno chamin che porta fora del dito Zulio." "The brothel was made this year in the *contrà* of S. Agnese in Ferrara. To make that big house the little street between the house of Antonio Grifuni and Giulio di Antiginni was closed off and walled up. That is, two walls were made, one on the side of the street toward Palazzo del Paradiso and the other wall on the other side of the canton behind the other side of the aforesaid house of Giulio, by commission of Mr. Tito Strozzi Judge of the Twelve Savi and the superior of the Bollette said Antonio Grifuni and Giulio di Antiginni were conceded and given said little street, that is, each man received half, and so said Giulio had half of the first wall built at his expense and the wall behind was done by the city of Ferrara and so said Antonio and said Giulio split said little street. Said Antonio got the wall on the side toward Palazzo del Paradiso and said Giulio got the other half on the side behind. The border is behind a chimney that emerges from [the house of] said Giulio."

[88] Gerolamo Melchiorri, *Nomenclatura ed etimologia delle piazze e strade di Ferrara (1918)*, ed. Eligio Mari (Ferrara: Liberty House, 1988), 175.

via della Lupa reportedly because of a *lupanara* (brothel) located there.[89] Perhaps more significantly, the first via della Lupa that breaks off from via delle Scienze (di S. Agnese) even earlier was called via del Gambaro: precisely the name of the street and brothel to the northeast of the Cathedral where the earlier, fifteenth-century brothel was located.[90] Perhaps the same prostitutes or the same proprietor transferred to the new brothel; in any case the persistence of the name from the earlier site is a strong indication that the brothel erected in 1501 was located within these streets, possibly at one of these sites.

Two rental contracts of June 1501 illustrate that more than one brothel now enlivened the area around S. Agnese. The notary records a two-story house on the contrada of S. Agnese adjacent to the Hospital of S. Agnese. To the rear, the house was bordered by a *postribolo*; a second house located on a corner on the contrada of S. Agnese describes its neighbor as a *stuffum*, or stew.[91] Together the two contracts suggest that as many as three brothels may have been located here, one of which sat either on via dell'Inferno, adjacent to Palazzo del Paradiso, or in the middle of the block; but neither appears to have been the one erected by di Antiginni and Grifuni. In 1510, the city paid for work on a wall in "la hostaria di Santa Agnese," which is probably the one between di Antiginni and Grifuni.[92]

Because so many records for the first five years of the sixteenth century are missing from state, city, and Este archives in Ferrara as well as in Modena, it has been impossible to make a more definitive determination.[93] The unusual decision to block off the street to enclose the most public of women no doubt reflected the personal interests of di Antiginni and Grifuni to enlarge their properties and gain income from the brothel, but it also offers the irony of turning a public thoroughfare into a brothel for women whose every movement on those very thoroughfares was, at least theoretically, controlled.

---

[89] Melchiorri, *Nomenclatura*, 48. *Lupanar* is the Latin term for brothel, from *lupa*, or she-wolf.

[90] BCA, Coll. Antonelli, n. 346, Giovan Battista Benetti, *Antichi nomi delle strade di Ferrara con annotazioni storiche,* 14.

[91] ASFe, ANA, Matr. 205, Filippo Pincerna, b. 1, f. 6, 16 June 1501, 37rv, "Locatio inter dominorum infra: Gabrieli de Plecenari et magistro Antonio delle Messe pretore"; and 26 June 1501, 38r–39v, "Affictus inter dominum Dominicum dicta Morgis civem Ferrarie et commendabile viro ser Petro de Pelipparis notario."

[92] ASMo, CD, Munizioni e fabbriche, b. 51, c. 67.

[93] The archive of surveyors (Archivio dei Periti) at the Archivio di Stato, Ferrara, contains very few sixteenth-century records, and none concern the two properties in question. Later documents at times include references to earlier property transactions for a particular site, so the possibility still exists that further records will turn up.

Placing the brothel here did not go unremarked or unnoticed by neighbors. Ercole's half-brother, Rinaldo Maria d'Este, then living in Palazzo del Paradiso, greeted the arrival of the public brothel with dismay. In a letter to Ercole in July 1499, Rinaldo complained bitterly about the recent decision to "... fare il bordelo qui contiquo a casa nostra, cossa che in verità mal me'l posso credere per havere qualche volta parlato ala Ex[cellenza] v[ost]ra...." Significantly, Rinaldo noted that "... in verita tal locho non serra ben suficiente per 10 o 12 femine...."[94] It may be no coincidence that Rinaldo died in April 1501, just when the decision was announced to place the brothel behind Sant'Agnese.

The decision to move the brothel to this location when the Herculean Addition was underway fixed the axis of prostitution in one of the oldest parts of the city, a district destined to endure as the city's center of prostitution for nearly five hundred years, until late in the twentieth century. In the sixteenth century, the brothels appear to have clustered in proximity to the one at Sant'Agnese, along via delle Volte, via del Bordeletto, and via dell'Inferno, adjacent to Palazzo del Paradiso. The proximity of the University, which by the late sixteenth century was housed in Palazzo del Paradiso, made for a ready client base, and the presence of several hostelries on via delle Volte no doubt served as magnets as well.

The only probable brothel identified in the Compendio Montecatini of 1597 was located on via dell'Inferno and was identified as a *stufa*, a public bath house or brothel, operated by Caterina Stovara, whose name indicated her occupation.[95] Although the Compendio did not identify specific locations, since the *stufa* is the last entry for via dell'Inferno, which ran along the western flank of Palazzo del Paradiso, it was probably the corner building. Equicola already referred to the *loco nella contra dell'Inferno* in 1537, and indeed, the *stuffum* mentioned in the 1501 rental contract may well still have been operating. Further evidence comes from Guarini, who noted that the church of S. Clemente, which sat on via del Bordelletto (now via Romiti) behind Palazzo del Paradiso, originally faced west. However, because "this part of the city had become an indecent place," and indeed, the doors would have directly faced Stovara's establishment, in 1574 the west entrance was

---

[94] ASMo, Archivio Estense, Casa e Stato 130, 3 July 1499, Rinaldo Maria d'Este to Ercole d'Este: "... put the bordello here next to our house, a thing which in truth I can hardly believe because I have talked with Your Excellency about it a few times ...," "in truth that place will not be big enough for ten or twelve women ..." Cited in Tuohy, *Herculean Ferrara*, 138–39.

[95] ASFe, ASC, Serie Patrimoniale, b. 30, f. 11, Fondo Montecatini, "Compendio di tutte le strade, case, palazzi e conventi," 58r.

ordered closed off and a new one opened where the main altar had been in order to shift the church's orientation east, away from such unpleasantness.[96]

The association of specific streets with prostitution in Ferrara has persisted throughout the succeeding five hundred years, even when the activity itself remained but a faint memory of the past: via del Gambaro is widely understood to have been the location of a brothel, and via delle Volte, just south of S. Agnese and S. Clemente, continued until recently — very recently — to house brothels.[97] Even in the fifteenth century, sites remained associated with brothels long after the brothels had disappeared. The ducal account books continued to refer to the site of the new stables as "dove era il bordello da San Biaxio" more than five years after the brothel had been leveled.[98] But the association of a site with a brothel was not necessarily tolerated. When a group of houses on via dell'Inferno was torn down to make way for the physics department of the University of Ferrara, builders found a closet stuffed with documents and licences to conduct a brothel dating back to the sixteenth century. Like most artifacts associated with women, these rare documents were not considered of any value, and were hence destroyed. The dean feared that the department would be tainted by the association.[99] Although the records are lost, their conservation by proprietors constitutes a remarkable testament to the persistence of a brothel in one building for nearly half a millenium.

The uncertainty about the precise location of Antiginni's brothel underscores the larger problem of understanding precisely the architectural character of Ferrara's brothels. They appear to have been ordinary in every respect; in neither plan nor elevation did they differ from other houses. Only the decision to construct a brothel by walling off a street and turning it into a house of prostitution marked it as different in the urban landscape, but even the scarce

---

[96] Marc'Antonio Guarini, *Compendio Historico dell'origine, accrescimento e prerogative delle chiese e luoghi Pij della Città e diocesi di Ferrara* (Ferrara, 1621), 227; *Atti della visita apostolica a Ferrara, (1574),* Parte II, Cap. XXV, ff 26v–28r. Filarete's description of a Casa di Venere as a bathhouse with upstairs office where "the craft that is practiced here will be controlled" illustrates the well-known link between bathhouses and prosti-tution. Antonio Filarete: *Treatise on Architecture*, trans. John R. Spencer (New Haven: Yale University Press, 1965), 128.

[97] In Giorgio Bassani, *The Garden of the Finzi-Contini*, trans. William Weaver (Orlando: Harcourt-Brace, 1977), Bassani writes about peering into the brothels, ". . . [their] doors left ajar, at the lighted interiors . . ." (174) still flourishing in via delle Volte during the 1930s and 1940s, and numerous conversations with Ferraresi indicate that they continued to do so until very recently.

[98] ASMo, CD, Minizioni e fabbriche, Reg. 26, 26 November 1493, c. 74.

[99] Personal communication, 30 May 2002.

urban documentation of Ferrara indicates that closing off small streets in this fashion was not at all unusual; via del Carbone offers at least one other example. By contrast with convents, patrician palaces, communal offices, churches, even shops, brothels left no special traces on the built landscape, at least none visibly different from a normal house: only street names and reputations far outlived their specific functions. Although this allowed brothels to remain inconspicuous, it also testifies to the ambiguous relationship of prostitution to other forms of relationships in Renaissance Ferrara. On the one hand, women inhabited the rooms as private spaces, using the rooms for casual sexual encounters along with other domestic activities; on the other, the relationships enacted there were not officially blessed by either church or state.

Finally, when a prostitute could no longer work, if her hopes of transforming concubinage into marriage failed, or if she had been converted away from her profession, by 1537 Ferrara offered the possibility for her to retire to a convent known as *Le Convertite* (the converted). The parish priest at S. Agnese, Don Giovanmaria Schiatti, apparently converted a number of his parishioners from their *mala vita* in 1537. After convincing them to leave the brothel, he first housed them in the Hospital of the Battuti Bianchi, following which, aided by generous contributions from Duke Ercole II and other citizens, they moved into a former monastery, S. Nicolò del Cortile, just off the Piazza Ariostea in Terranova.[100] On 7 April 1537, some of Ferrara's noble women accompanied approximately eighteen women, ten of whom came from the *loco nella contrà dell'Inferno* [brothel on via dell'Inferno], in solemn procession with crucifixes in their hands, from the Battuti Bianchi to S. Nicolò, henceforth known as the Convertite, referred to by some chroniclers as S. Maria Maddalena because the women were (appropriately) especially devoted to her.[101] Withdrawal from the brothel and a period of years laboring in a convent without taking final vows could effectively cleanse a prostitute of her former sins, and make her eligible for marriage once

---

[100] BCA, Ms Cl II, n. 355, Mario Equicola, *Annali della cita di Ferrara 1320–1582;* Guarini, *Compendio*, 221. Sandri gives the date as 17 March 1538, c. 86v. Antonio Sandri, *Dell'origine delle chiese e altri luoghi nella provincia di Ferrara*, BCA, ms. Cl.I, c. 89rv. However, this was the date that the complex received its new name of S. Maria Maddalena, not the date the Convertite occupied it. Nearly every convent erected in the sixteenth century was located in Terranova.

[101] Equicola, *Annali*, year 1537. For the post-Tridentine rule governing the convent, see *Regole et ordinationi per le suore convertite di Ferrara sotto il titolo di S. Maria Maddalena, riformate et ampliate da Mons. Revendissimo di Ferrara* (Ferrara: Vittorio Baldino, 1599).

she left the convent. Controls tightened throughout the century until 1597, when all the women were required to take permanent vows and to remain cloistered.[102]

The hard-won independence of a prostitute from direct, day-to-day control by men vanished upon her death in a very particular way. Even if she did not enter the Convertite, her goods did: in sixteenth- and seventeenth-century Italy, it was common practice to inventory the belongings of deceased prostitutes and turn them over to the local Convertite convent; usually this was done while her body still lay in her rooms.[103]

Marginal Spaces

Not surprisingly, Ferrara's prostitutes inhabited areas of the city also associated with other marginal groups, in particular Jews. The Este administrations from the fifteenth through the sixteenth centuries exhibited consistent tolerance for Jews, with Ercole I dining at the homes of prominent Jews and abolishing taxes and customs duties for Jews moving to Ferrara from elsewhere.[104] His grandson Ercole II invited Jews expelled from Portugal and Spain in 1537 to take up residence in Ferrara.[105] Most historians believe that such openness depended more upon the Estes' constant need to replenish their funds through loans from Jewish bankers than upon other noble sentiments.[106] Whatever the case, Ferrara enjoyed the reputation of being unusually hospitable

---

[102] Guarini, *Compendio*, 223.

[103] See, for example, ASFe, ANA, Mat. 1027, Not. Lorenzo Vacchi, b. 1, 16 October 1675, "Inventario de mobili ritrovati in casa della già Cecilia Polidori, publica meretrice." In 1677 alone, Vacchi inventoried the belongings of ten deceased prostitutes for the Convertite.

[104] Duke Ercole I agreed to such relief for Isacco da Fano, Jew, who was transferring his residence from Bologna to Ferrara in October 1500. Ercole exempted him from all taxes and fees on all his goods, and also granted him full freedom of movement: ASFe, Archivio Vendeghini, Secoli XV–XIX, Scatola 3, f. 25, 17 October 1500. When notified by his ambassador in Milan, Giacomo Trotti, that Spain had expelled the Jews, by 20 November 1492 Ercole had conceded the right to several families of Spanish Jews to live in Ferrara and join the city's already flourishing population of Jews: Antonio Balletti, *Gli ebrei e gli estensi* (Bologna: Forni, 1969 [1930]), 76.

[105] In May 1538, Ercole II was already making special arrangements regarding taxes and duties for Spanish and Portuguese Jews, and on 12 February 1550 he issued a general permission and guarantee of safety to those who came to Ferrara: Balletti, *Gli Ebrei,* 77–78.

[106] Balletti, *Gli Ebrei*, 59–72.

toward Jews during the fifteenth and sixteenth centuries. Nonetheless, laws on the books at various points required Jews to wear identifying garments similar to those of prostitutes, and forbade Christians and Jews from engaging in carnal relations.[107] Rumors and occasional uprisings against Jews occurred in Ferrara as they did elsewhere, a reminder that however tolerant the city's administration, Jews were still viewed with suspicion and as outsiders by many.[108] Just as prostitutes were seen as fulfilling an unfortunate need which protected other women's honor, so Jews were a necessary evil in Italy's growing cities: while Christians were forbidden to collect interest on loans, no such rules restrained Jews. Though they too were required to wear an identifying badge, at least in Ferrara, throughout the Estense period, the Jewish community was not confined to certain buildings or streets.

The very district that became the nexus of prostitution at the end of the fifteenth century was also an area widely inhabited by Jews, and when the ghetto was erected in 1626 it bordered the brothels of S. Agnese. As we have seen, the brothel near S. Biagio, Montealbano, was also located adjacent to the fifteenth-century Jewish cemetery near S. Giustina.[109] Although not formalized in the case of the Jews during the period of Estense rule, the proximity of brothels to areas where many Jews lived, or where the Jewish cemetery was located, unambiguously identified both groups as marginal. The gates of the ghetto came down only after Italian unification in 1860, but as with the streets near Sant'Agnese, the association of these two marginal groups with specific districts persisted for at least five hundred years. Where Guarini noted that the orientation of S. Clemente was altered in 1574 because this part of the city had become "an indecent place," a flourishing prostitution district, nearly two centuries later Giuseppe Antenore Scalabrini claimed that the change took place because "... da quella parte [occidente] era tutta asiepata da case di Ebrei Marani e Portughesi Giudei, prima che fosse fatto il circondario del ghetto."[110] Historians remark

---

[107] Luigi Napoleone Cittadella, *Notizie amministrative, storiche, artistiche relative a Ferrara* (Bologna: Forni, 1969), 298–99.

[108] Pardi, *Diario ferrarese*, 92.

[109] ASFe, ANA, Castelli, 25 November 1469, "Affictus Santini de Mediolano et Fratris . . . " (see n. 68 above).

[110] " . . . that [western] direction was all crowded with houses of Spanish and Portuguese Jews, before the ghetto was enclosed": G. A. Scalabrini, *Guida per la città e i borghi di Ferrara [ca. 1755]*, ed. C. Frongia (Ferrara: Liceo Classico Ariosto, 1997), 139. To prove his point, Scalabrini cited one property contract from the late fifteenth century, but the house noted in the contract was located on via Sabbioni, well removed from San Clemente. Jewish merchants lived throughout Borgo di Sopra, and as the political center of the city shifted north, many remained in the districts south of the cathedral, but episcopal

on the persistence of significant public sites such as the Campidoglio through centuries of profound political and social change, but as the case of prostitutes and Jews in Ferrara reveals, the sites associated with marginal groups have also remained remarkably consistent over time.

Threatened with expulsion, closure in brothels, and punishment in jails, being paraded through the streets and insulted, or pressured into the confines of a convent, Ferrara's public and occasional prostitutes found the spaces of the city riddled with spatial and discursive practices that aimed to restrict them to highly circumscribed places and activities, and which also were geared toward rooting out and isolating illicit sexual behavior. At the same time, the women confronted laws contravened by the behavior of civic officials and nobles themselves. Marquis Nicolò III d'Este had more lovers and concubines than even contemporaries could count, Ercole I and his brothers all had illegitimate children, and Alfonso I took Laura Dianti, daughter of a Ferrarese hat maker, as his concubine following the death of his wife Lucrezia Borgia in 1519. Laura was a concubine just like many others, but the status of her lover exempted her from the punishments inflicted on those of the lower classes, and indeed, many referred to her as Alfonso's wife.[111] The laws and formal spatial controls on the books in Ferrara, as in other places then and later, aimed not at upper-class women, or women who acquired upper-class prerogatives because of their relationships with noble men, but at women from the lower classes. Luigi

---

records document that the alteration of San Clemente was due to the presence of prostitutes mainly, and secondarily of Jews.: Mario Marzola, *Per la storia della chiesa ferrarese nel secolo XVI (1497–1590), Parte seconda* (Turin: Società Editrice Internazionale, 1978), 346.

[111] Unsubstantiated claims that Alfonso married Laura as he lay on his deathbed circulated particularly when the city was about to devolve to direct papal control in 1597 and the only male heir available descended precisely from their son Alfonso, and not from the legitimate line of Alfonso I and Lucretia Borgia. (See the essay by Jane Fair Bestor in this volume, above, 000–000). The problem was that she was not of noble extraction. Her family origins remain somewhat in dispute, although scholars agree that her father was Francesco Dianti and her brother Bartolomeo Dianti: anon., "Laura Dianti. La Donna del Duca Alfonso I d'Este," *Deputazione Provinciale di Ferrara di Storia Patria* n.s. 28 (1950): 82. Although some have argued for noble links, and specifically that the family changed its name from Boccacci to Dianti, and then Alfonso changed Laura's to Eustacchio, notarial records from 1520 point not only to Dianti as the family name prior to Alfonso's involvement, but to their plebian origins: ASFe, ANA, Giacomo Ziponari, Matr. 384, b. 1, f. 4, May 1520. The will of Francesco Dianti, *beretarius*, or hatmaker, son of Bernardino Dianti and living in the contrà of S. Maria di Bocca, designates as his heir Alberto, son of Bartolomeo Dianti, marangone, of the contrà of S. Antonio in Polesine.

Cittadella railed against the great injustice of the manner in which nobles and the wealthy maintained veritable stables of concubines and prostitutes for their own use while issuing ferocious proclamations against those very practices among the lower classes.[112]

Perhaps more to the point, Ferrara's aristocracy profited directly from the labor of prostitutes. When Cardinal Luigi d'Este died in 1587, he bequeathed the tax revenue on prostitution which he enjoyed to his nephew Cesare d'Este, future Duke of Modena and Reggio Emilia.[113] Despite the injunctions, the social and institutional arrangements of Ferrarese prostitution flourished even after the Este were banished to Modena and the papacy took direct control of the city. In fact, the only extant version of the medieval compact on prostitution in Ferrara is incorporated as part of the tax and licensing codes promulgated by the church in the seventeenth century.

The gendering of the city's spaces emerges with greater clarity when we examine how the city was structured to accommodate prostitutes, and how that city came to be understood. Although contemporaries were fully aware of the presence of *donne disoneste* and *postriboli*, they rarely wrote of them, and both have virtually disappeared from the Ferrara (and not only Ferrara) imaged by subsequent historians and architectural historians. And yet, as we saw with S. Clemente, public brothels not only figured in the lives of contemporary residents, their presence even influenced the architectural and spatial organization of ecclesiastical buildings. Ferrarese women and the spaces they inhabited were doubly effaced, then, both by their contemporaries and by later historians, whose profoundly gendered histories have robbed Quattrocento and Cinquecento Ferrara of much of its richness. Only in part are we now able to recover some of those histories.

---

[112] Cittadella, *Notizie*, 290.

[113] "Relatione sopra la Città e Stato di Ferrara," n. d. (1598 ca.), BL, Addl. MS. Ital. 28, 451, fol. 389v.

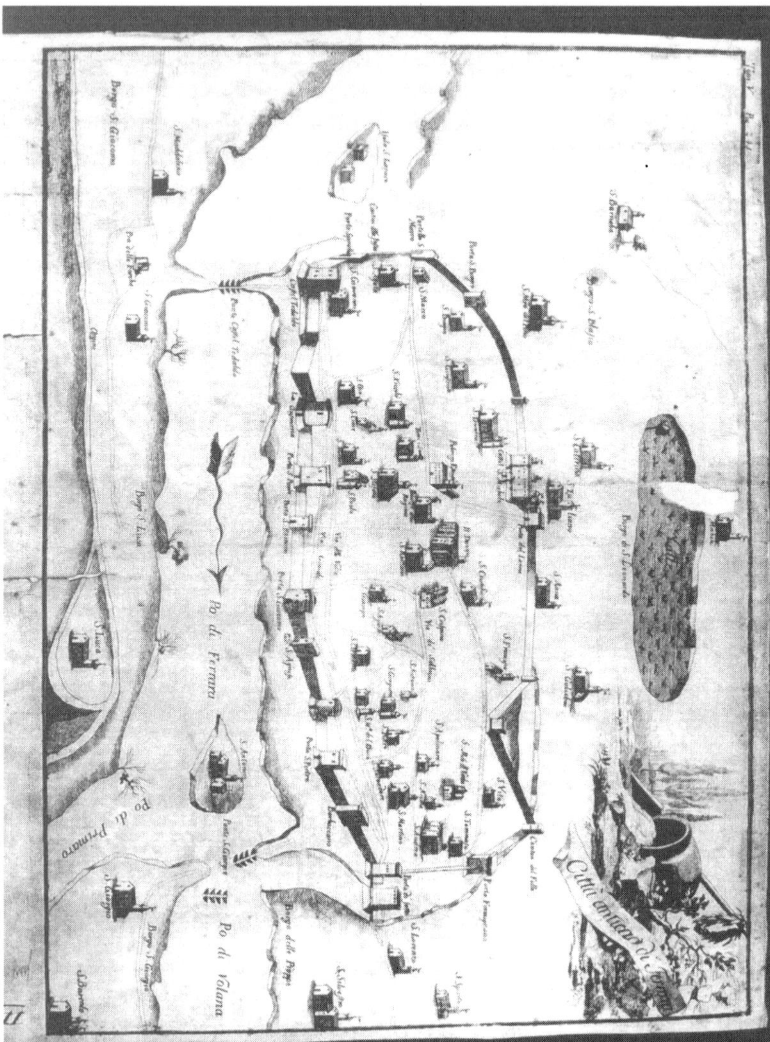

Figure 1. Antonio Frizzi, Ferrara in 1385, after Bartolino da Novara. Ferrara, Ariostea Communal Library.

Figure 2. Betrothal of a youth and a prostitute, 1474. *Decretum Gratiani Roverella*. Ferrara, Fototeca, Civic Museums of Ancient Art.

Figure 3. Statuto delle Bollette, Article 131: "Contra Blasfemantes, Sodomitas, Baratarios, Ludos, Concubinarios, Meretrices . . ." April 1496. Ferrara, State Archives.

Figure 4. A Prostitute leaning out her window and Two Gentlemen below. *Mores Italiae*, 1575. New Haven, Yale University, Beinecke Rare Book and Manuscript Library.

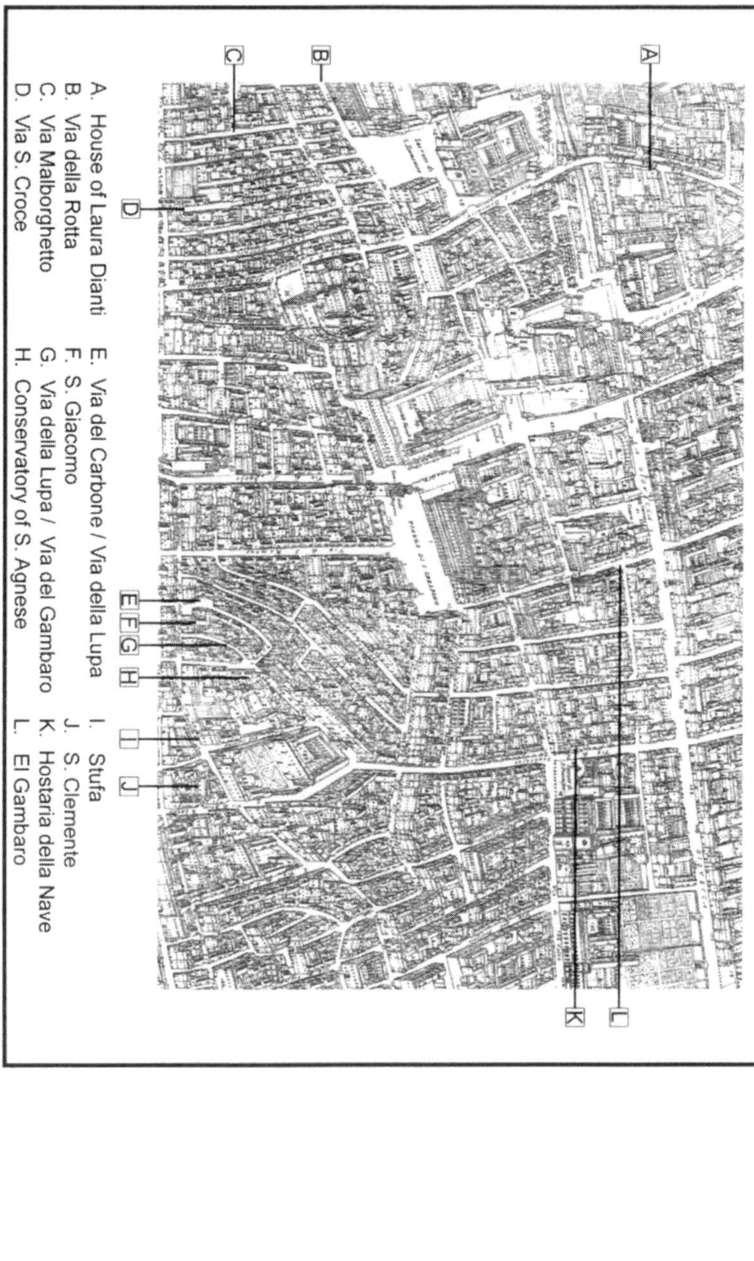

Figure 5. Andrea Bolzoni, Perspectival Map of Ferrara, 1782. Detail of area central square and southern section, including S. Agnese.

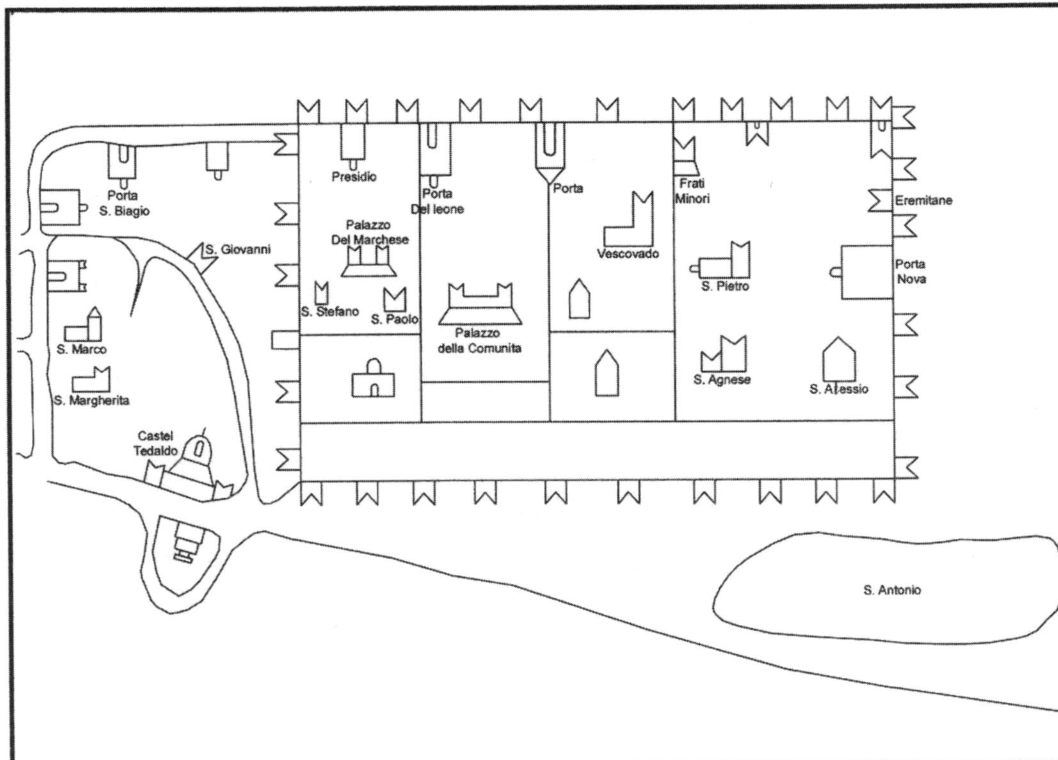

Figure 6. Transcription of Fra Paolino Minorita's Plan of the territory and city of Ferrara, 1322–1325, original in Biblioteca Apostolica Vaticana.

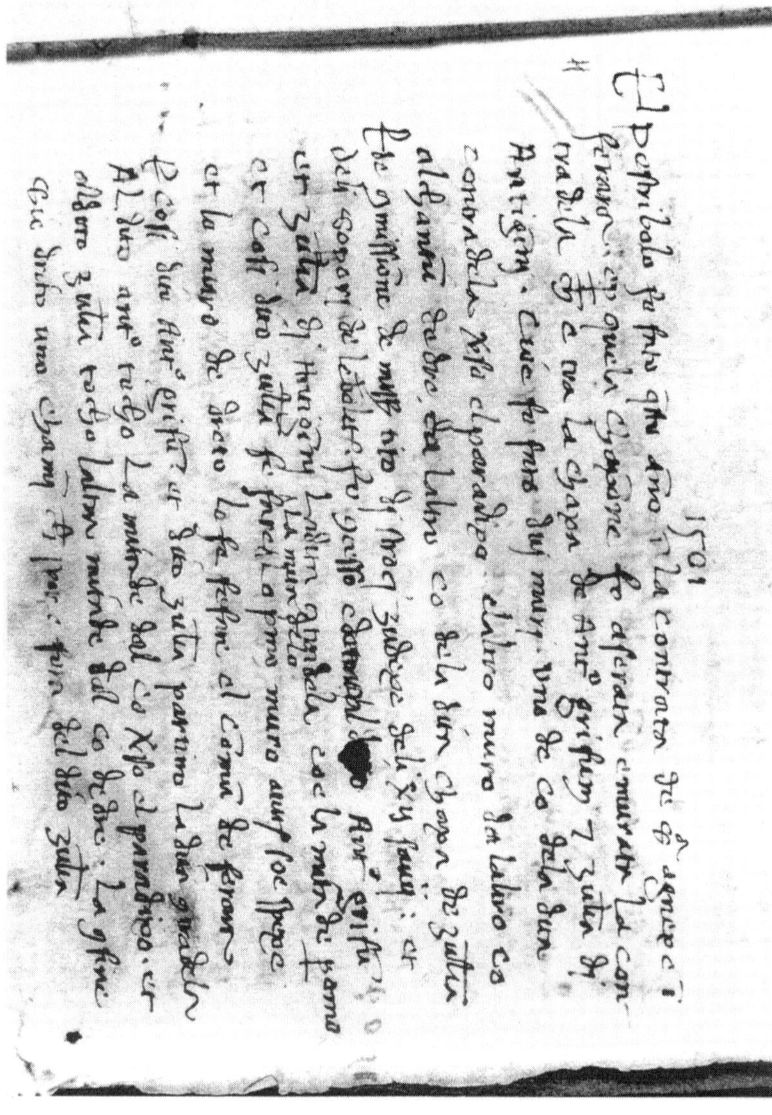

Figure 7. Giulio and Giacomo Antiginni, Entry for 1501, in *Annali di Ferrara dal 1384 al 1514*. Ferrara, Ariostea Communal Library.

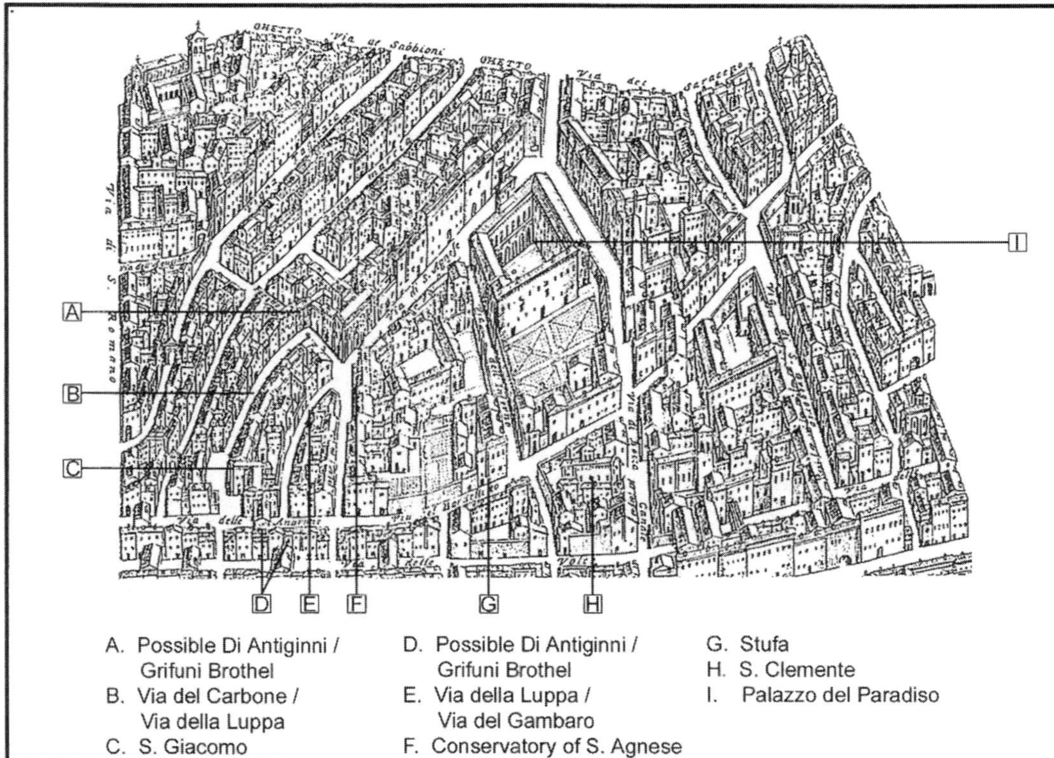

Figure 8. Andrea Bolzoni, Perspectival Map of Ferrara, 1782, detail showing S. Agnese area. Note gates to the ghetto to the left, on via Vignatagliata and via Gattamarcia.

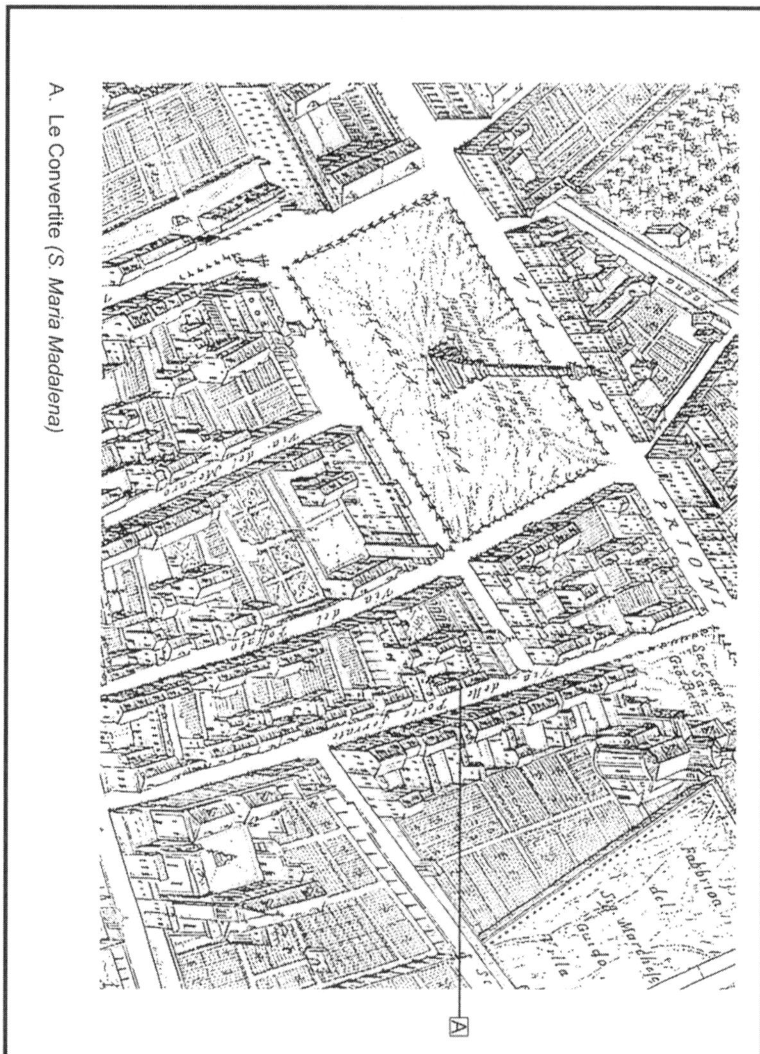

Figure 9. Andrea Bolzoni, Perspectival Map of Ferrara, 1782, detail showing the church of Le Convertite.

Figure 10. Antonio Sandri, Church of S. Maria Madalena, or Le Convertite. From *Dell' origine delle chiese e altri luoghi della Provincia di Ferrara*, nineteenth century. Ferrara, Ariostea Communal Library.

The *Istoria imperiale* of Matteo Maria Boiardo and Fifteenth-Century Ferrarese Courtly Culture[1]

Richard M. Tristano

In the Prologue to the *Istoria imperiale*, which is a dedication to Duke Ercole I d'Este, Matteo Maria Boiardo included this phrase: ". . . magnanimi gesti e prudentissimi governi degli antichi vostri passati. . . ." This could be translated as "magnanimous deeds and very prudent [or perhaps "very wise"] governance of your ancient forbears." What do magnanimous deeds have to do with wise rule, and what does either have to do with the past? The phrase hints at a complex relationship among proper aristocratic behavior, good government, and the study of the past, that is, the discipline of history. The code to understanding the relationship of these disparate things lies in the courtly culture of Ferrara, among the most vital and influential in Italy, and the history of the Estense state, the most ancient of all the signorie.[2] What was Boiardo's purpose in writing the *Istoria imperiale*? What does the text tell us about Ferrarese courtly culture? How competent is Boiardo as a historian? Is the text a Renaissance or medieval one, that is, is Boiardo inspired by classical or medieval models? What does the text reveal about the state of historical study in fifteenth-century Ferrara and its relationship to the state and politics? None of these questions has been satisfactorily answered because of a tendency to underestimate Boiardo's abilities as historian and to misunderstand his purpose for writing the text. This

[1] The research and writing of this essay were supported by the "Marvels of Rome" National Endowment for the Humanities Summer Seminar at the American Academy, Rome, directed by Dale Kinney and Birgitta Lindros Wohl, and by a sabbatical granted by Saint Mary's University of Minnesota. I would also like to thank Werner Gundersheimer, Albert Ascoli, and Dennis Looney for their comments and encouragement. A brief version of this essay was presented at the New College Conference on Medieval-Renaissance Studies, Sarasota, Florida, March 2000.

[2] The Estense signoria was "officially" established by Obizzo I in 1264, though Estense rule over Ferrara can be traced back to 1240, when Obizzo's grandfather, Azzo VII, took control of the city from the Salinguerra family and its supporters. Estense influence in the Ferrarese can be traced back to the eleventh century.

essay will attempt to answer these questions in the following way: first, I will present a critical review of the literature; second, I will explore the significance of the Prologue to the text; third, I will analyze two key sections of the text and assess Boiardo's competence as historian; and fourth, and I will assess the role of history in Ferrarese courtly culture.

I

Boiardo (1440/41–1494) was Count of Scandiano, one of the premier members of the Estense court, and governor of Modena and Reggio. Best known as the author of the epic romance *Orlando innamorato*, he has not been understood and appreciated as a historian because most scholars categorize him as a poet.[3] Through his poetics, especially the *Innamorato*, Boiardo is recognized as an Italian cultural icon, though something of a second-rate one, often condemned as an inferior precursor of Ariosto and his *Orlando furioso*. More often than not Boiardo has been evaluated less as an end and more as a means of understanding Ariosto.[4] This situation helps to explain why the *Istoria imperiale*, a historical text, has been examined nearly exclusively by literary scholars. They have been interested in the text as a literary work that shares at least two characters, Charlemagne and Roland, and certain chivalric ideas with the *Innamorato*.

But when it comes to the text as history, literary critics view it with some embarrassment, while historians have ignored it altogether, perhaps because they have believed the evaluation of their literary colleagues. Another important factor in understanding why the text has been so unappreciated is that Boiardo himself presented his work as a translation of one of Riccobaldo da Ferrara's works. Riccobaldo was born in Ferrara ca. 1245 and trained as a notary with connections to the Estense court.[5] In 1293 he was exiled and spent most of his life wandering around northern Italy, supporting himself through the com-

---

[3] On Boiardo's life see Giulio Reichenbach, *Matteo Maria Boiardo* (Bologna: Zanichelli, 1929), Gino Badini and Elio Monducci, eds., *Matteo Maria Boiardo, le vita nei documenti del suo tempo* (Modena: Aedes Muratoriana, 1997), as well as various articles in Giuseppe Anceschi and Tina Matarrese, eds., *Il Boiardo e il mondo estense nel Quattrocento* (Padua: Antenore, 1998).

[4] A relatively large amount of research on Boiardo has been published recently, much of it stimulated by the quincentennial of Boiardo's death in 1994. It remains to be seen if this research and its largely positive tone will be sustained.

[5] Most of this information is taken from A. Theresa Hankey, *Riccobaldo of Ferrara: His Life, Works, and Influence* (Rome: Istituto Storico Italiano per il Medio Evo, 1996). See also Gabriele Zanella, "Cultura, scuola, e storiografia a Ferrara tra XIII e XIV secolo," in *Storia di Ferrara*, Vol. 5: *Il Basso Medioevo, XII–XIV*, ed. Augusto Vasina (Ferrara: Corbo, 1987), 241–74; and Eric W. Cochrane, *Historians and Historiography in the Italian Renaissance* (Chicago: University of Chicago Press, 1981), 94–95.

position of mostly historical works for patrons. His most widely read work was the *Pomerium*, composed in 1297 and revised several times thereafter. The *Pomerium* is a universal history divided into six parts. Boiardo's "translation" is based on Part Four and is organized around lives of emperors beginning with Augustus and ending with Otto IV. As we shall see, it is in no way a faithful and literal translation of Riccobaldo's text, and Boiardo often writes virtually independently of Riccobaldo, incorporating information from other sources, especially in the last half of the work.[6] Given this fact, we shall also have to consider why Boiardo chose to call his work a translation. So, the evaluation of the *Istoria imperiale* is also influenced by the perception of modern scholars that it is not an original work, but one of lesser creativity: a translation.

Modern scholarship on the *Istoria imperiale* begins with Ludovico Muratori, who published parts of both Riccobaldo's and Boiardo's texts in Volume 9 of the *Rerum Italicarum Scriptores*.[7] It is difficult to overestimate Muratori's influence on perceptions of the *Istoria imperiale*. In the preface to his edition of the work, Muratori depicted Boiardo as credulous, as having produced more a romance than a history, and as having provided sources for the fables of both his poem and Ariosto's.[8] Most subsequent writers have been unable to free themselves from Muratori's judgment.[9] Even Giovanni Ponte, who has written on the *Istoria* for nearly twenty-five years, cannot fully disengage himself from a certain protective

---

[6] The six parts are: I. From Adam to Abraham; II. From Abraham to the Foundation of Rome; III. From the Foundation of Rome to the Birth of Christ; IV. The Roman Emperors from Augustus; V. Description of the Provinces of the World; and VI. The Roman Pontiffs. See Giovanni Ponte, *La personalità e l'opera del Boiardo* (Genoa: Tilgher, 1972), 76, n.1. See also Hankey, *Riccobaldo of Ferrara*, chap. 2. Hankey writes: "Its [the *Istoria imperiale*'s] first, unpublished section on classical antiquity and the early Middle Ages is based on a Pomerium codex. Slight use is made of the same text later, but most of the published section is a substantially independent production" (182).

[7] L. A. Muratori, *Rerum Italicarum Scriptores* (Milan: Typographia Societatis Palatinae, 1723–1738), hereafter *RIS*. Muratori published only the second half of part IV, the final chapter of part V, and most of part VI. See Hankey, *Riccobaldo of Ferrara*, 15. He published only the second half of the *Istoria imperiale*, from Charlemagne on. The manuscript copy of the *Istoria imperiale* is in Biblioteca Classense, Ravenna (hereafter BCR), MS. 424.

[8] I base this mostly on Ponte's reading of Muratori (Ponte, *La personalità*, 67): "Il Muratori non nascondeva le sue perplessità, notando che numerosi passi non corrispondevano e rintracciandone solo in parte le fonti; ed esprimeva un giudizio sfavorevole su un'opera che non soddisfaceva le sue esigenze di verità storica, ma piuttosto gli pareva un romanzo, fonte di favole per il Boiardo stesso e per Ariosto. . . ." ["Muratori did not hide his perplexity noting that numerous passages did not correspond and tracing them only in part to the sources; and he expressed an unfavorable judgment on a work that did not satisfy his requirements for historical truth, but rather the work seemed to him a romance, the source of fables for Boiardo and Ariosto."]

[9] Most of this section is based on the very useful summary by Ponte, *La personalità*, 67–68. It was Giulio Reichenbach who finally established Boiardo's authorship of the *Istoria imperiale*, Reichenbach: *Matteo Maria Boiardo*, 188–89.

embarrassment for Boiardo. Ponte concluded some time ago that the *Istoria* is indeed a translation of Riccobaldo's *Pomerium*, but with information added from several other sources. Ponte has gone a long way in identifying those sources. And while Ponte does not see Boiardo as being particularly rigorous and critical, he does recognize that Boiardo tones down some of the fantastic elements of his sources and demonstrates a genuine curiosity for some of the people he describes in the text.[10] But Ponte's later research also reveals a certain hardening and narrowing of his evaluation of Boiardo's text. In his recent essay on Boiardo's treatment of Frederick Barbarossa, Ponte writes:

> But his adaptation [of Riccobaldo] does not have historical value, since he does not succeed in imposing on himself a precise method, and this occurs exactly at a time in which a new documentary method of critical reconstruction of the past is established by Flavio Biondo whose *Italia Illustrata* Boiardo demonstrated he knew, but who used it only for some erudite knowledge, without demonstrating that he understood its innovative importance. . . .[11]

Ultimately Ponte can't help viewing the *Istoria* through the *Innamorato*, that is, as a historical text viewed through a modern literary perspective. This in turn produces the conclusion that Boiardo is a failed historian immune to the new Renaissance historical sensibility and rigor because he could not cease to be a poet. For Ponte, Muratori's judgment stands: the text is not true history but a romance.

But what makes Boiardo immune to the influence of the Renaissance? Are there social and cultural forces that would help explain what we might call Boiardo's "medieval" tendencies?[12] And what about Ponte's idea that Boiardo

---

[10] Ponte, *La personalità*, 75.

[11] "Ma il suo rifacimento non ha pregio storiografico, poiché egli non riesce a imporsi un metodo preciso; e questo avviene proprio nell'età in cui il nuovo metodo documentario di ricostruzione critica del passato si afferma con Flavio Biondo, la cui *Italia illustrata* il Boiardo dimostra di conoscere, ma che riprende solo per notizie erudite senza dimostrare di comprenderne la portata innovatrice": Giovanni Ponte, "Matteo Maria Boiardo dalla traduzione storiografica al romanzesco nella *Vita di Federico Barbarossa*," in Anceschi and Matarrese, *Il Boiardo e il mondo estense*, 443–59, here 444.

[12] I realize there are inherent problems in using the terms "medieval" and "Renaissance," but they are time-tested and useful concepts. I will use both mostly in terms of historicity. During the "Renaissance," writers developed the familiar tripartite division of Western history into Ancient, "Dark Ages," and Renaissance. As Breisach suggests, "They rejected any kinship with the medieval world and preserved continuity only between the ancient and their own period." Boiardo, working from Riccobaldo, demonstrates a "medieval" sensibility by constructing the *Istoria imperiale* as an unbroken succession of emperors from Augustus to Otto IV. Boiardo does make distinctions between "Roman," "Greek," "French," and "German" emperors, but his schema is one of essential continuity

somehow loses his way and "becomes a poet" ("diviene poeta")? Was Boiardo unable to distinguish between history and poetry?[13] Anna Soffientini would say yes, as she tends to see Boiardo's historical inquiry distracted by his imagination and his desire to flatter Ercole. "But beyond this intention of Boiardo to be responsive to his duke, the *Istoria* also responds to its author's desire to cloak events in a fabulous halo typical of heroic-chivalric poems every time the events of the past fire his imagination."[14] Finally, in the research of Alessandro Scarsella, the distinction between poetics and historical narrative is completely obscured. Scarsella focuses on what he calls "the fiction of Turpin," and while he is mostly concerned with the *Orlando innamorato* he also connects this "fiction" to the *Istoria*, thus suggesting once again Boiardo's inability to distinguish between poetry and history, pseudo and true sources, and fiction and fact.[15]

At the heart of the criticism of Boiardo's method is an anachronistic separation of history and literature that did not exist for medieval, classical, or Renaissance writers.[16] This tendency to judge Boiardo's history harshly because it does not conform to modern rules of historical writing has been countered by two scholars who have written not on the *Istoria imperiale*, but on Boiardo's translation of the *Histories* of Herodotus. This translation is different in that it is a "real," more literal translation of Herodotus, a classical and not medieval source. But the work of these two authors is central to this study: they rehabilitate Boiardo as a translator and historical thinker.

---

in the Empire. See Ernst Breisach, *Historiography: Ancient, Medieval, and Modern*, 2nd ed. (Chicago: University of Chicago Press, 1994), 159–60. On the other hand, as we shall see, Boiardo reveals a "Renaissance" sensibility in his "Prologue."

[13] "Come la supposta 'vera istoria' di Turpino 'move' il canto d'Orlando vinto da Amore, anche le 'istorie' lette e vagheggiate sulle pagine dei cronisti anteriori inducono Matteo Maria a fantasticare, al di là dei suoi compiti di traduttore e rielaboratore dei racconti altrui; e il manipolatore diviene poeta, in quella che al Muratori appariva una fabula romanensis, un romanzo": Ponte, "Matteo Maria Boiardo," 459.

[14] Anna Soffientini, "Le *Vite* di Enrico IV ed Enrico V nell'*Istoria imperiale* di Matteo Maria Boiardo," in Ancheschi and Matarrese, *Il Boiardo e il mondo estense*, 461–79, here 461 and n. 3.

[15] Alessandro Scarsella, "Boiardo traduttore parodista ovvero la finzione di Turpino," in Anceschi and Matarrese, *Il Boiardo e il mondo estense*, 387–98, here 397 and n. 25.

[16] See Nancy F. Partner, "The New Cornificius: Medieval History and the Artifice of Words," in *Classical Rhetoric and Medieval Historiography*, ed. Ernst Breisach (Kalamazoo: Medieval Institute Publications, 1985), 5–59, here 12–13, where she writes: "The very thing that made rhetoric so useful for all serious medieval literature could have been exactly what prevented its deeper application to the problems of historical argument and presentation — the fact of history as literature. The idea, so indubitable, that serious history was 'high' literature, with all the stylistic demands that that implied, would necessarily turn the author's fullest attention to the tropes and figures and, perhaps, distract him from the somewhat less obviously useful aspects of evidence and argument."

Edoardo Fumagalli believes that Boiardo translated Herodotus's text from the 1474 Venetian edition of Valla's Latin translation and not from the original Greek. This is an important point because it allows Fumagalli to point out that some errors are attributable not to Boiardo but to Valla, and that sometimes Boiardo catches mistakes and tries to remedy them.[17] In addition, Fumagalli, who considers Boiardo's translation thoroughly "professional," also reveals his technique of translation. Boiardo sometimes reorganizes the text into chapters, he tries to make the narrative more compact, and he often announces at the end of the chapter what will follow in the next. In other words, Boiardo uses several devices to make the narrative flow better and read more easily. He "translates" the text for his audience — Ercole and his fellow courtiers — by making it more accessible.[18] That Boiardo's audience was a courtly one can be demonstrated through the *Istoria imperiale* in three ways: 1) the Prologue is dedicated to the duke, Ercole; 2) the Prologue specifically states that Boiardo is translating for those who know only the vulgar tongue: this suggests educated people who don't know Latin, and it means the court, broadly construed; 3) we know that a copy of Riccobaldo's text was held in the ducal library and that the library was central to Ferrarese courtly culture, even acting as a lending library for courtiers.[19]

Dennis Looney, who also studied Boiardo's translation of Herodotus, shares Fumagalli's positive assessment of Boiardo's translation and also seeks to contextualize Boiardo's work as translator. According to Looney, fifteenth-century inventories suggest that two-thirds of the manuscripts and books in the Estense library were translations of Greek, Roman, and medieval historical texts.[20] This reveals important components of Ferrarese courtly culture, within which the *Istoria* should be interpreted. That culture was in large part a vernacular one, with an abiding interest in history, and no urgent need to distinguish between classical texts and medieval ones. Judging at least by the famous Estense library this was a culture "in translation." It is tempting to label this tendency not to distinguish between classical and medieval subjects as "medieval" since in the Middle Ages there was a tendency to appropriate the past in terms of the present for mostly moral ends. This contrasts with the well-known "Renaissance" tendency, more typical of cultures such as the Florentine, to historicize by reading classical texts in their original language, and to see "medieval" and "classical"

---

[17] Edoardo Fumagalli, "Il volgarizzamento di Erodoto," in Anceschi and Matarrese, *Il Boiardo e il mondo estense*, 329–428, esp. 411.

[18] Fumagalli, "Il volgarizzamento di Erodoto," 408–9. On Boiardo's translation of Herodotus see also Michael Murrin, *History and Warfare in Renaissance Epic* (Chicago: University of Chicago Press, 1994), Appendix Two.

[19] See Giulio Bertoni, *La Biblioteca Estense e la coltura ferrarese ai tempi del Duca Ercole I* (Turin: E. Loescher, 1903).

[20] Dennis Looney, "Erodoto dalle *Storie* al romanzo," in Anceschi and Materrese, *Il Boiardo e il mondo estense*, 429–41, here 429.

things in clear cultural contrast (without losing the interest in moral ends). This modern ("Renaissance") historical consciousness is less manifest in fifteenth-century Ferrarese courtly culture.[21] One historian has listed six "methodological assumptions" found in Renaissance history. It would be difficult to find any of them prominently present in the *Istoria imperiale*.[22]

Critics have misconstrued this cultural tendency to emphasize historical continuity and an unabashed eclecticism for a lack of coherence and an inability to distinguish fact from fiction. On the contrary, Looney points out that often Boiardo, by strengthening Herodotus's own admissions of doubt in the veracity of his sources, demonstrates a strong critical attitude.[23] Ultimately, Looney offers a much more positive assessment of Boiardo's historical translation: "... Boiardo was successful in transforming the narrative of Herodotus into a romance/chivalric narrative, carrying out a compromise between history and romance in which, perhaps, is contained the future development of the relationship between romance and epic in the Ferrarese literary tradition. . . ."[24]

Boiardo created a new hybrid historical narrative, influenced by chivalric romance and epic, but also by classical models. He did so not because he could not tell the difference between fiction and fact, poetry and history, but because he wished to translate not only from the ancient languages into the *volgare* but also from one culture to another. He devised his narrative from both classical

---

[21] Timothy Hampton writes: "... humanism aimed to read the past on the past's own terms, by returning to original textual sources and by attempting to recreate the cultural landscape which produced them": Timothy Hampton, *Writing from History: The Rhetoric of Exemplarity in Renaissance Literature* (Ithaca: Cornell University Press, 1990), 14. I am also thinking, for example, of manuscripts which transposed classical heroes such as Alexander the Great and Julius Caesar into medieval knights. See, for example, the discussion of the French manuscript described as "Libro uno chiamado le istorie de Alesandro, in francexe et in membrana. . . .": Pio Rajna, "Ricordi di codici francesi posseduti dagli Estensi nel secolo XV," *Romania* 2 (1873): 5–59, here 51.

[22] Herbert Weisinger, "Ideas of History During the Renaissance," in *Renaissance Essays*, ed. Paul Oskar Kristeller and Phillip P. Weiner (New York: Harper and Row, 1968), 74–94. The six assumptions are: the idea of progress, the theory of the plenitude of nature, the climate theory, the cyclical theory of history, the doctrine of uniformitarianism, and the idea of decline. The exception is the "Prologue" in which, as we shall see, there are some ideas of decline and revival.

[23] For example in the passage from the *Histories*, 3.115, Boiardo translates as follows: "E certamente questi duoi nomi Eridano e Chasiteride, che Greci sono, dimostrano questa essare fittione de Poeti *e non vera narratione di historici*." The last phrase in italics is added to the text by Boiardo. See Looney, "Erodoto dalle *Storie* al romanzo," 440.

[24] "... Boiardo riesce a trasformare la narrative di Erodoto in narrativa romanzesca, attuando un compromesso tra storia e romanzo in cui forse sta il futuro sviluppo dei rapporti tra romanzo e epica nella tradizione letteraria ferrarese, all'interno della quale gia da tempo l'eredità umanistica aveva condizionato la ricezione dell'uno e dell'altro genere": Looney, "Erodoto dalle *Storie* al romanzo," 441.

and medieval elements to speak to the court through peculiarly Ferrarese means. It remains to be demonstrated exactly how Boiardo did this and why.

II

One of the most peculiar things about the literature on the *Istoria* is the almost complete neglect of the Prologue. In fact, the Prologue is a key to understanding for whom Boiardo wrote the *Istoria* and why. It is addressed to Ercole, Duke of Ferrara, and begins with a praise of history as a teacher of many things in peace and in war. Boiardo then praises Ercole for his love of history and points out that in antiquity some princes, including Julius Caesar, Augustus, and Hadrian, not only praised history but also wrote it themselves. He also mentions Aurelian, who would not admit to his council of advisors anyone who had not studied the past. But the importance of history waned with the fall of Rome. This leads Boiardo to meditate on all the changes that occurred over the next thousand years: changes in place names, and the passing of the empire to the Greeks, then to the Franks, and finally to the Germans. Into this state of affairs came Riccobaldo, who revived the study of history by tending "... this little spark, almost spent, which was illuminating affairs of the past." Boiardo then mentions some of Riccobaldo's sources and his organization of his history by emperor, beginning with Augustus up to his own time. Boiardo concludes with two *topoi:* first his hope that Ercole will find his translation acceptable even though it is unadorned and unrefined in speech, and then a humanist *topos* of the literary work as archeological fragment:[25]

> But like the ancient marble statues of Praxiteles or Phidias which are customarily broken, with their heads and arms cut off, one is still grateful to whoever finds them because they were unknown for such a long time. And so this ancient history, newly rediscovered, because it contains many things in it, even though it is without any adornment, is pleasing to whoever reads it.[26]

---

[25] On medieval topoi or topics see Ernst Curtius, *European Literature and the Latin Middle Ages*, trans. Willard Trask (New York: Harper and Row, 1953). For similar practices among classical authors see Tore Jansen, *Latin Prose Prefaces: Studies in Literary Conventions*, Acta Universitatis Stockholmiensis (Stockholm: Almqvist and Wiksell, 1964).

[26] See Appendix I. I have consulted the following sources for the Prologue: Muratori, *RIS*, IX; Matteo Maria Boardo, *Tutte le opere di Matteo M. Boiardo*, ed. Angelandrea Zottoli (Milan: Mondadori, 1944), 719–20; and the MS. 424 in the Biblioteca Classense in Ravenna, Italy. All translations are mine. Generally I use the manuscript version; in this case, however, I use the edition of Muratori copied by Zottoli. Boiardo's "discovery" of Riccobaldo cannot be taken literally since the ducal library was in possession of a copy of the text. See Bertoni, *Biblioteca estense*, 250.

According to the research of Leonard Barkan, Boiardo's archeological topos is a precocious effort to bridge past and present, that is, a rather sophisticated notion of how one cobbles together a historical narrative.[27]

The Prologue also reveals a classical, Sallustian influence, and there is evidence that Sallust was read, in translation, at the Estense court.[28] But Sallust was also well known in the Middle Ages and greatly admired for his ability to combine rhetorical skill with historical truth, especially in his prologues. Boiardo, evoking Sallust, exhorts the reader to appreciate the value of studying history especially for the purpose of preserving good government, a theme, we shall see, of interest to Boiardo. It is no accident, therefore, that the critics who devalue the historical validity of Boiardo's text also ignore the Prologue, which so strongly asserts the dignity and necessity of history. Boiardo puts the value of studying history in the form of a Renaissance *topos*: the mastery of writing history by the ancients, its loss,

---

[27] Leonard Barkan, *Unearthing the Past: Archaeology and Aesthetics in the Making of Renaissance Culture* (New Haven: Yale University Press, 1999). I say precocious because Barkan begins his account in 1506, probably some twenty-five years after Boiardo wrote his Prologue. See also the review of Barkan's book by Zachary S. Schiffman, *Sixteenth Century Journal* 31 (2000): 944–46, who writes: ". . . how the fragmentary quality of ancient sculpture affected its Renaissance reception, how this reception illustrates ways of bridging past and present, and how the career of one sculptor (Baccio Bandinelli) reflects an artistic culture grounded (as it were) in the ancient statues that had issued from the soil beneath his feet" (945).

[28] The knowledge and influence of Sallust at the Estense court is strongly suggested by a translation of the *Conspiracy of Catiline* by Ludovico Carbone dedicated to Alberto d'Este, Ercole's half brother, around 1464. See Werner L. Gundersheimer, *Ferrara: The Style of a Renaissance Despotism* (Princeton: Princeton University Press, 1973), 166–67, and Appendix II for a transcription of Carbone's preface. Bertoni lists three unspecified works of Sallust in the ducal library, one in Latin and two vernacular translations: Bertoni, *Biblioteca estense*, 250. I don't mean to exclude other influences on Boiardo. My principal point is that Boiardo was well aware of a long tradition of the writing of historical prologues. An interesting question is the relative influence of ancient versus medieval sources. This may be a badly put question, since many medievals had long digested classical models of all kinds. For example, there are significant parallels between Boiardo's Prologue and those of Otto of Freising in both his *The Two Cities* and *The Deeds of Frederick Barbarossa*. See Otto I Bishop of Freising, *The Two Cities: A Chronicle of Universal History to the Year 1146 A.D.*, ed. Austin P. Evans, trans. Charles Mierow (New York: Columbia University Press, 1928; reprint, New York: Octagon, 1966), 93–97, and Otto I Bishop of Freising, *The Deeds of Frederick Barbarossa*, trans. Charles Mierow (New York: Columbia University Press, 1953; reprint, New York: Norton, 1966), 24–28. In the former, Otto cites a series of classical authors just as Boiardo does, views the Roman Empire as having fallen and been revived, focuses on a long line of emperors, and admits the rudeness of his style. Surely, these parallels are explained through a veritable model of prologue-writing that Boiardo knew well. On the medieval prologue as literary phenomena see Samuel Jaffe, "Gottfried Von Strassburg and the Rhetoric of History," in *Medieval Eloquence*, ed. James J. Murphy (Berkeley: University of California Press, 1978), 288–318.

and subsequent rebirth. But he presents his argument in what might seem to be the peculiar light of "... princes who not only did things worthy of eternal memory, but who also acquired eternal fame by means of writing."[29] By praising princes who not only performed deeds worthy of memory, but who also recorded them, Boiardo is able simultaneously to praise Ercole and justify his own authorial activity. For Ercole as prince not only performs deeds worthy of praise, he also is responsible for the Renaissance revival of the study of history to which Boiardo responds, thus becoming a "writer" ("But this perception of the importance of history, which was held in such honor by the ancients and is again esteemed worthy by Your Lordship...").[30] Boiardo's response — the translation of Riccobaldo — is thereby sanctioned by the usefulness of history as teacher, by the practice of ancient princes, and by Ercole himself, Boiardo's own lord. But why did Boiardo choose to translate Riccobaldo's history? Several answers can be suggested.

Some believe that it was Ercole who asked Boiardo to translate Riccobaldo, though Kristin Lippincott has suggested that we should be cautious in assuming courtly determination of creative activity.[31] A more concrete explanation for the translation is that it was available in the ducal library and was a well-known and respected historical text.[32] But the most important reason may have been that Riccobaldo was himself Ferrarese, and as such was interested in embedding Ferrarese developments in his universal history.[33] Two key passages of the

---

[29] "... gloriosissimi Principi, i quali non solamente hanno fatto cose degne di memoria eterna, ma scrivendo eziandio hanno aquistata gloriosa fama."

[30] "Ma questo scorgimento dela vita umana, che fu presso agli antichi in tanto onore, et hor di nuovo degnamente estimato da Vostra Eccellenza."

[31] Reichenbach spins an amusing yarn about Ercole's being wounded at the battle of Molinella and transported to the ducal palace to convalesce. To alleviate the boredom, Boiardo, whether on his own or at Ercole's suggestion, decided to tell stories of the deeds of past great leaders. ("... l'idea di alleviargli la noia delle ore interminabili col ricordo di gesta ..."). See Reichenbach, *Matteo Maria Boiardo*, 40–41. Out of this came the translation of the *Lives of Cornelius Nepos*. The story reflects the usual assumption that the purpose of Boiardo's translations was merely to amuse and entertain. In a private communication Dennis Looney has suggested the intriguing idea that the original tale could also reveal the healing power of history much like storytelling in the *Decameron* heals the suffering inflicted by the plague. On the question of courtly patronage see Kristen Lippincott, "The Neo-Latin Historical Epics of the North Italian Courts: An Examination of 'Courtly Culture' in the Fifteenth Century," *Renaissance Studies* 3 (1989): 415–28. While Lippincott limits herself to Latin historical epics, her comments on patronage would seem to be applicable to other forms of historical writing, at least as they refer to the question of actual commissions.

[32] Hankey, *Riccobaldo of Ferrara*, reports in chap. 8 that the *Pomerium* went through at least two revisions and is preserved in twelve manuscript copies, more than any other work of Riccobaldo. On the influence of Riccobaldo, see Bertoni, *Biblioteca estense,* 250, who lists an unspecified work of Riccobaldo in the ducal library.

[33] Riccobaldo is interested in Ferrarese history rather than a history of the Estense family. Therefore his references to the Estensi become common only when they enter into Ferrarese history around the year 1180. Thereafter, his references to them become very common. See, for example, *Historia imperatorum, RIS*, 9, col. 124.

Prologue need to be considered. The first reads, ". . . Riccobaldo, a new man from a new city . . ." (". . . Ricobaldo Ferrarese, huomo nuovo e da nuovo citade provenuto . . ."). The first part is probably a reference to Riccobaldo's relatively modest social status as notary. The second is a reference to Ferrara itself. Placing this phrase at the end of his meditation on the Middle Ages, Boiardo is acknowledging the medieval, probably seventh-century, origins of Ferrara itself as a "new city."[34] A subsequent passage puts Boiardo's relationship with Ercole in feudal terms (and in terms of another *topos*): it ties Boiardo's personal debt to Ercole to his translation of Riccobaldo (as a service owed to his lord), which is, in part, about Ferrara and the Estensi. "Besides the fact that I and everything I own is held from you, Riccobaldo, from whom this work is drawn, was of your city, and a good part of the book is filled with magnanimous deeds and the virtuous governance of your ancient forbears." ("Imperocché oltraché io con tutte le cose mie sia per obbligo di quella, fu Ricobaldo, da cui è tratta quest'Opera di vostra Cittade; e buona parte del Libro è ripiena de'magnanimi gesti, e prudentissimi governi degli antichi vostri passati.")

And so we come at last to the real purposes of the translation of Riccobaldo's text: surely to please Ercole, perhaps even to comply with some sort of commission. Here most of the commentators are content to remain on a level of Ercole's liking history and Boiardo's dutifully providing him with a text filled with chivalric fantasy for his entertainment. In this they underestimate the intelligence of both Ercole and Boiardo. If indeed Ercole was a devotee of history, isn't it likely that he had some understanding of its power and importance?[35] The hypothesis that the *Istoria imperiale* was commissioned by Ercole is best supported by what seems to be a conscious effort by the Estensi to document their history. Jane Bestor has traced a century of Estense genealogical activity beginning at the end of the fourteenth century.[36] Benvenuto da Imola dedicated

---

[34] Francesca Bocchi, *Istituzioni e società a Ferrara in età precommunale*, ser. 3, 26, *Deputazione Provinciale di Ferrara di Storia Patria, Atti e Memorie* (1979): 10–11, suggests that Ferrara originated as a Byzantine military post on the Po to defend against the Lombards.

[35] The standard argument is that Ercole liked history and asked Boiardo and others to translate historical works for him. For example Reichenbach, *Matteo Maria Boiardo*, 187, writes: "Forse nella relativa tranquillità di questi anni, nell'ozio di Scandiano, il Boiardo tradusse, a compiacenza di Ercole, due altre opere storiche . . ." ["Perhaps in the relative tranquility of these years, in the leisure of Scandiano, Boiardo translated, obliging Ercole, two other historical works"]. This remark is followed by an assumption that the alleged errors in Boiardo's text — indifference to fact versus fiction, uncritical methodology, incorporation of legendary material into the historical narrative — were encouraged by Ercole. In other words, I suppose, Ercole liked bad history and encouraged Boiardo to write bad history.

[36] For this paragraph I am indebted to Jane Fair Bestor, "Kinship and Marriage in the Politics of an Italian Ruling House: The Este of Ferrara in the Reign of Ercole I (1471–1505)" (Ph.D. diss., University of Chicago, 1992), 384–412.

his commentary on *The Divine Comedy* (completed between 1379 and 1383) to Niccolò II d'Este, inserting historical material and a genealogy of the House of Este in his discussion of *Inferno* 12.[37] The *Chronicon Estense*, also containing genealogical information, seems to have been written around the same time, and an inventory of 1436 refers to an illustrated family tree among Niccolò III's possessions. Genealogical activity increased during the reign of Ercole, probably in response to his dispute with Niccolò, the son of Leonello d'Este, over who would succeed Borso. In the 1470s two new genealogies were produced. The first is one usually referred to as the *Iconografia Estense,* and the second may have been compiled by the notary Ugo Caleffini. Caleffini also wrote a diary, a chronicle in rhyme, and a history, all in the vernacular. Finally, sometime in the 1490s, Pellegrino Prisciano produced his unfinished *Historiae*. Whether all or any of these genealogical and historical works were commissioned by the Estensi is uncertain. Still, they do illustrate considerable effort at court to explore the medieval Estense past. It is difficult to believe that the ruling dynasty did not encourage such efforts and understand their political value. One thing is certain: Boiardo's "translation" took place in the context of considerable historical activity which focused on the origins of the House of Este. Moreover, that activity reveals the diversity of Ferrarese courtly culture as it produced history in many forms: genealogies, chronicles in both Latin and the vernacular, a humanist Latin history, and the hybrid, vernacular *Istoria imperiale*.[38]

Boiardo chose to "translate" Riccobaldo's text not only because the author was Ferrarese and provided information on Ferrara and the Estensi, but most of all because it provided him with an opportunity to embed Ferrarese history, especially Estense history, in the history of the Empire. Ferrarese history could claim no ancient origins, as Ferrara and the Estensi were thoroughly medieval. When Boiardo meditates on the origins of the Middle Ages, the change of names, for example, from Cisalpine Gaul to Lombardy, he is contemplating the very origins of the Middle Ages, and of Ferrara and its ruling dynasty as well. This is what he means by "your [Ercole's] ancient forebears": the history of Ercole's ancestors. By embedding Estensi history in the affairs of the Empire and its rulers, Boiardo legitimates them legally, through feudal law, but also by means of their "magnanimous deeds and virtuous rule."[39] As we shall see, the very origins of the

---

[37] See Ernesto Milano, *Testimonianze dantesche: nella Biblioteca Estense Universitaria (sec. XIV–XX)* (Modena: Bulino, 2000), 38. My thanks to Dennis Looney for this reference.

[38] Bestor, "Kinship and Marriage," 427.

[39] In 1453 Borso d'Este, Ercole's half-brother, was legally invested as Duke of Modena and Reggio by the Emperor Frederick III. In 1471 Borso obtained a similar investiture from Pope Paul II as Duke of Ferrara. Boiardo is surely anxious to recall these events. In the *Istoria imperiale* the emphasis is, of course, placed on the imperial side of Estense authority. This raises questions of dating the composition of the *Istoria imperiale*. Internal evidence suggests that it was written while Ercole was duke, from 1471 to 1505, and of course before Boiardo's death in 1494. Reference in the "Prologue" to the present reign

dynasty and its rule are associated with the loyal conduct of the Estensi as imperial vassals and as affines of the emperor. This brings us back to the beginning of the Prologue and the legitimation of the discipline of history as a "... teacher of many things in peace and in war by means of examples..." Ercole activates the teaching power of history through his support of the writing of history and through his genealogical connection to those who did things worthy of memory ("magnanimi gesti"). And while Ercole does not literally write the history, it is his history ("antichi vostri passati") because it is about his family and because it is written through his instrument, the duke's vassal, Matteo Maria Boiardo.[40]

Why is the term "translation" chosen, even though we know that Boiardo based this part of the text mostly on other sources beyond Riccobaldo? First the *Istoria* is a "translation" in the time-honored medieval sense of a text which is not new but ancient and therefore authoritative.[41] Second, it is a "translation" for the court by Ercole and Boiardo because as courtiers the nobility need to understand the historical role of the dynasty in whose regime they play a crucial if subordinate part. In turn this project necessitates using a narrative form that makes the events of the past comprehensible and palatable to a feudal aristocracy. This is why, as we shall see, "magnanimous deeds" play such an important role in Boiardo's rhetorical strategy.[42] To use a schema identified by John O. Ward, Boiardo uses pieces of Riccobaldo's history as a basis for producing a finished, historical narrative.[43]

The political and "public" role of history is more explicitly treated in Boiardo's Prologue to his translation of Herodotus's *Histories*. There he talks about the public utility ("publica utilità") of the study of past deeds, of how through such study princes will know how to govern better in peace and in war.[44] But he also refers

---

of the Emperor Frederick III is not helpful since he ruled from 1440 to 1493. Ponte suggests a date of around 1483, because the Prologue refers to Ercole as count of Rovigo, a province lost by the Estensi in their war with Venice through the Peace of Bagnolo, signed in 1484: Ponte, *La personalità*, 69 and n. 19. In any case, the composition could not have been much more than fifteen years after the investiture of Borso d'Este as Duke of Ferrara in 1471 and was therefore a recent memory.

[40] Boiardo clearly associates the state with the person of the duke, which he makes clear through phrases such as "your city" and "your ancient forebears." He draws no distinction between the history of the city/state and the dynasty.

[41] A. J. Minnis, *Medieval Theory of Authorship*, 2nd ed. (Philadelphia: University of Pennsylvania Press, 1988), chap. 1.

[42] I had originally hoped to include in this essay a discussion of the "Life" of Frederick Barbarossa, where "deeds" play a very significant role, but space limits prevented me from doing so. I hope to be able to complete this analysis in a future study. In the meantime, the sections on Charlemagne and Otto I, discussed below, will have to suffice.

[43] John O. Ward, "Some Principles of Rhetorical Historiography in the Twelfth Century," in *Classical Rhetoric and Medieval Historiography*, ed. Breisach, 104–11.

[44] "Prologue" to Boiardo's translation of Herodotus, *Histories*, in Matteo Maria Boiardo, *Tutte le opere di Matteo M. Boiardo*, ed. Angelandrea Zottoli (Milan: Mondadori, 1944), 722.

to the "delightful utility to the listeners" ("dilettevole utilità a gli ascoltanti") of the strange and marvelous things, the frequent and good maxims and teachings that Herodotus provides.[45] For Boiardo, as for Sallust, history has a public end and a rhetorical means. So, in the Prologue to the *Istoria imperiale* he writes: "I decided to translate for vernacular speakers from the Latin, because knowledge of the past serves common usefulness [better] the more widely it is possessed."[46] Boiardo's end is a public one — the preservation of the princely, dynastic, and aristocratic state. The rhetorical means is the development of a historical narrative that communicates widely, not narrowly, to the "public." Of course in a Ferrarese context the "public" is not the humanists, nor even probably others outside the Estensi realm, but the Ferrarese court, and the "vulgar gente" are not commoners but the courtiers who spoke the "vulgar," Emilian tongue.[47] As one of the most highly ranked members of the court and as the court's principal cultural star, Boiardo is delegated a crucial political and educational role by Ercole. Boiardo defines good government (". . . magnanimi gesti e prudentissimi governi") and identifies it with the prince, whose function as "author," in the sense of authorizing voice/"writer" of history, in turn promotes good government.

By emphasizing his debt and service to Ercole and the fact that the history is truly the dukes', Boiardo uses his authorial activity to turn Ercole into a ruler/historian, like Julius Caesar. The role of the courtier is to advise the prince, but in order to do so the courtier/advisor must be educated in history.[48] So, Boiardo as courtier/historian has the special role of historical actor, as the person who activates history's potential power to teach.[49] In order to accomplish this necessary political task, Boiardo must pursue this end through an effectual rhetorical means: a "delightful" ("dilettevole") narrative.[50] Thus he "translates" Riccobaldo, emphasizing the Estensi in the historical narrative, while associating great deeds with proper moral development.[51]

---

[45] Zottoli, ed., *Tutte le opere di M.M. Boiardo*, 723.

[46] "ho deliberato tradurre alla vulgar gente da Lingua Latina, acciochè per conoscere delle passate cose, il quale è utilitade comune, più comunemente sia posseduta": Zottoli, ed., *Tutte le opere*, 720.

[47] One of the principal reasons for devaluing the *Orlando innamorato* is Boiardo's use of Emilian dialect. By the early sixteenth century this was considered such a serious defect that Berni produced his rifacimento, or reworking of the text into a proper Tuscan idiom. Boiardo seems to have both preceded and to lie outside of the circles that came to accept the Tuscanization of the vernacular.

[48] "Aurelian . . . held History in such esteem that he would not admit into his council of advisors anyone who had not read and considered the past." See Appendix I.

[49] "History has been praised by many people . . . as a teacher of many things. . . ." See Appendix I.

[50] I am also suggesting that Boiardo is emulating Herodotus here who, as Breisach suggests, wrote to inspire, to inform, but also to entertain: Breisach, *Historiography*, 18.

[51] The similarities with Castiglione's *The Book of the Courtier* are striking in that both texts explore the education and moral development of the courtier and his relationship with the prince. Much could probably be said about the relationship between the two texts.

III

It is time now to examine two sections of the *Istoria imperiale,* with two goals. The first is the section on Charlemagne, to demonstrate Boiardo's historical method; the second is the "Estensi interlace." This is Boiardo's practice of interposing in his narrative of imperial lives both a sub-narrative of the deeds of Ercole's ancestors and a meta-narrative on the transition of the ancient world to the medieval.

We have already seen that Alessandro Scarsella tries to link Boiardo's non-fiction translations to the *Orlando Innamorato*, suggesting even that Boiardo uses Turpin not only as a poetic narrative device but also as a historical authority.[52] Boiardo does indeed cite Turpin as a source used by Riccobaldo, and writes in the Prologue: "And in the affairs of Charlemagne and of the Franks he [Riccobaldo] followed Alcuin the tutor of the same Charles, who wrote at Paris, and Turpin, bishop of Rheims, assistant and counselor of that emperor." To which historical source by Turpin does Boiardo refer? Almost certainly to the *Historia Karoli Magni et Rotholandi*, which is often referred to as the *Pseudo-Turpin Chronicle* or simply the *Pseudo-Turpin*.

The interpretation of the *Pseudo-Turpin Chronicle* is a very complex subject.[53] For our purposes the following information is sufficient. The manuscript was written around 1150. Its subject matter is very similar to that of the *Song of Roland*: the story of the betrayal of Ganelon, the defeat of the French rearguard at Roncevaux, the death of Roland, and the final defeat of the Saracens at Saragossa. The author of the *Pseudo-Turpin* was surely a cleric, probably a monk somehow connected to St. James in Compostela. The work was written in Latin prose but drew upon the legends of a popular tradition about Charlemagne and

---

I am content here simply to point out that both share an interesting combination of medieval and Renaissance elements, as in an appreciation of traditional feudal warrior values of prowess combined with an appreciation of the *studia humanitatis*. Of course while the emphasis in *The Courtier* is on the development of an aesthetic appreciation, in the *Istoria imperiale* the emphasis is on developing a historical appreciation.

[52] Scarsella, "Boiardo traduttore," 396, where he writes: "Giustamente i volgarizzamenti del Boiardo sono stati studiati in connessione alla scrittura del poema . . ." And in n. 25 he quotes from the "Prologue" of the *Istoria imperiale*.

[53] I can only list a few references of the enormous bibliography. A good place to begin is Susan Farrier, *The Medieval Charlemagne Legend: An Annotated Bibliography* (New York: Garland, 1993), Section III, "The Pseudo-Turpin Chronicle," 56–68. For editions of the text and commentary, see Cyril Meredith-Jones, ed., *Historia Karoli Magni et Rotholandi; ou, Chronique du Pseudo-Turpin* (Paris: Droz, 1936; repr. Geneva: Slatkine Reprints, 1972), H. M. Smyser, ed., *The Pseudo-Turpin, edited from Bibliothèque Nationale, fonds latin, MS. 17656* (Cambridge, MA: Medieval Academy of America, 1937), and Ronald Walpole, *The Old French Johannes Translation of the Pseudo-Turpin Chronicle* (Berkeley: University of California Press, 1976). I base most of this section on Walpole's introduction to the last, xi–xxii.

was translated many times into the French vernacular. Of these the most popular and important is the "Johannes translation." According to Ronald Walpole three factors explain the translation's popularity: first, the "authenticity" of the text, since it was an "eyewitness" account by Archbishop Turpin himself. (Up to Boiardo's time the authenticity of the text was widely believed in.) Second, the text offered a series of high moral examples to the nobility; and third, Johannes reordered the narrative, making it more orderly and natural.[54] These factors are strongly paralleled in Boiardo's Prologue and text, in his decision to translate the "eyewitness" account of the Ferrarese Riccobaldo, in his evocation of "magnanimous deeds," and in his reorganization of the narrative. Another factor in explaining the translation's popularity is its combination with the *Descriptio qualiter Karulus Magnus*, a fictitious account of Charlemagne's journey to the Holy Land to restore the Holy Sepulcher to Christian control, which was eventually incorporated into the Johannes translation.

The entire *Descriptio-Turpin* tradition was fraught with political meaning. Gabrielle Spiegel has demonstrated a close political connection between the *Descriptio-Turpin* and the French-speaking Flemish nobility who used the text in their contest with Philip Augustus.[55] She has demonstrated that this aristocratic interest was not accidental. The lords found reassurance of their social status through the exploits of Roland and his comrades; they saw affirmation of their own participation in the Third and Fourth Crusades through Charlemagne's fictitious journey to the Holy Land; and they found legitimation through their own genealogies which were, in fact, more closely connected to Charlemagne than those of the Capetians were.[56] Similarly, Boiardo links the Estensi to Charlemagne through his poetic imagination in the *Orlando Innamorato*, and through history, as we shall see, to the Ottonians.[57]

We know from textual evidence that both Riccobaldo and Boiardo were acquainted with *Descriptio-Turpin* material, and that a French translation of the *Descriptio* still survives in the Biblioteca Estense in Modena and was catalogued in the Estense library in the fifteenth century.[58] We can use these facts to test the predominant interpretive framework that sees Boiardo as lacking

---

[54] Walpole, *Old French Johannes Translation*, xvi–xvii, where he writes, "In his sincerity and his warmer feeling, Johannes in his French comes nearer than the Pseudo-Turpin in his Latin to the drama and realism of epic poetry and so undoubtedly nearer to the mind and hearts of the lay people whom he had in mind as he made his translation."

[55] Gabrielle M. Spiegel, "Pseudo-Turpin, the Crisis of the Aristocracy, and the Beginnings of Vernacular Historiography in France," *Journal of Medieval History* 12 (1986): 207–23, esp. 208–11.

[56] Spiegel, "Crisis of the Aristocracy," 214–16.

[57] Boiardo, *Orlando Innamorato*, ed. Ross, 2.21.55–59.

[58] On the present state of the manuscript see Walpole, *Old French Johannes Translation*, 89–93. The manuscript is catalogued as MS. N.5.12. On the inventories of the fifteenth century see Rajna, "Ricordi di codici francesi," 49–58.

sufficient critical faculties to perceive the distinction between fact and fiction. Was Boiardo a mere composer of poetic romances, the producer of a historical "patchwork?"[59] Is his treatment of Charlemagne imaginative or historical?

Coming out of the *Descriptio-Turpin* tradition we should look for evidence of the following characteristics in Boiardo's narrative: acceptance of Turpin's account as authentic; the recounting of the story of Charlemagne's trip to the Holy Land; a general and widespread presence of fantastic and supernatural elements; and the confounding of historical and legendary elements, especially regarding the defeat and death of Roland, the key event in the *Descriptio-Turpin* tradition.

The evidence provided by the text suggests that Boiardo was a conscientious and critical historian with a firm grasp of the difference between fiction and fact. Neither Riccobaldo nor Boiardo mentions the story of Charlemagne's trip to the Holy Land, and neither uses the *Descriptio-Turpin* as the basis of their account of Roland's death.[60] Riccobaldo's account is as follows: "At that time, Roland count palatine and son of his [Charlemagne's] sister and others, whose deeds are known, perished in Spain. Charles twice conquered the Spanish; he subdued the Saxons, and other Germanic peoples; he built two bridges over the Rhine river."[61] The passage shows signs of using Einhard's *Life of Charlemagne (Vita Karoli)*, but no evidence whatsoever of the legendary material of Roland's defeat found in the *Pseudo-Turpin* material. It is terse in the extreme, omitting the names of those who perished in the battle with Roland and even omitting any mention of whom Roland was fighting. The narrative is perfunctory, even somewhat incoherent. In the last sentence Riccobaldo combines

[59] See Soffienti, "Le *Vite*," 479, who quotes Rajna's use of the term "raffazzonamento" or "patchwork."

[60] While Riccobaldo's facts are generally sound, he does make occasional mistakes, for example confusing Charlemagne with his father Pippin the Short. On the other hand, his narrative is somewhat rambling and confusing. He begins by introducing Charles Martel and his conquests, and then moves to Pippin and Charlemagne, whom he treats as brothers. Riccobaldo writes: "Mortuo Karulo Martelo successit in principatu ejus, Karulus Magnus primogenitus & Pipinus Secundus . . ." (*RIS*, 9, 108–9). Boiardo does not repeat this mistake. Riccobaldo then mentions Boniface's mission to the Germans. Next comes a discussion of Roman pontiffs, the kings of the Lombards, and the emperor at Constantinople. He then discusses Charlemagne's conquest of the Lombards, the succession of Pope Leo, and then back to the affairs of Constantinople. This is followed by a long meditation on world empires from the Assyrians to the Romans and a detailed discussion of Roman politics between Caesar and Pompey on the one hand and Octavian and Antony on the other. After describing the division of the Roman Empire, Riccobaldo concludes with a judgment of the superiority of the western empire ("Occidentale Imperium pater est, orientale est filius . . .": (*RIS*, 9, 112). This brings Riccobaldo to a section devoted, more or less, to Charlemagne. Boiardo's narrative is essentially independent of Riccobaldo's and in my opinion is much more coherent.

[61] "Ejus tempore fuerunt Comites Palatini Rotholandus ejus sororis filius & alii, de quibus gesta habentur, qui in Hispania perierunt. Karulus bis subegit Hispanos; Saxones subjugavit & gentem Germanorum: super Rhenum duos pontes construxit" (*RIS*, 9, 112).

three separate ideas into one sentence: defeating the "Spaniards," subjugating the Saxons, and building two bridges over the Rhine.

While Riccobaldo's account shows traces of Einhard, Boiardo's is a direct paraphrase. Indeed, almost the entire life of Charlemagne is paraphrased from Einhard's *Life of Charlemagne*, though attributed incorrectly to Alcuin, a mistake Boiardo picks up from Riccobaldo.[62] Boiardo's account of Roland's death is more than six times longer than Riccobaldo's; it is more coherent, and filled with detail.[63] The account states Charles's motivation for invading Spain: to secure the borders of his empire.[64] Basques (Guasconi) and not Muslims attack the rear of Charlemagne's army as it moved through the Pyrenees back to France, and they inflict a grave defeat because of the terrain, the lightness of their arms compared to the heavily armed Franks, and the Basques' knowledge of their native land.[65] Boiardo mentions the death of the commanders, just as Einhard does, and he also notes that revenge eluded the Franks due to the quickness of the Basques' retreat into the mountains.[66]

Boiardo offers a factual account of Roland's death. There is no mention of Roland's refusal to call for help, no mention of Turpin whatsoever; in fact there is no mention of the whole notion of "holy war" against the Saracens that is at the basis of the Roland legend. There is no revenge exacted by Charlemagne. Boiardo bases his account on one of the best historical sources available, Einhard, without making use of the Pseudo-Turpin material. In other words, Boiardo operates as a conscientious historian in this key section of the *Istoria imperiale*, not as an inventor of poetic romances. He clearly discerns a distinction between fact and fiction, history and romance, in what he writes and in which sources he uses.

---

[62] In his edition Muratori places the material in quotation marks, suggesting the direct copying of Einhard's text. In the Ravenna, Biblioteca Classense MS, Boiardo simply states: "De la vita e costume di Carlo non sapiamo come piu veramente poter descrivere che interporre quivi quello che di lui scrisse Alcuino Philosopho . . . si come esso medesimo nel prologo dichiara dicendo cussi" (fol.111r and v). The relevant section of Einhard is Book Nine. Riccobaldo writes: "... & ut Alcuinus ejus Doctor scribit de eo..." (*RIS*, 9, 113).

[63] I am thinking of Nancy Partner's remarks, "The difficulties in reading medieval histories are nearly all narrative. The plausibility of historical narrative is not a function of abstract truth and falsity, or even verifiability . . . certainly not of any fixed standard for reality . . . but of the telling, the connections and sequences of things": Partner, "The New Cornificius," 16.

[64] "... per le quale assicurò da tute parte il suo regno. . . ." All references to the Roland account are from BCR MS. 424, 11r–v and *RIS*, 9, 294.

[65] "Era in aiuto á Gasconi e la legerecia de lo arme, e il sito del locho a loro noto & opportuno; per il contrario á francesi la grave armatura, che usavano, & il paese scognosciuto dava grandissima molestia."

[66] "Forno in questa bataglia occisi Girardo preposto de la mensa reale, & Anselmo conte palatino, e Rolando prefetto de il passo britanico, & altri molti nobili baroni," and "Ni di tanta iniuria si potè al presente far vendetta: pero chè li nimici disparvero cum tanta prestecia. . . ."

One other section of the life of Charlemagne — the description of Charlemagne's appearance and eating habits — can further clarify Boiardo's historical method: how he "translated" Riccobaldo, what he accepted and rejected from him, which other sources he used, and how he distinguished between fact and fantasy. Here is the account of the Pseudo-Turpin Chronicle compared to Einhard's *Life of Charlemagne:*

The Life of Charlemagne[67]

Charles had a big and powerful body and was tall but well-proportioned. That his height was seven times the length of his own feet is well known. He had a round head, his eyes were unusually large and lively, his nose a little longer than average, his gray hair attractive, and his face cheerful and friendly. Whether he was standing or sitting his appearance was always impressive and dignified. His neck was somewhat short and thick and his stomach protruded a little, but this was rendered inconspicuous by the good proportions of the rest of his body [chap. 22]. Charles was a moderate eater and drinker, especially the

The Pseudo-Turpin Chronicle[68]

The Emperor was of a ruddy complexion, with brown hair; of a well-made handsome form, but a stern visage. His height was about eight of his own feet, which were very long. He was of a strong robust make; [his kidneys did their job and he was in agreement with his belly;] his legs and thighs very stout, and his sinews firm. [He was smart in battle, a very fierce soldier.] His face was thirteen inches long; his beard a palm; his nose half a palm; his forehead a foot over. His lion-like eyes flashed fire like carbuncles; his eyebrows were half a palm over. When he was angry, it was a terror to look upon him. He required eight

[67] I use the Latin-English edition, Einhard, *Vita Karoli Magni: The Life of Charlemagne*, trans. Evelyn Scherabon Firchow and Edwin H. Zeydel (Coral Gables: University of Miami Press, 1972; reprint, Dudweiler: AQ-Verlag, 1985), 86–87.

[68] Turpin, *History of Charles the Great and Orlando, Ascribed to Archbishop Turpin*, trans. Thomas Rodd (London: Privately printed, 1812), 36. Rodd does not indicate which particular manuscript or version he used for his translation other than the one printed in Spanheim's *Lives of Ecclesiastical Writers*. See the title page and p. viii. The Latin text as edited by C. Meredith-Jones, *Historia Karoli Magni*, 175–77 is as follows: "Et erat rex Karolus capillis brunus, facie rubeus, corpore decens et venustus, sed visu efferus. Statura vero eius erat in longitudine VIII pedibus, scilicet suis longissimis pedibus, humeris erat amplissimus, renibus aptus, ventre congruus, brachiis et cruribus grossus, omnibus artubus fortissimus, certamine doctissimus, miles acerrimus. Habebat in longitudine facies eius unum palmum et dimidium, et barba unum, et nasus circiter dimidium. Et frons eius erat unius pedis, et oculi eius similes oculis leonis scintillantes ut carbunculus. Supercilia oculorum eius dimidium palmum habebant. Omnis homo statim perterritus erat, quem ipse ira commotus apertis oculis respiciebat. Nullus ante ipsius tribunal fretus esse poterat, quem ille apertis oculis respiciebat. Cingulum namque quo ipse cingebatur, octo palmis extensum habebatur, praeter illud quod dependebat. Parum panis ad prandium comedebat, sed quartam partem arietis, aut gallinas duas, aut ansarem, aut spatulam porcinam, aut pavonem, aut grugam, aut leporem integrum edebat. Parum vinum, sed limpham sobrie bibebat. Hic tanta fortitudine repletus erat, quod militem armatum, inimicum scilicet suum, sedentem super equum a vertice capitis usque ad bases simul cum equo solo ictu propria spata trucidabat. Quattuor ferros equi simul manibus leviter extendabat. Militem armatum rectum stantem super palmam suam, a terra usque ad caput suum sola manu velociter elevabat." I have indicated omitted passages in the translation by means of brackets.

latter, because he abominated drunkenness in any man, particularly in himself and in his associates. But he could not easily abstain from eating and often complained that fasting was bad for his health. He rarely gave banquets and then only on special feast days for large numbers of guests. His daily dinner consisted of four courses, besides the roast which the hunters used to bring in on spits and which he loved more than any other food. [chap. 24]

spans for his girdle, besides what hung loose. He ate sparingly of bread; but a whole quarter of lamb, two fowls, a goose, or a large portion of pork; a peacock, crane, or a whole hare. He drank moderately of wine and water. He was so strong, that he could at a single blow cleave asunder an armed soldier on horseback from the head to the waist, and the horse likewise.[69] He easily vaulted over four horses harnessed together; and he could raise an armed man from the ground to his head, as he stood erect upon his hand.

The Pseudo-Turpin account parallels that of Einhard, but the whole tenor and purpose of the account is clearly different. Einhard's description is thoroughly human, the emperor cheerful and friendly; Charlemagne emerges as a real person, imposing yet flawed. Einhard is obviously describing a man in his old age. In the Pseudo-Turpin account Charlemagne is fearsome and terrifying. Physically, he becomes gigantic, with superhuman strength. The Pseudo-Turpin is obsessive in measuring parts of Charlemagne's face. In the Pseudo-Turpin the description of Charlemagne is combined with his eating habits; in Einhard's they are in separate chapters. Moreover, the whole purpose of each is completely different. Einhard emphasizes the moderation of Charlemagne; Pseudo-Turpin depicts the emperor's gargantuan appetite.

Here are the accounts of Riccobaldo and the *Istoria imperiale*:

Riccobaldo[70]

Charles wore a long beard down to his chest, with a comely body, a fierce visage. He was eight of his feet tall, his face a palm and a half, and his forehead a foot wide. With his sword he would break apart an

Istoria imperiale[71]

And so we come to the end of the life of the valorous Charlemagne, as much as has been written by the philosopher Alcuin. Having come upon a chronicle not ineptly written we find, in almost these exact

[69] Readers familiar with the *Song of Roland* will recognize this behavior occurring many times in that poem. Ariosto's description of Orlando as madman recalls these details as well; see *Orlando furioso 29* (private communication from Dennis Looney).

[70] *RIS*, 9, 113: "Karulus barbam prolixam ad pectus ferebat, formoso corpore, visu ferus, octo pedum ejus fuit statura, facies ejus palmum & dimidium habebat, frons pedis unius. Equitem & equum uno ictu spada armatum diffecuit, quatuor ferramenta pedum equorum manibus extendebat. Militem armatum stantem super manum suam à terra ad caput sola manu velociter elevabat. Leporem integrum aut duas gallinas vel anserem una refectione edebat, parcus in potu raro ultra ternam vicem potabat in coena, satis literis doctus, in quibus per singulos studebat; monasteria multa construxit. Inter quae Ecclesia Beati Jacobi in Gallecia."

[71] BCR MS. 424, fol. 115v; *RIS*, 9, 299: "Cussì faciamo fine ala vita del valoroso Carlo magno, per quanto scrive el philosopho Alcuino, sopragiugendo noi quello, che in una

armed man and his horse with one blow and he would unbend four iron horseshoes [at one time]. With his hand he lifted up speedily from the ground to his head an armed knight standing on his hand. He ate, all at one meal, a whole hare, two fowl, and a goose. He drank at dinner moderately, rarely more than three helpings. He was adequately learned in letters, which he studied every day. He built many monasteries, among which was the church of the blessed James in Galicia.

words, a description of his appearance and personal habits. Charles was of middling height, well formed, and very strong, chiefly in his hands, so that he was able to balance on one finger a broadsword that no one else could lift up. His sight was clear and with certain demonstrations of his great spirit he used to eat most of the time only once a day in the evening. In these meals he ate very often a whole hare, or two hens. In drinking he was temperate, rarely drinking twice as the cup was passed.

Riccobaldo's text is obviously derived from the *Pseudo-Turpin Chronicle*, though it is impossible to know if he used it directly or indirectly through some other text. The precise measurement of his face is preserved as is the account of his supernatural strength. Riccobaldo also retains the references to Charles's eating habits down to the "two fowls" and "whole hare." Riccobaldo also includes a reference to St. James of Compostela, whose glorification, as we have seen, was one of the main motivations for the composition of the chronicle.

Boiardo specifically chose not to use Einhard ("Alcuino") for his description of Charlemagne, but rather another chronicle "not ineptly written." Whichever chronicle Boiardo consulted, it seems to have taken a middle ground between Einhard and the Pseudo-Turpin, or else Boiardo reworked the material. Charles is of middling stature and not gigantic, yet he does possess strength prodigious enough to balance a broadsword on one finger, a feat no one else can duplicate. Still, he is raising a sword with his finger and not a man weighed down in armor with his hand, and he is not cleaving an armed knight and his horse with one blow or leaping over four horses. Boiardo also seems to suggest that Charlemagne was quite temperate in eating just once a day, though he does repeat the reference to his consuming an "entire hare" or "two fowls." All in all Boiardo is quite restrained in his description of the emperor, who while quite formidable is thoroughly human. Boiardo's Charlemagne is a historical rather than a romantic figure, and Boiardo's narrative is much more interesting than Riccobaldo's, as it is punctuated with details that make Charlemagne imposing yet not fantastic.

---

cronicha non ineptamente scripta troviamo del ventre [Muratori has "corpo"] suo, e culto de la persona: ne la quale sono quasi queste parole. Fu Carlo magno di meggiana statura, e ben formata, di forza grandissima, e ne le mane precipuamente, empero chè tenendo uno pomo cum uno solo dito, niuno ve lo potea levare. La vista hebe chiara, con certa demostratione del grandissimo animo, che havea: mangiava il più del tempo una sola fiata il giorno, cioè la sera: & in questa spesse volte una lepore integra, o doe galine; nel bere fu temperatissimo, pero chè rare volte passava le doe fiate."

Demonstrating Boiardo's competence and seriousness as historian does not suggest that his text is perfect: indeed there are considerable factual shortcomings in the following section of the *Istoria*, which runs from the death in 875 of Louis II, the last effective Carolingian ruler in Italy, to the death in 1056 of Henry III. One of these shortcomings is anachronisms, for example treating the College of Cardinals as if it existed in the tenth century. Boiardo also refers to four successive Berengars as emperors, though only two really existed, and he mixes up the numbers of the Henries, referring to Henry II as Henry I, Henry III as Henry II, and so on.[72] Boiardo repeats an anecdote about the youth of Henry III that is apocryphal, or at least dubious, and he depicts Berengar I as an Italian patriot and successful military leader while he really presided over the demise of royal power in northern Italy and was known for almost never winning a battle in his long career. Some of these shortcomings are justifiable, some are not. Certainly, the late ninth and first half of the tenth centuries were politically very confused in Italy, and Boiardo's numbering of the Henries was altogether typical among Italian writers, who didn't recognize Henry the Fowler as emperor.

Such things have led critics to devalue the entire *Istoria imperiale* and to question Boiardo's competence as a historian. This judgment is undeserved. Despite these factual lapses Boiardo's critical faculties allowed him to discern, with notable acuity, some of the most important historical developments of the time. While factual accuracy is a prime attribute of good history, the great historians are known for their ability to write simultaneously on many intersecting levels. Boiardo is probably not a great historian, but he was a thinker who, when confronted with a choice, chose good facts over bad, and whose critical faculties were highly developed.[73] He was clearly interested in the problem of historical change and was focused on the origins of the Middle Ages, an interest not at all in keeping with classicizing influences within humanist historiography.[74] Some of the long-term developments that Boiardo discerns

---

[72] Both of these errors are traceable to Riccobaldo.

[73] I make these remarks with the following ideas of Isaiah Berlin in mind: "If we ask ourselves which historians have commanded the most lasting admiration, we shall, I think, find that they are neither the most ingenious, nor the most precise, nor even the discoverers of new facts or unsuspected causal connections, but those who (like imaginative writers) present men or societies or situations in many dimensions, at many intersecting levels simultaneously...": Isaiah Berlin, "The Concept of Scientific History," in idem, *Concepts and Categories: Philosophical Essays* (New York: Viking, 1979), 103–42, here 141.

[74] Flavio Biondo is perhaps the first quintessential humanist historian. As such, he has a keen interest in the "fall" of the Roman Empire and the gap between that fall and his own time of classical revival. For this reason Denys Hay has called Biondo the "first medieval historian," one who realized that "there was a gap to be filled." But he also notes that such activity was not particularly "fashionable": Denys Hay, "Flavio Biondo and the Middle Ages," *Proceedings of the British Academy* 45 (1959): 97–128, here 116–17.

are: the failure of the state in northern Italy after Louis II; the devolution of power to the local level; the division of the "Italian" nobility into two factions, one supporting German candidates for emperor, the other French and Burgundians;[75] the change in place-names; and the growing autonomy of cities and the increasingly important role of bishops in governing them. The growth of these urban centers was the single most important development of Italian medieval history. Indeed, as Boiardo pointed out in his Prologue, it was during this period that place-names took on their medieval and modern forms, Etruria becoming Tuscany, Gallia Cisalpina becoming Lombardy, and so on. In other words, Boiardo is doing nothing less than chronicling the end of the ancient world and the creation of the medieval, a critical awareness we could label as "Renaissance."[76]

From the perspective of the Este family and Ferrarese courtly culture, the most important historical development of the time was the rise of a new aristocracy. The Carolingian aristocracy was facing extinction, being replaced with families who came to dominate late medieval and early modern European history. Among them was the Estensi, who came into being during this period and who ruled parts of north-central Italy until the nineteenth century.[77] This brings us to the "Estensi interlace."

In the section on "Berengar IV" (that is, the historical Berengar II), just after having introduced Otto of Saxony into Italian politics and having placed Hugh Capet and the throne of France, Boiardo wrote the following:

> In this part of our history we would like to interpose (*interponere*) in it that which we have seen in the ancient chronicles of the house of Este, things that surely happened that no other source would be able to affirm.[78]

I use the term "interlace" for two reasons: first, to connect Boiardo's narrative technique in the *Istoria imperiale* to that of his *Innamorato* and to medieval romances in general (but also, I will suggest below, to classical models as well),

---

[75] Geography was an important factor. Generally, the nobility of northwestern Italy supported French and Burgundian candidates while the nobility of the northeast supported German ones. See Chris Wickham, *Early Medieval Italy*, 2nd ed. (Ann Arbor: University of Michigan Press, 1989), 169.

[76] Donald J. Wilcox has noted that the meaning of change was a theme that fascinated Renaissance thinkers: "The Sense of Time in Western Historical Narratives from Eusebius to Machiavelli," in *Classical Rhetoric*, ed. Breisach, 167–237, here 167.

[77] Luciano Chiappini, *Gli Estensi*, 2nd ed. (Varese: Dall'Oglio, 1967).

[78] "In questa parte de la historia nostra ne pare de interponere quello che visto habiamo ne le croniche antiche de la casa da Este advenga che per fermeza di altro testimonio fermato non sia": MS. Classense, fols.128v–129r, *RIS*, 9, 314.

and second, to point out the skill with which Boiardo exposes the many strands of history in this key section of his work. Interlace carries the connotation of intertwining apparently unconnected narratives into a coherent whole. Indeed, as Charles Ross has suggested, it allows Boiardo to "create complex associations of themes . . . whenever he brings separate stories and characters together at carefully designed intersections."[79] In this case, Boiardo introduces the Este family at precisely the intersection of the development of key institutions (the translation of the empire to Germany, the rise of autonomous urban entities, the development of a new landed nobility, etc.) that explain the transition to the High Middle Ages in Italy.[80] The interlacing episodes can be sketched out as follows:[81]

IMPERIAL EPISODE	ESTENSI INTERLACE
Berengar IV	*Berengar IV*
Otto descends into Italy, defeats Berengar, signs an accord allowing Berengar to retain the imperial title and his domain.	Alberto Azzo returns to Germany with Otto. He grows up at the Austrian court. Otto delights in him and invests him with the County of Fausburg ("Fausburcho") in Saxony.
Otto I	*Otto I*
Otto comes to Italy three times, the first and second at the request of Pope Agapitus II, the third at the request	Alberto Azzo returns to Italy with Otto. He establishes himself in his ancestral castles of Calaone and Este.

[79] Boiardo, *Orlando Innamorato*, ed. Ross, 20.

[80] L. A. Muratori, *Antichità Estensi* (Modena: Stamperia ducale, 1717–1740), 79, traces this introduction of the Estensi genealogy back to Riccobaldo. I believe this to be erroneous. Muratori specifically cites the life of Otto I as the source of this information. This assertion does not appear in Muratori's subsequent (1724) edition of what he calls Riccobaldo's *Historia Imperatorum*. I believe what happened is that Muratori was working from a manuscript by Pellegrino Prisciani, ca. 1490, which in turn used the *Istoria imperiale*. Both Prisciani and Muratori assumed that this section on the Estensi was translated from Riccobaldo, though in fact it was interpolated into the text by Boiardo from another source, the "ancient chronicles of the house of Este." This practice of interpolating information from other sources into Riccobaldo's text and sometimes specifically identifying the source is, as we have seen, consistent with Boiardo's methodology. It could also be added that Riccobaldo was writing in Ravenna where it is doubtful that he would have had access to many sources on Estensi history, and that as an exile and a Ghibelline, he was ill-disposed towards the ruling family and unlikely to want to chronicle its origins and deeds, while Boiardo had obvious motivations to do so.

[81] See Appendix Two for text and translation.

of the College of Cardinals to reform the Church.

His wife Alda, the daughter of Otto, has her father invest her first-born son, Folco, with the castle of Fausburg. Alberto Azzo, loving both sons, leaves the marquisate of Este to his second-born, Ugo. Alberto Azzo returns to Germany and dies at Fausburg.

Otto II

Discourse on the changing of place-names. Italy is divided into Norman, Byzantine, and Saracen spheres. Otto unites and reforms Italy under imperial and papal auspices.

Otto II

Ugo accompanies Otto on his second descent into Italy. He is invested by the emperor with all of the fiefs possessed by his father in Italy. Ugo is made to renounce all claims to Fausburg, while Folco is made to renounce all claims to the family's Italian possessions. The two houses established by Alberto Azzo are divided.

Once again Boiardo's account seems on the surface defective because of certain errors of fact. Almost three hundred years ago Muratori demonstrated that there were two Alberto Azzos: father and son.[82] The one whom Boiardo narrates in the Estensi Interlace was the son, and Muratori labeled him Alberto Azzo II. He was born ca. 996 and died, a centenarian, in 1097, that is, half a century after Boiardo has him flourishing. He married at least twice and had three, not two, children. His first-born was Guelfo IV, son of Cunizza or Cunegonda, daughter of the count of Altdorf, while his second wife, Garsenda, the daughter of the Count of Maine, bore him Folco and Ugo. The descent of the marquises of Este issued from Folco and not Ugo.[83] The critics would probably use these significant discrepancies to illustrate the failure of Boiardo as historian, but a closer analysis suggests that Boiardo's account is essentially accurate.

Boiardo was undoubtedly following "the ancient chronicles of the house of Este" that he mentions. We have no knowledge of the content or composition of these sources. They push back the events of Alberto Azzo's life into the tenth century, either out of ignorance and/or out of an attempt to make the origins

---

[82] Boiardo notes this as well, referring to Alberto Azzo's father as "Azone." Both individuals were variously referred to in the documents as "Alberto," "Azzo," "Azzone," and "Alberto Azzo." He writes: "Emperoche Azone patre de il ditto Alberto Azo . . .": MS. Classense, fol.129r.

[83] Muratori, *Antichità Estensi*, chaps. 7–11.

of the marquises of Este seem older and therefore more prestigious. Yet they record essential truths. The Estensi were a branch of the Obertenghi clan, who were of Lombard origin.[84] Oberto I, from which they derive their name, flourished in the last half of the tenth century. He controlled vast parts of northern Italy from Pavia to Liguria to Tuscany. In 962 Otto I created him count palatine, the second highest title after king in the Italian aristocratic hierarchy. In fact it was Oberto who, with the bishops of Como and Milan, invited Otto to come to Italy against Berengar II.[85] So the close ties between Otto and the Obertenghi/Estensi are a historical fact, although Boiardo personalizes the relationship by having Alberto Azzo perform great acts of prowess and by his marriage to Otto's natural daughter, probably to supply motivation in lieu of the facts.[86] We also know that the historical Alberto Azzo II was closely connected to the imperial courts of Henry II and Conrad II through his marriage to the daughter of the count of Altdorf. While the story of Alberto Azzo's sojourn at the imperial court is probably apocryphal, a trans-alpine experience is confirmed in that Oberto II, the first Oberto's son who supported the pretender Arduin, was held captive by Henry II in Germany in the first years of the second millennium.[87] Also substantiated are the inheritance of Folco and Ugo in northeastern Italy in documents of 1077 and 1095, the inheritance of Guelfo IV as Duke of Bavaria, and the enmity not between Folco and Ugo but between Ugo and Folco on the one hand and Guelfo on the other. It was a conflict over wealth and power, not the result of a mother's preference for her first-born, but the conflict was real. In 1154 a document dates the reconciliation of the two branches of the family and establishes their separate identities, something Boiardo has fostered by the intervention of Otto II.[88] The imperial patronage, the Germanic origins of the clan, the origins of the houses of Welf and Este through Alberto Azzo II, the trans-alpine relationships, and the establishment of the house of Este in the Eugean hills in northeastern Italy are, therefore, historical fact.

For a very long time, scholars have interpreted much of fifteenth- and sixteenth-century Ferrarese literature and history as occasions for praising and flattering the Estensi princes. Muratori inventoried the various versions of the

---

[84] On the Obertenghi and the new aristocracy in general, see Wickham, *Early Medieval Italy*, 181–86.

[85] Chiappini, *Gli Estensi*, 17–18.

[86] Nancy Partner ("New Cornificius," 13) notes that most historians, medieval and classical, were taught to "suppress ignorance and fill in the gaps," a technique that Boiardo may be using here or that was used by the compiler of the chronicles he was using.

[87] Chiappini, *Gli Estensi*, 19–20.

[88] Muratori, *Antichità Estensi*, 271, and Chiappini, *Gli Estensi*, 20, 26. Muratori (341) notes that the first known use of the title "Marchiones de Este" was ca. 1170.

Estensi origins from Trojans and Romans, to the March of Friuli at the time of Attila, to the Carolingians. All but the last are spurious.[89] Muratori meticulously documented that the Estensi were of Lombard origins, and Boiardo affirms their Germanic identity through the story of Alberto Azzo's mastery of German at the court of Austria. Of course Boiardo's account is also flattering: Alberto Azzo is a robust youth, graceful and possessed of unparalleled prowess at courtly tournaments, but it is in its essence a historical, factual account. Boiardo also invites us to read Alberto Azzo's prowess and loyalty to his lord, the emperor, in connection to the Prologue and to the "magnanimous deeds . . . of your ancient forebears."[90]

Boiardo interposes into his narrative of imperial history the origins of the ruling dynasty of Ferrara whose descendant, Ercole, is his lord and patron. It is no accident that Boiardo interlaces this narrative with that of Otto I and his son, both because there is a real historical basis for the rise of the Obertenghi through the patronage of Otto and also because Boiardo embeds the Estensi narrative in the moral stature of the Ottonians. Boiardo contrasts the evil tyranny and chaos of Berengar with the "buon governo" of the Ottonians. Otto is legitimately crowned emperor in Rome by the pope and he restores peace to Italy while reforming the church. Indeed, Boiardo specifically associates Otto with Charlemagne as protector of the church.[91] The Obertenghi/Estensi are intimately linked to Ottonian legitimacy through the historic appointment of Oberto I as count palatine and inaccurately through the marriage of Alberto Azzo to Alda, the daughter of Otto. The Estensi thus become an extension of and are legitimized through Ottonian "buon governo."

Boiardo created the Estensi interlace to make a connection on several levels between the emperor and Ferrara's ruling dynasty. Eugene Vinaver has written, "The reminder is, as always, merely implicit; but once the two events become

---

[89] Both Muratori and Chiappini trace the Estensi back ultimately to a Boniface, who was Count of Tuscany in 813.

[90] Both Stephen Jaeger and Aldo Scaglione trace courtliness to the Ottonians. It is interesting to speculate that Boiardo may be recalling these Ottonians' origins and point out that the Estensi were, in effect, charter members. See C. Stephen Jaeger, *The Origins of Courtliness* (Philadelphia: University of Pennsylvania Press, 1985); Aldo Scaglione, *Knights at Court* (Berkeley: University of California Press, 1991).

[91] "Da poi Otto à Roma dove cesse a sancta chiesa tuto quello che per Carlo Magno e per li altri imperatori li era stato concesso, e fu legiptamente coronato à Laterano e confirmato nel romano imperio per mano de il beato Vigilio secundo": MS. Classense, fol.130r; *RIS*, 9, 316. References to Otto II include: ". . . e quivi incomincio cum il pontefice e cum il populo di Roma a tractare che un generale concilio fosse celebrato nel quale la unione d'Italia se havesse a riformare . . ." and "Ma quello che era pegio il minuto populo e li boni e quali di cio non haveano cagione alchuna magior pena ne portavano che li disturbatori de il buon governo de altrui . . .": MS. Classense, fols. 132v and 133r, respectively; RIS, 9, 320.

simultaneously present in our minds, each acquires an added depth through the other and their interaction brings to the fore, as no other device could have done, the underlying... theme."[92] Vinaver is referring to the "poetry of interlace" as applied to the story of Arthur and Lancelot, but it applies equally well to Boiardo's historical narrative. The underlying theme is the legitimacy of the good prince: on the highest level Otto I is chosen by God to rescue the church and to reform it, while establishing peace and security in Italy. Lower in the hierarchy are the Estensi, who function as loyal vassals, intimates of the emperor, and knights of prowess. The Estensi literally move back and forth over the Alps with their imperial lord, and Alberto Azzo, who loves his ancestral home in the Eugean hills and Italy, sacrifices both to serve the happiness of the emperor's daughter, eventually dying in Saxony. It is literally Otto's son, Otto II, who brings the family back with him to Italy (or who loyally follow their lord over the Alps, depending on which narrative you focus on) and who solemnly creates the two branches of the family. The story of the good prince and the faithful vassal would not be lost on Boiardo's courtly and feudal audience.

On top of this, Boiardo interlaces a third meta-narrative: the transformation of the ancient world into the medieval one. In his Prologue Boiardo offers this transformation as the main argument for the study of history, and in this section Boiardo makes good on his promise to relate the "... magnanimous deeds and the virtuous governance of your ancient forebears." And through the Estensi interlace he also fulfills his pledge to make the imperial history "truly yours," that is, truly a part of Estensi history.[93] The three narratives are so closely intertwined that, as Vinaver suggests, each one acquires added depth through the others.

As Vinaver also suggests, Boiardo's interlacing is firmly within the context of medieval (poetic) narrative and connected to the *Orlando innamorato*. But as Looney observes, there are classical narrative models, notably that of Herodotus, that Boiardo also imitates. Indeed, Looney identifies "interponere" (the verb Boiardo uses to introduce this section of the *Istoria imperiale*) as a Quintilianic, that is, classical, rhetorical device. He goes so far as to suggest that "interpositio" is the classical equivalent of the medieval "entrelacement" and that Boiardo "romancifies Herodotean narrative."[94] Boiardo seems to go out of his way to integrate, not juxtapose, medieval and classical influences and to place the text in narratives familiar to his audience. This integrating tendency seems to be an important attribute of Ferrarese courtly culture.

---

[92] Eugene Vinaver, *The Rise of Romance* (Oxford: Clarendon Press, 1971), 85.

[93] On the concept of "il bene publico," which I acknowledge is not precisely the same as "buon governo," see Gundersheimer, *Style of a Renaissance Despotism*, 272–73.

[94] Dennis Looney, *Compromising the Classics: Romance Epic Narrative in the Italian Renaissance* (Detroit, MI: Wayne State University Press, 1996), 70. See also Looney, "Erodoto dalle *Storie* al romanzo," 433.

As mentioned earlier, writers have put forward many fantastic origins of the Estensi. Boiardo himself participated in this tendency when he identified Ruggiero and Bradamante as the founders of the dynasty in his *Orlando innamorato* and included a genealogy tracing Ercole's lineage back to Hector himself.[95] But this was poetry and fantasy. In the *Istoria imperiale* Boiardo functions consciously as historian. The Estensi are not Trojans but Lombards, not refugees from the Trojan War but castellans from the Eugean hills, not ancients but medievals. Sometimes those facts are harsh. The Estensi were classic castellani. Their power was landed, lay, and dependent on the use of force. Eventually the family migrated from the Eugean hills, where Alberto Azzo was born, to the lowlands of Ferrara and established a *signoria*. But that is another story.

IV

The first purpose of this essay was to rehabilitate, perhaps I should say establish, Boiardo's reputation as a historian. We have seen that when given the opportunity to use a fictitious and fantastic account of Charlemagne and the ambush at Roncevaux, Boiardo opted instead to use a reliable factual historical source. Boiardo was not confused, as many scholars suggest, by differences between poetry and history. In fact, rather than viewing his talent as a poet as a detriment to historical study, it is more useful to see it as an aid. After all, it has always been necessary for the historian to tell a story effectively. In the section on Alberto Azzo and the founding of the Estense dynasty, Boiardo makes effective use of interlacing techniques that allow him to relate true history while developing the rhetorical purpose of his text and fulfilling his role as Ercole's client. Boiardo's skill in providing sound historical motivation is particularly strong and renders his narrative more plausible.[96] Ample attention has been paid to the role of pageant, art, and literature in Estense courtly culture, without much consideration of the role played by history, this despite repeated acknowledgment that Ercole d'Este was a devotee of historical works.[97] While

---

[95] Boiardo, *Orlando Innamorato*, ed. Ross, 2.21.55–59 and 3.5.18–40.

[96] I am thinking here, for example, of the motivation of Charlemagne for the incursion into Spain, namely defense of his empire, and the use of the preferences of Alda for her first-born as motivation for dividing the dynasty into Welfs and Estensi. Obviously this last motivation is not so sound historically, though it does represent an attempt on Boiardo's part to explain this important event.

[97] The principal exception is Gundersheimer, who cites the historical references (albeit weak ones) in Decembrio's *De Politia Litteraria*. See *Ferrara: The Style of a Renaissance Despotism*, 109–13. On pageant, see Richard Gordon Brown, "The Politics of Magnificence in Ferrara, 1450–1505: A Study in Socio-Political Implications of Renaissance Spectacle" (Ph.D. diss., University of Edinburgh, 1982). On art and archi-

Boiardo's central role in Estense courtly culture has long been recognized, his translations of Herodotus's *Histories* and other semi-historical works have been undervalued, and the *Istoria imperiale*'s originality and creativity has been ignored. Recognizing the quality and importance of Boiardo's historical works allows us to begin to meditate more broadly on the role of history in fifteenth-century Ferrarese courtly culture.

In 1973 Werner Gundersheimer published *Ferrara: The Style of a Renaissance Despotism*, thus establishing Ferrarese historical studies in the United States. Gundersheimer defines "Renaissance" in purely objective, chronological terms as the period from around 1300 to around 1600.[98] But since the publication of Burckhardt's *The Civilization of the Renaissance in Italy* the term has been anything but objective, and Gundersheimer uses it, at least implicitly, as an analytical tool that goes well beyond mere chronological considerations. I offer three examples of this tendency. First, the whole conceptualization of his book rests on the observation that something significant happened ca. 1400 that altered the way the Estensi ruled Ferrara, and that this process continued and was perfected through the reigns of Niccolò III (1393–1441) and his three sons Leonello (1441–50), Borso (1450–71), and Ercole (1471–1505). Gundersheimer's rather precise analysis of the fifteenth century distinguishes it from what preceded and followed and undermines the very idea of the unity of the chronological period ca. 1300–1600.[99] Second, Gundersheimer depicts Niccolò III in essentially Burckhardtian terms.[100] Third, and most importantly, Gundersheimer tends to identify Ferrarese courtly culture with Latinate humanism. When discussing the famous Estense library he produces a long list of the ancient authors contained in the library, while asserting that "romances of chivalry" were "popular with the ladies," that is, not popular with the men and therefore

---

tecture see T. Tuohy, *Herculean Ferrara: Ercole d'Este (1471–1505) and the Invention of a Ducal Capital* (Cambridge: Cambridge University Press, 1996), and most recently Charles M. Rosenberg, *The Este Monuments and Urban Redevelopment in Renaissance Ferrara* (Cambridge: Cambridge University Press, 1997). On literature see the huge literature on Boiardo, Ariosto, and Tasso.

[98] Gundersheimer, *Style of a Renaissance Despotism*, 12.

[99] I acknowledge that I do not do justice to the very subtle arguments Gundersheimer makes on 68–69, but I believe my generalization to be on the whole accurate.

[100] "And in perhaps more subtle ways, we see the despotism cultivating a new style, an operational tone rather different from that of his predecessors. Niccolò is the first truly princely figure in Ferrarese history. He cannot in any sense be regarded as just another Emilian petty tyrant. His vices and virtues, his excesses and repentances, his largesse and parsimony, all of these appear on a grand scale. He is a recognizable figure, an individual man, full of unresolved complexity": Gundersheimer, *Style of a Renaissance Despostism*, 90. I don't wish to suggest that Gundersheimer accepts Burckhardt's ideas uncritically, for example, 55.

marginalized, and he consigns his discussion of "chivalric traditions" to a footnote.[101]

In sum, Gundersheimer tends to overemphasize the new Latinate humanistic strains of Ferrarese courtly culture at the expense of the traditional vernacular and chivalric ones, and suggests a disconnectedness between the two. He also tends to define courtly vernacular culture too narrowly, identifying it with "Arthurian and Carolingian fables and romances" and "religious works." As we have seen, Boiardo expands a vernacular historical tradition by freely combining classical, Latinate elements with medieval and vernacular ones.

Gundersheimer's synthesis fits nicely into the traditional "Renaissance Paradigm" which the medievalist Giovanni Tabacco sees as a persistent historiographical problem:

> Our past has divided spontaneously into the concepts of ancient and modern as it acquired awareness of its own development, and between these concepts, in turn, is interposed the idea of a thousand-year-long crisis which ended in a "gloriously" innovating Renaissance. This tripartite model, too, has suffered from two centuries of intolerance, which arose when certain areas of late-medieval civilization were perceived to coincide with the first development of the national experiences we consider as modern, which varies according to where one places the emphasis among the socio-economic, political, and cultural structures that underwent deep changes in western Europe from the thirteenth century onwards. Despite this inconsistency, the tripartite model is destined to withstand any attempt to demolish it.[102]

Tabacco's political analysis lies outside the scope of this essay, but it can be noted that Part Five of *The Struggle for Power in Medieval Italy* is entitled "Cities and Fortresses as Centres for Hegemonic Development." Essentially Tabacco argues that both cities and fortresses, that is, both the urban communal governments and the rural "co-ordination of feudal and territorial power" in the process of *incastellammento* (castle-building) provided the socio-political basis for "modern" state-formation. The Estensi represent the leading force in synthesizing these two foci of political power, as they translated the feudal power of the fortresses

---

[101] Gundersheimer, *Style of a Renaissance Despotism*, 95–97 and note 10. In that footnote, however, Gundersheimer produces an astute analysis of the role of those traditions as ". . . an essential element in . . . [Ferrara's] cultural continuity and conservatism." He also suggests a synthesis of the chivalric and humanistic strains of Ferrarese culture, culminating in the works of Boiardo and Ariosto.

[102] Giovanni Tabacco, *The Struggle for Power in Medieval Italy: Structures of Political Rule*, trans. Rosalind Brown Jensen (Cambridge: Cambridge University Press, 1989), 2.

of Calaone and Este into their domination of the Ferrarese commune. As Gundersheimer stresses the "Renaissance style" of Latinate humanistic culture and new administrative structures, Tabacco and others emphasize the "medieval" feudal structures which underlay Estense rule.[103] But as Tabacco notes, there are cultural as well as socio-economic and political structures that underwent deep changes. Ferrarese courtly culture seems to have both a strong continuous and conservative vernacular tradition and a capacity to synthesize elements of innovative Latinate culture into that tradition.

The Renaissance paradigm is essentially disjunctive. In Tabacco's terms it depicts the Middle Ages as a "thousand-year-long crisis" ending in a "'gloriously' innovating Renaissance." In cultural terms the increased interest in and identification with ancient authors is "natural" and forward-looking. In historiographical terms Biondo provides the model of a decline in classical culture precipitated by a crisis caused by the invasion by barbarians, and an eventual recovery through the development of autonomous cities. Within this paradigm Boiardo suffers by comparison because he writes out of a different model: a history that focuses on the Middle Ages, an emphasis on continuity both within the Middle Ages and between them and his own time, and an integration rather than a juxtaposition of medieval and classical models. From the perspective of the Renaissance paradigm the *Istoria imperiale* seems either aberrant, merely curious, or not properly Italian. Marco Praloran articulates this bias clearly when he writes of Boiardo's translations into the vernacular: "It is curious to observe the translation of a medieval author, Riccobaldo, in a climate of humanism. But it is not astonishing in Ferrara or elsewhere in some northern court, where the classical and medieval elements compete with each other without much coherence, simply to satisfy the taste for the unusual or marvelous."[104]

And so the entire historical process is turned on its head: the medieval socio-economic and political structures which fashion culture, and which in turn are influenced by culture, are disconnected. In their place is a reified Renaissance, as some ideal, immutable, and ahistorical force. Boiardo's *Istoria imperiale* becomes a remedy to this fantasy, a dialectic to reconnect culture to history. For as we acknowledge that during the Renaissance there were valid, indeed deeply rooted cultural reasons for studying the Middle Ages, so can we shed the pre-

---

[103] See, for example, Richard Tristano, "Ferrara in the Fifteenth Century: Borso d'Este and the Devvelopment of a New Nobility" (Ph.D. diss., New York University, 1983), 43–64; idem, "Vassals, Fiefs, and Social Mobility During the Middle Ages and the Renaissance," *Medievalia et Humanistica* 15 (1987): 43–64; and Trevor Dean, *Land and Power in Late Medieval Ferrara*, Cambridge Studies in Medieval Life and Thought (Cambridge: Cambridge University Press, 1988).

[104] Marco Praloran, "Matteo Maria Boiardo," in *Storia di Ferrara VII. Il Rinascimento. La letteratura*, ed. Walter Moretti (Ferrara: Corbo, 1987), 215–64, here 220.

judices of the critics, and reevaluate and appreciate the motivations and historical method of Matteo Maria Boiardo. And as we better understand Boiardo's historical method and dedication to the discipline of history, so can we appreciate the conjuncture between medieval and Renaissance, vernacular and Latinate elements in Ferrarese courtly culture. Indeed we have the opportunity to re-historicize that culture.[105] Boiardo's *Istoria imperiale* was a notable effort to integrate Renaissance classical exemplars, a sense of the revival of the study of history, and a greater sense of historicity, with the medieval origins of the Este dynasty embedded in the very continuity of a text that runs from Augustus to Otto IV. It is also possible to see Boiardo's narrative as an attempt to integrate classical, Herodotean narrative devices with medieval interlacing ones. Through these processes I have suggested the existence of a distinct Ferrarese courtly culture that for good historical reasons did not want to, indeed could not, disconnect itself from the Middle Ages, and could not, for equally good historical reasons, connect itself to a Roman past, except through a more generic association of Ercole with Roman imperial patronage of history.[106]

Since the purpose of this collection of essays is to introduce Ferrarese studies, to make a case for the value of studying Ferrara, and to suggest directions for future research, I will conclude broadly and somewhat speculatively. One of the burdens of doing Ferrarese studies is freeing oneself from the Florentine model. Fortunately, this yoke is not as heavy as it was when Gundersheimer published his book more than thirty years ago. Still, the burden is there, especially for historians.

Eric Cochrane, a distinguished historian of Florence, published a book on Italian Renaissance history and historians in 1981. Not surprisingly he begins the book with Florence, with what he calls the "birth of humanist historiography," and with Leonardo Bruni. Indeed, Cochrane concludes his very long book with the "demise of humanist historiography," thus conceptualizing Renaissance historical studies in terms of the life cycle of humanist historiography. So when Cochrane finally gets to Ferrara, in chapter four, it is in the guise of "the diffusion of humanist historiography from communes to principalities," that is, in Florentine terms not Ferrarese, where

---

[105] I say "re-historicize" because it is clear that Boiardo saw the intimate connections and continuity of Ferrarese history which have been disconnected by the modern critics using the modern Renaissance paradigm.

[106] Trevor Dean, "Notes on the Ferrarese Court in the Later Middle Ages," *Renaissance Studies* 3 (1989): 357–69, and idem, "The Courts," in *The Origins of the State in Italy, 1300–1600*, ed. Julius Kirschner (Chicago: University of Chicago Press, 1996), 136–51. In the latter, Dean compares those who take a structuralist and interdisciplinary approach with those who emphasize "historical varieties and variables." I identify with the latter and the distinctiveness of Ferrarese culture.

the flow was just the opposite. The "Renaissance Paradigm" is alive and well in Cochrane's book. Cochrane's thesis, that humanist historiography revived and transformed municipal historiography, is undisputed. But he articulates it with such clarity as to obscure the multi-faceted composition of Ferrarese courtly culture. In discussing that rather remarkable triumvirate of sixteenth-century Ferrarese historians, Gasparo Sardi (d. 1564), Giovambattista Giraldi (1504–1573), and Giovan Battista Pigna (1529–1575), Cochrane offers a series of clichés as truisms:

> And Ferrara finally achieved in the late sixteenth century what it had considered unimportant in the late fifteenth: a body of historical writing worthy of its astonishing production in the realm of epic and dramatic poetry.... Nevertheless, all these historians were at the same time the victims of the Quattrocento predecessors — of Platina and Francesco Vigilio in Mantua and of Prisciano and Battista Guarino in Ferrara, from whom they admittedly (Giraldi) or secretly took many of their theses as well as much of their information. The historians of Ferrara were also victims of the literary preferences of their fellow citizens, who, they feared, would always overlook their own prosaic histories in favor of the poetic history of "our most famous, peerless poet, Lodovico Ariosto" (Sardi). They therefore felt obliged to invent even more fantastic stories to replace the ones they rejected as "myths...".[107]

Let us dissect Cochrane's evaluation of Ferrarese historiography one step at a time: 1) that historical writing was considered unimportant in fifteenth-century Ferrara; 2) that sixteenth-century Ferrarese historians were "victims" of their Quattrocento predecessors; 3) that Ferrarese courtly culture was so literary, poetic, and creative that historical, factual prose was inevitably subsumed into a poetic, mythical, and fantastic version of history. And so we come back full circle to the very same mentality by which Boiardo was dismissed as historian. This is a view that focuses quite understandably on the poetic, chivalric, and epic achievements of Ferrarese courtly culture, while incomprehensibly reducing that culture to a merely poetic one. How do we rectify this tunnel-vision? By reading the texts and by understanding their meaning within the distinctive context of Ferrarese courtly culture.

---

[107] Cochrane, *Historians and Historiography*, 264.

APPENDICES

The following appendices are translations and transcriptions of the Prologue to the *Istoria imperiale* and the sections of the text I refer to as the "Estensi interlace." The translations are my own and are quite literal.

Appendix I

To the Illustrious and Most Excellent Lord
Messer Hercule
Duke of Ferrara, Modena, and Reggio,
Count of Rovigo, Marquis of Este
Prologue
to the translation of Riccobaldo by Matteo Maria Boiardo

Variously and with different judgments has History been praised by many people, my Illustrious Lord, as a teacher of many things in peace and in war, by means of examples of events in the administration of ancient principalities. Among others Your Excellency deserves the highest praise, as has been well proven to us, as considering History to be deserving of praise. But at the same time there have been princes who not only did things worthy of eternal memory, but who also acquired eternal fame by means of writing. And among these were Lucius Lucullus, Asinius Pollio, Cornelius Nepos, Gaius Caesar, and his successor Octavian Augustus, and Elius Hadrian who all wrote History. These are men worthy of the highest praise. If they are to be praised who recorded the memory of magnificent deeds, and even more worthy of praise are those who performed magnificent deeds, how must we exalt those who deserve glory for doing both? Aurelian Alexander, the twentieth emperor of Rome, held History in such esteem that he would not admit into his council of advisors anyone who had not read and considered the past. But this perception of human life, which was held in such honor by the ancients and is again esteemed worthy by Your Lordship, has suffered great harm in the ruin of the Roman Empire, in such a way that in the thousand years that have passed from that fall, almost all of the land [of the Empire] has been transformed into something very different from what used to be the names, governments, and customs, and since no one has written about what has intervened we are not only ignorant of the battles that were fought, but it is also hard to understand how even the names of regions have been changed. Neither is how Cisalpine Gaul changed its name to the Lombardy of today known by many, nor how Germania was changed to Allemagna, and how Gaul became France is not known and understood by men who are moderately learned in our day. It is not known to every man how the Empire of Italy passed into the hands of the Greeks, and few know how it was divided between the Greeks and the Franks, and very few know how the Empire was transferred from France to the Germans, of how much evil has been the cause of adversity in past times. So, with the occupation of Italy and Greece (where letters flourished) by the Barbarians, the writing of History together with many other laudable works ceased for a long time. But in this bad state of affairs Riccobaldo of Ferrara, a new man and from a new city, attended this little spark, almost spent, which was illuminating affairs of the past. And so beginning with the Roman Monarchy until his own time, which was for more than thirteen hundred years, he went through all of the goings-on of the Empire, taking from the ancients ancient things and new things from the moderns. And in the beginning he followed Suetonius, Capitolinus, Eutropius, and Marcellinus, followed by the writings of the Saracens and the Koran of Muhammad, and the five Books of the History of Arabia. And in the affairs of Charlemagne and of the Franks he followed Alcuin the tutor of the same Charles who wrote at Paris, and Turpin, bishop of Rheims, assistant and counselor of that emperor. He also translated histories of the Goths and Lombards from their own language found in the archive of Ravenna, where the government of the barbarians was located for many years. In such a way is woven the summary of Riccobaldo of one hundred and thirteen emperors, of whom forty-three were in Italy from Octavian to Galerius; and in Constantinople forty-six from Constantine to Nicephorus; eight in France from Henry the Saxon to Berengar IV; and in Germany up to his own time eighteen from Otto I of Saxony to Henry VII. Then there are the succeeding emperors up to our own time: Charles IV, Wenceslaus I, Sigismund I, Albert II, and Frederick III, who reigns today. The total sum of emperors, therefore, is one hundred and eighteen. The succession of these emperors having been demonstrated by our Ferrarese native, I decided to translate it from Latin for those who know only the vulgar tongue, so that they could learn about the past, for the more commonly known it is the more useful is the past for all. And I address this translation to Your Lordship not so much moved by the will and desire of pleasing you, which I desire and which I am bound to desire, so much as by the propriety of not giving it to anyone else, since I am indebted to Your Lordship. Besides the fact that I and everything I own is held from you, Riccobaldo, from whom this work is drawn, was of your city, and a good part of the book is filled with the magnanimous deeds and the virtuous governance of your ancient forbears. And so if you love his writings and find them pleasing, Your Lordship will be pleased by this work which is truly yours. You will not have a full history with adorned speeches and with refined passages. This is to be blamed on the evil times in which your fellow-citizen wrote before the time of Dante and Francesco Petrarca, when any elegance of expression was completely alien. But like the ancient marble statues of Praxiteles or Phidias which are customarily broken, with their head and arms cut off, one is still grateful to whoever finds them because they were unknown for such a long time. And so this ancient history, newly rediscovered, is pleasing to whoever reads it, even though it is without any adornment, because it contains many [valuable] things in it.[108]

[108] Based on the transcription by Muratori, *RIS*, 9, which is reproduced in Zottoli, ed., Boiardo, *Tutte le opere*.

Appendix II

The "Estensi Interlace"

[Life of Berengario IV] Neli anni de Cristo Novecento e quaranta nove Otto primo ritorno in Sansogna havendo le terre de italia tutte radutte sotto suo dominio excepto il friuoli a La Lonbardia orientale la quale Marcha Tarvisiana se appellava. E queste doe provintie lascio liberamente in Signoria di Berengario il quale per lo adietro era stato in italia imperatore. Ma Paduani e Veronesi e quali de la rebellione prima contro a ditto Berengario erano statti promottori e cagionevoli restarno malissimo contenti di esser subietti a tal dominio. E molti di loro principali citadini passarno cum Otto in Sansogna per non patir pena de la oltragio facto al signore che novamente pigliare se doveano. Tra questi Alberto Azo che da il Castello di Calaone che havea rivoltati li habitatori de li monti Euganei che hora se appellano paduani a Le parte de Sasonesi sopra a tutti li altri havea da temere perche nominatamente era da Berengario minaciato. Emperoche Azone patre de il ditto Alberto Azo havea seguito lo exilio di Berengario tertio in germania cum la moglie gravida, et era quivi in Austria nasciuto questo fanciulo e levato da il batesimo per Sigismondo Duca era da poi accresciuto ne la corte insieme cum questo Berengario quarto dicui ragionamo. La cui perverssa natura li fece non solamente costui nimico, ma la piu parte de li domestici soi. Insieme adunque cum Otto primo ando Alberto Azo in Sansogna & avenga che multi altri nobilissimi homini andassero anchora cum lo imperatore. Niuno fu a lui ne la gracia pare impero che oltro a la lingua germanicha la quale esso in Austria perfectissimamente imparata havea in ogni altra generatione di virtute era a tutti li italiani superiore e ne li armegiamenti barbarici che giostre e torneamenti sono appellati. Sempre mai sopra a tutti li baroni di corte era il vincitore. Di queste cose molto di sua persona e per questo ne prese tanta gracia il taliano che meritò di havere Alda figlia naturale de lo imperatore insieme cum la contea di Fausburch in Sansogna e gia prima li havea donato esso imperatore un castello quando insieme cum lui vestiti de una insegna celestra cum il Leoncorno de oro havea vinto il torniamento contro al re di Dacia. Queste cose in Germania se faceano.[109]

In the year of Our Lord 949 Otto I returned to Saxony, having reduced all of Italy to his domain except Friuli and eastern Lombardy which is called the Trevisan March. And these two provinces were left under the control of Berengar who had been the emperor in Italy. But the Paduans and the Veronese, who were the first promoters of rebellion against Berengar, were very unhappy to remain part of his domain. And many of their principal citizens went with Otto to Saxony in order not to suffer punishment at the hands of Berengar, who once again controlled them. Among these was Alberto Azzo who, from the castle of Calaone, had led the inhabitants of the Euganean hills, who are now called

[109] BCR, fols. 129r–129v.

Paduans, to the party of Otto ["the Saxons"], above all due to fear because they were threatened by Berengar. Since Azzone, the father of Alberto Azzo, had followed Berengar III into exile in Germany with his pregnant wife, the boy was born in Austria; he was the godson of Duke Sigismund, and was raised at court with this same Berengar IV, whom we have discussed. The latter's perverse nature turned not only Alberto Azzo into an enemy, but also all of his followers as well. Together with Otto, Alberto Azzo went to Saxony and many other very noble men also came with the emperor. No one was Alberto Azzo's equal in grace since in addition to the German language, which he had learned perfectly in Austria, he was superior to all the Italians in every other skill; and in the martial arts practiced by northerners, called jousts and tournaments, he was always victorious over the other barons of the court. All of these things delighted Otto, together with the youth's robust physique and the grace in which he comported himself, that Otto awarded many favors to the Italian. He gave him for wife his own natural daughter Alda, together with the county of Fausburg, in Saxony, and even before this the emperor had given him a castle, and a coat of arms with a field of blue with a golden unicorn when he defeated the King of Dacia in a tournament. These events happened in Germany.

[Life of Otto I] Otto primo figliolo de henricho Duca di Sansogna & imperatore in germania ottene solo tuto lo imperio occidentale ne li anni de il Signor nostro Iesu Cristo Novecento e cinquanta e fece cum molta prosperitate e prudentia le cose di sopra dette tre volte fu in italia. La prima e la secunda chiamato da Agabito contro a Berengario per la salute de italia e de la romana chiesa. La tercia per il mal governo di ioane pontefice di quel nome duodecimo adimandato dal collegio de Cardinali per riformare li ordini ecclesiastici. Tuta la nobilitate de li homini la quale ditalia ne la sua prima partita se ne era gita cum lui rimeno ne la patria de quali erano la parte magiore veronesi e paduani. E tra li altri Alberto Azo del quale disopra ragionato habiamo e da cui la progenie de li Marchesi estenssi e poi diffesa ritorno la secunda fiata cum lui e preso da lo amore del luoco nativo ottene da esso imperatore non solo il picholo castello di Calaone dove nato era. Ma Adusto che Este al presente è nominato sito ne la radice del monte, il quale da Attila disfatto in quel tempo a riffarssi incominciava. In questo castello fu fatto il capo de il Marchesato di Alberto Azo e monte silice che prima fu citade, e montagnana da autore a noi incerto edifficata li forno subiecti. E ritornato esso Alberto Azo cum lo imperatore in germania non potè per alcun modo ala moglie persuadere che in italia volesse habitare e per questo resto lui a complacimento de lei in Saxonia nel contato di Fausburcho & hebe di lei in un solo parto dui figlioli, e forno Folcho il primo et Ugo il secundo. E ne Lo anno octavo de lo imperio do Otto primo ritornando in Italia vi fece dimora per dieci mesi nel castello di Este. La qual cosa portando la moglie cum pocha pacientia, fece investire alo Imperatore suo patre Folcho primo genito de il contato di Fausburcho, e questo contro ala voluntate del marito. Emperochè Alberto Azo equalmente tutti dui li amava, ma esso instituite herede solo nel Marchesato di Este Ugo il secundo figliolo e tre anni da poi che fu lo undecimo de lo imperio di Otto rese lanima a Dio nel castello di

Fausburcho lasciando i figliuoli heredi nel modo che è dispora mostrato. Restarno pero ambi doi in Saxonia insino al sexto anno del sequente imperatore Otto secundo, che Ugo vene in italia come narraremo nel loco suo. Ma lasciando di loro al presente ritorno ala nostra principale historia.[110]

Otto, first-born son of Henry Duke of Saxony and Emperor in Germany, obtained control of the entire Western Empire in the year of Our Lord 950, and he ruled with much prosperity and prudence. Three times Otto came to Italy: the first and the second he was called by [Pope] Agapitus against Berengar and for the well-being of Italy and the Roman Church. The third time he came because of the bad government of Pope John XII, sent for by the college of Cardinals to reform the ecclesiastical orders. Of all the nobility, the ones from Italy who accompanied the emperor on his first trip who were stirred to return to their native land, the greatest number were Veronese and Paduans. And among the others was Alberto Azzo, who we have discussed above, and from whom the progeny of the Marquises of Este are descended. He returned with the emperor on his second trip, and on account of his love for his native place he obtained not only the castle of Calaone, where he had been born, but also Este from which the Estensi are named at present, situated at the foot of the mountains where when Attila was defeated he went to recoup himself. This castle was made the head of the Marquisate by Alberto Azzo, and Monselice that had been earlier a city and Montagnana, which authorities say was built at some unknown time, were also made subject to his rule. And when Alberto Azzo returned with the emperor to Germany he was unable to persuade his wife that he wanted to live in Italy, so to please her he stayed in Saxony in the county of Fausburg and he had with her two sons, Folco, the first and Ugo, the second. And in the eighth year of the reign of the Emperor Otto, he returned to Italy and made the castle of Este his home for ten months. This his wife bore with little patience, and she asked her father the emperor to invest Folco the first-born with the county of Fausburg against the desire of her husband. Since Alberto Azzo loved his sons equally, he invested his second son Ugo with the Marquisate of Este. Three years later, namely the eleventh year of Otto's reign, Alberto Azzo rendered his soul to God in the castle of Fausburg, leaving his sons as heirs in the above-mentioned manner. They both remained in Saxony up to the sixth year of the reign of the following emperor, Otto II, when Ugo came to Italy as will be narrated in its proper place. But leaving them at present, I return to our principal history.

[Life of Otto II] Questa seconda fiata che passo lo imperatore in italia che fu lo anno sexto de suo imperio. Vene cum Ugo figliolo di Alberto Azo Marchese de Este essendo lo anno davanti Alda sua genetrice morta in Sansogna. E fu per Otto secundo novamente investitio de il marchesato di Este e deli pheudi paterni e dapoi per solenne stipulatione la quale dicono anchora e prefatti

---

[110] BCR, fols. 130v–131r.

Marchesi havere presso di se renuncio Ugo ad ogni ragione che havere potesse nel contato di Fausburcho in Sansogna, renunciando Folcho per simigliante modo a quanto se pretendesse di ragione nel marchesato di Este. E cussi bipartitamente sono le doe case discese da una medesima origine come disotto ne li loci e tempi soi faremo mencione.[111]

This second time that the emperor came down into Italy was in the sixth year of his reign; coming with him was Ugo son of Alberto Azzo, Marquis d'Este, being the year before the death of his mother Alda in Saxony. And Otto II invested him again with the marquisate of Este and all the fiefs possessed by his father. There was one solemn stipulation placed on the two Marquises. Ugo had to renounce all claims to the county of Fausburg in Saxony; and Folco similarly had to renounce all claims to the Marquisate of Este. And so the two houses were divided that were descended from common origin, as we will mention below in both the proper place and time.

[111] BCR, fol. 134r.

Ferrarese Chroniclers and the Este State, 1490–1505

Trevor Dean

My starting point is the microhistorical principle that great issues can be examined and great questions decided through observation of small details. The small detail in this case is the death of the renowned gentleman poet Matteo Maria Boiardo in December 1494. This death was not an event that registered widely on the consciousness of Ferrarese citizens. Of the two major printed chronicles for the period, only one mentions it (but under the wrong date): Bernardino Zambotti was aware not only that Matteo Maria was "much loved by our duke," but also that he had written, among other things, "the book of Orlando in love, a fine and beautiful thing to be read to any lord."[1] The anonymous *Diario ferrarese,* on the other hand, has nothing to say about Matteo Maria, at the moment of his death or for much of the reign of Duke Ercole d'Este (1471–1505).[2] Nor is Boiardo's death mentioned in a third diary, that of Ugo Caleffini.[3] This difference in one small detail seems representative of these texts as a whole: though two were written by officials close to the duke and the court, on the whole they do not show extensive interest in the artistic and literary life for which Renaissance Ferrara has become famed. It has often been remarked that, when they do pay attention to theatrical performances in the city, they show more enthusiasm for

---

[1] Bernardino Zambotti, *Diario ferrarese dall'anno 1476 sino al 1504*, ed. Giuseppe Pardi, Rerum Italicarum Scriptores, 2nd ed., 24/7 (Bologna: Zanichelli, 1934), 231–32, misdating the death to 20 February 1494.

[2] Giuseppe Pardi, ed., *Diario ferrarese dall'anno 1409 sino al 1502 di autori incerti*, Rerum Italicarum Scriptores 24.7 (Bologna: Zanichelli, 1928–38), 2nd ed.

[3] Giuseppe Pardi, ed., *Diario di Ugo Caleffini (1471–1494)*, 2 vols. (Ferrara: R. Deputazione di Storia Patria per l'Emilia e la Romagna, 1938), 1: xxvii.

the intermissions of dancing than for the plays themselves.[4] The great achievement of Este court culture, that "creation . . . of imaginary worlds and structures of fantasy,"[5] to be found in the paintings at Schifanoia, in the poems of Boiardo and Ariosto, and in chivalric rituals, all seem to have made little impression on those members of Ferrarese citizenry recording events in their diaries.[6] It is precisely this divergence between what now is thought to be of value and what impressed literate contemporaries that this essay will investigate, by focusing on Ferrarese diarists or chroniclers of the 1490s and early 1500s.

These chronicles have, of course, been widely used by historians for many years. Even when two out of the three were still unpublished, they were used by historians such as Frizzi and Gardner for detail, narrative and color, and for the conditions of life in Ferrara.[7] Both of the two more recent historians of the Estensi, Chiappini and Gundersheimer, have also used them in similar ways, with Gundersheimer adding an analysis of one of Caleffini's lists of annual officeholders (that for 1476).[8] Historians with more particular interests — whether in town-planning, or demography, or theater, or crime — have also referred to and quoted from these sources.[9] However, what has so far been lacking

---

[4] Luciano Chiappini, *Gli Estensi*, 2nd ed. (Varese: Dall'Oglio, 1967), 348.

[5] Werner L. Gundersheimer, "Ferrarese Studies: An Agenda for the Future," in *La corte di Ferrara e il suo mecenatismo 1441–1598*, ed. Marianne Pade, Lene Waage Petersen, and Daniela Quarta (Copenhagen/Modena: Museum Tusculanums Forlag/Panini, 1990), 353–61, here 354.

[6] Cf. Dale Kent's argument for a common popular culture shared by participants and plebeians in fifteenth-century Florence, in *Cosimo de' Medici and the Florentine Renaissance* (New Haven: Yale University Press, 2000).

[7] Antonio Frizzi, *Memorie per la storia di Ferrara*, 5 vols. (Ferrara: F. Pomatelli, 1846–1848); Edmund Garratt Gardner, *Dukes and Poets in Ferrara: A Study in the Poetry, Religion and Politics of the Fifteenth and Early Sixteenth Centuries* (London: A. Constable, 1904).

[8] Werner L. Gundersheimer, *Ferrara: The Style of a Renaissance Despotism* (Princeton: Princeton University Press, 1973), 285–96.

[9] See for example F. Bocchi, "La 'Terranuova' da campagna a città," in *La corte e lo spazio: Ferrara estense*, ed. Giuseppe Papagno and Amedeo Quondam (Rome: Bulzoni, 1982), 167–92; E. Guidoboni, "Aspetti della campagna estense: famiglie e nobiltà territoriale tra il XV e XVI secolo," in *La corte e lo spazio*, ed. Papagno and Quondam, 193–219; and F. Ruffini, "Linee rette e intrichi: Il *Vitruvio* di Cesariano e la Ferrara teatrale di Ercole I," in *La corte e lo spazio*, ed. Papagno and Quondam, 365–429, here 170–72, 180, 200, 202, 205, 206, 209, 378, 382. See also W. L. Gundersheimer, "Crime and Punishment in Ferrara, 1440–1500," in *Violence and Civil Disorder in Italian Cities, 1200–1500*, ed. Lauro Martines (Berkeley: University of California Press, 1972), 119–27.

is any sort of focused study of the texts of the chronicles themselves.[10] This essay should go some way towards remedying that neglect.

The three diaries already referred to — the anonymous and those of Caleffini and Zambotti — form, as G. Pardi put it, the "spinal column" of Ferrarese history in the fifteenth century. From a small number of further, unpublished diaries has recently been added a fourth, the "chronicles" of Paolo Zerbinati for the years 1500–1527, as transcribed and abridged by his descendant in the seventeenth century, Giovanni Maria Zerbinati.[11] The relative values of these diaries, and the personal histories of their authors, have been well investigated by their earlier editors, especially by Pardi, and it is not clear that anything new can be said in this regard.[12] Caleffini is the only extended narrative source for the early years of Ercole's reign, and is valuable for the war against Venice of 1482–1484, and for political and economic material up to the end of 1494, when it terminates. Pardi singled out for special mention two types of information in Caleffini: the almost weekly lists of food prices, and the complete lists of ducal officeholders announced at the beginning of each year; but he also noted Caleffini's limitations, his lack of interest in intellectual and cultural matters, and his inattention to urban life, remaining "closed in the environment of the court." Zambotti, by contrast, is useful for his interest in the life of the university, and in theatrical performances staged by the duke, but he too has little to say about the social or economic life of the city, while in the 1490s his Ferrarese material thins out and becomes inaccurate (as with the death-date of Boiardo) owing to his terms of office outside the city. Both Caleffini and Zambotti, then, have their limitations for the 1490s. The anonymous diary, conversely, was probably started only in 1482 (with the years since 1409 filled in from a variety of sources), and offers

---

[10] See the exiguous bibliographies in B. Andreolli et al., *Repertorio della cronachistica emiliano-romagnola* (Rome: Istituto storico italiano per il Medio Evo, 1991), 201–5. Luciano Chiappini, "Indagini attorno a cronache e storie ferraresi del sec. XV," *Atti e memorie della Deputazione ferrarese di storia patria* 14 (1955): 3–46 is more useful for the supplementary texts published than for analysis of them.

[11] Giovanni Maria Zerbinati, *Croniche di Ferrara: quali comenzano del anno 1500 sino al 1527*, ed. Maria Giuseppina Muzzarelli (Ferrara: Deputazione provinciale ferrarese di storia patria, 1989). On the unpublished diaries, see Chiappini, "Indagini," 6–10.

[12] Petrucci follows closely Pardi's introduction to his summary edition of the *Diario:* F. Petrucci, "Caleffini, Ugo," in *Dizionario biografico degli italiani*, ed. Alberto M. Ghisalberti (Rome: Istituto della enciclopedia italiana, 1973), 16: 647–50. Pardi in turn added little to A. Cappelli, "Notizie di Ugo Caleffini notaro ferrarese del secolo XV con la sua cronaca in rima di casa d'Este," *Atti e memorie della Deputazione di storia patria per le provincie modenesi e parmensi* 2 (1864): 267–69.

a varied menu of material only from 1493. For the last decade of Ercole's reign, this diary becomes the only narrative source, meagerly supplemented by Zerbinati.

Of the authors, we know least about the anonymous diarist: Pardi deduced from internal evidence that he was a notary with property at Fiesso and working in some office connected with food supply, but this remains a conjecture.[13] The Caleffini family had (like many ducal officials) recently migrated to Ferrara from Rovigo, a former Este possession occupied since 1482 by Venice. Like his father, Ugo was a notary. Again like his father, he took office in the financial administration of the Ferrarese communal or civic government, before eventually being appointed, in 1471, as recording notary for the ducal *spenditore* or household paymaster. This post he apparently continued to hold until the end of 1494, though he continued to work as a notary, and did not die until 1503. Bernardino Zambotti came from a family more well-established in Ferrara: his grandfather a rich spicer, his father a notary, his brother a wealthy physician familiar to the duke, Bernardino himself later married a widow from the important Costabili family. Zambotti had a humanist education, followed by a full legal training, which helps explain his continuing interest in university life and in literary culture. His legal qualifications led him to take up judicial posts first in Ferrara, later in the neighboring cities of Mantua and Reggio Emilia. All three authors came therefore from the notarial-legal milieu, and all three owned properties in the Ferrarese countryside: the question that immediately poses itself is how far their membership of the propertied, professional class determined their priorities in what to record and what not to record. In working out the answer to this and other questions, it is proposed to begin with the anonymous diary, which offers the fullest narrative for the 1490s, and then to compare the material of Zambotti and Caleffini.

First, however, two more general questions must be addressed: how do we explain the sudden and uncharacteristic presence of four diary-writers in late fifteenth and early sixteenth-century Ferrara, and what is the nature of this form of historical record? For the fourteenth and first half of the fifteenth century, Ferrara is marked more by the paucity of narrative sources: the *Chronicon estense* comes to an end in 1393, and Jacobo Delayto's *Annales,* which start in that year, reach only 1409.[14] Moreover, unlike Delayto, who was explicitly commissioned by Niccolò d'Este to write the history of his reign,[15] our three diarists invoke no commissioning patron. None of them can be said to have written for a particular

---

[13] Pardi, *Diario ferrarese dall'anno 1409*, xvii–xviii.

[14] G. Bertoni and E. P. Vicini, ed., *Chronicon Estense*, 2nd ed., Rerum Italicarum Scriptores 15, pt. 3(Città di Castello and Bologna, 1908), and L. A. Muratori, ed.,*Annales estenses Jacobi de Delayto*, Rerum Italicarum Scriptores 18 (Milan, 1731).

[15] "iussu ipsius": *Annales estenses*, col. 906.

readership — there is little evidence of their chronicles circulating — though they might have thought of themselves as collecting material for more formal histories. So what was the stimulus that led each of them to record events during their lives? It has been suggested that "narrative in general . . . from the annals to the fully realized history has to do with the topics of law, legality, legitimacy, or, more generally, authority," and that it is the transgression of law, or the challenge to authority, that creates the need to record events and tell stories.[16] This certainly holds true for Delayto's *Annales,* which start in the year of the contested accession of Niccolò III, and end in the year of successful recovery of disputed territory. But what transgressions or challenges were our four diarists responding to later in the century? The answer, for three of them, lies in the legitimacy of Ercole's rule: Caleffini began his diary in 1471, the year of Ercole's forcible accession at the expense of his nephew, Niccolò di Leonello; Zambotti began his in the year of that nephew's attempted coup d'état; and the anonymous in the opening year of the Venetian military attack on Ferrara. All three thus responded to the contested legitimacy of Ercole's authority, and two of them ended in fact by adding doubt and challenge to its legality, as we shall see.

To address the second general question, we should note that these authors' works have been called "diaries" by their editors, but as always with such writing it is not clear how far they were written contemporaneously or how far in later, more retrospective blocks. They seem to stand at the midpoint between two forms of historical record: "histories" proper, which dealt with public affairs, and shaped and ordered their material into books and chapters, often with clear political or moral purposes; and "ricordanze" or records of personal and family affairs, mostly of sales and purchases for business and household, and of births, marriages, and deaths. Less purposeful than the former, more miscellaneous than the latter, these diaries were, nevertheless, impregnated with moral and social attitudes, which this essay aims to uncover.

A useful starting point might seem to be legal and judicial issues, given that all three authors came from a legal milieu. The anonymous diarist, it has long been noticed, pays considerable attention to the crimes of violence and theft committed in Ferrara in the 1490s. However, the full contours of criminality, as reported by this diarist, have not before been drawn or analyzed, and it is those contours that most concern the argument here.[17] A first point to make is that the

[16] Hayden V. White, "The Value of Narrativity in the Representation of Reality," in idem, *The Content of the Form: Narrative Discourse and Historical Representation*, (Baltimore: Johns Hopkins University Press, 1987), 1–25, here 13, 19.

[17] For further treatement of Ferrarese crime and punishment, see D. S. Chambers and T. Dean, *Clean Hands and Rough Justice: An Investigating Magistrate in Renaissance Italy* (Ann Arbor: University of Michigan Press, 1997), 147–57.

violence and theft he records fall into a number of categories: brawls and fights on the piazza,[18] woundings and killings,[19] street robbery,[20] nocturnal burglary (especially from shops on the piazza).[21] His interest in crime does not extend much beyond these: occasionally he reports rapes, and he notes arrests and executions for other sex crimes too (incest, sodomy).[22] We should see this attention to particular categories not necessarily as an accurate reflection of criminality in Ferrara, but as an expression of the author's particular concern regarding property crime and public crimes of violence. Public authority was expected to repress these crimes above all others; the author reflects that expectation.

Within these categories, a number of patterns are discernible. First, prominently recorded in public brawls are servants of members of the ducal family: Sigismondo and Rinaldo, Ercole's brothers; Alfonso and Ippolito, Ercole's sons. These servants fought each other, they fought the ducal archers, they attacked others.[23] Brawls and fights within the court or involving members of the ducal staff were also numerous: there were brawls in the *cortile*, and ducal men-at-arms and footmen figure both as victims of public assault and as perpetrators of robbery, wounding, and counterfeiting.[24] Although these are reported in a matter-of-fact way, it will be argued here that they fall into the moral dimension of the failure of princely authority. The author expected the prince and his entourage to prosecute and prevent crimes, not to participate in them.

This moral dimension is evident in further aspects of the diarist's crime-reporting: where he is aware of the cause of murder or wounding, it is related either to sexual jealousy or desire,[25] or to enmity,[26] or to gambling and debt.[27] Again the moral message is not stated but can be inferred: such killings illustrated the dangers of the sins of lust, anger, and avarice. They acted as exemplary tales.

This line of argument can be taken further: other woundings and killings can, by implication, be related to patterns of authority and of resistance to them — thus, the farm laborers who killed their citizen employer, the servants

---

[18] *Diario ferrarese*, 166, 207, 220, 224, 248, 266.

[19] *Diario ferrarese*, 151, 163, 167, 171, 173, 178, 181, 196, 197, 198, 202, 207, 208, 210, 212, 213, 215, 219, 220, 221, 224, 242, 244, 245, 247, 259, 263, 265, 267, 268, 271, 279.

[20] *Diario ferrarese*, 217, 243, 251, 265.

[21] *Diario ferrarese*, 166, 221, 222, 223, 226, 243, 247, 249, 266, 272.

[22] *Diario ferrarese*, 157, 162, 174, 199, 200, 245, 252, 259, 272.

[23] *Diario ferrarese*, 154, 208, 211, 215, 220, 223, 261, 263, 279.

[24] *Diario ferrarese*, 191, 212, 213, 242, 247, 248, 263, 267.

[25] *Diario ferrarese*, 213, 245.

[26] Examples of men killed or wounded by their enemies; *Diario ferrarese*, 215, 219, 242, 245, 259.

[27] *Diario ferrarese*, 208, 268.

of officials who were wounded, the police and judicial officers who were killed or assaulted.[28] These attacks were recorded because they represented challenges to the authority of the city, its employers and officers, and pointed again to the failure of princely government to uphold these.

Finally, crime is made to seem seasonal: the bulk of the diarist's entries regarding crime each year fall in the winter months, from November to March. He reports few crimes in the spring and summer. The winter period included, of course, Carnival, a period of licensed violence, to which should perhaps be attributed the non-fatal cuts to arms and legs.[29] However, although violence among the nobility and wealthy was perhaps attracted into the winter months by Carnival, the recurrent outbreaks of burglary and thieving had a more obvious root in poverty and hunger over the winter.[30] The diarist almost makes the connection for us when he notes, in subsequent entries during 1500, "Winter began at the start of November, because it began to snow hard," and "Homicides, thefts and robberies are committed in great number by day and night . . . such that it is necessary to go home early in the evening."[31] Two years earlier, he likewise speaks in the same breath of bad winter weather and more frequent theft and violence.[32] The onset of winter meant the onset of more intense criminality that eased only with the spring. It is the historian, however, who has to provide the causal link. As has been noted of weather reporting in twelfth- and thirteenth-century chronicles, "the link of causation or signification is often manifested only in a conjunction *(et)* or a significant juxtaposition."[33] In the way that the diarist writes about these matters, he resembles annalists for whom "social events are apparently as incomprehensible as natural events . . . [and] seem merely to have occurred."[34] This leveling of social and natural events is a significant part of the author's sense of a malaise beyond human repair.

This seasonal pattern is repeated, it must be said, only in the years after the death of Ercole's Captain of Justice for Ferrara, the chillingly effective Gregorio

---

[28] *Diario ferrarese*, 211, 244, 265, 271.

[29] *Diario ferrarese*, 242, 263.

[30] *Diario ferrarese*, 198, 199, 207, 221, 222, 239, 243, 247, 265, 266. Cf. Gundersheimer, "Crime and Punishment," 122: "[T]here does not appear in Ferrara to be any particular correlation between periods of scarcity or famine, and outbreaks of crime by individuals."

[31] *Diario ferrarese dall' anno 1409*, 262.

[32] *Diario ferrarese dall'anno 1409*, 218.

[33] I. Draelants, "Le temps dans les textes historiographiques du Moyen Age," in *Le temps qu'il fait au Moyen Age: phénomènes atmosphériques dans la littérature, la pensée scientifique et religeuse*, ed. Claude Thomasset and Joelle Ducos (Paris: Presses de l'Université de Paris-Sorbonne, 1998), 91–138, here 122.

[34] White, "Value of Narrativity," 7.

Ciampanti from Lucca, known in Ferrara as "il Zampante," with a play perhaps on the word *zampa,* the animal hoof or claw with which this judge trampled and devoured the duke's subjects. For the author of the *Diario* he was "the greatest ribald, without pity or remorse, who proceeded de facto, without observing the provisions of law or statute, and always sought to arrest and to put to torture, giving four, six, ten or more drops of the rope, before asking questions, such that whoever fell into his hands did not escape with life and property intact; and if he did not take life, he took property. . . . " When he was killed by students in 1496 while Ercole was out of the city, songs and verses were composed in joyous celebration, and three of these the diarist copied down.[35] The diarist is, of course, inconsistent here, looking for law enforcement, but objecting to the methods used to achieve it. In the absence of this exceptional judicial force, crime came to resemble the seasons: beyond man's control, to be endured and recorded only.[36] Much the same perception is to be found in Zerbinati's diary for the year 1504: after recording plague deaths, poor harvest, fire, flooding and earthquake, as well as an angry servant's killing of her mistress, he notes that the world was "upside down" ("alla roversa"), with natural disasters, enormous crimes, and unseasonal weather.[37]

These thoughts on crime lead us in two directions in exploring the narrative of the *Diario:* towards comments on food and weather, and towards concern for respectable civic society (the "persone da bene"). Food supply is one of this author's major concerns. Many times each year he lists food prices on the Ferrarese market, and he frequently adds comments on factors affecting supply. Like Caleffini, he frequently records the price not only of wheat, but also of a wide range of agricultural produce (other grains, such as barley and millet, as well as meat, beans, oil, wine, fish, and so on).[38] In only one year of the period 1494–1502 did the diarist note that the harvest was abundant.[39] For most other years there were difficulties. In the spring of 1495, fear of war drained supplies off to Venice and Bologna.[40] Rain, snow, and cold in April and May 1496 led to a bad harvest that summer, causing immediate shortages.[41] An unusually wet

---

[35] *Diario ferrarese*, 182–86.

[36] Chiappini makes a similar point: *Gli Estensi*, 181.

[37] Zerbinati, *Chroniche di Ferrara*, 47–50.

[38] Cf. the graphs, constructed on Caleffini's figures, in Maria Serena Mazzi, "La fame e la paura del fame," in *A tavola con il principe*, ed. Jadranka Bentini et al (Ferrara: Gabriele Corbo: Banca nazionale dell'agricoltura, 1988), 153–69, esp. 160–64.

[39] *Diario ferrarese*, 215, 218.

[40] *Diario ferrarese*, 144.

[41] *Diario ferrarese*, 186.

winter in 1496/1497 was accompanied by large numbers of sheep and livestock deaths: as a result, the duke had to limit meat prices, and everyone lived on "snails, bitter vetch, grasses and other rubbish."[42] Capping the retail prices of meat was not always successful, however: when the duke tried this in 1499, the butchers shut up shop in protest.[43] In 1497, the harvest fell below expectations because of excessive rainfall in the spring, followed by a dry summer and autumn.[44] Poor harvest followed too in 1499, because of rain, and in 1500, and in 1501 excessive heat and the lack of rain dried the fields such that many crops did not grow, while the vines were eaten by aphids.[45]

It was damage done to crops that largely explains the diarist's continuous concern with the weather, though he does also record weather damage in town: the winds and storms that toppled chimneys, blew down rustic houses and barns, and uprooted trees (1494, 1495, 1496, 1501); the mild winters and wet springs that waterlogged the fields and multiplied pests (1494/1495, 1496); the dry summers that left the ground hard and the rivers and wells dry (1497, 1498).[46] The level of water in the river caused many anxieties: too little interrupted milling, too much generated fear of flooding (which would prompt daily processions by the clergy, suspension of the law-courts, and compulsory duties of river-watch).[47]

This constant attention to the fate of the fields, under the twin vagaries of the weather and the river, stands in contrast to the diarist's lack of interest or concern for commerce, business, or manufacture. Guilds and guildsmen are seldom mentioned. The only effect that the great building boom of the 1490s seems to have had on the diarist's experience was to increase the price of building materials.[48] He mentions but rarely the price of non-agricultural goods.[49] Poverty and unemployment he did notice, though. The urban population, he observed in 1497, had multiplied so much that houses to rent could not be found.[50] Later in the same year, he thought that poverty in the Ferrarese countryside was

---

[42] *Diario ferrarese*, 199.

[43] *Diario ferrarese*, 277; see also 199.

[44] *Diario ferrarese*, 202, 204, 207.

[45] *Diario ferrarese*, 235, 256, 270.

[46] *Diario ferrarese*, 134, 136, 137, 140, 143, 161, 168, 173, 178, 187, 203, 204, 215, 224–25, 267.

[47] *Diario ferrarese*, 137, 145, 166, 189, 191, 192.

[48] *Diario ferrarese*, 144.

[49] *Diario ferrarese*, 239, 261, 262.

[50] *Diario ferrarese*, 204. On this, see Charles M. Rosenberg, "The Erculean Addition to Ferrara: Contemporary Reactions and Pragmatic Considerations," *ACTA: The Fifteenth Century* 5 (1978): 49–67, here 62, n. 5.

"greater than it has ever been."[51] In 1499 he noted that the guilds were without work ("le arte non fanno covelle": a phrase he repeated in 1501).[52] In 1500 his diagnosis of economic ills went deeper: on the one hand, it was impossible to collect debts ("when you demand what is yours from your debtor, he wants to kill you"), and on the other, it was impossible to find servants ("the young today are worse than the old . . . you cannot find maids willing to serve: if they are young, they are whores, and if old, pimps, and they would rather go begging than serve others").[53] These comments on employment, debts, and servants coincide with notes of high prices for agricultural and other goods, suggesting that seasonal price movements were causing repeated seizures in economic activity, as surplus money for buying manufactures or paying debts disappeared, while the wages offered to servants were too low to sustain them.

The character and social position of the anonymous diarist thus starts to emerge: a landowner himself, he was firmly embedded in the non-business world, with his frequent reporting of food prices and agricultural fortunes; he was enough of an employer to be shocked that the young preferred begging to service but not enough of a property owner to take profit from high rents or food prices. In other words, he was typical of the middling stratum of society in a city without a strong commercial or manufacturing base.[54] This would explain too his attitude to credit. He reports in 1497 the death and strange burial of one Vesconte Policia, whose coffin was found to contain only stones: many said that the devil had carried him off in body and soul because during his illness he had never wanted to confess his sins, but had always asked for the devil, and this because throughout his life he had practiced usury boldly, also hiring out oxen and vats, and loading his soul with sin.[55] Likewise, the diarist records the death in 1498 of "a great usurer and enemy of the people," Francesco Corezzari, a clothes-dealer, and his burial "amid much cursing."[56]

Here and elsewhere, the diarist presents himself as a "man of the people." Talk among the populace is often his immediate source of information and opinion: for example, the recall of the duke's envoy to the victorious king of France in Naples caused much talk among the people, uncertain what this meant

---

[51] *Diario ferrarese*, 207.

[52] *Diario ferrarese*, 228, 272.

[53] *Diario ferrarese*, 263.

[54] On this see T. Dean, "Venetian Economic Hegemony: The Case of Ferrara, 1200–1500," *Studi veneziani* 12 (1986): 45–98.

[55] *Diario ferrarese*, 196.

[56] *Diario ferrarese*, 215.

for its sympathies towards the French.[57] He often records in these years popular discontent at civic taxation, and at civic and ducal officials. Civic taxes to complete the new wall-circuit in 1497 caused "so much blasphemy, complaint, and cursing that it was astounding."[58] In subsequent years the annual setting of new rates for the *colta* (direct tax) generated protest, much of it directed at the president of the communal council, Tito Strozzi: in 1500 the rate caused "enormous outcries and popular malevolence towards Messer Tito, universally hated, and towards his sons . . . such that scurrilous writings about him were found around the city."[59] There were no kind words either for the chief ducal financial officials, the *fattori generali:* they were "loathed more than the devil by the people," he observed of some of them.[60] The people also had cause to curse ducal monetary policy, especially Ercole's repeated efforts to ban all coins except Venetian ducats and coins from his own mint.[61] Were these complaints justified? It is worth pointing out that protest at even moderate direct taxation was characteristic of medieval property-owners, and it would be difficult to argue that Ferrara was over-taxed in this period, given that it was not at war, and as other taxes were actually reduced in the 1490s.[62] Nevertheless, the danger of popular disaffection was perceived by the diarist: he attributes the fall of the Sforza regime in Milan in 1500 to that duke's "wanting to tyrannize his people beyond measure, [such that] he turned them into his enemies." And the nature of that tyranny he clearly saw as fiscal: the sudden imposition of huge taxes caused such popular clamor that the duke of Milan dared not leave his court, and had armed guards posted around a raised platform whenever he gave audience.[63]

Such loss of trust in the people did not appear in Ferrara in these years, but the diary is evidence of distance between court and populace. The diary of course tells us much about the Este family, its residences, its public spectacles, its visitors. Almost every page records the arrival or departure of members of the Estensi, or members of other princely families, or ambassadors from other states. Sometimes such visitors were escorted by the duke and his companions into or out of the city, to the sound of trumpets and pipes. The diarist also seems to have had ready access to ambassadorial reports and speeches: "letters came to the duke

---

[57] *Diario ferrarese*, 146; see also 205.

[58] *Diario ferrarese*, 199.

[59] *Diario ferrarese*, 247; and see 223, 267, 285–86.

[60] *Diario ferrarese*, 278.

[61] *Diario ferrarese*, 137, 195, 206, 208–9.

[62] *Diario ferrarese*, 202–3.

[63] *Diario ferrarese*, 189–90, 254. Similarly, under the year 1488, he recorded the words of the assassin of Girolamo Riario, lord of Forlì: "Questo è il traditore che metea tante graveze" (124).

that . . . " or "it was heard from Rome that . . . " are frequent formulations for introducing such material.[64] This should cause no surprise, as ambassadors spoke not only to the prince but also to his subjects, gaining information and opinion in return for selected diplomatic news. On one occasion a French envoy made a letter from Naples freely available, and the diarist duly copied it down.[65] The diarist also notes Ercole's cultural projects (the building of palaces and churches, the staging of classical comedies) and his involvement in a regular calendar of religious spectacles (the *ventura* of Epiphany, the washing and feeding of the poor on Maundy Thursday, the offerings to Saint George the city's patron, and so on). He regards as noteworthy the marriages and funerals of the Este family, of leading gentlemen of the city, and of prime ducal officials and servants.[66] Occasionally, too, he attempts to describe, not without some derision, the fashions in dress adopted by young male courtiers: for example, their close-fitting, quartered jackets and little caps in the Spanish manner, which made them look like buffoons; or their lady-like, closed cork-shoes, large and round at the front, narrow at the back.[67] Yet of the internal life of the court he tells us little or nothing: he comments only when members of the ruling family emerge from the court, to meet ambassadors, to go to mass or sermon in the cathedral, to attend horse races, to dine in the houses of favored citizens. The only exception comes with acts of violence at court, as when a young Milanese nobleman left court in dudgeon after a Ferrarese count gave him a slap in the duke's bedchamber, or when one of Ercole's chamberlains, on leaving the ducal chamber to go to bed, had a vase of excrement thrown in his face.[68] Usually the diarist is vague regarding what happened in the palace: he admits, for example, that of the great "maestri" (physicians) whom Ercole had around him in 1500 "it is not known who they are, nor can it be found out."[69] The same distance from the court explains the diarist's occasional ignorance of the reason for processions or celebrations or ambassadorial visits.[70]

Although he presents himself as a man of the people, it is really the respectable part of society that he refers to. It is the "persone da bene" whose fortunes particularly concern him, and this can be seen in a number of key judicial episodes: it is these people who hated the effective police methods of Gregorio Zampante; it was the unnecessary torture of an "uomo da bene" that caused the

---

[64] For example, *Diario ferrarese*, 135–36, 143.

[65] *Diario ferrarese*, 153.

[66] *Diario ferrarese*, 134, 140, 149, 151, 182, 195–96, 203, 204, 205–6, 207–8, 215, 248, 259, 273ff.

[67] *Diario ferrarese*, 144, 277; also 256.

[68] *Diario ferrarese*, 181, 249.

[69] *Diario ferrarese*, 263.

[70] *Diario ferrarese*, 147, 181, 189, 254, 258, 259.

downfall of a prominent official; and it was the death on the scaffold of a man from a "good" Modenese family that made everyone cry (in contrast to the peasant who refused to "die well").[71]

As this last example suggests, religious devotion was important in respectable society. Hence the diarist's recording of extensive church-building and refurbishment in these years, of the importation of prestigious foreign nuns for the duke's new nunneries, of the issue of indulgences in Ferrarese churches, of the activities of preachers, and of the popularity of Savonarola. Modern research, using other sources, has of course vastly expanded the state of our knowledge on many of these themes,[72] and there is no need here to rehearse the many building projects referred to, save to note how the diarist's attention is drawn more to the major, traditional religious centers — the cathedral, the mendicant churches — than to newer ones.[73] Preaching in Ferrara has not attracted much modern study, but two aspects of it are evident in the diarist's record: the attendance of the duke, and the impact of individual preachers in persuading the people to fast so as to ward off misfortune, in converting Jews, and in inspiring the duke to issue edicts on morality.[74] Like his contemporary Florentine diarist, Luca Landucci, our author also records the popularity of Savonarola, or "Girolamo Savonarola from Ferrara," as he points out, recalling the great Dominican preacher's Ferrarese birth. In 1498 the diarist makes a long entry on Savonarola's demise in Florence and on the miracles performed after his death. Savonarola's popularity in Ferrara was such, he says, as to bring the Dominican order as a whole into hatred because its General had participated in the unjust sentence of death.[75]

However, in religious matters our diarist was no Landucci: no miraculous statues, no moralizing asides about the vanity of palace-building, no ominous reading of falling masonry.[76] Only once does he attribute unexplained misfortune to God acting "to punish the false Christians in the world today"; only once does he mention a procession in connection with the weather.[77] And apart from the

---

[71] *Diario ferrarese*, 162, 175, 191–92.

[72] See for example Gabriella Zarri, ed., "Pietà e profezia alle corti padaue: le pie consigliere dei principi," in *U Rinascimento melle corti padaue: società e cultura*, ed. P. Rossi (Bari, 1977), 201–37), and T. Tuohy, *Herculean Ferrara: Ercole d'Este (1471–1505) and the Invention of a Ducal Capital* (Cambridge: Cambridge University Press, 1996).

[73] *Diario ferrarese,* 161, 164, 172, 177, 210, 214, 215–16, 218–19, 220, 240, 260, 274.

[74] *Diario ferrarese*, 134, 135, 143, 145, 167, 174, 175, 255.

[75] *Diario ferrarese*, 209–12.

[76] Iodoco del Badia, ed., *Diario fiorentino dal 1450 al 1516 di Luca Landucci* (Florence: G. C. Sansoni, 1883), 13, 41–42, 44, 47–48, 61–62, 63–64, 68.

[77] *Diario ferrarese*, 149, 189.

miracles attributed to Savonarola, he reports only two marvels in these years: an episode in which two large stones, each weighing twenty pounds, fell out of the sky to a great burst of noise, "and it seemed that the sky opened and was seen to be full of stars and sun-rays"; and an anti-Semitic "miracle" in which wheat-seed grew as millet.[78] Neither story, however, originated in Ferrara: one came from the Romagna, the other from Padua. Why, we might ask, is this author's explicit moralizing so muted? Was religious devotion in Ferrara so controlled and directed, or so insufficiently stimulated, for the miraculous to happen there? Was there little popular interest in the fantastic and the marvelous?

In all this, one dimension of the Este state is glaringly absent: the territories beyond the Ferrarese borders. Modena and Reggio, the other main cities of the Este dominion, hardly feature in the diarist's experience or his view of Italy. It is almost as if Ferrara were still a lone city-state. There is abundant detail of life in Ferrara and plentiful narration of the major military and political events in the rest of Italy, but of Modena and Reggio almost nothing. The only piece of extended narrative regarding Modena tells of a popular tumult which followed the capture by passing French soldiers of an innkeeper and his nubile daughters. For all that modern historians have devoted their attention to the "regional states" of late medieval Italy, this contemporary chronicle tells us nothing about the nature or development of political, institutional, or economic relations between the dominant city and its subjects. This absence might, of course, reflect a genuine failure of the Este state to integrate its constituent parts, but it more likely reflects the prejudicial attitude that whatever happened in the subject cities was not worthy of record in the capital.

This characteristic the anonymous diary shares with the diary of Bernardino Zambotti, the other major narrative source for the history of Ferrara in these years, to which we now turn. There are, it has to be said, several superficial similarities between these two diaries. Both report the same sort of news: the arrival of princes and ambassadors; the births, marriages, and deaths of members of the Este family; and religious rituals. They share the same type of source in letters and reports received by the duke. They also share, to some extent, the same attitudes and sympathies: Zambotti reports in similar tones the death of Savonarola — his death grieves all good Christians, he says, especially the Ferrarese and their duke.[79] As with the anonymous diary, marvels, miracles, and omens are largely absent. One rare example occurs when Pope Alexander VI

---

[78] *Diario ferrarese*, 170, 201.

[79] Zambotti, *Diario ferrarese dall'anno 1476* (hereafter Zambotti, *Diario ferrarese*), 279, 281. On Ercole's support for Savonarola, see Luciano Chiappini, "Girolamo Savonarola ed Ercole I d'Este," *Atti e memorie della Deputazione ferrarese di storia patria* 7 (1952): 32–45.

had his head fractured and his arm broken by a falling beam hit by lightning: this was ascribed by many to God's judgment, Zambotti pregnantly remarks.[80] Explicit moralizing too is infrequent. Only once, following the death of an old soldier in a joust, apparently from exhaustion in the summer heat, does Zambotti launch into an extensive moral: this event, he writes, "teaches that no one should trust in strength or bravery or the Lord's favor, because fortune ceases when a man believes he will prosper and have her as his friend, but finds her his enemy and falls. Whoever thinks he is rising, falls with shame and damage to his honor, property, and soul."[81]

In other respects the differences between these two diaries are more apparent. Zambotti's narrative lacks the clutter of knifings and thefts, food prices and weather reports that fill out the anonymous. Secondly, Zambotti tells us much more about himself and his family: his marriage and that of his sister; the judicial offices he held in Ferrara, Reggio, and Mantua; the fortunes of his farm at Marrara.[82] He tells us more too about the interior of court life, such as public exchanges with ambassadors in the ducal chamber, or the tearful reunion of Ercole and his son, Ippolito, in the court hall;[83] though in the 1490s, when Zambotti was absent from Ferrara for several years, this aspect of his diary fades away. However, he was still sufficiently connected to court circles to have access to original documents, many of which he copied into his diary: the papal excommunication of the king of France, intercepted letters from the pope to the Turkish sultan, Cesare Borgia's letter recounting events at Sinigaglia, and so on.[84] Zambotti records too those events at which he was present — the burial of Gianfrancesco Gonzaga at Mantua, the publication of officeholder lists in the Ferrarese chancery, and a horse race, for example.[85] Even when he does not specifically note his own presence, he writes with the detail of an eyewitness, as in his account of classical comedies performed in Ferrara: he describes the dancing and eating that preceded the performances, the seating arrangements, the stage sets, the length of the plays and their division into parts divided by

---

[80] Zambotti, *DF*, 300.

[81] Zambotti, *DF*, 291. A brief moral is also drawn following his account of Cesare Borgia's deception used to oust the duke of Urbino from his lands in 1502: "from this other lords can reflect whether they should lend munitions, artillery, and soldiers to others at war": 340.

[82] Zambotti, *DF*, 192, 199, 200, 209, 216, 224–25, 234, 251, 254, 262, 263, 286, 290, 350.

[83] Zambotti, *DF*, 234.

[84] Zambotti, *DF*, 239–42, 254–57, 259–62, 263–64, 265–66, 269–72, 287–88, 295, 318–33, 344–45.

[85] Zambotti, *DF*, 263, 258–59, 268, 307.

moresche. He even comments once or twice on the content of the plays: Plautus's *Menaechmi,* he recalled, was about twins, and was "very fine and pleasing."[86]

As is by now apparent, Zambotti does not reflect or express the opinions and sentiments of the populace. On the rare occasions that he records protest at taxation, it is the action of the nobility that he reports, not the murmurings of the people: in 1503 the "gentlemen" seem to have marched into the civic council chamber and demanded to re-negotiate their personal tax assessments; on another occasion, they went straight to the duchess, and got the taxes lowered.[87] What is equally surprising, given Zambotti's tenure of judicial offices, is his relative lack of interest in reporting crimes and punishments. Just as significant is his marginal interest in the affairs of Modena and Reggio, cities which he certainly knew well, as he served as appeals judge in Reggio for two years, from August 1499 to August 1501. Yet in that time he reports little news from that city (troop movements, the Jubilee indulgence, an aristocratic wedding).[88] Likewise, during an earlier term of office in Reggio, he described at length the reception given to the city's bishop, on a rare visit bearing an indulgence for the cathedral, and the welcoming ceremony in which Matteo Maria Boiardo took a primary role, as captain of Reggio and as the bishop's foremost feudatory.[89] He does report a little more from Modena in these years, especially the popular tumult against French soldiers, the damage done by an earthquake, and the killing of the cathedral's archpriest.[90] Generally, however, instead of local news, he attempts to trace Ercole's movements, the calendar of major ducal activities in Ferrara, and the despatch and arrival of its ambassadors. His historiography is to a large degree centralized. And when he does give attention to the subject cities, it is in fact attention to their major aristocratic families, especially the Rangoni in Modena. Just as Zambotti is less concerned for the Ferrarese people, so too in the subject cities he sees significance only in the deeds of the noble elite.

Our third diarist, Ugo Caleffini, by contrast to Zambotti adopts a critical stance as regards ducal policies, and in this he resembles the anonymous diarist. Though Caleffini shares with them both an eye for Ercole's movements and devotions, for the arrivals and departures of ambassadors and princes, for the ceremonies of matrimony and burial, for *feste, balli,* and tournaments, his sensitivity to popular distemper is more nuanced and extensive. In one breath in 1490 he notes

---

[86] Zambotti, *DF*, 285, 315–16, 346–47.

[87] Zambotti, *DF*, 225, 349.

[88] Zambotti, *DF*, 302, 303, 306.

[89] Zambotti, *DF*, 223–24.

[90] Zambotti, *DF*, 304, 306, 307, 343, 358.

discontent at taxes, a great shortage of money, and delinquency in robbing, killing, and usury.[91] Throughout the rest of the diary, these three elements, usually separately, form a recurrent refrain. All Ferrara is "upside down," "crying out in anger," in 1490 at Ercole's demands for gifts for the wedding of his daughter Beatrice; and all the "populo grasso e menudo" cried out to the sky in 1491 when the new *colta* was announced, because it had never been so high.[92] Resentment at taxation lay behind Caleffini's recording of the violent behavior of the sons of Filippo Cestarelli, then *Giudice de' Savi*: they came to blows on the piazza with members of the nobility, they wantonly cut down a man's fruit trees, they hit their creditors in the mouth when they asked for payment.[93] Fiscal demands were made no easier by ducal monetary policy: Ercole's decree that only Ferrarese and Venetian coins be spent was mocked by the people because nine out of ten coins came from elsewhere.[94] Such a policy, though, had two outcomes: it encouraged counterfeiting, and it forced people to turn to moneylenders. Hence Caleffini's recording of the heavy punishments meted out to counterfeiters,[95] and his sardonic views on the social worth of usurers: "whoever knew best how to rob and cheat his neighbor, he was more respected."[96] Hence too Caleffini's post-mortem denigration of Galeazzo Trotti, famed Ferrarese "cash-king" ("Re de' dinari"), who, he alleges, exploited other people's need in order to make himself rich, while also recommending tax increases to the duke. Some of the people, Caleffini claims, attended Trotti's funeral "because they could not believe that he was dead, and they let themselves believe that he would come back to life and sink his teeth into their sides, to devour what little was left of them."[97] Galeazzo and his brother Paolo Antonio were so much in ducal favor that people said they had cast a spell on Ercole, and under them the Jews had more authority in Ferrara than the gentlemen. The anti-Semitism of those forced by ducal taxes into dependence on Jewish moneylenders is more clearly expressed here than in Zambotti or the anonymous, in an image which plays on the exaggerated fears of Christian flesh and blood as prey to voracious Jews.[98]

---

[91] Biblioteca Apostolica Vaticana, MS. Chigi I.I.4, *Cronaca di Ferrara 1471–1494,* fol. 270; Caleffini, *Diario*, ed. Pardi, 282.

[92] *Cronaca,* fols. 273v–274, 281v; Caleffini, *Diario*, 291–92, 308.

[93] *Cronaca,* fols. 296, 311–v; Caleffini, *Diario*, 336–37, 370–71.

[94] *Cronaca,* fols. 275v, 292, 298v–299; Caleffini, *Diario*, 296, 327, 344.

[95] *Cronaca,* fols. 271, 285v; Caleffini, *Diario*, 285, 312.

[96] *Cronaca,* fols. 270, 287, 305v; Caleffini, *Diario*, 282, 315–16, 358.

[97] *Cronaca,* fols. 287v–288v; Caleffini, *Diario*, 317–19.

[98] See also his reference to "uxurarii e inganaturi de homini e mangiaturi de sangue de poveri": *Cronaca,* fol. 287.

These recurrent elements of complaint at taxation and scarcity of coin also explain other features of Caleffini's diary in these years: the frequent thefts from churches, shops, and houses (including Caleffini's own), the thieving during ducal dances, the cutpurses "working" the crowd watching theatrical performances.[99] Every morning there was news of a fresh nocturnal burglary.[100] Thieves even snatched women's cloaks and cut pieces off their clothing. Caleffini implies criticism of the duke in his repeated phrase that Ercole attended only to his own pleasures or his building works, while "the Ferrarese have never had it so bad."[101] And his praise of the duchess is, by contrast, a sort of transfer or displacement of loyalist sentiment: she alone was "holy," dismissing buffoons from her presence, praying and hearing mass every day, visiting the convents, giving alms and audience, expediting petitions. She provided dowries for many poor girls. She disliked dancing, singing, and festivities. Hence the popular grief when she died, towards the end of 1493.[102]

It was Eleonora, not Ercole, who most struck this chronicler as an embodiment of Christian ideals of governance: sober and devout in her personal life, accessible and active in the people's interest. It was religion that, for Caleffini more than for our other authors, offered the only solace to the people: he makes note of the good preachers, and, when one of them died, he commented that "his death was grieved by all the people, so much was he loved, and so useful and good were his sermons."[103] By contrast, the enemy of the people and friend of the Jews, Galeazzo Trotti, could no more easily be got to sermons than a dog to a beating.[104] This contrast points, finally, to the principle of exemplarity that underlies Caleffini's choice of noteworthy material: Eleonora was a good example, Ercole and his advisers were not, and bad princely government was marked by high taxation, sharp practice, and widespread criminality. The same point was understood by the anonymous diarist in his reporting of the downfall of the Sforza and Riario regimes. Here, then, was a deep sense of moral crisis: criminality had become like the weather, unstoppable; the weather itself was predominantly cruel; the duke's fiscal and monetary policies, and his Jew-loving advisers, were

---

[99] *Cronaca,* fols. 270, 271v–272, 275v, 276, 280, 294, 297, 297v–298; Caleffini, *Diario*, 283, 287, 288, 295, 297, 305, 332, 340, 343.

[100] *Cronaca,* fol. 275; Caleffini, *Diario*, 294.

[101] *Cronaca,* fols. 274, 291; Caleffini, *Diario*, 292, 325.

[102] *Cronaca,* fols. 293, 313; Caleffini, *Diario*, 330, 376–77. See also W. L. Gundersheimer, "Women, Learning and Power: Eleonora of Aragon and the Court of Ferrara," in *Beyond Their Sex: Learned Women of the European Past*, ed. Patricia H. Labalme (New York: New York University Press, 1980), 46–54.

[103] *Cronaca,* fol. 269v; Caleffini, *Diario*, 280.

[104] *Cronaca,* fol. 288v.

forcing people into greater dependence on usurers; blasphemy, cursing, hatred, and violence arose from tax demands; members of the ruling family bore direct responsibility for public outbreaks of violence. The diarists' vision approached that of a Venetian observer, for whom Ferrara was "as under tyrants."[105] For this reason, it is difficult to agree with Gundersheimer that "the political and social structure," in fifteenth-century Ferrara, "was sound enough to weather all but the most serious political uprisings without any real strain,"[106] that the Este maintained popular affection through an extreme care to observe certain expected forms of conduct, or that "very occasional grumbling about high prices or the exactions of certain despised functionaries" was neither implicitly nor explicitly anti-Estensian.[107] Strains were all too evident in the chroniclers' records of the 1490s: they lay bare two fault-lines in the Este state, one between Ferrara and its subject cities, and one between the ducal entourage and the Ferrarese people. The former was to lead, within a few years, to the loss of Modena and Reggio to Pope Julius II; that the latter did not also cause political damage in this turbulent period is perhaps due more to chance than to the solidity of the political structure.

---

[105] Marino Sanuto, *I Diarii di Marino Sanuto*, ed. Rinaldo Fulin et al., 58 vols. (Venice: Visentini, 1879–1903), 4: 1449. On the author of this remark, Girolamo Donà, see T. Dean, "After the War of Ferrara: Relations between Venice and Ercole d'Este, 1484–1505," in *War, Culture and Society in Renaissance Venice: Essays Presented to Sir John Hale*, ed. David S. Chambers, Cecil H. Clough, and Michael E. Mallett (London: Hambledon Press, 1994), 73–98, here 79, 97.

[106] Gundersheimer, "Crime and punishment," 128. A similar point is made by Chiappini, *Gli Estensi*, 181.

[107] W. L. Gundersheimer, "Toward a Reinterpretation of the Renaissance in Ferrara," *Bibliothèque d'humanisme et Renaissance* 30 (1968): 267–81, here 273, 277, 278–79.

Ariosto's "Fier Pastor": Structure and Historical Meaning in *Orlando Furioso*

Albert Russell Ascoli

I. Questions

It has now been almost two decades since a wave of historical and cultural criticism and theory reversed the dominant "textualist" trend in North American literary studies that had led us from the New Criticism through Structuralism and into the theoretical arcana of post-Structuralism. This shift, true to its own historical character, has never been absolute or "pure." At its best, in fact, the imperative to "always historicize" has been complemented by a lingering textualist awareness of the complex and pervasive mediations that language and other forms of signifying representation must be accorded in any attempt to reestablish the bonds referential, ideological, or other between world and literary work. And as the genealogical and methodological links that still join the New Historicism and cultural critique to their formalist precursors and ancestors (New Criticism and Structuralism) have become more apparent over time, the need to understand the relationship between the form of a literary work and its multiple historicities has become more and more pressing, though no less difficult to satisfy.

In this essay I will consider a text, Ariosto's *Orlando Furioso,* which benefited immensely from the proliferation of sophisticated methods of formal analysis in the 1960s and '70s precisely because its structure is so extremely complex, its mode of signification so elaborate and, often enough, so oblique. At the same time, the *Furioso* displays its author's keen awareness of the forms of cultural and political crisis which he individually, the Ferrarese society of which he was a part specifically, and the Italian peninsula generally were each undergoing in the first third of the sixteenth century. The poem offers anachronistic fictions of chivalric heroism and errant desire as a means of at least temporarily eluding and even forgetting imminent threats not only to particular regimes (like that of the Este family that ruled Ferrara and patronized Ariosto, however inadequately), but also to an entire way of life (the aristocratic humanism that had flourished under the political equilibrium that persisted during much of the Quattrocento among the several autonomous states dotting the Italian peninsula).[1] The *Furioso*, then, presents an especially challenging test case for exploring the intricate relations between linguistic-poetic structure and historical circumstances, in a way that — I will argue — can take account of both textualist and historicist concerns, while qualifying the claims of both to methodological superiority.

This essay will further elaborate my account of the *Furioso* as poem of "crisis and evasion," now with a special focus on questions of historical, political, and military crisis.[2] It begins with a synoptic review of important recent work on the immense poem's hybrid form, then offers a general description of the *Furioso*'s basic signifying structures and procedures, emphasizing the ways in which historical materials are incorporated side by side with "intertextual" literary references and "intratextual" connections linking one part of the poem with another. This is accomplished — we will see — in a uniquely Ariostan adaptation of the romance compositional technique of *entrelacement*, or interlace, that he had inherited from a long and well-established tradition, and especially from his great Ferrarese precursor, Matteo Maria Boiardo, whose unfinished *Orlando Innamorato* the *Furioso* sets out to complete. I will then suggest (via a close reading of a single, exemplary canto) how those structures and procedures can be seen not only as the means of representing and containing (containing by representing apotropaically) cultural crisis,[3] but also as a response to and a product of extreme historical pressures — above all the threat to Italy generally from the violent incursions of European nation-states and from its own foolish

---

[1] Cf. Emilio Bigi, ed., *Orlando furioso di Ludovico Ariosto*, 2 vols. (Milan: Rusconi, 1982), 10 et passim.

[2] In *Ariosto's Bitter Harmony*, I argued that there are "three versions of crisis to which the *Furioso* may be referred: crises of an historical epoch (whether political, cultural, or religious), crises of the self caught in its temporal predicament, and crises of the process of reference itself": Albert Russell Ascoli, *Ariosto's Bitter Harmony: Crisis and Evasion in the Italian Renaissance* (Princeton: Princeton University Press, 1987), 15. I took as a methodological premise, in polemic with deconstruction, the claim that "it will not do to privilege the 'crisis of reference' in Ariosto over possible reference to various crises — historical, psychological, or literary as may be" (42). I would add in this context that it will not do to privilege "historical crisis" over questions of form, either.

[3] Cf. Franco Fortini, "I silenzi dell'Ariosto," *Rassegna della letteratura italiana* 69 (1975): 12–14, here 14; D. S. Carne-Ross, "The One and the Many: A Reading of Orlando Furioso," *Arion n.s.* 3 (1976): 146–219, here 153.

and ambitious leaders and the threat to Ferrara specifically from the imperial papacy that emerged in the early Cinquecento.[4]

Important work on the form of the *Furioso* has recently been done on at least three fronts. The first is the intertextual question of Ariosto's borrowings — of episode, character, image, phrase, and narrative technique — from a variety of literary precursors.[5] Notable, for my purposes, are the debts to Boiardo's long chivalric poem, *Orlando Innamorato*;[6] to Vergil's imperial epic, which furnishes the model for the dynastic fable of Bradamante and Ruggiero, and which competes formally with Boiardan romance for generic dominance throughout the poem;[7] and to Dante's *Commedia* which, despite its prominent role as a target of Ariostan irony against theological solutions to human problems, also functions as a highly productive model of a poem that confronts and absorbs historical crisis.[8] The

---

[4] Charles Stinger, *The Renaissance in Rome* (Bloomington: Indiana University Press, 1985), esp. 235–254.

[5] Pio Rajna, *Le fonti dell' "Orlando furioso"*, 2nd ed. (Florence: Sansoni, 1975 [1900]); Patricia Parker, *Inescapable Romance: Studies in the Poetics of a Mode* (Princeton: Princeton University Press, 1979); Daniel Javitch, "The Imitation of Imitations in *Orlando furioso*," *Renaissance Quarterly* 38 (1985): 215–39; idem, "The *Orlando furioso* and Ovid's Revision of the *Aeneid*," *Modern Language Notes* 99 (1984): 1023–36; Ascoli, *Ariosto's Bitter Harmony*; Dennis Looney, *Compromising the Classics: Romance Epic Narrative in the Italian Renaissance* (Detroit: Wayne State University Press, 1996); Ronald L. Martinez, "Two Odysseys: Rinaldo's Po Journey and the Poet's Homecoming in Orlando Furioso," in *Renaissance Transactions: Ariosto and Tasso*, ed. Valeria Finucci (Durham, NC: Duke University Press, 1999), 17–55.

[6] Rajna, *Le fonti*; David Quint, "The Figure of Atlante: Ariosto and Boiardo's Poem," *Modern Language Notes* 94 (1979): 77–91; Paolo Baldan, *Metamorfosi di un orco: un'irruzione foclorica nel Boiardo esorcizzata dall'Ariosto* (Milan: Unicopli, 1983); Riccardo Bruscagli, "'Ventura' e 'inchiesta' fra Boiardo e Ariosto," in *Stagioni della civiltà estense* (Pisa: Nistri-Lischi, 1983), 87–126; Peter Marinelli, *Ariosto and Boiardo: The Origins of "Orlando Furioso"* (Columbia, MO: University of Missouri Press, 1987); Matteo Maria Boiardo, *Orlando Innamorato*, trans. and ed. Charles Stanley Ross (Berkeley: University of California Press, 1989); Giuseppe Sangirardi, *Boiardismo ariostesco: presenza e trattamento dell' "Orlando innamorato" nel "Furioso"* (Lucca: Pacini Fazzi, 1993); Jo Ann Cavallo, "Denying Closure: Ariosto's Rewriting of the *Orlando innamorato*," in *Fortune and Romance: Boiardo in America*, ed. Charles S. Ross, MRTS 183 (Tempe, AZ: Medieval and Renaissance Texts and Studies, 1998), 97–134.

[7] Andrew Fichter, *Poets Historical: Dynastic Epic in the Renaissance* (New Haven: Yale University Press, 1982); Joseph Sitterson, "Allusive and Elusive Meanings: Reading Ariosto's Vergilian Ending," *Renaissance Quarterly* 45 (1992): 1–19.

[8] Cesare Segre, "Un repertorio linguistico e stilistico dell'Ariosto: *La Commedia*," in *Esperienze Ariostesche* (Pisa: Nistri-Lischi, 1966), 51–83; Luigi Blasucci, "*La Commedia* come fonte linguistica e stilistica del *Furioso*," *Studi su Dante e Ariosto* (1969): 121–62;

second, and perhaps most highly developed, critical tendency focuses attention on the intratextual question of narrative structure, and specifically the poem's deployment of a variant of the practice of narrative *entrelacement* developed in the tradition of medieval romance, that is, the simultaneous unfolding and juxtaposition of multiple characters and plots, interspersed with autonomous or semi-autonomous "episodes."[9] The last trend, to which I will turn very briefly at this essay's end, is reflected by a growing body of criticism exploring the significance of the changes introduced between the first and last editions of the *Furioso*, typically correlating those changes to dramatic shifts in socio-political conditions between 1516 and 1532.[10]

Much of the best recent criticism on the *Furioso* has in fact focused on its problematic relationship to the category of romance in either an intertextual or an intratextual sense, or both, with special attention to the way that narrative

---

Carlo Ossola, "Dantismi metrici nel *Furioso*," in *Ludovico Ariosto: Lingua, Stile e Tradizione*, ed. Cesare Segre (Milan: Feltrinelli, 1976), 69–94; Parker, *Inescapable Romance*; Ascoli, *Ariosto's Bitter Harmony*; Miranda Johnson-Haddad, "Gelosia: Ariosto Reads Dante," *Stanford Italian Review* 11 (1992): 187–210; Douglas Biow, *"Mirabile dictu": Representation of the Marvelous in Medieval and Renaissance Epic* (Ann Arbor: University of Michigan Press, 1996); Martinez, "Two Odysseys"; Ascoli, "Ariosto," in *The Dante Encyclopedia*, ed. Richard Lansing (New York: Garland, 2000), 60–61.

[9] On romance *entrelacement* generally, see Ferdinand Lot, *Étude sur le Lancelot en prose* (Paris: Champion, 1918), and Eugene Vinaver, *The Rise of Romance* (Oxford: Clarendon Press, 1971). For Ariosto's relationship to the tradition see Daniela Delcorno-Branca, *L' "Orlando furioso" e il romanzo cavalleresco medievale* (Florence: Olschki, 1973); Bigi, ed., *Orlando furioso*; and Marina Beer, *Romanzi di cavalleria: il "Furioso" e il romanzo italiano del primo Cinquecento* (Rome: Bulzoni, 1987), as well as Rajna's catalogue of romance sources in *Le fonti*. For influential discussions of Ariosto's narrative technique in related terms, see D. S. Carne-Ross, "The One and the Many: A Reading of *Orlando Furioso*, Cantos 1 and 8," *Arion o.s.* 5 (1966): 195–234; idem "The One and the Many" (1976), esp. 164, 201; and Eugenio Donato, "'Per selve e boscherecci labirinti': Desire and Narrative Structure in Ariosto's *Orlando furioso*," in *Literary Theory/ Renaissance Texts*, ed. Patricia Parker and David Quint (Baltimore: Johns Hopkins University Press, 1986), 33–62. Javitch, "Ovid's Revision," has rightly stressed that Ovid also offers a model for Ariostan interlace. For another account of the *Furioso*, see Clare Carroll, *The "Orlando Furioso": A Stoic Comedy*, MRTS 174 (Tempe, AZ: Medieval & Renaissance Texts & Studies, 1997).

[10] Lanfranco Caretti, "Codicillo ariostesco," in idem, *Antichi e moderni* (Turin: Einaudi, 1976), 103–9; Walter Moretti, *L'ultimo Ariosto* (Bologna: Patron, 1977); Eduardo Saccone, "Prospettive sull'ultimo Ariosto," *Modern Language Notes* 98 (1983): 55–69; Walter Moretti, "L'ideale ariostesco di un'Europa pacificata e unita e la sua crisis nel terzo *Furioso*," in *The Renaissance in Ferrara/Il Rinascimento a Ferrara*, ed. J. Salmons and idem (Ravenna: Mario Lapucci, 1984), 223–44; Alberto Casadei, *La strategia delle varianti: le correzioni storiche del terzo "Furioso"* (Lucca: Pacini Fazzi, 1988).

structures generate and complicate the process of poetic signification. The problem has typically been explored through two interrelated topics: first, the tension between what is called the romance tendency to an inconclusive openness and evasiveness of structure, on the one hand, and, on the other, the epic drive to closure;[11] second, the technique of narrative interlace itself.[12]

Though both topics can be understood as intratextual features of the *Furioso*, they have most often been explored in the intertextual, literary-historical terms of the crucial relationship of Ariosto to his precursor Boiardo, whose *Innamorato* was left unfinished at its author's death in 1494, which the *Furioso* ostensibly completes (although Ariosto, invidiously, never makes explicit reference to his precursor).[13] Seen from the point of view of romance *entrelacement*, Ariosto imitates and even considerably elaborates Boiardo's already derivative narrative praxis, a praxis which seems to be most responsible for the effects of openness and endlessness that characterize the *Innamorato* as it has come down to us. On the other hand, Riccardo Bruscagli has shown that while in Boiardo the knights move across the landscape driven by an open-ended "ventura" (chance, happenstance), in Ariosto, by contrast, they are motivated by goal-oriented "inchieste" (quests) that tend toward closure. Quint has subsequently extended this point by showing that in the *Furioso*, Ariosto, especially over the last twelve cantos of the poem, acts to impose epic, neo-Vergilian conclusion on the romance structure he took over from Boiardo.[14]

---

[11] Parker, *Unescapable Romance*; Quint, "Figure of Atlante"; Remo Ceserani, "Due modelli culturali e narrativi nell'*Orlando furioso*," *Giornale storico della letteratura italiana* 161 (1984): 481–506; Sergio Zatti, *Il "Furioso" tra epos e romanzo* (Lucca: Pacini Fazzi, 1990); Alberto Casadei, "Breve analisi sul finale del primo *Furioso*," *Studi e problemi di critica testuale* 44 (1992): 87–100.

[12] Elissa Weaver, "Lettura del intreccio dell'*Orlando furioso*: il caso delle tre pazzie d'amore," *Strumenti critici* 11 (1977): 384–406; Daniel Javitch, "*Cantus Interruptus* in the *Orlando furioso*," *Modern Language Notes* 95 (1980): 66–80; Giuseppe Dalla Palma, *Le strutture narrative dell' "Orlando furioso"* (Florence: Olschki, 1984); Daniel Javitch, "Narrative Discontinuity in the *Orlando furioso* and its Sixteenth Century Critics," *Modern Language Notes* 103 (1988): 50–74.

[13] Few critics have taken the *Furioso*'s character as "sequel" quite as literally as Torquato Tasso who, in his *Discorsi dell'Arte Poetica* insists (perhaps for his own invidious purposes) that the two *Orlando*s must be considered formally as a single entity. see Lawrence F. Rhu, *The Genesis of Tasso's Narrative Theory: English Translations of the Early Poetics and a Comparative Study of Their Significance* (Detroit: Wayne State University Press, 1993), 111, 115–17, 120–21.

[14] Quint, "Figure of Atlante"; cf. Carne-Ross, "The One and the Many" (1976), 205; Sitterson, "Allusive and Elusive Meanings." Cavallo, "Denying Closure," argues with conviction and good evidence that Ariosto's rewriting, and suppression, of various Boiardan

In the drive to characterize the connections and discontinuities between the two *poemi* in narrative and generic terms, however, critics have tended to overlook some of the most substantive ways in which both the form and the content of the *Furioso* depart from those of the *Innamorato*. The first major claim of this essay is that the attempt to make *narrative* — romance, epic, or both — definitional for the poetics of the *Furioso*, for all its usefulness, has not fully and adequately described the formal specificity and novelty of the *Furioso*, or its basic modes of signification, and in particular has not understood the degree to which that specificity is both historically produced and linked tightly to historical content. In fact, notwithstanding the foregrounding of the Vergilian genealogical plot in the *Furioso*, especially at the beginning (canto 3) and the end (cantos 44–46), and the empirical accident of the *Innamorato*'s unfinishedness, the later poem is more similar to the earlier poem in its use of narrative interlace than it is different from it — indeed it has been recognized since Rajna that Boiardo clearly excelled Ariosto in sheer narrative inventiveness. Instead, I argue, the most cogent differences, both formal and semantic, between the two are not primarily narratological. In fact, the issue of narrative structure might best be placed under the larger rubric of figure and trope, specifically the master trope of perspectival irony with which the poem has been consistently associated at least since DeSanctis and Croce.[15]

In formal terms, the *Furioso* is significantly more complex than the *Innamorato*, largely because, in addition to the interweaving of narrative strands and free-standing episodes, Ariosto's interlace extends to include, as integrally constituent elements, a number of non-narrative structures, most notably:

---

episodes is designed to efface signs that the third book of the *Innamorato* was tending toward closure. But Cavallo's point, though an important corrective to dismissive treatments of Boiardo's artistry, does not cancel two basic facts. First, that the *Innamorato* was never finished and thus is necessarily experienced as "open." Second, that whatever conclusions the poem might have reached if its author had lived, they are not foreseen from the outset or integrated into its structure throughout, as they are in the *Furioso*. Here Ariosto's recourse to the form of genealogical epic (Fichter, *Poets Historical*), as against imitation of and/or allusion to specific passages from Vergil, clearly separates the *Furioso* from its precursor. It is perhaps relevant to note that just as Ariosto tends to make us forget the very real advances in the integration of epic and romance carried out by Boiardo, so Tasso's later and more rigid use of epic form — which he specifically opposes to the hybrid monster of Boiardo plus Ariosto — has tended to conceal the fact that, up to its own day, the *Furioso* was perhaps the closest thing to Vergilian epic ever written in the Italian vernacular. On Tasso's invidious treatment of Ariosto, see Margaret Ferguson, *Trials of Desire: Renaissance Defenses of Poetry* (New Haven: Yale University Press, 1983); and Sergio Zatti, *L'Ombra del Tasso: Epica e romanzo nel Cinquecento* (Milan: Bruno Mondadori, 1996).

[15] Cf. Zatti, *Il "Furioso" tra epos e romanzo*, 10–11 and n.

1) the authorial proems which invariably precede each canto and comment on what has gone before and what comes after;[16] 2) the numerous other authorial digressions and interventions so well discussed by Durling in *The Figure of the Poet in Renaissance Epic*; 3) the major encomiastic and ekphrastic interludes in cantos 3, 26, 33, 42, 46;[17] 4) the principal allegorical episodes (of Alcina's island and the lunar surface) which participate in but also gloss the surrounding narrative lines.[18] These features are either entirely absent from Boiardo's poem or not a continuous and integral part of it — in particular, the use of proems for ethical, political, and/or social commentary emerges only in the latter part of the *Innamorato*. At the same time, the intertextual pattern of allusions to prior works in the *Furioso* is also more complicated and more systematic than it is in Boiardo.[19] As we shall see, Ariosto places verbal and thematic repetitions in the foreground among all these interlaced elements, intratextual and intertextual alike, to challenge and even to arrest the forward movement of plot and character.

The result is that one can legitimately trace interpretive paths through the poem in any of several ways: intratextually, by focusing on individual characters,[20] or narrative episodes,[21] or images,[22] or themes;[23] intertextually, by focusing on

---

[16] Durling, *Figure of the Poet*, 132ff.; Ascoli, *Ariosto's Bitter Harmony*, 97–98.

[17] Katherine Hoffman, "The Court in the Work of Art: Patronage and Poetic Autonomy in the *Orlando furioso*, Canto 42," *Quaderni d'Italianistica* 13 (1992): 113–24.

[18] Ascoli, *Ariosto's Bitter Harmony*, 123–24, 264–65.

[19] That is not to deny a significant intertextual dimension to the *Innamorato*, however. On this score see, for example, Cavallo, *Ethics of Desire*; Riccardo Bruscagli, "Introduzione," in *Orlando Innamorato*, ed. idem (Turin: Einaudi, 1995), v–xxxiii; Looney, *Compromising the Classics*; Manuele Gragnolati, "Love, Lust, and Avarice: Leodilla between Dante and Ovid," in *Fortune and Romance*, ed. Cavallo and Ross, 151–73; Claudio Micocci, "La presenza della tradizione classica nell' *Orlando innamorato*," in *Il Boiardo e il mondo estense nel Quattrocento*, ed. Giuseppe Anceschi and Tina Matarrese (Padua: Antenore, 1998), 43–61; and James Nohrnberg, "Orlando's Opportunity: Chance, Luck, Fortune, Occasion, Boats and Blows in Boiardo's *Orlando innamorato*," in *Fortune and Romance*, ed. Cavallo and Ross, 31–75.

[20] E.g., Peter De Sa Wiggins, *Figures in Ariosto's Tapestry: Character and Design in the "Orlando furioso"* (Baltimore: Johns Hopkins University Press, 1986).

[21] E.g., Dalla Palma, *Le strutture narrative*.

[22] E.g., A. Bartlett Giamatti, "Headlong Horses, Headless Horsemen: An Essay in the Chivalric Romances of Pulci, Boiardo, and Ariosto," in *Italian Literature: Roots and Branches*, ed. K. Atchity and G. Rimanelli (New Haven: Yale University Press, 1976), 265–307.

[23] E.g., Eduardo Saccone, "Cloridano e Medoro, con alcuni argomenti per una lettura del primo *Furioso*," in idem, *Il soggetto del "Furioso" e altri saggi tra Quattro e Cinquecento* (Naples: Liguori, 1974), 161–200.

the poem's citations/transformations of any one of several major precursors;[24] historically and culturally, by focusing on Ariosto's encomia of his Estense patrons, his accounts of the Italian wars,[25] his variations on any one of several cultural discourses (the "querelle des femmes" for example).[26] Unfortunately, each structurally-sponsored shift in focus also drastically shifts the interpretive results obtained, and the attempt to construct an interpretive calculus which could account for all possibilities, reducing multiplicity to unified significance, falters before the excessive number of signifying variables. Nonetheless, it is clear that isolating one structure or interpretive focal point to the exclusion of others obscures the essentially interlaced character of the poem, which incessantly juxtaposes its constituent elements with one another and with the literary texts and cultural discourses to which they refer in a volatile game of ironic perspectives. At the same time, it is also clear that the prominent historical-cultural materials, and their intricate positioning with respect to literary narrative and themes, are among the most distinctively innovative aspects of Ariosto's textual practice.

In this ceaseless play between one piece of writing and another, the text/context distinction and the literature/history opposition both lose much of their clarity. Within the *Furioso* pieces of poem take turns as text and context for one another, while the numerous contexts evoked by Ariosto's text, literary and historical alike, both determine its meaning and are recontextualized and reinterpreted by it. In short, neither a formalist, textual approach that strives to reduce the poem to a closed system of self-generating significances or anti-significances, or a historical, contextual analysis that attempts to find the work's meaning by submitting it to the determinations of external formations (literary, political, generally cultural, as may be) is sufficient to account for the *Furioso*'s signifying practices. In order to approximate the incessant dynamic of reciprocal appropriation and ironization

---

[24] E.g., Javitch, "Ovid's Revision"; and idem, "The Imitation of Imitations in *Orlando furioso*," *Renaissance Quarterly* 38 (1985): 215–39.

[25] E.g., Leonzio Pampaloni, "La guerra nel *Furioso*," *Belfagor* 26 (1971): 627–52; and Michael Murrin, *History and Warfare in Renaissance Epic* (Chicago: University of Chicago Press, 1994).

[26] E.g. Durling, *Figure of the Poet*; Pamela Benson, *The Invention of the Renaissance Woman: The Challenge of Female Independence in the Literature and Thought of Italy and England* (University Park, PA: Pennsylvania State University Press, 1992); Valeria Finucci, *The Lady Vanishes: Subjectivity and Representation in Castiglione and Ariosto* (Stanford: Stanford University Press, 1992); Albert Russell Ascoli, "Il segreto di Erittonio: politica e poetica sessuale nel canto XXXVII dell'Orlando furioso," in *La rappresentazione dell'altro nei testi del Rinascimento*, ed. Sergio Zatti (Lucca: Pacini Fazzi, 1998), 53–76; Deanna Shemek, *Ladies Errant: Wayward Women and Social Order in Early Modern Italy* (Durham, NC: Duke University Press, 1998).

within the *Furioso* and between the *Furioso* and its external interlocutors and historical circumstances, we should recognize that Ariosto's adaptation of romance interlace has explicitly broadened beyond narrative and theme to encompass both literary "intertextuality" and cultural "discursivity."[27] In other words, Ariosto both allusively interweaves macro- and micro-textual elements of the romance-epic tradition,[28] and, far more explicitly, incorporates social and historical references and discourses within the internal structures of his poem.

My second major point is that the emergence of a new, complex, and dynamic mode of interlace in the *Furioso* is closely correlated with equally striking shifts in semantic content with respect to the *Innamorato*. Zatti, building on the work of Durling, has recently suggested that the primary innovations of Ariosto with respect to Boiardo are moments of poetic self-reflexivity, particularly at the points of suture and transition from one narrative segment to another.[29] He is, of course, right — a point my own work on the multiple and contradictory figurations of poetry, poet, and reader in the poem tends to support.[30] On the other hand, I would like to stress here that the *Furioso* is equally innovative in the way that it systematically introduces historical and cultural materials that link the world of the poem to the circumstances of Estense Ferrara and of Italy in the throes of a dramatic crisis motivated by the foreign interventions (beginning with that of Charles VIII) and internecine violence (with particular attention to the papacy under Julius II [1503–1512] and then Leo X [1512–1521]).[31]

---

[27] I use "intertextuality" here in a specifically literary-historical sense. My notion of "discursivity" derives from the work of Michel Foucault, especially *The Archaeology of Knowledge*, with an assist from Stephen Greenblatt's notion of Shakespearean "negotiations" with social discourses. The phenomenon I am describing is what I have previously dubbed "cotextuality": Ascoli, *Ariosto's Bitter Harmony*, 45.

[28] Javitch, "Imitation of Imitations," convincingly shows how Ariosto's imitative practice typically and deliberately brings together at least two earlier variants of a given episode; Nohrnberg, Quint, Parker, Ascoli, Zatti, Looney, and Javitch, among others, discuss how, from the first line forward, the poem intentionally interweaves romance and epic elements: Nohrnberg, *Analogy*; Parker, *Inescapable Romance*; Quint, "Figure of Atlante"; Ascoli, *Ariosto's Bitter Harmony*; Zatti, *Il "Furioso tra epos e romanzo*; Looney, *Compromising the Classics*; and Daniel Javitch, "The Grafting of Virgilian Epic in *Orlando furioso*," in *Renaissance Transactions: Ariosto and Tasso*, ed. Finucci, 56–76. See also note 14 above.

[29] Zatti, *Il "Furioso tra epos e romanzo*, esp. chap. 1.

[30] Ascoli, *Ariosto's Bitter Harmony*, 37–39 et passim.

[31] On the presence of historical materials, see Durling, *Figure of the Poet*; Pampaloni, "La guerra"; David Marsh, "Ruggiero and Leone: Revision and Resolution in Ariosto's *Orlando furioso*," *Modern Language Notes* 96 (1981): 144–51; Roger Baillet, "L'Ariosto et les princes d'Este: poésie et politique," in *Le pouvoir et le plume* (Paris: Université de la Sorbonne nouvelle, 1982), 85–89; Bigi, ed., *Orlando furioso*; Moretti, "L'ideale ariostesco";

Although the two kinds of new material might seem to be antithetical — the one pointing toward poetic ficticity, the other toward historical reality — they are in fact mutually conditioning and determining. The presence of historical materials points up, by contrast, the fictions of poetic narrative.[32] But the more we notice the poem *qua* poem, the more we will consider the reality of poetry itself as a historically situated mode of discourse. Furthermore, and this point is crucial to my argument, *both* kinds of semantic novelties, poetic and historical, are closely intertwined with the formal innovations of the poem, since they make their appearances primarily in the proems, digressions, and ekphrases. The last step to be taken, and my third major claim here, is to suggest that the emergence of important new structural and semantic elements in the *Furioso*, brought together in Ariosto's expanded use of traditional romance interlace techniques, can be understood at least in part as a response to the pressure of historical crisis.

II. Examples

To illustrate these three central points (the innovative structure and semantics of the *Furioso* and their function as response to historical crisis), I will focus on

---

Hoffman, "The Court in the Work of Art"; Murrin, *History and Warfare*; Robert Davey Henderson, "The First *Orlando furioso*: Compositional Seasons and Political Strategies" (Ph.D .diss., University of California, 1995); Biow, "*Mirabile Dictu*"; Katherine Hoffman, "'Un così valoroso cavalliere': Knightly Honor in Artistic Representation in *Orlando furioso*, Canto 26," in *Renaissance Transactions: Ariosto and Tasso*, ed. Finucci, 178–212. In many ways, Carlo Dionisotti is the patron saint of contemporary interest in historicizing Ariosto and his poem: Carlo Dionisotti, "Appunti sui *Cinque canti* e sugli studi ariosteschi," in *Atti del Convegno di studi e problemi di critica testuale nel centenario della Commissione per i testi di lingua*, (Florence: Olschki, 1961), 368–82; idem, *Geografia e storia della letteratura italiana* (Turin: Einaudi, 1967). Casadei, *La strategia delle varianti*, offers an excellent review of the literature to that date in his careful accounting of the additions and revisions of the material between 1516 and 1532. On the historical circumstances in Ferrara at the time of Ariosto see Michele Catalano, *Vita di Ludovico Ariosto, ricostruita su nuovi documenti*, 2 vols. (Geneva: Olschki, 1931); Riccardo Bacchelli, *La congiura di Don Giulio d'Este*, 2nd ed. (Milan: Mondadori, 1958); Luciano Chiappini, *Gli Estensi*, 2nd ed. (Varese: Dall'Oglio, 1967); Werner L. Gundersheimer, *Ferrara: The Style of a Renaissance Despotism* (Princeton: Princeton University Press, 1973); E. Sestan, "Gli Estensi e il loro stato al tempo dell'Ariosto," *Rassegna della letteratura italiana* 69 (1975): 19–31; Beer, *Romanzi di cavalleria*; Casadei, *La strategia delle varianti*; Stefano La Monica, "La politica estense nel *Furioso* e negli *Ecatommiti*," *Rassegna della letteratura italiana* 96 (1992): 66–83; idem, "Realtà storica e immaginario bellico ariostesco," *Rassegna della letteratura italiana* 89 (1985): 326–58.

[32] Cf. Durling, *Figure of the Poet*, 133–34; Bigi, ed., *Orlando furioso*, 43.

canto 17, which offers a particularly interesting example of interlacing several different formal elements. Among these are two major narrative segments (the tale of Rodomonte's devastating, Turnus-like foray into Paris and the story of Grifone's ill-fated love for Orrigille and its unhappy denouement at the tournament of Norandino); the semi-autonomous episode of Norandino, Lucina, and the Orco; a moralizing proem on the plight of Italy subjected to tyrants and scourged by foreign invaders; and a digressive authorial apostrophe to the Christian European princes (and above all Pope Leo X).[33] As the last two items suggest, this is a canto with a strong topical, historical-political interest.

Canto 17 is also, and very much to my purposes, one of the most richly Boiardan of all the *Furioso*. The tournament of Norandino recalls the tournament of the King of Cyprus at which he, Norandino, battled for the love of Lucina (*Innamorato* 2.19.52–55); the story of Grifone and Orrigille continues a narrative begun in the earlier poem (2.3.62–65); the story of the Orco gives both the prequel and the sequel to the Boiardan story of Lucina chained, Andromeda-like, to a seaside cliff and rescued by Gradasso and Mandricardo (3.3.24–60).[34] Most

---

[33] David Quint, "Narrative Interlace and Narrative Genres in *Don Quijote* and the *Orlando Furioso*," *Modern Language Quarterly* 58 (1997): 241–68, discusses the question of interlace in this canto and those that surround it in terms different from my own, though complementary to them.

[34] Ariosto, in fact, is both borrowing and transforming multiple elements from Boiardo (Boiardo, *Orlando innamorato*, ed. Ross). Cf. Rajna, *Le fonti*, 266–88. The amorous treachery of the lovely and fraudulent Orrigille remains the same, but where in Boiardo Orlando was the betrayed lover and Grifone the object of Orrigille's desire, now Grifone has become the victim. The way in which Ariosto's Grifone is made by Orrigille's trickery to assume the disgraced armor of Martano and thus put his life at risk in fact echoes precisely the episode which introduces Orrigille in the *Innamorato* (2.19, esp. 17 and 31). In Boiardo, Norandino is a participant in a tournament; in Ariosto, he is the host (Rajna, *Le fonti*, 281) — in both Grifone is present. See Charles Ross, "Damsel in Distress? Orrigille's Subjectivity," in *Fortune and Romance*, ed. Cavallo and idem, 175–90, for a detailed reading of the Boiardan episode. As for the Orco episode, the focal point of the Boiardan original, the exposure of a naked woman to the dangers of the sea in loose imitation of the myth of Andromeda, recurs in Ariosto, but displaced into the episode of Angelica exposed to a (feminine) Orca and rescued by Ruggiero and Orlando (that episode is, in turn, doubled by the addition of the parallel Olympia episode in 1532). Ariosto takes up hints from Boiardo to write the antefact of Lucina's danger as a variation on Odysseus' encounter with Polyphemus: Boiardo's Orco has no eyes, as against one (3.3.28) and he throws a mountain after his tormentors/victims as they escape by sea (55–58). See Rajna, *Le fonti*, 282; cf. Baldan, "Metamorfosi di un orco." Micocci, "La presenza della tradizione classica," 48–54, demonstrates that Boiardo already had the Homeric model clearly in mind.

intriguing, from the perspective of this study, is that the *narrative* interlace of the stories of the Orco, Lucina, and Norandino, with those of Grifone and Orrigille, as well as of the monstrous Orrilo, is already in place in the *Innamorato*: what we do not find there are the topically historical interpolations, nor the further juxtaposition of these tales with the siege of Paris. This last addition also tends to historicize the material of romance by bringing it into contact with an epic world (on the one hand the Carolingian "matter of France," and on the other the Vergilian poetry of imperial Rome) which embraces the great sweep of military and political history.

Let me begin a specific illustration of the differences between the *Furioso* and the *Innamorato* by juxtaposing two passages whose content is analogous, but which, as we shall see, occupy very different positions structurally in their respective poems, and consequently establish very different relations to the historical world:

> But while I sing, redeemer God [Iddio redentore], I see all Italy on fire, because these French — so valiant! — come to lay waste who knows what land, so I will leave this hopeless love of simmering Fiordespina. Some other time, if God permits, I'll tell you all there is to this. (3.9.26)[35]

The stanza is the very last of the *Innamorato*. The pathos of this passage which signals the poem's premature end derives from the clear sense that historical events — the opening of the so-called "Italian crisis" with the invasion of the peninsula by the French king, Charles VIII, in 1494 — have overtaken Boiardo and his poem in ways he did not anticipate and that he clearly found unbearable. Such events have no coherent relation with the world of the poem, from which they have, until this decisive point of rupture, largely been excluded.[36] That is not to say that the *Innamorato* does not have a cultural role and hence a fundamentally political, or at least ideological, meaning, but rather that that role

---

[35] "Mentre che io canto, o Iddio redentore, / vedo la Italia tutta a fiama e a foco / per questi Galli, che con gran valore / vengon per disertar non so che loco; / però vi lascio in questo vano amore / de Fiordespina ardente a poco a poco; / un'altra fiata, se mi fia concesso / racontarovi il tutto per espresso." Citations of the *Orlando innamorato* are taken from the Bruscagli edition cited above, n.19. Translations are taken from Ross's edition, cited in n. 6. Citations of the 1532 *Furioso* are from Bigi (see n. 1 above); citations of the 1516 and 1521 *Furioso* are from Ludovico Ariosto, *Orlando furioso*, ed. Santorre Debenedetti and Cesare Segre (Bologna: Commissione per i testi di lingua, 1960). Translations of the *Furioso* and other Ariostan texts are my own.

[36] Cf. Bigi, ed., *Orlando furioso*, 26, 40; Casadei, *La strategia delle varianti*, 9–10.

and that meaning reflect the relative stability and compactness of Ferrarese and Italian culture in the later Quattrocento.[37]

Consider by contrast the proem of *Furioso*, canto 17:

> When our sins have passed beyond the limits of remission, God the just often gives reign to atrocious tyrants and to monsters — endowing them with the force and the wit to do evil — in order to show that his justice is equal to his mercy. (1.1–6)[38]

A lengthy list of classical tyrants is then presented, followed by the observation that in this way God also punished late antique Italy, but with barbarian invaders rather than with home-grown monsters, invaders who "made the earth fat with blood — [thus God] gave Italy in distant days as prey to the Huns and Lombards and Goths" (2.6–8). Finally, the poet observes that the situation has not changed much in his own day, when the Italian peninsula is afflicted *both* by tyrants *and* by foreigners:

> Of this we have not only in ancient times but also in our own clear proof, when to us, useless and ill-born flocks, he gives as guardians enraged wolves: to whom it seems that their hunger is not great enough nor their bellies capacious enough for such meat — and so they call wolves with even more ravenous appetites from beyond the mountains to devour us.... Now God permits that we should be punished by peoples perhaps worse than ourselves on account of our multiple, endless, nefarious, damnable errors. A time will come when to despoil *their* shores *we* will go, if ever we become better and if their sins should reach those limits which move the eternal Good to wrath. (3.5–8, 4.1–4, 5.1–8)[39]

---

[37] On the cultural politics of Boiardo's milieu, see Bertoni, *Biblioteca estense*; Chiappini, *Gli Estensi*; Gundersheimer, *Style of a Renaissance Despotism*; Bruscagli, "Ventura e inchiesta"; idem, "Introduzione"; Tuohy, *Herculean Ferrara*; Stephen J. Campbell, *Cosmè Tura of Ferrara: Style, Politics, and the Renaissance City* (New Haven/London: Yale University Press, 1997); Odoardo Rambaldi, "Lo stato estense e Matteo Maria Boiardo," in *Il Boiardo e il mondo estense nel Quattrocento*, ed. Anceschi and Matarrese, 549–606; Jody Cranston, "Commemoration, Self-Representation, and the Fiction of Constancy in Este Court Portrayal," in *Fortune and Romance*, ed. Cavallo and Ross, 271–77.

[38] "Il giusto Dio, quando i peccati nostri / hanno di remission passato il segno, / acciò che la giustizia sua dimostri / uguale alla pietà, spesso dà regno / a tiranni atrocissimi et a mostri / e dà lor forza e di mal fare ingegno."

[39] "Di questo abbian non pur al tempo antiquo; / ma ancora al nostro, chiaro esperimento, / quando a noi, greggi inutili e mal nati, / ha dato per guardian lupi arrabbiati: / a cui non par ch'abbi a bastar lor fame, / ch'abbi il lor ventre a capir tanta

Though more obvious literary precursors than Boiardo for these lines are Petrarch and Dante,[40] Ariosto does clearly refer to the series of devastating historical events, the Italian wars set in motion by Charles's invasion, which by his time had far exceeded in horror anything Boiardo could have imagined twenty years earlier. Again like Boiardo, he invokes divine causality ("Iddio redentore" / "Il giusto Dio") to explain and, perhaps, to remedy those events.

Despite the similarities in content, however, what is most striking is the very different formal positions that this material has in the two poems. The terminal outburst of Boiardo has only one precedent in the *Innamorato*, which also comes at the end of a large textual unit and presents itself as a formal rupture (2.31.49).[41] By contrast, a relatively large number of Ariostan proems treat analogous topics, usually linking them very closely to the specific circumstances of Ferrara and the Este (e.g., 14.1–19; 15.1–2; 34.1–3).

---

carne; / e chiaman lupi di più ingorde brame / da boschi oltramontani a divorarne . . . / Or Dio consente che noi sian puniti / da populi da noi forse peggiori, / per li multiplicati et infiniti / nostri nefandi, obbrobriosi errori. / Tempo verrà ch'a depredar lor liti / andremo noi, se mai saren migliori, / e che i peccati lor giungano al segno, / che l'eterna Bontà muovano a sdegno."

[40] For Petrarch see, for example, *Rime Sparse*, canzone 128, "Italia mia, benché il parla sia indarno" (see esp. 2.39–41): "Or dentro a una gabbia / fiere selvagge et mansuete gregge / s'annidan sì che sempre il miglior geme," as well as the iterated motif of foreign invasion met by the ineptitude of Italian princes. This and all other quotations from Petrarch are taken from Francesco Petrarca, *Rime, Trionfi, e Poesie latine*, ed. Ferdinando Neri et al. (Milan-Naples: Ricciardi, 1951). For Dante see, for instance, *Paradiso 27,* esp. ll. 55–59: "In veste di pastor lupi rapaci / si veggion di qua su per tutti i paschi: / o difesa di Dio, perchè pur giaci? / Del sangue nostro Caorsini e Guaschi / s'apparecchian di bere. . . ." This and all other quotations from Dante are taken from Dante Alighieri, *La Commedia secondo l'antica volgata*, ed. Giorgio Petrocchi (Milan: Mondadori, 1966). Behind Dante, of course, is Christ's indictment in the Sermon on the Mount of false prophets as "wolves in sheep's clothing" (Matthew 7:15; cf. Jeremiah 23:1). The relevance of the anti-clerical strain in these precursor texts will become apparent as we proceed.

[41] This is the penultimate stanza of Book 2 and apparently refers to the war with Venice in 1482. The first edition of the poem was published in 1482 or 1483 (cf. Ross, ed., *Orlando innamorato*, "Introduction," 14) and the third book was not added until significantly later and was published only after the author's death. In any case, this earlier interruption of poetic narrative by military crisis simply confirms Boiardo's reluctance to textualize historical violence. On the importance of the Venetian materials for Ariosto, see Sestan, "Gli Estensi e il loro stato"; Casadei, *La strategia delle varianti*; and Dennis Looney, "Ariosto's Ferrara: A National Identity between Fact and Fiction," *Comparative and General Literature* 39 (1990–1991): 25–34.

In short, Ariosto introduces structural means for representing within his poem, in continuity with its fictions, the historical violence that threatens him, his city, his patrons. Such means are, by contrast, virtually absent from the *Innamorato*. In the particular case under consideration, the poet's reflections on his own time grow out of Rodomonte's destructive rampage inside the walls of Carolingian Paris. Along with the adoption of a formal mechanism to facilitate the textualization of violence goes an intertextual recourse to literary topoi and to specific textual models for representing such material. The phenomenon of internal tyranny and external invasion is made familiar by placing it in a sequence of historical examples well known from much humanist literature; the attempt to explain God's apparently incomprehensible toleration of evil as a "divine scourge" is equally commonplace. More specifically, the plea for divine mercy on behalf of ravaged Italy goes back to Petrarch's "Italia mia, benchè il parlar sia indarno" (*Rime Sparse* 128), the canzone also cited by Machiavelli at the end of the *Principe* in exhortation of the Medici princes (chapter 26). We will soon see that the subsequent apostrophe to Leo X and company blends elements from two Petrarchan *canzoni* and his *Trionfo della Fama*, as well as invoking a complex network of Dantean intertexts.

The degree to which the proem draws upon prior textual sources in the representation of historical material already suggests that Ariosto's confrontation with history is heavily mediated and qualified, in a way that buffers him and his poem from the shock of violent, direct encounter that resonates in the last stanza of the *Innamorato*. In the proem alone we find indications of a strong parodic motive, characteristic of what Pocock has called the "Machiavellian moment", that undercuts the theological politics of Dante and Petrarch. Rather than imagining a divinely inspired political redeemer who will restore Italy to virtue and political stability, Ariosto simply foresees a day when Italians will get to take their historical turn as violent scourges to the peoples who now devastate the Italic peninsula — violence begets reciprocal violence in an endless spiral of unredeemable devastation — in a vision far more cynical than Machiavelli's.[42]

I now want to suggest how this complex process of acknowledging, textualizing, and ironizing historical-political crisis is subsequently played out in the interlaced structure of the canto, thus subordinating the movement of Ariostan narrative to an allusive political critique that gives specific shape — as it were, a local habitation and a name — to what the proem to canto 17 states in the most general terms. Already the transition from narrative strand to narrative

---

[42] This is not the only historical proem with a subversive agenda. A suggestive example, as Durling, *Figure of the Poet*, 140–44, noted some time ago, is the proem to canto 14 (stanzas 1–10).

strand is suggestive. At stanza 17, the narrator says that he wants to exchange the rage and death of the pagan-Christian battles for something more pleasant, a tale set in the Edenic city-garden of Damascus, which at first seems to be the anti-type of besieged Paris:

> For God's sake, my Lord, let us cease to speak of wrath and to sing of death . . . ; because the time has come to return to where I left Grifone, having arrived at the gates of Damascus with Orrigille and . . . her lover [Martano]. Damascus is said to be among the richest cities of the Levant, and among the most populous and most ornate. Seven days' distance from Jerusalem it lies, in a fruitful and abundant plain, no less jocund in the winter than in the summer. . . . Through the city two crystalline rivers run, watering an infinite number of gardens, which never lack either flowers or fronds. (17.1–2, 5–8; 18.1–6; 19.1–4)[43]

Before we know it, however, Grifone and company are listening to the story-within-the-story of the Orco's savage cannibalism. Shortly thereafter the festive tournament of Norandino dissolves into a slaughter virtually indistinguishable from that taking place inside Paris,[44] when the Syrian king mistakenly attempts to punish Grifone for the pusillanimous behavior of the treacherous Martano, Orrigille's latest lover (passed off as a brother to her feckless suitor) who had recently disgraced himself at Damascus while disguised in armor stolen from Grifone (17.116.8). Already at the end of canto 16, the Ariostan narrator had focused the reader's attention on the paradoxical process by which the representation of inhuman destruction gives rise to the pleasures of poetic verse: "He hears the din, views the horrible signs / of cruelty, the human members scattered. / No more now — come back another time, / you who gladly listen to this lovely tale [istoria]" (89.5–8).[45] In fact, the "bella istoria" — which in the proem to canto 17 comes to mean both story and history — does not depart for

---

[43] "Ma lasciam, per Dio, Signore, ormai / di parlar d'ira e di cantar di morte; / . . . / che tempo è ritornar dov'io lasciai / Grifon, giunto a Damasco in su le porte / con Orrigille perfida, e con quello / ch'adulter era, e non di lei fratello. / De le piú ricche terre di Levante, / de le piú popolose e meglio ornate / si dice esser Damasco, che distante / siede a Ierusalem sette giornate, / in un piano fruttifero e abondante, / non men giocondo il verno, che l'estate . . . / Per la città duo fiumi cristallini / vanno inaffiando per diversi rivi / un numero infinito di giardini, / non mai di fior, non mai di fronde privi . . . "

[44] Pampaloni, "La guerra nel *Furioso*," 644–49; La Monica, "Realtà storica," 330–31.

[45] "Ode il rumor, vede gli orribil segni / di crudeltà, l'umane membra sparte. / Ora non più: ritorni un'altra volta / chi voluntier la bella istoria ascolta."

long from a violence that overtly mimics the invasiveness of foreign armies mixed with the failure of leadership that we have just been told characterizes the contemporary Italian scene.

The structural crux of canto 17, however, is the placement of the episode of Norandino, Lucina, and the Orco in between the proem and the narrator's long digression on the evils of warfare among Christians that has led to Italy's present subjection. In this tale, Ariosto elaborates on the Boiardan intertext to create a knowing conflation of the Homeric Polyphemus with Jack-and-the-Beanstalk and the pastoral tradition.[46] The ostensible purposes of the story are, at one level, to justify the celebratory tournament of Norandino by recounting how he and Lucina were finally reunited and, at another, to complete one more of Boiardo's unfinished narratives as part of the project of continuing and bringing to closure the *Innamorato*. But the episode has a thoroughly overdetermined place in the *Furioso*'s economy of interlace, bearing a significant relationship to several different narrative and thematic strands of the poem. For instance, it clearly constitutes a diptych with the earlier episode of the monstrous female Orca devouring a series of naked female victims tied to a cliff. Furthermore, by making the Orco a shepherd who plays pastoral ditties on his "sambuca" or "zampogna," Ariosto places him in a long line of peculiar poet-figures who traverse the poem (17.35.8 and 47.5–8).[47]

What I will highlight now, however, is the calculating way that the episode echoes the political imagery of the proem, and also anticipates the later authorial digression, forming a kind of fictional bridge between the two moments when contemporary history intrudes into the canto. The Orco as "blind monster [mostro cieco]" (33) recalls the "tiranni atrocissimi et . . . mostri" (1) to whom God periodically gives reign. Moreover, since this monster is also a shepherd, a "pastor" (32.8, 34.6, 47.8, 54.6), he enters into the metaphorics of pastoral care that were used to characterize the failed leadership of contemporary Italy (3.5–8). In other words, the political violence which Ariosto sees ravaging the historical world, and which he repeatedly describes as a cannibalistic devouring of human flesh and blood (2.6, 3.7–4.8), is surprisingly echoed by the Orco who feasts on the flesh of Norandino's men (35).

The political significance of the Orco's cannibalism is given further stress by a verbal echo from one of Dante's most terrifying depictions of the spiritual consequences of the civil wars ravaging the Italian peninsula in his own day: the vision of the deposed Pisan leader, Count Ugolino, gnawing away at the skull

---

[46] Rajna, *Le fonti*, 282–84; Baldan, *Metamorfosi*, 29 et passim; Micocci, "La presenza della tradizione classica," 48–54.

[47] Cf. Ascoli, *Ariosto's Bitter Harmony*, 392 and n. 228.

of his archenemy Ruggieri, Archbishop of Pisa, in *Inferno* cantos 32 and 33. Emilio Bigi, in his excellent commentary on the *Furioso*, notes that the verse which describes Norandino returning to the cave to be near the hapless Lucina after his own Odysseus-like escape is a transformation of a famous line which hints that Ugolino may have devoured his own children: Ariosto's "poté la pietà piú che 'l timore" ("devotion did more than fear": 48.5) clearly echoing Dante's "piú che 'l dolor, poté il digiuno" ("hunger did more than sorrow": *Inferno* 33.75). Taken together with the proem these echoes could be said to constitute nothing more than a lingering memory of historical violence in the poem, with the additional, and non-trivial, irony that the Orco, whose solicitousness toward his flock is what permits Norandino's escape and who "mai femina . . . non divora" ("never eats women": 40.8) is considerably more discriminating and civilized than the monsters and "enraged wolves" running amok in Italy. That the episode has a more precise, and scandalous, political meaning, however, becomes apparent in the next formal segment of the canto.

As the narrator closes this episode and turns back to Norandino reestablished in Damascus, he almost immediately enters into a lengthy topical digression, occasioned by the observation that in that time the Syrian Moslems were armed like the European Christians:

> The Syrians in those days had the custom of arming themselves in the fashion of the West. Perhaps they were led to it by the continuous proximity of the French, who then ruled the holy place where omnipotent God lived in the flesh — and which now the proud and miserable Christians, to their everlasting discredit, left in the hands of [pagan] dogs (73).[48]

This indictment then gives way to a tirade against internecine Christian conflicts and particularly the wars, led by the Spanish and French, which have subjugated and humiliated Italy:

> If you want to be called "Most Christian" and you others "Most Catholic," why do you kill the men of Christ? Why are they despoiled of their goods? Why do you not take back Jerusalem? . . . Are you, Spain, not near to Africa, which has offended you far more than this Italy? And

[48] "Soriani in quel tempo aveano usanza / d'armarsi a questa guisa di Ponente. / Forse ve gli inducea la vicinanza / che de' Franceschi avean continuamente, / che quivi allor reggean la sacra stanza / dove in carne abitò Dio onnipotente; / ch'ora i superbi e miseri cristiani, / con biasimi lor, lascian in man de' cani."

> yet, to increase the poor wretch's travail, you abandon your first, so lovely, enterprise. O stinking bilge, full of every vice, you sleep, drunkard Italy — and does it not weigh on you that, once served by this people and by that, you are now their handmaiden? (75.1–5, 76.1–8)[49]

This attack on the internal wars of European Christians, with its call for a reconciling Crusade against the pagan Other, has, again, an obvious Petrarchan precedent, and perhaps a Dantean intertext as well.[50]

The digression culminates in an apostrophe, both monitory and hortatory, to Pope Leo X, during whose papacy both the first (1516) and second (1521) editions of the *Furioso* appeared, and whose imprimatur authorized its publication.[51] The narrator addresses Leo as the the one leader who could both

---

[49] "Se Cristianissimi esser voi volete, / e voi altri Catolici nomati, / perché di Cristo gli uomini uccidete? / perché de' beni lor son dispogliati? / Perché Ierusalem non riavete . . . / . . . / Non hai tu, Spagna, l'Africa vicina, / che t'ha via più di questa Italia offesa? / E pur, per dar travaglio alla meschina, / lasci la prima tua sì bella impresa. / O d'ogni vizio fetida sentina, / dormi, Italia imbriaca, e non ti pesa / ch'ora di questa gente, ora di quella / che già serva ti fu, sei fatta ancella?"

[50] The last two lines of stanza 73, and first four of stanza 75, clearly derive from Petrarch's *Trionfo della Fama*, 2.137–144: "poi venia solo il buon duce Goffrido / che fe' l'impresa santa e' passi giusti. / Questo (di ch'io mi sdegno e indarno grido) / fece in Jerusalem colle sue mani / il mal guardato e già negletto nido; / gite superbi, o miseri Cristiani / consumando l'un l'altro, e non vi caglia / che 'l sepolcro di Cristo è in man dei cani." Note especially the cannibalistic motif in the Petrarchan original ("consumando l'un l'altro") that suggests an associative link to the Orco episode. The passage, incidentally, may well have been an inspiration for Tasso's *magnum opus, Gerusalemme liberata.* Also relevant, however, are these lines spoken by the false counselor, Guido da Montefeltro, in Dante's *Inferno* 27.85–90: "Lo principe d'i novi Farisei, / avendo preso guerra presso a Laterano, / e non con Saracin né con Giudei, / ché ciascun suo nemico era cristiano / e nessun era stato a vincer Acri / né mercatante in terra di Soldano." The Dantean connection becomes more evident when Ariosto brings the papacy into picture at stanza 79, and with it additional echoes of the *Commedia.* See also n. 40 above.

[51] Leo's license to publish is given in a prefatory letter to the 1516 edition signed by the humanist Jacopo Sadoleto and dated 27 March 1516. That letter in turn was based on a version drafted by Ariosto's friend Pietro Bembo, dated 20 June 1515. The license was then renewed in 1521. The licenses are described in Giuseppe Agnelli and Giuseppe Ravegnani, *Annali delle edizioni ariostee* (Bologna: Zanichelli, 1933), 1: 17–21. Catalano, *Vita*, gives the background (1: 428) and reprints Bembo's letter (document 256, in 2: 149–50). I am indebted to Dennis Looney for bringing this information to my attention and for a number of other useful suggestions that have made a significant impact on this essay.

protect the Italian peninsula against her neighbors and, presumably, redirect European energies into a new Crusade:

> You, great Leo [gran Leone=Lion], on whom presses the heavy burden of the keys to heaven — do not allow Italy to be swallowed up in sleep, if you have your hands in her hair. You are Shepherd; and God has given you that staff to carry and has chosen that fierce name, so that you might roar, and raise up your arms, in order to defend your flock from wolves (79).[52]

Leo is explicitly treated as a potential force for good, a pastoral protector of sheep from ravening beasts, a presumed antidote to the "enraged wolves" who now guard the "useless and ill-born flocks" of Italy. Curiously, however, this apostrophe is immediately preceded by a reference to the Donation of Constantine, the spurious document by which the Emperor Constantine had allegedly ceded political jurisdiction over the Western Empire to the bishop of Rome (78.3–4). The point explicitly made is that the Germans and other ravagers of Italy should seek Roman wealth in the East, where Constantine moved it at the transfer of imperial riches from Rome to the Empire's new capital, Byzantium. Nonetheless, we can hardly miss its allusive relevance to the perennial critique of the papal usurpation and abuse of secular authority, which was developed by Dante (especially *Inferno* 19.90–116 and 27.55–111; *Paradiso* 27.40–66), Petrarch (*Liber sine nomine*), Valla (*De falsa et ementita donatione Constantini*), and even Ariosto elsewhere in the *Furioso* (34.80). Such a critique, it need hardly be said, was now more pressing than ever, in the aftermath of Alexander VI's nepotistic imperialism (1492–1503) and Julius II's adventurism, and on the eve of the Lutheran Reform.

---

[52] "Tu, gran Leone, a cui premon le terga / de le chiavi del ciel le gravi some, / non lasciar che nel sonno si sommerga / Italia, se la man l'hai ne le chiome. / Tu sei Pastore; e Dio t'ha quella verga / data a portare, e scelto il fiero nome, / perché tu ruggi, e che le braccia stenda, / sì che dai lupi il gregge tuo difenda." There is another Petrarchan echo here, this time from *Rime Sparse* 53.10–14, 19–23: "Che s'aspetti non so, né che s'agogni / Italia, che suoi guai non par che senta, / vecchia oziosa e lenta; / dormirà sempre et non fia chi la svegli? / Le man l'avess'io avolto entro' capegli / . . . / ma non senza destino a le tue braccia / che scuoter forte et sollevar la ponno / è or commesso nostro capo Roma. / Pon man in quella venerabil chioma / securamente, et ne le trecce sparte, / si che la neghittosa esca dal fango." As we shall see, however, Dante is a far stronger presence — consider, for example, the echoes of the passages cited previously in notes 40 and 50 above, both of which specifically link Italy's predicament to the failures of the papacy, as the Petrarch does not, at least not in the two canzoni echoed by Ariosto.

What we may also have noticed, simply from reading through the passage just cited, is that it contains a subterranean yet distinctive thematic, and even verbal, connection to the Orco episode with which it is so closely juxtaposed by the magic of Ariostan interlace. That juxtaposition brings with it an irony that reverses the basically hopeful thrust of the passage, turning Leo from potential solution into part of the problem delineated both in the digression and in the proem before it: "You are Shepherd [Tu sei *Pastore*]; and God has given you that staff to carry and has chosen that fierce name [scelto il *fiero* nome]." Like the Orco, Leo is a shepherd with a capacity for bestial ferocity. In retrospect, the reference to the pope's role as keeper of the "keys of heaven" connects with the pastoral Orco who "opened and closed [apriva e tenea chiuso]" the sheepfold (34.7). Both images derive from the passage in Matthew (16: 18–19), where Jesus confers "papal" powers on Peter: "thou art Peter and upon this rock I will build my church and the gates of Hell will not prevail against it. And I will give thee the keys of . . . heaven. And whatsoever you thou shalt bind upon the earth, it shall be bound also in heaven; and whatsoever thou shalt loose upon the earth, it shall be loosed also in heaven." The two principal tropes of the passage (of the keys and of loosing and binding) were often conflated in a composite figure of locking and opening, as in these lines from Dante's *Purgatorio* (the speaker is an angel): "I hold these [two keys] from Peter, who told me that I should err rather in opening [the gate] than in keeping it locked" ("Da Pier le tegno; e dissemi ch'i'erri / anzi ad aprir ch'a tenerla serrata": 9.127–128). Even more to our point, the biblical passage was regularly invoked to suggest the *abuse* by popes of their sacred office, particularly for purposes of simonistic profiteering (e.g., *Inferno* 19.97–205) and, notably, of waging war against fellow Christians. Dante has St. Peter pronounce the following anti-papal screed: "It was not our intention that on the right hand of our successor a part of the Christian people should sit, while the others sit on the other side, nor that the keys which were given to me should become the device on a battle-standard raised against baptized souls" ("Non fu nostra intenzione ch'a destra mano / d'i nostri successori parte sedesse, / parte dall'altra del popol cristiano; / né che le chiavi che mi fuor concesse, / divenisser signaculo in vessillo / che contra battezzati combattesse": *Paradiso* 27.46–51; cf. *Inferno* 27.100–105).

All of these potentially subversive elements were in place in the first, 1516, edition of the *Furioso,* when what we are calling canto 17 was in fact canto 15. For the 1521 edition, Ariosto made a small but crucial revision to his text that brought out the full force of the equation between the Orco and the Pope. To the first allusive reference linking the Orco to Dante's Ugolino and Ruggieri, he added a second (not noted by Bigi) in the preceding stanza. In 1516, stanza 47, line 8, reads: "the horrible shepherd [orribile pastor] who follows behind them." In 1521 it has become: "the fierce shepherd [fier pastor] who came along behind them." The phrase "fier pastor" ("fierce shepherd": 47.8) recalls Ugolino's first, explicitly cannibalistic, appearance: "la bocca sollevò dal *fiero pasto*" ("he raised his mouth from the fierce meal": *Inferno* 33.1; emphasis added). The change renders plain the thematic connection that motivated the original allusion by restoring the motif of bestial hunger excised in the shift from Dante's "piú che 'l dolor, poté il digiuno" to Ariosto's "poté la pietà piú che 'l timore." The shift from "pasto" to "pastor" brings with it a calculated comic irony, at once focusing attention on the Orco's cannibalism and on the fact that the monster actually is — as far as his sheep are concerned — a "good shepherd."

The force of the added phrase, however, is not confined to its significance within the confines of the Orco episode proper: it has a broader intratextual resonance as well, one which will become obvious if we consider again the apostrophe to Leo: "You are Shepherd [Tu sei Pastore]; and God has given you that staff to carry and has chosen that fierce name [fiero nome], so that you might roar [perché tu ruggi], and raise up your arms, in order to defend your flock from wolves." Separated by a single line we find the two constituent elements of the Orcan epithet, "fier pastor [fierce shepherd]."[53] The further element of a roaring ("perché tu ruggi" ["so that you may roar": 79.7]) may evoke Dante's treacherous ecclesiastic, Ruggieri, now cast as Leo's spiritual ancestor.[54] The pope with an animal's name is thus grotesquely metamorphosed into an alter ego of the monstrous Orco. In his case, however, the irony of the allusion is single and devastating: where the Orco is both shepherd ("pastor") and cannibal ("pasto"), Leo, it would seem, is a "pastor" turned cannibal, a ravening wolf in shepherd's clothing.

The procedure of ironic qualification through Ariosto's amplified, historicized adaptation of romance interlace is then comically confirmed later in the canto when, in the narrative of Norandino's disastrous error, Orrigille's lover, Martano,

---

[53] The description of Leo in these terms was present from the first edition, raising the question of whether Ariosto was already at that stage obliquely echoing, consciously or not, *Inferno* 33.1. The question, of course, cannot be answered definitively. But the insertion of the locution "fier pastor" in 1521, with its evident connection both to the Dantean echo in stanza 48 and to the description of Leo in stanza 79, surely means that by 1521 the poet had recognized not only the possible allusion, but its full, violently anti-papal, implications.

[54] In an earlier martial proem, Ariosto speaks of Ippolito's defeat of another roaring lion, Venice: "quando al *leone*, in mar tanto feroce . . . faceste sì, ch'ancor *ruggier* l'oda" (15.2; emphasis added). As is often noted, the papacy and the Venetians were the primary threats to Ferrarese security in both Ariosto's time and Boiardo's, the two joining forces at the battle of Ravenna. See n. 41 above.

encased in the armor he has stolen from Grifone, is described as "he who put on a pelt not his own, like the jackass once did that of the lion" ("Colui ch'indosso il non suo cuoio, / come *l'asino* già quel del *leone*" [112]) — an Aesopian image which not only connects back to Norandino and company escaping from the Orco, à la Homer, wrapped in goat skins and slathered in ovine grease, but also, evidently, conjures the leonine, that is asinine, Leo as well.[55]

Dante's nightmare made real of eucharistic community turned to cannibalistic, neo-Theban civil war, in Pisa, Florence, and the Italian peninsula generally, is characteristically focused in the *Commedia* on the struggle between Guelf and Ghibelline, ecclesiastical and secular powers, as it clearly is in *Inferno* 27, 32, and 33 — and it is indeed out of this tradition that both the proem and the Ariostan digression of canto 17 emerge, with the additional pathos of their prescient prolepsis of the conflicts between the Catholic church and Protestant sects. The fantastic narrative of the *Furioso*, as filtered through the complex evolutions of Ariostan interlace, thus become the vehicle of an indirect, sheltered commentary, not only on the general political crisis of the day, but also on the specific complicity of the papacy in that crisis. Along with the public crises in Italy and Ferrara, of course, these passages may reflect a motive of personal revenge against the pope, from whom Ariosto had expected but not received patronage, a point to which I will return shortly.[56]

In political and military terms, Leo could become for Ariosto, and his Estense masters, a convenient focal point for a collection of problems in which he was complicitous, even though he could rarely be given exclusive blame for them. In the years leading from 1494 to the publication of the first *Furioso* in 1516 the parade of foreign intruders — French, Spanish, and imperial — had continued unabated. The years of Julius II's papacy had been especially dangerous for Ferrara. The Estense state was set precariously near the point of encounter

---

[55] The later episode is dotted with images that reinforce a connection to the earlier part of the canto — for example, Martano is twice linked with "lupi" (88.8; 91.3), while two of the "extras" in the tournament have names pointedly derived from the pastoral tradition: "Tirse e Corimbo" (96.3).

[56] Catalano, *Vita*, discusses Ariosto's relationship with Leo at length (vol. 1, esp. 352–87) and gives particular prominence to the Pope's failure to provide patronage (354–57, 385–87, 476). Ariosto discusses his disappointment in *Satire* 3, esp. ll. 82–105, 151–206, and 7.55–69, 88–114, while *Satires* 2, esp. ll. 1–9, 58–96, 196–234, and 4, esp. ll. 79–102, contain anti-clerical and anti-Medicean diatribes. See also note 61 below. On Ariosto's attitude toward the clergy in general, see Dionisotti, *Geografia e storia*; and Thomas F. Mayer, "Ariosto Anticlerical: Epic Poetry and the Clergy in Early Cinquecento Italy," in *Anticlericalism in Late Medieval and Early Modern Europe*, ed. Peter Kykema and Heiko Oberman (Leiden/New York/Köln: E.J. Brill, 1993), 238–97.

between the shifting macro-forces of France, Spain, the Emperor, Venice, Milan, and the papacy, and its territories were divided between those with traditional feudal attachments to the papacy (Ferrara itself) and to the Empire (Reggio and Modena). This season of the Italian wars culminated in the bloody battle of Ravenna in 1512 that pitted France and Ferrara against Julius, the Venetians, and the Spanish and which, despite victory, left the Estensi shaken.[57] In addition, Julius had been responsible for depriving the Este of two of their most cherished territorial holdings, Reggio and Modena, in 1510, and had repeatedly threatened to depose them from their rule over the papal fiefdom of Ferrara, as he had earlier done to the Montefeltro in Urbino. In the years leading up to 1516 the memory of these losses and threats, with which Giovanni de' Medici had been associated as papal legate in Bologna during the last years of Julius's reign, were still fresh. They were made more vivid still by Leo's bad faith in failing to restore Modena and Reggio to Este control despite promises to do so. The Medici pope's own direct attempts to unseat the Este would not come until 1519.[58] It may well be that the outbreak of open hostilities at that point at least partly accounts for the insertion of the key locution, "fier pastor," in the 1521 edition.

Though the proem and digression avoid local Ferrarese and Estense concerns (which are taken up elsewhere, at a safe remove from references to Leo), they certainly constitute the open recognition that what for Boiardo had appeared to be an apocalyptic disruption of social and political normalcy, for Ariosto and his generation had itself become the norm, a fact which Ariosto is able to confront in representable, and hence tolerable, form within the body of his text as his predecessor could not.[59] But Ariosto's politically charged use of interlace takes the poem's relation to its historical circumstances a step further — allowing a corrosive, structurally determined irony to play over the poet's apparently pious celebration of patrons and potentates, creating at least the illusion that the poem afforded a refuge and a point of vantage from which history could be viewed, interpreted, and contingently mastered. At the same time, the very evasiveness and indirection of Ariosto's political critique, which he willingly offers under cover of its opposite, namely a courtly encomium of those most to blame for Italy's ills, suggests precisely how precarious, inefficacious, and fundamentally illusory such mastery really is.

---

[57] Ariosto makes repeated reference to this battle, notably in the proem to canto 15 (1–10), as well as at 3.55 and 33.40–41. The battle and its effects on the peninsula as a whole are memorably recounted by Francesco Guicciardini in books 10 and 11 of the *Storia d'Italia*.

[58] For the impact of the Modena/Reggio question on Ariosto's relationship to Leo, see Catalano, *Vita*, 1: 387, 478, 490, 501, 533–34.

[59] Cf. *Figure of the Poet*, 134.

This point might be less compelling if the viciously ironic textualization of Leo X through his symbolic name in canto 17 should somehow prove to be an isolated incident in both the *Furioso* and the period as a whole. It is clearly not, however. Charles Stinger, among others, has shown the positive typological-symbolic valences that were attached to papal names in official documents and through public displays of the iconography of power.[60] In the *Satires*, Ariosto explicitly vents his feelings about Leo and the Church in terms close to those of canto 17, though far more explicit,[61] and in the *Furioso* itself the ekphrastic allegory of Avarice and Liberality in canto 26 clearly draws on the motifs of canto 17 to turn an apparent encomium of Leo into another allusive, structurally implied indictment, directed specifically against the decidedly illiberal Pope who failed to provide the poet Ariosto with patronage at a time when he desperately felt the need of it.[62]

---

[60] Stinger, *The Renaissance in Rome*, 91–92. Machiavelli's fox-lion symbolism derived from Dante and Cicero in *The Prince,* chap. 18, also conceals a veiled and highly ambivalent reference to Leo, from whom he too vainly sought liberating patronage: Albert Russell Ascoli, "Machiavelli's Gift of Counsel," in *Machiavelli and the Discourse of Literature*, ed. idem and V. Kahn (Ithaca: Cornell University Press, 1993), 219–57, esp. 242–45. Ariosto would later pick up the Machiavellian image in attacking the tyrannical rule of Leo's nephew, Lorenzo, Duke of Urbino, the dedicatee of *The Prince* (*Satire* IV.94–102, cf. 7–12). For additional discussion of Ariosto and Machiavelli, see Albert Russell Ascoli, "Faith as a Cover-Up: Ariosto's *Orlando furioso*, Canto 21, and Machiavellian Ethics," *I Tatti Studies* 8 (2000): 135–70.

[61] *Satire* 2 indicts all prelates, from priest to pope, of ambition and avarice, simony and nepotism. Lines 205 and following depict a generic pope who will "triumph, filthy with Christian blood" (221) and is prepared to "give Italy in prey to France or Spain" (223) recalling 17.3–5, 73–79. For pastoral metaphorics linked to Leo in one way or another, see 3.115–121; 4.7–12. For comparable animal imagery, see 2.2–3; 5.25; 7.49–54, 93. For plays on Leo's name, see 3.97; 4.9, 154–156; 7.88–93. Cf. also note 56 above. The *Satires* were not intended for immediate publication and hence were franker in their criticisms than the *Furioso*. See I. A. Portner, "A Non-Performance of *Il negromante*," *Italica* 59 (1982): 316–29, for the idea (not entirely persuasive) that Ariosto's *Negromante* was not performed in Rome because Leo saw in it an unflattering allusion to himself. On Leo's positive reaction to a Roman performance of Ariosto's *Suppositi* and to the *Negromante* episode, see Catalano, *Vita*, 1: 376–85.

[62] In the ekphrastic representation of an allegorical intaglio, Avarice, personified as a chimerical beast combining features of ass, wolf, lion, and fox, is depicted ravaging the world. Also depicted are European rulers from the early Cinquecento, including Leo, who slay the monster with their liberality (34.6; 36.1). The language in which Leo is presented, however, identifies him with the beast he ostensibly opposes. The worst depredations of the beast are among "cardinali e papi" and have "contaminated the lovely

The issue of patronage brings us to the crucial point that Leo is not the only historical figure textualized in this way, nor likely the most important from Ariosto's perspective. Leo's patronage had seemed especially valuable to Ariosto in the years leading up to the publication of the first *Furioso* because his patron at that time was Cardinal Ippolito d'Este, in whose service he remained until the Cardinal's departure for Hungary in 1517. Ippolito is the man to whom the *Furioso* is addressed and the object of its most fulsome and central encomia, most notably in cantos 3 and 46. However, Ippolito's failings as a patron, and in particular his inability to appreciate or adequately reward Ariosto's artistic talents, are the explicit subject of *Satire* 1 and of at least one embittered letter,[63] as well as of biographical legend. In *Ariosto's Bitter Harmony*, I argued that Ariosto's treatment of Ippolito is subjected to a systematic subversion throughout the *Furioso*,[64] and in particular that the etymological, and mythological, resonances of his classicizing name are, like Leo's, made into a key structuring principle of the poem.[65] I hope that the strong evidence that analogous procedures are

---

seat of Peter" (32.6–8). In language like that associated with pope and Orco in canto 17, the beast arrogates "the keys . . . of heaven and of the abyss" (33.7–8). The beast is part lion, while Leo appears depicted allegorically as his bestial namesake. Two of the other three animals that constitute Avarice, the wolf and the ass, also appear in canto 17. The intaglio depicts Leo in the curious act of biting the ass-ears of the monster (36.2). In the first, 1516, redaction the image is made even more curious by the ambiguous language in which it is described: "avea attaccate l'asinine orecchie." Since "attaccate" can mean "attached" as well as "attacked," we are free to see the ass-ears on Leo as much as on Avarice (cf. 17.112.2: "come l'asino già quel del leone"), with a possible allusion to the Ovidian Midas, the mythical paradigm of avarice with the ill-concealed asses' ears who, incidentally, is a very poor judge of art (*Metamorphoses* 11.146–193). For a reading of this ekphrasis in light of its interlace with the rest of canto 26, see Hoffman, "'Un così valoroso cavalliere'." For other examples of such bivalent grammatical constructions in the poem, see Ascoli, *Ariosto's Bitter Harmony*, 355–56 and 359–60 and n. 172.

[63] Letter #26 in Angelo Stella, ed., *Lettere di Ludovico Ariosto* (Verona: Mondadori, 1965). Catalano, *Vita*, documents Ariosto's relationship to Ippolito extensively; see esp. 1: 434–54.

[64] Cf. David Quint, *Origin and Originality in Renaissance Literature: Versions of the Source* (New Haven: Yale University Press, 1983), 88–89; Zatti, *Il "Furioso" tra epos e romanzo*, 147–49; Looney, "Ariosto's Ferrara." Durling, *Figure of the Poet*, 135–50, argues for the seriousness of the encomia, though with important qualifications. Baillet, "L'Ariosto et les princes d'Este," makes a less subtle case for this position.

[65] The symbolically charged imagery of "cavalleria" and horsemanship (Giamatti, "Headlong Horses"; Dalla Palma, "Le strutture narrative") is subtended by the classical myth of Hippolytus, with its thematics of blind desire and mad violence (Ascoli, *Ariosto's Bitter Harmony*, 382–89). Ariosto's procedure of fusing classical myths and contemporary

at work in canto 17 vis-à-vis Leo will lend greater credence to a case — Ippolito's — that is far more central to Ariosto's world at the time of the poem's first publication, and hence far more carefully relegated to the occulted byways of ironic interlace, than the one that occupies center stage in this essay.

Let us now return to the question of narrative structure with which I began. If *Orlando furioso* does indeed make a turn away from the openness of romance to the closure of epic — and in so doing identifies itself and its author closely with the ideological values and political interests of the Este court — nonetheless, the voice of resistance and of critique, oscillating between personal *ressentiment* and acute political analysis, still persists. We can locate it specifically at the points of juncture and fracture between the disparate elements, of history and fiction, narrative and commentary, story and figure, that the poet weaves together into a mobile web of shifting and reciprocally qualifying perspectives. Though it is easy enough to say that such an enterprise ultimately serves the master discourse of courtly ideology, it is also worth noting that no more direct criticism was possible, at least not in a form that commanded a significant readership. Ariosto could not have openly attacked the man upon whom he, and through him a large number of brothers and sisters, depended for their livelihood, a man who was known for his impetuous recourse to violent methods — no more than he could indict Leo openly in a poem destined for wide circulation in the Italian courts and which — as noted earlier — required and bore Leo's imprimatur for publication. In other words, for Ariosto and his contemporaries it was a choice between an occulted and perhaps therefore unhearable irony, and "the silence of the lambs," to take our poet's pastoral motif one, unpleasant, step further.

III. Conclusions

As suggested near the beginning of this essay, Ariosto extends the Boiardan practice of narrative *entrelacement* to include and to emphasize non-narrative formal elements. This technique permits the suggestive juxtaposition of Ariosto's chivalric fictions with the world of contemporary history, whose materials enter the poem through proems, ekphrases, prophecies, and other "asides." These juxtapositions are often not simply formal. That is, the proems often make explicit a moralizing analogy between the narratives of the poem and some contemporary issue of note. Usually, however, what is made explicit is culturally normative or positive, in the sense that the views expressed are compatible with those of a dominant culture, not that they are always or even mostly couched in the

---

persons with the poem's characters is described in Ceserani, "Due modelli," 485.

affirmative mode. Culturally negative or subversive outcomes are, on the whole, left implicit — at the level of structure. Attacks on patrons, or on figures of unassailable prestige, such as the pope, can be deduced only by an active interpretation of ostentatious formal features — such as those discussed above. Ariosto,therefore, can have it both ways. He can enjoy the patronage and cultural prestige that a poem celebrating chivalric values and Estense genealogy affords, while still engaging in an implied critique of those values and that regime.

Because the activity of critique is largely present in the form of structural possibility, and not as explicit utterance, it is always possible to doubt its existence as a product of authorial intention. And yet many of the formal features of the *Furioso*, including those just mentioned, seem gratuitous if such a critical counter-narrative is not being deployed through them. Nonetheless, though I would insist that these features do, in effect, insistently invite the sort of speculative reading that I have given to them, I would also argue that they cannot be treated as keys to a straightforward political allegory. Their interpretation is left to the individual reader's judgment and is thus ambiguous by nature. For example, the limited framework of this analysis offers two sets of polar oppositions through which to evaluate significance that would allow different interpreters to arrive at very different conclusions. One might stress the status of canto 17 as a serious interrogation of the causes and cures of political crisis, or one might insist on the personal and venal vendetta of Ariosto against the pope who failed to make good on promised patronage. One might see Ariosto's recourse to oblique and allusive techniques of political-social criticism as a cunningly subversive strategy, calculated to undermine the powers that be — or one could see it instead as a failure of nerve, as an unwillingness to stand up for what one believes, combined with a courtier's readiness to be appropriated by a power structure whose vices one knows all too well (cf. Castiglione, *Il libro del cortegiano*, especially 4.6–10). The reading offered here suggests that we should not be too quick to opt for either pole in either of the two oppositions just sketched. We might go further to imagine that Ariosto, among other things, is precisely dramatizing the conflicting motives that operate in a work such as his, making it at once petty and public-spirited, bold and pusillanimous. But even this "open" reading is guided by personal preferences (mine) rather than by any ultimate certainty about Ariosto's intentions.

Moreover, I should like to stress, it is not simply a question of what Ariosto did or did not wish to express. The formal innovations of the *Furioso* were not only a response to historical circumstances; they were also a response made available and even necessary by such circumstances. If Ariosto went beyond Boiardo, it was because Boiardo had taught him the basics and refinements of narrative interlace to which he could add the intertextual and historical dimensions that I have pointed to here. And if he was able to face historical crisis by textualizing it, this was because Vergil, among others, had already found a vehicle for doing so. This vehicle had not been fully available to Boiardo, but it was for Ariosto's culture — where the Latin humanist tradition was able to find more direct expression in Italian vernacular texts than it typically had in the previous century.[66] If he was able to explore the breakdown of the ideological givens of the Quattrocento and before — such as a theologically grounded politics, the secure differentiation between Christian and pagan, and so on — it was at least partly because external events had made the arbitrary nature of such assumptions all too apparent, as it had also made evident the need to recuperate, reform, and/or revolutionize them.

I hope it is clear by now that the formal innovations I have pointed to are freighted with ideological significance, that historically-determined ruptures in cultural meaning are making themselves felt at the level of form. Machiavelli, one might posit heuristically, faced much the same crisis as Ariosto, but tackled it directly at the semantic level, while Ariosto's response was preponderantly syntactic and formal.[67] But such an opposition falsifies both the complex rhetoricity of Machiavelli and the high political content of the *Furioso*. The theoretical claim of this essay, then, is that the opposition — common equally to "textualist" and "historicist" scholarship — between structure and history, form and content, is both false and pernicious. Historical understanding moves through formal analysis; form is bound inextricably to history.

As a final consideration, let me suggest that a historical analysis of the *Furioso's* form which is also a formal analysis of the poem's representations of history will necessarily do for the transition from the first and second, forty-canto, editions (1516 and 1521) to the final, forty-six-canto, version of 1532 what I have

---

[66] Due exception made for Poliziano's *Stanze per la Giostra* and *Favola d'Orfeo*. Recent work by Looney, *Compromising the Classics*; idem, "Erodoto dalle *Storie* al Romanzo," in *Il Boiardo e il mondo estense*, ed. Anceschi and Matarrese, 429–41; and Tristano (in this volume, 129–68) has stressed the significant humanistic dimension in Boiardo's career. As noted earlier, criticism has shown consistent engagement in the *Innamorato* with not only Ovid but also Vergil and other classical poets (n. 19 above). Still, there is a world of difference between, say, Boiardo's translation of a Latin translation of Herodotus and Machiavelli's detailed, if idiosyncratic, commentary on Livy, or between Boiardo's occasional Vergilian allusions and Ariosto's adaptation of a Vergilian model (on the last point see n. 14 above). Bruscagli, "Introduzione," argues convincingly that Boiardo deliberately subordinates his use of classical and canonical vernacular materials (e.g., Boccaccio) to the world of Carolingian romance, which may account for the differences from Ariosto, who ostentatiously imitates the classics.

[67] See also Ascoli, "Faith as a Cover-Up."

already done for the shift from the *Innamorato* to the first *Furioso*. While I do not have the space to include extended reflections on this topic here, my sharp focus on the figures of Leo and Ippolito invites speculation on the crucial fact that by 1532 the former had been dead for eleven years and the latter for twelve. By the final edition, references to these two, and to many other people and events, had lost most of the topical, historical force they had had in 1516 or even 1521.[68] Yet Leo and Ippolito retain, and even expand, their decisive structural-thematic roles in 1532, suggesting how basic they had been to the internal structure of the poem from its inception. Defunct or not, Leo still remains the focus of cantos 17 and 26; while the late Ippolito continues as the poem's explicit dedicatee and the focal point of the principal Este encomia, especially in cantos 3 and 46.[69] This is so, notwithstanding increased references to Ariosto's second patron, Duke Alfonso d'Este, and to the Emperor Charles V, the figure who dominated Italian and European politics in the 1520s and 1530s as Julius and Leo had during the first twenty years of the century.

The tendency of the final *Furioso* to include figures from different historical moments side by side, referring to them in a newly generalized present tense that belies historical chronology and topicality, has been aptly dubbed "synchronization" by Alberto Casadei.[70] Against Casadei's insistence on the full historical engagement of the 1532 edition, however, I would argue that this process furthers the larger process of the textualization of history at work in the first *Furioso* by reinforcing the reader's sense of a poetic temporality increasingly distinct from historical chronology. This point then leads us toward the distinctly unfashionable notion that the 1516 edition was more immediately a response to historical crisis than the final version.[71]

It has been a topos of Ariosto criticism that the 1532 poem is more aware of crisis than its precursor,[72] but, as we have seen, that is only partially true. Historically, in fact, the 1520s and early 1530s were less immediately threatening

---

[68] Casadei, *La strategia delle varianti*, 17 n. 20, astutely observes that the changed context of the 1532 edition changes the significance of segments that are not changed in themselves — the notion deserves considerable attention and development.

[69] The changes in the treatment noted by Casadei, *La strategia delle varianti*, 24–27, 55, 75–76, are significant but do not alter Ippolito's fundamental place in the poem.

[70] Casadei, *La strategia delle varianti*, 50–56, 153.

[71] See Henderson, "The First *Orlando furioso*," for an interesting attempt to demonstrate Ariosto's hypersensitivity to his immediate historical context during various phases of composition of the first *Furioso*.

[72] E.g., Caretti, "Codicillo ariostesco"; Saccone, "Prospettive"; but cf. Bigi, ed., *Orlando furioso*, 33; and Ascoli, *Ariosto's Bitter Harmony*, 9–10 contra.

to Ferrara and to Ariosto personally than the earlier period.[73] Furthermore, by 1532 the outlines were emerging of a new order, social and political, that tended to guarantee stability for the Italian peninsula, even if at the cost of the loss of political autonomy and of a certain openness of cultural possibilities that had been a *conditio sine qua non* for the achievements of such as Machiavelli and Ariosto.[74] The underlying point is that the crisis that dominated the first two decades of the sixteenth century was such not only because it was a time of military-political upheaval — in this sense, it is hard to find a time in human history which is not in crisis — but also because it saw a radical destabilization of ideological assumptions, of naturalized cultural boundaries (Bourdieu's *doxa*).[75] By the time of the appearance of the third *Furioso* the project of ideological recuperation and reinstantiation was well under way — brilliantly represented by such transitional works as Castiglione's *Cortegiano* and Bembo's *Prose della volgar lingua*.[76]

Nonetheless, although the 1532 edition is a far less direct product and representation of historical crisis than the 1516 edition, it is, for this very reason,

---

[73] To this extent I agree with Casadei, *La strategia delle varianti*, 154, who distinguishes between the local Ferrarese concerns in 1516 and the national, Italian concerns of 1532. However, in doing so he trivializes 17.73–79 (41) and understates the international character of the battles that were being fought in and around Este territory, thus misunderstanding the significance of a crisis of the local (nothing less than the end of a way of life in the peninsula based on small regional states — Ferrara, Urbino, Florence, to name just a few).

[74] In 1532 the long-term negative outcome of the epoch of crisis in the peninsula was clearly visible — Italy was at the mercy of foreign invaders and especially the Emperor Charles V; the papacy's authority was under attack by Lutheran reforms and subject to the violent indignity of the Sack of Rome; and so on. Yet Ariosto and Ferrara were rather better off than they had been in 1516, not to mention the late 'teens when the dark *Cinque Canti* were apparently composed (see Casadei, "Alcune considerazioni"; David Quint, "Introduction," in *Cinque Canti / Five Cantos of Ludovico Ariosto* [Berkeley: University of California Press, 1996], 1–44; and Zatti, *L'Ombra del Tasso*, chap. 2). Having sided with Charles against Clement and the League of Cognac in 1527, Alfonso had finally recovered Reggio and Modena. While the reconciliation of the Pope and the Emperor in 1529–1530 may have been worrisome, it had created no serious problems for the Ferrarese by 1532. Moreover, Ariosto personally was particularly shown favors by the Emperor — and in general had begun to enjoy more of the fruits of fame that his immensely successful poem, as well as his various plays, now afforded him. Cf. Bigi, ed., *Orlando furioso*, 34–35.

[75] Pierre Bourdieu, *Outline of a Theory of Practice*, trans. R. Nice (Cambridge: Cambridge University Press, 1977), 164–71.

[76] Cf. Bigi, ed., *Orlando furioso*, 66.

more able to thematize crisis and to transform it from a series of *ad hominem* attacks and *cris de coeur* into an analysis of ideology in more general and reflective terms.[77] Returning to our example, it can be shown that even as Leo and Ippolito tend to lose their historical specificity and to function exclusively within the intratextual dynamics of the *Furioso*,[78] they are being redeployed within complex explorations of the problematic relationship of poetry and power, poet and patron, in general. In fact, one of the main principles of revision visibly at work in 1532 is the extension and transformation of key episodes from 1516, including episodes with significant topical content, in a process that hovers between the intertextual and intratextual.[79] For example, language and imagery that is closely linked to Ippolito and Leo becomes a primary building block of the one major addition to the genealogical narrative, the story of Ruggiero, Bradamante, and Leone told in cantos 44–46.

Although this point could be made in a variety of ways, one example must here stand for all — the fate of the intratextual echoes of *Inferno* 32–33 on which the critique of Leo hinges. In particular, the prominent stylistic device of "più che . . . poté" that marks derivation from *Inferno* 33.75, in 1532 also becomes an intratextual link between apparently unrelated episodes.[80] In 1516, there is a single use of this stylistic device, confined (as we have seen) to canto 17, the allusive force of which was then sharpened by the 1521 reference to the Orco as "fier pastor." In 1532, this stylistic device was introduced at two crucial junctures in canto 21. The canto offers a displaced version of the Hippolytus/Phaedra story in the tale of the faithful Filandro and the faithless Gabrina, and thus, like canto 17, constituted a crucial nexus between historical

---

[77] The major narrative additions to the poem address central ideological concerns — the politics of tyranny, the ethics of "fede," the cultural construction of gender identity — which, although present in 1516, are far more explicitly treated in 1532. See Dalla Palma, *Le strutture narrative*, 219–25.

[78] Cf. Ascoli, *Ariosto's Bitter Harmony*, 388.

[79] This phenomenon is more obvious in the case of two of the four major narrative additions: the Olympia episode doubles the earlier episode of Angelica and the Orca; the Marganorre episode is a palinodic rewriting of the episode of the "femine omicide" (cantos 19–20 in 1532 ed.). The "Rocca di Tristano" episode is less specifically linked to a single 1516 episode, though it does provide an oblique commentary on Bradamante's jealous despair, but it too has a function of rewriting — most especially in the ekphrastic-historical passage which recants the pro-French bias (however qualified) of 1516. Of the Ruggiero-Leone-Bradamante addition I shall speak below.

[80] M. Cabani, *Costanti ariosteschi* (Pisa: Scuola Normale Superiore, 1990) has recently given us a lengthy catalogue of various ways in which Ariosto uses verbal repetition to connect disparate episodes, though she does not discuss this particular example.

personage and literary narrative, as it also offers a variant on the Orrigille/Grifone story. The echoes appear in stanza 54 (ll.7–8), which signals Filandro's descent from exemplar of "fede" into willing pawn of Gabrina's lust, and in stanza 3 (ll. 7–8), which implicates Zerbino in the same foolish adherence to a rigid and self-destructive ethos of "fede" as Filandro.[81] Canto 21, in turn, became in 1532 the primary verbal and thematic source for the episode of Ruggiero, Bradamante, and Leone, and especially of its complex exploration of the ideology of faith.[82] Prominently featured are two additional echoes of *Inferno* 33.75, which are, within the intratextual economy of the poem, equally echoes of *Furioso* 17.48 and 21.3 and 54, at stanzas 34 and 56 of canto 45.[83]

Once the intricate verbal/thematic concatenation that leads from canto 17 through canto 21 to cantos 44–46 has been identified, one might then speculate that Ruggiero's misrepresentation of his identity when he wears Leone's armor into combat with Bradamante (45.55, 69) is indebted to the early episode of Grifone and Martano's exchange of armor and identity, which had similarly near-tragic consequences. One might wonder as well whether the character Leone's name is not derived from Leo's, and thus constitutes the most fitting emblem for the sublimation of a historical personage into the narrative economy of the poem.[84]

Here a crucial question arises. The addition of the materials in cantos 44 and 45 clearly gives the genealogical narrative, the purpose of which is to imagine an historical line leading from the time of the poem into the contemporary world

---

[81] For a detailed reading of canto 21, see Ascoli, "Faith as a Cover-Up."

[82] For additional elaboration of this argument see Ascoli, *Ariosto's Bitter Harmony*, 330–31 and n. 122. For debate concerning the value of (ethical) "faith" in the *Furioso*, see also Durling, *Figure of the Poet*, 167–76; Saccone, "Cloridano e Medoro"; and idem, "Prospettive"; Neuro Bonifazi, *Le lettere infedeli* (Rome: Officina Edizioni, 1975); Wiggins, *Figures in Ariosto's Tapestry*; and Zatti, *Il "Furioso" tra epos e romanzo*, esp. 91–111.

[83] Furthermore, key terms that appear in the earlier Ariostan echoings are found throughout the two cantos reinforcing thematic connections ("timor" 45.34–37 [5 times]; "ostinazione" 44.37.7, 44.45.1, 45.86.6, 45.107.6; "promesso" 44.35.4, 44.47.8, 44.53.3, 44.58.6, 44.69.2, 44.75.4, 45.6.1, 45.22.1, 45.60.1, 45.108.3, 45.109.3, 45.116.2).

[84] Possible further support for this hypothesis comes from: (1) the ostentatious linking of a nominal lion with a "roarer" which perhaps recalls Ariosto's earlier exegesis of the papal name ("scelto il fiero nome / perchè tu ruggi"); (2) the fact that Leone is the son of an emperor named after the original Costantino (both because of the earlier allusion to Constantine's donation in close proximity to Leo's name and because the memory of Constantine always evokes problems of papal authority); and, more tenuously (3) a series of locutions using the crucial adjective "fiero," one of which conflates the two Dantean passages echoed in canto XVII — "fiero dolore" (45.57.1; cf. 44.81.3; 85.7).

of Estense Ferrara, greater prominence and centrality in the 1532 edition, reinforcing the sense of epic closure.[85] How is it then possible to argue that the 1532 edition is *less* historical in orientation than that of 1516? My point, however, is that history has a different place in 1532 than 1516, not at all that it is absent (how could it be?). The difference is between a relatively direct experience of disruptive historical crisis, as well as an immediate sense of connection to the political-social world, on the one hand, and, on the other, the fantasy of cultural continuity and stability embodied in the marriage of Bradamante and Ruggiero.[86] The Ruggiero-Bradamante-Leone episode, then, sets the myth of Estense genealogy in sharp relief, but also tends to fold it increasingly into the plot of the poem, to make it part and parcel of the *Furioso*'s chivalric fictions.[87]

At the beginning of this essay I argued that the essence of Ariosto's strategy for confronting and absorbing historical crisis was the deployment of a combined intertextual and intratextual interlace which pitted non-narrative formal and thematic elements against narrative. By 1532, however, the non-narrative elements of historical crisis were being increasingly, though not completely, reabsorbed into the primary narrative of the *Furioso*, and specifically into the story which promotes the illusion of an unbroken and relatively untroubled link

---

[85] Marsh, "Ruggiero and Leone"; Bigi, ed., *Orlando furioso*, 53; Casadei, "Breve analisi." Cf. Quint, "Figure of Atlante."

[86] In 1516, the poem's penultimate episode (what became cantos 42 and 43 in 1532) was the futile journey of Rinaldo down through the Italian peninsula in order to join Orlando and co. at the battle of Lipadusa. The foci of the episode are an ekphrastic description of a castle near Mantua and two interpolated, neo-Boccaccian novelle. All of these materials evoke the origins and the culture of Ferrara and her sister city, Mantua (where Isabella d'Este reigned as Duchess). Cf. Casadei, "Breve analisi"; Ronald L. Martinez, "De-Cephalizing Rinaldo: The Money of Tyranny in Niccolò da Correggio's *Fabula de Cefalo* and in *Orlando furioso* 42," *Annali d'Italianistica* 12 (1994): 87–114; and idem, "Two Odysseys."

[87] Pampaloni, "La guerra nel *Furioso*," 644; and Marsh, "Ruggiero and Leone," both take the eastern locale of the Ruggiero-Leone encounter, and especially the city of Belgrade, as topically allusive to the Turkish threat of 1529. Even if this is so, its oblique approach is a far cry from the explicit presentation of such topics exemplified by the proem and digression of canto 17, perhaps because, however large in the abstract the pagan menace might seem, it did not have the scandalous immediacy that the Italian wars did (remember that in 17.73–79 Ariosto, like Dante, sees such extramural conflicts as normal and as a desirable alternative to inter-Christian warfare). A much more horrifying (and transparently allegorical) "eastern adventure" is the civil war of the *Cinque Canti* enacted in the heretical precincts of Prague. I would tend in any case to think that the emphasis should fall on the appearance of an imperial heir, the son of a namesake of Constantine, in an era of renewed imperialism.

between the chivalric past and the present-day Ferrara of Ariosto and the Este family. This turn to representation of history as narrative, which stabilizes the relationship between past and present, fiction and history, is the antithesis of the representation of history *as crisis* and *in crisis*. Curiously enough, although the neo-Vergilian model of genealogy is what turns the *Furioso* away from romance and toward epic, and thus, in Quint's terms, constitutes the fundamental rupture between Ariosto and Boiardo, this development also and equally constitutes a return to the *Innamorato* and a move away from the most radical innovations of the first *Furioso*. Not long after the episode of the Orco, Boiardo inaugurates the genealogical narrative in which Ruggiero and Bradamante become the founders of the Este dynasty (3.5). And the encomia of the Este line and their connections comprise the only historical materials that are integrated into Boiardo's poem (e.g., 2.21.55–60, 25.42–56, 27.50–59; 3.5.5–28).[88]

By 1532, then, Ariosto had begun to do what later readers almost always do to a text — reduce the undigested signs of its own and its author's historicity into the self-contained forms of narrative and into a generalizable, non-local, thematics of temporal existence. In the world of the 1532 *Furioso*, Leo X is no longer himself, or even the caricatured object of Ariosto's *ressentiment* — he is a figuration of the bestial abuse of power and the monstrous ingratitude of patrons. How great the difference between those two editions and those two moments in Ariosto's poetic career actually is may be seen in the very different treatment of the two historical figures who dominated the 1520s and 1530s and who were the protagonists of the Sack of Rome, symbolic culmination of the crisis that had opened with the French invasion of 1494: the Emperor Charles V and Pope Clement VII. Charles is given, in 1532, a glowing encomium (XV.23–36) that reflects the increasing Ferrarese attachment to him as well as his apparent patronage of Ariosto.[89] In a distinctly biblical and prophetic language with which we are now all too familiar, the Ariostan narrator imagines a new and greater imperium: "solo un ovile sia, solo un pastore" ("let there be one sheepfold, one shepherd only": 26.8, cf. John 10:16).[90] But here, to my knowledge, there is no subverting interlace at work, notwithstanding the convenient textual proximity of two Ariostan monsters, Caligorante and Orrilo. On the other hand

---

[88] Cf. Casadei, *La strategia delle varianti*, 22.

[89] Bigi, ed., *Orlando furioso*, 1.609–610 n. 18; Catalano, *Vita*, 1: 608.

[90] On the tendency to make Charles the object of apocalyptic prophecies previously applied almost exclusively to popes, see Stinger, *Rome in the Renaissance*, 120–21 and 324 n. 11. See also Casadei, *La strategia delle varianti*, 44–45; and Frances Yates, *Astraea: The Imperial Theme in the Sixteenth Century* (London/Boston: Routledge and Kegan Paul, 1975), chap. 1.

is Leo's cousin and eventual successor in the papacy, Clement, who in his reign certainly represented just as significant an historical problem for Ferrara as Leo had earlier, but who is never mentioned by name in the poem, and who receives only a single, glancing reference to his imprisonment after the Sack (33.55–56). The older Ariosto, one might argue, has retreated to the safety of a relatively uncritical position vis-à-vis contemporary history (again, much closer to Boiardo's stance) — where the powerful are praised when advantageous to the author, and ignored when they create problems. Still, the figure of Leo, the "pastor . . . [col] fiero nome," lingers on in the background — a subtle reminder that neither literary texts nor historical contexts are quite what they seem, and that the crisis out of which the *Furioso* first grew has left an indelible mark on Ariosto's pages.

Tears of Amber: Titian's *Andrians,* the River Po and the Iconology of Difference

Anthony Colantuono

Titian's *Bacchanal of the Andrians* (Madrid, Prado) (Fig. 1) was painted for Duke Alfonso I d'Este of Ferrara around 1523–1525, the last of a series of commissions for the decoration of his *camerino* or personal study.[1] The *camerino* was stripped of its paintings in 1598, but we know that the series also included two other pictures by Titian — *The Feast of Venus* (Madrid, Prado) and *Bacchus and Ariadne* (London, National Gallery) — and Giovanni Bellini's *Feast of the Gods* (Washington, D.C., National Gallery of Art), as well as a "bacchanal" and a painted frieze by the Ferrarese court painter Dosso Dossi. While the series was thus dominated by two of the most innovative exponents of Venetian naturalism, and by a Ferrarese artist whose style was itself atypical for Ferrara, it remains to be seen whether the peculiar bacchanalian subject matter of these paintings might be related to a specifically Ferrarese cultural discourse.

Scholars have come to consider Titian's *Andrians* the least problematic or even the "simplest" of Alfonso d'Este's "bacchanals." Franz Wickhoff long ago identified the classical text that is now generally regarded to be the principal — or,

---

[1] See principally H. E. Wethey, *The Paintings of Titian*, 3 vols. (London: Phaidon, 1975), 3:29–41 and 143–53 for Alfonso d'Este's bacchanals, and esp. 151–53, cat. no. 15 for basic information on Titian's *Andrians*. Andrea Bayer, "Dosso's Public: The Este Court at Ferrara," in *Dosso Dossi: Court Painter in Renaissance Ferrara*, ed. P. Humfrey and M. Lucco (New York: Metropolitan Museum of Art, 1999), 27–54, esp. 31–40, presents an elementary overview of what is known about the *camerino,* with up-to-date bibliography. See also K. Christiansen, "Dosso Dossi's Aeneas Frieze for Alfonso d'Este's Camerino," *Apollo* 151 (2000): 36–45, concerning newly discovered portions of the room's painted frieze.

for some, the sole — literary source of Titian's imagery: the elder Philostratus's rhetorical description of an ancient painting portraying a river of wine that flowed on the Greek island of Andros, and the Andrians who celebrate their river's magically inebriating powers.[2] Such a "simple" reading of this painting depends upon the methodological assumptions of modern "iconographical" methods, which define "meaning" in terms of the similarities between the image and its textual source, either setting aside as irrelevant anything in the image that happens to differ from what the text describes, or dismissing such differences as the product of the artist's mindless caprice. But as I have shown in an article of 1991, there exists explicit documentary evidence to prove that Alfonso d'Este had sent Titian detailed written instructions for the images he was to paint for the *camerino,* and there is good reason to believe that at least some of these instructions were authored by Mario Equicola, humanist preceptor and secretary to Alfonso's sister Isabella d'Este of Mantua.[3] If it was not the artist himself but a humanistically educated individual such as Equicola who conceived the argument of this painting, there is also reason to abandon the modern iconology of "similarity" in favor of another interpretative paradigm, which we may call the iconology of "difference."

---

[2] F. Wickhoff, "Venezianische Bilder, I: Die Andrier des Philostrat von Tizian," *Jahrbuch der Königlichen Preussischen Kunstsammlungen* 23 (1902): 118–20, esp. 119; cf., also in the *Jahrbuch*, R. Förster, "Philostrats Gemälde in der Renaissance," 25 (1904): 15–48, esp. 41–44. Charles Hope, *Titian* (New York: Harper and Row, 1980), emphasizes that Titian "took considerable liberties" (59) with this text (Philostratus, *Imagines* 1.25, trans. A. Fairbanks, Loeb Classical Library [London: Heinemann, 1931], 96–99), but nonetheless assumes that Philostratus was his only textual source, and that the painting is ultimately a simple evocation of the powers of wine ; and J. Shearman, *Only Connect — : Art and the Spectator in the Italian Renaissance* (Princeton: Princeton University Press, 1992), 257, while acknowledging that some of the bacchanals for Alfonso d'Este may have had more than one textual source, insists that *The Andrians* is "simpler" and "much less sophisticated" than the others, being based solely on Philostratus. Cf. H. David Brumble, *Classical Myths and Legends in the Middle Ages and Renaissance* (London: Fitzroy Dearborn, 1998), s.v. "Bacchus," 48–52. See Ruth Webb, "The Transmission of the *Eikones* of Philostratus and the Development of Ekphrasis from Late Antiquity to the Renaissance" (Ph.D. diss., Warburg Institute, University of London, 1992).

[3] Anthony Colantuono, "*Dies Alcyoniae*: The Invention of Bellini's *Feast of the Gods*," *Art Bulletin* 73 (1991): 237–56, esp. 238–41, concerning the instructions that Titian received from Alfonso d'Este, which are explicitly mentioned in letters from the artist and from the duke's Venetian diplomatic agent Giacomo Tebaldi, and concerning the implications of Equicola's probable role.

As is well known, the humanists of the early Renaissance theorized that painting was a form of poetry or rhetoric, whose "arguments" and "conceits" were expressed through visible images rather than words.[4] We do not have the written instructions with which Titian was provided, but where they do survive, such instructions (usually designated by the rhetorical term *invenzione)* were generally structured as rhetorical compositions, in which the description of the various images to be painted constitutes a type of rhetorically figured or poetical discourse — a discourse essentially identical to that of the proposed painting itself. This is not surprising, for the "humanist advisors" assigned to compose such instructions were merely following the same precepts of rhetorical invention and disposition that they employed in their literary writings.[5] However, these

---

[4] In addition to the famous passage in Alberti's *De Pictura* (3.53) where pictorial images are likened to rhetorical ornaments *(ornamenta),* and where it is recommended that painters seek the company of poets and orators who might aid in the invention *(inventio)* of the pictorial *historia,* see also for example Paolo Pino, "Dialogo di Pittura (1548)," in *Trattati d'arte del Cinquecento*, ed. P. Barocchi (Bari: Laterza, 1960), 1:95–139, esp. 115: "È anco invenzione il ben distinguere, ordinare e compartire le cose [i.e., the pictorial arguments] dette dagli altri, accomodando bene li soggetti agli atti delle figure, e che tutte attendano alla dichiarazione del fine. . . . E perché la pittura è propria poesia, cioè invenzione, la qual fa apparere [sic] quello che non è, però util sarebbe osservare alcuni ordini eletti dagli altri poeti che scrivono . . . ," that is: "Invention is also the [artist's] process of properly distinguishing, arranging and compartmentalizing [pictorial arguments] dictated by others, making the figures' actions appropriately accommodate the subjects [being portrayed], and [seeing that] all [of these figures] serve the clarification of the [desired rhetorical] purpose . . . "; and Giovan Battista Armenini, *De' veri precetti della pittura* (Ravenna: F. Tebaldini, 1587), esp. 25–26: " . . . per ciò si chiama la Pittura, Poetica che tace, et la Poetica, Pittura che parla, et questa l'anima dover esser, et quella il corpo, dissimile però in questo si tengono, perché l'una imita con i colori, l'altra con le parole . . . ," that is: " . . . for this reason Painting is called 'silent Poetry,' and Poetry 'Painting that speaks,' and while Poetry must be the soul, and Painting the body, they are held to be different in that the one imitates with colors, while the other [imitates] with words. . . ." I have pointed out elsewhere (Colantuono, "*Dies Alcyoniae*," 239), that in a letter of 1518 Titian similarly refers to one of his bacchanals for Alfonso d'Este as the pictorial "body" in which the incorporeal poetical "soul" provided by Alfonso's instructions will be contained.

[5] See for example Isabella d'Este's instructions for Perugino's *Battle of Love and Chastity* (Paris, Louvre), published in F. Canuti, *Il Perugino*, 2 vols. (Siena: La Diana, 1931), 2:212–13, esp. 212, where Isabella describes her proposed pictorial argument as "La poetica nostra invenzione. . . ." Cf. also J. Kliemann, "Il pensiero di Paolo Giovio nelle pitture eseguite sulle sue invenzioni," in *Atti del Convegno Paolo Giovio. Il Rinascimento e la memoria* (Como: Società a Villa Gallia, 1985), 197–223; C. Robertson,

rhetorical precepts differ markedly from the intentions attributed to painters and advisors by modern iconographers. For while an "iconographical" reading typically regards the pictorial image as an "illustration" of a given classical text, in which the similarities between image and text are deliberate and the differences accidental, the "rhetorical" mode of pictorial interpretation here proposed would instead regard the artist's use of textual sources as a form of rhetorical "imitation" — a process in which the orator both appropriates and *creatively transforms* the features of his literary models.[6] Thus, as in literary imitation, the painted image gains its force not merely by resembling a given source text, but also by *differing* from it: while the similarities between image and text enable the beholder to identify the artist's literary models, it is through the process of assessing the artist's transformation of and deviations from those models that the beholder discovers the new or "original" argument that the painting alone embodies. In this "iconology of difference," the most fundamental interpretative act is to determine which of the artist's figures were determined by his primary textual model, and which were not.

Certainly Philostratus's ekphrasis explains much of what we see in Titian's painting, for the ancient rhetorician explicitly mentions the river of wine that the artist has portrayed (in the foreground); the men singing (under the trees at the left); the men and women dancing (at the right); and the personification of the river as an old man lying on a "couch" of grapes, located on the distant knoll at far right (Fig. 2). It is for this reason that modern interpreters have invariably referred to Titian's painting by the title of *The Andrians* — the title of Philostratus's oration — as though the artist's references to this text announced the intention of creating an exact visual equivalent of the verbal argument. Yet Titian's "bacchanal" is not merely a straightforward illustration of this ancient text, for it also includes many details that Philostratus does not mention — details so utterly alien to the text that their inclusion seems deliberately enigmatic. Among these details we may count the figure of the voluptuously reclining nude female portrayed at lower right, whose pose recalls that of the famous ancient statue in the Vatican Museums now identified as representing Ariadne, but

---

"Paolo Giovio and the 'Invenzioni' for the Sala dei Cento Giorni," in *Convegno Paolo Giovio*, 225–37; idem, "Annibale Caro as Iconographer," *Journal of the Warburg and Courtauld Institutes* 45 (1982): 160–81; and Lina Bolzoni, "Parole e immagini per il ritratto di un nuovo Ulisse," in *Documentary Culture: Florence and Rome from Grand Duke Ferdinand I to Pope Alexander VII*, ed. G. Penni et al. (Bologna: Nuova Alfa, 1992), 317–48.

[6] See Colantuono, "*Dies Alcyoniae*," 238–55, esp. 244 where this rhetorical model is applied to another of the bacchanals of Alfonso d'Este's *camerino*.

considered by some early sixteenth-century antiquarians as a portrayal of Cleopatra; the nude infant who stands near her feet, urinating into the river (Fig. 3); and the diminutive, often-overlooked figure of the man with his dog, kneeling before a large wine vessel in the background, at center. While it is impossible to explain all of these figures in the context of this short essay, I should like to draw special attention to what I consider the strangest detail of all: the large, peculiar-looking bird — unmistakably identifiable as a Guinea fowl — perched high in the tree at the right (Fig. 4). In his description of the Andrians and their river of wine Philostratus makes no mention of such a creature; and nor does any other classical source connect the Guinea fowl to the island of Andros. But since Titian's painting was made for Duke Alfonso d'Este of Ferrara, it is of the most urgent interest that the Guinea fowl was associated in antiquity with the river Po — the river that geographically embraced, economically nourished, and strategically defended Alfonso's realm. As I shall suggest, Titian's painting does not actually represent the river of the Andrians at all, but instead employs Philostratus's oration as the basis for a new rhetorical invention whose subject is the Po itself.

Philostratus's collection of orations entitled *Eikones* ("Paintings," Latinized as *Imagines*) exemplifies the art of sophistic epideictic, that is, the ancient rhetorical genre involving the praise or condemnation of a specific person or object. Indeed, as classical scholars have all but unanimously concluded, the ancient paintings Philostratus purports to describe were not necessarily "real" paintings (though many of their details do have parallels in ancient art), but rather are rhetorical "images" that the orator himself has invented in order to praise some unstated but implied object; and as is also characteristic of sophistic oratory, the ultimate purpose of these praises is the display of sheer rhetorical technique, the ability to delight, instruct, and move the listener with the powerful expression of human sentiment and vivid, ingenious conceits. In the oration that provided Titian's imitative model, Philostratus praises the river of the Andrians as superior to all other rivers, adorning his speech with the brilliant rhetorical figures characteristic of his style. These figures or conceits often involve the use of rhetorical comparisons aimed at magnifying the importance of the object of praise. Specifically, I would like to draw attention to Philostratus's comparison of the Andrians' river to two other rivers, the Nile and the Ister (the latter is now known as the Danube), where he finds both of these mighty rivers lacking in the magical powers that only a river of wine could possess: " . . . he who draws from [the river of wine on Andros] may well disdain both Nile and Ister, and he may say of them that they would be more highly esteemed if they were small, provided their streams were like this one" (Philostratus, *Imagines*,

1.25.1).[7] As I shall demonstrate, Titian's transformative imitation of Philostratus's oration creates a variation on this rhetorical conceit, in which it is not the river of the Andrians, but the Po, that is found superior to all other rivers.

Philostratus's comparison of the Andrians' grapy stream to the Nile and Ister illustrates his own use of rhetorical *imitatio,* for as the later sixteenth-century humanist Blaise de Vigenère notes in his exhaustive commentary on the *Eikones,* Philostratus's conceit appears to have been imitated from a passage in Lucan's *Pharsalia* (2.416–420), where the Roman poet similarly praised the Po in comparison with the Nile and Ister. Blaise tells us: "This [comparison of the Andrians' river to the Nile and the Ister] is said in imitation of a passage in Lucan, speaking of the river Po, which Virgil calls the king of rivers."[8] He then quotes the relevant lines from Lucan, including these words: "The Nile would not be greater [than the Po], did it not flood the Libyan desert over the flats of low-lying Egypt; the Ister would be no greater, did it not in its course over the globe receive waters that might otherwise fall into any sea."[9] Since Lucan was plainly the earlier of the two authors, there can be no question that (at least within the scope of Blaise's knowledge) this comparison was originally conceived in praise of the Po, and was subsequently appropriated by Philostratus in order to praise the mythical river of the Andrians.

Blaise's conclusion that Philostratus's praises of the Andrians' river were modeled on Lucan's praises of the Po might well explain the relevance of Titian's obscure classical subject to his patron's interests. For the Este rulers of Ferrara counted the Po among their most precious geographical assets, not only on

---

[7] Philostratus, *Imagines,* trans. Fairbanks, 97.

[8] Blaise de Vigenère, *Les images ou tableaux de platte peinture des deux Philostrates . . .* (Paris: Guillemont, 1614), 206–9 (commentary concerning the oration on the Andrians), especially 209: "Cecy est dit à l'imitation d'un passage de Lucain parlant du Pau, que Virgile au premier des Georgiques appelle le Roy des fleuves. . . ." Although Blaise's commentary was published much later, he had originally begun studying Philostratus during his lengthy stay at the court of Mantua from 1566 to 1570, and it is likely that his interpretation of the text preserves local north-Italian philological traditions. See Gabriella Répaci-Courtois, "Blaise de Vigenère et l'expérience des arts visuels," in *Blaise de Vigenère poète et mythographe au temps de Henri III*, ed. Centre V. L. Saulnier (Paris: Ecole Normale Supérieure, 1994), 101–10, esp. 108 for Blaise's Mantuan period.

[9] Lucan, *Pharsalia* 2.416–420:

Non minor hic Nilo, si non per plana iacentis
Aegypti Libycas Nilus stagnaret harenas.
Non minor hic Histro, nisi quod, dum permeat orbem,
Hister casuros in quaelibet aequora fontes
Accipit, et Scythicas exit non solus in undas.

account of its material benefits, but also for its beauty, and for its reputation as Italy's mightiest river. Moreover, the Po was indeed a magical place, identified by ancient and contemporary writers with the river Eridanus — the woeful place where Phaethon fell to his death, having lost control of his father's fiery solar chariot. As a result, the Po/Eridanus appears not only in many works of art commissioned by the Estense court throughout the sixteenth century, for example in the *Venus on the Eridanus* attributed to Girolamo da Carpi (Fig. 5),[10] but also in many well-known Ferrarese literary products. The most famous example is of course to be found in the third canto of Ariosto's *Orlando Furioso,* where the poet presents the Po's mythical identity with the Eridanus as part of the dynastic legacy of Azzo VII d'Este, Ferrara's first Estense ruler: "[Azzo] shall hold with most-felicitous scepter this beautiful land, which is situated upon that river where with mournful plectrum Phoebus lamented his son, who steered the light off course, when the fabled amber was cried. . . ."[11] Ariosto's imagery is darkly figured, but was plainly legible to contemporaries such as Simone Fórnari, who identifies the unnamed river and Phoebus's unfortunate son in his comment on this passage: "The poet here uses periphrasis, a figure very familiar to poets, in describing Ferrara, a city built upon the Po. . . . Phaethon fell into the river Po, which in Greek is called the Eridanus. . . ."[12]

Ariosto also mentions a more obscure aspect of the myth: he says that Phaethon's passing had further occasioned the crying of tears of amber. As numerous classical, medieval, and humanist writers further explain, after Phaethon met his fate in the waters of the Po, his sisters, known as the Heliades ("daughters of the Sun"), mourned his passing with incessant tears, until at last

---

[10] Girolamo's painting is identified as *Venus on the Eridanus* by Girolamo Falletti, *Poemata* (Ferrara, 1546), 73–74r, where the poems are addressed to Anna d'Este, daughter of Duke Ercole II d'Este. Amalia Mezzetti, *Girolamo da Ferrara* (Milan: Silvana, 1977), 73–74, cat. no. 33, traces the picture's provenance to the *camera del poggiolo,* a room located near to Alfonso d'Este's *camerino.*

[11] *Orlando furioso* 3.34:

> Terrà costui con più felice scettro
> La bella terra, che siede sul fiume
> dove chiamò con lacrimoso plettro
> Febo il figliuol ch'avea mal retto il lume,
> Quando fu pianto il fabuloso elettro . . .

[12] Simone Fórnari, *La spositione da M. Simon Fórnari da Rheggio sopra l'Orlando Furioso di M. Ludovico Ariosto* (Florence: Lorenzo Torrentino, 1549), 146: "Usa il poeta in questo luogo la periphrasi figura molto famigliare a poeti, in descrivendo Ferrara, città edificata sovra il Po. . . . Nel Po, che Grecamente è chiamato Eridano, cadde Phetonte. . . ."

the gods took pity on them and transformed them into poplar trees, which stood on the banks of the Po, shedding tears of amber into the waters for all eternity.[13] The story of the Heliades and their amber tears is immediately relevant to the interpretation of the painting we know as Titian's "*Andrians.*" For since Blaise de Vigenère rightly recognized that Philostratus's praises of the Andrians' river were appropriated from Lucan's praises of the Po, it seems no coincidence that the Guinea fowl — that same creature which Titian has placed in the midst of Philostratus's Andrian riverscape — was associated not only with the river Po/Eridanus, but also with the myths of the Heliades and of the origins of amber.

In Strabo's *Geography,* first translated into Latin by Guarino da Verona in the 1450s, we read of an ancient myth according to which the Guinea fowl inhabited a place called the Amber Islands, located at the mouth of the Po on the Adriatic Sea, not far from where Phaethon fell, and where the Heliades were changed into poplars.[14] Strabo says: "Let the remaining mythical or false stories [regarding the region of the Adriatic] be set aside, such as that of Phaethon, and of his sisters the Heliades, who were turned into poplar trees near the river Eridanus, which exists nowhere on earth, even though it is said to be near the Po, and of the Amber Islands that lie before the Po, *which are also inhabited by the Guinea fowl. . . .*" [emphasis added].[15] When Strabo reports that Guinea fowl were

---

[13] See principally August Friedrich von Pauly and Georg Wissowa, eds., *Paulys Real-Encyclopädie der Classischen Altertumswissenschaft, neue Bearbeitung* (Stuttgart: J. B. Metzler, 1894–1963), 24 vols. 36:1, cols. 2178–2202, s.v. "Padus," esp. 2179–2183 for the river Po and its connection to this complex of ancient myths concerning the fall of Phaethon, the Heliades, and the origins of amber. Concerning the origins and significance of these myths, see also A. Violante, "Il fiume Eridano: mito e storia," in *L'uomo e il fiume*, ed. R. H. Rainero et al. (Settimo Milanese: Marzorati, 1989), 22–24; Aurelio Peretti, *Dall'Eridano di Esiodo al Retrone Vicentino* (Pisa: Giardini, 1994), esp. 148–293; and Dennis Looney's introduction to the present volume.

[14] See A. Diller and Paul Oskar Kristeller, "Strabo," in *Catalogus Translationum et Commentariorum: Mediaeval and Renaissance Translations and Commentaries: Annotated Lists and Guides*, ed. Paul Oskar Kristeller (Washington, DC: Catholic University of America Press, 1960–), 2:225–33 for the Renaissance translations of and commentaries on Strabo, esp. 225–30 for Guarino's translation of Strabo's first ten books under the patronage of Pope Nicholas V; and 230–32 for Gregorius Tiphernas's translation of the remaining books. Since Guarino was employed by the Ferrarese court from 1429 onwards, and taught at the university of Ferrara until his death in 1460, this translation was certainly well known among Ferrarese scholars of Alfonso I d'Este's generation.

[15] Strabo, *Geography* 5.1.9; Strabo, *Strabonis geographicorum commentarii, olim, ut putatur, a Guarino Veronese & Gregorio Tifernate latinitate donatos*, ed. Conrad Heresbach (Basel: Vualder, 1523), 149: "Reliqua vero permulta fabulis vulgata vel ficta alium in modum absint. Sicuti quae ad Phaethontem & sorores Heliades, in populos conversas

said to have inhabited the mythical "Amber Islands" of the Po delta, he designates the species by its Greek name (*meleagrides*), a name known to Renaissance humanists and agricultural writers, along with more common names such as the Italian *faraona* and the Latin *gallina africana*. Indeed, Renaissance humanists commonly cited the passage in Varro where the Guinea fowl's identity with the *meleagris* was plainly spelled out, and they also knew Clytus of Miletus's detailed description of the creature, quoted at length by Athenaeus: both passages are adduced, for example, by the sixteenth-century humanist Gilbertus Longolius in his *Dialogus de Avibus* (1543), which includes a lengthy discussion of this bird.[16] Moreover, as a comparison of Titian's bird (Fig. 4) with the Guinea fowl illustrated in Ulisse Aldrovandi's *Ornithologiae* (1599–1603) (Fig. 6) suffices to prove, there can be no doubt that this was the species the artist was instructed to portray.[17]

---

arbores, circa amnem Eridanum, qui nullibi terrarum existit, cum vicinis Pado dicatur. Itemque ferentes electra insulas, ante amnem Padum iacentes, in quibus & Meleagrides."

[16] For general orientation concerning these animals, see also R. A. Donkin, *Meleagrides: An Historical and Ethnographical Study of the Guinea Fowl* (London: Ethnographica, 1991). See also Marcus Terentius Varro, "Rerum Rusticarum Lbri Tres," in *Marcus Porcius Cato on Agriculture; Marcus Terentius Varro on Agriculture*, trans. William Davis Hooper, Loeb Classical Library (Cambridge, MA: Harvard University Press, 1934), 3.9.18: "Gallinae Africanae sunt grandes, variae, gibberae, quas Meleagrides appellant Graeci"; and Athenaeus, *The Deipnosophists*, trans. Charles Burton Gulick, Loeb Classical Library (Cambridge, MA: Harvard University Press, 1961), 14.665c–e, quoting a lost work of the Peripatetic philosopher Clytus of Miletus. Cf. Gilbert de Longueil, *Dialogus de Avibus* (Cologne, 1543), where the author is plainly aware of both Varro and Athenaeus, and translates Clytus's extremely detailed description of the animal (the description itself is too long to permit quotation here): "Sapis Pamphile, sed ut cognoscas me tibi verum dixisse, primò Meleagrides gallinas easdem cum Africanas esse, tibi describam, quemadmodum a veteribus, maxime Clyto Milesio Alexandri discipulo, pictae sunt. . . . ," that is: "You know this, Pamphilus, but that you may recognize that I have told you the truth in the first place — that these *meleagrides* are the same as the African hens *[gallinae Africanae]* — I shall describe them to you as they are portrayed by the ancients, and especially by Clytus of Miletus the disciple of Alexander. . . ." (This rare text is available in the Biblioteca Apostolica Vaticana, Stamp. Barb. N.I.54.) See J. F. Michaud, ed., *Biographie Universelle Ancien et Moderne,* 45 vols. (Paris: Louis Vives, 1854–1865), 25:78 for Longueil (not to be confused with the humanist Christophorus Longolius), who was born in Utrecht (1507) but studied extensively in Italy and knew many scholars in common with Equicola.

[17] U. Aldrovandi, *Ornithologiae*, 3 vols. (Bologna: N. Tebaldinus, 1637–1696), 2:336–38 (15.13: 'De Gallinis Guineis'), especially the illustration on 337. Aldrovandi cites the commonplaces from Varro and Athenaeus discussed above. An earlier illustration of the Guinea fowl may be found, for example, in the fourteenth-century *taccuino* of Giovannino de Grassi, BCB, Cod. 7.14, fol. 13r.

Thus, while Titian's portrayal of the Guinea fowl may be inconsistent with a portrayal of the island of Andros, it is perfectly consistent with a portrayal of the mythical landscape of the Po/Eridanus. Given Strabo's account of the ancient myths regarding this region, we may also picture the mythical Amber Islands at the mouth of the Po as a place where we find not only the Guinea fowl or *meleagrides*, but also numerous poplar trees — those resulting from the arboreal transformation of the Heliades. Moreover, as the name of these islands implies, we should also expect to find a great quantity of amber there, no doubt the amber tears these mournful poplars shed for Phaethon. Strabo was not the only ancient writer who associated the Guinea fowl with the Po or with the origins of amber, for Pliny discusses the same matter as part of a lengthier inquiry into the nature and physical properties of amber in the thirty-seventh book of his *Natural History*. Pliny recounts the story of the Heliades and of their metamorphosis, but then adds the rather significant detail that the birds known as the *meleagrides* — Guinea fowl — were similarly capable of crying tears of amber. The relevant passages in Pliny, far too long to quote here, are neatly summarized by the humanist Nicolò Perotti in his *Cornucopiae,* a lexical analysis of Martial's epigrams and *Liber Spectaculorum,* first published in 1478, and well known to early sixteenth-century humanists. Like Pliny, Perotti mentions the *meleagrides* and their amber tears in the same breath with the stories of the Heliades, the origins of amber, and the Po/Eridanus:

> They think, moreover, that the sisters of Phaethon . . . were changed into poplars, and with excessive bitterness they poured out tears of amber every year near the Eridanus, which we call the Po. Others say the Amber Islands are in the Adriatic Sea, into which the Po flows. . . . Others say that there is a lake in Africa called Sicyon, and the stream Cratina flowing from the lake into the ocean, in which birds called *"meleagrides"* or "Penelope birds" live, and that amber comes from there. . . . Socrates says that [amber] comes from the tears of the *meleagrides* birds as they mourn for Meleager. . . . [18]

---

[18] N. Perotti, *Cornucopiae* (Venice: Aldus, 1513), cols. 244–45: "Putant autem sorores Phaethontis fulmine icti nimio feltu in populos arbores mutatas lachrymis Electrum omnibus annis fundere iuxta Eridanum amnem, quem Padum vocamus. Alii Electridas insulas in Adriatico esse dixerunt, ad quas Padus dilaberetur, quod falsum esse manifestum est. . . . Alii Africae lacum esse Sicyonem appellatum et Cratinum amnem in oceanum fluentem e lacu, in quo aves, quas meleagridas, et penelopas vocant, vivere, ibi nasci electrum. . . . Socrates ultra Indiam fieri dixit [succinum] e lachrymis Meleagridum avium Meleagrum deflentium. . . ." Perotti here sums up numerous passages

Pliny's statement that the *meleagrides* birds or Guinea fowl cried tears of amber was well known to Renaissance humanists and literary writers. This classical topos is alluded to, for example, in Francesco Colonna's Renaissance romance *Hypnerotomachia Poliphili,* in the passage where Poliphilus praises the beautiful amber terraces in the gardens of Cythera by saying that "ne tale sono le lachryme delle Meleagride," that is, that even the amber tears of the Guinea fowl could not equal them.[19] It is my contention that Titian had been instructed to include the Guinea fowl in his so-called *Bacchanal of the Andrians,* not only in order to signal that the river he has portrayed is somehow similar to or identical with the Po, but also to imply the presence of amber in that river.

Alfonso d'Este must certainly have been aware of the classical commonplaces connecting the *meleagrides* to the natural history of the Po and to the origins of amber. Pliny was of course a widely-read author, and Alfonso's biographer Paolo Giovio tells us that the duke was accustomed to discourse with the scholar Nicolò Leoniceno, a professor at the university of Ferrara whose groundbreaking botanical research revolved around a painstaking and then highly controversial critique of Pliny's *Natural History*.[20] Moreover, Alfonso was apparently keenly interested in the Guinea fowl itself: he collected numerous exotic birds at his Villa del Belvedere, located on an island in the Po, and, in a poem probably composed shortly before 1530, the poet Scipione Balbi makes specific mention of the Guinea fowl with which Alfonso had artificially stocked the island: "You shall see . . . those African birds wandering in the open sunlight, distinguished by their speckles, and by the red crest on top of their heads. . . ."[21] Thus, not only

from Pliny, *Nat. hist.* 37, esp. 37.11.40–41, erroneously substituting "Socrates" for Pliny's "Sophocles" (the tragedian), in a passage from whose *Meleager* the Meleagrides or Guinea fowl are said to have cried their amber tears. (This passage does not correspond to any extant fragment of Sophocles.)

[19] Francesco Colonna, *Hypnerotomachia Poliphili*, ed. Giovanni Pozzi and Lucia A. Ciapponi (Padua: Antenore, 1980), 1:300; cf. 2 (commentary): 207 where Pliny is identified as Colonna's source for this reference to the *meleagrides'* amber tears.

[20] Paolo Giovio, *Liber de vita et rebus gestis Alphonsi Atestini* (Florence: Torrentinus Ducalis Typographus, 1551), esp. 59 for Alfonso's conversations with Leoniceno. For Leoniceno's revolutionary approach to Pliny, see A. Castiglioni, "The School of Ferrara and the Controversy on Pliny," in *Science, Medicine, and History: Essays . . . in Honor of Charles Singer*, ed. E. A. Underwood (London: Oxford University Press, 1953), 269–79, esp. 271–78.

[21] Balbi's text was originally published in a now-rare edition of ca. 1530. I have used the modern edition, Scipio Balbus, *Pulcher Visus Locus Illustrissimi Ducis Ferrariae* (Ferrara: Tip. Taddei condotta da Antonio Soati, 1897), esp. 10, where his description of the "Libyan birds" with their small spots and red crests identifies the Guinea fowl:

does Titian's imagery recall features of Alfonso's Belvedere with respect to its portrayal of the figure of the Guinea fowl in the environs of a river, and its consequent reference to the Amber Islands of the Po, but — more intriguingly — Alfonso's island retreat thus recalled the Amber Islands themselves, which Strabo specifically describes as being inhabited by Guinea fowl.

We recall that Strabo also mentions the presence of poplar trees on the Po's Amber Islands. Balbi also states that poplars grew on Alfonso d'Este's island of the Belvedere. He says: "Poplars are disposed in straight rows along the golden waters [of the Po], creating many pleasant shadows with their fronds . . ."; and he further notes that grapevines grew amongst those trees: "Beyond this, grapes dangle over the waters from their fecund vine-shoots, the soft shadows [of the poplars] enveloping their racemes. . . ."[22] Here, too, Titian's imagery recalls the

---

Prospicies . . .
Et volucres libycas sub aperta luce vagantes
Distinctas maculis, et rubra vertice crista . . .

The most common Latin name for the Guinea fowl was *gallina africana*. The word *libycus* was often used to signify things African, so that Balbi's unusual locution *volucres libycas* (probably chosen for metrical reasons) means "African birds." There were also turkeys *(Galline d'India)* on the island. See for example Agostino Steuco, *Augustini Eugubini Can. Regul. S. Salvatoris Cosmopoeia vel Mundano Opificio, Expositio trium capitum Genesis, in quibus de creatione tractat Moses* (Lugdini: Apud Sebastianem Gryphium, 1535), 131: "Eram Ferrariae cupidus visendi locum extra moenia, amoenissimum pomarium ducis eius urbis. . . . In nemore umbrifero lasciviebant diversorum generum animalia, Strutiones mirae magnitudinis, Gallinaeque quas Indicas dictitabant, Pavones item prodigiosae figurae . . . ," that is: "At Ferrara I desired to see that place outside the walls, the most-pleasant fruit-garden belonging to the duke of this city. . . . In a shady wood cavorted diverse kinds of animals, ostriches of marvelous size, those hens which they insisted were *gallinae Indicae,* and likewise peacocks of prodigious figure. . . ." Cf. the later sixteenth-century agricultural writer, Giovanvettorio Soderini, "Trattato degli animali domestici," in *Opere [di Giovanvettorio Soderini]*, ed. A. Bacchi della Lega (Bologna: Romagnoli dell'Acqua, 1902–1907), 4:297–98: "Sono [le Galline d'India] per certo trasportate dall'Indie. . . . Et sebbene alcuni contendono essere nel numero delle Meleagridi . . . l'indiane hanno solo i barbigli ma non le creste . . . ," that is: The [Galline d'India] were certainly brought here from the Indies. . . . And although some contend that these are to be included among the Meleagrides . . . the Indian ones have only the beards but not the crests. . . ."

[22] Balbus, *Pulcher Visus Locus,* 11:

Plurima, quae flavis in rectum fluctuat undis
Populus et mollis inducit frondibus umbras . . .
Praeterea pendent generosi palmitis uvae
Propter aquam, lenisque suos tegit umbra racemos.

island of the Belvedere. Several experts on plants have confirmed for me that all of the trees Titian has here represented belong to the Linnaean family of willows or Salicaceae — the family to which poplars belong. One of the trees at the left has an alternating pattern of lanceolate leaves typical of certain willows. The tall tree in the foreground at the right, where the Guinea fowl is perched, is very probably intended to portray a young poplar, as is suggested not only by its location on the bank of a river — as ancient writers were well aware, poplars characteristically grow near rivers and in marshy ground — but also by its sparse foliage, asymmetric, staggered branch pattern, self-pruning growth habit, and "suckers" (the still more slender shafts that spring up around the base of the tree).[23] What is more, grapevines can be seen growing on one of the trees at the left, near the top (Fig. 7). The practice of growing grapevines on poplar and willow trees is specifically discussed by Pliny in the *Natural History,* where it is further specified that the grapes growing nearest the top of the trees were believed to produce the best wines.[24] The practice of growing vines on poplar

---

[23] See for example Theophrastus, *Historia Plantarum* (1483), 4.1.1: "... some [trees] love wet and marshy ground, as [for example] the black poplar, the abele, the willow, and in general those that grow near rivers. . . ." Cf. the sixteenth-century observations of Soderini, *Opere,* 3:572–73, regarding the *pioppo* (poplar): "Ama luoghi acquosi e palustri, e però fa bene nei terreni umidi et arenosi. . . . Manda ancora fuori un'umore come ragia, il quale dicesi che stillando nel Po, intorno alla ripa del quale ne sono in gran copia, indura e rappiglisi in ambra gialla . . . ," that is: "It [i.e., the poplar] loves watery and marshy places, and therefore it does well in humid and sandy terrain. . . . It also sends forth a resinous liquid, which, they say, dripping into the Po — around which [poplars] grow in great numbers — hardens and turns into yellow amber. . . ." I thank Mr. Charlie Davis (Botanical Consultant, Baltimore, Maryland) and Dr. Frank Santamore (National Arboretum, Washington, D.C.) for confirming that the tree in which the Guinea fowl is perched, and the tree with the grapevine at the left, are both consistent with the growth habits and foliage patterns of certain varieties of poplar. Titian appears to have aimed for a general characterization of this type of tree and has not provided sufficient detail of the leaf anatomy to permit identification of the exact species. Since arboreal species have changed radically over time, and since individuals within a given species vary widely in form, it would probably be impossible to match this specimen with a specific modern counterpart.

[24] Pliny, *Nat. hist.* 17.23 (emphasis added): "Sequitur arbusti ratio mirum in modum damnata Sasernae patri filioque, celebrata Scrofae, vetustissimis post Catonem peritissimisque, ac ne a Scrofa quidem nisi Italiae concessa, cum tam longo iudicetur aevo nobilia vina non nisi in arbustis gigni et in his quoque laudatiora summis sicut uberiora imis . . . ," that is: "Next we shall discuss the method of growing grapevines on trees in the manner condemned by both the elder and the younger Saserna, and celebrated by Scrofa, the most ancient and, after Cato, the most knowledgeable [author

trees can still be observed today in the vast wine-growing region surrounding the river.[25]

That Titian's bacchanal might allude not only to the origins of amber in the Po/Eridanus but also to the viticultural fertility of the Po river valley is also suggested by allusions to the Bacchic fecundity of the Po valley found in the writings of Ferrarese court poets. For example, in a Latin epithalamium for Alfonso d'Este's marriage to his second wife, Lucrezia Borgia, Ariosto says: "[Ferrara] is now eminent among the neighboring cities, just as father Apenninus is among Bacchus's hills, or as the Eridanus is among rivers . . ."; and in his own epithalamium for Alfonso and Lucrezia, Alfonso's court historian and secretary Celio Calcagnini conjures up an image even more vividly recalling Titian's: "The oaks now flow with sweet waters, and the enfeebling Falernian wine flows in the streams. . . ."[26] This suggests another major point of comparison with Philostratus's oration: for Philostratus's description of the "river of wine" on Andros can be read as a rhetorical metaphor for the Andrians' own abundant vintage. Near the beginning of his oration (I.25.1), Philostratus in fact tells us that: " . . . by act of Dionysus the earth of the Andrians is so charged with wine that it bursts forth and sends up for them a river . . ." — an image that plainly alludes to the fertility of the Andrian soil, and to the large quantity of wine it yields. Philostratus all but completely unmasks this rhetorical metaphor at the end of his oration (*Imagines* 1.25.3), where he makes a somewhat more explicit reference to the rites and revelry of vintage-time: "Dionysus also sails to the revels of Andros. . . . He leads Laughter and Revel, two spirits most gay and most fond

---

on this subject]; and indeed Scrofa concedes this practice only to Italy, since long experience has proven that the noble wines can only be [produced from grapevines] grown on trees, and that among these the most-praised vintages come from [the grapes grown on] the highest branches, just as the most abundant wines come from the [grapes grown on the] lower ones. . . ."

[25] This modern viticultural practice is readily observed in the countryside surrounding Ferrara — for example on a summer's train ride from Ferrara to Modena. I also thank Professor Filippo Piccolo (University of Pisa) and Professor Fabio Garbari (University of Ferrara) for confirming this observation and for providing information on the widespread presence of poplars in the region.

[26] C. Calcagnini, *Epithalamium* (Ferrara, 1502): "Ilicibus iam mella fluunt: marcensq. Phalernum / Decurrit rivis . . ."; and Ludovico Ariosto, "Epithalamium," in *Opere di Ludovico Ariosto* (Trieste: Lloyd Austriaco, 1857), 112–13 (Carmina, IV), esp. 112 (praising Ferrara):

> Finitimas inter tantum nunc eminet urbes,
> Quantum inter bacchi colles pater Appeninus,
> Eridanusve inter fluvios . . .

of the drinking-bout, that with the greatest delight he may reap the river's harvest" (1.25.3). Just as Philostratus's selection of words — his allusion to the "reaping" of the river's "harvest" — suggests that his image of a "river of wine" indeed functions as a metaphor for an "abundant vintage," Titian's inclusion of the background figure of the old man who lies upon a pile of grapes and squeezes out their juices with his bare hands (Fig. 2) subtly but explicitly thematizes the production of wine.[27]

The figure of the infant urinating into the river (Fig. 3) near the reclining nude in the foreground similarly contributes to the theme of viticulture or vintage-time revelry. As Harry Murutes has shown in an important but often overlooked article, this *puer mingens* demonstrably refers to the god of Laughter mentioned by Philostratus as one of two spirits who had accompanied Dionysus to the island of Andros.[28] Indeed, it can be no accident that in the 1499 Aldine edition of Francesco Colonna's *Hypnerotomachia Poliphili,* we find an illustration of a similarly incontinent putto, inscribed with the Greek word ΓΕΛΟΙΑΣΤΟΣ — that is, "He who causes Laughter" (Fig. 8). In the *Hypnerotomachia,* this figure illustrates a statuary fountain located in the bath of the nymphs: when Colonna's protagonist Poliphilus approaches, the statue "raises its little priapus" (*priapulo*) and sprays ice-cold water in his face, as laughter echoes around him.[29] It is hardly superfluous to point out that the statue's effusion of water implies a pun on the Italian expression "fare acqua" — "to make water" — and that Titian's analogous infant is therefore similarly "making water" into the river of wine.[30] For Titian's advisor might thus have figured, with ironic understatement, the very essence of the Po valley's viticultural fecundity: its extraordinary abundance of water.

The ancient historian Polybius rehearses the whole set of classical topoi associated with the Po/Eridanus, including its geographical relationship to the Adriatic Sea, Phaethon's mythical fall into the river's waters, and the amber-weeping poplar trees that grew in the river's environs. However, in the same passage where he discusses these by now familiar commonplaces, he adds a brief natural-philosophical rationale for the extraordinary abundance of the Po's

---

[27] Concerning Titian's appropriation of this figure, see Rigas Bertos, "A Short Note on the *Bacchanal of the Andrians,*" *Mitteilungen des Kunsthistorischen Instituts in Florenz* 20 (1976): 407–10.

[28] H. Murutes, "Personifications of Laughter and Drunken Sleep in Titian's *Andrians,*" *Burlington Magazine* 115 (1973): 518–25, esp. 521; cf. Philostratus, *Imagines,* trans. Fairbanks, 1.25.3.

[29] *Hypnerotomachia Poliphili,* ed. Pozzi and Ciapponi, 1:72–80, esp. 77–78.

[30] See S. Battaglia, ed., *Grande dizionario della lingua italiana* (Turin: UTET, 1961–2000), 1:124–30, esp. 129–30 (no. 8): "Fare acqua: orinare."

waters: "[The Po/Eridanus]," he tells us, "has a larger volume of water than any other river in Italy, since all the streams that descend into the plain from the Alps and Apennines fall into it from either side, and is highest and finest at the time of the rising of the Dog-star, as it is then swollen by the melting snow on those mountains."[31] This passage was evidently known to Alfonso d'Este's secretary and court historian Celio Calcagnini, who alludes to it in a passage of his treatise *De re nautica:*

> In like manner Aristotle bears witness that all of the seas turn upside down at the rise of the Dog-star, and that both seaweeds and fish swim in the opposite direction.... *Our river Po also floods at the rise of the Dog-star, the snows having melted, flowing more violently for fields and ships alike.* Arrian writes that around the summer solstice the rivers of India are also overflowing and turbulent. . . ."[32] [emphasis added]

Calcagnini was thus aware of Polybius's observation that the Po/Eridanus floods annually at the heliacal rising of Sirius, the Dog-star, an astronomical event occurring around mid-July, and thus marking the height of summer.As we have seen, Polybius explains this natural phenomenon in terms of the summer's increasing heat, which melts the snows and, in turn, floods the river. But Calcagnini has broadened Polybius's observation by correlating it with a passage in the *Indica* of Arrian, where we learn that not only do the Indus and the Ganges flood at that time, also due to the melting of the snows, but further (as Calcagnini neglects to observe) that the Nile is similarly in flood around the summer solstice due to the torrential rains of Ethiopia.[33] If Titian's figure of the god of Laughter "making water" in the river of wine was intended to figure the natural-philosophical argument that the presence of water contributes to the viticultural fertility or abundance of the Po valley, his advisor has thus implied that this infusion of water must occur at the hottest time of the year.

This seems doubly probable when we realize that the artist's rather cryptic allusion to the origins of amber, implied by the figure of the Guinea fowl perched

---

[31] Polybius, *Histories*, trans. W. R. Paton, 6 vols., Loeb Classical Library (Cambridge, MA: Harvard University Press, 1960), 2:16.5–15, esp. 8–11.

[32] C. Calcagnini, "Commentatio de Re Nautica," in idem, *Opere Aliquot* (Basel: Froben, 1544), 301–16, esp. 315: "Caniculae item ortu omnia maria subverti testatur Aristoteles: & algas piscesque inversos natare.... Excrescit & Padus noster ad Canis ortus liquatis nivibus, agris quam navigiis torrentior. Scribit Arrianus, amnes Indorum circum aestivum solstitium plenos & turbulentos fluere. . . ."

[33] Arrian, *Indica*, trans. Iliff Robson, 3 vols. (Cambridge, MA: Harvard University Press, 1946–1949), 6:4–7.

in the poplar tree, necessarily also constitutes a reference to the rising of the Dog-star and therefore further alludes to the heat of summer. For it was at this time of year that the tree, and presumably also the bird itself, were thought to produce their amber tears. Amidst his observations on the origins of amber, Pliny repeatedly mentions the belief that it is the heat of the sun that causes amber to form. For example he tells of a lake called "Cephisis," which, "when thoroughly heated by the sun, produces from its mud amber, that floats upon the surface of its waters."[34] Pliny knew of ancient writers who specifically associated the production of amber with the rising of the Dog-star: he mentions "misguided" authors who reported that "on inaccessible rocks at the head of the Adriatic Sea there stand trees which at the rising of the Dog-star shed [amber] gum. . . ."[35] Since the geographical location that Pliny here describes obviously corresponds to the mythical "Amber Islands" of the Po delta, and since Titian has alluded to these Amber Islands by portraying the amber-producing *meleagris* or Guinea fowl that inhabits the region, the beholder familiar with Pliny's remarks might well have concluded that the painting itself was intended to allude to the rising of the Dog-star, and the consequent arrival of the sun's maximum summer heat.

This conclusion is reinforced by a passage in the influential mythographic handbook attributed to "Albricus philosophus," a medieval text that aroused new interest when it became available in its first printed edition in 1520 — shortly before Titian began work on his bacchanal.[36] Here the author interprets the myth of Phaethon's fall into the Eridanus as signifying the sun's proximity to the earth during the summer months, and attributes the formation of amber precisely to the combination of the sun's heat (Phaethon's solar chariot) with an abundance of water (that is, the Eridanus):

---

[34] Pliny, *Nat. hist.* 37.11.36–37: "Nicias solis radiorum sucum intellegi voluit hoc; circa occasum vehementiores in terram actos pinguem sudorem in ea relinquere, oceani deinde aestibus in germanorum litora eici. . . . Asarubas tradit iuxta Atlanticum mare esse lacum Cephisida, quem Mauri vocent Electrum. Hunc sole excalefactum e limo reddere electrum fluitans."

[35] Pliny, *Nat. hist.* 37.11.33: "modestiores, sed aeque falsum, prodidere in extremis Hadriatici sinus inviis rupibus arbores stare quae canis ortu hanc effunderent cummim. . . ."

[36] On Albricus's importance to Renaissance mythography, see Jean Seznec, *The Survival of the Pagan Gods: The Mythological Tradition and Its Place in Renaissance Humanism and Art*, trans. Barbara F. Sessions (Princeton: Princeton University Press, 1972), esp. 179.

> [Phaethon's] sisters, who are called the Heliades, that is, the daughters of the Sun, crying with gem-like tears (as Ovid tells in the *Metamorphoses*), bewail their brother's [death amidst the] flames; [and] their skin bursting open, they throw off golden amber. Helios indeed is interpreted as the Sun. The sisters are the trees, which therefore without doubt are one and the same with the virtue of plants and flowers, which are born amidst the raging heat and moisture. These trees, which then sweat out amber (while the Sun reaches Cancer and Leo, scorching the mature fruits in the hottest months of June and July) in the full strength of summer, with their bark split open, send forth their liquid sap into the river Eridanus, to be hardened into amber by the waters.[37]

When Albricus connects the formation of amber with the heat of the sun, he specifies that he means the extreme heat that arrives with the sign of Cancer, and continues under the sign of Leo. Since the sun's entrance into Cancer coincides with and defines the summer solstice (the same time of year marked by the rising of the Dog-star), Albricus is necessarily referring to precisely the same time of year when Polybius says the snows of the Apennines melt, causing the Eridanus to flood. But Albricus goes somewhat further than either Pliny or Polybius in arguing that it is the combination of the heat of the summer sun with the waters of the Eridanus that causes not only the formation of amber but also the growth of poplar trees — and indeed of all plants. It is this last point which suggests a more comprehensive way of interpreting Titian's conceit.

As we have seen, Titian's pictorial argument apparently involved the notion that the lands surrounding the Po/Eridanus were particularly well adapted to the growth of the grapevine, and thus produced an extraordinary quantity of wine. Albricus's allegorical reading of the Phaethon myth seems particularly relevant to that argument. For Albricus understood this bizarre ancient story

---

[37] Albricus, *Allegoriae Poeticae* (Paris: De Marnet, 1520), 29v–30r (De Phebi quibusdam appropriatis): "Huius [i.e., Phaethon's] sorores gemmeis guttis lucentibus (ut Ovidius in metamorphos. refert) fraterna plorant incendia succina diruptis iaciunt inaurata corticibus, quae etiam heliades id est solis filiae nuncupantur. Helios enim sol interpretatur. Herbarum igitur et florum procul dubio sorores sunt arbores, quae una eademque, fervoris humorisque frugalitate gignuntur. Arbores autem ille, quae succinum sudant (dum maturas fruges, sol torrens, Iunio, Iulioque mensibus incendiosior cancrum atque leonem attingerit) tunc estu valido, fissis corticibus, succum sui liquoris, in eridano flumine, aquis in electra durandum emittunt. . . ." Similar allegories are found in the mid-sixteenth-century mythographers, e.g., Natale Conti, *Mythologiae* (Venice, 1567), 167v–169r.

as a veiled reference to the sun's apparent proximity to earth at high summer, reading Phaethon's fall into the Eridanus as the combination of extreme heat with water, which causes both the formation of amber and the abundant growth of vegetation — necessarily including the growth of the grapevine itself.

In my view, this concept is summed up in the central image of Titian's composition — the figure of the man holding up a glass carafe filled with red wine, marveling at its radiant color. Indeed, this carafe of wine glows like a beautiful gem, capturing the soft sunlight amidst the shadows of the trees. Given the context of the pictorial argument at hand, which features the notion that tears of amber had fallen into the Po/Eridanus, and that the Po itself was a "river of wine," this unmistakably gemlike quality seems to suggest that the wine has somehow been infused not only with sunlight, but also with amber itself. Ancient, medieval, and Renaissance medical writers describe numerous medicinal preparations or "electuaries" featuring amber as an ingredient, and in many of these appalling concoctions the amber was actually dissolved in and/or taken with wine: for example, several of the electuaries recommended by Marsilio Ficino in *De Vita* feature these ingredients.[38] But for our present purposes it is perhaps more appropriate to point to a passage in Pliny's *Natural History,* where the author questions the ancient beliefs that jaundice and calculi could be cured by drinking amber dissolved in wine — or even by merely looking at such a solution.[39] With this in mind, it seems significant indeed that while Alfonso d'Este's personal friend the medical and botanical expert Giovanni Manardi was one of the first Renaissance physicians to reject outright the use of electuaries containing ground or dissolved gemstones, the duke's own personal physician, Antonius Musa Brasavola — a pupil of Manardi's — is known to have adopted a more moderate position regarding these practices.[40]

In any case, Titian's imagery suggests a natural-philosophical discourse on the Po/Eridanus, a discourse that alludes to the myths of Phaethon's fall and of the origins of amber in order to suggest that the wines produced in Alfonso's

---

[38] Marsilio Ficino, *Three Books on Life*, trans. C. Kaske and J. R. Clark, MRTS 57 (Binghamton: Medieval and Renaissance Texts and Studies, 1989), e.g., 154–55, 190–91, etc.

[39] Pliny, *Nat. hist.* 37.13.53: "falsum et quod de medecina simul proditur, calculos vesicae poto eo elidi et morbo regio succurri, si ex vino bibatur aut spectetur etiam," that is: "what is said about its medicinal value is also false, that by drinking it calculi can be removed from the urinary bladder, and jaundice cured, if it is taken with wine or even looked at." Cf. 37.12.51: "Callistratus prodesse etiam cuicumque aetati contra lymphationes tradit et urinae difficultatibus potum adalligatumque. . . ."

[40] E. L. Greene, *Landmarks of Botanical History*, 2 vols. (Stanford: Stanford University Press, 1983), vol. 2, esp. 2:596–97; and cf. 2:691–92.

domain and indeed in the whole region surrounding the Po were superior, with respect to both quality and quantity. It might well be asked how this recondite and densely figured discourse could have served Alfonso d'Este in the context of his personal study. I shall answer this question in more detail elsewhere, but for the moment it may suffice to consider this passage from Erasmus's *Ecclesiastes,* concerning the reasons why Christian scripture conceals the most profound wisdom under the cloak of allegory:

> In the *De Doctrina Christiana,* Augustine explains elegantly why God wanted scripture to be enshrouded in this sort of "covering," and with other obscurities. We neglect whatever is closest to hand. . . . We seek out hidden and remote things more avidly. . . . *Moreover, just as many things shine forth more beautifully through glass or amber, the truth brings us more delight when it shines through allegory.*[41] [emphasis added]

Faced with Titian's beautiful and apparently "simple" image, we are challenged to look beyond the translucent window of immediate appearances. Perhaps this is the significance of the famously mysterious lines inscribed on the sheet of music lying in the foreground of Titian's painting, on the river bank, at center: "Qui boyt et ne reboyt il ne scet que boyre soit," that is, "He who drinks and does not drink again does not know what drinking is."[42] For while our first draught from the cup of Titian's imagery is perhaps satisfying, it is only by returning to it again and again that we may begin to appreciate its wonders.

---

[41] Desiderius Erasmus, *Ecclesiastes*, ed. Jacques Chomarat, in *Opera Omnia: recognita et adnotatione critica instructa notisque illustrata* (Amsterdam: North Holland Publishing Company [ed. Union Académique Internationale and Académie Royale Néerlandaise des Sciences et des Sciences Humaines], 1969–), 5.5: 250: "Quamobrem autem deus voluerit Scripturam hoc genus involucris et aliis obscuritatibus opertam et involutam esse, eleganter explicat Augustinus in opere De doctrina christiana. . . . Quod in promptu est negligimus. . . . Ad recondita semotaque sumus avidiores. . . . Praeterea quemadmodum multa per vitrum aut succina pellucent iucundius, ita magis delectat veritas per allegoriam relucens."

[42] Scholars have generally dismissed these lyrics as a facile joke, but in my view they are integral to the painting's conceit. Concerning the music to which the lyrics are set, see principally D. Shinneman, "The Canon in Titian's *Andrians*: A Reinterpretation," *Studies in the History of Art* 6 (1974): 93–95; and Edward Lowinsky, "Music in Titian's *Bacchanal of the Andrians*: Origin and History of the Canon *per tonos*," in *Titian, His World and His Legacy*, ed. David Rosand (New York: Columbia University Press, 1982), 191–282.

Figure 11. Titian, *The Andrians* (Madrid, Museo del Prado) (Photo: Museo del Prado).

Figure 12. Old man squeezing grapes, detail from Titian, *The Andrians* (Photo: Museo del Prado).

Figure 13. Urinating infant, detail from Titian, *The Andrians*
(Photo: Museo del Prado)

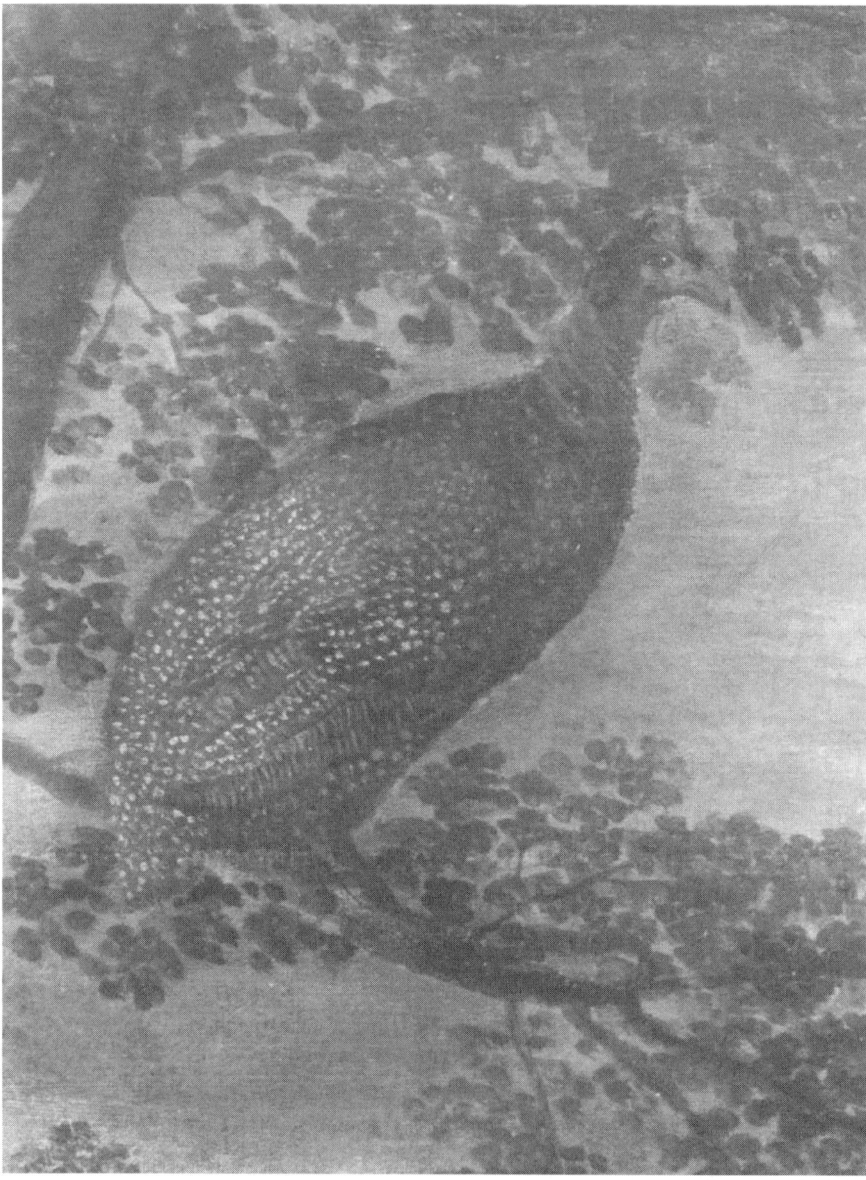

Figure 14. Guinea fowl, detail from Titian, *The Andrians*
(Photo: Museo del Prado)

Figure 15. Girolamo da Carpi, *Venus on the Eridanus* (Dresden, Staatliche Kunstsammlungen) (Photo: Staatliche Kunstsammlungen).

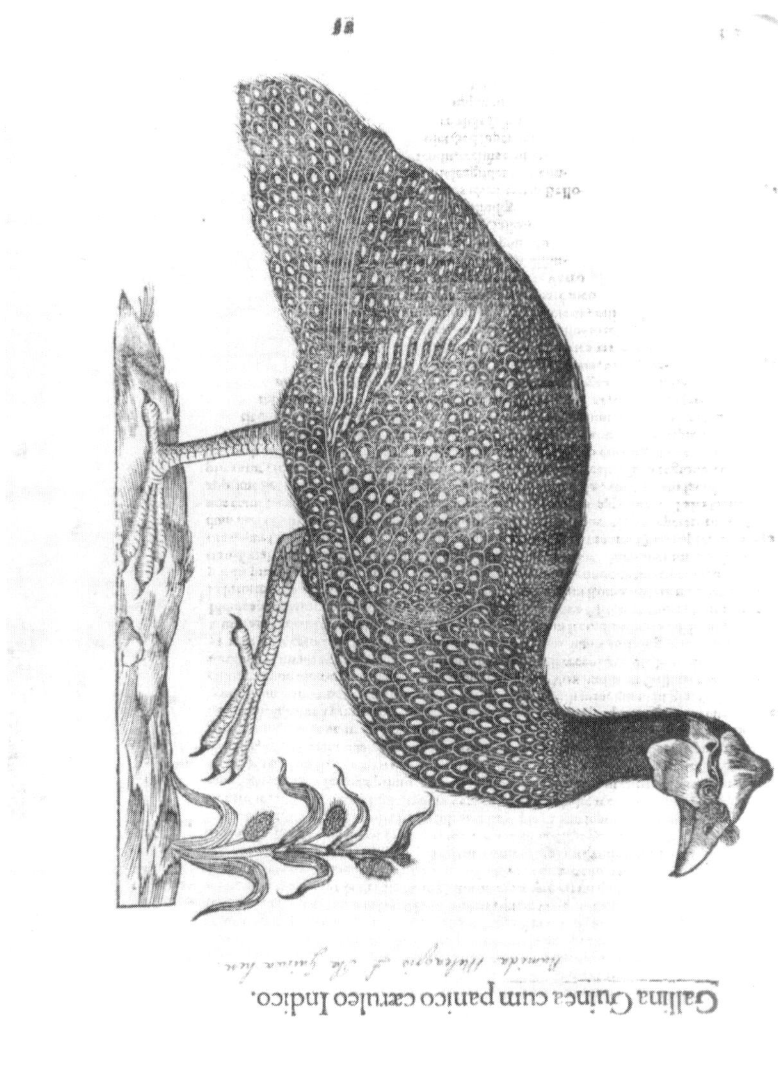

Figure 16. *Guinea fowl*, illustration from Ulisse Aldrovandi, *Ornithologiae* (Bologna, 1637–1646) (Photo: Milton S. Eisenhower Library, Special Collections, The Johns Hopkins University).

Figure 17. Grapevine climbing a tree, detail from Titian, *The Andrians* (Photo: Museo del Prado)

cogitato, Che ponendo ſopra el grado imo inſtabile, pondo alcuno, in giu el ſe moueua, & in ſu traheua lo inſtruméto puerile. Onde cum ſub tile examine inueſtigato la machina & curioſo artificio, mi fu molto gra tiſſimo. Et pero nel Zophorulo era inſcripto elegãte di Atthice formu le queſto titulo. ΓΕΛΟΙΑΣΤΟΣ.

Doppo molto iocoſo riſo balneati, & lauatone tutti, cũ mille & dolce amoroſe & piaceuole parolette, & uirginali ſcherci & bládiméti. Fora dl le termate aq̃ uſciſſimo, ſaliédo ſopra li aſſueti gradi cũ grãde tripudio &

Figure 18. *Geloiastos,* illustration from Francesco Colonna, *Hypnerotomachia Poliphili* (Photo: Author).

From Josquin Desprez to Cipriano de Rore: Tradition and Transformation in Sixteenth-Century Ferrarese Musical Culture

Lewis Lockwood

In 1521 Josquin Desprez died in the quiet glory of his old age in his native town of Condé-sur-Escaut in northern France. He was then the most acclaimed composer in Europe. For his legendary status the reasons were numerous, beginning with recognition by musicians and patrons that his Masses, motets, and chansons, plus some instrumental works, stood at the center of contemporary music.[1] Josquin's mastery of technique and breadth of expression had come to represent an absolute model for composers as early as around 1500, and his artistic stature was linked to his prominence in the new domain of music printing, which had begun in Venice in 1501.

A recent revolution in Josquin biography has revised the accepted picture of his career that had been in place until a few years ago.[2] To make a long story

---

[1] Josquin's prominence in Petrucci's early publications of motets and Masses, including his own First and Second Books of Masses, of 1502 and 1515, contributed strongly to the composer's great reputation. On the other hand, we have ample reason to believe that his stature was recognized before 1502, and that it was not merely the result of fame through publications. I offer this as a modest corrective to some current tendencies to regard his reputation as more or less a "construction" created by the nascent musical market for Petrucci's prints, rather than as having an inherent basis in the quality of his music as recognized by contemporaries.

[2] The new portrait is based on recent archival research by various hands, including Herbert Kellman, Richard Sherr, Pamela Starr, Adalbert Roth, and, most conspicuously, Paul and Lora M. Merkley. The Merkleys' research has been reported in articles and conference talks, but most fully in their book, Paul Merkley and Lora Matthews, *Music*

short, it now appears that the previously accepted notion that Josquin Desprez spent his early years (1459–1472) as a singer at the Duomo of Milan, followed by a period in the 1470s as a singer in the ducal chapel of Galeazzo Maria Sforza, is invalid. There *was* a singer in the Sforza chapel in the 1470s by the name of "Josquin" (spellings vary) who was from Picardy, as was the composer, but this singer was a different person. The Merkleys' discovery that the "Joschino di Picardia," also known as "Josquin de Kessalia," who was in Milan in the 1470s, died in 1498, clinches the case that there were two musicians by the name "Josquin," of whom one was the composer, the other apparently not a composer but a singer. It appears that the "real" Josquin was born around 1450, probably spent his earlier career in France, served in the court chapel of René d'Anjou in Aix-en-Provence c. 1475–1480, then served in some capacity to Cardinal Ascanio Sforza c. 1484–1485, followed by his membership in the Papal Chapel c. 1489–1495. As more facts emerge the picture will undoubtedly change again, but for the present this should suffice.

In any case, none of these recent discoveries have shaken the identity of the Josquin who was recruited by Ferrarese agents in 1502 and came to Ferrara as ducal maestro di cappella in April 1503, remaining for just about a calendar year.[3] There is no doubt that this was Josquin Desprez. In April 1504 Josquin left Ferrarese service to return to Condé, where he spent his remaining years as cathedral canon.

Two Ferrarese agents, writing in 1502, show us how Josquin was then seen. One, Gian de Artiganova, said in 1502, in a much-quoted letter, that Duke Ercole I d'Este, then looking for a new chapel leader, should hire Isaac rather than Josquin because "he is of a better nature among his companions and will compose new works more often." "It is true," added Gian, "that Josquin composes better but he composes when he wants to, and not when you want him to; and he is asking for 200 ducats while Isaac will come for 120." Gian's rival, Girolamo da Sestola, called "il Coglia," a friend of Ariosto's, told Ercole that, if he were to send for Josquin, "neither Lord nor King would have a better chapel than yours

---

and Patronage at the Sforza Court (Turnhout: Brepols, 1999). See the summary of known biographical facts (as of 2000) in Richard Sherr, ed., *The Josquin Companion* (Oxford: Oxford University Press, 2000), 11–20.

[3] On Josquin's stay at Ferrara see Lewis Lockwood, *Music in Renaissance Ferrara 1400–1505: The Creation of a Musical Center in the Fifteenth Century* (Cambridge, MA: Harvard University Press, 1984), 202–7, and earlier studies cited there. On Josquin at Condé see Herbert Kellman, "Josquin at the Courts of the Netherlands and France," in *Josquin Desprez: Proceedings of the International Josquin Festival-Conference*, ed. E. Lowinsky (Oxford: Oxford University Press, 1976), 181–216.

. . . [and] by having Josquin in our chapel I want to place a crown upon this chapel of ours."[4] So Ercole had hired Josquin in 1503, and Josquin in turn enshrined Ercole's name indelibly in the annals of patronage through his Mass entitled *Missa Hercules dux Ferrarie,* published just a few months after Ercole's death in 1505, in Josquin's Second Book of Masses.

In Ferrara in the first half of the sixteenth century, through thirty years of the rule of Alfonso I (1505–1534) and twenty-five (1534–1559) of Ercole II, the name of Josquin continued to symbolize the musical glories of the earlier years of Ercole I. Other patrons might have busts and portraits, but only this one, up to now, had had his name literally worked into the fabric of a famous composition.[5] How keenly this was understood is clear from some of the surviving sources of the *Missa Hercules Dux Ferrarie* that were copied into expensive manuscripts for other patrons; it appears in a Hapsburg-Burgundian source of about 1510 for Philip the Fair as *Missa Philippus Rex Castiliae,* and in a German source of about 1525 for Frederick the Wise as *Missa Fridericus Dux Saxoniae.* Of course the music was unchanged, so that the cantus firmus drawn from the syllables of Ercole's name had to be adjusted to fit the names of the new patrons: but glory counted more than accuracy.[6]

Ferrarese musical patronage after Ercole I soon fractured into rivalries among his children — Alfonso I, Cardinal Ippolito I, Isabella, and Sigismondo d'Este, to name only the four who remained active as music patrons.[7] The various

---

[4] On Gian's and Coglia's letters see Lewis Lockwood, "Josquin at Ferrara: New Documents and Letters," in *Josquin Desprez: Proceedings of the International Josquin Festival-Conference*, ed. Lowinsky, 103–37. See also idem, *Music in Renaissance Ferrara*, 200–7.

[5] On the *Hercules* Mass see Lockwood, *Music in Renaissance Ferrara*, 241–49.

[6] The full name appears as Tenor text throughout also in a newly found early sixteenth-century manuscript in Prague, Národni Muzeum, MS (no signature) of south German or Bohemian origin, which contains the name "Hercules Dux Ferrarie" throughout the Mass in the Tenor part. Of course the rigid structure of the Tenor part only permits either the singing of syllables "Her-cu-les Dux Fer-ra-ri-e" or the equivalent solmization syllables (re ut re ut re fa mi re) during the entire work.

[7] For a very partial picture of the patronage of Alfonso I (not yet fully studied) and on his brother Sigismondo see Lewis Lockwood, "Jean Mouton and Jean Michel: New Evidence on French Music and Musicians in Italy, 1505–1520," *Journal of the American Musicological Society* 32 (1979): 191–246. On Ippolito I, a good deal of material is assembled in Lewis Lockwood, "Adrian Willaert and Cardinal Ippolito I d'Este: New Light on Willaert's Early Career in Italy," *Early Music History* 5 (1985): 85–112. On Isabella see, most recently, William F. Prizer, "Isabella d'Este and Lucrezia Borgia as Patrons of Music: The Frottola at Mantua and Ferrara," *Journal of the American Musicological Society* 38 (1985): 1–33.

elements of Este patronage, and to some extent that of other north Italian centers, divided into contending factions just at the same time that new forms of expression were coming rapidly into Italian secular and sacred music, from about 1510 to about 1550. This was spearheaded by the rise of the Italian madrigal as the new indigenous art form blending music and poetry, but the same expansion was felt in the large domains of Latin-texted polyphonic forms — the Mass and above all the motet, in which Josquin remained a model for the next generation.

Under Alfonso I the court chapel was smaller than in Ercole's time but still international. It included French and Savoyard members such as the copyist and agent Jean Michel, the singer Bidon (praised extravagantly by Castiglione), and for a time the important composer Antoine Brumel. The rival group of musicians paid by Cardinal Ippolito I, Ariosto's patron, included instrumentalists and singers and also the young Adrian Willaert. In 1517, when the quietly defiant Ariosto made his famous refusal to go with Ippolito to Hungary — "a me piace abitar la mia contrada" — Willaert and several other musicians obeyed orders and went along. After about 1520 more Italian musicians became prominent at the court, among them Alfonso della Viola and others of his clan, but there remained a continued preeminence of French or Franco-Flemish master musicians in north Italian circles. One is the composer Jacques Collebaudi, called Jacquet of Mantua after his place of service; another, at Ferrara, was elusively named "Maistre Jhan," a prolific composer of madrigals, motets, and Masses, whose works were issued in Ferrarese music prints. In this line the culminating figure at mid-century was certainly Cipriano de Rore, who served Ercole II from 1546 to 1559. Taken all in all, Ferrara in the decades of Alfonso I and Ercole II remained a key center of north Italian musical life, possessing a rich tradition.

Inevitably Ferrara could not rival the major cities, Florence, Venice, Rome, and Naples, in breadth and productivity and could never be a center for music printing though its local printers were reasonably productive. Its narrower patronage base was limited by the court's domination and by economic constraints. Yet a good part of its distinction lay in its coherent civic culture and the continuity of the Este line, down to the end of the century, a condition that differentiated it from its nearer rivals, especially Milan and Mantua.

In musical matters, accordingly, the linked legacy of Josquin Desprez and Ercole I remained a matter of considerable local pride. Josquin's works, especially motets, continued to be copied in local manuscripts. They included several works that Josquin apparently wrote for Ercole I during his year of residency. One of them, the famous *Miserere,* reflects Ercole's own piety, and has also been shown to be associated with Savonarola's sermon on Psalm 50. The other is a motet for the Virgin on a poem by the Ferrarese poet Ercole Strozzi.[8] Most influential of all was the Mass *Hercules Dux Ferrarie,* which may have been written during 1503–1504, and which served as a direct model for similar works written later in the century. One surviving Mass was apparently written by Willaert for Ippolito I, and several others were composed in honor of Ercole II. We also see Josquin mentioned by Ferrarese writers and musicians long after his death.

In the visual arts one painting literally shows us how the legend of Josquin interacted with symbols of Este hegemony and the family's own mythology about itself, a theme that finds its way prominently into the *Orlando Furioso* and other Ferrarese literature. This is the celebrated *Allegory of Music* by Dosso Dossi (c. 1490–1542) in the Museo Horne, about which there has been considerable discussion, some of it almost as fanciful as the picture itself.[9]

This allegory, apparently painted c. 1524–1534, and centered on the theme of the origins of music, was brilliantly elucidated some years ago by H. Colin Slim, who was able to transcribe the two actual compositions that are presented in the picture and attribute one of them unquestionably to Josquin himself. Slim revealed for the first time that the triangular canon on the partially concealed stone slab at the bottom right of the picture is a famous three-part canonic Agnus Dei from Josquin's Mass *L'homme armé super voces musicales,* first published in 1502. It is clearly a companion to the four-part circle canon on the other, more visible slab, for which no composer has yet been identified.

In this painting Dosso draws on traditional accounts of Pythagoras's discovery of musical consonances upon hearing a blacksmith strike hammers of various weights. Dosso blends the Pythagoras figure with that of the Biblical Tubalcain, the mythical inventor of music, sometimes confused with his half-brother Jubal, also a musician. In the picture the hefty blacksmith, heeding a spirit at the far left, is in the act of creating musical sounds (and thus, fancifully, music) by hitting the anvil with a hammer while another hammer lies at his feet. As Slim writes, "Dosso even fancifully scatters a few stylized notes on the anvil of his Hebraic-

---

[8] On the *Miserere* see Patrick Macey, "Savonarola and the Sixteenth-Century Motet," *Journal of the American Musicological Society* 36 (1983): 422–52.

[9] On Dosso Dossi see F. Gibbons, *Dosso and Battista Dossi: Court Painters at Ferrara* (Princeton: Princeton University Press, 1968) and more recently, Luisa Ciammitti, Steven F. Ostrow, and Salvatore Settis, eds., *Dosso's Fate: Painting and Court Culture in Renaissance Italy* (Los Angeles: Getty Research Institute for the History of Art and the Humanities, 1998); also Peter Humfrey and Mauro Lucco, *Dosso Dossi: Court Painter in Renaissance Ferrara* (New York: The Metropolitan Museum of Art, distributed by Andrea Bayer, 1998). On the music, as indicated, the basic study is now H. Colin Slim, "Dosso Dossi's Allegory at Florence about Music," *Journal of the American Musicological Society* 43 (1990): 43–98, esp. 58–62.

Greco blacksmith" (50). The use of circle and triangle for the two canons associates these examples of notated music with classic geometric forms and thus with symbols of mathematical perfection. Further, as Slim has shown, the painting contrasts at least two aspects of time, raising the issue of music and temporality. The blacksmith is creating sounds in actual and present time: thus his work represents the making of music in the moment of its creation, music that is not fixed or written down but improvised and heard. The two tablets, on the other hand, which are on the ground (grass is growing from the earth on the more central one) present music in another time-frame, that of music notated, fixed, visible and unchanging because established once and for all. In the new age of music printing this new status of music was more palpable than ever before, that is, its capacity to be written down and preserved (established then for centuries past, but now for the first time *printed*), thus embodying both past creation and present fixed form. Slim cites Leonardo's remark in his *Paragone,* namely that music is lost to sound as soon as it is born (Leonardo does not think of notation as preservation), and says that this paradox "lies at the very heart of Dosso's . . . allegory" (83).

I might also suggest that the two music examples on the tablets represent the domains of secular and sacred music, the latter being chosen from the one composer, Josquin, whose connection to the Este dynasty symbolized the permanence of both music and the family line. A comparable project was the Palazzo de' Diamanti in the "new addition" to Ferrara, built in 1495, with its thousands of diamond-shaped stones referring to the diamond as Ercole's personal symbol, the embodiment of hardness, endurance, rarity, and value.

Contemporary images of the reigning duke as knight and as religious penitent characterize Ercole I in his public persona, combining his roles as one-time condottiere and as serious religious devotee, whose adherence to ritual and the power of faith contrasted sharply with the more secular-minded princes of his generation. Of course the portrayal of each reigning duke as military leader was also a reminder of the perpetual need to defend the small state, and so Alfonso also had himself portrayed by Dosso in full armor and in battle.[10] Alfonso's militant pose not only reflected his early struggles with Venice and his role as military tactician, but it also carried associations with his long-drawn-out confrontation with the Papacy, first under Julius II and then Leo X, over Ferrarese political independence and especially over Modena and Reggio.

The theme of the Duke in armor leads us onward to Duke Ercole II. Between 1534 and 1559, Ercole's burdens of office included not only the normal ones

---

[10] For a reproduction of the painting, owned by the Galleria Estense in Modena, see Luciano Chiappini, *Gli Estensi*, 2nd ed. (Varese: Dall'Oglio, 1967), facing page 224.

of managing civic and external affairs but, for the first time in the history of the duchy, he also had to engage with a religious and domestic crisis in the immediate ducal household. This was provoked by the outspoken support of Protestant reform by his wife, Princess Renée of France, Duchess of Ferrara.[11] Renée not only harbored French refugees, including Clément Marot (who was her secretary in 1535–1536), but also collaborated in the clandestine visit of Jean Calvin to Ferrara, which probably took place in 1536. For Ercole II, as fourth Duke of Ferrara, legally a papal vassal, the outbreak of religious opposition in his own house created a domestic and political crisis of the first order, rendering him intensely vulnerable to pressure from Rome and from neighboring Italian states to vigorously root out the heresy. Against this background Ercole's portrayal in armor may not have been just another routine depiction that upheld tradition but also carried the assurance that he too, like his father and grandfather, was a warlike servant of the Catholic faith.

Ercole's use of music to dramatize his unyielding opposition to the Protestant camp around Renée is well documented.[12] The strongest evidence is the overtly anti-Lutheran motet, on the text *Te Lutherum damnamus,* probably written sometime after Calvin's visit and set to music by Maistre Jhan, Ercole's court composer. The text, beginning "Te Lutherum damnamus, te haereticum confitemur," while it eloquently condemns Luther as the leader of heresy, is also a parody of the *Te Deum,* the hymn of praise sung on special occasions to celebrate state events. As Nugent suggests, *Te Lutherum* could well have been sung during Pope Paul III's state visit in 1543. It would have reassured the Pope of Ercole's loyalty during a visit that was designed to stiffen local resistance to heresy and to deal with the political dangers aroused by the defection of a reigning duchess and French princess who was also under the protection of the French throne.[13]

---

[11] On Renée and her espousal of Protestantism there is a substantial literature, but the basic study is still Bartolommeo Fontana, *Renata di Francia, duchessa di Ferrara, sui documenti dell'Archivio estense, del mediceo, del Gonzaga e dell'Archivio segreto vaticano (1510–1536)* (Rome: Forzani, 1889). Recent studies include: Charmarie Webb Blaisdell, "Politics and Heresy in Ferrara, 1534–1559," *Sixteenth-Century Journal* 61 (1975): 67–93; eadem, "Renée de France between Reform and Counter-Reform," *Archiv für Reformationsgeschichte* 63 (1972): 196–216; eadem, "Royalty and Reform: The Predicament of Renée de France, 1510–1575" (Ph.D. diss., Tufts University, 1969)

[12] Edward Lowinsky, "Music in the Culture of the Renaissance," *Journal of the History of Ideas* 15 (1954) 509–53: here, 522–23; and George Nugent, "Anti-Protestant Music for Sixteenth-Century Ferrara," *Journal of the American Musicological Society* 43 (1990): 228–91. The music of the motet is found in Winfried Kirsch, ed., *Das Chorwerk*, vol. 102 (Wolfenbüttel: Möseler Verlag, 1967).

[13] Nugent, "Anti-Protestant Music," 280.

Nugent also identified another motet, *Cantemus domino,* a four-voice motet by Jacquet of Mantua published in 1544, that includes a prayer for the safeguarding of Giulio Boiardo, Count of Scandiano, a descendant of the poet, who was evidently sympathetic to Renée and may have had a hand in her clandestine protection of heretics. The text, perhaps a warning to the count, calls on Saints Michael, Peter, and Paul, with other apostles and evangelists, to watch over Giulio and protect him. Nugent plausibly proposes that such a motet could have been commissioned at Mantua by Cardinal Ercole Gonzaga, Jacquet's master and Duke Ercole's cousin. This son of Isabella d'Este and Francesco Gonzaga was a leading defender of orthodoxy, an enlightened traditionalist, a perpetual candidate for the Papacy, and a close observer of the scene in neighboring Ferrara. He may have been instrumental in getting Jacquet of Mantua to pay tribute to Este family members in various works, including motets for Ippolito II and Jacquet's own *Missa Hercules Dux Ferrarie* for Ercole II, also modeled on Josquin's but now with a cantus firmus on the text "Hercules vivet usque in aeternum." Nugent has also called attention to Jacquet's Mass on the text *La fede unque debbe esser corrotta,* which might be based on an unknown madrigal but which in any event makes use of a line known from Canto 21, Stanza 2 of the *Orlando Furioso,* and also from Ariosto's *Rime,* 15, lines 37–48. In the *Rime* Ariosto tells that "Faith must never be broken, whether to one or a hundred ears, within mansion or cave: by common folk an oath is sworn, but with nobler spirits a simple promise holds as a sacrament." Nugent plausibly suggests that the Mass could have been written in the wake of a "final great showdown" between Ercole and Renée at which she was forced publicly to recant (278). The verbal warning to stand firm in the faith could well have been intended by Ercole Gonzaga for Duchess Renée but also in a sense for his cousin the duke.

In the last part of this essay I want to tie these threads together with the help of some further works that connect to Josquin. They have long been accepted as formal musical tributes to Ercole II, but can also be interpreted as supporting and symbolizing his role as defender of the faith amid his shattered household. These are the two great Masses for Ercole II, written by Cipriano de Rore (1516–1565), principal court composer in the later years of Ercole II, long acknowledged as the central figure of his generation in the composition of madrigals and sacred music. Since Alfred Einstein's classic study of the Italian madrigal, Rore's central place in the evolution of the genre has been manifest.[14]

---

[14] Alfred Einstein, *The Italian Madrigal,* 3 vols. (Princeton: Princeton University Press, 1949), 384–422. On Rore's sacred music see Alvin Johnson, "The Masses of Cipriano de Rore," *Journal of the American Musicological Society* 6 (1953): 227–39, and idem, "The Liturgical Music of Cipriano de Rore" (Ph.D. diss., Yale University, 1954).

Born in Flanders, Rore had come to Italy by the late 1530s; he almost certainly studied with Willaert at Venice in the 1540s and became *maestro di cappella* at Ferrara by 1546, emerging as the central figure in Ferrarese music in the late 1540s and 1550s. In 1559 he left, when Ercole death and Renée's departure for France brought in a new phase of musical taste under Alfonso II. His stay in Ferrara is Rore's longest single period of service in any one post, and it must have been a productive one for him.

Among other Rore works that bear direct connection to Ferrarese literary and political figures are these two Masses for Ercole II, namely the *Missa Vivat felix Hercules* for five voices and the *Missa Praeter rerum seriem* for seven voices. The Mass *Vivat felix Hercules* is a large and weighty polyphonic work in which the Tenor primus continually sings a basic melody with the text "Vivat felix Hercules secundus, dux Ferrariae quartus." Modeling the work in a broad sense on Josquin's *Hercules* Mass, Rore modernizes Josquin's spare four-voice sonorities in favor of the denser textures characteristic of the 1530s and 1540s. He also implies a rivalry with other tributes to Ercole II, such as that of Jacquet; in 1536 Ercole II had paid Jacquet of Mantua for an unspecified Mass, most likely Jacquet's *Hercules* Mass.[15] And still another Mass, apparently used for his accession in 1534 though, it appears, written for another state occasion in 1529, had been written by Maistre Jhan.[16]

But by the time of Rore's arrival at Ferrara in 1546, Ercole's public image as duke stood in a very different light from what it had been when he had risen to the ducal throne in 1534, then twenty-six years old and admired throughout Italy for his personal qualities and seeming readiness to succeed. By now he was tired, beleaguered, vulnerable, trying to contain a confessional and domestic crisis that had far-reaching political implications. That the Rore *Hercules* Mass was written by at latest the mid-1550s seems certain, thanks to source datings, but Alvin Johnson speculated that it could have been written earlier, in fact soon after Rore's arrival in Ferrara in 1546.[17] If so, it would have reflected Ercole's pride in hiring Rore as his new *maestro di cappella,* and would also have directly implied the second Ercole's allegiance to the memory of his grandfather and namesake.

---

[15] See Philip Jackson, "Two Descendants of Josquin's 'Hercules' Mass," *Music and Letters* 59 (1978): 188–205, esp. 192–93, following George Nugent, "The Jacquet Motets and their Authors" (Ph.D. diss., Princeton University, 1973), 45.

[16] See Joshua Rifkin, "Ercole's Second-Hand Coronation Mass," in *Music in Renaissance Cities and Courts: Studies in Honor of Lewis Lockwood*, ed. Jessie Ann Owens and Anthony Cummings (Warren, MI: Harmonie Park Press, 1996), 381–90.

[17] Johnson, "The Masses of Cipriano de Rore," 231. The two Rore Masses are available in Bernard Meier, ed., *Cipriani Rore Opera Omnia*, vol. 2 (Rome: American Institute of Musicology, 1966), 7, 32–90.

Whatever its date, it puts Rore squarely in the tradition inaugurated by Josquin in the *Hercules* Mass.

More powerful and significant is the other, larger work, the *Missa Praeter rerum seriem*. This Mass, written for the large complement of seven voices (it is the first Mass for seven voices yet written in the century), combines a number of important features. First, its Quintus part sings thirteen times throughout the Mass a cantus firmus with the text, "Hercules secundus, dux Ferrariae quartus, vivit et vivet." Second, the whole work is explicitly drawn from a famous six-voice motet by Josquin on the text *Praeter rerum seriem,* drawn from a medieval rhymed office.[18] Accordingly, Rore's Mass combines two genres. One is the *Hercules* Mass-type, that is, the Mass in praise of the ruling figure based on a cantus firmus. Josquin's had drawn its cantus firmus directly from the vowels of the eight syllables of the name *Hercules Dux Ferrariae,* applying solmization syllables for each vowel (thus "Her-cu-les Dux Fer-ra-ri-e" becomes *re ut re ut re fa mi re)*. The great theorist Zarlino later called this type of subject a *soggetto cavato delle parole*. The other aspect of the *Praeter* Mass belongs to the much more widely cultivated Mass-type, that of the so-called "imitation" Mass (often called "parody mass") in which the basic material of a Mass is drawn from a preexisting polyphonic model, whether a motet, chanson, or madrigal, reworking and elaborating the material in various ways. The "imitation-Mass" is the predominant Mass type in continental polyphony from about the 1520s on, and for prolific composers such as Palestrina and Lasso it becomes the principal Mass category.

Rore's approach in the Missa *Praeter* is symbolic in several ways. Most obviously it is a tribute to his patron and to the tradition of Hercules Masses, which Rore is now continuing. It also represents a gesture of affiliation by Rore to Josquin Desprez, who is artistically a grandfather to him, in a way that is figuratively parallel to Ercole I as grandfather to Ercole II. Ercole II was proud of the *Praeter* Mass. He sent a copy of it to Duke Albrecht V of Bavaria in 1557 and received a warm letter of thanks. The *soggetto* in this Rore Mass is not "carved from the words," as in Josquin's Mass, but that is because the melody is partially drawn from the motet's melodic material, which also permeates all the other voices of the Mass, thus giving the whole work a higher degree of organic unity (See Ex. 1). Again and again in the work we see Rore enriching the texture by interweaving his large number of voices. He operates from a very different and more complex premise regarding vocal ranges, harmony, and sonority than Josquin had done, and, as in all similar cases of "imitation Masses," the basic mixture of obligation and independence is clear. Example 2 gives the opening measures of Josquin's motet.

---

[18] On the motet see Helmuth Osthoff, *Josquin Desprez* (Tutzing: H. Schneider, 1962), 2: 72–76.

Missa Praeter rerum seriem

Kyrie

Example 1: Cipriano de Rore, *Missa Praeter rerum serium*, Kyrie I, mm. 1–14, (from Bernhard Meier, ed., *Cipriani Rore Opera Omnia*, Vol. 2. Rome: American Institute of Musicology, 1966).

33. Praeter rerum seriem.

Example 2: Josquin Desprez, motet *Praeter rerum serium,* mm. 1–11 (from *Josquin Desprez: Werken*, ed. Albert Smijers. Amsterdam, 1921–). *Motetten*, Deel ii, Afl. 18, No. 33.

In Josquin's setting the basic procedure is to build a series of balanced segments, contrasting an upper group of three voices with a lower group. In the first and higher group, the basic melody is in the soprano; in the lower-voiced group, it is in the first Tenor. Balance and equilibrium of groups and forces is of the essence in Josquin, the master of well-crafted and well-distributed polyphonic textures. By the time of Rore's Mass, about a half-century later, a much stronger sense of harmonic contrasts through full sonorities is beginning to dominate, the more so since, following the lead of Rore's teacher Willaert, full triadic harmonies have come to prevail, as they increasingly do in the course of the century in all genres.

Rore begins his Kyrie 1 with a three-voice group as in Josquin, but at bar 13 he brings in the upper group and quickly six voices are in action. Following tradition, the cantus firmus voice is the last to enter, at bar 19, bringing the text in honor of *Hercules secundus*. Now the full seven-voice chorus is active in almost every measure to the end of the section. The Christe, following Mass traditions, omits the *Hercules soggetto* but uses Josquin's main melody, and is a freer motet-like setting for five voices. The Kyrie II, in a more rapid triple-time meter, partly alternates antiphonal subgroups, introduces the *Hercules soggetto* again, and, in its resounding choral effects and clear periodic phrases, anticipates the massive block-like writing of later Venetian composers such as Giovanni Gabrieli.

At a more subtle level, Rore's Mass reflects the tradition of the original *Hercules* Mass but also adds symbolic features. Not to be overlooked is that the *cantus firmus* voice, the Quintus, always gives the full separate text with its tribute to *Hercules secundus, dux Ferrarie quartus.* In the Ferrara of the mid-forties and early fifties there were still living courtiers who could remember the last years of the old duke, Ercole I, who had knelt in his chapel and prayed and sung with his singers on every possible occasion. There is a strong likelihood that the original *soggetto* for Josquin's Mass, *Hercules Dux Ferrarie,* was sung with its separate text while the remaining three voices in Josquin's setting sang the text of the Mass Ordinary. In this way the name and persona of the Duke would have been part of the polyphonic complex, and his participation in the Mass as rite and as musical setting would have been fused in the same symbolic act. Could this be the case with Rore's Mass? Can we imagine Ercole II witnessing or taking part in a performance of the Mass with his chapel of singers and hearing his name resounding against the text of the Mass? There is a reasonable possibility that this could have been done, since the text of the *soggetto* is always given in full in the source.[19]

---

[19] The source is Munich, Bayerische Staatsbibliothek, Mus. MS. 46, fols. 137v–189.

There is also another potential meaning in the work. The original Josquin motet, *Praeter rerum seriem,* is an expression of wonder at the mystery of the Virgin Birth. The text begins:

Praeter rerum seriem	Beyond the order of things
Parit Deum hominem	The Virgin Mother bore God
Virgo mater.	in the form of man.
Nec vir tangit virginem	Untouched by man, still a virgin,
Nec prolis originem	Nor was the origin of the child
Novit pater.	Known to the father.
(etc.)	(etc.)

The whole spirit of this text derives from the Marian adoration that permeates so much late fifteenth-century religious feeling, tellingly reflected by Josquin and his contemporaries in hundreds of motets for the Virgin (his two famous Ave Marias are only the best-known) and dozens of Masses reflecting the same cult. With Josquin they range from his *Missa de Beata Virgine,* one of the most widely copied, to his *Missa Mater Patris,* derived from a Brumel motet. The text of the *Praeter* motet declares that the Virgin Birth not only is a mystical event, but also that it took place out of normal human time and space — "beyond the order of things," that is, things of the world and as perceived by human capacities. In choosing such a motet and combining it with the tribute to Ercole II, Rore combines the worldly praise of a ruler with the other-worldly experience of the veneration of the mother of Christ as virgin, a paradox that lies at the heart of Catholic doctrine. Since it was essential to the Protestants' view of Christianity that what they called Mariolatry be put aside, that images and pictures of the Virgin be reduced in importance or eliminated, it is more than likely that Rore's work is not just another stone in a wall of tradition but is a deliberate reaffirmation of Catholic doctrine raised against an overtly Protestant spirit. Certainly in Ercole's tense and embattled court, with its divided factions at the top, such an interpretation would have been readily understood. We might make the same case for Rore's great cycle of madrigals on Petrarch's canzone for the Virgin, first published in 1548 and then revised over the next four years. Martha Feldman has identified the cycle as a turning point for Rore as madrigalist, and it may also have been influenced by the religious crisis in Ferrara in these years.[20]

On Good Friday in 1536 one of Renee's singers, Jehannet de Bouchefort, scandalized and affronted the chapel of musicians and the entire court by openly

[20] Martha Feldman, *City Culture and the Madrigal at Venice* (Berkeley: University of California Press, 1995), 407–26.

refusing to venerate the crucifix during the liturgy and walking out of the service.[21] Such an incident, which apparently coincided exactly with the end of Jean Calvin's stay in Ferrara, speaks volumes. So does the motet *Te Lutherum damnamus,* hurled back at him and all the Protestants by the ducal singers. Against a background like this, Rore's two Masses for Ercole II glorify the Duke's place in the family line, reflect his role as defender of the faith, and reinforce Catholic doctrine and practice. They present Cipriano de Rore as the heir of Josquin, brilliantly articulating these elements. The local courtly pride that carried the legacy of Josquin forward at Ferrara had begun in Alfonso's time and it continued in the time of Ercole II in the same way, linking the second Hercules to his grandfather and namesake. In that sense Rore's Mass could be interpreted as a conservative bow to tradition. But in the light of the confessional, domestic, and political crisis surrounding Renée and her clan of reformers, the Josquin legacy in the hands of Rore became enmeshed in the local struggle between orthodoxy and heresy.

[21] First reported by Fontana, *Renata di Francia,* 1: 312–29; and see Nugent, "Anti-Protestant Music," 248, who corrects some factual details in Fontana's account and brings references to later studies.

In Continuous Expectation: Isabella d'Este's Epistolary Desire

Deanna Shemek

Isabella d'Este Gonzaga (1474–1539) lived only her first sixteen years in the city to which this volume is devoted, but through her close contacts with the court of her parents and her reign with Francesco II Gonzaga over the neighboring court of Mantua, her presence at Ferrara was felt long after her childhood there.[1] Ferrara's place in early modern Italian culture can best be understood through its sustained relations to other major courts on the peninsula, including those

---

[1] Isabella has been the subject of numerous biographical studies in Italian, English, and French (several of them for popular audiences) since the early twentieth century. See Julia Cartwright, *Isabella d'Este Marchioness of Mantua 1474–1539: A Study of the Renaissance* (London: John Murray, 1907); Titina Strano, *Isabella d'Este, Marchesa di Mantova* (Milan: Ceschina, 1938); Jeanne Boujassy, *Isabella d'Este, Grande Dame de la Renaissance* (Paris: A. Fayard, 1960); Edith Patterson Meyer, *First Lady of the Renaissance: A Biography of Isabella d'Este* (Boston: Little, Brown, and Company, 1970); George Marek, *The Bed and the Throne: The Life of Isabella d'Este* (New York: Harper and Row, 1976); Massimo Felisatti, *Isabella d'Este la primadonna del Rinascimento* (Milan: Bompiani, 1982); Daniela Pizzagalli, *La signora del Rinascimento. Vita e splendori di Isabella d'Este alla corte di Mantova* (Milan: Rizzoli, 2001). All of the above are enormously indebted (as is my own research) to the many publications of early twentieth-century Gonzaga archivist Alessandro Luzio and his associate Rodolfo Renier, a number of which will be cited below. For fuller bibliography, see Silvia Ferino-Pagden, ed., *"La prima donna del mondo": Isabella d'Este, Fürstin und Mäzenatin der Renaissance* (Vienna: Ausstellungskatalog des Kunsthistorisches Museum, 1994). See also the archivally-based novel by Maria Bellonci, *Rinascimento privato* (Milan: Mondadori, 1985), which takes Isabella as its protagonist, and the rather unflattering, more fanciful portrait of Isabella in another recent novel, Jacqueline Park, *The Secret Book of Grazia de Rossi* (New York: Simon and Schuster, 1997).

at Rome, Naples, and Venice. But in addition to those centers, the northern court circle that included Mantua, Urbino, and Milan formed an especially intricate network of alliances by marriage and political interdependence: Isabella's parents and then her brother Alfonso (who married first the Milanese Anna Sforza and then Lucrezia Borgia, natural daughter of Pope Alexander VI) ruled Ferrara. Her sister Beatrice married the Duke of Milan (Ludovico "il Moro" Sforza). Her husband's sister, Elisabetta Gonzaga Montefeltro, was Duchess of Urbino and became mother-in-law to Isabella and Francesco's daughter Elionora, who herself became Duchess of Urbino as a young woman. This geographic, political, and familial honeycomb of courts was the immediate sphere of influence for Isabella d'Este and all the members of her dynasty.

Connecting the elements of that sphere, for Isabella as for other members of those courts, was one specific, crucial practice: the frequent exchange of letters. This essay will focus on a single aspect of Isabella's extensive epistolary activity, presenting several examples that illustrate the importance of epistolary exchanges in her efforts to bridge the distance between Mantua, Ferrara, and the wider world. These letters explicitly engage themes of absence and desire, adopting a standard epistolary rhetoric that emphasizes writing's relation to the body, to memory, and to authenticity. Of particular interest to me here will be Isabella's intense desire for correspondence as such, and the temporal condition of "continuous expectation" in which she saw herself poised. The language of desire and expectation, as we shall see, remains in Isabella's correspondence throughout her life; its function, however, evolves from the early years of her marriage (when her requests for correspondence were often couched in personal concerns) to her maturity (when a similar rhetoric of longing for communication touched on a wider sphere of worldly issues). The contiguous space where these two dimensions meet, where private and public concerns converge, marks exactly the powerful but limited sphere in which dynastic women of Isabella's century operated.

My general aim in what follows is to bring to bear on the correspondence of Isabella d'Este not the skills of the historian, the biographer, or the archivist, but those of the reader of literary texts. I do not mean to suggest that Isabella's letters are particularly "literary," however, for they are not. Nor will I argue that she was exceptional for writing letters as a woman: quite the contrary. It is clear that Isabella d'Este was an extraordinary figure, for many reasons. Nonetheless, I present her letters not only as vehicles for the activities and personal expression of one remarkable woman, but also as examples of a *shared* epistolary culture in which both women and men participated, and which merits our attention precisely in its conventionality, perhaps even its banality. The routine correspondence of Isabella and her contemporaries has not been studied by literary specialists. It beckons neither from the literary heights of Machiavelli's humanist ruminations nor from the iconoclastic edge at which Pietro Aretino invented the new commodity of the published letter collection. But letters like Isabella's inform us about Renaissance communicative networks, about the routine tropes of epistolary exchange, about relations between the cultures of orality and literacy, and about the letter as a medium for personal contact, political agency, news-gathering, and self-construction. These matters, which I will discuss more fully in an extended study of Isabella's correspondence, should interest us for all Cinquecento producers of letters, but they are especially important for the history of women's writing, for reasons I will note below.

I

As the daughter of Duke Ercole I of Ferrara and the royal princess Eleonora d'Aragona, Isabella was raised by two of the most privileged, intelligent, and progressive public figures of the Italian sixteenth century. Eleonora was a strong model for the young Isabella, and she and Ercole graced their daughter with the finest education available to children of her class, male or female.[2] Isabella's life as an adult reflects this upbringing in countless ways. As a voice of authority in her city and a clear protagonist in the very construction of high Renaissance culture through her role as a patron of the arts, she does not number among those women for whom, as Joan Kelly argued many years ago, "there was no Renaissance."[3] Though her life pursuits were those of a co-regent and not of an intellectual, she received a thorough humanist education and avidly read both vernacular and Latin literature throughout her life.[4] Her substantial library

---

[2] On Eleonora, see W. L. Gundersheimer, "Women, Learning and Power: Eleonora of Aragon and the Court of Ferrara," in *Beyond Their Sex: Learned Women of the European Past*, ed. Patricia H. Labalme (New York: New York University Press, 1980), 46–54.

[3] Joan Kelly, "Did Women Have a Renaissance?," in *Women, History, Theory*, ed. eadem (Chicago: University of Chicago Press, 1984), 19–50.

[4] Letters from her tutors indicate that Isabella had significant training in Latin and was prodigiously adept in her childhood studies. She never attained the status of a "learned woman," however (a reputation she occasionally longed for), since marriage and childbearing duties interrupted her studies. Indeed, she most regretted that her Latin was not better, and as an adult she quite probably read most Latin literature in Italian translation. See Alessandro Luzio, *I precettori di Isabella d'Este* (Ancona: Gustavo Morelli, 1887), as well as idem and Rodolfo Renier, "La coltura e le relazioni letterarie di Isabella d'Este Gonzaga," *Giornale storico della letteratura italiana*, (hereafter *GSLI*), 33–42 (1899–1903). *I precettori* (12–13) includes Luzio's transcription of a mournful letter to Isabella from her tutor, Jacopo Gallino, sent on 25 March 1490 shortly after her departure

included a traditionally feminine collection of religious writings, romances, and tracts on astrology and dreams, but also numerous fruits of the classical and contemporary humanist culture for which the period is best known: Latin writings in many genres; Greek texts translated into Latin, manuscript and presentation copies of works by many living poets, and a complete set of the Aldine editions made to her exacting orders.[5]

Typically for women of her station, Isabella's management of Gonzaga family relations was extensive. She personally brokered the marriages and careers of her three sons: Federico succeeded Francesco as head of the Mantuan state, Ferrante distinguished himself as a military officer, and Ercole obtained the coveted cardinal's hat. Arranging, as well, for the marriage of her eldest daughter, Elionora, to the future duke of Urbino (Francesco Maria della Rovere), she placed her younger daughters, Hippolyta and Paula, in monastic communities, according to the girls' express wishes.[6] Within her court she facilitated marriages for a large

---

for Mantua as a bride. There we see some of the same rhetoric on memory and longing that appears in Isabella's letters: "Sometimes I think of when Your Ladyship listened with such attention to a tale of mine, or a history, and how much pleasure you used to take in it. And when with such studiousness you would compose those cute little declamations [*declamaciunzelle*] of ours, and when you scanned the verses of Vergil, and when you reassembled his scrambled verses, and when you fashioned some fair *sententiae* into verse. . . . And then I remember the accurate and deep memory that Your Ladyship has, who on Saturdays would translate [*rendere*] for me all of this: all of Vergil's *Bucolics*; the first, second, and part of the third book of Vergil; several of Cicero's epistles; part of the *Herotimate* [the Greek grammar of Crisolora]; and many other grammar materials. And then with what charm and grace you explicated the lessons you heard me read, especially from Terence and Vergil. Certainly when I recall these things, I am beside myself and insensate, and then when I come back to myself, I greatly lament being deprived of them." Gallino's evocative letter provides as well a precious record of humanist pedagogical style for children. All translations appearing in this essay are mine.

[5] On Isabella's library see especially the first and last installments of Luzio and Renier, "La coltura e le relazioni letterarie." On her correspondence with Aldo Manuzio, see part 1 of that series, in *GSLI* 33. Letters documenting Isabella's lending and borrowing of books assure us that she was no mere collector, but rather a constant reader of intense and sustained curiosity. As Cecil H. Clough also notes, the Gonzagas' library, though one of the richest of its time, was "created less by wealth than by literary interest." See Cecil H. Clough, "The Library of the Gonzaga of Mantua," *Librarium* (1972): 50–63. On the splendid library of Isabella's parents, see Giulio Bertoni, *La Biblioteca Estense e la coltura ferrarese ai tempi del Duca Ercole I* (Turin: E. Loescher, 1903).

[6] Isabella did not, in general, force her plans on candidates for marriage or other life choices. Hippolyta's unexpected request to take the veil in fact awkwardly thwarted a project to send her to the French court and was followed by her sister Paula's also

number of her dependents, often choosing spouses for them or providing funds for their dowries.[7] On the wider public horizon, she followed her mother's Ferrarese example and governed Mantua alone, both during Francesco's frequent absences from the court and during his year-long imprisonment by the Venetians.[8] She later again reigned unofficially after his death until Federico's coming of age.

Given her talents and interests, Isabella has long been considered a feminine counterpart to the "Renaissance men" who define the spirit of her century in traditional historiography.[9] She was a skillful dancer, an expert horsewoman, and

---

unanticipated choice to enter the convent. The two girls commenced monastic life on the same day. See Archivio Gonzaga F.II.9. 2996 libro 29 for various correspondence regarding this change of plans. Isabella's will (Archivio Gonzaga, Serie D, Busta 332) observes a strict hierarchy of primogeniture among her sons and leaves to each of her daughters the minimum income required to assure their financial security. She names her eldest son Federico her universal heir, leaving to her second son Ferrante the court at San Matteo with all of its livestock (as well as several large jewels) and to her third son Ercole the castle at Solarolo (along with an emerald, a bed frame (or headboard), a trunk filled with silks, and a set of silver altar dressings). On the other hand to her daughter Elionora, duchess of Urbino, Isabella left the traditional one-sixth of her own dowry of 25,000 ducati ("la sesta parte de ducati vinticinque millia, ad essa Signora testatrice datti in dote"). Her second daughter, Hippolyta, received a mill and an ivory carving of the Christ child; while the third daughter, Paula, inherited an ivory crucifix and an annual donation (*per elemosina*) of twenty-five sacks of grain. Isabella sets out a careful chain of inheritance to be followed in the event of any single heir's death, and she stipulates at some length that no bastards be admitted to this succession under any conditions. On the question of bastardy and legitimacy for the Estes, see Jane Fair Bestor, "Bastardy and Legitimacy in the Formation of a Regional State in Italy: The Estense Succession," *Comparative Studies in Society and History* 38 (1996): 549–85; eadem, "Gli illegittimi e beneficiati della casa estense," in *Il Rinascimento. Situazioni e personaggi*, ed. Adriano Prosperi (Ferrara: Corbo, 2000), 77–102; and Bestor's essay in this volume, above, 49–85. For Isabella's own concerns with this question, see Deanna Shemek, "Aretino's *Marescalco*: marriage woes and the duke of Mantua," *Renaissance Studies* 16, no. 3 (2002): 366–80, especially 373–76.

[7] For two rather spectacular example cases, see Rita Castagna, *Un Vicerè per Eleonora Brognina alla corte di Isabella d'Este Gonzaga* (Mantua: Moretti, 1982); eadem, "Una donzella di Isabella d'Este e la ragion di stato," *Civiltà Mantovana* 11 (1977): 220–31.

[8] See Alessandro Luzio, "La reggenza d'Isabella d'Este durante la prigionia del marito (1509–1510)," *Archivio storico lombardo* 4 (1910): 5–104.

[9] Luzio, whose archival publications have furnished the materials for virtually every modern biography written on Isabella, is certainly the greatest proponent of this view. See also Burckhardt's more condescending treatment: Jacob Burckhardt, *The Civilization of the Renaissance in Italy* (Oxford: Phaidon, 1981), 28–29; 233–34.

an able vocalist and musician.[10] Her passion for collecting gave rise to a legendary Gonzaga inventory of jewelry, clocks, maiolica, musical instruments, and antiques, all of which were acquired under her meticulous scrutiny and close supervision.[11] She owned artworks by Andrea Mantegna, Leonardo da Vinci, Raphael, Michelangelo, Titian, Giulio Romano, and many others; and she was herself the subject of numerous portraits by the luminary artists of her day. She made drawings for the design of her own jewelry and clothing (including millinery) and received requests from abroad for dolls dressed in exact replicas of her garments, right down to the underwear, so that French and Spanish women could copy them.[12] She maintained a perfume laboratory of renown, where she assisted

---

[10] Isabella was already dancing at the age of seven, "con una grazietta tutta sua" ["with a grace all her own"] under the instruction of the converted Jew, "Ambrogio." See Luzio, *I precettori*, 12. On her early dabblings in poetic composition, see 51–55; and Claudio Gallico, "Poesie musicali di Isabella d'Este," *Collectanea Historiae Musicae* 3 (1963): 109–19. Pietro Bembo's letter of 1 July 1505 records a memory of Isabella's singing and playing, published in Vittorio Cian, "Pietro Bembo e Isabella d'Este Gonzaga. Note e documenti," *GSLI* 9 (1887): 81–136, here 102. See also Iain Fenlon, "Music and Learning in Isabella d'Este's Studiolo," in *La Corte di Mantova nell'età di Andrea Mantegna: 1450–1550/ The Court of the Gonzaga in the Age of Mantegna: 1450–1550*, ed. Cesare Mozzarelli, Robert Oresko, and Leandro Ventura (Rome: Bulzoni, 1997), 353–67; William F. Prizer, "Isabella d'Este and Lucrezia Borgia as Patrons of Music: The Frottola at Mantua and Ferrara," *Journal of the American Musicological Society* 38 (1985): 1–33; idem, "'Una virtù molto conveniente a madonne': Isabella d'Este as a Musician," *Journal of Musicology* 17 (1999): 10–49; idem, "Isabella d'Este and Lorenzo da Pavia, 'Master Instrument Maker'," *Early Music History* 2 (1982): 87–127.

[11] See Ferino-Pagden, "*La prima donna del mondo*", as well as *I luoghi del collezionismo*, *Civiltà Mantovana,* n.s. 30 (1995), which is devoted to Isabella. See also Roberta Iotti and Leandro Ventura, *Isabella d'Este alla corte di Mantova* (Modena: Il Bulino, 1993); Rose Marie San Juan, "The Court Lady's Dilemma: Isabella d'Este and Art Collecting in the Renaissance," *Oxford Art Journal* 14 (1991): 67–78; and Andrew Martindale, "The Patronage of Isabella d'Este at Mantua," *Apollo* 79 (1964): 183–91.

[12] I thank Clifford M. Brown for informing me that a letter written by Federico Gonzaga to his mother requesting these dolls is printed in Raffaele Tamalio, *Federico Gonzaga alla corte di Francesco I* (Paris: Honoré Champion, 1994), 127–28, and that further documentation indicating the Spanish court's similar request appears in Raffaele Tamalio, *Ferrante Gonzaga alla corte spagnola di Carlo V* (Mantua: Arcari Gianluigi, 1991), 199–203. On Isabella's engagement with fashion, see Alessandro Luzio and Rodolfo Renier, "Il lusso di Isabella d'Este, marchesa di Mantova," *Nuova antologia* ser. 4, 63 (1896): 441–69; 64 (1896): 294–324; 65 (1896): 666–88; and Chiara Zaffanella, "Isabella d'Este e la moda del suo tempo," in *Isabella d'Este. La primadonna del Rinascimento*, ed. Daniele Bini, *Civiltà Mantovana,* Supplemento al n. 112 (Modena: Il Bulino, 2001), 209–23.

in the formulation of scents and cosmetics for herself and her closest friends (male and female).[13] And she loved to travel, as a rule without her husband and on occasion incognita to facilitate her free movement.[14] The subject of literary tributes by Ariosto, Castiglione, Bandello, Bembo, Trissino, and others, she was proclaimed by her kinsman, the diplomat and poet Niccolò da Correggio, as "la prima donna del mondo": an understandable, if obvious, employment of hyperbole that has carried over into much of the literature on Isabella.[15]

But herein lay the key to Isabella's limitations as well as her considerable powers. For "first lady" in fact has always meant not first, but *second to* the sovereign, a rank politically fraught with the risks of excess if the first lady forgets her secondary status, no matter what her skills or merits.[16] Francesco Gonzaga himself was occasionally embarrassed by his wife's inability fully to contain herself in this role. By numerous accounts, in the aftermath of Isabella's successful government of Mantua during his imprisonment by the Venetians (August 1509–July 1510), the marchese and marchesa became increasingly estranged from each other. In 1513, Francesco wrote bitterly about Isabella's overdue return from Milan, where he believed she had become a topic of widespread gossip due to her independent ways. He complained to Ludovico Guerriero, "[H]avemo vergogna di avere per nostra sorte una mogliere che sempre vol fare di suo cervello." ["We are chagrined at our fortune of having a wife who always wants to do things according to her own mind."][17]

---

[13] Cian records Bembo's request for "uno Bossoletto, o bussolino, non so come chiamarlo cortegianamente, di quella sua excellente mixtura," which Cian surmises may be a hair tonic. See his "Pietro Bembo e Isabella d'Este Gonzaga," 119.

[14] On Isabella's many travels, see especially Alessandro Luzio and Rodolfo Renier, *Gara di viaggi fra due celebri dame del Rinascimento* (Alexandria: Chiari, Romano e Filippa, 1890), and their *Mantova e Urbino*.

[15] Ferino-Pagden, "*La Prima donna del mondo*", 71–75, "Isabellas Persönlichkeit: Isabella als Frau." Speaking of this epithet, the author remarks, "so versuchte [Isabella] auch für den Rest ihres Lebens, diesem Ruf gerecht zu werden. Dabei schien für sie die Betonung nicht auf *donna* zu liegen, sondern auf *prima*" (71).

[16] See remarks to this effect regarding another Renaissance "first lady" in Francis W. Kent, "Sainted Mother, Magnificent Son: Lucrezia Tornabuoni and Lorenzo de' Medici," *Italian History and Culture* 3 (1997): 3–33, esp. 13. For discussion of Tornabuoni's "meddling" in political affairs, see the editor's introduction to Lucrezia Tornabuoni, *Sacred Narratives*, ed. and trans. Jane Tylus (Chicago: University of Chicago Press, 2001), 21–53.

[17] For a modern paraphrasing of much of this letter, see Pizzagalli, *La signora del Rinascimento*, 341. The letter is cited also, more briefly, in Maria Bellonci, *Segreti dei Gonzaga: Il duca nel labirinto (1562–1612); Isabella fra i Gonzaga (1474–1539); Ritratto di famiglia (1474)* (Milan: Mondadori, 1963 [1946]), 355.

Isabella d'Este's "own mind" comes most readily into view for readers of her enormous epistolary archive, which reveals her as an inveterate writer of letters. To survey Isabella's correspondence is to find her rising late in the night to compose notes for delivery to her husband by a suddenly available courier; pausing during her travels to dictate descriptions for friends of the pleasures of eating fresh trout or of watching her dogs run; noting minutely the details of pageants and plays she witnessed at distant courts; and even writing from her birthing bed, conducting urgent business within hours of delivering her children. The letters preserved in her secretarial copybooks, held in the State Archives of the city of Mantua, leave little doubt that Isabella d'Este approached the task of letter writing routinely, as the most efficient means through which to conduct her affairs. The many letters she received, which are held in the archive as well, suggest that she spent nearly as much time reading correspondence as she did dictating it to her secretaries. These numbers are significant not only because they indicate the influence and the communicative resources Isabella had at her disposal, but also because they leave us a remarkably full portrait of a woman who adopted the letter as a key arena of her political influence and her affective relations.

Like every young bride transported to a distant court, Isabella confronted the necessity of living far from her childhood home. As she recast her Ferrarese identity in a new, Mantuan setting, she also spent considerable time without her husband who, as a *condottiere*, was often away on military and political missions for their state.[18] As we shall see, Isabella's communications in this circumstance are important to her not only because they transmit news, but also because they have special value as material objects. Moreover, in their evident function to integrate Isabella's old world with her new one and to project her toward future reunions with absent loved ones, these letters reveal epistolary time as a dimension where expectation, desire, and memory converge. Their particular temporality creates some of the non-discursive functions of letters, their capacity to encompass bodies, feelings, and material tokens in a world of words and waiting. Before turning to the letters themselves, I begin with a few words about Isabella's archive as a collection and some considerations on letters as an object of scholarly study.

---

[18] For biographical and patronage information on Francesco II Gonzaga, see Mary Harris Bourne, "Out from the Shadow of Isabella: The Artistic Patronage of Francesco II Gonzaga, Fourth Marquis of Mantua (1484–1519)" (Ph.D. diss., Harvard University, 1997); eadem, "Renaissance Husbands and Wives as Patrons of Art: The *Camerini* of Isabella d'Este and Francesco II Gonzaga," in *Beyond Isabella: Secular Women Patrons of Art in Renaissance Italy*, ed. David G. Wilkins, Sixteenth Century Essays & Studies (Kirksville, MO: Truman State University Press, 2001), 93–123.

II

The Gonzaga papers in the Archivio di Stato di Mantova constitute an extraordinarily rich and well-preserved resource for scholars not only of Mantuan culture specifically, but also of literary, political, and diplomatic activities on the peninsula as a whole. Its density of materials has made it a major source of information regarding the theater, music, and art history of the period as well. Isabella's correspondence files, which remain virtually intact, contain over twenty-eight thousand communications she received between 1490 and 1539, and some twelve thousand duplicates for letters she sent, the latter gathered in the bound volumes of her secretarial copybooks or *copialettere*.[19] These are most of the written remains of her life, and they provide an unusually large window to both her individual life history and the culture in which she operated. But faced with this staggering number of boxes, fascicles, and files more or less charted by centuries of previous investigators, the reader of Isabella's letters also confronts a question: What is the specific nature of the epistolary "window"?

Recent years have witnessed a small boom in the scholarly study of the letter, both as a narrative element within fiction (as in epistolary novels) and as a historical medium of communication with its own generic constraints and assumptions. Studies of Renaissance letter writing have long explored the transmission of generic models from classical antiquity (especially visible in the letters of humanists after Petrarch); but more recent work has investigated the relations between letters and nascent print culture (especially the phenomenon of published personal letter collections) and the historic importance of letter writing for women.[20] As Claudio Guillén and others have noted, letters — both

[19] See Anna Maria Lorenzoni, "Contributo allo studio delle fonti Isabelliane dell'Archivio di Stato di Mantova," *Atti e memorie*, n.s. 47 (1979): 97–135. The fullest description of the Mantuan archive appears in Pietro Torelli, ed., *L'Archivio Gonzaga di Mantova*, vol. 1 (Ostiglia: Mondadori, 1920) and Alessandro Luzio, ed., *L'Archivio Gonzaga di Mantova*, vol. 2 (Mantova: Sartori, 1920). See Clifford M. Brown and Anna Maria Lorenzoni, *Isabella d'Este and Lorenzo da Pavia: Documents for the History of Art and Culture in Renaissance Mantua* (Geneva: Librairie Droz S.A., 1982), 9, for a brief but useful description in English of this archive.

[20] A valuable theoretical discussion of the letter remains Janet Gurkin Altman, *Epistolarity: Approaches to a Form* (Columbus: Ohio State University Press, 1982). See also John M. Najemy, *Between Friends: Discourses of Power and Desire in the Machiavelli-Vettori Letters of 1513–1515* (Princeton: Princeton University Press, 1993). On the ancient letter and its transmission, see Cecil H. Clough, "The Cult of Antiquity: Letters and Letter Collections," in *Cultural Aspects of The Italian Renaissance: Essays in Honor of Paul Oskar Kristeller*, ed. idem (Manchester: Manchester University Press, 1976), 33–67; Adriana

as literature and as documents — reside at the boundary between orality and literacy, and between the literary and the documentary. This dimension of the letter has also engaged cultural anthropologists like Jack Goody and Walter Ong, who have brilliantly studied the passage of Western cultures over the divide from orality into literacy.[21] Letters beg the question of distinctions between literary and non-literary language, [22] but they also exhibit regular formal features as a genre. Molly Whalen identifies six of these in her study of early modern English women's letter-writing: [23] the foregrounding of address (letters are always written to a stated addressee);[24] actual sending and arrival at destinations (stamps, seals, and dates are among the material features of letters);[25] presence and absence

Chemello, ed., *Alla lettera. Teorie e pratiche epistolari dai Greci al Novecento* (Milan: Guerini, 1998); Stanley K. Stowers, *Letter Writing in Greco-Roman Antiquity* (Philadelphia: Westminster Press, 1986); Patricia A. Rosenmeyer, *Ancient Epistolary Fictions: The Letter in Greek Literature* (Cambridge: Cambridge University Press, 2001). For discussions of women's letter writing, see Maria Luisa Doglio, *Lettera e donna. Scrittura epistolare al femminile tra Quattro e Cinquecento* (Rome: Bulzoni, 1993); eadem, "Scrittura e 'offizio di parole' nelle *Lettere familiari* di Veronica Franco," in *Les femmes écrivains en Italie au moyen âge et à la Renaissance* (Aix-en-Provence: Publications de l'Université de Provence, 1994), 103–18; Mario Pozzi, "'Andrem di pari all'amorosa face': Appunti sulle lettere di Maria Savorgnan," in *Les femmes écrivains,* 87–101, and Gabriella Zarri, ed., *Per lettera. La scrittura epistolare femminile tra archivio e tipografia secoli XV–XVII* (Rome: Viella, 1999).

[21] Jack Goody, *The Domestication of the Savage Mind* (Cambridge: Cambridge University Press, 1977); idem, *The Interface Between the Written and the Oral* (Cambridge: Cambridge University Press, 1987); Walter J. Ong, *Orality and Literacy* (New York: Routledge, 1991); idem, *Rhetoric, Romance, and Technology: Studies in the Interaction of Expression and Culture* (Ithaca: Cornell University Press, 1971).

[22] See the fundamental work of Roman Jakobson, "Closing Statement: Linguistics and Poetics," in *Style in Language*, ed. Thomas A. Sebeok (Cambridge, MA: Technology Press of Massachusetts Institute of Technology, 1960), 350–77.

[23] Molly Whalen, "The Public Currency of the Private Letter: Gender, Class, and Epistolarity in England, 1568–1671" (Ph.D. diss., University of California, Santa Cruz, 1994). See in particular her chap. 2, "Mapping Epistolarity: A Formal Consideration of the Familiar Letter," 27–41, from which I draw here.

[24] Whalen, "Public Currency," 33, invokes in this regard Genette's distinction between intra-diagetic and extra-diagetic narratees, noting that in the cast of the epistle, the latter "is always explicitly acknowledged by the structure of address itself and so is precariously fixed both 'within' the structure of the text and 'outside' the structure." See Gérard Genette, "D'un Récit Baroque," in *Figures II*, ed. idem (Paris: Editions du Seuil, 1969), 195–222.

[25] Guillén, "Notes," observes that the genre reflects this trait thematically, insofar as letters often discuss their own composition, sending, delay, and arrival. He considers this self-referentiality to be "a radical of presentation" that defines the authentic examples of the form.

mediated by the text (letters aim, by definition, to overcome distance and compensate for absence); tension between privacy and publication (letters stage intimacy, but as gestures outward from interiority they may undermine the privacy they represent);[26] tension between orality and literacy (since antiquity, letters have been conceived as "halves" of conversations); and the mark of the hand as metonymic figure (whether handwritten, typed, or dictated, letters conventionally refer to the writing hand and the body for which it stands as part).[27] Isabella's letters are typical in observing all these regularities; as we shall see in particular, she presented them especially often as substitutes for conversation and as metonymic signs for the bodies of absent interlocutors.

As a culturally coded genre, the female-authored letter mediated many of the constraints governing women's social experience as well as their literacy skills.[28] Guillén writes of the vernacular Renaissance letter as a locus of tension with other "new" genres. Women's practice of letter writing perhaps built on this tension, as Cinquecento society exhibited broad and increasing anxiety about

---

[26] This character of the letter text is often exploited by mystery and suspense genres of fiction. See Jacques Lacan, "Seminar on The Purloined Letter," in *The Poetics of Murder: Detective Fiction and Literary Theory*, ed. Glenn W. Most and William W. Stowe (San Diego: Harcourt Brace Jovanovich, 1983), 21–54.

[27] See Whalen, "Public Currency," 41; Jonathan Goldberg, "Rebel Letters: Postal Effects from Richard II to Henry IV," *Renaissance Drama* 19 (1988): 3–28; idem, *Writing Matter: From the Hands of the English Renaissance* (Stanford: Stanford University Press, 1990); and Stephanie H. Jed, *Chaste Thinking: The Rape of Lucretia and the Birth of Humanism* (Bloomington: Indiana University Press, 1989).

[28] Isabella d'Este herself was not exempt from such constraints, despite her privileged status as patron and ruler. On other female letter writers, see James Daybell, ed., *Early Modern Women's Letter Writing, 1450–1700* (New York: Palgrave, 2001); Doglio, *Lettera e donna*; Ottavia Niccoli, "Forme di cultura e condizioni di vita in due epistolari femminili del Rinascimento," in *Les femmes écrivains*, 13–32; and in the same volume: Doglio, "Scrittura e 'offizio'"; Mario Martelli, "Lucrezia Tornabuoni," 51–86; Pozzi, "'Andrem di pari all'amorosa face'"; Carlo Vecce, "Vittoria Colonna: Il codice epistolare della poesia femminile," 213–32. On letter writing by courtesans see Théa Picquet, "Profession: Courtisane," in *Les femmes écrivains*, 119–37; Romano, *Lettere di cortigiane*; and Fiora Bassanese, "Selling the Self; or, The Epistolary Production of Renaissance Courtesans," in *Italian Women Writers from the Renaissance to the Present: Revising the Canon*, ed. Maria Ornella Marotti (University Park, PA: Pennsylvania State University Press, 1996), 69–82. For English letters, see Anne Crawford, ed., *Letters of the Queens of England 1100–1547* (Phoenix Mill, UK: Sutton, 1997). On medieval women's letters, see Karen Cherewatuk and Ulrike Wiethaus, eds., *Dear Sister: Medieval Women and the Epistolary Genre* (Philadelphia: University of Pennsylvania Press, 1993).

female entry into the public discursive sphere.[29] Women themselves, moreover, like vernacular and personal letters, appeared poised in the sixteenth century to exceed their traditionally restricted sphere and to act in the public domain; indeed, one of the ways they achieved this entrance in some small measure may have been through the practice of letter writing. While the letter is a traditionally sanctioned genre of female writing, its legitimacy for women (like that of the diary) was predicated upon its definition as a private, domestic literary form. Women's epistolary activity in its broadest dimension suggests a parallel between letters as communicative exchange — as solidifiers of relations — and the similar role women themselves played in the economy of early modern marriage. Like their authors, however, women's letters were expected to circulate in a bounded sphere policed by fathers, husbands, and brothers. Humanists like Alberti, Castiglione, and Vives, who wrote important statements on women's proper relation to society, all associated feminine speech with female sexual openness. Women's writing and even their conversation thus stood in consistent tension with feminine honor, as "Popular wisdom aligned silence with chastity in opposition to frank speech and promiscuity."[30] Given this perception, which renewed its force in Counter-Reformation orthodoxy, it is no wonder that few women letter writers ventured into publication.[31] This fact, however, need not

---

[29] Such tension was already cause for complaint among the women humanists of the Quattrocento. See for example Margaret L. King and Albert Rabil Jr., eds., *Her Immaculate Hand: Selected Writings by and about the Women Humanists of Quattrocento Italy*, MRTS 20 (Binghamton: Center for Medieval & Early Renaissance Studies, 1983).

[30] Jones, *Currency of Eros*, 17. For similar associations, see Boccaccio's tale of Madonna Filippa in *Decameron*, 6.7.

[31] Though letter writing was probably practiced by virtually all literate women of the age, this writing rarely connected with the literary world. Of the published "libri di lettere" indexed by Amedeo Quondam and his associates, we find collections by ninety-four men and only seven women. Also notable regarding this roughly one-thirteenth share is the fact that of the seven women (Isabella Andreini; Madonna Celia, romana [love letters]; Vittoria Colonna [meditations written to another woman on Saint Catherine]; Madonna Emilia N., nobile fiorentina [written to Cavaliere Bernardo N.]; Veronica Franco; Chiara Matraini; and Angelica Paola Antonia de' Negri, religiosa), only the collections of the actress Andreini and of Madonna Celia were published more than one time (17 and 10 editions, respectively). Two other entries, a collection published as the letters of Lucrezia Gonzaga and the *Lettere di molte valorose donne*, turn out, as Novella Bellucci has discussed, to be compositions not by women but by the humanist Ortensio Lando. Bellucci presents the survey figure of nine letter volumes by women to one hundred and sixty by men. See Amedeo Quondam, ed., *"Carte messaggiere": Retorica e modelli di communicazione epistolare. Per un indice di libri di lettere del Cinquecento* (Rome: Bulzoni, 1981), 255. The situation for women writing a bit later

dissuade us today from recognizing the cultural importance of women's epistolary writing and the social impact of their development of the form.

Margaret Ezell observes that the organization of traditional literary history renders especially difficult the discernment of women's activities as writers. The history of literature has, for example, been conventionally linear in its narrative. It concentrates on locating events in time, aims to discover cause-and-effect relations between these events, and establishes ties of kinship and genealogy as well as ranks of quality among texts.[32] Historians look, according to this logic, for "origins," for "the best," "the first," and the most influential works, discarding or subordinating what they find to be derivative. They accordingly favor whole works over fragments, as the rhetorical force of this linear orientation moves researchers to fill in "gaps." Perhaps most importantly, such history relies on a notion of authorship that recognizes overwhelmingly the public spaces of writing and thus, by definition, casts women as absent or anomalous. Collapsing productivity into publication, literary histories locate Cinquecento women's writing in Italy in forms like the lyric, the romance, and the treatise.[33] Yet if we consider a broader horizon, on which writing appears not only as the succession and the relations of influential texts but also as a cultural practice, then the letter's position at the interface of literary and cultural productivity comes into sharper focus. It is here, at this point of interface, that we find a large community of writers, both men and women, whose texts, while not elaborated with literary aims, nonetheless merit attention and call for analysis. In Isabella's case, for example, key *topoi* return repeatedly in her correspondence, marking habits of mind and signaling the powerful role played by the rather routinely written word in the experience of the marchesa and her contemporaries. I take up several of these *topoi* in the following section.

---

in English was quite different, as Whalen's study of seventeenth-century letter writing shows. On France, see also Michèle Longino Farrell, *Performing Motherhood: The Sévigné Correspondence* (Hanover, NH: University Press of New England, 1991).

[32]Margaret Ezell, *Writing Women's Literary History* (Baltimore: Johns Hopkins University Press, 1993), 21.

[33]The pronouncements of Carlo Dionisotti, *Geografia e storia della letteratura italiana* (Turin: Einaudi, 1967), 227–54, have for decades been a principal point of reference regarding women's literary activity in Cinquecento Italy. For a reconsideration of Dionisotti's analysis, see Deanna Shemek, "The Collector's Cabinet: Lodovico Domenichi's Gallery of Women," in *Strong Voices, Weak History*, ed. Pamela Joseph Benson and Victoria Kirkham (Ann Arbor: University of Michigan Press, forthcoming).

III

Letters and Longing

As a princess, Isabella functioned in a wider and freer context than ordinary women of her time, and her epistolary archive reflects a sweeping range of activity. Even the most rapid perusal of her correspondence reveals that letters served a number of important purposes for the marchesa of Mantua. Many are the letters of government, of course, and these have numerous functions. There are letters of congratulation and of condolence; of condemnation and of reprieve; of negotiation and of official reportage; letters that snoop and letters that hide Mantuan affairs from the snooping of others. This is the correspondence in which Isabella d'Este speaks as a princess both to her subjects and to those of her own class. In a separate category may be considered the marchesa's much-studied letters of artistic patronage and those that document her "insatiable appetite" (the adjective is her own) as a collector. These include her requests for antiquities newly unearthed in Greece and Rome and for paintings, marbles, bronzes, and tapestries to decorate her legendary *camerini* (the *studiolo* and *grotta*); but also for medallions, clocks, musical instruments, sculptures, and books to fill that little haven with beautiful objects and pleasures of every sort. Other missives of great interest attest to Isabella's love of lavish self-presentation, as she shops by mail through her various agents for belts of silver and countless yards of cloth; tiaras and *beretine;* rubies, pearls, and gold chains; "acque odorifere et perfumi"; musk oil, pomades, breath fresheners, and "stecchi di denti."

But the letter became a space of crucial personal contact for Isabella as well, a device that structured the longing of a woman who often described herself as living "in continuous expectation" of correspondence. The very first letters the young marchesa wrote after her marriage and relocation in Mantua in February of 1490 give evidence of this function. Isabella's family visited her at the Gonzaga palace of Marmirolo immediately after her marriage. In her loneliness after their departure, she dictated several nearly identical letters to be sent to her family members. In these early missives, the sixteen-year-old bride appears overwhelmed by this novel separation from her family, and she resorts to letters as the pale substitutes for a crowd of people she has left behind. She writes to her sister, Beatrice:

> Most Illustrious Lady. My displeasure at your departure was so great that I was quite beside myself and could not use with you those words and terms that befit such an occasion and that were called for by the tender love we bear each other. And if I weren't certain that Your Ladyship must know this resulted from the tenderness in my heart,

which prevented me from speaking, I would try to make my excuses. But leaving that aside, I say that I so regret being deprived of Your Ladyship's sweetest company that I feel my soul has left my body. Nor do I know how to think of anything but Your Ladyship, whose image appears before me at every hour and in every place. And even though here my illustrious lord looks well on me, and no pleasure is lacking, nonetheless I don't enjoy these things with the contentment I would feel if I had Your Ladyship near. Since I cannot visit you personally I will do so continuously with my soul, and often with letters, begging Your Ladyship to wish to treat me similarly. For I could have no greater pleasure than hearing of Your Ladyship daily. I pray you will want to commend me every day to our most illustrious mother, and that every night when you go to receive her blessing you will take it also for me and kiss her hand in my name. I offer her nothing, since it seems to me superfluous to give her that of which she is just as much mistress as I am. Your Ladyship will excuse me if I don't write now in my own hand, for I am much occupied. But another time I will make good on this omission. I offer myself and commend myself to Your Ladyship.[34]

---

[34] F.II.9. 2904 libro 136 cc. 1v–2r. Translations and transcriptions are mine, unless otherwise noted. I have modernized punctuation, word division, and accents, and regularized capitalization. Round brackets indicate illegibility due to document damage; where possible, reconstruction appears within the brackets. Square brackets enclose my editorial insertions for clarification. Conventional abbreviations have been expanded. Stricken words in the manuscript appear stricken in my transcriptions. This letter is undated but is flanked in Isabella's *copialettere* by others dated 27 February 1490. "Illustrissima. Tanto fu el despiacere che hebbe de la partita de la Signoria Vostra che era cussì fora de me, che non potte usarli quelle parole et termini che in simile atto se convenea, et como recircava el tenero amore che se portiamo. Et se non fuse certa che Vostra Signoria debbe cognosere che questo procedeve da tenereza de cuore, che non me lassò parlare, cercaria fare la scusa mia. Però lasando questa parte dico che tanto me rincrese essere priva de la dulcissima compagnia de la Signoria Vostra che me pare l'anima sia partita dal corpo. Ne scio pensare de altro cha de la Signoria Vostra, la quala ogni hora et ogni punto se me representa inanti. Et benché qua da l'illustrissimo signor mio sia benveduta et non me manca alcuno piacere, nondimeno non gli godo cum quella contenteza che farria se havesse a presso la Signoria Vostra, la quale non potendo personalmente, La visitarò continuamente cum l'animo et spesso cum lettere, pregandola voglia similmente fare Lei meco. Che cosa alcuna de mazor piacere non poteria havere cha da intendere a la zornata de la Signoria Vostra, la qual prego voglia ogni zorno raccomandarme a la illustrissima nostra matre et ogni sera quando andarà a tuore la benedictione da la eccellenza sua per Lei [voglia] et piliarla per me et basarli la mane in nome mio. Io non li facio offerte parendomi superfluo offerirli quello de che La è cussi ma[dama] come sun io. La Signoria Vostra me haverà

Following this text in Isabella's copybook is the secretarial note to send similar letters to other members of her family: her brothers Alfonso, Ferdinando, and Sigismundo, her natural brother Giulio, another Sigismundo (perhaps her uncle [1480–1524]), and her half-sister Lucrezia.[35] Through this small postal campaign, Isabella aimed to fill the space of her family's absence with text, in a production of letters that could aptly be called elegiac, so filled is her language with images of mourning. In each of these missives, she evokes the scene of loss and separation as one that struck her silent and cast her into a state of spiritual disintegration. Her soul (as she puts it) having departed from her body in this detachment, Isabella turns — as she will often in the future — to the device of the letter to join them together again. Like many of her humanist contemporaries, Isabella draws on commonplaces from antiquity, professing a desire to "visit [an interlocutor] with words" or to enter into "conversation" with others through letters. Also present in this correspondence are Christian resonances that underscore the interface of body and soul as she does in the letter above, and lyric ones that recall Dante's overtures to Beatrice in the *Vita nuova* and Petrarch's to Laura in his *Canzoniere*. Like Petrarch with Laura (Canzone 129), Isabella remarks that Beatrice's image "appears before [her] at every hour and in every place."[36] She responds to this perception by composing letters to bridge the gap between an absent sister and the spirit that lingers as a presence in Isabella's life. Externalizing a highly subjective sense of connection with an absent interlocutor, the letter then travels to its reader as a material testament to the writer's affection, standing in for that writer's self to another who is urged to reciprocate.

The exchange of manual traces recalls the sender's conventional bodily contact with the letter, and Isabella's regular apologies for not writing in her own hand underscore the metonymic value added to any letter by this aura of corporeality. References to the hands and bodies of correspondents now out of each other's reach reinforce the work of mourning that Isabella's early letters seem to be performing, but they also add the dimension of personal guarantee, or of testament to the sender's sincerity. In the first months of her marriage, the memorial, sensual, and testimonial functions of the letter are especially consistent in Isabella's correspondence with her mother. On 2 March 1490, she sent a basket of fish to the duchess Eleonora in "demonstration" of her affection and her filial memories:

---

per excusata se non li scrivo adesso de mia mane per esser occupata. Ma un'altra volta satisfarò a questo mancamento et a la Signoria Vostra me offero et raccomando."

[35] Lucrezia was the illegitimate daughter of Ercole d'Este; she married Count Annibale Bentivoglio in 1487. The only sibling to whom Isabella appears not to have written at this time was her brother, the future Cardinal Ippolito d'Este.

[36] My thanks to Dennis Looney for our exchanges on this point.

Most Illustrious Lady. As I was unable to obtain fish from Lake Garda to send you as I had wished, in demonstration that I remember you and have you constantly in my heart, I had some fish caught in the rivers here. And since a certain small number of lampreys were caught, I thought immediately of sending them to you. I hope you will excuse me if they are not so beautiful and so numerous as you deserve, and accept my great affection [my large soul] in supplement. I commend myself always to the good grace of his Illustrious Lordship my father and you, praying you will deign to commend me to my illustrious brothers and sister. As I finished writing the above, my messenger from Garda returned with some salted carp, fifty of which I am sending along for you and equally as many for the illustrious lord, my father, as well as some citrons and lemons for Your Excellency. I will make every effort to have some fresh carp another time and will send them to Your Ladyship, to whom I commend myself once more.[37]

Again the letter functions as mnemonic token — as souvenir — and as material evidence of the affection its sender bears the recipient. Adding to the anticipated pleasures of its arrival are the fish Isabella sends along with it; but as though the lampreys don't suffice to fill the breach between daughter and mother, Mantua and Ferrara, she supplements them with other delicacies as the package leaves her door, so that salted carp, citron, and lemons add pungent notes to the already savory message Isabella sends her parents. This concoction of gastronomic pleasures aims to reinforce fond memories of a distant daughter, and indeed gifts of food continue to travel with Isabella's letters over the coming years, truffles, oysters, artichokes, wine, cheeses, and fish being among her favorite

---

[37] F.II.9. 2904 Libro 136 c. 3v. "Illustrissima. Non havendo possuto havere pisci del laco de Garda per mandare a la Eccellenza Vostra como era el desiderio mio per dimonstrarli che me ricordo de Lei et l'ho continuamente nel core, ho facto piscare in questi fiumi. Et presa certa poca quantità de lampredelle m'è parso subito mandarle a la Eccellenza Vostra quale se degnaria haverme per excusata se non sono belle et tante como La meritaria, acceptando in suplemento l'animo mio grande. Et a la bona gratia de l'ilustrissimo signor mio patre et de Vostra Signoria me raccomando sempre, supplicandoLa se digni racommandarme ali illustrissimi mei fratelli et sorella. Scripto fin qua è retornato uno mio messo da Garda che me ha portati certi carpioni sallati, de' quali mando cinquanta a Vostra Signoria et altritanti a lo illustrissimo signor mio padre, et alcuni cedri et limoni pur a la Eccellenza Vostra. Usarò ogni diligentia per haver di carpioni freschi una altra volta et mandaroli a la predetta Vostra Signoria, a la quala iterum me raccomando."

postal accompaniments. Such packages are clearly markers of an early modern food economy that prized the diversity of dietary offerings only the very elite could afford, but they also play a part in Isabella's efforts to reconstitute corporeal presence over distances. She sends food as an extravagant kindness and a memento of meals together, but these are also missives that enter the body, joining her to others through direct intervention in their physical well-being.

Isabella's family did not regard her letters with the same urgency in which she sent them, however. On 4 March, just five or six days after showering recipients at Ferrara with letters, she wrote again to Lucrezia. Isabella's frustration at her perceived neglect now moved her to sour-grapes petulance in compensation for the affection she sought: indeed, we can almost hear the marchesa of Mantua stamp her foot:

> Most Illustrious Cousin who is like a delightful sister to me. The courier we sent there returned with no reply to the letter we wrote you, which would have much amazed us if we had not already anticipated that you would be caught up in so many pleasures that you no longer remembered us. And it seems to us that you have verified the proverb that says 'out of sight, out of mind.' We had not written you in our own hand, since we doubted you would trouble yourself to respond, and we guessed well. Because if you did not deign now to send the courier with a tiny little letterlet, much less would you have written in your own hand. And so, having written you that we intended to write you in our own hand, we changed our mind upon confirming what we suspected. Yet we thought to confuse you by writing yet another letter to ask you, if you don't care to honor us with one of your letters, at least to kiss the hand of our mother every day in our name, and keep us commended [to her] and also to our illustrious lord father. And greet all the ladies of the court on our behalf. We dispose ourselves to your pleasure.[38]

[38] F.II.9. 2904 Libro 136 c. 4v. "Illustrissima consobrina et tamquam soror dilectissima. El cavallaro che mandassimo là è retornato senza risposta de la litera che ve scrivessimo, del che haveressimo preso grande admiratione, se non havessemo già pronosticato che staresti di là in tanti piaceri che non ricordaresti piu di nui, e parne che in (vui) sia verificato el proverbio che se dice che longe da ( ) occhi è longe da cuore. Non ve scrivessimo de nostra mane, dubitando che ve agravasse la fatica da rispondere, et bene indivinassimo, perché se adeso non vi seti dignata de comettere al cavallaro una litteruza, tanto manco haveresti scripto de propria mane. Unde nui che come ve scrivessimo havevamo intentione de scrivervi di nostra mane, esendo mo certificate de quello che dubitavemo, havemo facto altra deliberatione. Tuttavia c'è parso a vostra confusione scrivervi questa altra nostra et pregarvi se già non volevi farne degne de vostre lettere vogliati almanco ogni zorno basiare

Lucrezia stands accused of erasing a sister from her heart while carrying on the merry life for which Ferrara was known. Isabella's petty claim that she considered sending an autograph letter but changed her mind marks again the high value assigned to the bodily connection to letter writing, as she covers the wound left from Lucrezia's withheld response with an immobile hand that now refuses to write. The pleasures Isabella attributes to her sister's existence in Ferrara are a key psychic element in her life as a letter writer, for letters become the space of transmission for vicarious experiences that texture her solitary periods in Mantua. Indeed, what appears to be at issue generally is not only the absence of familiar people from her daily life, but Isabella's *own* absence from Ferrara; and the odd temporality represented in the letter to Lucrezia is symptomatic of her exertion to project herself back into Ferrarese relations. Isabella complains about not receiving a reply she purportedly never expected. She claims she did not write in autograph for her own reasons but that, having not received the autograph she did *not* expect to receive, she has now revised a plan to send one herself in return. This ostentatious withholding is a struggle within and against conditions of space and time that become a significant dimension of Isabella's epistolary life. As desire and memory are forced to accept reality and lack, Isabella tries to forge new relations with the world whose distance at times provokes her to rage. The language of this process of mourning becomes even more explicit in Isabella's letters to her parents.

Hands, Memory, and Mourning

One person who did apparently hear the cries of the forlorn Isabella was the woman whose hand she instructs Lucrezia to kiss, her mother. Isabella's missive of 9 March to the Duchess of Ferrara makes explicit the young marchesa's conception of letters as partial objects, displaced but powerful reminders of what once was present and what now must be strenuously evoked through memory and imagination. She wrote to her mother after a day of recreation with her sister-in-law, the duchess of Urbino:

> Through the reply Your Excellency made, I learned of your well-being, which I desire more than my own. You need not have explained why you did not respond to me in your own hand, because any letter from

---

la mane a la eccellenza de madama in nome nostro et a lei et alli illustrissimi nostri fratelli et sorella tenerce arraccomandate, et cussì alo illustrissimo signor nostro padre. Et confortate tutte le done de casa da parte nostra et ali vostri piaceri ne offerimo."

> you suffices for me. And I would not want you to suffer any inconvenience on my account, though when I do have letters from Your Excellency's hand I keep them as holy relics. I beg you, for my part, to excuse me if this letter is not written in my hand, for I was with the most illustrious duchess of Urbino all day and had no time. My illustrious consort came here yesterday, and today after dinner he went back to Gonzaga en route to arriving there [in Ferrara]. Perhaps Your Excellency will see him before I do.
>
> [. . .] Your Excellency once charged that I would soon forget everyone there [in Ferrara]. But it seems to me that just the opposite is true, because I have written to twelve people and have had not one reply, except that of Gianmaria Trotto. Whence I have cause to complain of that whole court. . . . And so if I wrote no more in the future, Your Excellency could not accuse me of haughtiness or of forgetting Ferrara. I enclose here the list of all those to whom I gave, so that Your Excellency will be apprised of my every action. And to your good grace and that of my illustrious father I commend myself. Mantua, 9 March 1490.[39]

Since most of the letters Isabella and her correspondents exchange are in fact dictated, the personal writing hand that repeatedly surfaces in their discourse is an absent ideal, symptomatically marked as desirable but paradoxically dismissed as expendable. Isabella's implicit, Christian assumption of the body's interface with the soul through the writing hand also returns in the rhetoric of

---

[39] F. II.9 2904 Libro 136 c. 7r. "Per la resposta che me ha facto la Eccellenza Vostra ho inteso el suo benstare, el quale desidero più chal mio proprio. Non bisognava che La me faceste intendere la causa perché non me respondeva de sua mane, perché a me basta ogni lettera pur che la sia da parte sua. Né voria che per me pigliasse uno disconzo, benché quando ho lettere de mane de la Eccellenza Vostra le conser( )e com(e) reliquie sancte. Supplicola ben io se digni haverme per excusata se questa non è de mia mane, perché essendo stata tutto hozi cum la illustrissima duchessa de Urbino, non ho havuto tempo. Lo illustrissimo consorte venne heri sera qua et hozi doppo disnare retornoe a Gonzaga, per venirsene poi là. Forsi che Vostra Eccellenza lo (ꝑ) vederà più presto che questa mia.

"... [L]a Eccellenza Vostra me imputava (~~me~~) che me scordaria subito de quelli là. Ma parme ch'el sia tutto el contrario, perché havendo scripto a più de dodece persone, non ho havuto resposta da veruna, salvo cha do Zohanmaria Trotto. Unde ho causa de dolermi di tutta quella corte. . . . Siché seben per l'advenire non scrivesse, la Vostra Eccellenza non me poterà più imputare de superbia, né che me habia scordato de Ferrara. Mando annotati in la lista qui inclusa quelli a chi ho donato, aciò che la Vostra Eccellenza sapia ogni mia actione. Et in sua bona gratia et del illustrissimo mio patre me raccomando."

the letter above: if the personal hand is the conduit of the writer's authentic inner voice, then the mediation of voice through dictation and a secretarial writing hand weakens the desired, direct spiritual contact through the letter. Letters from Isabella's mother — autograph or not — appear in this context as "holy relics," metonymic objects that encapsulate and transmit the powerful presence of a body to which they were once "attached." The conventionality of this language also surfaces constantly, as above where, after extolling the significance of a handwritten letter, Isabella explains that she herself was too busy to pen a coveted autograph text. She goes on to expose two other epistolary conventions as well, for she ignores both the intimacy and the voluntary nature of affectionate letter writing by providing a report to the duchess on all recipients who have failed to satisfy her demand. Thus if the longing for contact with others produces in Isabella's letters a frequent set of references to the hand as a guarantor of her sincerity, these references often mark instances of her bad faith: if these are deictic gestures, they point in the wrong direction.[40] Isabella in effect appears, in moments of reference to her own hand, not to be gesturing toward any real desire to abandon her secretary but to be sending "hand signals" that correspondence

---

[40] Several recent studies have explored the hand's role as a symbol in early modern culture, where it functioned as an especially powerful metaphor for agency, sovereignty, commitment, and personal faith, and where its relation to the arts of memory was crucial. See Katherine Rowe, *Dead Hands: Fictions of Agency Renaissance to Modern* (Stanford: Stanford University Press, 1999); Goldberg, *Writing Matter*; and Claire Richter Sherman, ed., *Writing Hands: Memory and Knowledge in Early Modern Europe* (Seattle: University of Washington Press, 2000). Clinical neurology also takes this crucial relation into account. Neurologist Frank R. Wilson, who specializes in hand disorders, argues that "[A]ny theory of human intelligence which ignores the interdependence of hand and brain function, the historic origins of that relationship, or the impact of that history on the developmental dynamics of modern humans is grossly misleading and sterile." Wilson not only argues an evolutionary connection between human intelligence and the development of the hand, a connection he insists is at least as important as that between intelligence and language use. He also underscores that the hand has been historically — indeed anthropologically — a conduit of emotion and passion specific to human experience. Wilson's work thus considers the hand as a learning tool (in child development), as an instrument of communication (in gesture and in technologies like writing and keyboard use), and as a mediator for totally nonverbal, body/mind expression (as in the playing of musical instruments). See Frank R. Wilson, *The Hand: How Its Use Shapes the Brain, Language, and Human Culture* (New York: Vintage, 1998), 7. Wilson's research suggests a particular way of understanding the ambivalence in letters by Isabella and others and the highly mediated relation between letter authors and their writing. That relation appears especially important as we consider a historical moment when the letter was the primary mode of communication across distances.

is important to her. The recurrent emphasis in these letters on memory — the memory of others and that of Isabella — further suggests the affective dimension in which letters were coming to play such a large part in Isabella's life. Her requests for letters that will solidify precious memories *and* elicit her future contacts with correspondents create an interwoven temporality. Expectations anticipate the contents of letters before they arrive; the letters once received evoke both reminiscence and the promise of future pleasures; and postal delay dilates time into a yawning realm of wanting.

Medicinal Missives

It follows as a matter of course that letters from one's closest loved one should be as frequent and informative as possible. A regular refrain in letters from Isabella to Francesco is her request for more correspondence. A note from 30 April 1490 records the loneliness of the young bride who turns to letter writing as a substitute for spousal company. Declaring that his parting remark to her that he didn't feel well was "a knife in [her] heart" ["una cortella al cuore"], Isabella attempts to soothe the wound from that knife with a familiar salve of words applied to paper. In this reflexive image, Francesco's letters appear as an unguent for the "knife" wound he put in Isabella's heart when he suggested his own possible illness. She notes the subjective nature of the time of waiting with a conventional phrase that recurs often in her correspondence: "Though it is not yet ten hours since Your Excellency left here, nonetheless since it seems to me ten years I wanted to visit you with these few words." ["Benché non sia sino dece hore che partesse la Eccellenza Vostra de qua, nondimeno parendome dece anni ho voluto cum queste poche parole visitarla."][41] A month later (28 May) she assures Francesco that he can do her "no greater favor" than to write to her frequently.[42] Well after Isabella's days as a new bride, moreover, this pattern continued. In February of 1496, she wrote to Francesco on the day of his departure for the war in Naples:[43]

> My Illustrious Lord. The last time Your Excellency left for the field I took displeasure, but I consoled myself that you were not going so far away, and soon word of your activities returned to me almost daily. But now I don't know where to take comfort, considering the distance and

[41] F.II.6. 2106 c. 375.

[42] F.II.6. 2106 c. 364.

[43] On Francesco's role in aiding Ferdinand II against the French, see Leonardo Mazzoldi, ed., *Mantova. La storia* (Mantua: Istituto Carlo d'Arco, 1961), 2:77–204, esp. 108–14.

> the danger of the place where you are being transferred; and Your Lordship's absence seems not one day but a thousand. Think now what lies ahead for me. I know no better remedy to keep me alive with little trouble than to have frequent confirmation of your well-being; and I pray you content me in this by sending me word of it every day. I have no other news for this letter, save that I wanted to visit you as is my duty. I would have satisfied you with [a letter by] my hand if it were not for a bit of fever that came upon me yesterday evening. I was not in discomfort, but I hope it goes no further. Elionora is well. I commend myself to Your Excellency's good grace. Mantua, 24 February 1496.[44]

Here, for all her pain, Isabella again excuses herself from writing in autograph, this time by returning to the theme of illness with the suggestion that she herself is not well.

Isabella seems to have appreciated that others needed letters from her as much as she needed to hear from them. On 4 April of the same year, she remarks that she remains "in continuous expectation" for news of Francesco's safe arrival in Rome; but on the 27th of that month, she assures him that, though she has not received replies to all the letters she has sent him, she will keep writing, assuming delays in delivery and "knowing that a person who is away from home never receives so many letters from his family that he does not desire to have more" ["sapendo che la persona, quale è fora de casa non ha mai tante lettere da li soi che non desiderano haverne più"].[45] In June, she thanks her husband profusely for his correspondence and "supplicates" him not to desist;[46] and in

[44] F.II.6. 2111 Fasc. V c. 208r. "Illustrissimo Signor Mio. L'altra volta quando la Eccellenza Vostra andò in campo io ne presi dispiacere, ma pur non essendo ita troppo lontana me confortava, sì che presto ritornò como de cottidiano aviso de li progressi soi. Ma adesso non scio in che parte me possa confortare, consyderando la longheza et periculosità del loco dove La se transferisse, per modo che non uno giorno ma mille me pare l'absentia de Vostra Signoria. Pensi mo quello che per lo advenire me intervenirà. Io non cognosco altro remedio megliore a farmi vivere cum manco fastidio, cha havere spesso certeza de la bona valitudine de Vostra Signoria la quale prego voglia in questa contentarmi facendomene a la zornata dare aviso. Altro non me occorre per questa se non che per debito mio ho voluto visitarlo. De mia mane haveria satisfacto, se non per un poco de febre che me sopragionse heri ser. Non me sentisse disturbata, ma spero non passarà più oltra. La Elionora sta bene. Raccommandome in bona gratia de Vostra Eccellenza." See also F.II.9.2992 libro 6 cc. 30r–v for a copy of this letter.

[45] F.II.6. 2111 Fasc. V c. 240r.

[46] F.II.6. 2111 Fasc. V c. 254r.

July, she notes to Francesco that she writes often, "so as not to allow a void of letters from me" ["per non lassare venire vacuo de mie lettere"].[47]

This mutual need for letters as surrogates for physical presence is also articulated in Isabella's letters to her closest friends. On 19 February 1495, she writes from Milan to Francesco's ailing sister, Chiara Gonzaga, that she hopes her letters will act as medicine:

> Since I cannot speak with you by my own mouth, my desire induces me to be satisfied with letters, knowing very well that they will be so welcome to you that each time you read them you will feel some improvement in your condition. I certainly think this is possible, because I write them with such love that they should lift all your illness away, and in order to do this I would spill my own blood.[48]

For Chiara too, letters heal. In this spectacular interiorization and somaticization of the spiritual tie that binds her to Chiara, Isabella evokes the opening of her own body to spill blood as a variation on the more conventional imagery of the soul poured out as ink on paper. As with the letter to Francesco, Chiara's suffering becomes Isabella's own in an extreme form of participation in the illness of her interlocutors.

The theme of letters as medicine is a frequent one. Just about a year later, she wrote to the duchess of Urbino, in the wake of the latter's departure from Mantua. Chiara Gonzaga remained at Mantua with Isabella, and Isabella asked Elisabetta for letters as an antidote to the two women's pain at Elisabetta's departure:

> I well believe Your Ladyship took displeasure in departing from here, since you are so sweet and loving, but I won't believe that your displeasure is greater than mine. For though you take leave of your brothers and sisters, you are on your way to see and enjoy your illustrious consort. But I am left deprived not only of your faithful and welcome conversation but also of my husband's presence, who is leaving on a

---

[47] F.II.6. 2111 Fasc. V c. 264r–v. Francesco's letters in this folder indicate that he felt the same need for letters as did Isabella.

[48] F.II.9 2992 Libro 5 c. 15r. "[E] l desiderio che ho de parlare cum Lei, non lo potendo far a bocha, mi induce a satisfar cum lettere. Intendo maximamente che le sonno tanto grate a la Signoria Vostra che ogni volta che La le lege sente meglioramento di la persona sua. Certamente io creddo ch'el sia el vero, perché le scrivo cum tal amore che voria poterli in tutto levarli el mal da dosso, et per questo spargeria el proprio sangue."

difficult and dangerous mission, as Your Ladyship knows. It is true that the illustrious lady, the archduchess, our sister, remains here and will be of great refreshment to me. But I don't know now which of us has greater need of comfort, and without someone between us who is less taken by passion, we are not well and cannot feel much consolation. And so we deservedly say we feel the greater pain. One remedy will relieve it: if you write to me often. Because in reading your letters I will see before me the thousand pleasures we shared together in your sweet conversation. I commend myself to Your Ladyship and pray you commend me to your illustrious lord consort and to signor Ottaviano, not forgetting also Madame Emilia. Mantua 22 February 1496.[49]

IV

These themes and topoi persisted as Isabella turned letters into a medium also for accessing a world outside the intimate confines of the family. As her "continuous expectation" grew in its political and historical orientation, she employed letters deftly in the construction and maintenance of Gonzaga power relations at multiple levels. This was possible, of course, because noble and dynastic families themselves were the principal scaffolding on which Cinquecento political relations were constructed. Family politics (in which Isabella could legitimately take direct interest) thus functioned frequently as a rhetorical curtain that thinly veiled Isabella's news-gathering throughout the Italian peninsula and beyond, even in spheres where her presence might be perceived as intrusive.

---

[49] F.II .9 2992. Libro 6 c. 29r. "Credo ben che Vostra Signoria habia preso displicentia assai de la partita Sua de qui per esser tutta dolce et amorevole, ma non voglio già credere che la sia magiore de la mia. Perché se Lei parte da soi fratelli et sorelle, va a vedere et godere lo illustrissimo suo consorte. Ma io resto non solum priva de la fidele et grata conversatione sua, ma anchora de la persona del'illustrissimo signor mio consorte, quale va ad impresa periculosa et difficile como scia Vostra Signoria. L'è vero ch'el resta qua la illustrissima madama archiduchessa nostra comune sorella che serrà ad me de grande refrigerio. Ma non scio mo' qual de nui habia magiore bisogno de essere confortate. Perhò senza una persona de mezo che non sia in tanta passione non stiamo bene, né poteremo pigliare troppo consolatione. De la partita dunque de Vostra Signoria meritamente dovemo sentire magiore dolore. Uno remedio sarà a levarlo: se la Vostra Signoria me scriverà spesso. Perché leggendo le lettere sue me vedurò à memoria mille piaceri che per la dolce conversacione nostra havemo preso inseme. Racommandome a la Signoria Vostra et pregola me racommandi alo illustrissimo signore suo consorte et signor Octaviano, non se scordando de madama Emilia."

As I observed above, women of Isabella's class frequently stayed at home while husbands went on military campaign, as Francesco Gonzaga is said to do in the letter cited above. In such a milieu, visits to and from neighboring courts (the former being possible only when the consort was at home to mind domestic affairs) were key conduits for information about happenings outside the restricted sphere of the single city-state as well as opportunities to cultivate social and familial relations. Intimate bonds formed during these extended visits, and the separations that interrupted them took on intense significance as well, so that in times of separation letters became crucial for maintaining the health of both mind and body. On the one hand, they reinforced memories that would have served as entertainment until another such visit took place. On the other, they constituted the space of political and familial relations that were crucial to stay-at-home consorts — male or female — in small city states.

Francesco's letters were especially important to Isabella, since they served not only to assure her of his well-being during his absences but also to inform her about the world. Active and aware as she was, the more experienced Isabella sought thicker and thicker correspondence from her husband during his many military campaigns. Her late twenties are marked by an increasing interest in the world around her and a desire for letters as a means of vicarious participation in the spheres of life that remain closed to her as a woman. In this period, information from Francesco takes on particular urgency, as her fears for his safety as head of state and her desire to produce a male heir with him intertwine with Isabella's ever more insistent curiosity about matters military and political in the courts of Italy. We see develop what we might even call an ideology of the letter for Isabella: an understanding of politics and history predicated on action within an epistolary arena. That arena of letters, in its vulnerability to delay and detour, appears to have functioned in the temporality of Machiavellian *occasione* (opportunity) and was manipulated and maintained as such.

Part of this manipulation involved Isabella's presenting her inquiries about public matters as though they were strictly personal and familial. The more we learn about the lives of women in the Italian courts, the more we are moved to revise the notion that they had no institutional power; but it remains the case that the kinds of power women had were specific ones, often related to dynastic concerns, and that women's activism in the broader political sphere was usually unwelcome. Isabella understood this and was often careful to screen her political interests with familial ones. She tells Francesco in a letter of 13 November 1502, "I am in a state of continuous desire for letters from Your Lordship, which put my soul at peace" ["Sto in continuo desiderio de havere lettere di Vostra Signoria che me fanno stare quieta cum l'animo"].[50] Yet clearly her orientation in this period is a civic, political one. The same letter informs Francesco of her intention to send a robber to the gallows ["dare supplicio de la forcha"]; recounts other criminal unrest in Mantua; communicates news of a local marriage; reflects on the political situation of the Urbino dukes, who have been left out of the Bolognese peace; and finally offers her opinions on the Florentine political situation.

In July of 1503, addressing Francesco as "Illustrissimo Signor Mio Unico" she pleads for him to send more and more letters.[51] On 29 August, she asks him to be still more detailed in his writings to her, but she typically presents her desire for news as concern for Francesco's health:

> Your Excellency sends post informing me in two words that you are well and happily dispatched. I took singular pleasure at the news, but to tell the truth I was not entirely satisfied. I would like to understand your successes and fortunes more particularly, because since you only recently recuperated from illness and are not yet entirely well, I will be ever anxious and fearful for your health. Hence I beg you for now and for the future to keep me most minutely informed of Your Excellency's every progress.[52]

Francesco appears to have been inconsistent in satisfying his wife's wish for letters. On 31 August, Isabella expressed gratitude for his copious missives from Bologna and assured him that he could do her no greater favor than to keep the letters coming.[53] But on 15 September she begged him not to subject her to a "famine" of his letters ["La prego a non mi fare carestia de lettere"]. Clearly by this point what Isabella wants is news, as she contrasts her own time with his, almost envying his dangerous adventures: "Don't be amazed at having so little news, for our affairs are proceeding with such peace that I can only write you

---

[50] F.II.6 2115 cc.186r–187r.

[51] F.II.6 2115 Fasc. VII c.349r.

[52] F.II.6 2115 Fasc. VII c.358r. "La Eccellenza Vostra per uno posta me significa in due parole che La sta bene et se ne va allegramente. Io ne ho recevuto singulare piacere, ma a dire el vero non sono però rimasta in tutto satisfacta. Però ch'io voria intendere più particularmente li successi et accidenti suoi, perché essendo fresca dil male, et non bene convaluta, starò sempre anxia et dubiosa de la salute Sua. Però La supplico che et per adesso et per lo advenire voglij ordinare che sij tenuta informata minutissimamente de ogni progresso de Vostra Eccellenza."

[53] F.II.6 2115 Fasc. VII c.359r–361r.

letters of well-being" ["Ne se maravegliarà de avere pochi avisi, perché le cose nostre passano cum tanta quiete, che non mi resta scriverli se non lettere de sanità"].[54]

Once the Gonzaga children grew and began to move about the world, Isabella mobilized them personally to their epistolary duties; but she also relied on their guardians and associates to dilate the commentary and offer multiple perspectives on all events. When the future marchese, Federico, was taken voluntary hostage at the court of Pope Julius II as assurance of Mantua's loyalty to Rome in the political conflicts of 1510–1513, he was accompanied by a personal staff, all of whom were enlisted as informants to supplement the letters Isabella received from the ten-year-old Federico. To the majordomo Matteo Ippoliti she wrote immediately after Federico's arrival that she wanted constant news of her son's well-being, while of his governess Magdalena she requested letters on the same subject, but highlighting "certain details that men do not write" [certe particularità che li homini non scriveno].[55] Nor was such mobilization without need of reinforcement. To Gonzaga agent Francesco Grossino Isabella wrote in July of 1511:

> We see that you are silent with us and have set aside your natural and thorough diligence, perhaps in the belief that we will be pleased if you do not bother us with letters, since you know that others too are writing to us. And so we thought we would disabuse you of this error by explaining that the more letters we receive that speak of our son and of events at court, and the longer the letters are, the happier we are to read them. So prepare to be diligent. Give Federico and Magdalena our greetings. Mantua 5 July 1511.[56]

Correspondents like Grossino were in fact major suppliers of news, and Isabella managed them deftly. On the one hand, since many of these figures

---

[54] F.II.6 2115 Fasc. VIII c. 368r–369r.

[55] F.II.9.2996 libro 28 cc. 23r–v, 41v. See also Alessandro Luzio, "Federico Gonzaga ostaggio alla corte di Giulio II," *Archivio della società romana di storia patria* 9 (1886): 509–92.

[56] F.II.9.2996 libro 29 c. 38v. "Poi che vedemo che tu usi tanto silentio cum noi et che hai posto da canto la tua naturale et accurata diligentia, credendo forsi farni piacere a non fastidirni cum lettere, sapendo che li altri ce scriveno, ni è parso levarti da questo error declarandoti che quante più lettere et più longe havemo che parlano di Federico nostro figliolo et de le altre occurentie de corte, tanto più voluntieri le legemo. Sì che apparechiati di fare il dilligente. Saluta Federico et la Magdalena da parte nostra."

were in her employ, she freely specified constant letter writing as one of their duties. On the other hand, as we may infer from the letter to Grossino, the quality and frequency of the news she would get ultimately depended on not only the reliability but also the willingness of her sources to engage substantially and continuously in such contact with her. For this reason, she treats her best correspondents carefully, coasting between command and plea in relationships that were crucially important to her. In this relation of coercion and consent, which required constant renewal in order to be effective, we recognize again Isabella's subtle vein of Machiavellianism, for she holds out the options of reward and punishment offered by any effective prince, hinting at her own capacities as centaur, who functions according to reason but may turn to cruelty if moved to do so.

Since as early as her bridal departure from Ferrara, the courtier Bernardino Prosperi, too, was a key informant from her native city. The letters Isabella wrote to family members at that time (as we have seen) are sometimes whining and peevish, but with Prosperi she is always gracious. It is easy for her to be so, of course, since Prosperi is an obliging correspondent and an excellent reporter. As Isabella wrote to him on 20 March 1498:

> If it were not for your letters, we would never have news of our homeland again, as though we were a foreigner, because we have no one else but you who tells us about it. For this reason your letters are all the more dear to us, and you merit praise and thanks for them. We refer to the reports you provided in your letter of the 18th, especially about the arrival [at Ferrara] of the most illustrious lord our consort, and the endearments that were shown him by the illustrious lords our father and brother. And the other parts of your letter were all extremely appreciated as well. If you continue thus, we will gratify your work all the more.[57]

[57] F.II.9.2992 libro 9 c. 38v. "Se non fussino le littere vostre, nui non haveressimo mai piu noticia de quella nostra patria, como se fussino forestera. Perché non habiamo altra persona che ce ne rendi conto se non vui. Però tanto più ne sono chare le lettere vostre, et meritatine commendatione et gratie. Questo dicemo per li avisi quali per la vostra de xviij ce haveti dato, maxime de la giunta lì dell'illustrissimo signor nostro consorte, et careze gli sono state facte per li illustrissimi signori nostri patre et fratello et altre parte, quale tutte ne sono state gratissime. Et continuando magiormente gratificaremo le opere vostre."

Isabella's use of the word *gratificaremo* — to reward, gratify, or to satisfy — is important in the letter above, because together with the word *gratissime* in the previous sentence it suggests her strategy of consistently repaying good correspondence. She replies enthusiastically with thanks and praise for her best reporters, and she is willing to make it worth Prosperi's while to compose flavorful, detailed letters that put her in touch with distant arenas of activity. On the other hand, she is quick to scold or dismiss correspondents who do not perform well for her purposes.

Her other strategy was to be well organized, as we see in a communication to Donato de Preti (then in the service of Isabella's brother, cardinal Ippolito d'Este) on the same day as the letter above:

> From your most recent letters we are fully informed of the order of our most reverend and most illustrious monsignor the cardinal our brother's entry into Milan and of the departure of the most illustrious and most excellent lord duke of Milan. We communicated it all to our most illustrious lord, and each of us took great satisfaction in it. We commend you most highly. And since we wish to understand the order of entry and other observances in Genoa to honor the above-mentioned lord duke, we are sending you this courier, through whom you will write in detail all that happens there.[58]

Here again, Isabella fishes for news about current events under the pretext of seeking information about the well-being (or at least the success) of her relatives in their endeavors. The courier system and her network of correspondents were far from perfect, but they were the only means available for gathering news, and Isabella wanted very much to keep informed of political and social developments abroad without appearing to overstep her bounds as a mere woman. Hence her frustration when mail failed to arrive, for reasons that were not always so easy to determine as they were with the letters I cited at the beginning of this essay.

---

[58] F.II.9.2992 libro 9 c. 38v. "Per le ultime vostre restamo diffusamente avisate dil' ordine de la intrata in Milano del reverendissimo et illustrissimo monsignor cardinale nostro fratello, et de la partita dell' illustrissimo et eccelentissimo signor duca de Milano. Il tucto habiamo communicato cum lo illustrissimo signor nostro, che a l'uno et l'altra è stato de grandissima satisfactione. Et commendiamovine summamente. Et perché desyderamo intendere l'ordine della intrata et altro mo' servato lì in Genoa per honorare el predetto signor duca, mandiamovi questo cavallaro, per el quale scrivareti minutamente quanto ve occorerà."

On 23 January 1522, for example, she wrote to several parties in the papal court. Pope Leo X had died in December, and Isabella wanted news about his successor, not least because she would continue with this person her campaign for a cardinal's hat for her son Ercole. She writes to him:

> Not without enormous displeasure, we marveled that after a first letter from the magnificent messer Baldesar Castiglione about the creation of the new pontiff, we never heard another thing. This made us very anxious, given our desire to hear the news from there, especially regarding the well being of the most reverend and most illustrious lord cardinal, our brother-in-law and honored father, and also news about you. We cannot believe — in fact we are certain — that you have not all neglected to write several times regarding what has happened, just as we have continuously sent news there of what we were hearing here daily. We are certain that the same cause that has not permitted your letters to fall into our hands must have delayed ours to you.[59]

There was a "same cause," perhaps; but what that cause was is less evident. If, as I have suggested, Isabella came to intuit something like Machiavellian *occasione* in the need to seize available means and moments of communication, she also experienced the fickleness of Fortuna, as letters fell prey to chance detours and even treacherous thefts within the delivery system upon which she relied. The flip-side of this dynamic was that Isabella's success in generating correspondence was sometimes greater than she herself would have wished. A letter she wrote on 8 October 1524 to Gonzaga agent Giacomo Suardo ("Suardino") after her son Ferrante Gonzaga had been successfully installed in the court of Charles V laments:

> Though for a time we were in continuous desire for letters from Spain to have news of the illustrious don Ferrante our son, we are now of

---

[59] F.II.9.2998 libro 38 cc. 66v–67r. "Non senza summa displicentia siamo state in gran maraviglia che dopo la prima lettera del magnifico messer Baldesar Castiglione circa la creatione del novo pontefice mai havemo inteso cosa alcuna, dil che veramente ne stiamo molto anxiose, per il desiderio tenemo de intendere de le cose de la, at maximamente dil ben star dil reverendissimo et illustrissimo signor cardinale nostro cognato et patre [honoran] ed dil vostro. Ne possemo credere, anzi siamo certe, che da voi altri lì non sij mancato in scriverci più volte di quanto è accorso, sì come anchor noi di qua havemo continuamente facto in dar noticia lì di quello che si intendeva qui alla giornata. Ma tenemo per certo che la medema causa che non ce ha lassate capitar in mano le vostre, haverà anchor intertenute de nostre lettere."

> another mind, because we feel much more vexation than pleasure at them. This is because the letters contain nothing but complaints of his poverty and hardship. And despite the fact that we never fail to do the impossible by supplying him with money, these troubles don't end; in fact more of them keep piling up.[60]

We have seen that the young bride Isabella sought copious communication from her loved ones as a way of compensating for their absence and filling her solitary time, while the more mature marchesa adopted this medium to build an extensive network of correspondents to inform her of the realm of war and politics in which her presence was largely superfluous. If by the time she reached middle age, she had assured that her "continuous expectation" would seldom go unsatisfied, Isabella had also come to recognize (for example in exchanges like that with Ferrante, cited above) that her demands for constant correspondence might result in too much of a good thing. More importantly, we see in Isabella's negotiation of the sentiments and the hard realities of epistolary communication an emergence of the non-literary letter as a space of experience, of understanding, and of action on both the personal and the political planes. As the aristocratic-domestic sphere in which Isabella d'Este was sovereign spills over into the contingencies of a historical realm through the postal activism of the marchesa of Mantua, the letter emerges as one more space in which the powers of such dynastic families as hers were destined to rise and fall.

---

[60] F.II.9.2999 libro 46 cc. 70r–71r. "Se per un tempo siamo state in continuo desiderio di havere lettere di Spagna per sentir nove del'illustrissimo don Ferrante nostro figliolo, siamo hora constrette ad esser di altro animo, perché sono molto più li fastidij che ne sentimo che non sono li piaceri. Questo procede che esse lettere non contengono se non lamenti di povertà et miserie. Et se bene noi dal canto nostro non mancamo di fare possibile lo impossibile in fargli avere denari, per questo non ne cessano li soliti fastidij, anci sempre si ni accumulano di novi."

Judeo-Christian Cultural Relations in Cinquecento Ferrara

Robert Bonfil

Toward the conclusion of his essay on the memorable earthquake that shook Ferrara in 1570, Azariah de Rossi,[1] who has been termed the first modern Jewish historian, sketched the following picture of the Jewish community:

> May their memory live on for eternity, those many of the noble representatives of our people, the leaders of the community of Ferrara [here follows a list] . . . as well as the distinguished leaders of the Sephardi community. May all of them be blessed by my God, Amen. For all of them, together with other generous men who owned within

[1] Readers not proficient in Hebrew may consult the following with profit: Salo W. Baron, "Azariah de' Rossi: A Biographical Sketch," in *History and Jewish Historians: Essays and Addresses*, ed. Arthur Herzberg and Leon A. Feldman (Philadelphia: Jewish Publication Society, 1964), 167–73, 405; and in the same volume, idem, "Azariah de' Rossi's Historical Method," 205–39, 422–42; and idem, "Azariah de' Rossi's Attitude to Life," 174–204, 406–22; Joanna Weinberg, "Azariah dei Rossi: Towards a Reappraisal of the Last Years of His Life," *Annali della Scuola Normale di Pisa*, ser. 3, 8 (1978): 493–511; eadem, "The *Me'or 'Enayim* of Azariah de' Rossi: A Critical Study and Selected Translations" (Ph.D.diss., University of London, 1982); eadem, "Azariah de' Rossi and the Septuagint Traditions," *Italia: Studi e ricerche sulla storia, la cultura, e la letteratura degli ebrei d'Italia* 5 (1985): 7–35; eadem, "The Quest for the Historical Philo in Sixteenth-Century Jewish Historiography," in *Jewish History: Essays in Honor of Chimen Abramsky*, ed. Ada Rapaport-Albert and Steven J. Zipperstein (London: Peter Halban, 1988), 163–87; eadem, "The Voice of God: Jewish and Christian Responses to the Ferrara Earthquake of November 1570," *Italian Studies* 46 (1991): 69–81; Robert Bonfil, "Some Reflections of the Place of Azariah de Rossi's *Meor Enayim* in the Cultural Milieu of Italian Renaissance Jewry," in *Jewish Thought in the Sixteenth Century*, ed. B. D. Cooperman (Cambridge, MA: Harvard University Press, 1983), 23–48; and idem, "Accademie rabbiniche e presenza ebraica nelle università," in *Le università dell'Europa*, ed. Gian

> their house or elsewhere among their possessions a capacious court or garden, or any other spacious place, opened their doors to whoever sought refuge, be he or she poor or rich, so that each of them offered refuge to more than one hundred people. And although confusion reigned in the hearts of them all, for they were also deeply grieved, they did not refrain from caring for the poor and the distressed, so that they would not lack bread and food, as well as fire and abundant wood to defend themselves from the cold of the snow and to cook for themselves and their offspring. This they did, always with smiling faces and gently, notwithstanding the fact that they bore this burden for a long time and the refugees were very numerous.[2]

Anyone who would stop reading here would no doubt attribute these lines to the familiar stance of nationalistic chauvinism, so common in the sixteenth century, particularly among the Jews.[3] Azariah de Rossi's entire book may in a sense be considered as a sophisticated expression of that kind of world view.[4] However, should one continue reading, the picture that emerges would show significant evidence of just how complex such a perception might be:

> So did the Christians. All the areas of the town, the streets and the courts, the parks and the gardens, whether fenced in or not, were filled with tents, cabins, and huts where the rich and the poor took refuge together, and they also generously bestowed upon the poor, for that was the time for every nation to seek God and bring before Him his good deeds as an expiatory offering and act of atonement.[5]

Paolo Brizzi and Jacques Verger, 6 vols. (Milan: Amilcare Pizzi, 1990–1995), Vol. 2, *Dal Rinascimento alle riforme religiose*, 133–51. One may also find the following useful: Lester A. Segal, *Historical Consciousness and Religious Tradition in Azariah de' Rossi's Me'or 'Enayim* (Philadelphia/New York/Jerusalem: The Jewish Publication Society, 1989). Readers of Hebrew will find a more detailed discussion and bibliography in Robert Bonfil, ed., *Kitve Azariah min ha-Adumim (Azariah de' Rossi, Selected Chapters from Sefer Me'or 'Einayim and Matsref la-Kessef)* (Jerusalem: Bialik Institute, 1991).

[2] Azariah de' Rossi, *Me'or Einayim* (Mantua: s.n., 1573–1575); idem, "Kol Elohim," in *Me'or Einayim*, ed. David Cassel (Jerusalem: Makor, 1970 [Vilna, 1866]), 20–21; Bonfil, ed., *Kitve*, 202. Further references will be to these two editions.

[3] For some examples of that view among sixteenth-century Italian Jews, see Robert Bonfil, *Jewish Life in Renaissance Italy* (Berkeley: University of California Press, 1994), 164.

[4] I have already called attention to this aspect of de' Rossi's work in my previous studies of his writings (above, n. 1).

[5] Rossi, "Kol Elohim," ed. Cassel = Rossi, *Kitve*, ed. Bonfil, 202–3. See also Rossi, *The Light of the Eyes*, trans. J. Weinberg (New Haven: Yale University Press, 2001), 7–32, here 29.

Thus, however positive the Jews might appear in de Rossi's proud self-perception, he did not see the Christians among whom they lived to be lacking in those very same merits. In all that concerns intense human solidarity, reassuring religiosity, and civic responsibility, de Rossi believed that Jews and Christians exhibited close affinity.

De Rossi's depiction comes toward the end of a lengthy and, in modern eyes, boring discussion of the earthquake and its causes. As has very aptly been shown, his account contains recognizable features of other contemporary tracts dealing with the earthquake, and as such is indicative of the extent to which a Jew living in Ferrara could be part of its intellectual community and partake of its scholarly endeavors.[6] This impression may be reinforced by further pointing to the well-known explicit testimonies of de Rossi's contacts with his Ferrarese contemporaries, such as the learned priest who suggested that he translate the *Letter of Aristeas* into Hebrew.[7]

At first glance, then, the resulting picture would almost faithfully represent a particular case of what has time and again been described as the felicitous integration of Italian Renaissance Jews into the non-Jewish context. Indeed, although the history of the Jews of Ferrara has not been explored as fully as it deserves,[8] one may safely affirm that up to the end of the sixteenth century Ferrara was one of the most attractive places in Italy where Jews chose to live. Spanish

---

[6] Weinberg, "The Voice of God," 70–71.

[7] Rossi, *Me'or Einayim*, 22–23 = Rossi, *Kitve*, ed. Bonfil, 205–6.

[8] Yosef Hayim Yerushalmi, *A Jewish Classic in the Portuguese Language* (Lisboa: Fundação Calouste Gulbenkian, 1989), 67. To the titles listed by Yerushalmi one may add the following: Aron di Leone Leoni, "Gli ebrei sefarditi a Ferrara da Ercole I a Ercole II: Nuove ricerche e interpretazioni," *La rassegna mensile di Israel* 52 (1986): 406–43; Robert Bonfil, "Ferrare: Un port sur et paisible pour la diaspora séfarade," in *Les Juifs d'Espagne—histoire d'une diaspora*, ed. Henry Mechoulan (Paris: Liana Levi, 1992), 295–303; idem, "The History of the Spanish and Portuguese Jews in Italy," in *The Sephardic Legacy*, ed. Haim Beinart (Jerusalem: Magnes Press, 1992), 217–39; A. di Leone Leoni, *La nazione ebraica spagnola e portoghese negli stati estensi* (Rimini: Luisè, 1992); idem, "Documents inédits sur la Nation portuguaise de Ferrare," *Revue des études juives* 152 (1993): 137–76; idem, "La diplomazia estense e l'immigrazione dei cristiani nuovi a Ferrara al tempo di Ercole II," *Nuova rivista storica* 78 (1994): 293–326; idem, "Nuove notizie sugli Abravanel," *Zakhor—Rivista di storia degli Ebrei d'Italia* 1 (1997): 153–206; idem, "I marrani di Coimbra denunciati al papa dall'Inquisizione portoghese nel 1578: Il loro status giuridico in diversi stati italiani," *Zakhor* 2 (1998): 73–109; Herman Prins Salomon and Aron di Leone Leoni, "Mendes, Benveniste, De Luna, Micas, Nasci: The State of the Art (1532–1558)," *Jewish Quarterly Review* 88 (1998): 135–211.

and Portuguese New Christians who wished to revert to Judaism considered it — in the words of Samuel Usque, one of the most remarkable *converso* historians of the sixteenth century — as "Italy's safest port, where God's mercy had ordained" that they "might rest from the distressing journeys" they had made from Portugal and Spain.[9] In this author's most original representation of Jewish history as a sequence of regenerations in the wake of tragedies, the distressing past suffered by himself and by his Iberian brethren was left behind in the shining Ferrarese present and the future that Usque's imagination, remarkably lacking in messianic overtones, sketched as even more luminous. Viewed from the rich houses in which Usque and the newly-settled Portuguese merchants were frequent guests, such as Doña Gracia's prestigious salon where erudites met in a cosmopolitan atmosphere reminiscent of distant Spain, the Ferrarese context seemed to be even more charming than that sketched by Azariah de Rossi. Indeed, what Usque sensed appears to be thoroughly justified on the basis of the extant documentation concerning the zealous efforts of Ercole II to secure the safe settlement of New Christians in his province. As the Duke overtly stated, his desire was to follow the example of Antwerp and fill Ferrara with merchants, especially New Christians ("empir questa nostra cittade di mercanti spetialmente di quella natione").[10]

And yet, however attractive that context might appear to contemporary Jews, it manifested itself concretely in two clearly distinct spheres: the Jews with the Jews, and the Christians with the Christians. This trait is even more neatly portrayed by De Rossi's depiction of the outstanding solidarity shown by the Sephardi community — a community that, for him as well as for everyone else, displayed clearly separatist tendencies. It is to this ambivalent, in many senses ambiguous, aspect brought to light by reality that I would like to draw attention. A proper understanding of it may help us comprehend the complexities of pre-modern Jewish-Christian relationships and of the dynamics of change that emerged precisely during the lifetime of Usque and De Rossi, as well as the paradigmatic role played then by Ferrara, and the paradoxical convergence of Jewish and Christian aspirations to overcome some of their reciprocal inherited disabilities.

For Ferrarese society, and particularly for the ducal court, the inherited willingness to tolerate a Jewish presence in town was still, as elsewhere, utilitarian. Since the thirteenth century, the Jews had been allowed to settle there mainly in order to execute the socioeconomic function of money lending to the poor. Yet *socioeconomic* should be interpreted narrowly, i.e. that their economic function

---

[9] Samuel Usque, *Consolation for the Tribulations of Israel*, trans. from the Portuguese and ed. with an introd. by Martin A. Cohen (Philadelphia: The Jewish Publication Society of America, 1977), 213.

[10] di Leone Leoni, "La diplomazia estense," 325–26.

was intended specifically for relief of the poor, by providing petty loans enabling them to overcome cases of economic distress.[11] The Ferrarese economy, greatly dependent on the agricultural development of the *contado,* made poor *contadini* a quite frequent occurrence. And although recourse to the Jews was by no means absolutely necessary, it was widespread. So far, then, the Ferrarese rulers were no different from other rulers who opted for the Jewish solution to the problem of poverty in their states. However, I would argue, the dukes' policy concerning the Jews faithfully reflects what seems to have been one of their most momentous problems: how to overcome the constraint inexorably imposed on the town by the almost medieval underlying socioeconomic and cultural structure in order to play an appropriate role in the creation of the vibrant new European Renaissance outlook, one that was essentially urban, bourgeois, and cosmopolitan, engaging in trade and industry. Although contemporaries were certainly not aware of all the ramifications of the problem, it was one of expedient mediation between the pre-mercantilist mode and mercantilism; in generically cultural terms, between the aristocratic court mode and civic humanism;[12] in strictly literary terms, between representation of reality and fiction, history and myth; in sociocultural terms, between learned elite cultural practice and its popularization,[13] between courtly and bourgeois "good manners."[14] In this sense, one and the same thread links the Court's support of the diffusion of the "entertainment literature" produced by Boiardo, Ariosto, and Tasso to Alfonso's idea of imitating Venice by having a Bucintoro cruise on the Po to please his young wife — too young and beautiful for him in the opinion of Monsieur de Montaigne.[15]

Montaigne's *Journal de voyage* offers, indeed, one of the most vivid pictures of the places he visited toward the turn of the century. Ferrara was one of them, although he limited his stay there to less than forty-eight hours. One cannot really

---

[11] Although in many descriptions of medieval Jewish money lending this statement may be taken as implicitly granted, in many more it is, not always unintentionally, left unqualified. For a more detailed discussion, see Bonfil, *Jewish Life*, 19–97.

[12] One should bear in mind that during the Quattrocento Ferrara was a most important center of humanistic studies headed by Guarino Guarini.

[13] Gian Mario Anselmi, Luisa Avellini, and Ezio Raimondi, "Il Rinascimento padano," in *Letteratura italiana: Storia e geografia, II: L'età moderna* (Turin: Einaudi, 1988), 521–91, here 533: "se si volesse un po' ragionare per estremi, mentre a Bologna 'si commenta', a Ferrara 'si volgarizza'."

[14] Norbert Elias, *The Civilizing Process*, 3 vols., vol. 1: *The History of Manners* (Oxford: Blackwell, 1978). Elias's pioneering and still fundamental book is also quoted by Anselmi et al., "Il Rinascimento padano," 585, although not precisely in the sense it is quoted here.

[15] Michel de Montaigne, *Journal de voyage en Italie par la Suisse et l'Allemagne en 1580 et 1581*, ed. Charles Dedeyan (Paris: Société des Belles Lettres, 1946), 180–82.

say if he did so because he was in a hurry to reach Rome or rather out of fear that he would once again suffer from his chronic colic because of the turbid wine and water that he was offered to drink. Be that as it may, and although it does not seem that the city's sights left a great impression upon him, Montaigne did not refrain from noting that the duke 's extraordinary politeness in the course of the audience granted him — "le Seigneur Duc ne s'étant jamais couvert" — and the Ferrarese custom of serving fruit on plates.[16] If I am not mistaken in reading between the lines, Montaigne was struck by the contrast between the Ferrarese aspiration to exhibit the latest in good manners and thus align with the most progressive spirit of the century,[17] and the daily "business as usual," that still conveyed a sense of being highly medieval. This was probably heightened by the effect conveyed by the mighty palaces and the wide, straight streets of a town that to Montaigne appeared to be as big as Tours, yet "fort peu peuplée."

The uniqueness of Ferrara may be variously evaluated, depending upon the vantage point of the observer. One may consider the Ferrarese literary production, associated with the courtly context of the century, as a notable exception to the "rule" that the major products of humanist culture were created in the free republics and did not depend upon the patronage of princely courts. This being the case, one may thus consider Ferrara's literary production to be a most eloquent testimony of negation of the courtly context, as one most authoritative scholar has in fact argued quite recently, referring to Ariosto's "transfer of knightly matter to the imaginary Carolingian world."[18] Be that as it may, beyond such an extreme and perhaps debatable contention one cannot deny that one of the most remarkable traits of the Ferrarese literary production, from Boiardo — an important feudal lord himself — to Ariosto and Tasso, is indeed the fantastic transformation of distant medieval mirrors of reality into entertaining ways of bridging the gap between the tedious norm of everyday life, unbridled imagination,[19] and — as we learn from David Quint's work[20] — actual political discourse dressed in sophisticated allegory.[21]

---

[16] Montaigne, *Journal*, 180–82.

[17] See Elias, *History of Manners*, chap. 4 (84–129): "On Behaviour at Table."

[18] Cf. Alberto Asor Rosa, "Apogeo e crisi della civiltà letteraria italiana," in *Letteratura italiana: Storia e geografia, II: L'età moderna*, 3–21, here 10–11; cf. the essay by Albert Russell Ascoli in this volume, 189–224.

[19] See, e.g., F. Forti, "Matteo Maria Boiardo," in *Dizionario Biografico degli Italiani*, ed. Alberto M. Ghisalberti (Rome: Istituto della Enciclopedia italiana, 1969), 11:211–23.

[20] David Quint, "Political Allegory in the *Gerusalemme liberata*," *Renaissance Quarterly* 43 (1990): 1–29; reprinted as chap. 5 of idem, *Epic and Empire: Politics and Generic Form from Virgil to Milton* (Princeton: Princeton University Press, 1993).

[21] This did not remain an exclusively Ferrarese trait. The numerous sixteenth-century

The "Jewish aspect," I will argue, was but one particular facet of the general picture. Despite the inherent bias affecting Christian attitudes toward the Jews, the dukes of Ferrara were among the first — perhaps the very first — after Ferdinand of Naples to perceive the possibility of departing from the already well-established practice and assigning the Jews a more comprehensive positive role in the dukedom. The king of Naples had in fact, at least a decade before the fatal year of 1492, undertaken a very ambitious plan of transforming his kingdom into the most progressive Renaissance state. Ferdinand considered the Jews to be a crucial component of that plan. Since he looked forward to the settlement of Jewish merchants, he therefore encouraged the establishment of Jewish academies of learning and of Jewish printing establishments, just as he encouraged humanist scholarship. In 1492 he welcomed the mass settlement of Spanish refugees, in whom he placed great hopes that they would give an impetus to the kingdom's commercial and cultural life. But, alas, Charles VIII's descent, which marked the beginning of Italy's transition from stability to turbulence,[22] and the plague that raged throughout the region in those years, also marked the sad epilogue of the forced departure of Spanish Jewry from Western Europe.[23] Instead of turning into a haven for the thousands of exiles who might have proved a valuable source of enrichment, Italy itself became a springboard for mass emigration toward the golden Eldorado of the Great Turk. Very few Spanish Jews did not leave then for the Orient. Among those who stayed were the three or four dozen refugees whom Ercole I permitted to settle in Ferrara in 1492. Yet, viewed in retrospect, that quite insubstantial settlement proved to be the most significant survivor of Ferdinand's unrealized vision.

In fact, one may say that the precedent set by Ferdinand was adopted by the dukes of Ferrara. Whenever the Jews were expelled from some Italian state,

---

editions of Ariosto's *Orlando furioso* are clear proof not only that Ariosto's fantasy was ready to adopt Boiardo's world, but also of the widespread positive response throughout Italy to the cultural message emanating from Ferrara. They are also indicative of how the humanist reception of the French narrative tradition of the fanciful and courtly, characteristic of the Carolingian *épopée*, finally opened the way for transforming the idealization of medieval situations and figures into an inexhaustible source of *libretti* and *intermezzi*. Cf. Paul Renucci, "La cultura," in *Storia d'Italia*, ed. Ruggiero Romano and Corrado Vivanti, 6 vols., 2.2: *Dalla caduta dell'Impero romano al secolo xviii* (Turin: Einaudi, 1988), 1081–1466, here 1287, 1292, 1346.

[22] Francesco Guicciardini, *Storia d'Italia* (Milan: Garzanti, 1988), 1.1: "Ma le calamità d'Italia . . . cominciorono con tanto maggiore dispiacere e spavento negli animi degli uomini quanto le cose universali erano allora più liete e felici."

[23] Robert Bonfil, "Italia: un tríste epílogo de la expulsión de los judíos de Espana," in *Judíos, Sefarditas, Conversos: La expulsión de 1492 y sus consecuencias*, ed. Ángel Alcalá (Valladolid: Ámbito, 1995), 246–68.

Ferrara presented itself as the natural potential haven. This was repeated again and again as Ferrara opened its doors to refugees from the Kingdom of Naples in 1540s, from Venice and Ancona in the fifties, and from the Papal State in 1569. The phenomenon is particularly remarkable if one focuses upon the Iberian newcomers. Although they did not achieve outstanding importance until their community was substantially reinforced by the Portuguese *conversos* who settled in Italy after the establishment of the Inquisition in Portugal in 1536, their merging with those new immigrants came to symbolize the persistence of a new attitude toward the Jews, who were no longer considered to be mere suppliers of socioeconomic relief to the poor, but rather as true agents of the substantial development of the state.[24] While the Papal State definitely reversed its former attitude toward the Jews and particularly toward the so-called *marranos* under Pope Paul IV, and while the Republic of Venice and the few other Italian states that displayed some openness toward the new attitudes[25] were unable to develop an effective and definitely unambiguous policy concerning the *conversos* until the final years of the sixteenth century, Ferrara emerged as a firm exception to the rule. That was the city Usque had in mind when he described Ferrara as "Italy's safest port, where God's mercy had ordained" that the new immigrants "might rest from the distressing journeys" they had undertaken from Portugal and Spain. In the sixteenth century, everybody knew that, as far as the *conversos* were concerned, Ferrara was "different." It was common knowledge that in Azariah de Rossi's time a standard procedure for Portuguese New Christians was to go to Ferrara, have themselves circumcised there, adopt a Jewish name, and then find their way out as Jews.[26]

---

[24] Bonfil, "The History of the Spanish and Portuguese Jews in Italy."

[25] For Venice see Benjamin Ravid, "A Tale of Three Cities and their Raison d'État: Ancona, Venice, Livorno and the Competition for Jewish Merchants in the Sixteenth Century," *Mediterranean Historical Review* 6 (1991–1992): 136–62, also published in book form with the same pagination in *Jews, Christians and Moslems in the Mediterranean World after 1492*, ed. Alisa Meyuhas Ginio (London: Frank Cass, 1992). For Florence, see Umberto Cassuto, *Gli ebrei a Firenze nell'età del Rinascimento* (Florence: Olschki, 1965 [1905]), 89–90. For Savoy, see Haim Beinart, "Hityashevut ha-Yehudim be-duksuth Savoia be-ʿikvot ha-privilegia shel shenat 1572 (La venuta degli ebrei nel ducato di Savoia e il privilegio del 1572)," in *Scritti in memoria di Leone Garpi: Saggi sull'ebraismo italiano*, ed. Daniel Carpi, Attilio Milano, and Alexander Rofé (Jerusalem: Fondazione Sally Mayer, 1967), 72–117.

[26] Brian Pullan, *The Jews of Europe and the Inquisition of Venice, 1550–1670* (London: Blackwell, 1983), 172, 213; Robert Bonfil, "Yediot Chadashot le-toledot chayyav shel R. Menahem Azariah mi-Fano (New Information on Rabbi Menahem Azariah da Fano and his Age)," in *Studies in the History of Jewish Society in the Middle Ages and in the*

Like Ferdinand half a century earlier, in 1556 Ercole II acceded to the Jews' request and granted them permission to establish a *yeshivah* in town. In the duke's document, the *yeshivah* is termed *studium,* being thus equated with the Christian university. He moreover assumed that such an institution enhanced the city, as did the university ("ciò non può tornare se non ad honore et ornamento di essa nostra Cittade"), due to the profit and benefit that many students, both Jewish and Christian, foreigners as well as citizens, would obtain from it ("per il profitto che ne potranno trarre molti Hebrei et Christiani scolari sí forestieri come sudditi nostri").[27] Thus, in favoring the development of Jewish academic life on a fairly equal footing with that of the Christians, the duke almost explicitly invited foreign Jewish intellectuals to settle in Ferrara. Moreover, in noting the potential benefit that Christian students might get from the Jewish *studium*, he also quite explicitly welcomed the establishment of Judeo-Christian cultural relations in the town. The duke did not even oppose the establishment in Ferrara of the well-known so-called "Marrano Press" precisely at the time when the Venetian government was severely restricting Jewish printing.[28] By so doing, he was favoring the diffusion of Jewish culture among New Christians, of course more outside Ferrara than within the town's walls.

In a sense, Ercole's policy may be seen as bringing to a conclusion the process initiated several decades earlier, when Jewish students were permitted to obtain in the University of Ferrara the doctoral degrees that they were prevented from getting elsewhere. Such, for instance, was the case of the well-known Rabbi Obadiah Sforno, then resident in Bologna.[29] But there was more to it than that. For perhaps the first time, Ercole's policy was an explicit avowal that the humanist encounter of Christians with the *Hebraica veritas* was in fact a shared interest and joint venture, to be pursued not only by encouraging Christians to take advantage of the Jews' learning, but also by helping Jews to develop their own cultural institutions, and this by means of encouraging a cultural dialogue devoid of religious polemic overtones. Azariah de Rossi's close cultural relations

---

Modern Period Presented to Professor Jacob Katz, ed. E. Etkes and Y. Salmon (Jerusalem: Magnes, 1980), 98–135.

[27] Antonio Balletti, *Gli ebrei e gli estensi* (Bologna: Forni, 1969 [1930]), 97; Robert Bonfil, *Rabbis and Jewish Communities in Renaissance Italy* (Oxford: The Littman Library for Jewish Civilization, 1990), 19.

[28] See Cecil Roth, "The Marrano Press at Ferrara, 1552–1555," *Modern Language Review* 38 (1943): 307–17; Yerushalmi, *A Jewish Classic in the Portuguese Language*, 67–91. On the Venetian attitude toward Jewish printing during that period, see Paul F. Grendler, *The Roman Inquisition and the Venetian Press, 1540–1605* (Princeton: Princeton University Press, 1977).

[29] Bonfil, "Accademie," 131–51.

with Christian intellectuals during the rule of Alfonso II may then be considered as the natural outcome of that policy, as formulated less than two decades earlier. Amatus Lusitanus, the New Christian physician appointed in 1540 to teach at the University of Ferrara, sketched a vivid scene of everyday intellectual practice:

> Some time ago, I met one of my best friends whose fate is to be living now in Rome, in most unfortunate conditions. He is a man of wide experience and eager for new knowledge. We entered a bookshop at the same time. Looking over some books, he came across the volume of Galatinus against the Jews, a very splendid piece of book-work and full of erudition. Just as we began to discuss the work, Azariah, the Jew of Mantua, a great scholar both in Hebrew and in Latin letters, happened to come in. He entered as the third in our party ["terzo fra cotanto senno," one would say] and gave his view, especially concerning the two Jesuits that appear in this work in the defense of the famous Reuchlin, who at the time was in prison. They defended him from calumnies and endeavored to vindicate him.[30]

The fact that Amatus relied on memory while writing these lines caused him to make more than one error, as justly pointed out by Harry Friedenwald, from whose learned article I quote the above translation. But he remembered the episode itself very well, not to mention the patient and his illness, to which the entire chapter of his book is devoted. Although there is some uncertainty as to where the meeting took place, it is quite probable that it was in Ferrara, sometime between 1540 and 1547, the year in which Amatus left that town.[31]

---

[30] Amatus Lusitanus, *Centuriae*, curatio 42. I quote here the translation given in Harry Friedenwald, *Jews and Medicine* (Baltimore: Johns Hopkins University Press, 1944), 392–93.

[31] My conclusion here stands as a partial correction to my writing elsewhere — following Friedenwald — that the encounter took place in 1547 or 1548: Rossi, *Kitve*, ed. Bonfil, 25. That inference was based on the conjecture that Amatus correctly assumed that at the time of the encounter Azariah was thirty-five years old. However, such a statement should not be taken at face value, especially since in this case Amatus exhibits a great degree of inaccuracy. In any case, the patient was first sent for cure to the Calderic springs, near Ferrara. It is therefore quite safe to conclude that they met in Ferrara, as I was inclined to argue in the above-mentioned work. The book by Galatinus, still available in the bookshop, must therefore have been the 1518 edition of the *De arcanis*, for its second edition was published in 1550, one year after Amatus wrote the text quoted above.

Much may easily be read between the lines of that text. A few examples are the cautious concealment of the name of the friend living in Rome "in most unfortunate conditions," not unlikely a New Christian, like Amatus himself; the nonchalant mention of that "very splendid piece of book-work . . . full of erudition," but unfortunately also full of inflammatory anti-Jewish propaganda that is barely mentioned *en passant* by noting that the book was in fact "against the Jews"; the vague reference to Azariah's view on the book, one that — as I argued elsewhere — was probably among the most pressing reasons that led him to compose his own book in defense of Judaism.[32] But more than anything else, I would call attention to the relaxed intellectual discussion conducted inside a Christian bookshop displaying anti-Jewish literature on a topic that was of Christian, no less than Jewish, interest at the time: the significance of the Dominicans' defense of Reuchlin's stand concerning the Talmud, i.e., a stance adopted by Christians undoubtedly unsympathetic toward the Jews and Jewish culture, yet opposing the burning of the Talmud. In other words: the setting and climate of the cultural encounter conveys an impression of peaceful serenity, in contrast to a sense of impending jeopardy conveyed by the issue discussed on that particular extemporaneous occasion. All this conveys a strong impression of an almost ambiguous inception of change, hesitantly seeking to burst forth and yet unable to make a breakthrough, very much a faithful mirror of the general setting.

The fact remains, however, that notwithstanding such manifestations of a benevolent attitude toward the Jews, and particularly toward the Iberian newcomers, Este Jewish policy was never formulated in a clear-cut programmatic manner so as to give the impression of a conscious, careful departure from the current conceptions concerning the Jews. Of no specific element in that policy might one say that it was really new. In a word, with all Ferrara's strong appeal, its rulers' normative attitude concerning the Jewish community was still governed by the standard utilitarian medieval ethos — one that had not yet accepted the Jews as full partners and an organic element of the town. Nonetheless, what is notable is the ostensibly nonchalant deviation from the norm and its consistent maintenance as a coherent line of action. Viewed in retrospect, this appears to be much more than the usual medieval practice of princes exercising discretionary political power. When deviation from a norm becomes hardly discernible from the norm itself, one may say that a process of change is taking place, no matter how furtively. In this sense, the Estes' proceeding is indicative of another *sui generis* aspiration to bridge as smoothly as possible the gap between tradition and change by favoring a setting that radiates a vague sense of nuanced ambiguity rooted in some kind of heedless, perhaps hesitant, open-mindedness.

---

[32] Bonfil, "Some Reflections"; Rossi, *Kitve*, ed. Bonfil, 47–59, 120–25.

The Jewish response was, not surprisingly, rather analogous. I will try to make the point focusing on two very significant fields, *prima facie* quite indirectly related to our topic, and yet — precisely because of that — deeply revealing.

Let us first look at the aspiration of the Jews for autonomy in the exercise of juridical and judicial power. I have described elsewhere how such aspirations to develop a great degree of autonomy were prevented by the opposition of the Christian authorities.[33] This was rooted primarily in the Christian religious attitude of the ecclesiastical authorities who explicitly opposed granting the Jews permission to exercise power independently: not only were the Jews condemned to perpetual servitude because they had failed to recognize Christ's divinity, but it would be blasphemous for a Christian prince to recognize as binding within the area of his sovereignty the abrogated Old Testament, still followed by the infidel Jews in the exercise of judicial authority. One should, of course, also not forget the possible concern for loss of income and fees to city courts and lawyers. Furthermore, a good deal of opposition can no doubt be attributed to considerations of a vaguely "constitutional" nature, since obviously the more or less complete independence of the Jewish communities would have implied limiting the powers of the state in the exercise of its sovereignty — a sort of *de facto* recognition of the Jews' right to constitute a city within a city. I will not recall here the variety of expedients devised by the communities to disguise their activities in this field and overcome the impediment. Yet one example may be of considerable importance for our discussion here. It pertains to the disguised rabbinical tribunal established in Ferrara in 1575 and very significantly opposed by two Jews who submitted to the duke their reservations of a "constitutional" character.

In their petition, those Jews stressed that in authorizing the creation of a rabbinical tribunal the duke was ceding his sovereignty over some of his subjects, who in turn were being deprived of part of their freedom.[34] Much of their argument may well have been specious, quite probably dictated more by the feeling that their cause would have a more favorable outcome before a non-Jewish court than before a Jewish one. It was inevitable that when Jewish law clashed with the non-Jewish body of law followed by the local judicial authorities, personal interests would play a significant role in choosing one over the other. It is nonetheless remarkable that these Jews, or perhaps their Christian attorney, did not consider it implausible that arguing the importance of defending the freedom of the Ferrarese Jews might make sense in the context of appealing to the duke to apply his justice equally to all his subjects. In other words, one would

---

[33] Bonfil, *Jewish Life*, 204 ff.

[34] Bonfil, *Jewish Life*, 207–8.

not be entirely unjustified in reading between the lines an admittedly feeble echo of the Jews' sensing some potential of being admitted to the same standing as the other citizens of Ferrara. Yet, if in this case the stand adopted by the Jews was tainted by quite transparent interests, the way in which the issue manifested itself in some rabbinic *responsa* reveals how deeply ambiguous was the entire situation. One simple example will suffice to make the point.

According to Jewish law, legal documents drawn up by non-Jewish officials, such as Christian notaries, are to be considered valid, unless there is some reasonable suspicion that they are fraudulent. The Italian rabbis of this period therefore assumed a priori that documents drawn up by Christian notaries were definitely valid. Bearing this in mind, let us now focus on a particular case concerning a dispute on the collection of a woman's dowry. According to Jewish law, a woman is not entitled to collect her dowry unless her husband has died or divorced her. However, a centuries-old practice had made it possible to deviate from the strict norm by resorting to "local custom." Accordingly, explicit mention of that practice was introduced into the legal documents that accompanied the wedding formalities. Italian Jews used to have such documents drawn up by Christian notaries as well, in order to secure their validity before Christian courts. As one might easily imagine, litigations and controversies were not infrequent. Records have survived about a legal controversy concerning a certain dowry document drawn up in a Gentile court which did not contain the phrase required by Jewish law to validate non-Jewish practice, namely "to collect it according to the local custom." In that case the question was whether, according to Jewish law, the woman could still materialize her dowry on the basis of the document during her husband's lifetime, "as was the custom." Several Italian rabbis took part in the learned controversy.[35] Now, what is significant for our topic is the stance adopted in that case by the leading figure among those responding in the affirmative, Rabbi Baruch Uzziel Chazzachetto (Forti) of Ferrara. In order to understand the implications of the question, we must turn briefly to the socioeconomic context of the litigation.

When might a woman appeal to a court to collect her dowry during her husband's lifetime? Possibly when she had been denied a divorce and was living outside her husband's house. Yet from the documentation brought to light up to now, such a case never occurred in the period under discussion here. The next most plausible prospect is an appeal rooted in some socioeconomic reason: just as happens today in cases of bankruptcy, couples might then also have wished

---

[35] The case has already been mentioned in my general discussion of the judicial function of Italian rabbis during that period: see Bonfil, *Rabbis and Jewish Communities*, 249–50.

to transfer registration of the household's capital from the husband's name to that of his wife, in order to safeguard it from creditors who could, of course, have been Jews as well as Christians. In principle, then, the debate would not refer to specific situations of Jews resorting to that stratagem in order to escape exclusively Christian creditors. Yet Rabbi Chazzachetto's *responsum* seems to point quite significantly in that direction. Indeed, one of the rabbi's main arguments was that "this was the custom of the generations, from the beginning, also to be saved there from the kingdom and the other duties of the Gentiles."[36] In other words, adhering to the custom of the generations which, we should recall, was to gain advantage from and validate non-Jewish legal practice, was envisaged by our Ferrarese rabbi in a context of supporting fiscal evasion and extrication from debts to Christian creditors. The legal confrontation assumes, then, an apparently paradoxical configuration. According to Rabbi Chazzachetto, the support of fiscal evasion and extrication from debts to Christian creditors justified deviation from the strictly orthodox legal practice advocated by those who hold the principle that "one must rule only according to Jewish law."

The complex nature of this conclusion may be stressed further by reflecting on the fact that this rabbi is considered by modern scholars as one of the most telling examples of Jewish humanists. Focusing upon his vivid biographical sketch of Isaac Abravanel, written in 1551, one scholar has indeed argued that Rabbi Chazzachetto should be considered a representative of "a humanist movement among Jews."[37] Although I do not endorse this view, I nonetheless consider it significant that it could be formulated. In other words, our rabbi's image is not *prima facie* incompatible with openness toward current humanist patterns of writing and thought. Approving deviation from strictly orthodox legal practice and advocating compliance with local custom might then, from this perspective, be considered part of that image. And yet, the overall context is in fact overtly one of a separatist double standard favored by the extraordinarily ambiguous options offered by the situation at hand. What would then appear at first glance to be a symptom of openness toward a non-Jewish practice turns out to be a device supporting an anti-integrationist trend, while what would appear to be a strongly separatist principle would paradoxically favor the contrary. In a situation in which confronting the issue of basic definitions governing mutual recognition of the Other's sociocultural space was carefully avoided, the result could not but remain ambiguous, and therefore open to conflicting interpretations.

---

[36] Bonfil, *Rabbis and Jewish Communities*, 249, n. 147.

[37] Arthur Lesley, "Hebrew Humanism in Italy: The Case of Biography," *Prooftexts* 2 (1982): 163–77.

My second example will come from the Portuguese *conversos*. We have already mentioned the Ferrara Portuguese press. We need not list here the books produced by the Portuguese printers, among which was the famous Ferrara Bible published by Duarte Pinel (alias Abraham Usque ben Selomoh Usque Portuguez) and Jeronimo de Vargas (alias Yom Tob Atias hijo de Levi Atias Español). Rather it is to the paradigmatic value of that enterprise that I would like to call attention. For during the years in which the Jewish printing enterprise in Italy was undergoing strongly menacing vicissitudes, in the very same decade in which the Talmud was doomed to go up in flames, "Ferrara was to be the true cradle of Jewish printing in the Iberian vernaculars, firmly establishing the tradition that would later flourish in Holland and elsewhere."[38] The significance of this development was not only that it supplied the uninstructed *conversos* returning to Judaism with the necessary instruments to enable them to explore the Jewish literary heritage and shape accordingly their new Jewish identity, but also in its several byproducts. First, it opened a window through which Christian readers could look directly at the conceptual foundations of Jewish religious practice and eventually could criticize them. Second, it compelled the traditional Jewish outlook and vocabulary to come to grips with the Christian spiritual background that the *conversos* had already learned to appreciate and would not easily forego. Finally, in addressing the Spanish- and Portuguese-speaking audiences, this kind of literary production established a linguistic and, consequently, a cultural bridge between the Western community of the Iberians and the Eastern one, already firmly settled in Ottoman lands. If we now add to this picture the other examples of felicitous incorporation of the *conversos* into the body of Ferrarese Christian society such as, for instance, the already-mentioned appointment of Amatus Lusitanus as professor at the university, in striking contrast to the previous practice of excluding Jews from such prestigious functions, we may get the impression of a steady and vigorous advance toward bridging the gap between Judaism and Christianity. Viewed in retrospect, one might then get the impression that the Ferrara sixteenth-century setting did represent some kind of precursor of what would indeed transpire during the next century, particularly in Holland.

And yet, the image is not that unambiguous. First, as far as the press is concerned, the number of titles published was certainly not particularly large. In fact the enterprise almost immediately came to an end. Moreover, although it is true that the *conversos* were returning *en masse* to Judaism in Ferrara, it is nonetheless also true that the practice was not at all without danger. Rabbi Menahem Azariah da Fano, who circumcised many of them, did not risk

---

[38] Yerushelmi, *A Jewish Classic*, 73.

registering them by their full names in his notebook: the memory of Joseph Saralvo, burnt at the stake in Rome, was still in the air when Rabbi Menahem circumcised Joseph's grandson.[39] Finally, Usque himself, who contributed so effectively to conveying the image of Ferrara as "Italy's safest port, where God's mercy had ordained" that the *conversos* "might rest from the distressing journeys" they had made from Portugal and Spain, painted a dark picture of the episode of the expulsion of the Portuguese Jews recently settled in Ferrara in 1549, this in the wake of alarmist rumors that the newcomers were carriers of the plague.[40] The port, then, was not as safe as his panegyric might suggest. Y. H. Yerushalmi has recently very aptly suggested interpreting in this spirit the iconography of the title-page of the famous Ferrara Bible: "In the top center of the ornate woodcut frame we see the head of a bearded man, apparently Neptune, who, with bulging cheeks, is blowing a storm. Beneath the lines of text a ship flounders in the waves of a raging sea, its sails torn, its mast broken."

Contrary to the optimistic interpretations which see in the woodcut a symbol of miraculous deliverance, of great significance to the victims of the Inquisition, Yerushalmi suggested — in my opinion quite rightly — that the scene depicted is not optimistic, but tragic, and that the ship represents the afflicted Jewish people — particularly the Spanish and Portuguese exiles — in their perilous search for a safe haven. Yerushalmi concludes: "Seen in this light the title-page of the Ferrara Bible becomes truly emblematic of the entire era."[41] I fully concur with this view.

Appearances, then, were definitely not clear. In view of what has been said thus far, one should not be content with interpreting the situation in categories of ups and downs. I submit that, in fact, all these traits testify to the main characteristic of the epoch, for which the setting of Ferrara has been presented here as paradigmatic: the impossibility of clearly perceiving and defining the essence of change. That impossibility was built into that setting, desperately longing to restructure received configurations of reality and yet unable to take a clear stand and make unequivocal decisions.

---

[39] Bonfil, "Yediot Chadashot," 129.

[40] In Usque's work, the episode is said to have taken place in the Hebrew year 5311, i.e., 1550–1551 C.E. The presumably typographical error caused perplexity among the scholars who were well aware that the plague had already struck Ferrara the previous year and felt compelled to conclude that in the absence of independent documentation it is hard to know what actually occurred (Yerushelmi, *A Jewish* Classic, 69–70). Such documentation has now been brought to light in Aron di Leone Leoni, "La nazione portughese corteggiata, privilegiata, espulsa e riammessa a Ferrara (1538–1550)," *Italia: Studi e ricerche sulla storia, la cultura, e la letteratura degli ebrei d'Italia* 13 (2001): 211–47.

[41] Yerushelmi, *A Jewish Classic*, 81.

The resort to literature and theater as agents of sociopolitical discourse and to allegory and metaphor as literary instruments of that very same discourse appear, then, to be almost natural manifestations of the trend favoring the inception of change. As is often the case, poets and intellectuals are among the first to perceive the necessity of change, yet they lack the power to translate their vision into clearly-defined political programs. If I am not mistaken, some of Tasso's insights in his *Gerusalemme liberata* might well also be relevant for my topic, and particularly the various elements constitutive of the almost positive image of the "infidel." Would it be too far-fetched to read into the love stories of the Christian heroes for infidel women, and particularly the story of Clorinda, subtle allusions to the other "infidels," more near at hand in Tasso's Ferrara?[42]

To be sure, the overall plot is brimmong with ideas stemming from popular *topoi*. There is the myth of the good Saladin and that of enlightened Ottoman sultans conducting exemplary lives that stood in striking contrast to those of the Christian rulers of Western Europe; there is the *topos* of love as a unifying force able to overcome all kinds of adversities; there is the belief that infidels would in any case ultimately be converted to Christianity. Clorinda indeed dies a Christian, yet her death emphasizes the tragic sense of the facts of life, as sketched by Tasso. Clorinda's death discloses the fate of that woman: she was born "different"; she was raised as a Saracen although secretly baptized by her mother; she jealously kept the secret that her mother revealed to her on her deathbed; she did not choose Christianity during her lifetime — rather she heroically fought for the victory of Islam, until the agony of death "reconciled" her with her mother's faith.

If I am not misled by some subconscious tendency to uncover New Christians everywhere, I would submit that Clorinda's story may well also be read as subtly alluding to the poet's longing for love as a mediator between men and women divided by religious rivalry in Ferrara as well as in the Christian West — yet still being unable to suggest a viable mechanism to overcome that rivalry.[43]

---

[42] I believe that, although it points in a specific direction, my suggestion does not conflict with the general picture offered in Sergio Zatti, *L'uniforme cristiano e il multiforme pagano: Saggio sulla* Gerusalemme Liberata (Milan: il Saggiatore, 1983).

[43] In a different approach, Valeria Finucci offers a brilliant and sophisticated psychological interpretation of Clorinda that, to my mind, may well support the one suggested here. In Finucci's study, Clorinda is indeed a model of a non-woman and a non-white person who is healed through baptism so that order may be reestablished. Finucci interprets Clorinda's "monstrosity" as stemming from her being black and discusses the theme as pointing to the instinctive reception by Italians of information concerning the Ethiopians and their world within the framework of their own traditional and conventional learning and wisdom. See Valeria Finucci, "Maternal Imagination and Monstrous Birth:

Perhaps there is even more to it than that: perhaps also a longing for human mediation between the male and female domains, as through the suggestion that a woman may enter the male domain as a warrior, not just as a whore — though, to be sure, in the "Other" camp, not yet within the "proper order of things." Clorinda is nonetheless absolutely lacking in satanic beauty, for her attractive beauty is most human. The message she conveys is, therefore, that the Other may well be human, may well be appreciated as standing on an equal footing with the Self, that reality may be construed on a basis of equality rather than on one of superiors and inferiors. In this sense, it would perhaps not be far-fetched to argue that in essence the figure of Clorinda brings to culmination the message already subtly introduced by that of Alete, a model of a fine diplomat of the kind Alfonso d'Este would certainly have fully appreciated at his court.[44] No doubt, one may also find in the "Other" camp diplomats like the ill-mannered Argante and sorcerers like Idroate, as well as other repulsive people — but is the Christian camp really devoid of such negative figures? What is more, appearances are misleading. Idroate, although a sorcerer, was not only famous but also noble ("famoso e nobil mago");[45] and his granddaughter Armida, of whom we read that "gli accorgimenti e le più occulte frodi / ch'usi o femina o maga a lei son note," is perhaps one of the most attractive figures in Tasso's work. In any case, Armida's discourses certainly deserve to be more thoroughly analyzed from this perspective: her appeal for an alliance with an "infidel" against her own unfaithful relatives, so much reminiscent of Western Christian rulers appealing to the Great Turk against their Christian rivals; her mentioning God, *sic et simpliciter*, as common to Christians and Moslems — "ch'a tutti e Giove"; and so on and so forth.[46] In sum, what appears to be clearly established is in fact wrong, for more acute introspection and observation would reveal a different order of things, perhaps the proper one.

However, the time was not yet ripe for that. Clorinda dies, killed — although unintentionally — by Tancredi, while Tancredi resumes a struggle that only love might have annulled, but alas did not. Should we, in this case, interpret *time* in the sense given to its Hebrew equivalent — *zeman* — by Tasso's Jewish contemporaries, time would mean *destiny*. The destiny incumbent upon men

---

Tasso's *Gerusalemme Liberata*," in *Generation and Degeneration: Tropes of Reproduction in Literature and History from Antiquity through Early Modern Europe*, ed. eadem and Kevin Brownlee (Durham, NC: Duke University Press, 2001), 41–77. My thanks to Valeria Finucci for having shared her study with me before publication.

[44] Cf. Giovanni Getto, *Nel mondo della* Gerusalemme (Rome: Bonacci, 1977), 15–19.

[45] Lanfranco Caretti, ed., *Gerusalemme liberata* (Milan: Mondadori, 1979), 4.20.

[46] Caretti, ed., *Gerusalemme liberata*, 4.23; 4.42

and women of Tasso's time ruled out the possibility of a clear-cut union between Clorinda and Tancredi. The theme of the illusions harbored by the tranquil human soul would again vanish into bitter and fatal disappointment.[47] One scholar wrote some ninety years ago that even should Tasso have written nothing but the duel of Clorinda and Tancredi, he would be deserving of immortality.[48]

Viewed in retrospect, the tone conveyed by Tasso's literary discourse would then be in tune with the one conveyed by the examples presented above. In a sense it may be said that it is even more explicit. The time had not yet come for the definitive abolishment of the social barrier separating people of opposite religious beliefs. As Azariah de Rossi depicted Jews and Christians in his beloved Ferrara, the Jews were still to be kept apart from the Christians. As Rabbi Barukh Chazzachetto implicitly maintained, a double standard concerning the Jews' commitment to fairness toward their Christian neighbors was still deep-rooted among Jews.

The luminous Italian Renaissance revealed an inability to enlighten contemporary minds to that extent. In order to reach its goal, diffusion of enlightenment still required the Baroque's intermingling of reality and dream, of overt disclosure and dissimulation. But the new era was already at the door, heralded by the intellectual efforts of men such as the Jew Azariah de Rossi, the New Christian Samuel Usque, and the Christian Torquato Tasso. Even the replacement of enlightened Renaissance princes, such as the Dukes of Este, by the pontifical regime of the Counter-Reformation would prove unable to stop the process once it had been initiated.

---

[47] Getto, *Nel mondo della "Gerusalemme,"* 128. According to Getto's analysis, this theme is central and pervasive in *Gerusalemme*.

[48] A. Mezières, "Le mystère de la vie du Tasse," *Revue des deux mondes* 1 (1909), quoted in Eugenio Donadoni, *Torquato Tasso: saggio critico* (Florence: La Nuova Italia, 1946), 244.

Olympia Morata: From Classicist to Reformer

Janet Levarie Smarr

Lisa Jardine and Anthony Grafton in their book *From Humanism to the Humanities*[1] entitle their chapter on women humanists "Education for What?" and cite Bruni's argument that women should not receive too much rhetorical education because they will never use it. They succinctly sum up the problem for humanist women: if education were only for the sake of civic action, women would not have been given a humanist education; but if such education were purely for individual moral improvement, there would be nothing problematic about their education. Jardine and Grafton consider specifically the case of fifteenth-century humanist women in the Nogarola family. But in the sixteenth century a new channel for humanist energies created possibilities of public action for the educated woman, as the case of Olympia Morata demonstrates.

Olympia's short life — she died at the age of twenty-nine — breaks into two main phases: her early life at the court of Ferrara and her five years of married life in Germany in a time of widespread turmoil. In a letter to one of the friends of her youth, she wrote: "Since by the singular kindness of God I first left the idolatry of Italy, and, having married the doctor Andreas Grunthler, moved into Germany, it is incredible how God has altered my mind."[2] I intend here to trace

---

[1] Lisa Jardine and Anthony Grafton, *From Humanism to the Humanities* (London: Duckworth, 1986), 29–57.

[2] "Nam ut primum Dei singulari benignitate ab illa idololatria Italiae discesi meque nuptam medico Andreae Grunthlero in Germaniam contuli, incredibile est quam Deus mutaverit animum meum" (115–116). All quotations from Olympia's letters are from Olympia Morata, *Opera Omnia*, ed. Lanfranco Caretti, vol. 1: *Epistolario (1540–1555)*, 2: *Orationes. Dialogi et Carmi*, R. Deputazione di Storia Patria per l'Emilia e la Romagna, sezione di Ferrara (Ferrara: Premiata Tipografia Sociale, 1940), hereafter Caretti, ed., when cited in notes. As Caretti notes (2: 17), he has omitted the translations, both of Boccaccio and of the Psalms; for the omitted materials and letters from others to her, I have used the

some of these alterations, and also continuities, in the outlook of this learned woman from Ferrara, and to set her personal changes in the context of the wider changes of political and religious climate in Ferrara and in Europe more generally.

Morata's father, a university professor, was invited by Duke Alfonso of Ferrara around 1530 to tutor his sons. Olympia, born in Ferrara in 1526, the oldest of five children (only the youngest a son), was taught Greek and Latin at home from childhood. Admired by her father's scholarly friends, Olympia was not the isolated freak that some earlier humanist women had been, for she lived in a time and place with other learned women. Renée of France, who had married Ercole II and become duchess of Ferrara at Alfonso's death in 1534, was similarly learned and encouraged her daughter Anne, five years younger than Olympia, to study Greek and Latin. She invited Olympia, probably in 1540, to come to court as a companion for Anne.[3] Together they studied with a pair of German brothers named Iohan and Chilian Senf, or Sinapius in Latin.[4] Also at court and a few years older than Olympia was another learned woman, Lavinia della Rovere Orsini (recently married to Paolo Orsini), who became friends with both Olympia and Anne. In sum, it did not have to feel strange to Morata to be a learned woman, for she had at the court of Ferrara her own small community of similarly educated female friends.

As a teenage student Olympia translated the first two tales of the *Decameron* into Latin, wrote some Greek verses about her love for the Muses rather than for the usual female pleasures, composed in Greek an essay in praise of Mutius Scaevola, and in Latin a defense (now lost) of Cicero against detractors. She was also encouraged to give public performances of her learning, and wrote three

---

1580 edition of her *Opera omnia* (hereafter cited as such in notes). All translations are my own. Another edition of the letters alone without other materials is in Giuseppe Paladino, ed., *Opuscoli e lettere di riformatori italiani del Cinquecento*, vol. 2, Scrittori d'Italia 99 (Bari: Laterza, 1927). The University of Illinois library Rare Book collection contains three of the four sixteenth-century editions of Morata's works (all except the 1570), which I have also consulted. Caretti has arranged the letters in chronological order (and made a persuasive effort to date the other writings), whereas the original editor Curione and Paladino both present a chronologically jumbled collection. For the most thorough bibliography of studies pertaining to Olympia Morata,, see John Tedeschi and James Lattis, *The Italian Reformation of the Sixteenth Century and the Diffusion of Renaissance Culture: A Bibliography of the Secondary Literature (ca. 1750–1994)* (Modena: Panini, 2000), 366–72, and supplement, 19.

[3] Anne would then have been nine years old, Olympia fourteen. For the dating of Olympia's arrival at court, see Caretti, ed., 1: 37. Curione in a letter comments that the duchess wanted Anne to have a companion in her studies "ut haberet qui cum honesta emulatione certaret": *Opera Omnia*, 96–97.

[4] Paladino, ed., *Opuscoli e lettere*, 234–35.

introductory speeches to her series of readings and explications at court of Cicero's *Paradoxes*. The scholar Calcagninus, who had probably helped to arrange her position at court,[5] in a letter of praise, called her studies the work of a soldier in Cicero's camp ("militiam . . . in castris Ciceronis").[6]

Her own self-image is reflected in the Greek letter which accompanied her composition on Mutius Scaevola sent to Chilian Senf.[7] She expresses her gratitude to her teacher, comparing it to Alexander's gratitude to Aristotle. As for Alexander, so for her too the value of learning and virtue lies not in mere knowledge but in action: "For not in knowledge but in practice and action is both the beginning and end of virtue." Then, with a probable play on her own name, she mentions the Olympic contests, whose crown went "not to the most handsome or the strongest but to those who competed and won." So too the crown goes to not the learned but to those who use their learning in order to live rightly. The example of this is Mutius Scaevola, "that outstanding man, who endured so much hardship for his country, whose story I am sending you, which I recently wrote."[8] Here is a teenage girl taking Alexander and Mutius Scaevola as her models, and admiring, in good humanist fashion, a man who can turn his learning into patriotic action. There is very little explicit feminism in Olympia's writings,[9] but also not much sense of there being a problem for her in having such models.

In the preface to her readings of Cicero's paradoxes, she reflects on the Aristotelian pair of dangers she must guard herself against during her series of

---

[5] Caretti, ed., 1: 37.

[6] Olympia Morata, *Opera omnia* (Basel: Petrus Perna, 1580), 79–81.

[7] Caretti, ed., 1: 58–61.

[8] "Neque enim in scientia, sed in exercitatione atq; actione et initium virtutis est et finis. Ac quemadmodum ludis Olympicis non formosissimi & valentissimi quique sed qui certant coronantur, quippe quorum aliqui vincant, sic et bonorum huius vitae compotes fiunt, qui recte vivunt, sicuti Mutius ille vir praestans, qui pro patria tantum laborem pertulit. Cuius ego tibi historiam mitto, quam nuper conscripsi": Caretti, ed., 1: 60. I quote here the published Latin translation of her Greek.

[9] As compared, for example, to Renée's reported exclamation: "Had I a beard I would have been the King of France. I have been defrauded by that confounded Salic law": Roland Bainton, *Women of the Reformation in Germany and Italy* (Minneapolis: Augsburg Publishing House, 1971), 235. Olympia's earliest extant letter, however, expresses her rejection of the usual female occupations and silence in favor of the humanist value placed on studies and eloquence: "Cum tantum igitur literae inter caeteras res humanas excellant, quae quaeso me muliercularum fusa et acus (ut tu ais) a mansuetoribus Musis avocare poterunt? ego enim illarum magiis [1580: magis] tanquam Ulysses Syreneis scopulis aures clausi meas. Quid? colus et fusa valebunt ad persuadendum mihi hoc quo non loquuntur?": Caretti, ed., 1:, 57. One can note here once again her identification with the male hero, this time along with explicit rejection of the female role.

intellectual performances at court: on one hand incapacitating fear, on the other foolish vainglory.[10] The Roman conquerors during their triumphs, she observes, had an official beside them in the chariot whose duty it was to remind the victor to behold his groaning captives and to remember that but for Fortune their places might be reversed. Aware of the ever-remaining possibility of future failure, the victor should not become insolent in his pride. This identification with Roman conquerors is like her identification with Alexander and Mutius Scaevola, and her warning to herself about pride indicates her consciousness of the success of her performances and of the admiration of the learned men around her. The mix of erudition and humor reveals a bright, ambitious, and self-aware young lady, enjoying her skills. By the end of the decade, however, everything had changed.

Morata had grown up among men not only learned but also keenly interested in religious reform. Her father had been actively involved in the discussion and spread of Lutheran and Calvinist ideas along with those of Erasmus and Valdes, especially during a period of years in Vicenza and Venice that interrupted his sojourns in Ferrara (1532–1538) but also in Ferrara, where he remained in touch with his Vicentine acquaintances.[11] Her teacher Senf corresponded with Calvin while maintaining an interest also in Luther's ideas. Celio Secondo Curione, an old friend of Morata's father and like him a classical scholar at Ferrara, had already been arrested twice in connection with religious matters. He was familiar with writings of Melanchthon and Zwingli as well as of Luther and Calvin, and became personally acquainted with Bernardino Ochino in Venice.[12] Morata's father in a letter to Curione called him "my divine teacher, sent to me by God, for my instruction and conversion."[13] Morata's early translations from the *Decameron,* especially the second tale with its attack on the papal court, already showed some influence of the reformist movement, or at least of the sentiments of her teacher, who may have suggested the project.

---

[10] Caretti, ed., 2: 21–25.

[11] Achille Olivieri, "Alessandro Trissino e il Movimento Calvinista Vicentino del Cinquecento," *Rivista di Storia della Chiesa* 21 (1967): 55–57.

[12] G. K. Brown, *Italy and the Reformation to 1550* (Oxford: Basil Blackwell, 1933), 63–77. See also Salvatore Caponetto, *La Riforma Protestante nell'Italia del Cinquecento* (Turin: Claudiana, 1992).

[13] Quoted in translation by Robert Turnbull, *Olympia Morata: Her Life and Times* (Boston: Massachusetts Sabbath School Society, 1846), 18. After her father's death, Olympia turned to Curione, who affectionately embraced her "quasi filiam," corresponding with her regularly and encouraging her writings.

The first sign of trouble for this group was the establishment in 1542 of the Roman Inquisition. At this point some of Fulvio Morata's friends, including Curione, left Ferrara for Germany and Switzerland. That Bernardino Ochino also fled from Italy at this moment was certainly known to Olympia, for on his way he came through Ferrara to be a guest of the duchess Renée; Olympia comments in later letters on his wanderings.[14] The visit of Pope Paul III to Ferrara in 1543 brought the Inquisition even closer to home. The duke of Ferrara was in need of better relations with the pope, and the atmosphere for reformers grew steadily more hostile. When in 1545 Pope Paul ordered the investigation of persons of suspect faith in Ferrara, Olympia's family was on the list.

In 1548 the rest of her circle fell apart. The Senf brothers left for the North. Olympia's father became ill and died. Suddenly Olympia, as the oldest child (she was then twenty-two), felt responsible for a family without having the means to support it. For in the same year Anne married the Duc de Guise and moved to France, leaving Olympia without a place at court. In fact, when Olympia returned to the court after tending her father's final illness, expecting to find aid there for her family's financial troubles, she was coldly sent away. Her potentially influential friend Lavinia was in Rome with her husband's family. The duchess Renée, who had been harboring Protestant refugees from France, was restricted to her palace under hostile scrutiny and continual pressure to return openly to Catholic practices. In Ferrara a whole subcommunity had vanished. Olympia's connections to her father and his friends, once the source of her success, now became a terrible liability. It was for her a moment of profound disillusionment and upheaval.

In a letter to Curione she described her situation:

> all at once I was deserted by my princess, and received in an unworthy manner. Nor did this happen to me separately from my sisters, but we all reaped this fruit from our princes, that for our service truly we received hatred. How smitten I was with grief, you can imagine. There was no one who would look out for us, and all our affairs were beleaguered at the same time. There was no visible way out.[15]

---

[14] See, e.g., her letter to Vittoria (Caretti, ed., 1: 102); and Curione conveys Ochino's greetings to her: *Opera omnia*, 168–70.

[15] "... statim a Principe mea desertam indignisque acceptam modis fuisse. Neque mihi hoc separatim a meis sororibus accidit, sed hos fructus omnes a nostris Principibus retulimus, nimirum pro labore tulimus odium. Quanto vero fuerim dolore affecta, tu existimare potes. Nullus erat qui nos respiceret et tot nos res eodem tempore circumvallabant, unde emergi nunquam posse videbatur": Caretti, ed., 1: 70.

Her personal solution, both economic and spiritual, came two years later from a marriage, probably in 1550,[16] to a German, similarly learned in Latin and Greek, who had been studying medicine in Ferrara, and had found his way into the circle of German scholars that had taught and admired Olympia since her childhood. German students in Italy, corresponding with their friends in the North, were frequently a conduit for reformist books and ideas, and Andreas Grunthler was a devoted Protestant.[17] In her troubled state, Morata began to pay serious attention to the religious discussions which had always surrounded her. No doubt her affection and gratitude towards Grunthler, who loved her dearly,[18] also played an influential role in this new interest.

But women too were involved in Olympia's turn to religion. After all, her former patroness, Renée, had been educated by LeFevre and spent much of her life protecting French Protestants and corresponding with reformers. Lavinia too was making serious efforts through her Roman family connections to help Fannio Fanini, one of Ferrara's first victims of counter-reform persecution, who was just then languishing in Ercole's jail under a death sentence from the church. While Olympia was still in Ferrara, she and Lavinia sympathetically visited the imprisoned Fanini,[19] and after Olympia had moved to Germany, she encouraged and thanked Lavinia for continuing to work on his behalf.

---

[16] Jules Bonnet, *Vie d'Olympia Morata, épisode de la Renaissance et de la Réforme en Italie*, 3rd ed. (Paris: Charles Meyrueis, 1856), 78, dates the marriage to 1550 since at Olympia's death in 1555 her husband wrote that they had been married barely five years. Paladino, *Opuscoli e lettere* 2: 271, however, points out that Olympia after her marriage was encouraging Lavinia to help Fanini; as he was killed in 1550, and it is unlikely that she would have asked Lavinia to help him after his death, Paladino dates her marriage to 1549, thereby supporting the unexplained dating by Turnbull (*Olympia Morata*, 81). Caretti, noting both Andrea's reference to their five years of marriage and Olympia's comment that she had two bad years after her father's death, returns to the 1550 date. Since Fannio was killed in August 1550, Olympia could have married and left Ferrara earlier that year, and thus still have written to Lavinia as she did.

[17] Olympia simply calls their faith "Christi puram religionem" (Caretti, ed., 1: 68), and says they belong "to Christ" rather than to any particular sect. On the Italian-German connection see R. Kössling, "Die Korrespondenz der Olympia Fulvia Morata (1526–1555) als Dokument italo-deutscher Begegnungen," in *Acta Conventus Neo-Latini Bariensis*, ed. R. Schnur et al., MRTS 184 (Tempe: Medieval and Renaissance Texts and Studies, 1998), 371–77.

[18] "Tantus vero est eius amor in me, ut nihil supra possit esse": Caretti, ed., 1:71. Cf. Andreas's pained letter to Curione soon after his wife's death: *Opera Omnia*, 187–92.

[19] *Vie d'Olympia Morata*, 73–74; Thomas M'Crie, *History of the Progress and Suppression of the Reformation in Italy in the Sixteenth Century* (Edinburgh/London: William Blackwood and Sons, 1827 [repr. 1856]), 167; Brown, *Italy and the Reformation*, 103; Turnbull, *Olympia Morata*, 75.

While waiting in Ferrara for her husband to come back for her after making arrangements in Germany, Olympia composed a dialogue between herself and Lavinia in which she gives Lavinia credit for urging her to shift from classical to religious studies:

Lavinia: For divine studies are a most healthy and fertile field, in which the friends of God pluck joyful and abundant and immortal fruits; they are different indeed from the pleasure of human letters to those who do not yet understand with the mind the truths perceived with the eyes, so that they may look up at the heavens and contemplate heavenly matters: and therefore from these blossoms they pick the ones which quickly wither.

Olympia: Would that I had not for some time been involved in this great error and this ignorance of the most important things. For I, who thought myself very learned because I used to read such writers and teachers of all the good arts and used to wallow in their writings as in the mud, then, although I was raised to the sky by everyone's praises, found myself to be tested and ignorant of all erudition. Meanwhile I was carried off by the error of thinking that everything happens by chance, nor did I believe that any God cared about mortal affairs. So thick was the fog in my mind, which already began to be dispersed by God, and some bit of the light of his singular and divine wisdom arose in me, and I made trial within myself that all human affairs are managed by his wisdom. For he so took up my protection when I was abandoned, as you know, and dashed to the ground, that I might learn by experience that he is the father and protector of orphans, nor does any parent, believe me, show such indulgence for his children as God showed to me. Ah, finally after much difficulty I have become aware of my foolishness!

Lavinia: Yet it was commonly held by many that you were endowed with remarkable piety and virtue.

Olympia: You heard it, and it was the common report; but if men listened to what is said about princes and their servants, their opinion of me would not be so great. For flatterers, in order to influence the way to princes, are wont to praise not only the princes but their servants as well, the ones which they think are in best favor. You could bear witness to how much I shrank away from Christian matters.

Lavinia: I remember; yet if not all the things said were true, still this opinion that we received about you wasn't false: that you were learned in Greek and Latin.

Olympia: Rumor usually mixes falsehoods with truths so as to elicit trust in the account. I (for it is permissible to tell the truth) never shunned labor nor interrupted my zeal for learning even in the busiest times; but that I was not so brilliant in erudition and learning anyone can easily perceive who reads my writings.

Lavinia: I used to hear from your teachers how much effort and work you spent on these things; and in my opinion indeed you did wisely, if as much time as others give to arranging their hair and adorning themselves, to other pleasures, and to the resting of mind and body, you spent safely in cultivating these studies. Moreover, what stirs in me the greatest admiration is that although you were a girl, yet despite the urging of small-minded women and the pressures of men, who kept shouting that you ought to engage in some other employment, and that no husband could be found for you who would prefer your being learned to your being rich, you never departed from your intent.[20]

Olympia: Although I thought the matter over carefully again and again, I could find no other cause than that *it was God's will*[21] to dedicate myself to these studies. He gave me this intelligence and this disposition such that I was so burning with the zeal for learning that no one could deter me from it. For he, the omnipotent, is the best of all orators who without any art of rhetoric impels our mind to wherever he will and leads it away from wherever he will. Therefore all these things are

---

[20] Olympia proved her critics wrong, for, as she wrote to Curione, "me etiam illi viro nuptum dedit, qui magnopere hisce meis studiis delectatur": Caretti, ed., 1: 71. ["(God) even gave me in marriage to that man, who greatly delights in these studies of mine"].

[21] A table of translations from Greek at the front of the 1580 volume, giving the wrong page number for this phrase, offers the meaning "Dei ad pedes iacebat, hoc est Deo ita visum est." Caretti, ed., 2: 35, identifies this as a borrowing from the *Iliad* 17.514 or 20.435. But the Greek as printed in Curione's edition is not quite right. Giuseppe Cammelli, in a review of Caretti's edition, comments on the frequent errors in Greek phrases in Curione's editions, lamenting that some further Greek errors were introduced in the editions of Paladino and Caretti. Giuseppe Cammelli, "Olympia Morata," *Rinascita* 4 (1941): 456–57. However, the gist of this Greek phrase is clear enough from the context in any case.

done 'by his nod and counsel,' nor does he do anything without cause or imprudently. These things will perhaps be for his glory, and for my benefit.

Lavinia: It is as you say, my Olympia: 'by his nod and judgment' are all things done, nor could you find a better cause than this, nor could I look for another. So much shall I urge you on to the cultivation in human life of divine studies. For if you received some pleasure from those, in which surely there is neither enduring usefulness nor any delight other than childish, these will make you steeped in a joy in which no grief ever intervenes. These studies have their own particular pleasures. Therefore, if you listen to me, you will attach your studies to the divine as handmaids and followers. *For we know that for those who love God all things work together for good*[22] which we pray to God may happen for us.[23]

The image of quickly fading flowers, once used by Calcagnini in a letter of praise to Olympia to represent fading physical beauties set in opposition to the unfading adornment of learning,[24] now represents that same secular learning in opposition to sacred studies and the desire for salvation. However, when Olympia refers to her former studies as "mud," Lavinia does not encourage her to forsake them altogether but rather to subordinate them as handmaids to the pursuit of spiritual wisdom. This is precisely what Olympia did.[25]

She began a project which carried over from Ferrara into Germany: she translated psalms into classical Greek meters. The first reference to this work comes in a letter from Morata to Curione, describing the events since her father's death: she says she is sending him some "carmina" which she had written the year before, i.e., during her time of troubles in Ferrara.[26] Curione replied:

> I much applaud the hymn or ode worked out in Greek; for in it you interpret the forty-sixth [lit. forty-fifth] psalm of David. I wish you would

[22] A quotation of Romans 8:28.

[23] Caretti, ed., 2: 33–38, here 33–35: See Appendix for original text.

[24] *Opera omnia*, 79–81.

[25] Cf. the printer's verses at the beginning of the volume: "Qui Musas Christi iunctas bene religioni / Imbibis, hunc librum, quem te mitto, lege." ["You who drink the Muses well mixed with the religion of Christ, read this book, which I send you."]

[26] "Carmina, quae superiore anno feci, quae subscripta eo ad te mitto ut videas ocium mihi, tot calamitatibus oppressae, literis operam dandi Deum praestitisse": Caretti, ed., 1: 71.

> treat many more in this manner, for then we would not envy the Greeks their Pindar. Go on, therefore, my Olympia, whither your Muse already calls you. Set a sacred laurel on your divine head: for you drink poetic inspiration from a more sacred spring than Pindar or Sappho.[27]

Eight of her psalms, in heroic and Sapphic meters, were printed in the volume of her works; any others were lost in the fires of Schweinfurt.[28] Her husband apparently set these verses to music, and the couple may have sung them with groups of friends, for Morata received letters requesting copies of both text and music.[29] Carolus Molineus, apologizing for writing to her when they barely know each other, comments that her Greek songs are being praised by poets in Italy.[30] In short, the songs were circulating beyond the circle of her acquaintances.

Now the psalms were certainly a favorite part of the Bible for Reformers. Olympia cites them repeatedly in her letters, especially letters to her sister Vittoria and madonna Cherubina.[31] She may have been aware of Marot's French translations, as Marot was employed for a while by Renée in Ferrara. His psalms were similarly given musical settings, and one scholar speculates that Olympia may have heard them sung. But there is a peculiar difference between Marot's or later Mary Sidney's rendering the psalms in vernacular meters, as an encouragement to popular piety, and Morata's translating them into classical Greek,

---

[27] "Hymnum sive oden Graece elaboratam, valde probo: in eam enim Davidis Psalmum xlv coniecisti. Utinam plures hoc modo tractares, Pindarum Graecis non invideremus. Perge igitur mea Olympia, quo te iamdudum tua Musa vocat. Laurum sacram tuo divino capiti impone: da sacratiore enim fonte spiritum poeticum, quam Pindarus aut Sappho illa hausisti": *Opera omnia*, 100.

[28] The volume of her works includes translations of Psalms 1, 2, 22 (23), 33 (34), 45 (46), 69 (70), 124 (125), and 149 (150).

[29] E.g., the letter from Andreas Rosarius: "quos Psalmos Graecis carminibus, in quibus te operam, quam Suinphurdiae incoeperas, navare tuam & audio & credo: vel si Doct. Andreas maritus tuus dilectissimus, & mei amantissimus, musicis numeris donavit, ad me velim perscribatis. Hoc enim gratius facere mihi nihil poteritis": *Opera Omnia*, 155.

[30] "Graecis etiam carminibus, in media Italia a Poetis nuper celebratam": *Opera Omnia*, 156.

[31] Vittoria, with Lavinia's help, found a position in the household of madonna Cherubina Orsini; Olympia wrote to both women in Italian. One letter to Vittoria was published, however, in a Latin translation, which Paladino assumed to be by Curione, but which Caretti, ed., 1: 17–23, argues may have been by Olympia herself, implying the thought already on her part of possible publication.

which would be accessible to far fewer readers than the Latin.[32] Why would she undertake such a project?

Curione suggests one reason in his letter of encouragement: the modern era should produce its own Greek poets so that we no longer have to envy the ancients for Pindar and Sappho.[33] This is the humanist dream, but it seems not to be Olympia's way of thinking about her work. A hint comes in her letter to a young student of her husband's, Michael Weber. Praising his zeal for his studies, she reminds him that it is a great gift from God and cites a Greek verse that divine gifts should not be the object of our scorn. To waste this gift would be ungrateful to God. Therefore she urges him by continuing his studies "isthuc Deo acceptum referas," to pay back, as it were, what you have received from God.[34] This is a very different motivation from rivaling the Greeks. It is in part a way of bringing the Greek poets into Christian use.[35] It is also a way of perceiving her own early life of humanist studies as something given her by God in order that she might use it in his service. As her dialogue with Lavinia asserts, her own zeal for study came from God; thus she does not reject but converts her earlier pursuits: what she had done previously for her own glory will now be done for his. Dedicating her Greek verses to God is a part of dedicating her whole self to God, as she repeatedly urges her friends to do.

In Germany Olympia turned with zeal to religious studies, and became more and more a reformer herself. Two letters to Curione shortly after her move express her sense that her change of life has been providentially granted for the good of her soul:

---

[32] Olympia apparently translated from the Vulgate, as she did not know Hebrew and as her numbering accords with the Vulgate. But Curione changed her numbering to the Hebrew system, notes Paladino (*Opuscoli e lettere*, 270).

[33] Cf. an earlier letter from Calcagninus (in re her humanist phase at court), who expounds a certain feminism in the service of rivalry with the ancients (*Opera Omnia*, 79–81): "te hortor, ut tuos istos profectus naviter promoveas, eosque quotidie meliores auctioresque facias: ut nostra quoque secula intelligant, magni numinis beneficentiam non cessare, neque bonarum artium studia foeminis abiudicasse: multoque minus naturam effoetam esse, ut nonnulli suae patrocinantes desidiae arbitrati sunt, quae nostra enim aetate Aspasias & Diotimas non possit excitare, si modo cura & diligentia adhibeatur. Cuius rei facile fidem feceris, si constanter in coepta studia incumbas, et pro colo calamum, pro lino libros, pro acu stylum exerceas."

[34] Caretti, ed., 1: 83.

[35] This is interesting in comparison with late antiquity. In the fifth century A.D. a Christian Greek poet rendered the Septuagint Greek psalms into Greek hexameter verse so as to bring them into the school curriculum. See J. Golega, *Der homerische Psalter* (Ettal: Kunstverlag, 1960).

> for had I remained attached longer at the court, my self and my salvation would have been at stake. . . . Nor did we come here with the intent of returning to Italy. For it does not escape you how dangerous it may be there for a Christian openly to profess his faith, where the Antichrist has so much power.[36]

To Lavinia she identified herself with the Jews who had left Egypt.[37] To Vergerio she mentions her prayer that her mother and sisters might join her in Germany "ex illa Babylonia."[38]

Matters in Germany, meanwhile, had also become unsettled. If we compare the letter Olympia wrote to her husband from Ferrara early in 1550 with one she wrote to him at the end of that same year, when he had once again gone ahead to make arrangements for their moving, we can see her anxiety at the increasing dangers in Germany and along with that a notable increase in religious sentiments. Where the first letter begs him by their mutual love for his speedy return, without any reference to God at all,[39] the second letter refers repeatedly to God, who alone can return him safely to her, emphasizing their dependence on God's protection and her faith in the efficacy of the prayers of pious persons.[40] Within the first few months of her life in Germany, the combination of continuing danger and the opportunity to read intently the writings of reformers and the Scripture had altered her manner of thought and expression.

Instability dominates her subsequent vision of life, not without reason. The collapse of her situation in Ferrara was followed only a few years later by the siege and destruction of Schweinfurt, her husband's native town where they had settled.[41] Several of her letters recount how her family barely escaped with their

---

[36] "Ego enim, si diutius in aula haesissem, actum de me ac de mea salute fuisset": Caretti, ed., 1: 71. "Non enim hoc animo huc venimus, ut iterum Italiam petamus. Nam te non fugit quam sit periculosum illic christianum se profiteri, ubi potestatem habet tantam Antichristus": Caretti, ed., 1: 77.

[37] Caretti, ed., 1: 93.

[38] Caretti, ed., 1: 120.

[39] Caretti, ed., 1: 64–65.

[40] Caretti, ed., 1: 72–73. This letter is dated December. Although earlier editors had assumed it was written from Ferrara, Caretti's dating of the marriage makes that impossible; he therefore concludes that it was written in Germany, possibly while Andreas went temporarily ahead to Schweinfurt. The difference in Olympia's manner of writing bears out his redating, for it shows the effects of her intense readings in Germany earlier that year.

[41] According to Caretti, ed., 1: 45–46, the siege began in April 1553, less than two years after Olympia and her husband had settled there, and the city was burned in May 1554.

lives, walking barefoot and fevered for miles. All their possessions, including her books and writings, were destroyed in the fire.[42] At last, with the help of some kind aristocrats, they resettled in Heidelberg, where, at requests from her friends, Olympia tried to rewrite from memory at least some of her verses.

She saw these catastrophes as simply a part of the chaos and war all around. Writing to Chilian from Heidelberg, she follows the mention of Schweinfurt with news from Italy: "I hear that in Ferrara Christians are cruelly harassed: neither the highest nor the lowest are spared; some are imprisoned, others are driven out, and others advise themselves to flee."[43] To her sister Vittoria she writes, with reference to Queen Mary's accession in England (1554): "In England too there is great persecution and I hear that father Bernardino [Ochino] has fled from England to Geneva, so that in every place those who wish to belong to Christ must bear the cross."[44] At about the same time she writes to Lavinia: "Here everything is burning with war, and holy men are pressed down with many hardships everywhere: even from England many have fled: so cruelly the Devil rages."[45]

Her letter to Anne, written from Heidelberg, describes in a mixture of Christian and Horatian terms for the companion of her youth her change of heart and its relation to her experiences of upheaval:

> just as I previously kept far away from divine letters, now I delight myself in them alone, and place in them all my zeal, work, concern, and my whole mind, as much as I can. I scorn all these things: riches, honors, pleasures, which once I even used to admire. This is what I want you, best of princesses, to reflect on over and over. Nothing, believe me, is stable here, all things change, and all of us (as he says) must one day tread the road of death, and soon; for the span of life flies by. Wealth

---

[42] See esp. her letters to Curione, Vittoria, and Cherubina Orsini (Caretti, ed., 1: 94–96, 100–9). If we can guess at the contents of her library from the works that either she or Curione mentions her knowing, it apparently included Homer and Cicero — her favorite authors (Curione comments in the dedicatory letter to Isabella Bresegna that she wrote a commentary on Homer as well as a defense of Cicero, both now lost), Pindar, Plato, Sophocles, Plutarch's *Lives,* Pliny the Younger, Vergil, Horace, Avicenna, and the books of "theology" which she mentions enjoying the liberty to read in Germany.

[43] "Ferrariae crudeliter in Christianos animadverti intellexi; nec summis, nec infimis parci; alios vinciri, alios pelli, alios fuga sibi consulere": Caretti, ed., 1: 118.

[44] "L'è ancora gran persecuzione in Anglia e intendo che padre Bernardino è fuggito a Geneva, sicchè in ogni loco bisogna portare la croce che vole esser di Cristo": Caretti, ed., 1: 102.

[45] "Hic omnia bello ardent et ubique multis aerumnis premuntur sancti viri; etiam ex Anglia multi sunt fugati: ita saevit diabolus": Caretti, ed., 1: 98.

> is of no use, nor honors, nor the favor of kings; but only that faith, truly, by which we embrace Christ can snatch us away from that eternal death and damnation, faith which, as it is a gift of God, you must seek for from him with your greatest prayers.[46]

The instability of life in the world becomes a frequent theme in her letters. Thus, writing from Heidelberg, she warns her sister, with clear reference to her own recent past, not to trust or fear

> the appearance of this world, whether threatening or even smiling and flattering. For everything that you see, what is it all but a thin vapor, or evanescent smoke, or stubble or straw soon to be consumed by fire?[47]

Indeed, by the time Morata was in Heidelberg, she seems to have expected the whole world to end very shortly; for the letter to Lavinia concludes: "Cito praeterit figura huius mundi" ["Soon the figure of this world shall pass"].[48]

---

[46] "Utpote quae prius longissime a divinis literis abhorruerim, iam illis solis me oblectem et omne meum studium, operam, curam, mentem denique omnem, in eo locem, ut quantum fieri possit, haec omnia contemnam, divitias, honores, voluptates, quae quondam adeo admirari solebam. Quae sane vellem, optima princeps, etiam atque etiam tu considerares. Nihil est, mihi crede, stabile hic: omnia mutantur, et omnibus (inquit ille) calcanda semel via laeti [I agree with Turnbull (*Olympia Morata*, 61) in reading this word as "leti" rather than "laeti"] et cito. Volat enim aetas: nihil divitiae prosunt, nihil honores, nihil regum favor; tantum vero illa fides, qua Christum amplectimur, nos ab illa sempiterna morte ac damnatione eripere potest. Quae cum sit donum Dei, eam ab illo maximis precibus petere debes": Caretti, ed., 1: 116. "Calcanda semel via leti" is a quotation from Horace, *Odes* 1.28.16. My thanks to Leslie MacCoull for help in tracing this and other citations.

[47] ". . . huius mundi speciem, quantumvis minitantem, aut etiam arridentem & blanditientem. Nam quae cernis omna, quid sunt quam tenuis quidam vapor, aut fumus evanescens, aut stipula foenumque igni mox absumenda?": *Opera Omnia*, 179. Caretti presents only the Italian version, which is somewhat different and omits these sentences, referring instead to "un pezzo di carne, la quale è come il ferro, un poco di fiato che presto uscisse fuora": Caretti, ed., 1: 102; but if Caretti is right that the Latin version is Olympia's, then she enhanced this emphasis. Cf. also the letter to Lavinia (Caretti, ed., 1: 98): "homunciones . . . quorum vita umbrae, foeno, flori, fumo in divinis literis comparari solet"; and, already before the fall of Schweinfurt, her second dialogue: "Homo bulla; et Petrus hanc vitae brevitatem quam congruenter vaporem esse dixit . . . caetera omnia fluunt, labuntur nec diu esse uno et eodem statu possunt": Caretti, ed., 2: 45–46. Caretti notes (46) that the citation is not actually from Peter but from James 4: 14. Cf. also Horace, *Epistles* 1.15.38–39; Isaiah 5:24, 47:14.

[48] Caretti, ed., 1: 99. Cf. 1 Corinthians 7: 31.

This letter too mixes a classical and Christian message, combining Horace's inescapable self with inescapable sin and the devil:

> We are often forced to wander, yet we can never escape from the devil and the world; rather, as that man said: Dark care does not leave the bronzed ship and sits behind the horseback rider. So we always draw with us our familiar enemies: the old Adam and sin. Therefore it behooves us, without missing any jot of time, to pray to God that we be not broken among so many evils; otherwise, if we yield to lassitude and sloth while we have so many wars to wage, we will easily succumb, and so we shall perish in eternity."[49]

Surrounded by physical wars, Olympia feels herself engaged in a spiritual battle, no longer "a soldier in Cicero's camp" but a "soldier of Christ," as she wrote to Hermann's son.[50] To her sister Vittoria she wrote: God "strengthens and fortifies me so that I may not yield a hair's breadth in the cause of religion to his enemies, who are everywhere. . . . "[51] And to madonna Cherubina she wrote as she had long before about the Greek Olympics: "The crown is not given except to those who fight."[52]

Curione, in a work published at this time, expressed his optimism that Italy would soon be reformed.[53] Morata, who was in continual correspondence with him, may have shared his hopes. In any case, as a soldier of Christ, she was doing her best to help make it happen. She sent to Lavinia along with another of her

---

[49] "Nos saepe peregrinari cogimur, sed tamen nusquam diabolum et mundum effugere possumus; imo, quod ille inquit: — Neque decedit aerata triremi et post equitem sedet atra cura — Ita nos domesticos hostes veterem Adamum et peccatum semper nobiscum vehimus. Proinde nullo temporis puncto intermisso Deum comprecari oportet, ne in tantis malis frangamur; alioqui si languori desidiaeque nos dederimus, cum nobis tot bella sint gerenda, facile succumbemus et ita in perpetuum peribimus": Caretti, ed., 1: 98. The quotation is of Horace, *Odes* 3.1.38–40.

[50] "Nos sub Christo merere eiusque militiae sacramento ita obligatos esse": Caretti, ed., 1: 81. (From Schweinfurt, 1552.)

[51] "Sentio enim me sic roborari et obfirmari, ut eius adversariis, quorum plena sunt omnia, ne latum quidem pilum in causa religionis cesserim": *Opera Omnia*, 178. Or in the Italian version: "lui mi dia grazia che io perfin qui, a laude sua, fra gl'impii delli quali ogni cosa è piena, mai ho ceduto un pelo quanto alla religione": Caretti, ed., 1: 102.

[52] "Non si dà la corona se non a colui che combatte": Caretti, ed., 1: 107, cf. 110, 111: "egli non vuole che siamo pegri & ociosi, ma che di continuo stemo in esercitio, armati di quelle arme che scrive san Paolo alli Ephesi . . . (priego che) abbiate la corona, la quale solo si darà a colui che averà vinto." The allusion is to Ephesians 6:11–17.

[53] Caelio Secundo Curione, *De amplitudine Beati Regni Dei dialogi* (Basel, 1554).

own dialogues, "also some writings of Dr. Martin, which when I read them pleased me greatly, so that they may also affect and refresh you."[54] To the "pious and erudite Matthew Illyrico," she writes more formally, urging him to translate Luther's writings for the sake of converting the Italians. Write in Italian rather than Latin, she urges, "because many of them do not know their letters."[55] When Vergerio sent her a letter, she seized the opportunity of replying with a similar request: that he translate Luther's work "for our Italians."[56] Here was her chance, like Mutius Scaevola, to do something *pro patria,* "nostris Italis."

Her early expression of impatience with knowledge not turned into action recurs in her exhortations to her influential female friends in France and Italy (Anne and Lavinia) to act openly against the persecution of reformers, even at the cost of martyrdom. Thus she writes to Anne (my emphases):

> For it is not enough to *know* the story of Christ, which even the devil is not ignorant of, but it is necessary to have that faith which *acts* through love, which enables you to dare to profess Christ among his enemies.[57]

To take action in the midst of the enemy is to fulfill the model of Scaevola as well as of the Christian martyrs.

Her letters from Germany, especially to other women, continually urge the entrusting of oneself to God, the daily reading of Scripture, if possible its discussion with friends and family, and prayer to God for enlightenment in understanding it. She exhorts all three, Lavinia, Vittoria, and madonna Cherubina, to read and discuss Scripture with each other.

---

[54] "Mitto etiam D. Martini scripta quaedam, quae cum legerem, valde me delectarunt, ut te quoque afficere & recreare possint": Caretti, ed., 1: 80. A number of subsequent letters ask repeatedly whether Lavinia has received them.

[55] ". . . quippe ipsorum multi literas nesciunt": Caretti, ed., 1: 89.

[56] Bainton, *Women of the Reformation*, 230, notes that in the early 1560s Vergerio was still trying to smuggle Lutheran writings into Italy. He visited in Switzerland the reform-minded Isabella of Brisegna to whom Curione dedicated the first edition of Olympia Morata's works.

[57] "Non enim sat est Christi historiam nosse, quam et diabolus non ignorat, sed eam fidem habere oportet, quae operatur per dilectionem, quae efficit ut Christum profiteri audeas inter illius hostes . . .": Caretti, ed., 1: 116. Cf. her letter of encouragement to Lavinia in re her work for Fanini: "tantum te hortor ut ne malevolentissimis hominum obtestationibus magnitudinem animi tui inflectas in his, quae ad Christi puram religionem pertinet": Caretti, ed., 1: 68 ["so much I urge you not to turn aside, because of the malevolent entreaties of men, the greatness of your resolve in matters which pertain to the pure religion of Christ"]. Cf. Galatians 5:6.

What she envisions going on among them back in Italy looks somewhat like her old situation at court: again a group of women will read the same texts and discuss them. These women do not all know the ancient languages, however, and they are reading religious texts rather than the classics. There is neither an explicit feminism nor any apparent need for the presence or authority of men. Indeed, she requests Cherubina to tell Vittoria to govern her life by Scripture and "non l'autorità di persona alcuna" [and not the authority of any person].

> Do you think he is a liar when he says "Verily, verily I say unto you, that if you will ask anything of the Father in my name, he will give it to you"?[58] And "if two or three shall gather on the earth and pray for something, I will do it"?[59]

Therefore, she urges,

> Read the Scripture, by yourself and together with the Lady Lavinia, and with Vittoria, and exhort her to piety; pray together, and you will see that God will give you such strength that you will conquer the world and will not do out of fear anything against your conscience.[60]

As an ambitious teenager Olympia had identified with Alexander and the Roman heroes; now in her twenties, she piously altered the meaning of that confidence: three women with God on their side can conquer the world.

It is interesting to see how Curione, gathering all the writings of hers he could find into a memorial volume after her death in October 1555, presents his young friend. On one hand, he uses the volume to further the religious cause, as she would have been pleased no doubt to see. Thus he dedicated the first edition to Isabella of Brisegna (or Breseña), who had been influenced while in Naples by Ochino[61] and Valdes, had harbored and employed several persons

---

[58] Cf. John 16: 23.

[59] Cf. Matthew 18: 20.

[60] "Pensate ch'egli sia bugiardo quando ei dice: 'In verità in verità vi dico che se domandarete cosa alcuna al Padre nel nome mio, che ve la darà, e se saranno due o tre congregati sopra la terra, e pregaranno di qualche cosa, io la farò'? . . . leggete la Scrittura da per voi, e insieme con la signora Lavinia, e con la Vittoria; essortatela alla pietà: pregate insieme, e vederete che Dio vi darà tanta fortezza che vincerete il mondo, e per paura non farete cosa alcuna contra la vostra conscienzia": Caretti, ed., 1: 107–8. Cf. also John 16: 33.

[61] Ochino dedicated to her a treatise on the sacraments (Bainton, *Women of the Reformation*, 229).

suspected of heresy, and had eventually fled to Zurich from where she refused to return despite her family's pleas, and where she received as a guest the same Vergerio that Olympia had urged to translate Luther for the Italians. This first dedication, then, was to someone who, like Morata herself, had left Italy and was trying to further the Italian Reformation from abroad. When the first edition of Morata's works quickly sold out, the second and subsequent editions,[62] published after the accession of Elizabeth in England, were dedicated to a more powerful figure, the new Protestant Queen, who is specifically requested to be helpful to religious refugees.[63]

Despite the clearly Protestant use of these dedications, Curione's dedicatory letters to Isabella and Elizabeth stress two other aspects as well which reflect his own humanist interests more, probably, than the outlook of Morata herself. One is his emphasis on Morata's classical writings. He lists proudly the works she produced in her humanist mode, including those lost at Schweinfurt: commentaries on Homer and Cicero, translations of Homer, Greek and Latin dialogues after the model of Plato and Cicero, and public declamations on Cicero's *Paradoxes*. Thus, unlike the religious historians who focus mainly on the letters from Germany, Curione focuses on the writings — many of them lost — which Morata had produced in Ferrara as a classicist. He wishes to immortalize precisely the period of success at court which Olympia herself had put behind her as a peril to her soul. He adds to her collected writings the "judgments and praises about her by learned men,"[64] recreating that circle of humanist praise which Olympia had come to associate with court flattery and which she felt had dangerously seduced her away from acknowledging her need for God.[65]

The other divergence from Morata's own self-presentation, related to this same humanist focus, is his emphasis on her being a woman. The letter to Elizabeth begins with several pages on the defense of women's intellectual abilities, with reference to Plato's arguments in the *Republic* and *Laws* and with

---

[62] There were altogether four editions: 1558, 1562, 1570, and 1580. The last, after Curione's death, is a reprint of the 1570. While alive, Curione kept adding materials to each new edition, the first having been compiled of whatever he could hastily obtain. For a comparative table of the contents, see Caretti, ed., 1: 151–56.

[63] "erga eos qui veritatis causa in exilio vitam degunt, charitas": *Opera Omnia*, tenth unnumbered page of preface.

[64] "Statui enim Olympiae nostrae quae sunt apud me monumenta, quamprimum edere una & doctorum virorum de ea iudicia & laudes": *Opera Omnia*, 193.

[65] See esp. her first dialogue and her letter to Curione (Caretti, ed., 1: 71), both cited above.

the standard list of classical examples: Semiramis, Zenobia, Aspasia, Sappho, Praxilla, Corinna, plus some more recondite cases: Telesilla, Anyte, Erinna, Cleobulina, and the daughters of Stesichorus. From the Old Testament Judith and the Queen of Sheba are named, followed by the Roman virgins Paula and Eustochium, and one single recent example: Cassandra Fedele. Despite his appending the praises of learned men, Curione says explicitly that he has picked a learned and pious female dedicatee for the writings of this learned and pious female writer. So, too, he oddly adds one totally unrelated item at the end of the volume: a secular Latin verse epistle by Hippolyta Taurelli to her husband Baldassare Castiglione.[66] Thus the volume ends with an emphasis on the learned woman, not the reformer. Despite Morata's basic lack of interest in explicit feminist debate, her easy identification as a youngster with male models, and her sure sense as a reformer of a religious mission for which gender differences are irrelevant, to the men of letters who wrote in her praise she remained first and foremost a female, and a remarkable example for that reason.[67]

It is with mixed feelings that I am compelled to acknowledge the similar basis of my own interest in her, and to wonder to what extent that does her justice. Perhaps, despite her lack of explicit interest in women as a category, she perforce gave the matter some thought. I trace here a few clues to that aspect of her work.

Her earliest letter blithely dismisses female roles, summed up in the traditional spindle, in favor of a life of learning and eloquence, embodied in the pen.[68] Early Greek verses, probably also written during her teens,[69] declare that God gives each person different pleasures, and that hers consist in the flowery fields of the Muses rather than the usual female concerns.[70] But the preface to

---

[66] Turnbull seems convinced that this epistle is also by Morata, although Curione makes quite clear who its author is, and even includes her epitaph, just as he includes Morata's. One dead woman writer is set beside the other in a double funeral monument to female learning and virtue. It is noteworthy that both Olympia and Hippolyta combine the roles of classically learned writer and loving wife, possibly an implicit demonstration against the common argument that learning would make a woman less fit for wifehood.

[67] The French feminist writer Catherine des Roches enlists her along with — interestingly — Hippolyta Taurella and Laura Terracina as examples of learned Italian women. Olympia is mentioned in Catherine Des Roches, *Les Secondes Oeuvres*, ed. Anne Larsen (Geneva: Droz, 1998), 219; and by Anne Larsen in her introduction to Catherine Des Roches, *Les Oeuvres*, ed. Anne Larsen (Geneva: Droz, 1993), 22–23. Presumably Catherine was aware of Curione's volume containing both Olympia and Hippolyta along with his defense of women's learning.

[68] See note 9.

[69] Caretti, ed., 2: 14–15, dates them 1540 because of their similarity to the letter.

[70] Caretti, ed., 2: 50.

her court performances rejects also the image of the Amazon queen who might challenge the learned men in her audience.[71] Rather she claims her performance to be a matter of dutiful obedience to her mistress Anne. Thus not only is her attitude one of properly female humility and obedience, but also her speech is directed primarily at another female: "to you, I say, professors of humanities, but especially to you, royal Anna, as friendly as you are illustrious."[72] Yet along with this modest deferral comes the implication that Anne, a female, is a "princeps" whose command can summon not only Olympia but also this audience of learned men. Moreover, a reference later in these prefaces to obedience as the virtue God loves best marks it as a male and not just a female virtue, for the example offered is Abraham.[73] We can see the carefulness with which Olympia had to negotiate her situation.

Her letters also vary in tone. To learned men she shows continual deference, while with her female correspondents — even those of much higher social status — she takes an authoritative tone of preaching and exhorting which she rarely takes with men; two exceptions are the letter to a young male student[74] and the admonishment of an irresponsible German official who remains unnamed.[75] The second dialogue, dedicated like the first to Lavinia, is similarly between two females: Theophila who counsels in faith the more worldly Philotima.[76] Although the first dialogue clearly puts Lavinia in the position of a Theophila, it is more ambiguous in the second dialogue which woman is which; perhaps that is why allegorical names replaced the real ones. A letter to Lavinia[77] mentions that this dialogue was written in order to draw Lavinia's mind away from worries; thus Olympia is now the advisor and consoler. In any case, the audience for female preaching is again female.

Moreover, this second dialogue, written in Germany,[78] offers a female heroine who can substitute for the male heroes of her early writings: Queen Esther, of whom "it is established that neither riches nor honors nor the love of a king could turn her aside from God, but rather, for the salvation of her people and all their

---

[71] ". . . ego tanquam rudis tyruncula non deberem, qualis Pentesilea furens, cum tantis viris concurrere": Caretti, ed., 2: 21.

[72] ". . . a vobis, inquam, humanitatis professoribus, praecipue vero a te, Anna princeps tam comis quam illustris": Caretti, ed., 2: 21.

[73] Caretti, ed., 2: 25.

[74] Caretti, ed., 1: 83–84.

[75] Caretti, ed., 1: 89–92.

[76] Caretti, ed., 2: 39–46

[77] Caretti, ed. 1: 79–80.

[78] Caretti, ed., 2: 11, dates it to the autumn of 1551.

goods. she ignored even the peril to her own life."[79] Esther, whose story Theophila narrates at length, is a female figure of public action. Living at court, she made courageous use of her position to defend the victims of unjust religious persecution. She bears out Olympia's persistent concern to make active use of her abilities for a similar public good. Since Olympia not only allows herself this active role, but also urges other women as well to turn their knowledge into action, perhaps the introduction of the female model Esther is part of an underlying argument for such a possibility specifically for women.

We can see how humanist values were both carried across and transformed as Olympia's focus shifted from a secular to an ever more intensely devotional life. Apart from feminist issues, we can see through Olympia's case the swift change of religious climate in Ferrara, the suddenness with which an entire subculture was endangered and dispersed, and the importance for reformers of travels and communications between Ferrara and northern Europe. Olympia's years of writing further allow us to glimpse the alterations in subjective experience of one individual living through this period of upheaval.

[79] ". . . neque divitiae neque honores neque regis amor eam a Deo abstrahere potuerint; imo prae populi sui salute omnium bonorum illorum et capitis etiam periculum neglexisse eam constat": Caretti, ed., 2: 43.

Appendix

"From the Dialogue between Olympia and Lavinia"

Lav: Studia enim divina, dico, sunt agri saluberrimi et maxime fertiles, e quibus amici Dei laetos et uberes et immortales ferunt fructus; alia vero humanarum literarum voluptati sunt his, qui sensum nondum habent animi oculorum vera cernentium, ut caelum suspicere et coelestia contemplari possint: itaque ex his flosculis quosdam celeriter decidentes carpunt. *Olymp*: Utinam neque ego in hoc summo errore et in hac maximarum rerum ignoratione versata aliquando fuissem! Ego enim, quae me ipsam doctissimam arbitrabar quia omnium artium bonarum scriptores tales et doctores legebam et in eorum scriptis tanquam in luto volutabar, tunc cum ad caelum laudibus ab omnibus efferebar me omnis eruditionis expertem atque ignaram esse comperi. Interdum enim in eum errorem rapiebar ut omnia casu fieri putarem neque Deum crederem curare mortalia quenquam. Tanta animo meo offusa erat caligo, quae iam a Deo discuti coepit et aliqua mihi eius singularis et divinae sapientiae lux oborta est et in me ipsa periculum feci illius sapientia omnes res humanas geri. Tantum enim mei desertae et abiectae, ut nosti, patrocinium suscepit ut eum patrem et pupillorum patronum esse re ipsa sim experta, nec ulli parentes, mihi crede, ea indulgentia sunt in liberos suos qua Deus in me fuit. Ah, vix tandem sensi stolida! *Lav*: Tamen increbuerat apud multos te commemorabili pietate & virtute praeditam esse. *Olymp*: Audieras et fama fuit; sed si homines attenderent quae de principibus & eorum familiaribus dicuntur, non tam magna fuisset eorum opinio de me. Adulatores enim, quia ad principes affectant viam, non modo principibus adulari solent, sed etiam eorum familiaribus, quos apud illos gratiores esse putant. Tu testimonium dare poteris quam abhorrens fuerim a re Christiana. *Lav*: In memoria habeo; sed tamen, si non omnia vera fuerunt quae praedicabant, non tamen hanc falsam de te opinionem accepimus, te literis Graecis et Latinis eruditam esse. *Olymp*: Fama veris falsa quaedam semper solet adiungere, quo eius testimonio fides tribuatur. Ego (licet enim verum dicere) nunquam laborem fugi neque in maximis occupationibus intermisi studia doctrinae, sed me non tam praeclara eruditione et doctrina esse facile qui mea scripta leget intelligere poterit. *Lav*: Audivi de tuis praeceptoribus quantum laboris et operae in his consumpseris et, mea quidem sententia, sapienter fecisti, si quantum coeteris [1580: caeteris] ad capillum componendum et se ornandum, quantum ad alias voluptates et ad ipsam animi requiem et corporis conceditur temporis, tantum tibi tute ad haec studia recolenda sumpsisti. Hoc autem mihi maximam admirationem movet quod, cum esses puella, tamen neque hortatu mulier-cularum neque virorum impulsis, qui clamitabant, alia munera obeunda tibi fore neque virum tibi inveniri posse qui te doctam quam ditem mallet, unquam a tua sententia discesseris. *Olymp*: Ego sane, cum etiam atque etiam quam diligenter considerarem, nullam aliam causam reperire potui, quam ϑεοῦ μετὰ ποσσὶν ἔκιτο me his studiis operam dedisse. Ille mihi ingenium et hanc mentem dedit, ut studio discendi adeo incensa fuerim ut nemo me ab his deterrere potuerit. Nam ille omnipotens est omnium oratorum optimus, qui nulla dicendi arte mentes nostras quo vult impellit, unde vult deducit. Quare haec omnia eius nutu atque consilio gesta sunt neque vero quidquam temere aut imprudenter facit. Haec fortasse illi gloriae erunt et mihi emolumento. *Lav*: Est ut dicis, mea Olympia, illius nutu et arbitrio omnia geri, nec meliorem causam hac invenire poteris nec amplius ego aliam quaeram. Tantum te hortabor ut in vita humana divina studia colas. Si enim ex illis aliquid voluptatis cepisti, in quibus certe nulla solida utilitas delectatioque est nisi puerilis, haec gaudio te delibutam reddent cui nulla unquam aegritudo intercedit: horum enim studiorum voluptates propriae sunt. Quare, si me audies, illa studia divinis tanquam ancillas pedissequasque adiunges, Οἴδαμεν γὰρ ὅτι τοῖς ἀγαπῶσι τὸν ϑεὸν πάντα συνεργεῖ εἰς ἀγαϑόν quod nobis ut eveniat, Deum comprecabimur.

Olympia Morata, *Opera Omnia*, ed. Lanfranco Caretti, vol. 1: *Epistolario (1540–1555)*, 2: *Orationes. Dialogi et Carmi*, R. Deputazione di Storia Patria per l'Emilia e la Romagna, sezione di Ferrara (Ferrara: Premiata Tipografia Sociale, 1940), 2: 33–35. Also in *Opera omnia*, 42–46.

Staging Ferrara: State Theater from Borso to Alfonso II

Louise George Clubb

I

Theatrical activity in Ferrara emanated from a theatrical Ferrara that was itself a stage, a protagonist, a producer and generator of theater, an object of representation. In Ferrara modern comedy came into its own, tragedy was first fully performed, pastoral drama was invented, drama theory was nourished. Ludovico Zorzi called the city a crossroads of experimentation; his treatment of the municipal attitude toward the common space[1] is part of the illuminating scrutiny that has documented the Ferrarese self-representational spirit. Less attention has been given to the way that "Ferrara palcoscenico" was perceived and portrayed elsewhere. In my *cavalcata* through Ferrarese drama I shall introduce and linger on three dissimilar examples of the way Ferrara was theatrically projected from outside the city itself.

The Ferrarese tradition of literature, dramatic and other, is so star-studded that we tend naturally to define its theatrical span as from Boiardo to Tasso. But the tradition was not begun by Boiardo nor ended by Tasso, nor in fact did the weight of Ferrara's illustrious writers, almost overpowering in other regards, determine the climate and create the agenda of the stage. Ferrara called forth the powers of her *literati* great and small and made them dramatists, and then *they* made "Ferrara palcoscenico." The demand came first from the court, and the staging of Ferrara is more usefully ordered according to Estensi rulers than to their poet-playwrights, the greatest of whom wrote to more than one court climate. For this reason I prefer to set the boundaries from Borso to the second Alfonso and the aftermath of the latter's reign.

---

[1] "Il sipario ducale" in Ludovico Zorzi, *Il teatro e la città: Saggi sulla scene italiana* (Turin: Einaudi, 1977), 5–59.

The marquis Borso d'Este, whose pursuit of *magnificenza* caused an ideal dramatic image of feudal Ferrara to be played out in paint on the walls of Palazzo Schifanoia, expanded the apparatus of spectacle with public ceremonies and *giostre,* processions with floats, machines, tableaux vivants, and courtiers in romanticized armor and classical costume. The ducal grandeur of Borso's court was expressed by his style long before the title of Duke of Ferrara was granted just before his death in 1471.

Borso's successor and brother Ercole I put humanistic pedagogy into state service, adding to Ferrara's representational and musical splendor, ordering Latin plays performed and translated. When Ercole's son Alfonso I came to power in 1505 the stage literally and figuratively was set for modern vernacular drama, and Ludovico Ariosto was at hand to write the earliest classics of *commedia erudita.*

The second Ercole, son of Alfonso, ruling from 1534 to 1559, saw the launching of the Council of Trent, and presided over a Ferrarese theatrical scene dominated by Giambattista Giraldi Cinzio, professor of rhetoric at the Studio, ducal secretary, and prolific playwright and theorist. The first performances of modern tragedy were of his Senecan works by his students, under his direction and in his home.

The reign of Alfonso II, the last duke of Ferrara, was the longest and, in sheer quantity and variety, the most theatrical. Pastoral drama triumphed in the decades preceding his death in 1597, Tasso's *Aminta* and Guarini's *Pastor fido* the supreme examples. Even more intensely than his predecessors, Alfonso II patronized music and the gestation of music drama. Jousts and *tornei* continued to be Ferrarese specialties, while *commedia dell'arte* troupes were regularly welcomed. Taxes went up in these years and then down in 1598, when the papacy took Ferrara away from the Estensi.

II

It has been thought that Ferrara became a theatrical model to other cities by answering a widespread contemporary need for form and norms. Thus Mario Apollonio could narrate the appearance of regular comedy as a response to fragmenting wars and cultural crisis in Italy.[2] The troubled times of Ercole I and Alfonso I would constitute the first two chapters of such a narrative. But a remarkable Florentine Griselda play, surviving only in manuscript until 1993, shows that the theatrical exemplarity of Ferrara was established even before

---

[2] Mario Apollonio, *Storia del teatro italiano*, 3rd ed., 2 vols. (Florence: Sansoni, 1954), 1: 272–73.

classical norms were excavated. Called a "sacra rappresentazione profana" by its modern editor,[3] this dramatization of the Griselda story in the ottava rima form of the medieval *sacra rappresentazione* sheds all claim to the supernatural, though Griselda is treated as an exemplum of saintly patience.

An audience familiar with Griselda's story from Boccaccio, Petrarch, or other version, would expect Griselda's insatiably experimental husband to test her by sending away her children to a nobleman in Bologna and returning them like packages for the final unwrapping; instead, the play transports the audience to Ferrara and introduces the "Marchese" and his court, where the two children are reared in learning and grace, and Griselda's daughter is given an aristocratic finish that stands her in good stead when she is betrothed to the Marchese's heir in the last scene.

This is secular drama, astoundingly early, possibly written by Feo Belcari for Lorenzo il Magnifico's marriage festivities in June 1469, or for the *giostra* in which he triumphed earlier that year, or for some other event while the Estensi were still *marchesi* in Ferrara, though *duchi* in Modena and Reggio since 1453. Relations between Florence and Ferrara were serene in these years; a peace had been ratified in 1468, and Borso had graciously sent his horse (named, of course, Baiardo) to young Lorenzo for his *giostra*.[4]

While both the rambling medieval form of the *rappresentazione* and the Boccaccian source are Tuscan, the unwontedly secular subject and the introduction into the play of a major and flattering role for the "Marchese di Ferrara" (only once referred to as "duca") are diplomatic compliments to the image of elegant worldly entertainment at the court of Borso d'Este, who would live to see his Ferrarese marquisate elevated to a duchy in 1471.

The part of the action that takes place in Ferrara is theatrically courtly, suggesting scenes from the Schifanoia frescoes: ladies play and sing, banquets are spread, the Marquis and his court *perform* the roles of a marquis holding court. In short, the music, banquet, and dancing that would actually have been part of the performance in Florence are fictionally set in a Ferrara that existed in the imagination as a source and image of theatrical spectacle. Borso would doubtless have been pleased by the evidence that it was so. We need not agree with André Chastel that Ferrara constituted an anti-Firenze[5] to see here early signs of a theatrical *concorso di eleganza,* between Medici and Estensi, with Ferrara in the lead.

---

[3] Raffaele Morabito, ed., *Una sacra rappresentazione profana: Fortune di Griselda nel Quattrocento italiano* (Tübingen: Max Niemeyer, 1993).

[4] For the dating and further historical context of the Griselda *rappresentazione,* see Riggero Stefanini, "Formazione e dilegno del dittongo nei possessivi preposti del fiorentino," *Letteratura Italiana Antica*, 1(2000): 17–40, esp. 27, n. 21 and 22.

[5] André Chastel, *I centri del Rinascimenti* (Milan: Feltrinelli, 1965), 177 (originally published as *Renaissance méridionale* [Paris: Gallimard, 1965]).

III

At the court of Ercole I the theatrical ventures were of many kinds, some with more future than others. In celebration of a family wedding in 1487, the duke's half-brother Niccolò da Correggio wrote the *Fabula di Cefalo,* an Ovidian *favola mitologica* which would be re-evoked in Tasso's *Aminta*. Ercole's programmatic encouragement of avant-garde humanistic theater spurred Boiardo about 1490 to write his *Timone,* dramatizing and moralizing a Lucianic dialogue. Ariosto was involved in Ferrarese theater from the beginning of his career, even while he was still a law student. When Ludovico Sforza requested a theatrical loan in 1493, among the youths Ercole took to Pavia to play comedies of Plautus in Latin was nineteen-year-old Ariosto. On the way they stopped at Reggio Emilia, where Boiardo rehearsed them for performance.[6]

IV

Though the logical classical structure of Ariosto's own plays, a natural progression from acting Latin and translated scripts, was hailed as the foundation of modern vernacular comedy, what really electrified audiences in 1508 and 1509 were his settings, namely contemporary Italian cities: his second comedy, *I suppositi,* brought onstage the bourgeois Ferrara of merchants, customs officers, and travelers, with the offstage court invoked as a guarantor of order. Above all, this was the Ferrara of university students, from whom the actors for court productions, like Ariosto himself, were drawn. The *jeune premier* is a young Sicilian law student who turns himself instead into a "studente di amore" (1.1), exchanging identities with his servant and getting a job in his beloved's house. The local references and flavor, the prologue, spoken by Ariosto himself, punning on the title's suggestion of sodomy, belong to the campy in-joking of an undergraduate cum court/club atmosphere, transferable, however, to similar locales, such as the papal court of Ariosto's not very faithful friend Leo X, where Ferrarese drama was in demand. Both Ariosto's admired classical construction and his takeover of Plautine/Terentian vehicles for representation of his own Ferrara were natural consequences of Ercole's humanistic theatrical program and of Alfonso's succession to his father's place.

---

[6] Michele Catalano, *Vita di Ludovico Ariosto, ricostruita su nuovi documenti*, 2 vols. (Geneva: Olschki, 1931), 1:123.

V

Although tragedy had been broached in the classical program of Ercole I, in this genre Ferrara may have appeared to lag behind Florence, in that the most admired early experiments in vernacular tragedy (on the page and in declamation, if not in actual performance), Giangiorgio Trissino's *Sofonisba* and Giovanni Rucellai's *Rosmunda,* came from the Medici circle, its perimeter enclosing Rome and Florence. But Ferrara took the lead in tragedy when Giraldi Cinzio began writing for the Ferrarese court and had his blood-soaked neo-Senecan *Orbecche* first performed in 1541, for Ercole II and other friends. This led not only to further performances of *Orbecche* but also to the composition and performance of other tragedies, many by Giraldi himself, and to the Aristotle-based polemics on the theory of tragedy, involving Giraldi's neighbors at the University of Padua, and the rival academic playwright Sperone Speroni, among others. Some of Giraldi's tragedies after *Orbecche* — such as the romantic or chivalric *Antivalomeni, Arrenopia,* and *Epitia,* which end with rewards and punishments distributed according to strict justice — were really experiments with tragicomedy and exemplify the genre he championed as *tragedia di fin lieto* in his theoretical *Discorsi.*

With Giraldi Ferrara laid a weighty and early claim on the new science of literary criticism. From our vantage point in the critical tradition, the importance of these events in the reign of Ercole II and the youth of Alfonso II is huge, whether for

1. what they disclose of the direction the *speculum principis* tradition had taken — we see the Estensi, whose dungeons had more than once held other Estensi, watching enactments of exotic displacements of Senecan mayhem in royal families; or for

2. what they reveal of the approach to and retreat from the political tragedy of engagement that might have been created from Machiavelli's framing of the conflict between power and morality — Riccardo Bruscagli has written penetratingly on this subject;[7] or for

3. the vein of dramatic theory they uncover, flowing toward intensified Aristotelian experiments in stagecraft and Counter-Reformation ideology as it felt its way to its true goal, the expression of the idea of the world as a great theater directed by the Prime Mover of the universe. Again Ferrara is the nurturer of new theater as well as of the theater where the new is seen.

---

[7] "La corte in scena. Genesi politica della tragedia ferrarese," in Riccardo Bruscagli, *Stagioni della civiltà estense* (Pisa: Nistri-Lischi, 1983), 127–59; and idem, "Thrones of Blood: Machiavellian Politics and the Rebirth of Tragedy on the Italian Renaissance Stage," The Berkeley Chair of Italian Culture Lecture, 1993, unpublished.

VI

The pastoral play was the newest and most original dramatic genre of the Renaissance. It is not a coincidence that the genre which staged the landscape of the mind should arise in the city that had become a theatrical landscape in the minds of contemporaries. The process of shaping and disseminating was lengthier for pastoral drama than it had been for the Ariostean model of comedy. From the ancients' fragmentarily defined and exemplified genre of satyr play and from Quattrocento *favole mitologiche* — Poliziano's *Orfeo* gestated during his sojourn among humanists in Venice, Ferrara, and Mantova, and Niccolò da Correggio's *Cefalo* followed in Ferrara in 1487 — the Estense theater culture developed the Arcadian play, the *favola satirica, silvestre, boscareccia,* and the *tragicommedia pastorale.*

Giraldi's *Egle, satira,* dedicated to Ercole II and performed in 1545 for him and Cardinal Ippolito in Giraldi's house, though rejected as a specific model by subsequent pastoral dramatists, was recognized as the opening of a new theatrical phase. Giraldi applied evolving neoclassical theory to fashion a modern satyr play: five acts in hendecasyllable verse about some satyrs' attempted gang rape of nymphs who elude them by turning into plants, concluding with a moral:

> Non si dee desiar cosa, che neghi
> Il ciel, ne cosa a l'honestà contraria;
> Che non sen puo veder felice fine. (5, Choro)[8]
>
> [One must not desire that which heaven forbids or that which is contrary to chastity; from this no happy outcome can be foreseen.]

The pastoral wave of the next decades is sometimes interpreted as a predictable expression of the climate of Alfonso II's reign: aesthetic and enervated, quaking at the looming specters of the Inquisition and the Papal States, holding back the grim dawn, drowning out the thunder of impending devolution with Arcadian music, escapist, elitist, exquisite. In the many Ferrarese places of delight, in palaces and those gardens which Gianni Venturi has described as "tramite necessario tra paesaggio e città, luogo di contemplazione estetica e di forza politica insieme" [necessary connection between landscape and city, a place of both aesthetic contemplation and political power],[9] the pastoral experiments multiplied: in 1563

---

[8] Quotation from the Folger Library copy of the original edition, Giambattista Cinzio Giraldi, *Egle: satira* (Florence: n.p., 1550?).

[9] Gianni Venturi, "Scene e giardini a Ferrara," in *Il rinascimento nelle corti padane: Società e cultura* (Bari: De Donato, 1977), 553.

Alberto Lollio's *Aretusa* at Schifanoia for Alfonso II and Cardinal Luigi, financed by "scolari delle leggi"; in 1567 Agostino Argenti's *Sfortunato* for Cardinal Luigi, also paid for by the university. This phase culminated in the *Aminta* of 1573, directed by Tasso himself in the gardens of the Isoletta di Belvedere del Po, with the professional company of Zan Battista Boschetti; it would become a standard repertory piece for the renowned Gelosi troupe. The permutations of the *favola boscareccia* now grew numberless and ubiquitous, and the Este court saw a steady stream of them. Giovanni Da Pozzo regards their proliferation as no longer dependent on ducal initiative: at this point in Ferrarese artistic production, he writes, "il genio originario locale non ha bisogno di essere incentivato, continua da solo, per sua forza di riproduzione" [native local spirit needs no incentive, continues by itself, through its own reproductive power].[10]

But certainly the mature pastoral drama reflects the climate of Alfonso II's reign, although I think both are susceptible of a more searching reading. True, these plays supplied the demand for sophisticated recreations in gardens and offered theatrical mirrors at which the Este courtiers preened themselves and spied on one another, but that the pastoral play could accommodate more than gossamer and gossipy court-masquerade is clear, on the one hand from the fact of its easy fusion with popular forms of comedy and its success on the playbills of commercial troupes, and on the other from the Aristotelian debates that Guarini's *Pastor fido* nourished and the philosophical and religious content that could be dramatized in this form. The intellectual atmosphere at Ferrara was, after all, charged with the spirit of inquiry into dramatic theory and into questions of orthodoxy and heresy, moved by reforming and synthesizing impulses toward Catholic unity, and in the 1580s and 1590s the capacity of the pastoral for such content was increasingly manifested. The pastoral play filled a need for a structure of hope, a scene out of time, court, and city, as a landscape of the mind allowing representation of fantasy and of otherwise invisible "realities" of life, primarily the internal psychological scene of the heart and the external design of a divine providential plan.[11]

Guarini's super-*contaminatio* of Sophocles, Tasso, and the Old Testament, and the many *trattati* concerning it all germinated in Ferrara's pastoral plantation. Angelo Ingegneri, himself the author of *Danza di Venere, pastorale,* published

---

[10] Giovanni Da Pozzo, *L'ambigua armonia: Studio sull' 'Aminta' del Tasso* (Florence: Olschki, 1983), 26.

[11] These general premises are developed at length in Louise George Clubb, *Italian Drama in Shakespeare's Time* (New Haven: Yale University Press, 1989), chaps. 4–6; and eadem, "Pastoral Elasticity on the Italian Stage and Page," in *The Pastoral Landscape,* ed. J. D. Hunt (Washington, DC: National Gallery of Art, 1992), 110–27.

his *Della poesia rappresentativa* there in 1598, and Cesare Cremonini, university professor and *oratore di stato* until 1590, dedicated *Le pompe funebri, overo Aminta e Clori, favola silvestre* to Alfonso and printed it in Ferrara that year. At the end of the decade Cremonini would pronounce Alfonso's funeral oration and would also speak the welcome to Clement VIII on his triumphant arrival the following year.[12] In 1590 Cremonini had not yet been investigated for heresy by the Inquisition, but he was already a free-thinking philosopher to watch, and his pastoral play is an intellectually weighty excursus on religion, nature, and society served up playfully with echoes of Giraldi and Tasso. Using the genre that was the most Ferrarese of all Renaissance theatrical products, he celebrated its famous practitioners and dramatized the city as a new Athens by propounding philosophical principles in pastoral terms.[13]

VII

Approaches to Italian Cinquecento tragedy — Bruscagli's to Giraldi's returns to mind[14] — provide clues to the celebratory intentions of representations of ruling-class ethos and to the fault-lines beneath their surfaces. Comedy also was used politically to celebrate and, less often, to advise. Sforza Oddi's "court comedy," *Prigione d'amore,*[15] set in the environs of the Este dungeons and treating the loves of courtiers under the aegis of the benign but exacting *duchi* in the castle above, is a case of heavily pro-establishment propaganda (with perhaps a titillating echo of the unforgotten scandal of the first Alfonso's keeping his treacherous kinsmen in the very same prison, or even, depending on the date of composition, a suggestion of Tasso's incarceration at Sant'Anna). This comedy, *not* a Ferrarese one, rests upon an idea of Ferrara as an appropriate setting for *commedia grave,* a genre originally bourgeois but gradually opened up to treat subjects of moral elevation and romantic exaltation, without loss of laughter, and to present characters of somewhat higher social standing — in this case minor courtiers, a pair of refined and musical boy-girl twins and their friends and lovers,

---

[12] Elvira Garbero-Zorzi and Daniele Seragnoli, "Lo Studio e lo spettacolo in Ferrara estense," in *La rinascita del sapere: Libri e maestri dello studio ferrarese*, ed. Patrizia Castelli (Venice: Marsilio, 1991), 307–28; see 308 and 316.

[13] See Clubb, "Pastoral Elasticity, " 115–16.

[14] See note 7.

[15] Sforza Oddi, *Prigione d'amore, commedia . . . recitata in Pisa da scolari l'anno secondo del felice Rettorato del S. Lelio Gavardo Asolano* (Fiorenza: Filippo Giunti, 1592). The work was first printed in 1590, colophon 1589, and was written some years earlier.

summoned by the duke from Padua, Mantua, and Bologna to contribute their talents to the superior culture of Ferrara. The city is represented as a place where private actions, disguises, and dramatic gestures, fine points of honor, emotional conflicts, and glamorous attitudes were at home, carried out in the middle of town, watched by the entire municipality, and watched over by the benevolent *duchi,* powerful spectators whose displeasure at an act of apparent *lèse majesté* is the threat that moves the action but who interfere with it only to seal and applaud its happy ending.

Oddi, a Perugian jurist, was an ideologue for the reformed stage, and wrote *Prigione d'amore* not *for* Ferrara but *about* Ferrara because of what its theatrical image in the late Cinquecento contributed to the thematic design of his play. The Ferrara setting provided an atmosphere of guaranteed law and order, absolute but just and responsive to chivalrous gestures and popular humors, combined with courtly elegance and leisure, compassionate paternalism, and a social scene that was simultaneously intimate and hierarchical — a Counter-Reformation utopia, but with room for irony. Changes in the "moralità" (we remember that at its first performance Ariosto's *Suppositi* was praised as "moderna tuta deletevole e piena de moralità" [modern, thoroughly delightful, and filled with moral lessons])[16] expected of comedy may be illustrated by contrast with *Suppositi* and its ethos of the laughing sodomite — Ariosto had laced his comedies with this topos jestingly, as had Aretino and other *commediografi* of the earlier Cinquecento. But when it came to rearing his son, Ariosto's strictures to Bembo in *Satira VI* on choosing a tutor looked forward rather to Oddi, whose comedy makes a pointed condemnation of homosexuality. This is communicated in *Prigione d'amore* through comic theatergrams — quarrels between a clownish underling named Grillo and a Latin pedant, misunderstandings arising from eavesdropping and cross-dressing — but the lesson is no less grave for that. Grillo's horror at the idea of forbidden love, "cose brutte" [ugly things] (3.4.5) or "vizio" [vice] (5.5), between Lelio and Flamminio, with hellfire as its consequence, reflects a serious ethical shift in regular comedy.

VIII

The first play performed in Ferrara after the devolution, by command of the pope's cardinal-legate and nephew Pietro Aldobrandini, was a Jesuit sacred

---

[16] Guido Davico Bonino, ed., *Il teatro italiano. II. La commedia del Cinquecento*, 2 vols. (Turin: Einaudi, 1977–78), 1:415, quoted from Catalano, *Vita*, 2:88.

tragedy on Judith and Holofernes played by students in the Castello in 1598,[17] a choice of entertainment usually interpreted as a complete break with the past and a recipe for the future. Sacred drama, however, although not the most characteristic feature of the Ferrarese theatrical tradition, was nevertheless part of it from Borso's time and thereafter: witness the Good Friday Passion played before Ercole I in Piazza Duomo. During the reign of Alfonso II as well, the flourishing Counter-Reformation genre of *tragedia sacra* was used to stage Ferrara, as I propose to demonstrate by revisiting a text that I have presented heretofore only in the context of the career of Galileo's rival, the Neapolitan "mago" and dramatist Giambattista Della Porta.[18]

Unlike Sforza Oddi, Della Porta was no ideologue, nor was his pen generally for hire, but he used it for more than one purpose. He always referred to his plays as *scherzi* — of youth or of leisure — and although we recognize this stance as a conventional topos, it is obvious that what he held to be serious was his incessant investigation of the physical world; call it science or magic, his life's work was among the secrets of nature. His plays stemmed from various causes, but it may be conjectured that he reserved for them the task of cushioning his scientific career against unyielding contexts or of demonstrating his orthodoxy. He must often have felt his safety threatened by his other works, so diverse were their directions, and potentially so suspect in an era of programmed reunification and reconsolidation of Catholic power over the acquisition of knowledge, and the Neapolitan Inquisition once enjoined him to leave off predicting the future and write plays instead.

Della Porta reputedly wrote three sacred dramas, but the only one known among his seventeen extant plays is *Il Georgio,* printed in 1611.[19] Labeled "tragedia" and proceeding by means of familiar combinations of characters and events of the favored neoclassical kind, compact of such Oedipal commonplaces as a kingdom under a curse and a mysterious oracle, together with the Agamemnonian elements of the sacrificing of a royal maiden to her father's

---

[17] Bonner Mitchell, *1598: A Year of Pageantry in Renaissance Ferrara*, MRTS 71 (Binghamton, NY: Medieval and Renaissance Texts and Studies, 1990), 41 and [130], [C3 verso] of Facsimile V, *Relatione dell'entrata solenne fatta in Ferrara a dì 13 di November 1598* (Roma: Nicolò Mutij, 1598).

[18] Louise George Clubb, "Ideologia e politica nel teatro dellaportiano," *Lettere Italiane* 3 (1987): 329–45.

[19] Giovanni Battista Della Porta, *Il Georgio, tragedia* (Naples: Gio. Battista Gargano & Lucretio Nucci, 1611). My quotations are from Giovanni Battista Della Porta, *Teatro, I. Le tragedie*, ed. Raffaele Sirri, Pubblicazioni della Sezione romanza (Napoli: Istituto Universitario Orientale, 1978).

ambition and the society's safety, the action disposed according to the supposedly Aristotelian unities and by means of encounters with messengers, narrating counselors, chorus and semi-chorus, *Il Georgio* turns out in the final analysis to be *San Giorgio, tragedia sacra,* or *tragedia di fin lieto* in the manner of Giraldi — in short, *tragicommedia*. Capping and redirecting the *contaminatio* of classical motives is the familiar story (known in the *Legenda Aurea* and the old popular *sacre rappresentazioni)* of the Cappadocian warrior St. George and the dragon and of how the holy "cappadoco duce" (5.3.478) or "cavalier di Cristo" (5.1.134), as Della Porta calls him, saves a king's daughter and converts the realm to Christianity — in this version not one but two realms, for a Moroccan king, a knight errant, passes by on a quest for his destined bride and, with Georgio's backing, gains both the princess and a new religion to take home to his people.

The action assigned to the holy hero is a prescribed miracle performed by what might be called a *machina ex Deo,* while that of the princess and her royal lover is an episode from a *romanzo cavalleresco;* what classically *tragic* action there is belongs to the king caught in a crossfire of conflicting duties, ambition and affections. His position is carefully made morally perplexing: the *antefatto* is narrated to emphasize that he is historically responsible for the continuing disaster in his state and for the toll it now threatens to take in his own family. At the time when the dragon first began devouring the populace, there arose a motion to disperse, but the king, desiring to maintain his power, persuaded his subjects to stay together and agreed to uphold a law destining victims drawn by lot to appease the dragon (1.1.153–156; 1.2.322–330). Now that the lot has fallen to his only child, the king claims to be above the law:

Dunque, il popol co 'l re concorrer deve?
e commun sia la sorte all'uno e all'altro?
E qual distinzion sarebbe mai
tra 'l popolo e 'l suo regge, s'alla legge
fusse l'un sottoposto come l'altro? (1.2.308–312)

[So, must the people and the king equally compete?
can they share a common lot?
Then what distinction would there be
between people and ruler
were they alike subject to the law?]

Della Porta designs a government more complex than a mere despotism: this kingdom includes a Senate and a Prefetto *vox populi,* with ideas about the uses of power, laws, and political responsibilities. The king opposes the populace;

their response is to take the law into their own hands and seize the princess. He sends his secretary of state to persuade the Senate that kings are not subject to the common lot and should not be deprived of their daughters. The answer he receives from a senator is the standard topos of advice to princes:

> vinci te stesso, e l'ira che ti bolle
> intorno 'l cor intiepidisci e molci,
> e soffri di fortuna il duro colpo.
> Ché non convien a un re che gli altri regge
> esser d'un cuor sì tenero. . . . (1.2.420–424)
>
> [conquer yourself, cool down and soften that rage that boils in your heart, and bear the hard blow of fortune. For it is unseemly in a king who rules others to be so tenderhearted. . . .]

Like Oedipus Rex, this king must recognize that he has contributed to the curse on his realm and must face the consequences of his past mistake; like Agamemnon in *Iphigenia in Aulis,* he determines to deceive his wife and sacrifice their daughter for the sake of the state and of his own power.

By the end of the third act there has been no sign of the titular hero of the play or of a brake on the inevitable tragic movement downward to general woe. Both king and people are presented as being in the wrong, they to rebel seditiously against his power, he to abuse it and set himself above the law. Both are also in the right, he to oppose human sacrifice, they to demand justice and equality before the law. Attempts by the queen, the courtiers, and the royal Moroccan visitor to save the princess having failed, she is led away to be fed to the dragon, like the classical Andromeda and Hesione, like Ariosto's Angelica and Olimpia, and like all the maidens in all the versions of the St. George legend. Everyone is wrapped in error and doomed to suffer the consequences of the unmitigated human condition. At this pass a reconciliation between ruler and people would not save the future victims required by the law, and even the best humanistic advice to princes is useless.

Only a higher power can help, and in the middle of the chorus following the third act, the play shifts from pagan tragic into Christian comic gear. The error of belief in fate is unmasked, the Redeemer, "cavalier istrano e d'altra legge" [foreign knight of another law] (1.1.190), of the oracle is announced, and Georgio appears in the fourth act, stopping off on his way to missionary work in the Indies, a kind of lay Jesuit (a condition actually assumed by Della Porta himself after his reprimand by the Inquisition). After Georgio's miraculous rescue of the princess, a political accord is achieved together with a mass conversion

(5.5.667–690; 733–741). At first reading, Georgio's entrance suggests a naive awkwardness in Della Porta's dramaturgy: a chorus in six stanzas, the first three in classical accents, lamenting the inescapability of fate, the last three denying the premises just stated and substituting for them an enunciation of the doctrine of human free will and a rejection of any idea of fate or predestination except the providence of a divinity that guarantees that freedom. The lack of modulation, the sudden grafting of a Christian resolution onto a classical conflict might well appear both illogical and indecorous.

It does not make *Georgio* seem necessarily a better play but indubitably a more complex and communicative one to recognize, rather, that its startling generic juxtapositions and conflations are akin to the calculated assonances at work in otherwise dissimilar theatrical structures of these years. Change of genre could be a flaunting of technical versatility or a theatrical sign of a profound change of dispensation.

Both the general advice to princes and the representation of the sterility equally of good and evil intentions, absent the enlightenment and blessing of Christianity, which are intrinsic to the plot of *Georgio*, would have been suitable generalities for performance or reading at any school, academy, or court of the epoch. As it issued from the press the tragedy was dedicated to the Neapolitan Ferrante Rovito, but I think it was originally intended for another recipient, Cardinale Luigi d'Este, the patron whose circle Della Porta frequented in Ferrara and Rome between 1579 and 1581 and for whom he undertook experiments in optics and lens-making in Venice, assisted by the glassworkers of Murano. The cardinal also wanted plays for court performance and Della Porta furnished him with at least two, perhaps more.[20]

The tragedy of *Georgio* is full of marks of deference to Ferrarese culture; even the choice of the *tragedia di fin lieto* as a mold for casting this conflation of classical and chivalric motifs points to Giraldi. But the strongest indication is the choice of George as a subject. Della Porta's two other saints' plays, on the virgin martyrs Dorotea and Eugenia, are lost, known to us by name only. In the portrayal of a *cavaliere errante,* in a setting embellishing the popular hagiographical version with "armi e amori" from the chivalric epic genre, theatergrams from classical tragedy, and discussions of the duties of rulers and subjects, *Georgio* is an image of Este power that functions without explicit parallels drawn by the playwright; it is enough to know, as anyone likely to see the text in the 1580s would have known, that George was the patron saint of Ferrara and of the city's Estensi lords.

---

[20] See Louise George Clubb, *Giambattista Della Porta, Dramatist* (Princeton: Princeton University Press, 1965), 19–22.

Clement VIII also may have had this in mind in 1593 when he created his nephew Cinzio Aldobrandini Cardinale di San Giorgio in Velabro. The cardinal's cultivation of Ferrarese intellectuals and writers involved not only his well-known protection of Tasso in the 1590s but patronage also of Guarini and Ingegneri. In the event it was the other nephew, Pietro, who became papal legate of Ferrara, but Clement had not yet decided that in 1593. When he entered the city to take possession in May 1598, Cinzio and Pietro flanked him; the trio spent the night at the monastery of San Giorgio, then crossed the bridge by the Porta San Giorgio to proceed to the Duomo dedicated to San Giorgio and thence to the Castello.[21]

Even if no immediate references are posited, the total charge of *Georgio, tragedia* is complex. Della Porta transforms the commonplaces of classical tragedy of fate, within classicizing rules, into a Christian spectacle of providence. He depicts an ideal adjustment in the relation of ruler to subjects and to God by presenting a conflict and its resolution in terms familiar to the humanistic tradition of advice to princes (the same terms, incidentally or not, that Machiavelli presupposed as objects of subversion and that Counter-Reformation policy aimed to revalidate). Simultaneously he re-presents Christian redemption in his peripety and denouement: Georgio is insistently portrayed as a Messianic figure, his coming obscurely prophesied, who fights the dragon a mystical three times, calling on divine power to defeat it at last, not killing but temporarily subduing and sending back to the abyss the "orco," identified at last as a rebel "angiol dell'inferno" (5.3.468).[22]

As a celebration of a political patron, however, the play is still more subtly complex. It adds to the large number of representations in art, pictorial and literary, of the Ferrarese patron saint, in whom appears a combination of the chivalric attitudes and trappings long and insistently appropriated by the Este court with suggestions of both Christ and Michael the Archangel, functioning as Christian improvements on and fulfillments of the various classical ancestries and affinities claimed for the Estensi by their poets, not only in the artificial Trojan genealogy concocted by Boiardo but also in numerous thematically associative allusions to Perseus, to Hercules, and so on. Just as in the *Orlando Furioso* Ruggiero's and Orlando's performance of the Perseus action of rescuing a princess from an *orca marina* (also featured in the classical Hercules myth) tacitly unites them as Este heroes under the ensign of St. George; and as in the

---

[21] Mitchell, *A Year of Pageantry*, [A3–A4 verso] of Facsimile II, Felicissima Entrata di N.S PP Clemente VIII. nell'Inclita Città di Ferrara.

[22] The Saint George of the *Legenda Aurea* and the Quattrocento *sacre rappresentazioni* fights the dragon only once and kills it; Della Porta's Georgio, however, is related to the Archangel Michael and also resembles Spenser's figure of St. George the Redcrosse Knight in *The Faerie Queene* I.xi.

Gerusalemme Liberata, in addition to the ancestral hero Rinaldo, the African warrior princess Clorinda also is claimed for the Estes, having been born white by virtue of the prenatal influence of St. George (Patron of Ethiopia) on her Ethiopian mother; so in Della Porta's tragedy the first chorus, in the pagan and "tragic" part of the tragicomedy of conversion, prays for help against the dragon to Hercules the Hydra-killer:

> cala giú dal cielo
> o vincitor de mostri, . . .
> l'Idra, mirabil angue . . . uccidesti. . . .
> Vien, vincitor Alcide. . . . (I, Coro, 564–595)
>
> [descend from heaven, O conqueror of monsters . . . you killed the Hydra, awesome serpent. . . . Come, victor (Hercules) Alcides]

and with that invocation links the Este name of Ercole to Perseus and his Christian metamorph George and sets the stage for the Christian answer to a classical pagan prayer, for the Christian "comic" denouement to a classical pagan tragedy.

The date of *Georgio* is uncertain. The 1610 dedication to Rovito states vaguely that it was written "anni a dietro" ["years ago"].[23] If Della Porta originally drafted this play while he was in Este service, there was a lapse of some thirty years between composition and publication. We know, however, that many of his plays were written long before he published any, the first not appearing until 1589, when he was in his fifties. The subject of the knightly saint is unique in his theater and lends credence to the assumption that he chose it while employed by Cardinal Luigi and as a compliment to his patron, at a time when the Estensi still ruled in Ferrara and hoped for continuance, but that he published it thirteen years after those hopes were definitively quashed. It is possible, of course, that if *Georgio* was written around 1580 it may originally have contained partisan pro-Este sections which had to be excised in 1610, but this is unlikely, considering that Della Porta had had his troubles with the Inquisition before 1579 and that everything else in his career suggests that these made him careful to keep on good terms with the Vatican.

If the play in its only extant form was written while the Estensi were in power, it constitutes a triumph of ambiguity. In the act of depicting a fallible ruler who

---

[23] The manuscript sent to the censor in this year is indubitably the basis for the printing by Gargano and Nucci in Naples, 1611. Also see Clubb, *Giambattista Della Porta*, 62–63 and 101–21.

needs divine help, Della Porta celebrates the Estes through the redemptive deeds of their *santo protettore,* and does so at a moment when the family was obsessed with maintaining its hold on Ferrara, when the brother of Della Porta's patron had already contracted three marriages in hopes of an heir. Meanwhile the Vatican waited for the reversion of the city to the Holy See, as ultimately came about on the death without issue in 1597 of Alfonso II, when the Estense failure to obtain the right of succession in Ferrara forced his cousin Cesare d'Este to move the court to the family duchy of Modena.

In the absence of an earlier version substantially different from the printed *Georgio* of 1611, if we assume that the work was drafted for the Estensi between 1579 and 1581 and regard it as a patronage play, we find that it manages to serve two parties without commitment to the politics of either. *Georgio* can be read as divine providential confirmation and reformation of an existing government, but in a non-partisan way unobjectionable either to the Estes or to the papacy. In 1611 Georgio's conversion of the city could even have been equated with the devolution; the rescued princess is the king's only child and, as she presumably accompanies her new husband to Morocco (or Modena?), her father's dynasty would end in her homeland, now become a Christian state, whatever its form of government. In any case, once Ferrara was under the rule of a papal legate, the name of *Georgio* sounded no echo of dissent; perhaps as a knight George was identified with the Estes but, despite their efforts to claim him entirely, as a saint he belonged to the Church. Only in the late twentieth century would St. George be disavowed as uncanonical, the last of the Estensi to be dispossessed by Rome.

IX

I have mentioned the opinion that by the time of Alfonso II theater in Ferrara had become a municipal activity not requiring a ducal drive. After the dynasty's end, the year of the devolution was marked by theatrical pageantry, connoting union of church and state. Thereafter, *tornei,* horse ballets, and the developing music drama still held a place in municipal life, limited and directed by the policies of the new government, which relied on university circles for suitable texts.[24]

The Estes' claim on the iconic action associating them with Perseus and St. George was now disputed, as may be illustrated by a brief consideration of the musician and poet Benedetto Ferrari's *Andromeda . . . rappresentata in musica* (1637), the first of the Venetian commercial opera *libretti,* and the *Andromeda . . .*

---

[24] Paolo Fabbri, "Ferrara: Musica e Università," in *La rinascita del sapere: Libri e maestri dello studio ferrarese*, ed. Castelli, 331–32.

cantata e combattuta in Ferrara (1638) of Ascanio Pio, a Riformatore of the University of Ferrara .[25]

Although Ferrari's choice of subject, like that of his *Armida* two years later, may have originated in the remaining Estense duchy, where he was born in Reggio and died in Modena, his treatment of the myth has no Ferrarese connections, aside from some verbal echoes of Ariosto; rather, its representation of a sea rescue contributed to the Accademia degli Incogniti's campaign to glorify Venice.[26]

Pio's *Andromeda,* on the other hand, is concentrated on Ferrara and represents the new regime's determination to appropriate Estense imagery for the Papal States. First adducing a superabundance of reasons for staging this "festa" — the post-nuptial visit to Ferrara of Costanza Sforza and Cornelio Bentivoglio, the carnival season, the desire of the Ferrarese nobility to offer a special "segno di divozione" to Cardinal-Legate Ciriacco Rocci and because public theatrical productions "paiono proprie, ed innate a questa Città" [seem to belong innately to this city],[27] a commentary provides complete coverage of the production, describing the scenes and machinery, the music, dances, and choreographed skirmishes and "Euclidian" martial formations, and their effect on the spectators, narrating the plot and reproducing the *libretto,* which ends with Giove's confirmation of Perseo as his son, destined to rescue Andromeda and to rule. The father of the gods then concludes the occasion by revealing its primary cause in direct address to the three cardinals in the audience:

> Voi purpurati Eroi, ch'al Ciel Romano
> Sin dal Reno, e dal Po lume accrescete,
> E con l'opre magnanime rendete
> Di novo glorie adorno il Vaticano.[28]

> [You scarlet-robed heroes who brighten the Roman sky even from the Reno and the Po, and by your magnanimous works adorn the Vatican anew with glories.]

---

[25] Benedetto Ferrari, *L'Andromeda del Signor Benedetto Ferrari Rappresentata in Musica in Venetia l'anno 1637* (Venice: Antonio Bariletti, 1637); Ascanio Pio, *L'Andromeda di d. Ascanio Pio di Savoia; cantata e combattuta in Ferrara al carnevale dell'anno 1638* (Ferrara: Francesco Suzzi, 1639). Though printed in 1639, Pio's play was performed in 1638.

[26] Ellen Rosand, *Opera in Seventeenth-Century Venice: The Creation of a Genre* (Berkeley: University of California Press, 1991), 140–41.

[27] Pio, *Andromeda*, A–A2, 1–3.

[28] Pio, *Andromeda*, 125.

The spectacular machinery for the production was designed by Francesco Guitti, celebrated especially for his successes in Rome under the auspices of the Barberini papacy, and the Vatican doubtless paid the bill for this Ferrarese *Andromeda*.

Although not formally divided into five acts, the action has five phases and is longer and more intricate than the plot of Ferrari's Venetian *Andromeda*; the unities and other conventions of high tragedy are observed; and the text, too complex to be grasped through song alone, is obviously designed for reading as well. St. George and the Estes' epic heroes Ruggiero and Orlando are not alluded to, and the allegory is set forth in purely classical terms: Andromeda is Ferrara, Perseo her divinely-appointed rescuer and spouse. With a tinge of classical authority, Pio clinches the political allegory by the addition of a plot which unfolds after the rescue: Andromeda's uncle Fineo claims hereditary right to her hand and kingdom, challenges Perseo, and is defeated in a combat of seven against seven (the winning team clad all in white, the papal non-color). Perseo uses the Medusa's head to petrify Fineo, who thus joins the former Este rulers of Ferrara as a stone monument to the past.

In the same year that saw the production of *Andromeda* Pio also wrote *Ferrara trionfante,* the *libretto* for an elaborate open-air "festa" for the coronation of the Blessed Virgin of the Rosary, published twenty-four years later while the late author's son was bishop of Ferrara.[29] Presenting the rediscovered designs and description of the distant occasion, Giovanni Bascarini explained that the sacred "pompa" was inspired by municipal satiety even to the point of nausea with spectacles of chivalry, which had long and frequently filled the theaters and public spaces with "profane materie." These had earned for Ferrara superlative fame for arms and letters, but finally there prevailed a desire for nobler subjects: "quando collo sfoggio estremo della magnificenza le profane materie cominciarono à venir meno, & à nauseare l'appagata curiosità de Cavalieri, e de Cittadini: si mossero muse più solevate in traccia di soggetti più riguardevoli, e più eroici."[30]

Bascarini leaves no doubt that although spectacles and music drama on mythological subjects did not die out, Ferrarese theater dwindled after Estense rule ceased. If papal Rome was a great theater center in the seventeenth century, papal Ferrara was not. What was left of the Estes' staged Ferrara was in printed texts and in memories, a glorious "Ferrara palcoscenico" that went on — and goes on — playing in the mind.

---

[29] Ascanio Pio, *Ferrara trionfante per la coronazione dell B.ma Vergine del Rosario celebrata l'anno 1638. Con aparato di teatro, di machine, e di musica* (Ferrara: Per gl'heredi del Suzzi, 1662).

[30] Pio, *Ferrara trionfante*, 12.

The Debate Between Arms and Letters in the *Gerusalemme Liberata*

David Quint

It is well known that Tasso suppressed an episode that would have appeared in Canto 8 of the *Gerusalemme liberata*.[1] The Danish soldier Carlo has brought to the camp of the crusader army the sword of his slain prince Sveno, its blade indelibly stained by the blood of the infidel enemy. The bloodstain is, in fact, a kind of test: it will disappear only when the sword is picked up by its rightful new owner, the destined avenger of Sveno. Goffredo and then Raimondo are the first to try their hands at this "ventura," but the sword does not come clean; they realize that it is reserved for another — "ch'altrui si riserbava." This someone else, Carlo surmises, is probably the absent Rinaldo, whom Sveno had himself emulated and at whose side he had wanted to fight.

> Ahi! qual stata saria la coppia ardita
> s'era d'amor tanta virtude unita? —[2]
>
> [Alas, what daring couple would they have made,
> had so much valor been united by love?]

[1] The passage is reprinted by Lanfranco Caretti as an appendix to his edition of the *Gerusalemme liberata*: Lanfranco Caretti, ed., *Gerusalemme liberata* (Milan: Mondadori, 1979), 598–99. It is discussed in Riccardo Bruscagli, *Stagioni della civiltà estense* (Pisa: Nistri-Lischi, 1983), 215–16; see also Lawrence Rhu, "From Aristotle to Allegory: Young Tasso's Evolving Vision of the *Gerusalemme liberata*," *Italica* 65 (1988): 111–30.

[2] Caretti, ed., *Gerusalemme liberata*, 599.

Tasso cut the episode of the sword from his epic, noting in a letter that "I fear that the adventure of the sword has the flavor of romance."[3] Indeed, the passage seems reminiscent of the sword-in-the-stone that declared the legitimacy of Arthur.

But Tasso had another reason to excise this story of warriors competing for the arms of a dead companion. He was removing from his poem a direct allusion to one of its controlling models: the debate between Ajax and Ulysses over who should inherit the arms of Achilles, as it is recounted by Ovid in *Metamorphoses* 13.1–383. Tasso doubly covered his tracks by dismissing the classically inspired episode as savoring of romance.

The Ovidian text provides, as we shall see, a virtual outline for the *Gerusalemme liberata*. It well might, since in their respective speeches Ajax and Ulysses each recall episodes from the *Iliad* and the Trojan war, the larger epic story on which Tasso based his account of the siege and conquest of Jerusalem. Nonetheless, the debate between Ajax and Ulysses has a privileged status among the literary models of the *Liberata*. If Tasso's normal practice of imitation is to combine together, through the practice of *contaminatio,* a series of predecessor texts in order to construct an episode, a scene, even an individual octave, in this case Ovid's passage affords him a single overarching source for much of the narrative material of his poem. Moreover, the rivalry between the hero of intellect, Ulysses, and the hero of force, Ajax, provides the ideological model for Tasso's opposition of Goffredo and Rinaldo. At the heart of the *Liberata* is an uncertainty about which of these two heroes — and which of their respective kinds of heroism — is to be preferred, and this uncertainty, in turn, reflects a wide-ranging debate in sixteenth-century elite culture that was contained under the shorthand title of arms versus letters — a debate that had newly become topical in Tasso's Ferrara as the Estense duchy sought to assert its precedence over Medicean Florence. If I start by examining Tasso's imitations of Ovid, I want to show how, through these imitations, the *Liberata* and its poet are drawn into the larger preoccupations of late Renaissance culture.

In the contention over the arms of Achilles in *Metamorphoses* 13, Ovid's Ajax considers himself the obvious heir: he is related by blood to Achilles (30–31), and he is acknowledged to be the second champion of the Greek army. Ulysses, however, wins the day through his eloquence — "the skilled speaker took the arms of the strong man" (fortisque viri tulit arma disertus) (383) — and the

---

[3] "... la ventura de la spada dubito che senta del romanzo": letter to Luca Scalabrino, 24 May, 1575: Cesare Guasti, ed., *Le lettere di Torquato Tasso*, 5 vols. (Florence: F. Le Monnier, 1852–1855), 1:81.

dismayed Ajax commits suicide.[4] Ulysses claims an equally noble family as that of Ajax, tracing his genealogy back to the gods (141–147). But he also argues that the deeds of one's ancestors do not belong to oneself, and he bases his claim solely on his own exploits (140–141; 159–161). He displays the wounds he has suffered during the war (262–265), and he lists the works and good offices he has done the Greek side. In the company of Diomede, he brought back the young disguised Achilles from the island of Scyros (162–180); he went out on the night-exploit, killed Dolon, and stole the horses of Rhesus (242–252); and, on another occasion, he stole the Palladium from Troy (336–349); in the company of Menelaus, he went as an ambassador to Troy (196–204; see *Iliad* 3.205–224). Each of these episodes has its imitation in the *Liberata*. The stealing of the Palladium has its counterpart in Canto 2 in the theft of the image of the Virgin Mary from the Jerusalem mosque, a theft for which first Sofronia and then her companion from the supposedly stronger sex, Olindo, claim responsibility (2.5–53). The embassy of Ulysses and Menelaus to Troy is paralleled by the visit of the ambassador Alete, accompanied by the warrior Argante, to Goffredo and the crusader camp in the same canto (57–97). The episode of the Doloneia is recalled in the night-exploit of Canto 12, where Clorinda, in the company of the same Argante, burns down the Crusader siege-towers (12.2–48).[5] The conveying of Achilles from Scyros, where the young hero has been disguised as a girl, has its corresponding episode in the rescue of Rinaldo from Armida's island by Ubaldo and Carlo, where Tasso closely follows the version of the story in the *Achilleid* of Statius.[6]

---

[4] Citations from the *Metamorphoses* are taken from Ovid, *Metamorphoses*, trans. Frank Justus Miller, 2 vols., Loeb Classical Library (Cambridge, MA: Harvard University Press, 1968).

[5] These episodes are, of course, contaminated by other epic models. The embassy of Alete and Argante to the Crusader camp concludes (2.89–90) with an imitation of the declaration of war by the Roman envoys, Publicola and Fabius, to the Carthaginian senate in the *Punica* of Silius Italicus (2.380f.). The *Punica* also contains a night-exploit (9.66–177) that is an important, if little noted, model for the duel between Clorinda and Tancredi; in the darkness, Solimus unwittingly kills his father Satricus, and then commits suicide in turn: so Tancredi unknowingly slays the woman he loves. The night-exploit has a long history in epic after the Doloneia: from the Nisus and Euryalus subplot of *Aeneid* 9 to the Cloridano and Medoro episode in the *Orlando furioso* (18.165f.); all of these episodes find echoes in Tasso's version. For a discussion of the epic night-exploit from Virgil to Ariosto, see Barbara Pavlock, *Eros, Imitation, and the Epic Tradition* (Ithaca: Cornell University Press, 1990).

[6] The parallels to the *Achilleid* are discussed in Beatrice Corrigan, "The Opposing Mirrors," *Italica* 33 (1956): 165–79.

The Ulyssean model in Ovid's text explains why the characters in these episodes of the *Liberata* work in pairs. Either a woman — Sofronia or Clorinda — or a figure of Ulyssean guile and experience — the eloquent Alete, "a l'ingannare accorto" (2.58) or Ubaldo, whose pursuit of "virtute e senno" (14.28) invokes the Dantean Ulysses[7] — is paired with a man or warrior — Olindo, Argante, Carlo:

Sofronia-Olindo
Alete-Argante
Clorinda-Argante
Ubaldo-Carlo
[Vafrino-Erminia]

The first of this series of Ulyssean figures, Sofronia, is linked by her name (prudence, self-control) to the wily Alete and Ubaldo, and suggests that the heroism of intelligence is itself an attribute of the "men forte sesso" (2.42). To this series, Tasso adds one more figure, going beyond the list of exploits enumerated by Ovid's Ulysses. In Canto 19, Vafrino, the clever squire of Tancredi who has been sent to spy on the pagan camp, is recognized through his disguise by Erminia (80f.); Erminia does not betray him and reveals that she has just designed the false insignia with which the pagan soldiers plan to disguise themselves and infiltrate the crusader ranks to kill Goffredo in the upcoming battle. The episode recalls the story that Helen tells in the *Odyssey* (4.235–264) of having recognized Ulysses without giving him away, when he came disguised as a beggar to spy on Troy.[8] Tasso's final version of the cunning Ulyssean

---

[7] Dante's Ulysses tells his men to pursue "virtute e canoscenza" (*Inferno* 26.120). On Ubaldo and Ulysses, see David Quint, *Epic and Empire: Politics and Generic Form From Virgil to Milton* (Princeton: Princeton University Press, 1993), 262; Matteo Residori, "Colombo e il *volo* di Ulisse: una nota sul XV della *Liberata*," *Annali della Scuola Normale Superiore di Pisa, Classe di Lettere e Filosofia* 22 (1992): 931–42.

[8] In her exchange with Vafrino, Erminia once again takes up the epic role of Helen that she has earlier played in Canto 3, where she pointed out the leading Crusader soldiers to King Aladino (17–20; 37–40; 58–63) in a scene that recalls Helen's conversation with Priam about the Greek host, the *teichoskopia* of *Iliad* 3.161f. In her designing or making the false insignia, Erminia is also like the Helen who is first seen weaving a robe depicting the events of the Trojan War in *Iliad* 3.125f. and also like Helen's antithesis in the *Odyssey*, the weaving Penelope, who, for all of her faithfulness, nonetheless shares with Helen a feminine craftiness that matches the wits of her husband, Ulysses. On the scene in *Odyssey* 4 and Helen's duplicity, see William S. Anderson, "Calypso and Elysium," *Classical Journal* 54 (1958): 2–11; Mihoko Suzuki, *Metamorphoses of Helen: Authority, Difference, and the Epic* (Ithaca: Cornell University Press, 1989), 67–70.

figure — Vafrino's name means "tricky" — meets his match in an equally crafty woman.

Tasso's poem repeatedly pairs a figure of intellect and/or feminine guile working together with a figure of masculine force — a Ulysses with a Diomede or a Menelaus — in order to comment on the central heroic pairing of the *Liberata,* the commander-in-chief Goffredo with his lead warrior Rinaldo.[9] The action of the epic requires the cooperation of the two heroes that is achieved only when Rinaldo returns from self-imposed exile and submits himself to the rule and direction of Goffredo: an obvious rewriting of the *Iliad* in which Rinaldo plays the role of an Achilles angry and then reconciled with Agamemnon. The proper relationship that is to obtain between the two is spelled out to the dreaming Goffredo by the divine mouthpiece Ugone: "tu sei capo, ei mano / di questo campo" (14.13.6–7), that is, the hero of intelligence should direct the actions of the hero of force. Rinaldo is similarly instructed to let his fighting ardor be guided by the "senno" of Goffredo (17.63.5–8).

This is the same relationship of dependence that Ovid's Ulysses argues that Ajax bears to him and that is the ground of his superiority to his rival.

> tibi dextera bello
> utilis, ingenium est, quod eget moderamine nostro;
> tu vires sine mente geris, mihi cura futuri;
> tu pugnare potes, pugnandi tempora mecum
> eligit Atrides; tu tantum corpore prodes,
> nos animo; quantoque ratem qui temperat, anteit
> remigis officium, quanto dux milite maior,
> tantum ego te supero. . . . (13.361–368)

[Your good right arm is useful in the battle; but when it comes to thinking you need my guidance. You have force without intelligence; while mine is the care for to-morrow. You are a good fighter; but it is I who help Atrides select the time of fighting. Your value is in your body only; mine in mind. And, as he who directs the ship surpasses him who only rows it, as much as the general excels the common soldier, so much greater am I than you.]

---

[9] In his dialogue *Il Manso ovvero de l'amicizia,* Tasso offers a gloss on the relationship of Ulysses and Diomede that may also describe the heroic coupling of Goffredo and Rinaldo in his own epic: ". . . i poeti antichi congiunsero ne' pericoli Ulisse e Diomede affinché la prudenza de l'uno aiutasse l'altro e vicendevolmente ricevesse aiuto da la fortezza de l'altro": Torquato Tasso, *Opere*, ed. Bruno Maier (Milan: Rizzoli, 1965), 5:358–69. All citations of the *Liberata* and from Tasso's dialogues are taken from Maier's text.

Ulysses claims to be the master strategist of the Greek army and he virtually displaces Agamemnon as its general. Tasso makes Goffredo a combination of Agamemnon and Ulysses, but it is Ovid's Ulysses with whom he is identified from the third line of the *Liberata* — "Molto egli oprò co'l senno e con la mano" that recalls *Metamorphoses* 13 and Ulysses' vaunt of the deeds he has done "consilioque manuque" (205) for the Greek cause.[10] These deeds — his having fortified the Greek camp with trenches ("fossa munimima cingo" [212]), his having consoled his associates ("consolor socios" [213]), his having stopped the Greek rank and file from abandoning the war at Agamemnon's own ill-advised suggestion, and his putting down of Thersites (216–237) — find their parallels in the actions of Goffredo who has trenches dug around the Crusader tents ("le tende munite / e di fosse profonde e di trinciere" [3.66]), delivers a version of the "O socii" speech of Aeneas (5.90–92; cf. *Aeneid* 1.198–207) that consoles ("consola" [5.93.2]) his men,[11] and quells the popular rebellion of Argillano (8.76f). Tasso gives Goffredo further Ulyssean traits both in his immunity to the charms of Armida, who employs the arts of Circe and the voice of a siren to seduce his soldiers (4.86), and in his building of the siege machines that resemble the arch-stratagem of Ulysses, the Trojan horse.[12] It is then possible to view the relationship that Goffredo bears to Rinaldo in the *Liberata* not simply in terms of the Iliadic conflict between Agamemnon and Achilles — for Agamemnon, as Homer and Ovid's Ulysses make fairly clear, was not very bright. Goffredo is equally the poem's central Ulysses figure, and his opposition to the Achillean Rinaldo repeats a heroic contrast that belongs to the Homeric origins of epic itself.

---

[10] See Maier's notes to this passage in Tasso, *Opere*, 3: 9.

[11] Goffredo's actions most clearly repeat those of Aeneas (*Aeneid* 7.157–159; 1.198–203), whom Ovid may recall as well in these words of his Ulysses. But the "O socii" speech of Virgil's hero itself imitates the speech of Homer's Ulysses to his men at *Odyssey* 12.209f.; in turn, Dante, who did not know the *Odyssey,* would imitate the speech of Aeneas in the "orazion piccola" that *his* Ulysses uses to spur his men on into unknown seas (*Inferno* 26.112f.). By Tasso's arrival in the literary tradition, the eloquent, prudential dimension of Aeneas was thus easily recognized as Ulyssean: insofar as Goffredo is an Aeneas-like hero whose sphere of action is limited to that of commander and strategist he is also a kind of Ulysses; see below. On Dante's triangulation of Virgil and the Homer he could not read, see John Freccero, *Dante: The Poetics of Conversion* (Cambridge, MA: Harvard University Press, 1986), 140–45; David Thompson, *Dante's Epic Journeys* (Baltimore: Johns Hopkins University Press, 1974); Giuseppe Mazzotta, *Dante, Poet of the Desert: History and Allegory in the Divine Comedy* (Princeton: Princeton University Press, 1979), 89–90, 100–2.

[12] Compare the depiction of the siege machine at 18.45 and its model, the description by Virgil's Aeneas of the Trojan Horse at *Aeneid* 2.235f.

The Goffredo-Rinaldo relationship has a secondary version or reflection in the poem's association of Raimondo and Tancredi. Raimondo, the aging counselor figure who recalls Nestor,[13] is a kind of abstraction of the Ulyssean "senno" that Goffredo combines with martial prowess in his own person; Tancredi is second only to Rinaldo as military champion in the Crusader forces. The relationship of the four characters is summed up in a couplet spoken by Erminia about Goffredo in Canto 3.

> Sol Raimondo in consiglio, ed in battaglia
> sol Rinaldo e Tancredi a lui s'agguaglia. (3.58.7–8)
>
> [Only Raimondo in counsel, and in battle
> only Rinaldo and Tancredi are his equals.]

The relationship of Raimondo and Tancredi — a relationship of intellect to force — is also governed by the model of *Metamorphoses* 13, this time by Ajax's speech and side of the argument. In his claim to his right to the disputed arms, Ajax lists two of his exploits among others. Chosen by lot, he met Hector on the battlefield after Hector had challenged the Greek side to send out a champion to fight him in single combat (87–90), a battle, Ajax leaves his listeners to infer, that placed him on the same level as the Achilles who finally killed Hector. On another occasion, Ajax recalls, he had extended his great shield to protect none other than Ulysses himself when the latter found himself in distress on the battlefield (73–81; see *Iliad* 11.461f.). In the *Liberata,* Argante plays the role of Hector and issues a similar challenge to the Crusader army;[14] he is initially met

---

[13] The honey-tongued Nestor was traditionally paired with Ulysses on account of their eloquence. So Ovid's Ajax compares Ulysses to Nestor (13.63–65). See also Horace, *Odes* 1.15.21–22; Quintilian, *Inst.* 12.10.64–65; and, for Renaissance examples, Poliziano, *Manto* 23–24, referring to the oratory of Cicero, "pyliae non mella senectae / Nec jam dulichias audet conferre procellas"; and Shakespeare's Gloucester, the future Richard III, speaking of himself in *Henry VI, Part 3:* "I'll play the orator as well as Nestor / Deceive more slyly than Ulysses could" (3.2.188–189). Ovid, *Ars Amatoria* 2.736, juxtaposes the wisdom of Nestor with the might of Achilles. Tasso assigns Nestor's trait of honeyed eloquence to the ambassador Alete (2.61.5–6).

[14] In general, Argante plays out the role of Hector in the *Iliad,* while Solimano, the other male pagan champion, assumes that of Turnus in the *Aeneid*. Solimano the Turk, whose descendant will be Saladin — and perhaps will find another embodiment in Suleyman the Magnificent — has a historical dimension that Argante lacks and hence he is fitted out with a Virgilian typology as an enemy of Rome, modeled after Turnus and after the Hannibal of the *Punica* of Silius Italicus; on this latter point, see Quint, *Epic and Empire,* 112, 384 n. 22. Argante is a more purely literary figure; he is assimilated both

by Tancredi in Canto 6 (13–55), but when Tancredi, now the prisoner of Armida, fails to show up for the continuation of their duel in Canto 7, it is Raimondo who steps in, chosen by lot, to take his place (63–113). But Raimondo, a "debil vecchio" as he acknowledges himself to be in his prayer for divine aid (78.7), is not equal to the task on his own; he is assisted by his excellent horse (75–77) and — in answer to his prayers — by his guardian angel who interposes an invisible divine shield that shatters Argante's sword (92–93).[15] It will, however, be Tancredi who finally resumes the duel with Argante and finishes it by killing his pagan adversary in Canto 19. In Canto 20, moreover, the unarmed Tancredi rises from the bed in Jerusalem where he is still recovering from his battle with Argante, takes up his great shield and covers the unprotected Raimondo, who had fallen during the fighting inside the city. Tancredi acts as Raimondo's new guardian angel, and his shield, "il qual di sette / dure cuoia di tauro era composto" (86.1–2), clearly recalls the "sevenfold-ox-hide terrible shield" that Ajax carries in the *Iliad* as his trademark (*Il.* 7.245, 266) and beneath which the Ajax of the *Metamorphoses* reminds the Greeks that he had once sheltered the cowering Ulysses.

The Raimondo-Tancredi complex is another illustration of the need for cooperation between the hero of intelligence and the hero of force. But here the relationship is viewed from the point of view of an Ajax or Tancredi, the warrior hero who is the only one who can fight the decisive duel and who is required physically to protect the Ulyssean strategist. The Raimondo-Tancredi subplot thus opposes the central plot of the *Liberata* where the irascible warrior Rinaldo appears to be subordinated to the direction and wisdom of his captain, Goffredo. But the nature of this relationship is also called into question in the action of the last cantos of the poem. If Rinaldo does not rescue Goffredo himself, he does come to the aid of Eustazio, Goffredo's brother, as the two of them assault the walls of Jerusalem on ladders in Canto 18.

---

to Hector — and in Tasso's revised epic, the *Gerusalemme conquistata,* he will even be given a wife and infant son to play Andromache and Astyanax (22.51f.) — and to Ariosto's Rodomonte. Argante's death (19.21f.), however, like Rodomonte's, is a rewriting of the death of Turnus at the end of the *Aeneid*: see Lauren Scancarelli Seem, "The Limits of Chivalry: Tasso and the End of the *Aeneid*," *Comparative Literature* 42 (1990): 116–25.

[15] For an analysis of this episode, see Timothy Hampton, *Writing from History: The Rhetoric of Exemplarity in Renaissance Literature* (Ithaca: Cornell University Press, 1990), 94–110. Hampton shows how Raimondo's hesitation to finish Argante off (7.94–95) parallels Goffredo's later mistake in Canto 11, where he attempts to take Jerusalem without armor and without Rinaldo. Thus Raimondo, no less than Goffredo — both of them figures of prudential wisdom in the epic — are subject to error. On the later episode see Riccardo Bruscagli, "L'errore di Goffredo (G.L. XI)," *Studi tassiani* 40–41 (1992–1993): 207–32.

> Ed egli stesso a l'ultimo germano
> del pio Buglion, ch'è di cadere in forse,
> stesa la vincitrice amica mano,
> di salirne secondo aita porse. (18.79)
>
> [And he himself, extending his victorious hand in
> fellowship to the youngest brother of pious Goffredo,
> who was in risk of falling,
> gave him help to climb up second.]

We may see this Eustazio who comes in second behind Rinaldo as a kind of symbolic substitute for his brother; Rinaldo saves him from falling as Tancredi will later rescue Raimondo. Moreover, the assault that Rinaldo successfully leads on the city wall where it is highest and best fortified ("più munito ed alto") [72.8] is taken entirely on his own initiative, and is not part of the design of Goffredo who enters Jerusalem only to find Rinaldo already there before him — consigning him, like Eustazio, to second place. Similarly, in the final battle outside the city in Canto 20, Rinaldo exceeds Goffredo's orders to launch an attack on the enemy's left flank and cuts through the entire pagan army, killing Adrasto (103), Solimano (107), and Tisaferno (120) on its right wing and winning the battle single-handedly. To Goffredo is left the less glamorous task of vanquishing the opposing commander Emireno (139), just as the aged Raimondo, revived beneath Tancredi's shield, kills his even more decrepit counterpart Aladino (89).

When Tasso translated the debate over the arms of Achilles in the *Metamorphoses* into the action of the *Gerusalemme liberata,* he took a sufficiently ambivalent attitude toward the rivalry between the heroism of intelligence, the attribute of the commander-in-chief, and the heroism of force that belonged to the warrior. The official position of the *Liberata* notwithstanding, that, like Ovid's poem, awards superiority to the Ulyssean, thinking man's hero, Goffredo, Tasso's sympathies may lie with the prowess of Rinaldo and Tancredi, the soldier heroes whose combats may still generate the highest drama of his epic. It may have been, in part, to conceal or play down those sympathies that Tasso cut his romance version of Ovid's debate — the contention over who should inherit Sveno's marvelous sword — out of his poem. For in this version it was *Rinaldo,* the poem's Achillean fighter, who was destined to capture the arms which both Goffredo and Raimondo had tried to win.[16]

---

[16] Rhu, "From Aristotle to Allegory," 125, notes that the rivalry between Goffredo and Rinaldo over the sword of Sveno "threatens to undermine the allegorical hierarchy" of the *Liberata.*

The *Liberata* nonetheless restages the Ovidian debate between Ulysses and Ajax by repeatedly pairing and opposing two types of heroes and heroism. The central conflict of Goffredo and Rinaldo, which those other pairings mirror and comment upon, opposes intelligence and self-control on the one hand, force and ardor on the other. The opposition, as the Ovidian model suggests, is as old as the history of epic itself and goes back to the contrast of Ulysses and Achilles as heroes of their respective poems, even to the roles that each plays in the *Iliad* itself.[17] Ovid might be allegorizing in the *Metamorphoses* how the sequel to the *Iliad* will not be a similar poem in which an Achillean Ajax would be the protagonist but rather a new poem with a new type of hero — the man of many turns rather than the more one-dimensional warrior — who will visit both Achilles and Ajax in an underworld that is also the realm of an already superseded literary past. Furthermore, Ovid updates the heroism of Ulysses to the practice of Roman warfare, which gave importance to the strategist-general rather than the individual fighting man. Tasso may similarly give centrality to the commander-in-chief — his poem was to have been titled *Il Goffredo* — in an epic written for an age of artillery and mass warfare.[18] His Goffredo is supposed to combine both intelligence and martial prowess, and the evident model for such a combination of Ulyssean and Achillean traits is Virgil's Aeneas, who is both leader and principal warrior. But by explicitly assigning the latter role to Rinaldo, Tasso reduces his Aeneas-like hero to his Ulyssean, prudential dimension; as a fighter, Goffredo probably imitates Aeneas most closely at the moment when he is wounded and sent out of battle in Canto 11 (54f.; see *Aeneid* 12.318–319, 384f.)[19]

There are, however, contemporary contexts in which to read the opposition, however traditional it may be, of a Ulyssean Goffredo to an Achillean Rinaldo.

---

[17] Thomas Greene distinguishes "executive" and "deliberative" scenes and heroism in epic poetry in *The Descent from Heaven* (New Haven: Yale University Press, 1963), 12–21; see also James Nohrnberg, *The Analogy of The Faerie Queene* (Princeton: Princeton University Press, 1976), 58–65. In *The Best of the Achaeans*, Gregory Nagy takes as the starting point for his discussion of archaic Greek heroism the passage in Demodokos's song in the *Odyssey* (8.75–82) that describes a quarrel between Achilles and Ulysses: Gregory Nagy, *The Best of the Achaeans: Concepts of the Hero in Archaic Greek Poetry* (Baltimore: Johns Hopkins University Press, 1979), especially 42–58.

[18] See Michael Murrin, *History and Warfare in Renaissance Epic* (Chicago: University of Chicago Press, 1994), 179–96, for a discussion of how the methods and conduct of early modern war changed the way in which epic poetry represented battle: the commanding officers achieved new prominence. For Tasso's Goffredo, see 194–96.

[19] See Bruscagli, "L'errore di Goffredo," 213, 223; Fredi Chiappelli, *Il conoscitore di caos* (Rome: Bulzoni, 1981), 110–15.

Goffredo the captain is also the figure of a divinely-sanctioned authority to which Rinaldo, the mighty individual and independent soldier of fortune, must submit. This political scenario, as I have discussed elsewhere, primarily describes obedience to the Counter-Reformation Church.[20] But it also suggests the curtailing of feudal prerogatives by the nascent modern state whose princes enjoy — or claim to enjoy — absolute power over their subjects; such a state, as Tasso's dialogue, *Il Forno ovvero de la nobiltà,* asserts, was Ferrara itself where the "podestà assoluta o quasi assoluta e simile a quella de' re"[21] of the Este dukes required the unconditional obedience of their nobility, a nobility that could best show its noble character *through* its obedience.

> Talché niuno altro segno di nobiltà maggiore posson dimostrare che la servitù co' vostri principi e l'ubbedienza e la fedeltà dimostrata, per la quale sono stati degni di tutti que' gradi e di tutti que' titoli ch'a nobilissimi cavalieri son convenienti; e vivono con splendore e con ornamento eguale a quello de' baroni de' grandissimi regni. (4:507)
>
> [So that they can show no greater sign of nobility than the servitude, obedience, and loyalty they have shown to your princes, for which they have been worthy of all those ranks and titles that belong to the most noble cavaliers; and they live with a splendor and magnificence equal to that of barons of the largest kingdoms.]

In this social and political setting, where noble identity, with its titles and ranks, is conferred upon the nobleman by the prince in exchange for the nobleman's submission, the two types of heroism, intellectual and martial, of the *Liberata* acquire a particular resonance. For here they may correspond to two kinds of nobility, equally dependent on the prince. The speakers of *Il Forno* discuss how a new noble lineage may begin.

> A.B. E gli uomini famosi per valor di guerra o per lettere o per negozio ne le corti sono il più illustre principio che possa avere il nuovo legnaggio.
>
> A.F. Senza fallo.

---

[20] Quint, *Epic and Empire*, 213–47.

[21] Tasso, *Opere*, ed. Maier, 4:507.

A.B. Il quale suole essere in minor pregio de l'antico, perché l'istesse cose più lontane che vicine sono degne di gloria: laonde i nobili sprezzano ne' vivi quegli onori medesimi per li quali i maggiori sono onorati. (4:520)

[A.B. And men famous for valor in war or for letters or for the affairs of the court are the most illustrious beginning that a new lineage may have.

A.F. Without doubt.

A.B. Which is wont to be of less esteem than an old lineage, because the same things more distant rather than nearer in the past are worthy of glory: whence nobles disdain in the living the same honors for which their ancestors are honored.]

One may be ennobled either through arms or letters or through court business, and it is significant that Tasso, the *letterato,* tries to distinguish the latter two categories. For the two were generally linked together under the name of letters and helped to define the occupation of an emergent noble class of princely servants and bureaucrats often trained in the law — what in France would be the *noblesse de robe* — that was to be distinguished from an older martial aristocracy.[22] This

[22] In the *Discorsi* (1585) of Annibale Romei, written in Tasso's Ferrarese ambiance, the seventh and final dialogue on the precedence of arms and letters eventually identifies the profession of letters — including philosophy, poetry, oratory — with the jurisconsult: the lawyer Cati who takes up this argument not only argues for the subordination of arms to the rule of law, and hence to princely or civic authority, but also, in a remarkable passage, condemns war itself: "E io dirò all'incontro, che l'arme sono al mondo di maggior travaglio, che d'ornamento, sendo elle principio dell'occupar i beni altrui, e di metter le città libere in dura servitù, sforzando il più delle volte uomini savi obedir alla pazzia degli atrocissimi tiranni. Dirò ancora, che per abuso e ingiustamente si drizzano statue, si danno corone e i trionfi a' vincitori guerrieri; perchè qual può esser maggior abuso e cosa più inumana, che cercar la grandezza e la gloria dalle uccisioni, dagli incendi, dagli stupri, dai sacrilegi, dalle rapine, e finalmente trionfare delle miserie umane?" (277). One feels here as elsewhere in the *Discorsi* the presence of what Norbert Elias has called the "civilizing process" overtaking an aristocratic society that nonetheless liked to think of itself in feudal, chivalric terms. For the final verdict on the day's debate, although split, is delivered in favor of the profession of arms. Romei's text is reprinted by Angelo Solerti in *Ferrara e la Corte estense nella seconda metà del secolo decimosesto. I discorsi di Annibale Romei gentiluomo ferrarese* (Città del Castello: S. Lapi, 1900). For a discussion of Romei's work, see Stefano Prandi, *Il Cortegiano ferrarese: i Discorsi di Annibale Romei e la cultura nobiliare*

traditional nobility of arms looked down upon the newcomers, both, as Tasso indicates here, because they were new and because they were the products of a court culture that was unwarlike and even effeminate. So Ottaviano Fregoso famously complains in the fourth book of *Il Cortegiano* of a courtiership that often does nothing but "make their spirits effeminate . . . whence it comes about that there are few who dare, I will not say to die, but even to risk any danger" (4.4).[23] The debates between arms and letters encountered in the *Cortegiano* (see 1.45–46) and throughout the literature of the sixteenth century thus encode a rivalry between a new nobility rising at court through intellectual talents and an older aristocracy anxious about losing its position as a military caste; such anxiety was only increased by an emergent style of absolutism that divested the old magnates of their feudal autonomy and reduced them to princely servants and courtiers along with their new rivals, both dependent on the favor of the ruler.

The opposition in the *Gerusalemme liberata* between an Achillean heroism of martial prowess and the Ulyssean heroism of intelligence was in fact a *topos* of this debate between arms and letters — and over the nature of nobility. In 1571, Girolamo Muzio, the former schoolteacher of the young Tasso at the court of Urbino, published *Il Gentilhuomo,* a work "divided into three dialogues," in which "is treated the matter of nobility." Its third book contains a typical debate on arms and letters. Muzio's speakers take up a *topos* of this debate that had already appeared in the *Cortegiano:* the question of who was greater, Achilles, the greatest man of arms, or Homer, the greatest poet.

> *Nobile:* Ed io ti dico che di tanto maggior honore è degno Homero di Achille, quanto piu stimar si dee il vero, che il sogno. Fu Homero uno scrittor veramente eccellentissimo: Et Achille fu una favola. Et in questa favola fu egli descritto per un giovine furioso, & bestiale. Molto fu piu honorato Ulisse da Homero, che Achille: che oltra l'havere scritto una opera del nome di lui intitolata, & tutta di lui, ad Ulisse diede nome di vincitor di citta, il che non disse mai di Achille. Et dovete essere Ulisse uno huomo letterario: che Ovidio recita una oratio sua piena di arte oratoria. *Eugenio:* Quella oratione stata sarà piu di Ovidio che di Ulisse. *Nobile:* Qui non ci accade disputa.[24]

---

nel cinquecento (Florence: Olschki, 1990); for the issue of arms and letters and the nature of nobility, see 185–210.

[23] Baldassarre Castiglione, *The Book of the Courtier*, trans. Charles S. Singleton (Garden City, NY: Anchor Books, 1959), 289.

[24] Girolamo Muzio, *Il gentilhuomo* (Venice: Appresso gli heredi di Luigi Valuassori, & Gio. Domenico Micheli, 1575), 238.

> [*Nobile:* And I say to you that Homer is worthy of so much more honor than Achilles as one should esteem reality more than a dream. Homer was truly a most excellent writer: and Achilles was a fable. And in this fable he was portrayed as a furious and bestial youth. Ulysses was much more honored by Homer than Achilles: for beyond having written a work that took its title from the name of Ulysses and was totally about him, he gave to Ulysses the name of conqueror of cities, which he never said about Achilles. And Ulysses must have been a man of letters: for Ovid recites an oration of his full of oratorical art. *Eugenio:* That oration will have been more Ovid's than Ulysses'. *Nobile:* We have no argument on that point.]

Homer, the man of letters, has made a man of letters, Ulysses, into a hero, and both are superior to the *furioso* Achilles. Ulysses is a sacker of cities, specifically, one may infer, of the Troy which fell by his cunning stratagem. The clincher to this argument is Ovid's portrait of Ulysses as a skilled orator, winning the debate for the arms of Achilles, over Ajax, another Achillean man of arms. Muzio has put the argument into the mouth of a character named Nobile in dialogue with another named Eugenio: their names may seem to be synonyms, but in fact, Eugenio is "well-born." The claim for letters over arms is advanced against the traditional aristocracy of lineage and blood: it is the claim of a new noble class.[25]

Tasso himself offers complicated commentary on Achilles and Ulysses in *Il Forno*. He brings up the case of Achilles shortly after his speakers have remarked on the noble subject's duty to obey his prince, an obedience that is defined as a kind of self-control and thus as a form of prudence. Achilles was both king of the Myrmidons and subject to Agamemnon.

> A.B. Era dunque in Achille la virtù regia, la quale era la sua prudenza; ma non era peraventura la prudenza eroica, perch'egli ad Agammenone non avrebbe dovuto obbedire. Nondimeno da Pallade fu consegliato ch'egli cedesse, e da Nestore ripreso ch'egli contendesse.
>
> A.F. Non per mio giudizio.
>
> A.B. Ma la fortezza d'Achille fu eroica, come si dimostrò quando egli solo pose in fuga Ettore e spaventò il campo de' Troiani.

---

[25] Muzio, *Il gentilhuomo*, 21: "Et per parlar della Eugenia, et della Nobiltà, dico che molto più honorevole è questo, che quel nome, che in quello antichità di sangue, & in questo chiarezza di virtù si comprende."

A.F. Fu senza fallo.

A.B. Dunque Achille aveva la fortezza eroica, ma non la prudenza: era dunque e non era eroe: come stanno queste cose che paiono contrarie? Ma peraventura non sono, perch'in Achille non era la virtù eroica perfettamente: perch'egli avrebbe avuto insieme la prudenza e la fortezza in somma perfezione; o s'ella v'era, la virtù eroica consiste principalmente ne la fortezza e ne la magnanimità.

A.F. Così mi pare. (4:511–512)

[AB. Achilles thus possessed royal virtue, which was his prudence; but it was not perhaps heroic prudence, because he would not have had to obey Agamemnon. Nonetheless he was counseled by Pallas to yield, and he was rebuked by Nestor for his contentiousness.

A.F. Not in my judgment.

A.B. But the fortitude of Achilles was heroic, as was demonstrated when he alone put Hector to flight and terrified the Trojan army.

A.F. It was without doubt.

A.B. Thus Achilles had fortitude that was heroic, but not prudence: thus he was and was not a hero: how may these two things exist that appear contrary? But perhaps they are not contrary, for Achilles did not have heroic virtue in a perfect manner: for he would have had to have had together prudence and fortitude in highest perfection; or if he had perfect heroic virtue, heroic virtue consists principally in fortitude and magnanimity.

A.F. So it seems to me.]

The tortuous logic of this passage sees in Achilles' wrathful disobedience to Agamemnon a lack of prudence and thus of perfect heroism which is a combination of "la prudenza e la fortezza in somma perfezione." We can read the passage as a gloss on the heroes of the *Liberata:* like the similarly insubordinate Rinaldo, Achilles can singlehandedly win the field of battle, but both fall short of the ideal heroism of a Goffredo who possesses both prudence and martial prowess. Yet Tasso qualifies this scheme both through the demurral of Antonio del Forno (A. F.) and through the final concession of Agostino Bucci (A. B.) that perhaps heroism is largely a matter of fortitude and magnanimity, in which prudence plays little role. We may sense here not only an admiration for an old-style heroism, but, in the context of *Il Forno,* a nostalgia for a more traditional feudal idea of nobility whose highest expression would lie *not* in the nobleman's servitude and obedience to his prince but in his own hereditary claims — Achilles is a king in his own right — and deeds of arms.

A similar social conservatism colors Tasso's treatment of Ulysses in a passage that comes near the beginning of *Il Forno*. The Greek hero is here coupled with the ugly, plebeian Socrates as an orator, and both are contrasted to noble heroes who did not need words to manifest a nobility that was evident in the physical beauty of their faces.

> A.F. Socrate nondimeno aveva il volto come quello che si dipinge ne' satiri e ne' sileni, e usava quelle parole che sono in bocca del calzolaio e del sartore, con le quali s'egli persuadesse Alcibiade o no, sasselo quella notte che ricoperse il lor ragionamento; ma non persuase egli al popolo ateniese. E se la medesima maniera d'eloquenza che'egli usava fosse stata usata da Ulisse co' principi de la Grezia, non avrebbe conseguito il suo fine; ma il raccontar le cose prudentemente e con singolar fortezza in guerra adoperate, il mostrar le ferite del suo petto, il ridurre agli iddii non men la nobiltà paterna che la materna gli recarono la desiderata vittoria; ma non l'avrebbe già potuta aver al giudizio d'Elena, se con Paride avesse conteso; e se Circe avesse dopo lui veduto Aiace, così da quel novo amor sarebbe stata presa come fu poi Alcina da quel di Ruggiero. Ma io credo che Socrate e Ulisse non tanto per alcuna eloquenza persuadessero, quanto per alcuna arte incantassero, non ch'altri, l'incantatrici medesime. (4:435–436)

> [A.F. Socrates nonetheless had a face like those one depicts on satyrs and sileni, and he used those words that are in the mouths of cobblers and tailors, with which whether or not he persuaded Alcibiades is known only to that night that covered their conversation; but he didn't persuade the Athenian people. And if that same manner of eloquence that he used had been used by Ulysses with the princes of Greece, he would not have obtained his end; but the recounting of the deeds he prudently and with singular fortitude had performed in war, the showing of the wounds on his breast, the tracing back to the gods the nobility of the lineage not only of his father but of his mother as well, gave him the desired victory; but he would not have been able to obtain it in the

> judgment of Helen had he contended with Paris; and if Circe had seen Ajax after him, she would have been taken by that new love as Alcina later was by her love for Ruggiero. But I think that Socrates and Ulysses did not so much persuade by a kind of eloquence, as they enchanted by some magical art no others than the enchantresses themselves.]

In this retelling of Ulysses' speech claiming the arms of Achilles, Tasso acknowledges that Ulysses combined prudence and fortitude — what will later be defined as a perfect heroism. But the phrase, "le cose prudentemente e con singolar fortezza in guerra adoperate," already seem to tip the scale in favor of fortitude, and it seems to be Ulysses' further confirmation of that fortitude in the display of his wounds and his declaration of his aristocratic blue blood that win the day for him: it is specifically *not* an eloquence that would have linked him with the philosopher Socrates, who speaks the language of artisans. Moreover, in a final distancing of heroism and nobility from intellect and letters, Ajax, the old-style military hero whom Ulysses defeated in their debate, is fancifully made a victor over Ulysses in the domain of the latter's own epic: Circe would have fallen for the mere sight of the soldier Ajax and discarded the orator Ulysses.

In his treatment of both Achilles and Ulysses, then, the Tasso of the *Forno* seems to betray a sympathy for a traditional aristocracy of arms over a new nobility of letters. And yet Tasso was, like Homer in Muzio's text, a poet and man of letters himself; and, again like Muzio's Homer, he created in the *Liberata* an Ulyssean hero, Goffredo, a hero of prudence and intellect, whom the poem appears to exalt above its other Achillean hero, Rinaldo. But the *Liberata,* too, we have seen, wavers in the precedence it gives the heroism of mind over the heroism of force, and its poet may be suspected of upholding the claims of the latter, when, in the poem's final cantos of battle, he brings back both Rinaldo and Tancredi to the win the day for Goffredo and Raimondo. It is not surprising that the intellectual and writer Tasso should have chosen to identify as much, if not more, with a hereditary nobility, with its martial traditions, as with *letterati* who had newly risen through court service to nobility — the class to which he and his father more clearly belonged. He embraces the *sprezzatura* with which *Il Forno* describes the old nobility looking down on the recently ennobled; and this snobbery can be clearly perceived in his treatment of the various figures of Ulyssean intelligence in the *Liberata*.

If we turn away from Goffredo and Raimondo and look at the five other versions of the Ulysses figure that I have isolated — Alete, Sofronia, Clorinda, Ubaldo, and Vafrino — we find either men from lower social origins or women. The pagan ambassador Alete, the first in the series, is also the explicit representative of the new class of princely servants.

Alete è l'un, che da principio indegno
tra le brutture de la plebe è sorto;
ma l'inalzaro a i primi onor del regno
parlar facondo e lusinghiero e scorto,
pieghevoli costumi e vario ingegno
al finger pronto, a l'ingannare accorto. (2.58.1–6)

[Alete is one who has risen from an unworthy beginning
among the ugliness of the plebeian class;
but he was raised to the first honors of the realm
by eloquent and flattering and clever speech,
by adaptable manners and a mind of various nature,
quick to feign and skilled in deceit.]

This disparaging portrait of the court careerist who has risen from humble origins has been taken to be a satirical barb at powerful courtiers in the service of Alfonso II, Tasso's rivals.[26] Risen from the "brutture de la plebe," the eloquent Alete can be compared to the ugly, artisan Socrates with whom Tasso coupled Ulysses in *Il Forno*. This formerly lower-class character from the beginning of the poem is matched towards its end by Vafrino, the squire of Tancredi, who recalls, among other literary predecessors, the crafty Brunello of Boiardo and Ariosto, the "ribaldello" (*Innamorato* 2.3.39.6) who rises through royal service to become vassal king, before he is finally hanged in the *Furioso* (32.8) for the lowlife thief that he is. The knight-adventurer Ubaldo does not initially appear to belong in the same déclassé company as Alete and Vafrino, but Tasso's description of him, "come uom che virtute e senno merchi," links him and his Ulyssean intelligence with mercantile rather than aristocratic, heroic pursuits, mercantile pursuits that Goffredo, the poem's central hero of "senno," pointedly rejects in the last words spoken in the poem ("guerreggio in Asia, e non vi cambio o merco").[27] The capacity that both Alete and Vafrino share for fraud and which is perhaps a sign of their class origins is also shared by Sofronia, whose claim to have stolen the image of the Virgin Mary is a "Magnanima menzogna" (2.3.22), but a lie nonetheless, by Clorinda who stages the nighttime sneak attack on the siege

[26] See Maier's notes to Tasso, *Opere*, 3: 64, which suggest an identification of Alete with Giovanni Battista Pigna or Antonio Montecatini.

[27] On Ubaldo, Goffredo, and mercantile commerce, see Quint, *Epic and Empire*, 262–64. For the disdain towards such commerce in Este Ferrara see the report of the Florentine diplomat, Orazio dalla Rena, cited in Solerti, *Ferrara e la corte estense*, lix.

machines, and by the Helen-like Erminia with whom Vafrino is paired — even though she protests her unwillingness to be involved "in atto alcun di frodo" (19.89.8). Tasso remarks in *Il Forno* that the art of Ulysses seemed to match that of Circean "incantatrici" who were his adversaries, and the assimilation of these Ulyssean characters of the *Liberata* with feminine guile suggests their resemblance to the poem's central version of Circe, the fraudulent and seductive Armida.[28] If lower-class associations cling to the Ulyssean figure of intelligence and prudence, who, as the figure of Alete makes clear, is linked to the new nobility of letters, so do associations of effeminacy — and the two may seem to be much the same from the point of view of a traditional military aristocracy that saw the lower classes as unfit for the manly pursuit of arms and regarded the lettered peacetime culture of the court as potentially effeminizing. It is these associations — and the social bias that lies behind them — that may help to account for Tasso's reservations about the preeminence he grants Goffredo as the Ulyssean hero of his poem.

These reservations would have been heightened by the ideological climate in Ferrara during Tasso's composition of the *Liberata*. The struggle for precedence that the Este waged with the Medici rulers of Florence — a struggle that only intensified after the apparent victory of the Medici, who were named Grand Dukes of Tuscany in 1569 — was viewed by the apologists on both sides as a kind of large-scale debate between arms and letters.[29] Since the Medici banking family could not boast a long dynastic history, their defenders extolled the antiquity of Florence itself and praised a Florentine citizenry whose nobility did not depend so much on lineage as on the virtue of its deeds — and these included intellectual achievements. The Este, to the contrary, based their claim to precedence on long-held feudal dominion and an equally long, if sometimes imaginary, history of military feats; one version of this history is recounted on the shield portraying the deeds of Rinaldo's Este ancestors in the *Liberata* (17.64f.).

Tasso contributed further to this propaganda war between Ferrara and Florence. In *Il Nifo ovvero del piacere,* he included an insulting passage that

---

[28] On the dissimulation that links Armida to Sofronia, Erminia, even Clorinda, and Alete, see Sergio Zatti, "Il linguaggio della dissimulazione nella *Gerusalemme liberata*," in *Forma e parola: studi in memoria di Fredi Chiappelli*, ed. Dennis Dutschke et al. (Rome: Bulzoni, 1992), 423–47, and Francesco Erspamer, "Il 'pensiero debole' di Torquato Tasso," in *La Menzogna*, ed. Franco Cardini (Florence: Ponte alle Grazie, 1989), 120–36.

[29] For a discussion of the arguments over nobility that were employed by the Ferrarese and Florentine adversaries in the precedence controversy, see Robert Williams, "The Facade of the *Palazzo dei Visacci*," *I Tatti Studies* 5 (1993): 209–44, esp. 231–38. See also Venceslao Santi, "La precedenza tra gli Estensi e i Medici e *l'Historia dei principi d'Este* di G. Battista Pigna," *Atti e memorie della R. Deputazione di Storia Patria Ferrarese* 9 (1987): 37–122.

implied that Florentines were all lowborn tradesmen, "sarti" and "pizzicaruoli," who talked mostly about their goods.[30] *Il Forno* is itself an document of the precedence controversy: in it Tasso asserts that "antichissima oltre l'altre famiglie de' principi italiani è quella d'Este" (518), and the dialogue ends with the Este being declared to be worthy of the same title of "serenissimo," enjoyed by the Medici Grand Dukes (536).[31] The whole discussion of nobility in *Il Forno* may, in fact, find its raison d'être in the passage that immediately follows on the already cited exchange on the founding of new lineages and the disdain in which they are held by nobles of long standing.

---

[30] Tasso, *Opere*, ed. Maier, 4: 585–86. Williams, "The Facade," 233–34 n. 71, notes that the Florentine Filippo Valori singled out this work as well as Muzio's *Il gentilhuomo* for their disparaging treatment of Florence. See the opening of Valori's *Termini di mezzo rilievo e d'intera dottrina tra gli archi di casa Valori* (1604), reprinted in Filippo Villano, *De Famosis civibus...*, ed. G. C. Galletti (Florence: Mazzoni, 1847), 251. The offending passage in *Il gentilhuomo* appears to have been the following anecdote [115–16], mocking the Florentines' lack of nobility, told by the well-born Eugenio who is himself a Florentine: "Fra noi si recita, che passando per quà uno Ambasciatore del Re di Francia, il quale andava a Roma, & essendosi fermato per non so che poco male, che gli haveva in una natica, fatto forse cavalcando, fu medicato da un barbiere. Et guarito, havendo havuto commissione dal suo Re di trattare alcuna cosa con questa Republica, si abbattè ad andare alla Signoria, che quel suo barbiere era fatto de' Signori. & entrato nel luogo della udienza, & raffigurato colui seder pro tribunali, volte le spalle se ne usci dicendo, Non voler far relatione delle ambasciate del Re al medico del suo culo. *Nobile*. Adunque colui non riconosceva per nobile, tutto che quivi sedesse come Signore."

[31] On the disputed title of "serenissimo," in the precedence controversy, see Quint, *Epic and Empire*, 227, 400 n.38. In the dedicatory letter of the *Forno* written to Scipione Gonzaga in 1586, Tasso says that he originally wrote the work in 1579 to celebrate the marriage of Margherita Gonzaga to Duke Alfonso II d'Este. Freed from the imprisonment in which the Este had kept him for seven years and outside of their jurisdiction in Mantua, he now revised the dialogue to honor the marriage of Cesare d'Este to Virginia de' Medici, an event that signaled an uneasy truce in the feud between the two families and their cities. Noting that he would not keep silent "quel che allora non mi fu conceduto scriver de la casa de' Medici" (*Opere*, ed. Maier, 4: 428), Tasso included a fulsome encomium of the Medici noting that they could lay claim to a valor as high as that possessed by "gli antichi eroi di cui si fa menzione in questi dialoghi, o ne' principi e cavalieri moderni." As a further diplomatic gesture (429–30), he argued that the highest nobility lies in the soul's conserving the image of the divine in itself, and it is the souls of the religious that do this best: there are none nobler than the late Cardinal Ippolito d'Este, Cardinal Ferdinando de' Medici (the future Duke), and, from his patron's own family, Cardinal Giovan Vincenzo Gonzaga. In God all are equally noble, though some are more equal than others. Scipione Gonzaga himself was an ecclesiastic who aimed at the cardinalship that he would receive a year later in 1587.

> ... laonde i nobili sprezzano ne' vivi quegli onori medesimi per li quali i maggiori sono onorati.
>
> A.F. Sempre veramente le più antiche famiglie sogliono esser in maggior venerazione.
>
> A.B. E quando l'antichità s'aggiunge a la nobiltà reale, sono quasi adorate, come aviene de' principi d'Este, i quali conservano con gran riputazione quello stato che da' lor maggiori fu acquistato con gran valore.
>
> A.F. L'acquisto fu nobilissimo e la conservazione è onoratissima. (4.520)
>
> [... whence nobles disdain in the living the same honors for which their ancestors are honored.
>
> A.F. The oldest families are always wont to be held in the greater admiration.
>
> A.B. And when one adds regal nobility to antiquity, they are almost adored, as happens with the princes of Este, who conserve with great repute the state that their ancestors acquired with great valor.
>
> A.F. The acquisition was most noble and the conservation most honorable.]

The Este, who originally won their state through the valor of arms, are not only the oldest, but, the text lets us infer, also the noblest of Italian families: they clearly merit precedence over their parvenu Medici rivals.

Tasso never published the dialogue he specifically addressed to the conflict between the Este and the Medici, *Della precedenza,* though it has survived in manuscript.[32] The dialogue features the same speakers as *Il forno* and appears to have been intended as a sequel to it. Tasso defends the precedence of Ferrara and her Duke, Alfonso II d'Este, not only over Florence and the Medici Grand Duke Francesco I but also over the Republic of Venice and her Doge. Comparing Florence and Ferrara, his speakers are willing to concede a possible Florentine superiority only in letters.

---

[32] The text of *Della precedenza* is printed by Ezio Raimondi in his critical edition of Tasso's *Dialoghi* (Florence: Sansoni, 1958), 3: 471–506.

> Solo forse Ferrara a Firenze la gloria della poesia può invidiare: perciò, che non ha chi opporre al Boccaccio e mal può l'Ariosto a Dante paragonare; né al Petrarca ha chi opporre, se ben al Casa potrebbe opporre il Guarino; né co'l Guicciardino forse o co'l Machiavelli alcun Ferrarese può contendere. (497)
>
> [Perhaps Ferrara may envy Florence only for the glory of poetry: inasmuch as she has no one to hold up against Boccaccio and Ariosto can ill be compared to Dante; nor does she have anyone to counter Petrarch, although Guarino could counter della Casa; nor perhaps could any Ferrarese compete with Guicciardini or with Machiavelli.]

Tasso leaves himself out of this *paragone* of Ferrarese and Florentine men of letters: because of modesty, and perhaps because he was not himself a native of Ferrara. We may nevertheless feel that he is the poet to compete with and to overgo Dante and Petrarch. But if mercantile Florence is conceded an advantage in letters, chivalric Ferrara, with its "principe eroico" (495), is a city of arms: "Firenze così attende alla mercantia come Ferrara alla vita cavalleresca e militare" (496). The Venetians, inhabitants of another commercial city, are similar praised for prudence and eloquence, but disparaged as soldiers — "prudentissimi ed eloquentisssimi , ma poco guerrieri" (488). The Duke of Ferrara rules over a less populous city, but one whose citizens are accustomed to nobility and to the exercise of arms: "molto più essercitato in maneggiare le armi e molto ardito nelle zuffe particolari e nelle guerre e non senza molta cognizione delle cose di cavalleria per la pratica che ha con la nobiltà che nell'arte cavalleresca è ammaestratissima" (490).[33] In fact, Alfonso is willing to defend his precedence in single combat.

---

[33] What was the social reality behind this claim? The Ferrarese did at least affect chivalry and the way of life of a soldierly nobility. Della Rena, cited in Solerti, *Ferrara e la corte estense*, lix, takes the sardonic Florentine view that it was all a painted facade: "hanno assai amore in tener vita cavalleresca come principal loro professione, ma però non sono molto vaghi d'impiegarla in guerra; lor fine è di esser tenuti signori da splendore e gentiluomini di gran portata. Tengon quei che hanno il modo niente niente dei cavalli in stalla, e cavalcano e armeggiano bene. Universalmente tutti, piccoli e grandi, portan la spada a canto, infiniti piú per ornamento della vita che per occasion di far del male, perché sono amici della pace e rare sono le questioni e rarissimi gli omicidi che ne seguono.

Cercan sempre tutte le strade di parer cavalieri, a che s'aiutano ancora col farsi dipinger tali; ché ho osservato in molte imagini di private e mediocri persone aver visto dal ritratto, che, se non mi fosse stato detto il nome, arei pensato esser l'imagine di un Achille o di un Ettore, cosí fregiate d'oro son le dipinte armature del Dosso."

> E se nelle precedenze è alcuna considerazione la virtù eroica dell'animo e del corpo, Alfonso non solo a Francesco, ma a molti principi di lui maggiori deve senza contesa essere anteposto; e se la lite s'avesse con contesa a terminare, egli volentieri al giudicio della spada se ne rimetterebbe. (499)
>
> [And if any consideration is given in questions of precedence to the heroic valor of the mind and body, Alfonso should without any contest be placed before not only Francesco but many princes greater than he; and if the dispute should have to be decided with battle, he would willingly submit himself to the judgment of the sword.]

Continuing the military practices of their supposedly glorious feudal past, the Este surpass in nobility the rulers of Florence and Venice — with their more peaceable, republican, and mercantile traditions — to the extent that arms are nobler than letters, that martial valor is nobler than the intellectual virtues of prudence and eloquence. To the extent, one might add, that an Achilles or Ajax is nobler than a Ulysses.

For the pro-Este propaganda to which Tasso the courtier lent his pen must have posed a dilemma for Tasso the poet of the *Gerusalemme liberata*. He had written an epic that based its models of heroism on the debate between Ulysses and Ajax in Ovid's *Metamorphoses* and, in the figure of Goffredo, had chosen to make its central and apparently most important hero a Ulyssean hero of intelligence. The Ulysses of Ovid's debate had dismissed his ancestry as irrelevant — although he made sure to trace his genealogy on both paternal and maternal sides back to the gods — and he had based his claims to heroic preeminence solely on his deeds, primarily on deeds of intellect and prudence: he thus pointedly opposed the claims of Ajax that were based on lineage and sheer martial prowess. The Ulyssean nature of Goffredo's heroism in the *Liberata* thus went directly against the prevailing ideology of nobility in Este Ferrara, an ideology that had a particular application in the precedence controversy with Florence. To exalt Goffredo over Rinaldo might seem to recognize the claims of a new nobility like the Medicean upstarts themselves: a socially mobile class that could rise from non-noble origins through its intellectual talents and letters and whose clear representative in the poem is the devious, unwarlike Alete. Tasso, of course, draws back from the recognition of such claims — which may be the claims he could make for himself as a writer — by the snobbery with which he satirizes Alete and by the frequent inclination of his sympathies to the fighting man Rinaldo, the Este avatar. His poem incorporates its own version of the precedence controversy in its uncertainty about which of its heroes is the noblest of them all.

The presence of the Ovidian model behind the ideas of heroism in the *Liberata,* behind its systematic pairing and opposition of Ulyssean heroes of intelligence with Achillean heroes of force, may shed some light on the problem of the prose allegory that Tasso attached to his poem. In it he asserts that Goffredo represents the intellect and Rinaldo the irascible part of the tripartite human soul; and he cites Goffredo's dream where Ugone calls him the head and Rinaldo the right hand of the Crusader cause. There has been considerable controversy among scholars as to whether this allegory was composed *post-facto* when the *Liberata* was already substantially completed and when Tasso, it is presumed, was trying to appease the censors of the Roman inquisition, or whether the poet genuinely constructed his poem along allegorical lines.[34] A document that has been subject to divergent interpretations is a passage in Tasso's letter of June 1576 to Luca Scalabrino.

> Ma certo, o l'affezione m'inganna, tutte le parti de l'allegoria son in guisa legate fra loro, ed in maniera corrispondono al senso littterale de poema, ed anco a' miei principii poetici, che nulla più; ond'io dubito talora che non sia vero, che quando cominciai il mio poema avessi questo pensiero.[35]

> [But certainly, or else my affection deceives me, all the parts of the allegory are so linked together among themselves and correspond in such a manner to the literal sense of the poem and also to my poetic principles, that they could not do more; whence I sometimes wonder whether it is not true that I had this thought when I began my poem.]

It is difficult to determine the tone of this passage: is Tasso discovering that all along he had been writing a poem with allegorical consistency, or is he making a joke? Perhaps he is doing both at once. For the Ovidian debate between Ulysses

---

[34] The argument that Tasso's allegory was built into the composition of the *Liberata* is advanced in Michael Murrin, *The Allegorical Epic: Essays in its Rise and Decline* (Chicago: University of Chicago Press, 1980), 87–127; see also Rhu, "From Aristotle to Allegory"; Lucia Olini, "Dalle direzioni di lettura alla revisione del testo: Tasso tra 'Allegoria del Poema' e *Giudizio*," *Rassegna della letteratura italiana* 7 (1985): 53–68. For a counter-argument, see Walter Stephens, "Metaphor, Sacrament and the Problem of Allegory in *Gerusalemme Liberata*," *I Tatti Studies* 4 (1991): 217–47. An earlier, related discussion is found in William Kennedy, "The Problem of Allegory in Tasso's *Gerusalemme Liberata*," *Italian Quarterly* 15–16 (1972): 27–51.

[35] Tasso, *Lettere*, ed. Mazzali, 1: 185.

and Ajax had structured the *Liberata* into an extended meditation on the relationship between heroic intellect and heroic force — or between letters and arms. Even as Tasso concealed his Ovidian model by suppressing the episode of Sveno's bleeding sword, he was transforming it into the allegorical master plan of his epic.

The Experience of Ferrara: English and American Travelers and the Failure of Understanding

Werner Gundersheimer

You go from Bologna to Venice by Way of Ferrara and Padua. There is very little interesting to be seen at either of those Cities.[1]

Modern approaches to Florence, Venice, or Rome, while cluttered with the detritus of industrial and post-industrial construction, take the traveler through landscapes which would still be recognizable to an observer from the nineteenth century. Around those and almost all the other Italian cities, the topography has been inscribed, but not eradicated, by change. The surrounding landscape has become a palimpsest, on which the past remains dimly legible beneath the accretions of later hands. In this, as in many other respects, Ferrara is an exception. No one alive today can remember what it was like to reach the gates of Ferrara before the eastern regions of the Po Valley were transformed into some of Italy's most verdant farmland.

Even for those inured to the many rigors of pre-modern travel, the journey to Ferrara was unusually unpleasant, a depressing and alarming passage. Until the twentieth century, most visitors came by road, borne usually in the horse-

---

[1] From "Advice on Travel in Italy," by William Patoun, c. 1766, a manuscript in the Exeter Archives at Burghley House, published in John Ingamells, *A Dictionary of British and Irish Travelers in Italy, 1701–1800* (New Haven: Yale University Press, 1997), xlix. The compiler identifies over six thousand Englishmen known to have visited Italy during the eighteenth century. Of these, only a small minority can be definitively placed in Ferrara.

drawn carriage known as the *vetturino.* The roads were built along dikes and natural elevations, but they were always muddy and dangerous, and they gave way to deep panoramas of ancient swampland on all sides. Hamilton Geale, Esq., a perceptive young English expatriate whose book appeared in 1847, describes the journey as "an aquatic one," through "miserable and swampy country." He was not alone in thinking that the area presented hopeless environmental obstacles to prosperous agrarian life: "The wretched huts of the peasantry, built of reeds and mud, seem to rise out of the stagnant waters by which they are surrounded; the inhabitants looking miserable and agueish, as the occupiers of such habitations, in such a soil, may be supposed [i.e., *expected]* to look. Water is the great enemy of these tracts, and from their extreme flatness, draining would be difficult, or, perhaps, impossible."[2]

Whether coming from Bologna or Venice, the pre-modern visitor to Ferrara would have to have experienced similar rigors and depressing scenes. One would expect that it would therefore have come as something of a relief to reach the city itself. Yet for many travelers Ferrara provided the physical and emotional low point of an Italian journey. Historically, its associations tended to be negative, a site of petty tyranny symbolized by the cruel Alfonso's persecution of the noble genius, and by the jealous Niccolò's judicial murder of the young lovers, horrors lavishly commemorated by Romantic poets and painters. Physically, the town presented a depressing aspect. As the (not atypical) Geale tells us, "The entrance to the city of Ferrara is not calculated to dispel the gloomy impressions which the road to it inspires; its wide and grass-grown streets, its deserted and ruinous palaces, give an idea of desolation which must be witnessed to be understood." To make matters worse, the inns were exceptionally unpleasant, and the innkeepers unusually rapacious. Geale describes his hotel, aptly named "I tremori," as "one of the dirtiest and most extravagantly dear." In what was clearly a scene of great unpleasantness, he flatly refused to pay the full bill. Like most of his eighteenth- and nineteenth-century fellow travelers, Geale did not linger in the city of the Estensi.

I knew absolutely nothing about Ferrara before I first saw it, on one of those hazy, sultry Po Valley days in the summer of 1953. I had just turned sixteen, and was visiting Europe for the first time. As the child of refugees, born in Frankfurt and fortunate to have escaped in 1939, I grew up with my parents' memories of Italy, where they had gone for their wedding trip. In Germany, my father, an art historian, had been a museum curator specializing in the ceiling-painters of the German baroque, but in America he became a professor of the

---

[2] Hamilton Geale, *Notes of a Two Years' Residence in Italy* (Dublin: James McGlashan, 1847), 150 ff.

history of art. After the war was over and travel had resumed, he began to lead tours of college students around Europe during the summers, and it was with one of these groups that I came to Ferrara on that summer's day.

Like countless English and American travelers before me, I had made my Italian landfall at Naples. Having crossed the Atlantic on the brand new, stylish but ill-fated *Andrea Doria,* I was prepared for the reemergent energy and modernity of Italy. But nothing had prepared me for the rest of what I found — lingering devastation from the war, vast panoramas of homelessness and need, set amidst the powerful presence of a traditional and exuberant Mediterranean civilization, strikingly different from the pale, tranquil suburban America in which I was growing up. Following in the footsteps of earlier travelers, I went (in a bus filled with giggling, gum-chewing college girls) along the traditional route of the Grand Tour to Rome, and then through the towns of Umbria and Tuscany to Florence. The topography, the verdant countryside, the friendliness and vitality of the people, the energetic lilt and sheer music of the language, the magnificence of the art and architecture, the light, dry clarity of the air — all filled me with a sense of wonder.

From Florence, we proceeded to Ravenna. It felt like another country — flat, still, sparsely populated. It takes an act of will to recall, in the midst of today's massive and oppressive hordes of visitors, that in 1953 one could wander into the tomb of Gallia Placidia, or the cool recesses of Sant'Apollinare in Classe, and enjoy complete silence and virtual solitude. The next stop on our quite traditional itinerary was Venice, in those times a full day's drive. And so, we also made the traditional stop for lunch in the city of the Estensi. I can still remember stepping out of the bus in front of the Ristorante Italia, and running across the Largo Castello to gaze over the moat at one of the most imposing structures I had ever seen. In the eyes of an American teenager, the *castello* seemed the most complete expression of the medieval world — alien, closed, intriguing in its inaccessibility, at the same time inviting and repelling attention. After the usual good meal Da Giovanni, there was no time to see the city or even go into the *castello.* But I did make a few photographs of Bartolino da Novara's great building, and until losing the album in some much later move, often looked at them, recalling that initial, rather personal revelation that Italy and Tuscany are neither synonymous nor coterminous.

After that brief encounter, I seldom thought about Ferrara for the next five years. In 1958, though, I began to study the history of Renaissance Italy in an undergraduate course at Amherst College. Amherst is situated in what was then a small New England village, but it was a cosmopolitan little school, with a distinguished faculty. My teacher was Richard M. Douglas, a thoughtful and methodical scholar whose career had been delayed by his service in the officer corps of the United States Marines in World War II. When I first knew him he was just publishing his biography of Cardinal Jacopo Sadoleto, the eminent reforming prelate born in Ferrara, which remains the standard treatment of its subject.[3] His study of the Bishop of Carpentras had given Douglas an appreciation, unusual in American scholarly circles at that time, of the powerful intellectual crosscurrents sweeping over the northern Italian courts in the early *cinquecento*. Thus he was able to interpret the Renaissance as a trans-Alpine phenomenon, and the Reformation as a movement with deep Cisalpine implications. Of course, Douglas assigned the classic books by Jacob Burckhardt and Johan Huizinga, so that his students came to view early modern Europe not only as a series of isolated and discrete cultures, movements, and epochs, but also as a complex theater of continuous developments and evolving traditions and styles.

Douglas referred occasionally to the Estensi in his lectures, always using Ferrara as a foil, a kind of intellectual control, for the prevalent tendency in post-war American historical scholarship to assume that the Florentine experience was equivalent to the Italian experience. His approach, more anthropological than anecdotal, avoided the lurid stories of princely excesses which had long been the stock in trade of popular historians of the Renaissance (including Burckhardt), emphasizing instead the structural differences between princely states and merchant republics in the *quattrocento*.

In my last undergraduate year, I stayed with the plan and wrote an honors thesis on Machiavelli.[4] But one day, browsing among the recently published books newly arrived at the College library, I came upon a copy of Paolo d'Ancona's work on the Schifanoia frescoes.[5] I had rarely seen images of such strange and evocative beauty, rich with obvious and concealed meanings, alive with visual and local color, expressive of a lost world of great complexity, subtlety, and elegance. I could hardly believe that a few years earlier I had been in the city where these treasures existed, and had never heard of, let alone seen them.

Francesco del Cossa's sumptuous images stayed in my mind for years, while I pursued an entirely unrelated set of interests, relating to northern humanism and the late French renaissance, in graduate school. Then at last, in 1965, I found my way back to Ferrara, to the Palazzo Schifanoia, and to the many sites —

---

[3] Richard M. Douglas, *Jacopo Sadoleto (1477–1547): Humanist and Reformer* (Cambridge, MA: Harvard University Press, 1959).

[4] Werner Gundersheimer, "Machiavelli as an Empirical Humanist" (B.A. thesis, Amherst College), 1959.

[5] Paolo d'Ancona, *I mesi di Schifanoia a Ferrara* (Milan: Il Milione, 1958). A French translation appeared in the same year.

churches, palaces, convents, cemeteries, houses, gardens, ramparts, and cobbled and vaulted streets — which give the city its unique and mysterious atmosphere. The *trecento* frescoes in the Casa Minerbi had only just been uncovered, and the city was waking up to its history. Yet, at a meeting of the preservation society called *Ferrariae Decus*, only three other people appeared, and in the reading rooms of the archives and the Biblioteca Ariostea attendance was almost as light as it had been when Anglophone travelers had remarked on it in earlier times. At that time, too, the ecclesiastical archives were still closed, at least to foreign scholars, so a vital aspect of the city's past was practically inaccessible.

An additional, and rather uncommon, problem complicated the study of Ferrara's past. The vast preponderance of the surviving archival and literary remains of Estean Ferrara had been transferred to Modena as part of the devolution of 1597–1598, and therefore could not be studied in what might be called their natural habitat. It was as though the city, which had lost so much of its autonomy and vitality over the centuries, had also been stripped of its historical and intellectual birthright. Thus, if you want to study Florence, you go to Florence; if you want to study Boston, you naturally find most of what you need in Boston; but if you want to work on Ferrara, you must spend most of your time in Modena, yet another example of Ferrara's exceptionalism.

Having found my way to Ferrara through a combination of aesthetic pleasure, scholarly contrariness, intellectual curiosity, and dogged persistence, I was prepared to pursue a somewhat lonely enterprise, for my English, American, and Italian colleagues were focusing their energies on the larger and more celebrated city-states. Happily, though, I then discovered a remote, but appealing family tie to the city. My wife had a great-aunt whose husband, Max Ascoli, came from a Jewish family with ancient roots in Ferrara. He had settled in New York, where for many years he published and edited *The Reporter* magazine, an important bi-weekly review of politics, international affairs, and culture; but he maintained friendly ties with his childhood friends who had survived and remained in or returned to Ferrara. Max taught me to see Ferrara in ways that would otherwise have escaped me, and introduced me to a helpful and welcoming circle of *ferraresi*, who made the absences from my family and the long winter evenings at the Europa or the Astra much more pleasant than they would otherwise have been. Thus, for me personally, Ferrara has always been a friendly city, belying the gloomy, forbidding aspect upon which so many foreign visitors have remarked.

In fact, it is safe to say that the great preponderance of English and American travelers visiting Ferrara from the seventeenth through the early twentieth centuries — like Hamilton Geale — found themselves extremely disenchanted with the experience. The standard view was actually so negative that an understanding of the marginality of Ferrara to the awareness of the ordinary traveler may prove useful in accounting for its relatively late emergence as a widely accepted subject for historical investigation. Surely, anyone who read what the leading travel diaries and journals had to say about the city would have thought twice about visiting it. In reviewing some of the pertinent comments made by such visitors, I of course intend no offense to Ferrara and its civic traditions. On the contrary, I hope to demonstrate the nature of the obstacles Ferrara has had to overcome so as to produce its own, late-twentieth-century historiographical renaissance.

With the exception of a handful of discerning individuals who saw beyond first appearances, Ferrara has suffered over the centuries from a negative image, or what we might call a bad press. The theme begins early, undergoes only a few variations, and continues virtually uninterrupted into the early years of this century. In part, it is constructed out of negative commonplaces and stereotypes applied to many other parts of Italy, or leveled at Italy itself— anticlericalism; annoyance at the discomforts of inns and coaches; aspersions directed at the honesty of the people; complaints about the food and water; and other perennial travelers' laments. The stresses and vexations of travel in pre-industrial Europe were of course balanced by the intense pleasures which the northern visitors derived from musing on classical landscapes, enjoying the salubrious climate at the higher elevations, viewing the treasures of antiquity and the renaissance, escaping the miasmas of London or the rigors of American winters, living in grand style on very little money, and gossiping with their countrymen about their obvious superiority to the Italians, whom they recurrently viewed as debased descendants of a more heroic and accomplished people.[6] But such joys did not seem evident to those who came to, or passed through, Ferrara.

---

[6] For information on eighteenth-century English travelers, see Ingamells, *Dictionary*, and esp. the abbreviated list of titles (xvii–xxxiii), which includes many unpublished manuscripts and archival collections. The standard bibliography is R. S. Pine-Coffin, *Bibliography of British and American Travel in Italy to 1860* (Florence: Leo S. Olschki, 1974), followed by a volume of *Additions and Corrections* by the same author, published in *La Bibliofilia* 83 (1981): 237–61. See also Harold F. Smith, *American Travelers Abroad: A Bibliography of Accounts Published before 1900* (Carbondale: Southern Illinois University Library, 1969). Mildred Abraham, of the University of Virginia, is preparing a bibliography of Italian travel, 1860–1914. In addition, there is a growing body of work about the early travel accounts, of which the most prominent example remains Van Wyck Brooks, *The Dream of Arcadia: American Writers and Artists in Italy, 1760–1915* (New York: E. P. Dutton, 1958), in which the word Ferrara does not appear. William M. Johnson, *In Search of Italy: Foreign Writers in Northern Italy since 1800* (University Park: Pennsylvania State University Press, 1987) omits discussion of Ferrara, focusing on such other Emilian towns

It was all too easy for foreign visitors to find their prejudices about certain aspects of Italian history confirmed during their brief stops in Ferrara. Many visitors assumed that the fact that they came from well-established English-speaking nations with representative governments made them superior to the natives. An intellectual platform of privilege, superciliousness, and unassailable self-confidence does not allow for a sensitive appreciation of other societies or peoples, as we have seen in our own time. In establishing credibility as an historically and artistically significant destination, Ferrara suffered from disadvantages much greater than those of many other cities of comparable importance. In the first place, its climate was distinctly unhealthful, a point noted even as early as the seventeenth century. Second, it had become embarrassingly depopulated and run-down, so that both private residences and the urban infrastructure provided striking evidence of decay. Third, it lay astride what was for many decades one of the worst roads in Italy, a punishingly rutted, dank, and oozy trail across the malarial swamps and turbid tributaries of the Po. Fourth, its resources for hosting travelers were few, for virtually no foreign travelers actually perceived it as a destination. Ferrara and Rovigo were the towns where you stopped overnight on the way from Bologna to Venice, or *vice versa,* and most voyagers preferred Rovigo, noting the charm of its houses, and its relative cleanliness. Fifth, Anglo-American associations with Ferrara were almost entirely literary, and to a great extent negative. The Estensi were looked upon as vindictive tyrants whose untrammeled powers led them to mistreat Ariosto and imprison Tasso. Even worse, they were succeeded by papal administrators who systematically ruined the remaining elements of courtly and secular culture, dispossessed the leading families, and allowed the administrative and economic infrastructure to collapse, whether by their own malevolence (the prevailing view) or through incompetence and neglect. Perhaps, then, it is not too surprising that it took nearly four centuries to begin to arrive at a more balanced and comprehensive understanding of the Ferrarese contribution to Italian civilization, at least in the English-speaking world.

---

as Parma, Bologna, Rimini, and Ravenna. Paul R. Baker, *The Fortunate Pilgrims: Americans in Italy, 1800–1860* (Cambridge, MA: Harvard University Press, 1964) mentions only Byron in connection with Ferrara. More recent scholarship also elides the experience of Ferrara. See, for example, Chloe Chard and Helen Langton, eds., *Transports: Travel, Pleasure, and Imaginative Geography, 1600–1830* (New Haven: Yale University Press, 1996), a good series of critical essays most of which deal with Italy, where Ferrara is not mentioned; and Theodore E. Stebbins, *The Lure of Italy: American Artists and the Italian Experience, 1760–1914* (Boston: Abrams, 1992).

How can we account for this failure of understanding? It may be useful to consider some examples of the literate traveler's experience of Ferrara, in order to gauge its implications for modern scholarship. We begin with a notable English cleric, Gilbert Burnet, later Bishop of Salisbury, who published his impressions of Ferrara at Rotterdam in 1686. Burnet, a gifted historian and careful observer, drew a stark contrast between the Ferrara of the Estensi and that of the cardinal-legates:

> *Ferrara* was one of [Italy's] best Towns while they had princes of their own who for a course of some Ages were Princes of such eminent vertue, and of so Heroicall a Nobleness that they were really the Fathers of their Country, nothing can be imagined more changed than all this is now . . . . The Soil is abandoned and . . . we were amazed when we passed through that vast Town, which by its extent shews what it was about an age ago, and is now so much deserted that there are whole sides of streets without Inhabitants.[7]

Burnet seeks to uncover the cause of so precipitous a decline, and attributes it to confiscatory taxation by the church, which has "devoured many of the Families of *Ferrara*, [and] driven away many more." Burnet also noted a correlation between depopulation of the countryside and the proliferation of air- and water-borne diseases, which have reduced a formerly viable region to a northern facsimile of the Roman *campagna*.[8]

Joseph Addison, a more celebrated author than Burnet, published his *Remarks on Several Parts of Italy . . . In the years 1701, 1702, 1703.* It soon became one of the most popular of the pocket-sized English *ciceroni,* frequently reprinted over

---

[7] Gilbert Burnet, *Some Letters Containing An account of what seemed most remarkable in Switzerland, Italy, &c.* (Rotterdam: Abraham Acher, 1686), 164–66. For the complicated history of the early printings of this work, see Pine-Coffin, *Bibliography*, 90–91.

[8] "I could not but ask all I saw how it came that so rich a soil was so strangely abandoned, some said the Air was become so unhealthy, that those who stay in it were very short-lived; but it is well known that four-score years ago it was well peopled; and the ill Air is occasioned by the want of Inhabitants, for there not being people to drain the ground and to keep the Ditches clean, this makes that there is a great deal of water lies on the ground and rots, which infects the Air in the same manner as is observed in that vast and rich but uninhabited Champaign of *Rome*, so that the ill Air is the effect rather than the cause of the dispeopling of the Popes Dominions. The true cause is the severity of the Government, and the heavy Taxes, and frequent Confiscations by which the Nephews of several Popes, as they have devoured many of the Families of *Ferrara*, so they have driven away many more": Burnet, *Some Letters*, 165–66.

the entire eighteenth century. Addison was a confirmed Italophile, who in his Preface extolled the countryside, the Italian achievement in music, painting, sculpture, and architecture, the refinement of Italy's political systems, and so on.[9] Yet when he arrived in Ferrara, he could hardly wait to move on toward Ravenna. "At Ferrara," he writes, "I met nothing extraordinary. The Town is very large, but extreamly thin of People." Addison merely mentions the presence of a citadel and the city walls, and concludes by flatly stating that the Benedictines showed him Ariosto's monument. He cannot have stayed more than an hour or two, and developed no feeling for the place whatsoever.

Few if any of Addison's many readers would have been inspired to make an independent investigation. Having seen the space represented to them as Tasso's prison, and visited Ariosto's monument and perhaps his house, they were more than ready to hurry on to the next destination where, they believed, greater works of art awaited them. Whether their road went north to Venice, south to Bologna, east toward Ravenna, or west toward Cento (where the revered Guercino awaited them), they believed the revealed word of the guidebooks that greater sights were in store. Thus, the fact that Ferrara was a site of literary rather than artistic pilgrimage became something of a liability, particularly because the northern and western visitors came to Italy for its light and color, refracted both in landscape and in masterpieces of visual art.

A pertinent example was Anna Brownell Jameson, whose anonymously published *Diary of an ennuyée* chronicled her travels through Italy in 1821 as a governess. She notes on November 4: "We passed through Ferrara; only stopping to change horses and dine. We snatched a moment to visit the hospital of St. Anna and the prison of Tasso — the glory and disgrace of Ferrara." Tasso had become a literary martyr, and Jameson was not alone in considering the sad remains of Renaissance Ferrara as the appropriate end of an historical morality play: "How amply has posterity avenged the cause of the poet on his tyrant: . . . with what fervent hatred, indignation and scorn, do we gaze upon the towers of the ugly red brick palace, or rather fortress, which deforms the great square; and where Alfonso feasted while Tasso wept." Thus for her, and for hurried passers-by, Ferrara's decay was its just reward. Miss Jameson comments without emotion on the "grass growing in the wide streets . . . rank and long

[9] The first edition appeared in 1705. I use the second edition (London: J. Tonson, 1718). The relevant passages appear on 87–88. While Addison held a conventionally low opinion of contemporary Italians (cf. Pine-Coffin, *Bibliography*, 99), he tended to glorify the nation's past achievements. Hence his indifference to Ferrara stands in striking contrast to his views of other towns.

even on the thresholds of the deserted houses, whose sashless windows and flapping doors, and roofless walls, looked strangely desolate."[10]

It is worth recalling that for the vast majority of English and American visitors until relatively recent times, there would be only one visit to Italy in a lifetime. The distance, the expense, the time involved, and the rigors of travel meant that only a few might enjoy recurring opportunities to revise or refine their initial impressions. Even if one spent a season or two in Rome, Florence, or Venice, or took a year or two in one of the expatriate communities in those major cities, the *gita turistica* called for brief visits in the smaller centers. But in the case of Ferrara, there seems to have been a desire, shared among many writers, to settle an old score with the Estensi for Tasso's sufferings, and to punish the surviving remnants with recurrent expressions of contempt and obloquy.

Still, such hostile comments as Miss Jameson's might have been kinder than the offhand neglect of many other writers. It was one thing to have bypassed Ferrara altogether, as many travelers did, either by following a more westward course or by taking the sea route to or from Venice. It was something else to have absolutely nothing to say about it, like the popular Mrs. Piozzi, who on the second of her two visits only mentioned her departure from Bologna toward "empty and deserted Ferrara," and laments the breaking of a carriage-wheel on the road.[11]

Perhaps the conditions of travel yielded more exhausted, less receptive travelers to Ferrara than elsewhere. Certainly the roads and the climate presented more than the normal vicissitudes. Consider the experience of Robert Gray, an English country vicar not unacquainted with back roads and bad weather. In February of 1791, Gray had to make his way from Cento, where he had gone to see the Guercinos, to Ferrara. The roads, he found, "were so execrably bad that we were obliged to have eight oxen to our chaise, and eight horses to that of our friends . . . and notwithstanding this, we were detained for nine hours

---

[10] Anna Brownell Jameson is of course better known as Mrs. Jameson, whose extensive writings on Shakespearean heroines, Italian art, and sacred images became popular best-sellers in the mid-nineteenth century. Anna Jameson's *Diary* first appeared with the title *A lady's diary,* and was re-issued in the same year with its catchier title. I use the American edition (Philadelphia: E. Litell, 1718), unrecorded by Pine-Coffin.

[11] Piozzi was formerly Hester Lynch Thrale: Hester Lynch Piozzi, *Observations and Reflections made in the course of a Journey through France, Italy, and Germany*, 2 vols. (London: A. Strahan and T. Cadell, 1789), 2: 177. Mrs. Piozzi's fleeting and dismissive reference is all the more telling because she writes almost lyrically of the Guercino pictures in Cento, and has interesting things to say about Bologna, Rovigo, and Padua. Her first visit, which entailed an overnight stay (1: 23–47), seems to have been pleasant enough, although she disparages the modern *ferraresi*, who appear to be more enthusiastic about the recent visit of the Emperor of Austria than about their own great poets.

in a deep clay and stiff mud, through which, the persevering efforts of the poor animals could, with difficulty, drag the straining carriages, before we could accomplish the two posts and half. Such is the entrance to the country of Ferrara, once so flourishing under the paternal government of its dukes."[12] Understandably, perhaps, Gray chose not to prolong his stay, citing that it was there that he "felt, very seriously, the effects of a transition from the mild air of Naples to the severity of a northern latitude."

Another egregious example of such casual dismissiveness was Mary Wollstonecraft Shelley, who rambled around Italy on three separate journeys, apparently in even more of a rush. "I was sorry not to spend more time at Ferrara," she avers, without saying one more word about the place.[13] Normally an acute observer, Mary Shelley at least suspected, on the basis of her previous experience, that she might have missed something worthwhile. Perhaps such silence is preferable to the jejune comments of a breezy aristocrat like Lady Anne Miller, whose nearly 1200 anonymous pages of Italian travel letters included just thirteen lines on Ferrara, featuring such profundities as "Ferrara, where they shewed us some good pictures, is situated on a branch of the Po"; and "here is also the tomb of Ariosto."[14]

A few years after Lady Anne's visit, John Owen passed through Ferrara in April, using roads "hardened into the most inconvenient furrows by the action of a powerful sun." It was Easter Sunday, and the churches were filled with people dressed in "the best of their wardrobe." Frustrated by the crowds of

---

[12] Robert Gray, *Letters during the course of a Tour Through Germany, Switzerland and Italy in the Years MDCCXCI and MDCCXCII. With reflections on the manners, literature, and religion of those countries* (London: F. and C. Rivington, 1794). Pine-Coffin considers Gray one of the "thoughtful men whose accounts of Italy show that they were not content with a mere inspection of the surface." While generally true, the statement does not hold for Gray's comments on Ferrara. Ingamells, *Dictionary*, 425, regards Gray's letters as "largely statutory displays of learning," yet "of some interest." Gray became Bishop of Bristol in 1827 and died in 1834.

[13] Mary Wollstonecroft Shelley, *Rambles in Germany and Italy, in 1840, 1842, and 1843*, 2 vols. (London: Edward Moxon, 1844), 2: 132.

[14] Lady Anne Miller, *Letters from Italy, describing the Manners, Customs, Antiquities, Paintings, &c. of that Country, In the Years MDCCLXX and MDCCLXXI, to a Friend residing in France, by an English Woman*, 3 vols. (London: Edward and Charles Dilly, 1776), 3: 236. Anne Miller's letters were addressed to her mother-in-law. Ingamells, *Dictionary*, 660 justly remarks that "they convey the character of an indefatigable, slightly absurd, but tolerant tourist." Generally indefatigable, perhaps, but in Ferrara she did not seem to make her usual tireless effort.

worshippers and the clouds of incense, Owen found it impossible to "gaze upon the paintings," and quickly moved on towards Rovigo.[15]

It would be wrong, however, to assume that all of the Anglo-Saxon visitors to Ferrara were interested only in its cultural heritage. One of the interesting exceptions was John Moore, M.D., whose two-volume collection of letters, *A View of Society and Manners in Italy,* first printed in 1781, went through six editions before 1795. Moore went on the grand tour as governor to the Duke of Hamilton and to his own son, later to become a notable general in the British army. Moore writes with a clinician's clarity of expression and sharpness of observation. He notes the evidence of former magnificence, but finds the people few, and manifesting "every mark of poverty." This he attributes to its governance, as Dr. Burnet had done over a century earlier. "In the year 1597," Moore observes, "[Ferrara] was annexed to the Ecclesiastical State, and has ever since been gradually falling into poverty and decay. It must be owing to some essential error in the Government, when a town like this, situated in a fertile soil, upon a navigable river near the Adriatic, remains in poverty. Except the change of its Sovereign, all the other causes, which I have heard assigned for the poverty of Ferrara, existed in the days of its prosperity." Moore's sole recorded cultural visit was to Ariosto's tomb, which prompts a meditation on the mutability of fame: "This fine fanciful old bard has done more honour to modern Italy, than forty-nine in fifty of the Popes and Princes to which she has given birth, and while those, who were the gaze of the multitude during their lives, are now entirely forgotten, his fame increases with the progress of time." He concludes with the paradox that during Ariosto's lifetime his importance may have derived from his Este patrons, whereas "now he gives importance, in the eyes of all Europe, to the illustrious names of his patrons, and to the country where he was born."[16]

By the time James Wilson wandered through Ferrara in 1818, Ariosto's tomb had been moved from San Benedetto to the Palazzo Paradiso. Wilson took time to notice with appreciation the manuscripts of Ariosto and the *Gerusalemme*

---

[15] Owen (1766–1822) served as curate of Fulham, rector of Paglesham, and then as secretary of the British and Foreign Bible Society. He traveled in Italy at the age of twenty-six, as tutor to a sickly young man, and soon thereafter published his *Travels into different parts of Europe in the years 1791 and 1792 with familiar remarks on places — men — and manners* (London: T. Cadell Jun. and W. Davies, 1796). The brief remarks on Ferrara may be found in 2: 212–13.

[16] See John Moore, *A View of Society and Manners in Italy: With Anecdotes Relating to Some Eminent Characters*, 3 vols. (London: W. Strahan and T. Cadell, 1781), 1: 185–91, most of which is a disquisition on the conditions leading to happiness in despotic governments. Dr. Moore also comments on the Ferrarese custom of wearing swords, also observed by Mrs. Piozzi.

liberata, the *Pastor fido,* and the poets' letters. He also transcribed the inscription of Ariosto's tomb. Wilson was more curious and less judgmental than most of his fellow travelers. He actually bothered to notice the Palazzo dei Diamanti, "one of the most beautiful buildings in Ferrara," and was sufficiently modest to acknowledge, on departing, that he might not have exhausted the points of interest: "Probably there are several other objects worthy of notice at Ferrara, but we passed through it too hastily to certify to ourselves that we had seen all that is most remarkable." Wilson was one of the few who actually seems to have enjoyed and benefited from a visit to Ferrara.[17]

So, to a degree, did Joseph Forsyth, whose *Remarks on antiquities, arts, and letters during an excursion in Italy in the years 1802 and 1803,* first published in 1813, quickly established him as one of the more percipient observers. Intelligent, incisive, and articulate, Forsyth quickly went to the heart of Ferrara's problems and accomplishments. "By turning the Reno from its direct tendency to the Po, away through the Ferrarese, the Popes have not only desolated the plain, but also produced a confusion in private property," resulting also in disease and depopulation. The disease Forsyth identifies as "mephitism," or illness caused by noxious or contaminated air, or "malaria," to use the modern term. Forsyth notices, but is not deterred by, the evidence of Ferrara's decline, finding in it a nostalgic appeal consistent with the ethos of romanticism: "Yet melancholy as this city looks now, every lover of Italian poetry must view with affection the retreat of an Ariosto, a Tasso, a Guarini."[18] Forsyth's veneration of the great poets leads him to lament the decision to move Ariosto's bones: "The apotheosis, I understand, was magnificent; yet a friend to what is ancient will hardly approve this manner of translating poets." Ariosto, one suspects, would have liked Forsyth's pun.

Sydney Owenson, known as Lady Morgan, rivaled and in some ways superseded Forsyth as a knowledgeable and incisive, if perhaps less finely balanced, observer of the Italian scene. In her massive, two-volume *Italy* (1822), she devoted four pages to Ferrara, concentrating — as usual — on the literary monuments. While evoking the atmosphere of a quiet backwater without

[17] James Wilson, *A Journal of Two Successive Tours upon the Continent in the Years 1816, 1817, & 1818,* 3 vols. (London: T. Cadell and W. Davies, 1820), 3:257–63. Ariosto's remains were actually translated to their present site in 1801.

[18] I use the second edition, Joseph Forsyth, *Remarks on Antiquities, Arts, and Letters during an Excursion in Italy in the Years 1802 and 1803,* 2nd ed. (London: John Murray, 1816). The *DNB* (7:472–73) describes Forsyth's *Remarks* as "for style and matter . . . one of the best books on Italy in our language." It is in fact brisk, clear, and full of intelligent observations.

conjuring up the image of a sinister or repulsive place, she seems to be deliberately seeking the balance that eluded her competitors. Thus, she uses parallel clauses to create a more equilibrated view. Of the *castello,* for example, she writes: "This vast palace, or castle, was the scene of much crime, and much festivity. It contained the dungeons where the followers of Calvin perished; and the theater, where the dramas of Ariosto, and Tasso, and Guarini, were performed. . . . For the castle of Ferrara is a monument of recollections, at once terrible and delightful." The overheated rhetoric is typical of Lady Morgan's time; her wish to understand and interpret, rather than to pass judgment, is not.[19]

A more sober, politically aware, and socially prominent visitor was Richard Plantagenet Temple Nugent Brydges Chandos Grenville, first Duke of Buckingham and Chandos, who produced a three-volume journal of his travels in Italy between 1827 and 1829. The author had been a member of parliament between 1797 and 1813, and had held several important government offices. He favored the abolition of the slave trade. Tough and sophisticated, Buckingham commented on daily life, bunked down in some very rough places, went hungry on occasion, and missed nothing. In the big cities, he moved in the highest society, but contemporary affairs interested him far more than high culture. Heading from Bologna to Venice early one morning toward the end of June, he reports: "I passed through Ferrara, where I breakfasted. The town old and ugly, and remarkable only as the birthplace of Ariosto, and the prison-house of Tasso." Had he stopped there, Buckingham would have provided yet another instance of the perfunctory literary visit. But he went on to discuss the ecclesiastical government of Ferrara, focusing on its inadequacies and absurdities. His sympathies obviously lie with the "mad liberals" who had recently failed in an insurrection against the Church, and with the opponents of a regional revival of the Inquisition, which threatened to refuse absolution to any Catholic who had "dormito" with any Jew. Of this proclamation he writes, "I could not have believed this had I not seen it with my own eyes. . . . We shall see whether

---

[19] Pine-Coffin, *Bibliography*, 182, characterizes *Italy* as "at once one of the most comprehensive and most controversial works published on Italy at this time," owing to the author's liberal sympathies. Predictably, Byron considered it "a really excellent book." I cite the first edition, Lady (Sydney) Morgan, *Italy*, 2 vols. (London: Henry Colburn & Co., 1821), 2: 441–45. Morgan's political sentiments find relatively restrained expression here. She praises the French occupation, and merely offers a few archly disapproving references to the administration of the Cardinal-legate, e.g.: "The *Porporato* resides in the ancient palace, where he had lately ordered the picture-gallery to be closed against strangers; and seemed, for this and many other better reasons, to be sufficiently unpopular with all classes" (444).

the Papal Government tolerates this madness or not." Buckingham was aware of the history of relative tolerance of Jews under the Estensi. As a ranking member of the House of Lords, Buckingham took a keen interest in political and religious affairs. Yet he also manifested, almost everywhere he went except Ferrara, a vivid appreciation of the visual arts. His comments there seem indicative of the extent to which the Este city had come to be regarded from an exclusively political and literary point of view.[20]

It is with some sense of relief that one discovers now and again a visitor who genuinely enjoyed the experience of Ferrara, discovering that its amenities far outweighed the familiar aggravations and limitations. Such a traveler was Samuel Rogers, whose journal, written during the author's residence in Italy between 1814 and 1821, was found in 1954 in a London cellar by that congenial and accomplished historian John (later Sir John) Hale, and published with Hale's commentary two years later.[21] Rogers came to Ferrara on 25 October 1814. His stay got off to a good start — he loved his hotel, and he could afford the best: "The Three Moors, a magnificent Inn, exhibiting on each side of the gate a long list of its imperial and royal guests, from the Emperor Joseph downward." Rogers was an energetic tourist, who wrote brief but vivid notes on the sights. He walked through the cathedral, noting the major pictures; the *castello*; the Hospital of Saint Anne; Ariosto's house (where he observed "the natural politeness & anxiety to please of the young Lady at the house"); many palaces and gardens; and the theater (where he saw a comedy in three acts, performed by Andolfati's Company). On the next day, he visited the exterior of the cathedral; the library (where he remarked "the courtesy & intelligence of the Custode," who let him sit on Ariosto's chair!); and the *piazzetta,* where he enjoyed the cries of the street vendors, before an afternoon departure for Bologna. Rogers's comments are among the few places in the vast literature of Anglo-American travel that give evidence of Ferrara as a lively, if reduced, urban community with an active civic life.

---

[20] Buckingham's diary did not appear in print until 1862: Richard Plantagenet Temple Nugent Brydges Chandos Grenville, Duke of Buckingham and Chandos, *The Private Diary of Richard, Duke of Buckingham and Chandos, K. G.* (London: Hurst and Blackett, 1862), long after the author's death. It appears to have been prepared for publication by his son. The passage on Ferrara is in 3: 227–30. The work reads like a diary, and there is no evidence that either author or editor altered this section before publication. An unsigned Preface to the first volume remarks only that the diary "was printed as written, with some unimportant exceptions" (1: viii).

[21] Samuel Rogers, *The Italian Journal of Samuel Rogers, Edited with an Account of Rogers' Life and of Travel in Italy in 1814–21*, ed. J. R. Hale (London: Faber and Faber, 1956). Hale's introduction is full of useful information about the mechanics and *minutiae* of Italian travel in the early nineteenth century.

Thus a writer like Rogers may provide us with a useful corrective to the description of an academically-trained but unimaginative observer such as Professor Benjamin Silliman of Yale, the distinguished geologist who later became President of that College, and who went to Ferrara in 1851. Silliman was understandably interested in the topography of the region, and his comments on the landscape, while hardly original, tend to be usefully precise. His impressions confirmed the gloomy descriptions in his guidebook, and its perfunctory glosses seem to have persuaded him not to work too hard at seeing the sights: "It was impossible for us to afford time to range over this fallen city; and we were the less disposed to do it, because we saw enough to convince us that the above sombre picture is not shaded too deeply. Everything looks like decay . . . ."[22] Silliman goes on to mention the presence of the library and of Ariosto's house, but it does not appear that he managed to bestir himself to see those sights.

Yet he proved to be a better informant than his Harvard counterpart, Professor Charles Eliot Norton, an academic pioneer who introduced instruction in the history of art to the United States. The prestigious Norton lectures at Harvard still preserve his memory. Probably the most idiosyncratic passage in his travel journal, published in 1870 as *Notes of Travel and Study in Italy*, is the entry he made during his day in Ferrara — 16 June 1856. A five-page diatribe against the superstition and authoritarianism of Roman Catholicism, it attacks a number of anti-Protestant tracts published by the Church. There is nothing to indicate the slightest interest in, curiosity about, or awareness of Ferrara, or even the fact that Norton had been there, except for the name of the city at the beginning of the entry. A reader in search of insights about Italian art and architecture would conclude from this source that Ferrara had no monuments even worth mentioning, let alone discussing.[23]

The rising tide of nationalism and the political upheavals of 1848 produced the beginnings of a revitalization of Ferrara's energies, although the process was not a rapid one. As early as 1856, observant travelers noticed the signs of change. One of these was an American Episcopalian priest, the Reverend John E. Edwards. In his *Random Sketches and Notes of European Travel,* Edwards describes a fertile, abundant, well-tended countryside stretching in all directions on the alluvial plain between Bologna and Ferrara. Where his predecessors had slogged along virtually impassable roads, Edwards found a fine new road, one of many,

---

[22] Benjamin Silliman, *A Visit to Europe in 1851*, 2 vols. (New York: G. P. Putnam, 1854), 129–30.

[23] Charles Eliot Norton, *Notes of Travel and Study in Italy* (Boston: Ticknor and Fields, 1860), 181–86.

"kept up at very considerable expense by the government; a great many hands being constantly employed in hauling pebbles, and in breaking up rocks into small pieces, with which the road is kept in a firm and unyielding condition. Over these pebbles a thin coating of earth is kept deposited, and firmly pounded down, so as to preserve the surface in a smooth and even condition." It was about this time that many of the splendid rows of poplar trees which line the highways of Emilia were first installed, and Edwards is quite certain that these and other amenities are intended to protect travelers, and contribute to more agreeable journeys. Travelers who had made the trip even a few years before would have been incredulous at Edwards's description of the approach to Ferrara: "We entered, yesterday morning, upon this lovely road, stretching over this fertile plain, skirted with rich green fields, and vineyards, and gardens, and cottages. . . . A thousand elements combined to make the whole scene one of intoxicating delight, and untold loveliness." It had been a long time — many centuries in fact — since anyone had described the Ferrarese *contado* in such lyrical terms. True to the general practice, however, Edwards spent only a few hours in the city itself, guided around to see Tasso's cell and Calvin's room. His only other observation about contemporary Ferrara was that it had been a hotbed of revolutionary activity in 1848, and that many lives were lost in the process.[24]

Just fifteen years earlier, the gifted American novelist Catherine Maria Sedgwick had made her way to Ferrara from the north. It was November, and the Po had overflowed its banks. The winter wheat crop had been destroyed, and she read "anxiety and despair" in the faces of the people. Sedgwick was favorably disposed to Ferrara, because it was the home of her friend Felice Foresti, an imprisoned patriot whose character, in her view, "does [Ferrara] more honour than all this princely house [the Estensi] from beginning to end." Her mission to Ferrara was not to see the sights, but to express her solidarity with Foresti and his cause by visiting his family and friends. However, they escorted her to Santa Anna, where she was impressed by "its really Christian purpose of sheltering the sick and insane," and by the gentleness of the treatment provided to the mentally ill. She writes with evident delight of the newly erected statue of Ariosto

---

[24] John E. Edwards, *Random Sketches and Notes of European Travel* (New York: Harper and Brothers, 1857), 240. Edwards was equally alert to the contemporary political situation, of which he observes the following: "The spirit of revolution ran high in this place in 1848, and not a few lost their lives by the part which they took in the insurrectionary movements. It was here that Cardinal Bedini perpetrated the outrages upon the person of Hugo Bassi, which brought such a storm about his ears during his visit to the United States, as compelled him to leave without accomplishing the tour which he had projected."

on the Piazza Ariostea, taking particular pleasure in the unsuccessful opposition mounted by the Jesuits against the elevation of so secular a monument. One of the rare travelers to mention the Certosa, she appreciated its transition from monastery to cemetery, just as she applauded all those who opposed what she called "the imbecility of the papal government, the most imbecile in Italy." Sedgwick was completely fluent in Italian, so her use of the word *imbecile* may be understood to include all of its Italian connotations. Among the small circle of women travelers to Italy who included Ferrara in their comments, she was perhaps the most politically aware and the most socially astute observer.[25]

During the second half of the nineteenth century, Ferrara became increasingly accessible. The roads were improving, so that travel by horse and carriage became far less vexatious and dangerous than before. Banditry was declining, owing to the development of stronger local and national police and military forces. The railway offered an increasingly safe, reliable, and cost-effective means of transportation. And, toward the end of this period, the automobile eliminated the last barriers to rapid, unfettered travel. The most remote mountain village would soon be within easy reach of buses and cars. As Francis Miltoun put it to his adventurous readers in 1909, "The automobile, as a means of getting about, has opened up many old and half-used byways, and the automobile traveler

[25] Catherine Maria Sedgwick, *Letters from Abroad to Kindred at Home*, 2 vols. (New York: Harper and Brothers, 1841), 2:112–24. Sedgwick was impressed, like several other travelers coming from Venice, by Ferrara's cleanliness. Generally our authors attribute this to depopulation, and Sedgwick herself implies as much: "Ferrara is a *clean* fine old city, with immense, unoccupied houses, and wide, grass-grown streets, looking little like the seat of the independent and proud house of Este." Indeed, her interest in Ferrara lies mainly in its connection with Foresti, at the time so familiar a name that she saw no need to identify him further. Eleutario Felice Foresti (1793–1858) was born in Conselice, in the province of Ferrara. After receiving his doctorate in law at Bologna in 1809, he returned to Ferrara as an assistant judge, taught eloquence and letters at the *liceo,* and became a justice of the peace in the *polesine*. An early member of the Carbonari, he was betrayed by a colleague, denounced as a revolutionary, imprisoned and tortured in Venice, and ultimately condemned to death, his sentence commuted to twenty years' imprisonment. In time, he and other Italian patriots were released, and exiled to America. Foresti arrived in New York (where Sedgwick spent the winter months) in 1836. Three years later he became professor of Italian language and literature at Columbia, subsequently moving to New York University (then the University of the City of New York). He was Mazzini's official representative in America and remained active in Italian affairs for the rest of his life, even serving briefly as United States consul in Genoa. For further details, see H. R. Marraro's article in the *Dictionary of American Biography* or the more detailed and current essay, with useful bibliography, by G. Monsagrati in *DBI* (Rome: Istituto della Enciclopedia italiana, 1997), 48: 797–801.

of to-day may confidently assert that he has come to know the countryside of a beloved land as it was not even possible for his grandfathers to know it." Even the "modern railway," as Miltoun realized, could not begin to compete with the new mobility. "We used to go to the places marked on our railway tickets, and 'stopped off' as the regulations allowed. Now we go where fancy wills and stop off where the vagaries of our automobile force us to."[26] For Miltoun, and the modern travelers who constituted his audience, the old Grand Tour and its middle-class railway-based variants were obsolete. Travel could now be unbounded, and therefore far more engaging and picturesque than before.

Miltoun's approach to the *Ferrarese* is correspondingly quite original — he finds his way first to Comacchio, where he stops to watch the catching of eels, and deftly describes how they are processed for distribution to "Italian restaurants the world over." Miltoun's easy cosmopolitanism, his ability to elide the distances separating isolated villages from global horizons, alerts us to the irresistible onslaught of modernity. When he roars along the Via Cavour and parks alongside the *castello,* he sees a Ferrara where little has changed except the mentality he brings to the experience. For him, the absence of modern development in Ferrara has become its peculiar charm — it can still be discovered: "Of all the romantic Renaissance shrines of Italy none have a more potent attraction than Ferrara." Miltoun, unlike so many of the whining and blinkered travelers we have already encountered, understood that the paradox of Ferrara's decline provided its visitors with unique opportunities. While his description of Ferrara is conventional — he comments only on the *castello,* Ariosto's house, and Santa Anna — its reduced population and isolation from "contingent development" are clearly among its major assets. Realizing at some level that the world outside had changed in ways that Ferrara had avoided or resisted, he nevertheless lacked the vision to explore the implications of his perception. While Miltoun understood his advantage as a motorist, he thus failed to exploit it fully. How easy it would have been for him to familiarize himself with the walls of the city, to find his way to Sant'Antonio in Polesine, the Certosa, or even to the crenellated ruins of Belriguardo. But, like so many drivers who followed him, he took the road toward Padua after the briefest of visits.[27]

---

[26] Francis Miltoun, *Italian Highways and Byways from a Motor Car* (Boston: L. C. Page & Co, 1909), 2. Miltoun instructs his readers to take their time, rather than speeding along the Via Emilia at sixty miles per hour merely because they can. He sees excessive speed as an impediment to sightseeing, but his own impressions tend to be hurried and superficial.

[27] Miltoun, *Italian Highways and Byways*, 251–56.

Like the ancient roads they followed, this winding but representative survey of travelers to the city of the Este must draw to an end. As a final example of the emergent, modern Anglo-American mentality towards Ferrara it seems right to turn to William Dean Howells, the distinguished man of letters who, as United States consul in Venice at the age of thirty-four, wrote his *Italian Journeys* at the height of the *Risorgimento*. Howells stopped at Ferrara on his way to Genoa in 1864, and was immediately persuaded to make the standard literary pilgrimage to Tasso's cell, "in which was never imprisoned the poet whose works I had not read." Here we encounter a different voice from that of the typical sightseer. Skeptical, self-critical, and funny, Howells's archly youthful style brings a fresh, new tone to his discussion of the obligatory sights. He allowed the guides to offer their various explanations at Santa Anna and in the *castello,* but took all of their effusions with a grain of salt: "you paid your money, and took your choice of believing in them or not." Howells clearly regarded the Tassitean pilgrimage sites as a standard hoax for the tourists, and went along with it with a diplomat's observant good humor. He cites the standard Italian guidebook, Count F. Avventi's *Il Servitore di Piazza* (1838), as a support for his own skepticism. But, like Tertullian, he is not averse from believing inherited traditions *because* they are absurd: "I am afraid that if as frank caution were uttered in regard to other memorable places, the objects of interest in Italy would dwindle sadly in number, and the *valets de place* would be starved to death. . . . An Italian would rather enjoy a fiction than know a fact — in which preference I am not ready to pronounce him unwise."[28]

Howells coupled his skepticism concerning the accretions of legend with a high regard for the sad but impressive beauty of the cities of northern Italy, with their "reserved and dignified desolation." His sense of wonder at Ferrara's emptiness is remarkably positive; he sees no reason for this "city at rest" to evolve into a bustling modern metropolis. No one describes the feeling of walking about the Addizione Erculea better than Howells: "One may walk long through the longitude and rectitude of many of her streets without the encounter of a single face: the place, as a whole, is by no means as lively as Pompeii, where there are always strangers; perhaps the only cities in the world worthy to compete with Ferrara in point of agreeable solitude are Mantua and Herculaneum."[29]

Howells spent three days — an unusually long time — in Ferrara, and he writes about it more accurately and vividly than all but a handful of other

---

[28] William Dean Howells, *Italian Journeys* (New York: Hurd and Houghton, 1867), esp. 14–42: "The Picturesque, the Improbable, and the Pathetic in Ferrara." See p. 18 for his comments on the tour-guides ("valets de place").

[29] Howells, *Italian Journeys*, 23–24.

travelers. His appreciation of the cathedral, especially the Gothic exterior with its sculptural elements, and the Bastianino *Last Judgment* within, reveals a careful observer at work. His sharp eyes and vivid powers of description also extend to the urban scene in general, and he has some interesting observations concerning the Ghetto, through which he passed on his way to the Library, in those days a somnolent place: "We found that the dead *letterati* of Ferrara had the place wholly to themselves; not a living soul disputed the solitude of the walls with the custodians, and the bust of Ariosto looked down from his monument upon rows of empty tables, idle chairs, and dusty inkstands." Howells also visited Ariosto's house, now inhabited by a family, the *castello,* and some of the churches, which impress him only by the seriousness of the worshippers. These he contrasts with the "gay young dandies" who, when they go to church in Venice, "post themselves against a pillar, suck the heads of their sticks, and make eyes at the young ladies kneeling near them." The young American diplomat, notwithstanding his facile acceptance of national and religious stereotypes (Italians are dishonest rascals who will rob you at a moment's notice, Jews tend to be "foul" and exhibit "the universal Israelitish fondness for dealing in relics and ruins," etc.), appears open-minded and accepting in his dealings with individuals. His social attitudes, while typical of his time and heritage, seem to be held in check by a certain judiciousness. That serene certainty of judgment, combined with his easy assumptions about national differences, emerges in his fascinating description of his departure from Ferrara:

> Indeed, surprise at the presence of strangers spending two days in Ferrara when they could have got away sooner, was the only emotion which the whole population agreed in expressing with any degree of energy, but into this they seemed to throw their whole vitality. The Italians are everywhere an artless race, so far as concerns the gratification of their curiosity, from which no consideration of decency deters them. Here in Ferrara they turned about and followed us with their eyes, came to windows to see us, lay in wait for us at street-corners, and openly and audibly debated whether we were English or German. This interest rose almost into a frenzy of craving to know more of us all, when on the third day the whole city assembled before our hotel, and witnessed, with a sort of desperate cry, the departure of the heavy-laden omnibus which bore us and our luggage from their midst.

Howells, even at this early age, was already a far more talented writer than most of the other authors of travel journals cited in this essay. From a strictly literary standpoint, he belongs more in the company of such celebrated tourists as Goethe,

Dickens (who presented Ferrara to his multitude of readers as a "city of the dead"),[30] Henry James, and Edith Wharton than with the relatively less known and less talented writers with whom I consider him here. But in either circle, Howells stands out for the amount of time and space he devotes to Ferrara, his efforts to go beyond the standard clichés, and his evident enjoyment of the experience of Ferrara.

But Howells was swimming against the tide. As we have seen, generations — actually centuries — of English-speaking travelers, going back to the first years after the *devoluzione,* had fashioned a powerful negative stereotype of the city. Whether alienated by the legacy of "tyranny," outraged by "Popery" and what they saw as the evils of ecclesiastical governance, saddened by the inescapable evidence of decline, offended by the modest amenities, bored by the topography, annoyed by the hardships of travel, or righteously indignant at the sufferings of the late, great men of letters, every traveler had some reason to find fault with the city. Unable to see it on its own terms, they were all too ready to invoke invidious comparisons with the high spots on the tour.

It has taken a long time, and the slow leavening power of several long-term historical processes, to bring Renaissance Ferrara and its heritage back into the mainstream of our historical consciousness. Among these have been the growth of historical scholarship on the local and international levels; the revitalization of modern Ferrarese cultural achievement as evidenced by Futurism and the prominence of *ferraresi* in other literary and artistic movements; and the local effects of the post-World War II *boom economico* and its stimulative effects upon local industrial and commercial development, social and economic infrastructure, and strategic planning for the promotion of tourism as a dimension of Ferrara's civic and economic life. Howells would, perhaps, be disappointed if he were translated to modern Ferrara — no more grass in the streets, depopulated

[30] Charles Dickens, *Pictures from Italy* (London: Bradbury & Evans, 1846), 104. Dickens, perhaps the most widely read of all the travelers to Italy, has the most consistently unflattering things to say about Ferrara. He calls it solitary, depopulated, deserted, grim. The sun shines there with "diminished cheerfulness," and the best sights are the "long silent streets, and the dismantled palaces . . . where rank weeds are slowly creeping up the long untrained stairs." The town is "dreary, unreal, spectral . . . a desert of a place." The *castello* is a "sullen city in itself." Given the immense and long-lived popularity of this book, and the extraordinarily hostile vigor of the author's descriptions of Ferrara, its effects must have been damaging. Yet Dickens' originality should not be exaggerated. In 1831, the American painter Amasa Hewing visited Ferrara, and made much the same observation: "[It] is indeed what the Italians call a 'cittamorte,' or dead city." See Amasa Hewing, *A Boston Portrait-Painter Visits Italy: The Journal of Amasa Hewing, 1830–33*, ed. F. H. Allen (Boston: The Boston Atheneum, 1931).

neighborhoods, empty shells of palaces, or beggars. But most of us will not miss those relics of a long period in the shadows of historical change. The second, modern (or post-modern) Renaissance of Ferrara has brought new vitality and distinction to this grand old city. Now the challenge is to maintain some connection with the best of what has gone before, to preserve and record the meaning of that vanishing world.

Archival Sources and Abbreviations

ASFe: Archivio di Stato, Ferrara
ANA: Archivio Notarile Antico
ASC/SF: Archivio Storico Comunale, Serie Finanziarie
Archivio Vendeghini
Bollette: Statuti dell'Ufficio delle Bollette
Not.: Notaio

ASMn: Archivio di Stato, Mantua

ASMo: Archivio di Stato, Modena
AG: Archivio Gonzaga
Archivio per materie
ASE: Archivio Segreto Estense
Casa e Stato
Camera Ducale
Cancelleria Ducale
Fondo Inquisitione
Libri dei Malefici

ASR: Archivio di Stato, Rome
Trib Crim Gov: Tribunale Criminale del Governatore

ASV: Archivio segreto vaticano, Rome

BAV: Biblioteca Apostolica Vaticana

Bayerische Staatsbibliothek, Munich, Mus. MS. 46

BCA: Biblioteca Comunale Ariostea, Ferrara

BCB: Biblioteca Civica di Bergamo

BCR: Biblioteca Classense, Ravenna

BEM: Biblioteca Estense Universitaria di Modena

BL: British Library

Additional Abbreviations:

DBI *Dizionario Biografico degli Italiani*
GSLI *Giornale storico della letteratura italiana*
MRTS Medieval & Renaissance Texts & Studies
RIS *Rerum Italicarum Scriptores*
UTET Unione Tipografico-Editrice Torinese

Works Cited

I. Primary Sources

A. Manuscript Sources

Act of legitimation of Alfonso and Alfonsino by Cardinal Deacon Innocenzo Cibo, 17 April 1532. ASMo, A.S.E., Casa e Stato b. 355.

"Ad Dei Omnipotentis Laudem et Gloriam Contra Blasfemates, Sodomites, Baratarios Ludos, Concubinarios, Meretrices, Lenones, Datiarios, et Officiales Passium Ac Beccarios Vendentes Tempore Festivitatum." ASFe, *Bollette*, 25 April 1496, article 131.

"Affictus Baldino di Simone de Bergamo e Bono dei Danieli." ASFe, ANA, Matr. 7, Pietro Pincerna, b. 1, fol. 4, cc. 8rv, 8 April 1379.

"Affictus Federici de Flandria et Petri de Salandria magistro Zanini de Picardia."ASFe, ANA, Lodovico Portelli, matr. 217, b. 1, 6 August 1476, 37r–38v. 26 June 1501, 38r–39v.

"Affictus inter dominum Dominicum dicta Morgis civem Ferrarie et commendabile viro ser Petro de Pelipparis notario." ASFe, ANA, Matr. 205, Filippo Pincerna, b. 1, fol. 6, 26 June 1501, fols. 38r–39v.

"Affictus Santini de Mediolano et fratris a Simone et fratre de Mediolano," 25 November 1469. ASFe, ANA, Not. Giovanni Castelli, Matr. 128, b. 3, 12v–14v. Rental contract regarding the Montealbano brothel.

Aldobrandini, Cardinal Pietro. Letter to Pope Clement VIII, 9 February 1598. ASV, Armadio 46, 1, fols. 142v–144r.

Antigini, Giulio and Giacomo. *Annali di Ferrara dal 1384 al 1514*. BCA, MS. Cl. 1, 757.

Aragona, Eleonora d'. Letter to Francesco Gonzaga, 4 November 1484. ASMn AG b. 1183.

ASMo, ASE, Cancelleria, Carteggio di Principi Esteri, Rome b.1299/14.

Benetti, Giovan Battista. *Antichi nomi delle strade di Ferrara con annotazioni storiche*. BCA, Coll. Antonelli, n. 346.

Boiardo, Matteo Maria. *Istoria imperiale*. BCR, MS. 424.

Caleffini, Ugo. "Croniche facte et scripte per Ugo Caleffini notaio ferrarese." BAV, MS Chigiana I.I.4.

Canani, Baldessar. Memorandum to Ercole d'Este, 20 June 1488. ASFe, ANA, Mat. 165, Baldessare Canani, b. 2, fasc. 4.

———. Memorandum to Eleonora d'Este, 11 October 1488. ASFe, ANA, Mat. 165, Baldessare Canani, b. 2, fasc. 4.

———. Memorandum to Eleonora d'Este, 17 October 1488. ASFe, ANA, Mat. 165, Baldessare Canani, b. 2, fasc. 4.

Commissio ducalis contra meretrices publicas facientes et committentes insultum contra aliquem. ASFe, ASC, *Bollette*, article 114, 17 May 1476.

"Compendio di tutte le strade, case, palazzi e conventi." ASFe, ASC, Serie Patrimoniale, b. 30, fol. 11, Fondo Montecatini, 58r.

Complaints from citizens of Rome against the activities of prostitutes. ASR, Trib Crim, Atti di Cancelleria Miscellanea, b. 105, fols. 34; 36, 1624.

"Contra meretrices et hospites." *Bollette*, article 68, 23 April 1450, ASFe, (ASC/SF), Busta 9 (b), fascicolo (f) 17.

"Contra Moranda Magnanini di Fanano." ASMo, Fondo Inquisizione, b. 9, Processo 3, 2 August 1596, c. 2v.

"Contra Moranda Magnanini da Fanano, meretricem." ASMo, Fondo Inquisitione, b. 9, Processo 3, 22 August 1596, 5v.

"Contra Camillam Senens. curalem."ASR, Trib Crim Gov, Processi, Sec. XVI, b. 2, case 19, 23 October 1557.

"Contra Maddalena Prosperi et altri." ASR, Trib Crim Gov, Processi, Sec. XVII, b. 534, case 5, 28 June 1660.

Cronaca di Ferrara 1471–94. Biblioteca apostolica vaticana, MS Chigi I.I.4.

Decembrio, Angelo. *Politia letteraria*. MS. Vat. Lat. 1794.

"De meretricum banda." ASFe, ASC/SF, *Bollette*, article 3, 1438.

Descriptio-Turpin. BEM, MS. N.5.12.

Equicola, Mario. *Annali della cita di Ferrara 1320–1582*. BCA, MS. Cl II, n. 355.

Este, Alfonso I. Testament, 28 August, 1533. ASMo, A.S.E., Casa e Stato, b.325.

Este, Borso d'. Letter to Hieronymus de' Alegri da Verona, 2 March 1471. ASMo, A.S.E., Casa e Stato, Cancelleria C–2, c.32.

Este, Ercole d'. Letter to Duchess Eleonora d'Aragona, 26 October 1478. ASMo, Camera Ducale (CD), Leggi e decreti, C, V, f. 200.

———. Letter to Eleonora d'Aragona, Duchess of Ferrara, 12 November 1478. ASMo, CD, Leggi e decreti, C, V, f. 211.

Este, Isabella d'. Letters regarding her daughters' desire to enter monastic life. ASMn, AG F.II.9.2996 libro 29 (Copialettere).

———. Letter to Beatrice d'Este, 27 February 1490. ASMn AG F.II.9.2904 libro 136 cc.1v–2r (Copialettere).

———. Letter to Eleonora d'Aragona, Duchess of Ferrara, 2 March 1490. ASMn AG F.II.9.2904 libro 136 c. 3v (Copialettere).

———. Letter to Lucrezia d'Este, 4 March 1490. ASMn AG F.II.9.2904 libro 36 c. 4v (Copialettere).

———. Letter to Eleonora d'Aragona, Duchess of Ferrara, 9 March 1490. ASMn AG F.II.9.2904 libro 136 c. 7r (Copialettere).

———. Letter to Francesco II Gonzaga, 30 April 1490. ASMn AG F.II.6.2106 c. 375.

———. Letter to Francesco II Gonzaga, 28 May 1490. ASMn AG F.II.6.2106 c. 364.

———. Letter to Chiara Gonzaga, 19 February 1495. ASMn AG F.II.9.2992 libro 5 c. 15r (Copialettere).

———. Letter to Elisabetta Gonzaga, Duchess of Urbino, 22 February 1496. ASMn AG F.II.9.2992 Libro 6 c. 29r (Copialettere).

———. Letter to Francesco II Gonzaga, 24 February 1496. ASMn AG F.II.6.2111 Fasc. V c. 208r.

———. Letter to Francesco II Gonzaga, 27 April 1496. ASMn AG F.II.6.2111 Fasc. V c. 240r.

———. Letter to Francesco II Gonzaga, 5 June 1496. ASMn AG F.II.6.2111 Fasc. V c. 254r.

———. Letter to Francesco II Gonzaga, 1 July 1496. ASMn AG F.II.6.2111 Fasc. V c. 264r–v.

———. Letter to Bernardino Prosperi, 20 March 1498. ASMn AG F.II.9.2992 libro 9 c. 38v (Copialettere).

———. Letter to Donato de Preti, 20 March 1498. ASMn AG F.II.9.2992 libro 9 c. 38v (Copialettere).

———. Letter to Francesco II Gonzaga, 13 November 1502. ASMn AG F.II.6.2115 cc. 186r–187r.

———. Letter to Francesco II Gonzaga, 17 July 1503. ASMn AG F.II.6.2115 Fasc. VII c. 349r.

———. Letter to Francesco II Gonzaga, 29 August 1503. ASMn AG F.II.6.2115 Fasc. VII c. 358r.

———. Letter to Francesco II Gonzaga, 31 August 1503. ASMn AG F.II.6.2115 Fasc. VII c. 359r–361r.

———. Letter to Francesco II Gonzaga, 15 September 1503. ASMn AG F.II.6.2115 Fasc. VIII c. 368r–369r.

———. Letter to Matteo Ippoliti, 14 August 1510. ASMn AG F.II.9.2996 libro 28 cc. 23r–v (Copialettere).

———. Letter to Magdalena, gubernatrice, 9 September 1510. ASMn AG F.II.9.2996 libro 28 c. 41r (Copialettere).

———. Letter to Francesco Grossino, 5 July 1511. ASMn AG F.II.9. 2996 libro 29 c. 38v (Copialettere).

———. Letter to Ercole Gonzaga, 23 January 1522. ASMn AG F.II.9.2998 libro 38 cc. 66v–67r (Copialettere).

———. Letter to Giacomo Suardo, 8 October 1524. ASMn AG F.II.9.2999 libro 46 cc. 70r–71r (Copialettere).

———. Testament. ASMn AG Serie D, Busta 332.

Este, Niccolò d'. Testament. ASMo A.S.E., Casa e Stato, b.324, fasc.10, 26 December 1442 (1441).

Este, Rinaldo Maria d'. Letter to Ercole d'Este, 3 July 1499. ASMo, Archivio Estense, Casa e Stato 130.

Exemption of Isacco da Fano, Jew, from taxes and fees on all his goods. ASFe, Archivio Vendeghini, Secoli XV–XIX, Scatola 3, fol. 25, 17 October 1500.

Fines against prostitutes for leaving the city without permission. ASMo, *Maleficio*, 1459–1460, 35v, 23 July 1459; Bartolomea Fiorata, 25r, 20 April 1459.

Ferrara, Orlando de'. Complaint about prostitutes' unpaid debts. ASMo, CD, Libri Camerali Diversi, n. 2, 24 December 1426, c. 1.

Gride concerning the spatial limitations of *meretrici*. ASFe, *Bollette,* 25 April 1496, article 131.

Guarneri, Antonio Maria. *Letters*. ASMo, Cancelleria: Carteggi di Ufficiali Camerali, Busta I, 1487.

"Inventario de mobili ritrovati in casa della già Cecilia Polidori, publica meretrice." ASFe, ANA, Mat. 1027, Not. Lorenzo Vacchi, b. 1, 16 October 1675.

Letter to Duchess Eleonora, 16 September 1490, containing complaints about prostitutes in the city of Ferrara. ASMo, Cancelleria Ducale, Carteggio Fattorale (CD/CF), b. 22/1, fol. 25.

List of prostitutes living on the Strada della Campana in Rome. ASR, Trib Crim Gov, Atti di Cancelleria, Miscellenea, b. 105; Trib Crim Gov, Processi, Sec. XVI, 1557, b. 33, process 19.

"Locatio inter dominorum infra: Gabrieli de Plecenari et magistro Antonio delle Messe pretore." ASFe, ANA, Matr. 205, Filippo Pincerna, b. 1, f. 6, 16 June 1501, 37rv.

Martin V, Pope. Papal bull. ASMo, A.S.E., Casa e Stato, Membranacei, cass.24, no.4, 12 December 1430.

Names of prisoners in Ferrara's jail. ASFe, ASC, Ser. Pat. *Libro Commissioni,* B 7, f. 10, 8 November 1471, c. 101r.

Notarial records indicating plebian origins of the Dianti family. ASFe, ANA, Giacomo Ziponari, Matr. 384, b. 1, f. 4, May 1520.

"Obligatio Ursoline et Lucie Meretrices facta Magistro Jannino Franzexeno." ASFe, ANA, Not. V. Lucenti, matr. 201, b. 2, 13 January 1473.

"Obligatio Ursoline et Lucie meretricum facta Magistro Joannino franxoso." ASFe, ANA, Vitale Lucenti, Matr. 201, b. 1, 24r, 19 January 1473.

Paolino, Fra Minorita. "Plan of the territory and city of Ferrara, 1322–25." MS. Vat. Lat. 1960, 267r.

Payments for demolition of the Montealbano osteria and records of initiated construction of stables on the site. ASMo, CD, Munizioni e fabbriche, Reg. 21 (1488), cc. 5, 10, 35.

Payment for work on a wall in "la hostaria di Santa Agnese." ASMo, CD, Munizioni e fabbriche, b. 51, c. 67.

Prisciani, Giacomo. Letter to Duchess Eleonora d'Este, 27 February 1490. ASMo, Cancelleria Ducale, Carteggio Fattorale (CD/CF), b. 22/1, fol. 8.

———. Letter to Duchess Eleonora d'Este, 16 September 1490. ASMo, Cancelleria Ducale, Carteggio Fattorale (CD/CF), b. 22/1, fol. 25.

———. Letter to Duke Ercole d'Este, 4 May 1491. ASMo, Cancelleria Ducale, Carteggio Fattorale (CD/CF), b. 22/1, fol. 25.

"Proclama contra lenones ferrarienses et eos qui habitassent in civitate ferrariae per spatium decem annorum." ASFe, ASC/SF, *Bollette,* article 83, 29 April 1462.

"Proclama contra lenones ferrarienses et meretrices et contra illos quoscumque sibi domos locantes." ASFe, ASC/SF, *Bollette*, article 50, 5 October 1486.

"Proclama contra publicas meretrices euntes hospitiis et tabernis." ASFe, ASC/SF, *Bollette*, article 80, 28 December 1461.

Proclamation denouncing thefts by prostitutes. ASFe, ASC. *Bollette,* article 116, 29 November 1476.

Proclamation on *postriboli* and a *loco pubblico*. ASFe, ASC, *Bollette*, 18 May 1476.

Prohibition against the prostitute Giovanna of Venice from frequenting Ferrara's inns or hostelries, on pain of immediate expulsion. ASFe, ASC/SF, *Bollette*, article 68.

"Promisio facta per Joanna de Venezia meretricem et eius lenonem Johanni Cazano." ASFe, ANA, Not. Lodovico Portelli, Matr. 217, busta (b) 1, pp. 10v–11r, 6 August 1476.

"Quod non liceat alicui tabernario prestare domicilium alicui mulieri inhoneste viventi." ASFe, ASC/SF, *Bollette*, article 90, 23 August 1464.

Re: Beating of one prostitute by another, the Polish Caterina, with a club. ASMo. Memoriale 11, c. 131v, 8 June 1458.

Re: Clubbing of Franchino of Reggio by the prostitute Anna, for attempting to get away without paying. ASMo, *Maleficio*, 2, 3 December 1459.

Re: Collecting of taxes on the brothels of Ferrara. ASMo, Camera Ducale, Libri camerali diversi, Entrata et Spesa anno 1434, reg. 4, c. 2r.

Re: Donations made by Niccolò III d'Este to Stella Tolomei. ASMo, Camera, Notai camerali ferraresi, Jacobus Delaito, XXIII, cc.182r–186r.

Re: Former location of "bordello da San Biaxio." ASMo, CD, Minizioni e fabbriche, Reg. 26, 26 November 1493, c. 74.

Re: Grants to prostitutes to clear debts with brothel owners. ASMo, CD, Libri Camerali Diversi, "Entrata e spesa," 4; Memoriale n. 20 (1468–71), 271.

Re: Punishment of prostitutes for petty crimes. ASFe, ASC, Bollette, article 114, 17 May 1476.

Re: Punishment of the Slav prostitute Caterina for not wearing the yellow cloth. ASMo, Memoriale 11, December 1458; ASMo, Memoriale 14, 15 September 1461.

Re: Shaming ritual performed against a cuckolded husband. ASFe, ASC, Bollette, article 40.

Regulations against criminal activities of prostitutes. ASFe, ASC, Bollette, article 83, 29 April 1462, and 22 September 1462.

"Relatione sopra la Città e Stato di Ferrara," n. d. (1598 ca.), BL, Addl. MS. Ital. 28, 451, fol. 389v.

Report of Antonio de Paxi against his wife, Luciana Bianca, for her adultery. ASMo, CD, *Libri dei Malefici*, Reg. 2 (1451), 22 September, c. 111r.

Rodi, Filippo. *Annali di Ferrara a l'anno 1598*. BL. Additional Manuscripts It. 16,521. Vol. I, Book 1, 77v.

Sale of the Montealbano osteria and chiusi by Matteo da Milano to Ercole I d'Este. ASFe, ANA, Mat. 231, Gentile Sardi, b. 2, f. 2, 23 April 1488.

Sardi, Gaspare. Letter to Alessandro Marocello, 28 October 1553. ASMo, Archivio per materia, Letterati, b. 60.

———. "Genealogia delli Estensi accopiata per mi Guasparo di Sardi dal libro di Fra Paolo da Legnago," Miscellanea, BEM, F.3.3 (Ital. 410), c.8v.

Sogari, Leonello. Letter to Duke Ercole d'Este, 29 April 1491. ASMo, Cancelleria Ducale, Carteggio Fattorale (CD/CF), b. 22/1, f. 26.

B. Printed Sources

Addison, Joseph. *Remarks on Several Parts of Italy . . . In the Years 1701, 1702, 1703*. 2nd ed. London: J. Tonson, 1718.

Alberigo, J., et al., eds. *Conciliorum oecumenicorum decreta*. 3rd ed. Bologna: Istituto per le scienze religiose, 1972.

Alberti, Leandro. *Descrittione di tutta Italia*. Bologna: Anselmo Giaccarelli, 1550.

Alberti, Leon Battista. *On Painting*. Trans. John R. Spencer. New Haven: Yale University Press, 1966.

Albricus. *Allegoriae Poeticae*. Paris: De Marnet, 1520.

Aldrovandi, U. *Ornithologiae*. 3 vols. Bologna: N. Tebaldinus, 1637–1696.

Aleotti, Giovan Battista. *Della scienza et dell'arte del ben regolare le acque di Gio. Battista Aleotti detto l'Argenta architetto del Papa, et del pubblico ne la città di Ferrara,* ed. Massimo Rossi. Modena: Panini, 2000.

Alighieri, Dante. *La Commedia secondo l'antica volgata*, ed. Giorgio Petrocchi. Milan: Mondadori, 1966.

Andreini, Isabella. *Lettere d'Isabella Andreini padovana, comica gelosa et academica intenta nominata l'Accesa*. Venice: M. A. Zaltieri, 1607.

Aretino, Pietro. *Il terzo libro de le lettere di Messer Pietro Aretino*. Venice: Appresso Gabriel Giolito de Ferrari, 1546.

Arienti, Giovanni Sabadino degli. *De triumphis religionis: Art and Life at the Court of Ercole I d'Este*, ed. Werner L. Gundersheimer. Geneva: Droz, 1972.

———. *The Letters of Giovanni Sabadino degli Arienti (1481–1510)*, ed. Carolyn James. Florence and Perth: Olschki, 2001.

Ariosto, Ludovico. "Epithalamium." In *Opere di Ludovico Ariosto*. Trieste: Lloyd Austriaco, 1857.

———. *Lettere*, ed. Angelo Stella. Verona: Mondadori, 1965.

———. *Opere minori*, ed. Cesare Segre. Milan: Ricciardi, 1954.

———. *Orlando Furioso*. Trans. Allan Gilbert. 2 vols. New York: Vanni, 1954.

———. *Orlando Furioso*, ed. Santorre Debenedetti and Cesare Segre. Bologna: Commissione per i testi di lingua, 1960.

———. *Orlando Furioso*. Turin: Einaudi, 1971.

———. *Orlando Furioso*. Trans. Guido Waldman. Oxford and New York: Oxford University Press, 1974.

———. *Orlando Furioso*, ed. Emilio Bigi. 2 vols. Milan: Rusconi, 1982.

Armenini, Giovan Battista. *De' veri precetti della pittura*. Ravenna: F. Tebaldini, 1587.

Arrian. *Indica*. Trans. Edgar Iliff Robson. 3 vols. Loeb Classical Library. Cambridge, MA: Harvard University Press, 1946–1949.

Athenaeus. *The Deipnosophists*. Trans. Charles Burton Gulick. Cambridge, MA: Harvard University Press, 1961.

Atti della visita apostolica a Ferrara. 1574.

Badia, Iodoco del, ed. *Diario fiorentino dal 1450 al 1516 di Luca Landucci*. Florence: G. C. Sansoni, 1883.

Balbus, Scipio. *Pulcher Visus Locus Illustrissimi Ducis Ferrariae*. Ferrara: Tip. Taddei condotta da Antonio Soati, 1897.

Barberino, Andrea da. *L'Aspramonte*, ed. Marco Boni. Bologna: Per i Tipi dell'Antiquaria Palmaverde, 1951.

———. *Li reali di Francia*. Venice: Tipografia di Alvisopoli, 1821.

Barberino, Francesco da. *Reggimento e costumi di donna*, ed. Giuseppe Sansone. Turin: Loescher-Chiantore, 1957.

Baruffaldi, Girolamo. *Dell'istoria di Ferrara scritta dal dottor D. Girolamo Baruffaldi Ferrarese* . . . Ferrara: Bernardino Pomatelli, 1700.

Barzi, Benedetto de'. *Tractatus de filiis non legitime natis.* In *Tractatus universi iuris*. 29 vols. Vol. 8, Part 2, fols. 24ra–29vb. Venice: Societas Aquilae Renovantis, 1584.

Basinio. *Basini Parmensis poetae opera praestantiora nunc primum edita et opportunis commentariis illustrata*, ed. Drudi, L. Rimini: Typo Albertiniana, 1794.

Blessington, Marguerite, Countess of. *The Idler in Italy*. 2nd ed. 3 vols. London: Henry Colburn, 1839.

Boccaccio, Giovanni. *Genealogia deorum*. Venice: Augustinus de Zannis de Portesio, 1511.

Boiardo, Matteo Maria. *Tutte le opere di Matteo M. Boiardo*, ed. Angelandrea Zottoli. Milan: Mondadori, 1944.

———. *Orlando Innamorato*. Trans. Charles Stanley Ross. Berkeley: University of California Press, 1989.

———. *Orlando innamorato*, ed. Riccardo Bruscagli. Turin: Einaudi, 1995.

Bonino, Guido Davico, ed. *Il teatro italiano. II. La commedia del Cinquecento*. 2 vols. Turin: Einaudi, 1977–1978.

Buckingham and Chandos, Richard Plantagenet Temple Nugent Brydges Chandos Grenville, Duke of. *The Private Diary of Richard, Duke of Buckingham and Chandos, K. G.* London: Hurst and Blackett, 1862.

Burnet, Gilbert. *Some Letters Containing An account of what seemed most remarkable in Switzerland, Italy, &c.* Rotterdam: Abraham Acher, 1686.

Calcagnini, Celio. *Epithalamium*. Ferrara, 1502.

———. "Commentatio de Re Nautica." In *Opere Aliquot,* 301–16. Basel: Froben, 1544.

Caleffini, Ugo. *Diario di Ugo Caleffini (1471–1494)*, ed. G. Pardi. 2 vols. Ferrara: Premiata tipografia sociale, 1938–1940.

Carbone, Ludovico. "Oratio." In *Prosatori latini del quattrocento*, ed. Eugenio Garin, 379–417. Turin: Einaudi, 1952, repr. 1977.

Cereta, Laura. *Collected Letters of a Renaissance Feminist,* ed. and trans. Diana Robin. Chicago: University of Chicago Press, 1997.

Castiglione, Baldassarre. *The Book of the Courtier*. Trans. Charles S. Singleton. Garden City, NY: Anchor Books, 1959.

Chronicon Estense, ed. Giulio Bertoni and E. P. Vicini. 2nd ed. Rerum Italicarum Scriptores 15/3. Città di Castello and Bologna: S. Lapi, 1908.

Colonna, Francesco. *Hypnerotomachia Poliphili*, ed. Giovanni Pozzi and Lucia A. Ciapponi. Padua: Antenore, 1980.

Curione, Caelio Secundo. *De amplitudine Beati Regni Dei dialogi*. Basel, 1554.

Datini, Margherita. *Le Lettere di Margherita Datini a Francesco di Marco (1384–1410)*, ed. Valeria Rosati. Prato: Biblioteca dell'archivio storico pratese, 1977.

———. *Per la tua Margherita. Scrittura della distanza. Lettere di una donna del Trecento al marito mercante,* ed. Diana Toccafondi and Gianni Cascone. Prato: Comune di Prato-Archivio di Stato di Prato-Provincia di Prato, 2001.

Decembrio, Angelo. *Politia letteraria*. Augsburg: Heinrich Stayner, 1540.

———. *Politia letteraria*. Basel: Johann Hervagen, 1562.

Delayto, Jacobus de. *Annales estenses Jacobi de Delayto*, ed. L. A. Muratori. Rerum Italicarum Scriptores 18. Milan: Ex Typographia Societatis Palatinae, 1731.

Della Porta, Giovanni Battista. *Il Georgio, tragedia*. Naples: Gio. Battista Gargano & Lucretio Nucci, 1611.

———. *Teatro, I. Le tragedie*, ed. Raffaele Sirri. Naples: Istituto Universitario Orientale, 1978.

Des Roches, Catherine. *Les Oeuvres*, ed. Anne Larsen. Geneva: Droz, 1993.

———. *Les Secondes Oeuvres*, ed. Anne Larsen. Geneva: Droz, 1998.

Diario ferrarese dall'anno 1409 sino al 1502 di autori incerti, ed. Giuseppe Pardi. Rerum Italicarum Scriptores 24. Bologna: Zanichelli, 1928–1938. 2nd ed.

Dickens, Charles. *Pictures from Italy*. London: Bradbury & Evans, 1846.

Domenichi, Ludovico. *La nobiltà delle donne*. Venice, 1549.

———. *La nobiltà delle donne corretta, & di nuovo ristampata*. Venice, 1551.

Erasmus, Desiderius. *Ecclesiastes*, ed. Jacques Chomarat. In *Opera Omnia: recognita et adnotatione critica instructa notisque illustrata* 5.5. Amsterdam: North-Holland Publishing Company, 1969–.

Euripides. *Euripides' Phaethon*, ed. J. Diggle. Cambridge: Cambridge University Press, 1970.

Faletti, Girolamo. *Poemata*. Ferrara, 1546.

Fedele, Cassandra. *Letters and Orations,* ed. and trans. Diana Robin. Chicago: University of Chicago Press, 2000.

Ferrari, Benedetto. *L'Andromeda del Signor Benedetto Ferrari Rappresentata in Musica in Venetia l'anno 1637*. Venice: Antonio Bariletti, 1637.

Ficino, Marsilio. *Three Books on Life*. Trans. C. Kaske and J. R. Clark. MRTS 57. Binghamton: Medieval and Renaissance Texts and Studies, 1989.

Filarete, Antonio. *Treatise on Architecture*. Trans. John R. Spencer. New Haven: Yale University Press, 1965.

Fórnari, Simone. *La spositione da M. Simon Fórnari da Reggio sopra l'Orlando Furioso di M. Ludovico Ariosto*. Florence: Lorenzo Torrentino, 1549.

Forsyth, Joseph. *Remarks on Antiquities, Arts, and Letters during an Excursion in Italy in the Years 1802 and 1803*. 2nd ed. London: John Murray, 1816. 4th ed. London: John Murray, 1835.

Franco, Veronica. *Poems and Selected Letters*, ed. and trans. Ann Rosalind Jones and Margaret F. Rosenthal. Chicago: University of Chicago Press, 1998.

Frizzi, Antonio. *Memorie per la storia di Ferrara*. 5 vols. Ferrara: F. Pomatelli, 1846–1848.

———. *Diario di Antonio Frizzi in continuazione delle Memorie per la storia di Ferrara*. Ferrara: Abram Servadio, 1857.

Gatari, Galeazzo, and Bartolomeo Gatari. *Cronaca carrarese*. Ed. A. Medin and G. Tolomei, Rerum italicarum scriptores 17.1. Bologna: Zanichelli, 1909–1932.

Geale, Hamilton. *Notes of a Two Years' Residence in Italy*. Dublin: James McGlashan, 1847.

Giovio, Paolo. *Liber de vita et rebus gestis Alphonsi Atestini*. Florence: Torrentinus Ducalis Typographus, 1551.

———. *La vita di Alfonso da Este Duca di Ferrara*. Trans. Giovambattista Gelli. Venice, 1597.

Giraldi, Giambattista Cinzio. *Egle: satira*. Florence: n.p., 1550?

Giraldi, Lilio Gregorio. *De deis gentium*. 1548. Repr. New York: Garland, 1976.

Gratian. "Decretum." In *Corpus iuris canonici*, ed. E. Friedberg. Leipzig: Officina Bernhardi Tauchnitz, 1879.

Gray, Robert. *Letters during the course of a Tour through Germany, Switzerland and Italy in the Years MDCCXCI and MDCCXCII. With reflections on the manners, literature, and religion of those countries*. London: F. and C. Rivington, 1794.

Guarini, Marc'Antonio. *Compendio historico dell'origine, accrescimento e prerogative delle chiese e luoghi pij della città e diocesi di Ferrara*. Ferrara, 1621.

Guazzo, Marco. *Cronaca*. Venice: Francesco Bidoni, 1553.
Guicciardini, Francesco. *Opere*, ed. E. Scarano. Turin: UTET, 1970.
———. *Storia d'Italia*. Milan: Garzanti, 1988.
Hare, Augustus J. C. *Cities of Northern and Central Italy*. Vol. 2 (of 3). New York: George Routledge & Sons, 1876.
Herodotus. *Histories*. Trans. A. D. Godley. Loeb Classical Library. Cambridge, MA: Harvard University Press, 1981.
Hewing, Amasa. *A Boston Portrait-Painter Visits Italy: The Journal of Amasa Hewing, 1830–33*, ed. F. H. Allen. Boston: The Boston Athenaeum, 1931.
Howells, William Dean. *Italian Journeys*. New York: Hurd and Houghton, 1867.
Ingamells, John. *A Dictionary of British and Irish Travelers in Italy, 1701–1800*. New Haven: Yale University Press, 1997.
Jameson, Anna Brownell. *Diary of an Ennuyée*. Philadelphia: E. Littell, 1826.
Jerome. "Commentaria in Evangelium S. Matthaei." PL 26.15–228.
Jhan, Maistre. *Das Chorwerk*. Ed. Winfried Kirsch. Wolfenbüttel: Moseler, 1967.
King, Margaret L., and Albert Rabil Jr., eds. *Her Immaculate Hand: Selected Writings by and about the Women Humanists of Quattrocento Italy*. MRTS 20. Binghamton: Center for Medieval & Early Renaissance Studies, 1983.
Lassels, Richard. *An Italian Voyage, or A Compleat Journey Through Italy, In Two Parts*. 2nd ed. London: Richard Wellington, 1698.
Longueil, Gilbert de. *Dialogus de Avibus*. Cologne, 1543.
Machiavelli, Niccolò. *Opere*, ed. Rinaldo Rinaldi. Gen. ed. Alessandro Montevecchi. 4 vols. Turin: UTET, 1971–.
Maragna, Luciano, ed. *Gli statuti del Polesine di Rovigo durante il dominio estense*. Ferrara: Copy Express, 1996.
Meier, Bernard, ed. *Cipriani Rore Opera Omnia*. Vol. 2. Rome: American Institute of Musicology, 1966.
Meredith-Jones, Cyril, ed. *Historia Karoli Magni et Rotholandi; ou, Chronique du Pseudo-Turpin*. Paris: Droz, 1936. Repr. Geneva: Slatkine, 1972.
Miller, Lady Anne. *Letters from Italy, describing the Manners, Customs, Antiquities, Paintings, &c. of that Country, In the Years MDCCLXX and MDCCLXXI, to a Friend residing in France, by an English Woman*. 3 vols. London: Edward and Charles Dilly, 1776.
Miltoun, Francis. *Italian Highways and Byways from a Motor Car*. Boston: L. C. Page & Co, 1909.
Montaigne, Michel de. *Journal de voyage en Italie par la Suisse et l'Allemagne en 1580 et 1581*, ed. Charles Dedeyan. Paris: Société des Belles Lettres, 1946.
Montorsi, William. *Statuta Ferrariae anno MCCLXXXVII*. Ferrara: Cassa di risparmio di Ferrara, 1955.

Moore, John. *A View of Society and Manners in Italy: With Anecdotes Relating to Some Eminent Characters*. 3 vols. London: W. Strahan and T. Caddell, 1781.

Morata, Olimpia. *Opera omnia*. Basel: Petrus Perna, 1580.

———. *Opera Omnia*, ed. Lanfranco Caretti. Vol. 1: *Epistolario (1540–1555)*, 2: *Orationes. Dialogi et Carmi*. R. Deputazione di Storia Patria Per l'Emilia e la Romagna, sezione di Ferrara. Ferrara: Premiata Tipografia Sociale, 1940.

Morgan, Lady (Sydney). *Italy*. 2 vols. London: Henry Colburn & Co., 1821.

Muratori, L. A. *Antichità Estensi*. Modena: Stamperia ducale, 1717–1740.

———. *Rerum Italicarum Scriptores*. Milan: Ex Typographia Societatis Palatinae, 1723–1738.

———. *Chronicon Estense*. Rerum Italicarum Scriptores 15. Milan: Ex Typographia Societatis Palatinae, 1729.

Muzio, Girolamo. *Il gentilhuomo*. Venice: Appresso gli heredi di Luigi Valuassori, & Gio. Domenico Micheli, 1575.

Norton, Charles Eliot. *Notes of Travel and Study in Italy*. Boston: Ticknor and Fields, 1860.

Oddi, Sforza. *Prigione d'amore, commedia . . . recitata in Pisa da scolari l'anno secondo del felice Rettorato del S. Lelio Gavardo Asolano*. Fiorenza: Filippo Giunti, 1592.

Otto I, Bishop of Freising. *The Deeds of Frederick Barbarossa*. Trans. Charles Mierow. New York: Columbia University Press, 1953. Repr. New York: Norton, 1966.

———. *The Two Cities: A Chronicle of Universal History to the Year 1146 A.D.* Trans. Charles Mierow. Ed. Austin P. Evans. New York: Columbia University Press, 1928. Repr. New York: Octagon, 1966.

Ovid. *Metamorphoses*. Trans. Frank Justus Miller. 2 vols. Loeb Classical Library. Cambridge, MA: Harvard University Press, 1968.

Owen, John. *Travels into different parts of Europe in the years 1791 and 1792 with familiar remarks on places — men — and manners*. 2 vols. London: T. Cadell Jun. and W. Davies, 1796.

Paladino, Giuseppe, ed. *Opuscoli e lettere di riformatori italiani del Cinquecento*. Vol. 2. Scrittori d'Italia 99. Bari: Laterza, 1927.

Patoun, William. "Advice on Travel in Italy." In *A Dictionary of British and Irish Travelers in Italy, 1701–1800*, ed. John Ingamells, xxxix–lii. New Haven: Yale University Press, 1997.

Pedretti, Carlo. *Documenti e memorie riguardanti Leonardo da Vinci a Bologna e in Emilia*. Bologna: Editoriale Fiammenghi, 1953.

Perotti, N. *Cornucopiae*. Venice: Aldus, 1513.

Petrarca, Francesco. *Rime, Trionfi, e Poesie latine*, ed. Ferdinando Neri et al. Milan-Naples: Ricciardi, 1951.

Philostratus. *Imagines*. Trans. A. Fairbanks. Loeb Classical Library. London: Heinemann, 1931.

Piccolomini, Aeneas Silvius (Pope Pius II). *The Commentaries of Pius II*, ed. F. Gragg. 5 vols. Smith College Studies in History. Northampton, MA: Smith College, 1937–1957.

———. *De viris illustribus*, ed. Adrianus Van Heck. Stuttgart: Sumptibus Societatis Litterariae Stuttgardiensis, 1842. Repr. Vatican City: Biblioteca Apostolica Vaticana, 1991.

———. *Historia rerum Friderici Tertii Imperatoris*. Strasbourg: J. Staedelli et J. F. Spoor, 1685.

———. *I commentarii*. Ed. and trans. Luigi Totaro. Milan: Adelphi, 1984.

Pino, Paolo. "Dialogo di Pittura (1548)." In *Trattati d'arte del Cinquecento*, ed. P. Barocchi, 95–139. Bari: Laterza, 1960.

Pio, Ascanio. *Ferrara trionfante per la coronazione dell B.ma Vergine del Rosario celebrata l'anno 1638. Con apparato di teatro, di machine, e di musica*. Ferrara: Per gl'heredi del Suzzi, 1662.

———. *L'Andromeda di d. Ascanio Pio di Savoia; cantata e combattuta in Ferrara al carnevale dell'anno 1638*. Ferrara: Francesco Suzzi, 1639.

Piozzi, Hester Lynch. *Observations and Reflections made in the course of a Journey through France, Italy, and Germany*. 2 vols. London: A. Strahan and T. Cadell, 1789.

Pliny. *Natural History*. Trans. H. Rackham. 10 vols. Loeb Classical Library. Cambridge, MA: Harvard University Press, 1938–1963.

Polybius. *Histories*. Trans. W. R. Paton. 6 vols. Loeb Classical Library. Cambridge, MA: Harvard University Press, 1960.

Regole et ordinationi per le suore convertite di Ferrara sotto il titolo di S. Maria Maddalena, riformate et ampliate do Mons. Reverendissimo di Ferrara. Ferrara: Vittorio Baldino, 1599.

Riccoboni, Sister Bartolomea. *Spiritual Letters, Dialogues, & Poems*. Trans. Daniel Bornstein. Chicago: University of Chicago Press, 2000.

Rocca, Angelo. *De sacrosancto Christi corpore romanis pontificibus iter conficientibus praeferendo commentari antiquissimi ritus causam, et originem, ... Clemente VIII. Pont. Max. Ferrariem proficiscente*. Rome: Guillelmum Facciottum, 1599.

Rogers, Samuel. *The Italian Journal of Samuel Rogers, Edited with an Account of Rogers' Life and of Travel in Italy in 1814–21*, ed. J. R. Hale. London: Faber and Faber, 1954.

Romano, Angelo, ed. *Lettere di cortigiane del Rinascimento*. Rome: Salerno Editrice, 1990.

Roselli, Antonio. "Tractatus legitimationum." In *Tractatus universi iuris*. Venice: Societas Aquilae Renovantis, 1584.

Rosellis, Antonius de. "Tractatus legitimationum." In *Tractatus universi iuris*. Venice: Lichtenstein, 1584.

Rosmini, Carlo de'. *Vita di Francesco Filelfo da Tolentino*. 3 vols. Milan: Musi, 1808.

Rossi, Azariah de'. *Me'or Enayim*. Mantua: s.n., 1573–1575.

———. "Kol Elohim." In *Me'or Enayim*, ed. David Cassel, 20–21. Vilna: Bidefus Y. R. Rom, 1866. Repr. Jerusalem: Makor, 1970.

———. *Kitve Azaryah Min ha-Adumim : mivhar perakim mi-tokh sefer "Me'or 'enayim" ve-sefer "Matsref la-kesef"*, ed. Robert Bonfil. Jerusalem: Mosad Byalik, 1991.

———. *The Light of the Eyes*. Ed. and trans. Joanna Weinburg. New Haven: Yale University Press, 2001.

Sanuto, Marino. *I Diarii di Marino Sanuto*, ed. Rinaldo Fulin, Federico Stefani, Nicolo Barozzi, Guglielmo Berchet, and Marco Allegri. 58 vols. Venice: Visentini, 1879–1903.

Sardi, Gasparo. *Historie Ferraresi di Gasparo Sardi*. Ferrara: Francesco Rossi da Valenza, 1556.

———. *Libro delle historie ferraresi del Sig. Gasparo Sardi . . . Aggiuntivi di più quattro libri del Sig. Dottor Faustini sino alla devolutione del ducato di Ferrara alla Santa Sede*. Ferrara: Giuseppe Gironi, 1646.

Sardis, Ludovicus a. "Tractatus de naturalibus liberis, legitimatione, ac successione eorum." In *Tractatus universi iuris*. Venice: Lichtenstein, 1584.

Saxoferrato, Bartolus de. *Commentaria in primam Digesti veteris partem*. Venice: Baptista de Tortis, 1526. Repr. Rome: Il Cigno Galileo Galilei, 1996.

Scalabrini, G. A. *Guida per la città e i borghi di Ferrara [ca. 1755]*, ed. C. Frongia. Ferrara: Liceo Classico Ariosto, 1997.

Sedgwick, Catherine Maria. *Letters from Abroad to Kindred at Home*. 2 vols. New York: Harper and Brothers, 1841.

Sella, P. "Inventario testamentario dei beni della Biblioteca di Alfonso II d'Este." *Atti e memorie della Deputazione ferrarese di storia patria* 28 (1931): 131–395.

Silliman, Benjamin. *A Visit to Europe in 1851*. 2 vols. New York: G. P. Putnam, 1854.

Simeoni, Gabriele. *Commentarii di Gabriello Symeoni Fiorentino sopra alla tetrarchia di Vinegia, di Milano, di Mantova, et di Ferrara*. Venice: Comino da Trino di Monferrato, 1546.

Smyser, H. M., ed. *The Pseudo-Turpin, edited from Bibliothèque Nationale, fonds latin, MS. 17656*. Cambridge, MA: Medieval Academy of America, 1937.

Soderini, Giovanvettorio. *Opere*, ed. Bacchi della Lega. 4 vols. Bologna: Romagnoli dell'Acqua, 1902–1907.

———. "Trattato degli animali domestici." In *Opere*, ed. A. Bacchi della Lega, 4: 297–98.

Speroni, Sperone. *Opere*. Venice: Domenico Occhi, 1740.

Spoleto, Cherubino da. *Regole della vita matrimoniale*, ed. Francesco Zambini. Bologna: Commissione per i testi di lingua, 1888.

Starke, Mariana. *Letters from Italy*. 2nd ed. 2 vols. Vol. 2. London: G. & S. Robinson, 1815.

Statuta civitatis Ferrariae. Book 2, *Quod legitimati non succedant*. Ferrara, 1476.

Steuco, Agostino. *Augustini Eugubini Can. Regul. S. Salvatoris Cosmopoeia vel Mundano Opificio, Expositio trium capitum Genesis, in quibus de creatione tractat Moses*. Lugdini: Apud Sebastianem Gryphium, 1535.

Strabo. *Strabonis geographicorum commentarii, olim, ut putatur, a Guarino Veronese & Gregorio Tifernate latinitate donatos*, ed. Conrad Heresbach. Basel: Vualder, 1523.

Tasso, Torquato. *Le lettere di Torquato Tasso*, ed. Cesare Guasti. 5 vols. Florence: F. Le Monnier, 1852–1855.

———. *Rime*, ed. Angelo Solerti. Bologna: Romagnoli-dall'Acqua, 1898–1902.

———. *Dialoghi*, ed. Ezio Raimondi. Florence: Sansoni, 1958, repr. 1968.

———. *Gianluca overo delle maschere*. In *Dialoghi*, ed. Raimondi, 669–82.

———. *Prose*, ed. Ettore Mazzali. Milan-Naples: Ricciardi, 1959.

———. *Apologia della* Gerusalemme liberata. In *Prose*, ed. Mazzali, 411–85.

———. *Discorsi dell'arte poetica e in particolare sopra il poema eroico*. In *Prose*, ed. Mazzali, 349–410.

———. "Discorsi del poema eroico." In *Prose*, ed. Mazzali, 487–729.

———. *Opere*, ed. Bruno Maier. Milan: Rizzoli, 1965.

———. *Discourses on the Heroic Poem*. Trans. M. Cavalchini and I. Samuel. Oxford: Clarendon Press, 1973.

———. *Gerusalemme liberata*, ed. Lanfranco Caretti. Milan: Mondadori, 1979.

———. *Lettere poetiche*, ed. C. Molinari. Parma: Guanda, 1995.

Taylor, Catharine. *Letters from Italy to a Younger Sister*. 2 vols. London: John Murray, 1841.

Tesauro, Emanuele. *Historia dell'augusta città di Torino*. 2 vols. Turin: Zappata, 1679. Repr. Bologna: Forni, 1988.

Theiner, Augustin. *Codex diplomaticus dominii temporalis Sanctae Sedis*. 3 vols. Rome: Imprimerie du Vatican, 1861–1862.

Theophrastus. *Historia Plantarum*. Treviso: Bartholomaeus Confalonerius, 1483.

Tornabuoni, Lucrezia. *Sacred Narratives*. Trans. and ed. Jane Tylus. Chicago: University of Chicago Press, 2001.

Turpin. *History of Charles the Great and Orlando, Ascribed to Archbishop Turpin*. Trans. Thomas Rodd. London: Privately printed, 1812.

Usque, Samuel. *Consolation for the Tribulations of Israel*. Trans. from the Portuguese and ed. with an introd. by Martin A. Cohen. Philadelphia: The Jewish Publication Society of America, 1977.

Varro, Marcus Terentius. "Rerum Rusticarum Libri Tres." In *Marcus Porcius Cato on Agriculture; Marcus Terentius Varro on Agriculture*, trans. William Davis Hooper. Loeb Classical Library. Cambridge, MA: Harvard University Press, 1934.

Vasari, Giorgio. *Le vite de' piu eccellenti pittori, scultori e architettori, nelle redazioni del 1550 e 1568*, ed. Rosanna Bettarini and Paola Barocchi. Florence: Sansoni, 1966–1987.

———. *Le vite de' più' eccellenti pittori, scultori ed architettori*, ed. Gaetano Milanesi. Vol. 7. Florence: G. Barbera, 1906.

Vecellio, Cesare. *Habiti antichi et moderni di tutto il mondo*. Venice: Appresso i Sessa, 1598.

Vigenère, Blaise de. *Les images ou tableaux de platte peinture des deux Philostrates* . . . Paris: Guillemont, 1614.

Villano, Filippo. *De Famosis civibus* . . . , *ed.* G. C. Galletti. Florence: Mazzoni, 1847.

Wilson, James. *A Journal of Two Successive Tours upon the Continent in the Years 1816, 1817, & 1818*. 3 vols. London: T. Cadell and W. Davies, 1820.

Zambotti, Bernardino. *Diario ferrarese dall 'anno 1476 sino al 1504*, ed. Giuseppe Pardi. Rerum Italicarum Scriptores. 2nd ed. 24/7. Bologna: Zanichelli, 1934.

Zerbinati, Giovanni Maria. *Croniche di Ferrara: quali comenzano del anno 1500 sino al 1527*, ed. Maria Giuseppina Muzzarelli. Ferrara: Deputazione provinciale ferrarese di storia patria, 1989.

II. Secondary Works

Agnelli, Giuseppe. "I monumenti di Niccolò III e Borso d'Este in Ferrara." *Atti e memorie della Deputazione ferrarese di storia patria* 23 (1918): 1–32.

Agnelli, Giuseppe, and Giuseppe Ravegnani. *Annali delle edizioni ariostee*. Bologna: Zanichelli, 1933.

Altman, Janet Gurkin. *Epistolarity: Approaches to a Form*. Columbus: Ohio State University Press, 1982.

———. "The Politics of Epistolary Art." In *A New History of French Literature*, ed. Denis Hollier, 915–21. Cambridge, MA: Harvard University Press, 1989, repr. 1994.

Anceschi, Giuseppe, and Tina Matarrese, eds. *Il Boiardo e il mondo estense nel Quattrocento*. 2 vols. Padua: Antenore, 1998.

Anderson, William S. "Calypso and Elysium." *Classical Journal* 54 (1958): 2–11.

Andreolli, B., et al. *Repertorio della cronachistica emiliano-romagnola*. Rome: Istituto storico italiano per il Medio Evo, 1991.

Anselmi, Gian Mario, Luisa Avellini, and Ezio Raimondi. "Il Rinascimento padano." In *Letteratura italiana: Storia e geografia, II: L'età moderna*, 521–91. Turin: Einaudi, 1988.

Apollonio, Mario. *Storia del teatro italiano.* 3rd ed. 2 vols. Florence: Sansoni, 1954.

Ariani, Marco. *Il teatro italiano: La tragedia del '500*. 2 vols. Turin: Einaudi, 1977.

Ascoli, Albert Russell. *Ariosto's Bitter Harmony: Crisis and Evasion in the Italian Renaissance*. Princeton: Princeton University Press, 1987.

———. "Machiavelli's Gift of Counsel." In *Machiavelli and the Discourse of Literature*, ed. A. R. Ascoli and V. Kahn, 219–57. Ithaca: Cornell University Press, 1993.

———. "Il segreto di Erittonio: politica e poetica sessuale nel canto XXXVII dell'*Orlando furioso*." In *La rappresentazione dell'altro nei testi del Rinascimento*, ed. Sergio Zatti, 53–76. Lucca: Pacini Fazzi, 1998.

———. "Ariosto." In *The Dante Encyclopedia*, ed. Richard Lansing, 60–61. New York: Garland, 2000.

———. "Faith as a Cover-Up: Ariosto's *Orlando furioso*, canto 21, and Machiavellian Ethics." *I Tatti Studies* 8 (2000): 135–70.

Asor Rosa, Alberto. "Apogeo e crisi della civiltà letteraria italiana." In *Letteratura italiana: Storia e geografia, II: L'età moderna,* 3–21. Turin: Einaudi, 1988.

Bacchelli, Riccardo. *La congiura di Don Giulio d'Este*. 2nd ed. Milan: Mondadori, 1958.

Badini, Gino, and Elio Monducci, eds. *Matteo Maria Boiardo, le vita nei documenti del suo tempo*. Modena: Aedes Muratoriana, 1997.

Baillet, Roger. "L'Ariosto et les princes d'Este: poésie et politique." In *Le pouvoir et la plume*, 85–95. Paris: Université de la Sorbonne nouvelle, 1982.

Bainton, Roland. *Women of the Reformation in Germany and Italy*. Minneapolis: Augsburg Publishing House, 1971.

Baker, Paul R. *The Fortunate Pilgrims: Americans in Italy, 1800–1860*. Cambridge, MA: Harvard University Press, 1964.

Baldan, Paolo. *Metamorfosi di un orco: un'irruzione foclorica nel Boiardo esorcizzata dall'Ariosto*. Milan: Unicopli, 1983.

Balletti, Antonio. *Gli ebrei e gli estensi*. Reggio Emilia: Forni, 1930. Repr. Bologna: Forni, 1969.

Balsamo, Luigi. "La circolazione del libro a corte." In *La corte e lo spazio: Ferrara Estense*, ed. Papagno and Quondam, 670–71.

Barkan, Leonard. *Unearthing the Past: Archaeology and Aesthetics in the Making of Renaissance Culture*. New Haven: Yale University Press, 1999.

Baron, Salo W. "Azariah de' Rossi's Attitude to Life." In *History and Jewish Historians*, ed. Herzberg and Feldman, 174–204, 406–22.

———. "Azariah de' Rossi's Historical Method." In *History and Jewish Historians*, ed. Herzberg and Feldman, 205–39, 422–42.

———. "Azariah de' Rossi: A Biographical Sketch." In *History and Jewish Historians*, ed. Herzberg and Feldman, 167–73, 405.

Bassanese, Fiora. "Selling the Self; or, The Epistolary Production of Renaissance Courtesans." In *Italian Women Writers from the Renaissance to the Present: Revising the Canon*, ed. Maria Ornella Marotti, 69–82. University Park, PA: Pennsylvania State University Press, 1996.

Bassani, Giorgio. *The Garden of the Finzi-Contini*. Trans. William Weaver. New York: Harcourt-Brace, 1977.

Battaglia, Salvatore, ed. *Grande dizionario della lingua italiana*. 20+ vols. Turin: UTET, 1961–.

Baudrillard, Jean. "The System of Collecting." In *The Culture of Collecting*, ed. John Elsner and Roger Cardinal, 7–24. Cambridge, MA: Harvard University Press, 1994.

Baxandall, Michael. "A Dialogue on Art from the Court of Leonello d'Este." *Journal of the Warburg and Courtauld Institutes* 26 (1963): 304–36.

Bayer, Andrea. "Dosso's Public: The Este Court at Ferrara." In *Dosso Dossi: Court Painter in Renaissance Ferrara*, ed. P. Humfrey and M. Lucco, 27–54. New York: Metropolitan Museum of Art, 1999.

Bayle, Pierre. *Dictionnaire historique et critique*. Paris: Editions sociales, 1820, repr. 1974.

Beer, Marina. *Romanzi di cavalleria: il "Furioso" e il romanzo italiano del primo Cinquecento*. Rome: Bulzoni, 1987.

Beinart, Haim. "Hityashevut ha-Yehudim be-duksuth Savoia be-ʿikvot ha-privilegia shel shenat 1572 (La venuta degli ebrei nel ducato di Savoia e il privilegio del 1572)." In *Scritti in memoria di Leone Garpi: Saggi sull'ebraismo italiano*, ed. Daniel Carpi, Attilio Milano, and Alexander Rofé, 72–117. Jerusalem: Fondazione Sally Mayer, 1967.

Bellonci, Maria. *Segreti dei Gonzaga: Il duca nel labirinto (1562–1612); Isabella fra i Gonzaga (1474–1539); Ritratto di famiglia (1474)*. Milan: Mondadori, 1946, repr. 1963.

———. *Rinascimento privato*. Milan: Mondadori, 1985.

Benson, Pamela. *The Invention of the Renaissance Woman: The Challenge of Female Independence in the Literature and Thought of Italy and England*. University Park, PA: Pennsylvania State University Press, 1992.

Bentini, Jadranka, ed. *Gli Este a Ferrara: una corte nel Rinascimento*. Milan: Silvana, 2004.

Berlin, Isaiah. "The Concept of Scientific History." In idem, *Concepts and Categories: Philosophical Essays*, 103–42. New York: Viking Press, 1979.

Berra, Claudia, ed. *Fra satire e rime ariostesche*. Milan: Cisalpino, 2000.

Bertocchi, M. *La tirannia degli astri: Aby Warburg e l'astrologia di Palazzo Schifanoia*. Bologna: Cappelli, 1985.

Bertoni, Giulio. *Nuovi studi su Matteo Maria Boiardo*. Bologna: Zanichelli, 1904.

———. *La biblioteca estense e la cultura ferrarese ai tempi del duca Ercole I (1471–1505)*. Turin: Loescher, 1903.

———. "Notizie sugli amanuensi degli Estensi nel Quattrocento." *Archivum Romanicum* 2 (1918): 30–34.

———. "Una copista del Marchese Leonello d'Este." *Giornale storico della letteratura italiana* 7 (1918): 196–206.

———. *Guarino da Verona fra letterati e cortigiani a Ferrara (1429–1460)*. Geneva: L. S. Olschki, 1921.

Bertos, Rigas. "A Short Note on the *Bacchanal of the Andrians*." *Mitteilungen des Kunsthistorischen Instituts in Florenz* 20 (1976): 407–10.

Bertozzi, Marco, ed. *Alla Corte degli Estensi. Filosofia, arte e cultura a Ferrara nei secoli XV e XVI*. Ferrara: University of Ferrara Press, 1994.

Bestor, Jane Fair. "Kinship and Marriage in the Politics of an Italian Ruling House: The Este of Ferrara in the Reign of Ercole I (1471–1505)." Ph.D. diss., University of Chicago, 1992.

———. "Bastardy and Legitimacy in the Formation of a Regional State in Italy: The Estense Succession." *Comparative Studies in Society and History* 38 (1996): 549–85.

———. "Marriage Transactions in Renaissance Italy and Mauss's *Essay on the Gift*." *Past and Present* 164 (1999): 6–46.

———. "Gli illegittimi e beneficiati della casa estense." In *Il Rinascimento. Situazioni e personaggi*, ed. Adriano Prosperi, 77–102. Ferrara: Corbo, 2000.

———. "Family and Statecraft in Renaissance Italy: The Este of Ferrara, 1264–1598." Unpublished book manuscript.

———. "Titian's Portrait of Laura Eustochia: the Decorum of Female Beauty and the Motif of the Black Page" *Renaissance Studies* 17 (2003): 628–73.

Bigi, Emilio. "La poesia latina del Boiardo." In *Il Boiardo e la critica contemporanea*, ed. Giuseppe Anceschi, 81–96. Florence: L. S. Olschki, 1970.

Bini, Daniele, ed. *Isabella d'Este. La primadonna del Rinascimento. Civiltà Mantovana*, Supplemento al n. 112. Modena: Il Bulino, 2001.

Biow, Douglas. *"Mirabile dictu": Representation of the Marvelous in Medieval and Renaissance Epic*. Ann Arbor: University of Michigan Press, 1996.

Blaisdell, Charmarie Webb. "Royalty and Reform: The Predicament of Renée de France, 1510–1575." Ph.D. diss., Tufts University, 1969.

———. "Renée de France between Reform and Counter-Reform." *Archiv für Reformationsgeschichte* 63 (1972): 196–216.

———. "Politics and Heresy in Ferrara, 1534–1559." *Sixteenth-Century Journal* 61 (1975): 67–93.

Blasucci, Luigi. "*La Commedia* come fonte linguistica e stilistica del *Furioso*." In idem, *Studi su Dante e Ariosto*, 121–62. Milan-Naples: Ricciardi, 1969.

Bocchi, Francesca. *Istituzioni e società a Ferrara in età precomunale. Atti e memorie della Deputazione provinciale di Ferrara di storia patria*, ser. 3, 26. Ferrara: Deputazione provinciale, 1979.

———. "La 'Terranuova' da campagna a città." In *La corte e lo spazio: Ferrara estense*, ed. Papagno and Quondam, 167–92.

Bock, Friedrich. "Der Este-Prozess von 1321." *Archivum fratrum praedicatorum* 7 (1937): 41–111.

Bolzoni, Lina. "Parole e immagini per il ritratto di un nuovo Ulisse." In *Documentary Culture: Florence and Rome from Grand Duke Ferdinand I to Pope Alexander VII*, ed. G. Penni et al, 317–48. Bologna: Nuova Alfa, 1992.

Bonfil, Robert. "Yediot Chadashot le-toledot chayyav shel R. Menahem Azariah mi-Fano (New Information on Rabbi Menahem Azariah da Fano and his Age)." In *Studies in the History of Jewish Society in the Middle Ages and in the Modern Period Presented to Professor Jacob Katz*, ed. E. Etkes and Y. Salmon, 98–135. Jerusalem: Magnes, 1980.

———. "Some Reflections of the Place of Azariah de Rossi's *Meor Enayim* in the Cultural Milieu of Italian Renaissance Jewry." In *Jewish Thought in the Sixteenth Century*, ed. B. D. Cooperman, 23–48. Cambridge, MA: Harvard University Press, 1983.

———. *Rabbis and Jewish Communities in Renaissance Italy*. Oxford: The Littman Library for Jewish Civilization, 1990.

———, ed. *Kitve Azariah min ha-Adumim (Azariah de' Rossi, Selected Chapters from Sefer Me'or 'Enayim and Matsref la-Kessef)*. Jerusalem: Bialik Institute, 1991.

———. "Ferrare: Un port sûr et paisible pour la diaspora séfarade." In *Les Juifs d'Espagne—histoire d'une diaspora*, ed. Henry Mechoulan, 295–303. Paris: Liana Levi, 1992.

———. "The History of the Spanish and Portuguese Jews in Italy." In *The Sephardi Legacy*, ed. Haim Beinart, 217–39. Jerusalem: Magnes Press, 1992.

———. *Jewish Life in Renaissance Italy*. Berkeley: University of California Press, 1994.

———."Accademie rabbiniche e presenza ebraica nelle università." In *Le università dell'Europa dal Rinascimento alle riforme religiose*, ed. Gian Paolo Brizzi and Jacques Verger, 6 vols., vol. 2, *Dal Rinascimento alle riforme religiose*, 133–51. Milan: Amilcare Pizzi, 1990–1995.

———. "Italia: un tríste epílogo de la expulsión de los judíos de Espana." In *Judíos, Sefarditas, Conversos: La expulsión de 1492 y sus consecuencias*, ed. Ángel Alcalá, 246–68. Valladolid: Ámbito, 1995.

Bonifazi, Neuro. *Le lettere infedeli*. Rome: Officina Edizioni, 1975.

Bonnet, Jules. *Vie d'Olympia Morata, épisode de la Renaissance et de la Réforme en Italie*. 3rd ed. Paris: Charles Meyrueis, 1856.

Boujassy, Jeanne. *Isabella d'Este, Grande Dame de la Renaissance*. Paris: A. Fayard, 1960.

Bourdieu, Pierre. *Outline of a Theory of Practice*. Trans. R. Nice. Cambridge: Cambridge University Press, 1977.

Bourne, Mary Harris. "Out from the Shadow of Isabella: The Artistic Patronage of Francesco II Gonzaga, Fourth Marquis of Mantua (1484–1519)." Ph.D. diss., Harvard University, 1997.

———. "Renaissance Husbands and Wives as Patrons of Art: The *Camerini* of Isabella d'Este and Francesco II Gonzaga." In *Beyond Isabella: Secular Women Patrons of Art in Renaissance Italy*, ed. Sheryl E. Reiss and David G. Wilkins, 93–123. Kirksville, MO: Truman State University Press, 2001.

Boutet, Dominique, and Armand Strubel. *Littérature, Politique, et Société dans la France du Moyen Âge*. Paris: Presses Universitaires de France, 1979.

Breisach, Ernst. *Historiography: Ancient, Medieval, and Modern*. 2nd ed. Chicago: University of Chicago Press, 1994.

———, ed. *Classical Rhetoric and Medieval Historiography*. Kalamazoo: Medieval Institute Publications, 1985.

Bridgman, Nanie. "Un manuscrit italien au debut du XVIe siècle." *Annales Musicologiques* 1 (1953): 177–267.

Brooks, Van Wyck. *The Dream of Arcadia: American Writers and Artists in Italy, 1760–1915*. New York: E. P. Dutton, 1958.
Brown, Clifford M., and Anna Maria Lorenzoni. *Isabella d'Este and Lorenzo da Pavia: Documents for the History of Art and Culture in Renaissance Mantua*. Geneva: Librairie Droz S.A, 1982.
Brown, G. K. *Italy and the Reformation to 1550*. Oxford: Basil Blackwell, 1933.
Brown, Judith C., and Robert C. Davis, eds. *Gender and Society in Renaissance Italy*. London and New York: Longman, 1998.
Brown, Richard Gordon. "The Politics of Magnificence in Ferrara, 1450–1505: A Study in Socio-Political Implications of Renaissance Spectacle." Ph.D. diss., University of Edinburgh, 1982.
Brumble, H. David. *Classical Myths and Legends in the Middle Ages and Renaissance*. London: Fitzroy Dearborn, 1998.
Brundage, James A. *Law, Sex, and Christian Society in Medieval Europe*. Chicago: University of Chicago Press, 1987.
Bruscagli, Riccardo. *Stagioni della civiltà estense*. Pisa: Nistri-Lischi, 1983.
———. "'Ventura' e 'inchiesta' fra Boiardo e Ariosto." In idem, *Stagioni della civiltà estense*, 87–126.
———. "Vita d'eroe: L' *Ercole*." *Schifanoia* 12 (1991): 9–19.
———. "L'errore di Goffredo (G.L. XI)." *Studi tassiani* 40–41 (1992–1993): 207–32.
———. "Introduzione." In *Orlando Innamorato*, ed. idem, v–xxxiii. Turin: Einaudi, 1995.
———. "Matteo Maria Boiardo." In *Storia della Letteratura Italiana*, ed. E. Malato, 635–708. Rome: Salerno, 1996.
———. "Thrones of Blood: Machiavellian Politics and the Rebirth of Tragedy on the Italian Stage." Berkeley Chair of Italian Culture Lecture, 1993. Unpublished.
Buddensieg, Tilmann. "Die Statuenstiftung Sixtus' IV. im Jahre 1471: von den heidnischen Götzenbildern am Lateran zu den Rühmeszeichen des römischen Volkes auf dem Kapitol." *Römisches Jahrbuch für Kunstgeschichte* 20 (1983): 33–73.
Burckhardt, Jacob. *The Civilization of the Renaissance in Italy*. Trans. S. G. C. Middlemore. Oxford: Phaidon, 1944, repr. 1981.
———. *The Civilization of the Renaissance*. Intro. Benjamin Nelson and Charles Trinkaus. New York: Harper, 1958.
Cabani, Maria. *Costanti ariosteschi*. Pisa: Scuola Normale Superiore, 1990.

Calura, Mario. "Italo Balbo. Per la storia e per l'arte ferrarese." In *Atti e memorie della Deputazione di storia patria per l'Emilia e la Romagna,* 1–14. Ferrara: Premiata Tipografia Sociale, 1942.

———. "Il monastero di S. Romano sede della Civica Magistratura ferrarese." *Atti e memorie della Deputazione di storia patria ferrarese,* n.s. 14 (1944): 173–85.

Cammelli, Giuseppe. "Olympia Morata." *Rinascita* 4 (1941): 456–57.

Campagnoli, R. "Girolamo Naselli primo tradutore italiano di Montaigne." *Studi francesi* 16 (1972): 213–31.

Campbell, Stephen J. *Cosmè Tura of Ferrara: Style, Politics, and the Renaissance City*. New Haven-London: Yale University Press, 1997.

Campori, Giuseppe. "Sei lettere inedite di Fra Leandro Alberti a Gaspare Sardi ed una del Sardi a Iacopo Tebaldi." *Atti e memorie delle Reali Deputazioni di storia patria per le provincie modenesi e parmensi* 1 (1863): 413–20.

———. "Nuovi documenti per la vita di Leonardo da Vinci." *Atti e memorie delle Reali Deputazioni di storia patria per le provincie modenesi e parmensi* 3 (1865): 45–47.

———. "I miniatori degli Estensi." *Atti e memorie delle Reali Deputazioni di storia patria per le provincie modenesi e parmensi* 6 (1872): 6–11.

Canuti, F. *Il Perugino*. 2 vols. Siena: La Diana, 1931.

Cappelli, Antonio. "La Biblioteca Estense nella prima metà del secolo XV." *Giornale storico della letturatura italiana* 14 (1889), 1–30.

Caponetto, Salvatore. *La Riforma Protestante nell'Italia del Cinquecento*. Turin: Claudiana, 1992.

Cappelli, A. "Notizie di Ugo Caleffini notaro ferrarese del secolo XV con la sua cronaca in rima di casa d'Este." *Atti e memorie delle Reali Deputazioni di storia patria per le provincie modenesi e parmensi* 2 (1864): 267–69.

Caretti, Lanfranco. "Codicillo ariostesco." In idem, *Antichi e moderni,* 103–9. Turin: Einaudi, 1976.

———. *Antichi e moderni. Studi di letteratura italiana. Seconda serie*. Rome: Salerno, 1996.

Carne-Ross, D. S. "The One and the Many: A Reading of *Orlando Furioso*, Cantos 1 and 8." *Arion* o.s. 5 (1966): 195–234.

———. "The One and the Many: A Reading of *Orlando Furioso*." *Arion* n.s. 3 (1976): 146–219.

Carroll, Clare. *The "Orlando Furioso": A Stoic Comedy*. MRTS 174. Tempe, AZ: Medieval & Renaissance Texts & Studies, 1997.

Cartwright, Julia. *Isabella d'Este Marchioness of Mantua 1474–1539: A Study of the Renaissance*. London: John Murray, 1907, 2nd ed. New York: E. P. Dutton, 1923.

Casadei, Alberto. "Alcune considerazioni sui *Cinque canti*." *Giornale storico della letteratura italiana* 165 (1988): 161–79.

———. *La strategia delle varianti: le correzioni storiche del terzo "Furioso"*. Lucca: Pacini Fazzi, 1988.

———. "Brevi analisi sul finale del primo *Furioso*." *Studi e problemi di critica testuale* 44 (1992): 87–100.

Cassuto, Umberto. *Gli ebrei a Firenze nell'età del Rinascimento*. Florence: Galletti e Cocci, 1905. Reprint, Florence: Olschki, 1965.

Castagna, Rita. "Una donzella di Isabella d'Este e la ragion di stato." *Civiltà Mantovana* 11 (1977): 220–31.

———. *Un Vicerè per Eleonora Brognina alla corte di Isabella d'Este Gonzaga*. Mantua: Moretti, 1982.

Castelli, Patrizia, ed. La rinascita del sapere: Libri e maestri dello studio ferrarese. Venice: Marsilio, 1991.

Castiglioni, A. "The School of Ferrara and the Controversy on Pliny." In *Science, Medicine, and History: Essays . . . in Honor of Charles Singer*, ed. E. A. Underwood, 269–79. London: Oxford University Press, 1953.

Catalano, Michele. *Vita di Ludovico Ariosto*. 2 vols. Geneva: Olschki, 1930–1931.

Cavallo, Jo Ann. *Boiardo's Orlando Innamorato: An Ethics of Desire*. London: Associated University Presses, 1993.

———. "Denying Closure: Ariosto's Rewriting of the *Orlando Innamorato*." In *Fortune and Romance: Boiardo in America*, ed. eadem and Charles S. Ross, 97–134. MRTS 183. Tempe, AZ: Medieval and Renaissance Texts and Studies, 1998.

Cavallo, Jo Ann, and Charles S. Ross, eds. *Fortune and Romance: Boiardo in America*. MRTS 183. Tempe, AZ: Medieval and Renaissance Texts and Studies, 1998.

Ceserani, Remo. "Due modelli culturali e narrativi nell'*Orlando furioso*." *Giornale storico della letteratura italiana* 161 (1984): 481–506.

Chambers, David Sanderson. *Patrons and Artists in the Italian Renaissance*. Columbia, SC: University of South Carolina Press, 1971.

———, and T. Dean. *Clean Hands and Rough Justice: An Investigating Magistrate in Renaissance Italy*. Ann Arbor: University of Michigan Press, 1997.

Chard, Chloe, and Helen Langton, eds. *Transports: Travel, Pleasure, and Imaginative Geography, 1600–1830*. New Haven: Yale University Press, 1996.

Charity, A. C. *Events and their Afterlife: The Dialectics of Christian Typology in the Bible and Dante*. Cambridge: Cambridge University Press, 1966.

Chastel, André. *I centri del Rinascimento*. Milan: Feltrinelli, 1965.

———. *Renaissance méridionale*. Paris: Gallimard, 1965.

Chemello, Adriana, ed. *Alla lettera. Teorie e pratiche epistolari dai Greci al Novecento*. Milan: Guerini, 1998.

Cherewatuk, Karen, and Ulrike Wiethaus, eds. *Dear Sister: Medieval Women and the Epistolary Genre*. Philadelphia: University of Pennsylvania Press, 1993.

Chiappelli, Fredi. *Il conoscitore di caos*. Rome: Bulzoni, 1981.

Chiappini, Alessandra, ed. *Tasso tra sant'Onofrio e la biblioteca ariostea*. Ferrara: Corbo, 1995.

Chiappini, Luciano. "Girolamo Savonarola ed Ercole I d'Este." *Atti e memorie della Deputazione ferrarese di storia patria* 7 (1952): 32–45.

———. "Indagini attorno a cronache e storie ferraresi del sec. XV." *Atti e memorie della Deputazione ferrarese di storia patria* 14 (1955): 3–46.

———. *Gli Estensi*. 2nd ed. Varese: Dall'Oglio, 1967.

Christiansen, Keith. "Dosso Dossi's Aeneas Frieze for Alfonso d'Este's Camerino." *Apollo* 151 (2000): 36–45.

———. "Entry no. 78." In *Catalogo: Le muse e il principe. Arte di corte nel Rinascimento padano*, ed. A. Mottola Molfino and M. Natale, 311. Modena: Panini, 1990.

Ciammitti, Luisa, Steven F. Ostrow, and Salvatore Settis, eds. *Dosso's Fate: Painting and Court Culture in Renaissance Italy*. Los Angeles: Getty Research Institute for the History of Art and the Humanities, 1998.

Cian, Vittorio. "Pietro Bembo e Isabella d'Este Gonzaga. Note e documenti." *Giornale storico della letteratura italiana* 9 (1887): 81–136.

Cittadella, Luigi Napoleone. *Notizie amministrative, storiche, artistiche relative a Ferrara*. Bologna: Forni, 1969.

Clarke, John R. *The Houses of Roman Italy 100 B.C.–A.D. 250. Ritual Space and Decoration*. Berkeley: University of California Press, 1991.

Clough, Cecil H. "The Library of the Gonzaga of Mantua." *Librarium* 15 (1972): 50–63.

———. "The Cult of Antiquity: Letters and Letter Collections." In *Cultural Aspects of The Italian Renaissance: Essays in Honor of Paul Oskar Kristeller*, ed. idem, 33–67. Manchester: Manchester University Press, 1976.

Clubb, Louise George. *Giambattista Della Porta, Dramatist*. Princeton: Princeton University Press, 1965.

———. "Ideologia e politica nel teatro dellaportiano." *Lettere Italiane* 3 (1987): 329–45.

———. *Italian Drama in Shakespeare's Time*. New Haven: Yale University Press, 1989.

———. "Pastoral Elasticity on the Italian Stage and Page." In *The Pastoral Landscape*, ed. J. D. Hunt, 110–27. Washington, DC: National Gallery of Art, 1992.

Cochrane, Eric W. *Historians and Historiography in the Italian Renaissance*. Chicago: University of Chicago Press, 1981.

Cohen, Thomas V., and Elizabeth S. Cohen. *Words and Deeds in Renaissance Rome: Trials before the Papal Magistrates*. Toronto: University of Toronto Press, 1993.

Colantuono, Anthony. "*Dies Alcyoniae*: The Invention of Bellini's *Feast of the Gods*." *Art Bulletin* 73 (1991): 237–56.

Comitato Ariostesco dell'Ottava d'Oro. *L'Ottava d'oro. La vita e l'opera di Ludovico Ariosto*. Milan-Verona: A. Mondadori, 1933.

Corner, Paul. *Fascism in Ferrara: 1915–1925*. Oxford: Oxford University Press, 1975.

Corradini, Elena. "Le raccolte estensi di antichità. Primi contributi documentari." In *L'impresa di Alfonso II. Saggi e documenti sulla produzione artistica a Ferrara nel secondo Cinquecento*, ed. Jadranka Bentini and Luigi Spezzaferro, 163–92. Bologna: Nuova Alfa Editoriale, 1987.

Corrigan, Beatrice. "The Opposing Mirrors." *Italica* 33 (1956): 165–79.

Cranston, Jodi. "Commemoration, Self-Representation, and the Fiction of Constancy in Este Court Portrayal." In *Fortune and Romance,* ed. Cavallo and Ross, 271–77.

Crawford, Anne, ed. *Letters of the Queens of England 1100–1547*. Phoenix Mill, UK: Sutton, 1997.

Curtius, Ernst. *European Literature and the Latin Middle Ages*. Trans. Willard Trask. New York: Harper and Row, 1953. Repr. Princeton: Princeton University Press, 1990.

d'Ancona, Paolo. *I mesi di Schifanoia a Ferrara*. Milan: Il Milione, 1958.

Da Pozzo, Giovanni. *L'ambigua armonia: Studio sull' 'Aminta' del Tasso*. Florence: Olschki, 1983.

Dalla Palma, Giuseppe. *Le strutture narrative dell' "Orlando furioso"*. Florence: Olschki, 1984.

Davis, Robert C. "The Geography of Gender in the Renaissance." In *Gender and Society in Renaissance Italy*, ed. Judith C. Brown and idem, 19–38. London and New York: Longman, 1998.

Daybell, James, ed., *Early Modern Women's Letter Writing*, 1450–1700. New York: Palgrave, 2001.

de Tolnay, Charles. *Michelangelo, II: The Sistine Ceiling*. Princeton: Princeton University Press, 1945, repr. 1969.

———. *Michelangelo, III: The Medici Chapel*. Princeton: Princeton University Press, 1948, repr. 1970.

Dean, Trevor. "Venetian Economic Hegemony: The Case of Ferrara, 1200–1500." *Studi veneziani* 12 (1986): 45–98.

———. *Land and Power in Late Medieval Ferrara*. Cambridge Studies in Medieval Life and Thought. Cambridge: Cambridge University Press, 1988.

———. "Notes on the Ferrarese Court in the Later Middle Ages." *Renaissance Studies* 3 (1989): 357–69.

———. "Commune and Despot: The Commune of Ferrara under Este Rule, 1300–1450." In *City and Countryside in Late Medieval and Renaissance Italy: Essays Presented to Philip Jones,* ed. idem and Chris Wickham, 183–97. London: Hambledon Press, 1990.

———. "After the War of Ferrara: Relations between Venice and Ercole d'Este, 1484–1505." In *War, Culture and Society in Renaissance Venice: Essays Presented to Sir John Hale*, ed. David S. Chambers, Cecil H. Clough and Michael E. Mallett, 73–98. London: Hambledon Press, 1994.

———. "The Courts." In *The Origins of the State in Italy, 1300–1600*, ed. Julius Kirschner, 136–51. Chicago: University of Chicago Press, 1996.

Delcorno-Branca, Daniela. *L' "Orlando furioso" e il romanzo cavalleresco medievale*. Florence: Olschki, 1973.

Dersofi, Nancy. "Timon of Athens and Ferrara." Unpublished ms.

di Leone Leoni, Aron. "Gli ebrei sefarditi a Ferrara da Ercole I a Ercole II: Nuove ricerche e interpretationi." *Rassegna mensile di Israel* 52 (1986): 406–43.

———. *La nazione ebraica spagnola e portoghese negli stati estensi*. Rimini: Luisè, 1992.

———. "Documents inédits sur la nation portuguaise de Ferrare." *Revue des Etudes Juives* 152 (1993): 137–76.

———. "La diplomazia estense e l'immigrazione dei cristiani nuovi a Ferrara al tempo di Ercole II." *Nuova rivista storica* 78 (1994): 293–326.

———. "Nuove notizie sugli Abravanel." *Zakhor—Rivista di storia degli Ebrei d'Italia* 1 (1997): 153–206.

———. "I marrani di Coimbra denunciati al papa dall'Inquisizione portoghese nel 1578: Il loro status giuridico in diversi stati italiani." *Zakhor* 2 (1998): 73–109.

———. "La nazione portoghese corteggiata, privilegiata, espulsa e riammessa a Ferrara (1538–1550)." *Italia: Studi e ricerche sulla storia, la cultura, e la letteratura degli ebrei d'Italia* 13 (2001): 211–47.

Diller, A., and Paul Oskar Kristeller. "Strabo." In *Catalogus Translationum et Commentariorum: Mediaeval and Renaissance Translations and Commentaries: Annotated Lists and Guides*, ed. Paul Oskar Kristeller, 2:225–33. Washington, DC: Catholic University of America Press, 1971.

Dinshaw, Carolyn, and David Wallace, eds. *The Cambridge Companion to Medieval Women's Writing*. Cambridge: Cambridge UniversityPress, 2003.

Dionisotti, Carlo. "Appunti sui *Cinque canti* e sugli studi ariosteschi." In *Atti del Convegno di studi e problemi di critica testuale nel centenario della Commissione per i testi di lingua*, 368–82. Florence: Olschki, 1961.

———. "Review of P. R. Horne, *The Tragedies of G. B. Giraldi*." *Giornale storico della letteratura Italiana* 140 (1963): 114–21.

———. *Geografia e storia della letteratura italiana*. Turin: Einaudi, 1967.

Doglio, Maria Luisa. *Lettera e donna. Scrittura epistolare al femminile tra Quattro e Cinquecento*. Rome: Bulzoni, 1993.

———. "Scrittura e 'offizio di parole' nelle *Lettere familiari* di Veronica Franco." In *Les femmes écrivains en Italie au moyen âge et à la Renaissance,* 103–18. Aix-en-Provence: Publications de l'Université de Provence, 1994.

Donadoni, Eugenio. *Torquato Tasso: saggio critico*. Florence: La Nuova Italia, 1946.

Donato, Eugenio. "'Per selve e boscherecci labirinti': Desire and Narrative Structure in Ariosto's *Orlando furioso*." In *Literary Theory/ Renaissance Texts*, ed. Patricia Parker and David Quint, 33–62. Baltimore: Johns Hopkins University Press, 1986.

Donkin, R. A. *Meleagrides: An Historical and Ethnographical Study of the Guinea Fowl*. London: Ethnographica, 1991.

Douglas, Richard M. *Jacopo Sadoleto (1477–1547): Humanist and Reformer*. Cambridge, MA: Harvard University Press, 1959.

Draelants, I. "Le temps dans les textes historiographiques du Moyen Age." In *Le temps qu'il fait au Moyen Age: phénomènes atmosphériques dans la littérature, la pensée scientifique et religeuse*, ed. Claude Thomasset and Joelle Ducos, 91–138. Paris: Presses de l'Université de Paris-Sorbonne, 1998.

Dubois, Page. *History, Rhetorical Description and the Epic from Homer to Spenser*. Cambridge: Biblio Distribution Services, 1982.

Durling, Robert. *The Figure of the Poet in Renaissance Epic*. Cambridge, MA: Harvard University Press, 1965.

Edgerton, Samuel Y. *Pictures and Punishment: Art and Criminal Prosecution during the Florentine Renaissance*. Ithaca: Cornell University Press, 1985.

Edwards, John E. *Random Sketches and Notes of European Travel*. New York: Harper and Brothers, 1857.

Einhard. *Vita Karoli Magni: The Life of Charlemagne*. Trans. Evelyn Scherabon Firchow and Edwin H. Zeydel. Coral Gables: University of Miami Press, 1972. Repr. Dudweiler: AQ-Verlag, 1985.

Einstein, Alfred. *The Italian Madrigal*. 3 vols. Princeton: Princeton University Press, 1949.

Eisenstein, Elizabeth L. *The Printing Press as an Agent of Change: Communications and Cultural Transformations in Early Modern Europe*. Cambridge: Cambridge University Press, 1979.

Eisler, Colin. *The Genius of Jacopo Bellini: The Complete Paintings and Drawings*. New York: H. N. Abrams, 1989.

Elias, Norbert. *The Civilizing Process*. 3 vols. Vol. 1: *The History of Manners*. Oxford: Blackwell, 1978.

Erspamer, Francesco. "Il 'pensiero debole' di Torquato Tasso." In *La Menzogna*, ed. Franco Cardini, 120–36. Florence: Ponte alle Grazie, 1989.

Ezell, Margaret. *Writing Women's Literary History*. Baltimore: Johns Hopkins University Press, 1993.

Fabbri, Paolo. "Ferrara: Musica e Università." In *La rinascita del sapere: Libri e maestri dello studio ferrarese*, ed. Castelli, 331–32.

Faccioli, Emilio, ed. *Il teatro italiano: Dalle origini al '400*. 2 vols. Turin: Einaudi, 1975.

Farrier, Susan. *The Medieval Charlemagne Legend: An Annotated Bibliography*. New York: Garland, 1993.

Fava, Domenico. *La Biblioteca Estense nel suo sviluppo storico, con il catalogo della mostra permanente*. Modena: Vincenzi, 1925.

Feldman, Martha. *City Culture and the Madrigal at Venice*. Berkeley: University of California Press, 1995.

Felisatti, Massimo. *Isabella d'Este la primadonna del Rinascimento*. Milan: Bompiani, 1982.

Fenlon, Iain. "Music and Learning in Isabella d'Este's Studiolo." In *La Corte di Mantova nell'età di Andrea Mantegna: 1450–1550/ The Court of the Gonzaga in the Age of Mantegna: 1450–1550*, ed. Cesare Mozzarelli, Robert Oresko, and Leandro Ventura, 353–67. Rome: Bulzoni, 1997.

Ferguson, Margaret. *Trials of Desire: Renaissance Defenses of Poetry*. New Haven: Yale University Press, 1983.

Ferino-Pagden, Silvia, ed. *"La prima donna del mondo": Isabella d'Este, Fürstin und Mäzenatin der Renaissance*. Vienna: Ausstellungskatalog des Kunsthistorisches Museum, 1994.

Ferroni, Giulio. "Ludovico Ariosto." In *Storia della Letteratura Italiana*, ed. E. Malato, 353–455. Rome: Salerno, 1996.

Fichter, Andrew. *Poets Historical: Dynastic Epic in the Renaissance*. New Haven: Yale University Press, 1982.

Finelli, Luciana. *Il Duca Ercole I e il suo architetto Biagio Rossetti. Architettura e città nella Padania tra Quattro e Cinquecento*. Rome: Edizioni Kappa, 1995.

Finucci, Valeria. *The Lady Vanishes: Subjectivity and Representation in Castiglione and Ariosto*. Stanford: Stanford University Press, 1992.

———, ed. *Renaissance Transactions: Ariosto and Tasso*. Durham, NC: Duke University Press, 1999.

———. "Maternal Imagination and Monstrous Birth: Tasso's *Gerusalemme Liberata*." In *Generation and Degeneration: Tropes of Reproduction in Literature and History from Antiquity through Early Modern Europe*, ed. eadem and Kevin Brownlee, 41–77. Durham, NC: Duke University Press, 2001.

———. "Performing Maternity: Femaile Imagination, Paternal Erasure, and Monstrous Birth in Tasso's *Gerusalemme Liberata*." In eadem, *The Manly Masquerade: Masculinity, Paternity, and Castration in the Italian Renaissance*, 119–57. Durham, NC: Duke University Press, 2003.

Fontana, Bartolommeo. *Renata di Francia, duchessa di Ferrara, sui documenti dell'Archivio estense, del mediceo, del Gonzaga e dell'Archivio segreto vaticano (1510–1536)*. Rome: Forzani, 1889.

Förster, R. "Philostrats Gemälde in der Renaissance." *Jahrbuch der Königlichen Preussischen Kunstsammlungen* 25 (1904): 15–48.

Forti, Franco. "Matteo Maria Boiardo." In *Dizionario Biografico degli Italiani*, ed. Alberto M. Ghisalberti, 11:211–23. Rome: Istituto della Enciclopedia italiana, 1969.

Fortini, Franco. "I silenzi dell'Ariosto." *Rassegna della letteratura italiana* 79 (1975): 12–14.

Foucard, Cesare. "Proposta fatta dalla corte estense ad Alfonso il Re di Napoli (1445)." *Archivio storico per le provincie Napoletane* 4 (1879): 689–803.

Franceschini, Chiara. "La corte di Renata di Francia (1528–1560)." In *Il Rinascimento. Situazioni e personaggi*, ed. Adriano Prosperi, 185–214. Ferrara: Corbo, 2000.

Freccero, John. *Dante: The Poetics of Conversion*, ed. Rachel Jacoff. Cambridge, MA: Harvard University Press, 1986.

Friedenwald, Harry. *Jews and Medicine*. Baltimore: Johns Hopkins University Press, 1944.

Fumagalli, Edoardo. "Il volgarizzamento di Erodoto." In *Il Boiardo e il mondo estense*, ed. Anceschi and Matarrese, 1:329–428.

Gallico, Claudio. "Poesie musicali di Isabella d'Este." *Collectanea Historiae Musicae* 3 (1963): 109–19.

Gamba, Angelica. "La prostituzione a Ferrara nel tardo medioevo." Ph.D. diss., University of Ferrara, 1997.

Garbero-Zorzi, Elvira, and Daniele Seragnoli. "Lo Studio e lo spettacolo in Ferrara estense." In *La rinascita del sapere: Libri e maestri dello studio ferrarese*, ed. Castelli, 307–28.

Gardner, Edmund G. *The King of Court Poets: A Study of the Work, Life, and Times of Lodovico Ariosto*. London: Dutton, 1906.

———. *Dukes and Poets in Ferrara: A Study in the Poetry, Religion and Politics of the Fifteenth and Early Sixteenth Centuries*. London: A. Constable, 1904.

Gaudemet, Jean. *Le mariage en Occident: les moeurs et le droit*. Paris: Cerf, 1987.

Genette, Gérard. "D'un Récit Baroque." In *Figures II*, ed. idem. Paris: Editions du Seuil, 1969, 195–222.

Getto, Giovanni. *Nel mondo della* Gerusalemme. Rome: Bonacci, 1977.

Ghirardo, Diane. "Virtually Visible." *Thresholds* 19 (1999): 41–47.

———. "Women and Space: How Architectural History Erases Women." In *Intersections: Architectural History and Critical Theory*, ed. I. Borden and J. Rendell, 170–200. London: Routledge, 2000.

Giamatti, A. Bartlett. "Headlong Horses, Headless Horsemen: An Essay in the Chivalric Romances of Pulci, Boiardo, and Ariosto." In *Italian Literature: Roots and Branches*, ed. K. Atchity and G. Rimanelli, 265–307. New Haven: Yale University Press, 1976.

Gibbons, Felton. *Dosso and Battista Dossi: Court Painters at Ferrara*. Princeton: Princeton University Press, 1968.

Gilmore, Myron Piper. *Argument from Roman Law in Political Thought 1200–1600*. Cambridge, MA: Harvard University Press, 1941.

Giordano, Barbara. "Il monastero agostiniano di Santa Maria delle Grazie detto Mortara." B.A. thesis, University of Ferrara, 1998.

Goldberg, Jonathan. "Rebel Letters: Postal Effects from Richard II to Henry IV." *Renaissance Drama* 19 (1988): 3–28.

———. *Writing Matter: From the Hands of the English Renaissance*. Stanford: Stanford University Press, 1990.

Golega, J. *Der homerische Psalter*. Ettal: Kunstverlag, 1960.

Goody, Jack. *The Domestication of the Savage Mind*. Cambridge: Cambridge University Press, 1977.

———. *The Interface Between the Written and the Oral*. Cambridge: Cambridge University Press, 1987.

Gordley, James. *The Philosophical Origins of Modern Contract Doctrine*. Oxford: Oxford University Press, 1991.

Gragnolati, Manuele. "Love, Lust, and Avarice: Leodilla between Dante and Ovid." In *Fortune and Romance,* ed. Cavallo and Ross, 151–73.

Greenblatt, Stephen. *Renaissance Self-fashioning: More to Shakespeare*. Chicago: University of Chicago Press, 1980.

Greene, E. L. *Landmarks of Botanical History*. 2 vols. Stanford: Stanford University Press, 1983.

Greene, Thomas. *The Descent from Heaven*. New Haven: Yale University Press, 1963.

Greenstein, Jack M. "Alberti on *Historia:* A Renaissance View of the Structure of Significance in Narrative Painting." *Viator* 21 (1990): 277–82.

Grendler, Paul F. *The Roman Inquisition and the Venetian Press, 1540–1605*. Princeton: Princeton University Press, 1977.

Grierson, Philip. "Ercole d'Este and Leonardo da Vinci's Equestrian Statue of Francesco Sforza." *Italian Studies* 14 (1959): 404–8.

Grosser, Hermann. *La sottigliezza del disputare. Teorie degli stili e teorie dei generi in età rinascimentale e nel Tasso*. Florence: La Nuova Italia, 1992.

Guidoboni, E. "Aspetti della campagna estense: famiglie e nobiltà territoriale tra il XV e XVI secolo." In *La corte e lo spazio: Ferrara estense*, ed. Papagno and Quondam, 193–219.

Guillén, Claudio. "Notes Toward the Study of the Renaissance Letter." In *Renaissance Genres: Essays on Theory, History, and Interpretation*, ed. Barbara K. Lewalski, 70–110. Cambridge, MA: Harvard University Press, 1986.

Gundersheimer, W. L. "Machiavelli as an Empirical Humanist." B. A. thesis, Amherst College, 1959.

———. "Toward a Reinterpretation of the Renaissance in Ferrara." *Bibliothèque d'humanisme et Renaissance* 30 (1968): 267–81.

———, ed. *Art and Life at the Court of Ercole I d'Este: The 'De triumphis religionis' of Giovanni Sabadino degli Arienti*. Geneva: Droz, 1972.

———."Crime and Punishment in Ferrara, 1440–1500." In *Violence and Civil Disorder in Italian Cities, 1200–1500*, ed. Lauro Martines, 119–27. Berkeley: University of California Press, 1972.

———. *Ferrara: The Style of a Renaissance Despotism*. Princeton: Princeton University Press, 1973.

———. "The Patronage of Ercole I d'Este." *Journal of Medieval and Renaissance Studies* 6 (1976): 1–18.

———. "Women, Learning and Power: Eleonora of Aragon and the Court of Ferrara." In *Beyond Their Sex: Learned Women of the European Past*, ed. Patricia H. Labalme, 46–54. New York: New York University Press, 1980.

———. *Ferrara estense: Lo stile del potere*. Trans. Vittorio Vandelli (Italian translation of *Ferrara: The Style of a Renaissance Despotism)*. Modena: Panini, 1988.

———. "Ferrarese Studies: An Agenda for the Future." In *La corte di Ferrara e il suo mecenatismo 1441–1598*, ed. Marianne Pade, Lene Waage Petersen, and Daniela Quarta, 353–61. Copenhagen/Modena: Museum Tusculanums Forlag/Panini, 1990.

———. "Clarity and Ambiguity in Renaissance Gesture: The Case of Borso d'Este." *Journal of Medieval and Renaissance Studies* 23 (1993): 1–17.

Hampton, Timothy. *Writing from History: The Rhetoric of Exemplarity in Renaissance Literature*. Ithaca: Cornell University Press, 1990.

Hankey, A. Theresa. *Riccobaldo of Ferrara: His Life, Works, and Influence*. Rome: Istituto Storico Italiano per il Medio Evo, 1996.

Haskell, Francis. *History and its Images: Art and the Interpretation of the Past*. New Haven: Yale University Press, 1993.

Hay, Denys. "Flavio Biondo and the Middle Ages." *Proceedings of the British Academy* 45 (1959): 97–128.

Henderson, Robert Davey. "The First *Orlando furioso*: Compositional Seasons and Political Strategies." Ph.D. diss., University of California, 1995.

Hermann, Hermann Julius. "Zur Geschichte der Miniaturmalerei am Hofe der Este in Ferrara." *Jahrbuch der Kunsthistorischen Sammlungen des allerhöchsten Kaiserhauses* 21 (1900): 131–40.

Herzberg, Arthur and Leon A. Feldman, eds. *History and Jewish Historians: Essays and Addresses*. Philadelphia: Jewish Publication Society, 1964.

Heydenreich, L. H., and W. Lotz. *Architecture in Italy 1400–1600*. Harmondsworth: Penguin, 1974.

Hind, Arthur M. *Early Italian Engravings* .... Vol. 2. London: Quaritch, 1938.

Hoffman, Katherine. "Reading History in *Orlando furioso* and the *Faerie Queene*." Ph.D. diss., Northwestern University, 1991.

———. "The Court in the Work of Art: Patronage and Poetic Autonomy in the *Orlando furioso*, Canto 42." *Quaderni d'Italianistica* 13 (1992): 113–24.

———. "'Un così valoroso cavalliere': Knightly Honor in Artistic Representation in *Orlando furioso*, Canto 26." In *Renaissance Transactions*, ed. Finucci, 178–212.

Hope, Charles. "The Camerini d'Alabastro of Alfonso d'Este." *Burlington Magazine* 113 (1971): 716–21.

———. *Titian*. New York: Harper and Row, 1980.

Horne, P. R. *The Tragedies of G. B. Giraldi*. Oxford: Oxford University Press, 1962.

Hotchkiss, Valerie. *Clothes Make the Man*. New York: Garland, 1996.

Humfrey, Peter, and Mauro Lucco. *Dosso Dossi: Court Painter in Renaissance Ferrara*. New York: The Metropolitan Museum of Art, distributed by Andrea Bayer, 1998.

Isabella d'Este. I luoghi del collezionismo. Ed. Daniela Ferrari, intro. Leandro Ventura. Special issue of *Civiltà mantovana*, n.s. 30. Modena: Il Bulino, 1995.

Ianziti, Gary. *Humanistic Historiography under the Sforzas*. Oxford: Clarendon Press, 1988.

Iotti, Roberta, and Leandro Ventura. *Isabella d'Este alla corte di Mantova*. Modena: Il Bulino, 1993.

Jackson, Philip. "Two Descendants of Josquin's 'Hercules' Mass." *Music and Letters* 59 (1978): 188–205.

Jaeger, C. Stephen. *The Origins of Courtliness*. Philadelphia: University of Pennsylvania Press, 1985.

Jaffe, Samuel. "Gottfried von Strassburg and the Rhetoric of History." In *Medieval Eloquence*, ed. James J. Murphy, 288–318. Berkeley: University of California Press, 1978.

Jakobson, Roman. "Closing Statement: Linguistics and Poetics." In *Style in Language*, ed. Thomas A. Sebeok, 350–77. Cambridge, MA: Technology Press of Massachusetts Institute of Technology, 1960.

Jansen, Tore. *Latin Prose Prefaces: Studies in Literary Conventions*. Acta Universitatis Stockholmiensis. Stockholm: Almqvist and Wiksell, 1964.

Jardine, Lisa, and Anthony Grafton. *From Humanism to the Humanities*. London: Duckworth, 1986.

Javitch, Daniel. "Cantus Interruptus in the *Orlando furioso*." *Modern Language Notes* 95 (1980): 66–80.

———. "The *Orlando furioso* and Ovid's Revision of the *Aeneid*." *Modern Language Notes* 99 (1984): 1023–36.

———. "The Imitation of Imitations in *Orlando furioso*." *Renaissance Quarterly* 38 (1985): 215–39.

———. "Narrative Discontinuity in the *Orlando furioso* and its Sixteenth-Century Critics." *Modern Language Notes* 103 (1988): 50–74.

———. "The Grafting of Virgilian Epic in *Orlando furioso*." In *Renaissance Transactions*, ed. Finucci, 56–76.

Jed, Stephanie H. *Chaste Thinking: The Rape of Lucretia and the Birth of Humanism*. Bloomington: Indiana University Press, 1989.

Johnson, Alvin. "The Liturgical Music of Cipriano de Rore." Ph.D. diss., Yale University, 1954.

———. "The Masses of Cipriano de Rore." *Journal of the American Musicological Society* 6 (1953): 227–39.

Johnson, William M. *In Search of Italy: Foreign Writers in Northern Italy since 1800*. University Park: Pennsylvania State University Press, 1987.

Johnson-Haddad, Miranda. "Gelosia: Ariosto reads Dante." *Stanford Italian Review* 11 (1992): 187–201.

Jones, Ann Rosalind. *The Currency of Eros: Women's Love Lyric in Europe, 1540–1620*. Bloomington: Indiana University Press, 1990.

Kellman, Herbert. "Josquin at the Courts of the Netherlands and France." In *Josquin Desprez: Proceedings of the International Josquin Festival-Conference*, ed. E. Lowinsky, 181–216. Oxford: Oxford University Press, 1976.

Kelly, Joan. "Did Women Have a Renaissance?" In *Women, History, Theory*, ed. eadem, 19–50. Chicago: University of Chicago Press, 1984.

Kennedy, William. "The Problem of Allegory in Tasso's *Gerusalemme Liberata*." *Italian Quarterly* 15–16 (1972): 27–51.

Kent, Dale. *Cosimo de' Medici and Renaissance Florence*. New Haven: Yale University Press, 2000.

Kent, Francis W. "Sainted Mother, Magnificent Son: Lucrezia Tornabuoni and Lorenzo de' Medici." *Italian History and Culture* 3 (1997): 3–33.

Keuck, Karl. *Historia: Geschichte des Wortes und seiner Bedeutungen in der Antike und in den romanischen Sprachen*. Emsdetten: J. Lechte, 1934.

Kirschner, Julius, ed. *The Origins of the State in Italy, 1300–1600*. Chicago: University of Chicago Press, 1991.

Kliemann, J. "Il pensiero di Paolo Giovio nelle pitture eseguite sulle sue invenzioni." In *Atti del Convegno Paolo Giovio. Il Rinascimento e la memoria*, 197–223. Como: Società a Villa Gallia, 1985.

Knaack, G. "Phaëthon." In *Ausführliches Lexikon der griechischen und römischen Mythologie*, ed. W. W. Roscher, 2175–202. Leipzig: Teubner, 1902–1909.

Kohl, Benjamin G. *Padua under the Carrara, 1318–1405*. Baltimore: Johns Hopkins University Press, 1998.

Kolsky, Stephen. "Images of Isabella d'Este." *Italian Studies* 39 (1984): 47–62.

Kössling, R. "Die Korrespondenz der Olympia Fulvia Morata (1526–1555) als Dokument italo-deutscher Begegnugen." In *Acta Conventus Neo-Latini Bariensis*, ed. R. Schnur et al., 371–77. MRTS 184. Tempe, AZ: Medieval and Renaissance Texts and Studies, 1998.

Kostof, Spiro. *A History of Architecture: Settings and Rituals*. New York: Oxford University Press, 1985.

Kristeller, Paul Oskar, ed. *Catalogus Translationum et Commentariorum: Mediaeval and Renaissance Translations and Commentaries: Annotated Lists and Guides*. Washington, DC: Catholic University of America Press, 1960–.

Kuehn, Thomas. *Illegitimacy in Renaissance Florence*. Ann Arbor: University of Michigan Press, 2002.

La Monica, Stefano. "Realtà storica e immaginario bellico ariostesco." *Rassegna della letteratura italiana* 89 (1985): 326–58.

———. "La politica estense nel *Furioso* e negli *Ecatommiti*." *Rassegna della letteratura italiana* 96 (1992): 66–83.

La Via, Stefano. "Cipriano de Rore as Reader and as Read: A Literary Study of Madrigals from Rore's Later Collections." Ph.D. diss., Princeton University, 1991.

Labalme, Patricia. "Personality and Politics in Venice: Pietro Aretino." In *Titian: His World and his Legacy*, ed. David Rosand, 119–32. New York: Columbia University Press, 1982.

Lacan, Jacques. "Seminar on The Purloined Letter." In *The Poetics of Murder: Detective Fiction and Literary Theory*, ed. Glenn W. Most and William W. Stowe, 21–54. San Diego: Harcourt Brace Jovanovich, 1983.

Lamont, Michèle, and Annette Lareau. "Cultural Capital: Allusions, Gaps and Glissandos in Recent Theoretical Developments." *Sociological Theory* 6 (1988): 153–68.

Larivaille, Paul. *Pietro Aretino*. Rome: Salerno Editrice, 1997.

"Laura Dianti. La Donna del Duca Alfonso I d'Este." *Deputazione provinciale di Ferrara di storia patria,* n.s. 28 (1950).

Lesley, Arthur. "Hebrew Humanism in Italy: The Case of Biography." *Prooftexts* 2 (1982): 163–77.

Lewis, Andrew W. *Royal Succession in Capetian France: Studies on Familial Order and the State*. Cambridge, MA: Harvard University Press, 1981.

Lewis, C. S. *The Allegory of Love*. London: Oxford University Press, 1958, repr. 1975.

Lewis, Charlton T., and Charles Short, eds. *A Latin Dictionary*. Oxford: Clarendon Press, 1975.

Lippincott, Kristen. "The Neo-Latin Historical Epics of the North Italian Courts: An Examination of 'Courtly Culture' in the Fifteenth Century." *Renaissance Studies* 3 (1989): 415–28.

Lockwood, Lewis. "Dufay and Ferrara." In *Dufay Quincentenary Conference, Papers*, ed. A. Atlas, 24–25. Brooklyn: Dept. of Music, School of Performing Arts, Brooklyn College of the City University of New York, 1976.

———. "Josquin at Ferrara: New Documents and Letters." In *Josquin Desprez: Proceedings of the International Josquin Festival-Conference*, ed. Lowinsky, 103–37.
———. "Jean Mouton and Jean Michel: New Evidence on French Music and Musicians in Italy, 1505–1520." *Journal of the American Musicological Society* 32 (1979): 191–246.
———. "Musicisti a Ferrara all'epoca dell'Ariosto." In *L'Ariosto: La Musica e i Musicisti*, ed. Maria Antonella Balsano, 7–30. Florence: L.S. Olschki, 1981.
———. *Music in Renaissance Ferrara 1400–1505: The Creation of a Musical Center in the Fifteenth Century*. Cambridge, MA: Harvard University Press, 1984.
———. "Adrian Willaert and Cardinal Ippolito I d'Este: New Light on Willaert's Early Career in Italy." *Early Music History* 5 (1985): 85–112.
———. "Musica a corte e in chiesa nel XV secolo." In *Il Rinascimento. Situazioni e personaggi*, ed. Prosperi, 313–31.
———. "A Virtuoso Singer between Ferrara and Rome: The Case of Bidon." In *Papal Music and Musicians in Late Medieval and Renaissance Rome*, ed. Richard Sherr, 224–39. Oxford: Clarenden Press, 1998.
Longhi, Roberto. *Officina ferrarese*. Rome: Le Edizioni d'Italia, 1934.
———. *Ampliamenti*. Florence: Sansoni, 1940.
———. *Nuovi ampliamenti*. Florence: Sansoni, 1940–1956.
———. *Opere complete di Roberto Longhi*. Florence: Sansoni, 1956.
Longino Farrell, Michèle. *Performing Motherhood: The Sévigné Correspondence*. Hanover, NH: University Press of New England, 1991.
Looney, Dennis. "Ariosto's Ferrara: A National Identity between Fact and Fiction." *Comparative and General Literature* 39 (1990–1991): 25–34.
———. *Compromising the Classics: Romance Epic Narrative in the Italian Renaissance*. Detroit: Wayne State University Press, 1996.
———. "A Reading of Boiardo's Herodotus in the Late Quattrocento: Annotations to Modena MS α.H.3.22." *Manuscripta* 41 (1997): 127–32.
———. "Erodoto dalle *Storie* al romanzo." In *Il Boiardo e il mondo estense*, ed. Anceschi and Matarrese, 1:429–41.
———. "Tasso e la legislazione della narrativa." In *Torquato Tasso e la cultura estense,* ed. Venturi, 1:135–44.
———. "Ariosto and the Classics." In *Ariosto Today: Contemporary Perspectives*. Ed. Donald Beecher, Massimo Ciavolella, and Roberto Fedi. Toronto: University of Toronto Press, 2003.
Lorenzoni, Anna Maria. "Contributo allo studio delle fonti Isabelliane dell'Archivio di Stato di Mantova." *Atti e memorie*, n.s. 47 (1979): 97–135.
Lot, Ferdinand. *Étude sur le Lancelot en prose*. Paris: Champion, 1918.

Lowinsky, Edward. "Music in the Culture of the Renaissance." *Journal of the History of Ideas* 15 (1954): 509–53.

———, ed. *The Medici Codex of 1518: A Choirbook of Motets Dedicated to Lorenzo de Medici, Duke of Urbino.* Monuments of Renaissance Music 3. Chicago: University of Chicago Press, 1968.

———. "Music in Titian's *Bacchanal of the Andrians*: Origin and History of the Canon *per tonos*." In *Titian, His World and His Legacy*, ed. Rosand, 191–282.

———. *Cipriano de Rore's Venus Motet*. Provo, UT: Brigham Young University Press, 1986.

Ludwig, Walther, ed. *Die Borsias des Tito Strozzi: Ein lateinisches Epos der Renaissance*. Munich: Wilhelm Fink Verlag, 1977.

Luzio, Alessandro. "Federico Gonzaga ostaggio alla corte di Giulio II." *Archivio della società romana di storia patria* 9 (1886): 509–92.

———. *I precettori di Isabella d'Este*. Ancona: Gustavo Morelli, 1887.

———. "La reggenza d'Isabella d'Este durante la prigionia del marito (1509–10)." *Archivio storico lombardo* 4 (1910): 5–104.

———, ed. *L'Archivio Gonzaga di Mantova*. Mantova: Sartori, 1920.

Luzio, Alessandro, and Rodolfo Renier. *Gara di viaggi fra due celebri dame del Rinascimento*. Alexandria: Chiari, Romano e Filippa, 1890.

———. *Mantova e Urbino: Isabella d'Este ed Elisabetta Gonzaga nelle relazioni familiari e nelle vicende politiche*. Turin: Roux and Co, 1893.

———. "Il lusso di Isabella d'Este, marchesa di Mantova." *Nuova antologia* ser. 4 (1896): vol. 63: 441–69; vol. 64: 294–324; vol. 65: 666–88.

———. "La coltura e le relazioni letterarie di Isabella d'Este Gonzaga I. La coltura." *Giornale storico della letteratura italiana* 33 (1899): 1–62.

———. "La coltura e le relazioni letterarie di Isabella d'Este Gonzaga II. Le relazioni letterarie. 1: Gruppo mantovano." *Giornale storico della letteratura italiana* 34 (1899): 1–97.

———. "La coltura e le relazioni letterarie di Isabella d'Este Gonzaga. 2: Gruppo ferrarese." *Giornale storico della letteratura italiana* 35 (1900): 193–257.

———. "La coltura e le relazioni letterarie di Isabella d'Este Gonzaga 3: Gruppo lombardo." *Giornale storico della letteratura italiana* 36 (1900): 325–49.

———. "La coltura e le relazioni letterarie di Isabella d'Este Gonzaga. 4: Gruppo veneto." *Giornale storico della letteratura italiana* 37 (1901): 201–45.

———. "La coltura e le relazioni di Isabella d'Este Gonzaga. 5: Gruppo emiliano." *Giornale storico della letteratura italiana* 38 (1901): 41–70.

———. "La coltura e le relazioni letterarie di Isabella d'Este Gonzaga. 6: Gruppo centrale." *Giornale storico della letteratura italiana* 39 (1902): 193–251.

———. "La coltura e le relazioni letterarie di Isabella d'Este Gonzaga. Appendice: Inventarii di libri." *Giornale storico della letteratura italiana* 42 (1903): 75–111.

M'Crie, Thomas. *History of the Progress and Suppression of the Reformation in Italy in the Sixteenth Century*. Edinburgh-London: William Blackwood and Sons, 1827, repr. 1856.

Macey, Patrick. "Savonarola and the Sixteenth-Century Motet." *Journal of the American Musicological Society* 36 (1983): 422–52.

Mallett, Michael. *The Borgias: The Rise and Fall of a Renaissance Dynasty*. Chicago: Academy, 1987.

Manca, Joseph. *The Art of Ercole de' Roberti*. Cambridge: Cambridge University Press, 1992.

———. "What is Ferrarese about Bellini's *Feast of the Gods?*" In *Titian 500*, ed. idem, 303–4. Hanover, NH: University Press of New England, 1993.

Marcianò, Ada Francesca. *L'età di Biagio Rossetti. Rinascimenti di Casa d'Este*. Ferrara: Corbo, 1991.

Marek, George. *The Bed and the Throne: The Life of Isabella d'Este*. New York: Harper and Row, 1976.

Marinelli, Peter. *Ariosto and Boiardo: The Origins of "Orlando Furioso"*. Columbia, MO: University of Missouri Press, 1987.

Marotti, Ferruccio. *Lo spettacolo dall'umanesimo al manierismo*. Milan: Feltrinelli, 1974.

Marsh, David. "Ruggiero and Leone: Revision and Resolution in Ariosto's *Orlando furioso*." *Modern Language Notes* 96 (1981): 144–51.

Martelli, Mario. "Lucrezia Tornabuoni." In *Les femmes écrivains en Italie au moyen âge et à la Renaissance,* 51–86.

Martindale, Andrew. "The Patronage of Isabella d'Este at Mantua." *Apollo* 79 (1964): 183–91.

Martines, Lauro. *Power and Imagination: City-States in Renaissance Italy*. New York: Random House, 1980.

Martinez, Ronald L. "De-Cephalizing Rinaldo: The Money of Tyranny in Niccolò da Correggio's *Fabula de Cefalo* and in *Orlando furioso* 42." *Annali d'Italianistica* 12 (1994): 87–114.

———. "Two Odysseys: Rinaldo's Po Journey and the Poet's Homecoming in *Orlando Furioso*." In *Renaissance Transactions*, ed. Finucci, 17–55.

Marzola, Mario. *Per la storia della chiesa ferrarese nel secolo XVI (1497–1590)*. Turin: Società Editrice Internazionale, 1976.

———. *Per la storia della chiesa ferrarese nel secolo XVI (1497–1590). Parte seconda*. Turin: Società Editrice Internazionale, 1978.

Mastronardi, M. A. "L'immagine di Ferrara nella letteratura estense." In *Acta Conventus Neo-Latini Abulensis: Proceedings of the Tenth International Congress of Neo-Latin Studies, Avila, 4–9 August 1997*, ed. Roger Green et al., 423–30. MRTS 207. Tempe, AZ: Medieval and Renaissance Texts and Studies, 2000.

Mayer, Thomas F. "Ariosto Anticlerical: Epic Poetry and the Clergy in Early Cinquecento Italy." In *Anticlericalism in Late Medieval and Early Modern Europe*, ed. Peter Kykema and Heiko Oberman, 238–97. Leiden-New York/Koln: E.J. Brill, 1993.

Mazzi, Maria Serena. "La fame e la paura del fame." In *A tavola con il principe*, ed. Jadranka Bentini et al., 153–69. Ferrara: Corbo, 1988.

———. *Prostitute e lenoni nella Firenze del Quattrocento*. Milan: Il Saggiatore, 1991.

Mazzoldi, Leonardo, ed. *Mantova. La storia*. Mantua: Istituto Carlo d'Arco, 1961.

Mazzotta, Giuseppe. *Dante, Poet of the Desert: History and Allegory in the Divine Comedy*. Princeton: Princeton University Press, 1979.

McClure, George W. *Sorrow and Consolation in Italian Humanism*. Princeton: Princeton University Press, 1991.

McGough, Laura Jane. "'Raised from the Devil's Jaws': A Convent for Repentant Prostitutes in Venice, 1530–1670." Ph.D. diss., Northwestern University, 1997.

Meconi, Honey. "Does *Imitatio* Exist?" *Journal of Musicology* 12 (1994): 152–78.

Melchiorri, Gerolamo. *Nomenclatura ed etimologia delle piazze e strade di Ferrara (1918)*, ed. Eligio Mari. Ferrara: Liberty House, 1988.

Merkley, Paul, and Lora Matthews. *Music and Patronage at the Sforza Court*. Turnhout: Brepols, 1999.

Meyer, Edith Patterson. *First Lady of the Renaissance: A Biography of Isabella d'Este*. Boston: Little, Brown, and Company, 1970.

Mezières, A. "Le mystère de la vie du Tasse." *Revue des deux mondes* 1 (1909).

Mezzetti, Amalia. *Girolamo da Ferrara*. Milan: Silvana, 1977.

Michaud, J. F., ed. *Biographie Universelle Ancien et Moderne*. 45 vols. Paris: Louis Vives, 1854–1865.

Micocci, Claudio. "La presenza della tradizione classica nell' *Orlando innamorato*." In *Il Boiardo e il mondo estense*, ed. Anceschi and Matarrese, 1:43–61.

Milano, Ernesto. *Testimonianze dantesche nella Biblioteca Estense Universitaria (sec. XIV–XX)*. Modena: Il Bulino, 2000.

Miner, Earl. "Allusion." In *The New Princeton Encyclopedia of Poetry and Poetics*, ed. A. Preminger and T. V. F. Brogan, 38–40. Princeton: Princeton University Press, 1993.

Minnis, A. J. *Medieval Theory of Authorship*. 2nd ed. Philadelphia: University of Pennsylvania Press, 1988.

Mitchell, Bonner. *1598: A Year of Pageantry in Renaissance Ferrara*. MRTS 71. Binghamton, NY: Medieval and Renaissance Texts and Studies, 1990.

Morabito, Raffaele, ed. *Una sacra rappresentazione profana: Fortune di Griselda nel Quattrocento italiano*. Tübingen: Max Niemeyer, 1993.

Moretti, Walter. "L'ideale ariostesco di un'Europa pacificata e unita e la sua crisis nel terzo Furioso." In *The Renaissance in Ferrara/Il Rinascimento a Ferrara*, ed. J. Salmons and idem, 223–44. Ravenna: Mario Lapucci, 1984.

———. *L'ultimo Ariosto*. Bologna: Patron, 1977.

———, ed. *Storia di Ferrara, VII. Il Rinascimento. La letteratura*. Ferrara: Corbo, 1987; repr. Ferrara: Edizioni Líbrit, 1994.

Muller, Gerhard. *Die Romische Kurie und die Reformation 1523–1534. Kirche und Politik während des Pontifikates Clemens VII*. Heidelberg: G. Mohn, 1969.

Murray, Peter. *The Architecture of the Renaissance*. New York: Schocken Books, 1966.

Murrin, Michael. *The Allegorical Epic: Essays in its Rise and Decline*. Chicago: University of Chicago Press, 1980.

———. *History and Warfare in Renaissance Epic*. Chicago: University of Chicago Press, 1994.

Murutes, H. "Personifications of Laughter and Drunken Sleep in Titian's *Andrians*." *Burlington Magazine* 115 (1973): 518–25.

Nagy, Gregory. *The Best of the Achaeans: Concepts of the Hero in Archaic Greek Poetry*. Baltimore: Johns Hopkins University Press, 1979.

Najemy, John M. *Between Friends: Discourses of Power and Desire in the Machiavelli-Vettori Letters of 1513–1515*. Princeton: Princeton University Press, 1993.

Niccoli, Ottavia. "Forme di cultura e condizioni di vita in due epistolari femminili del Rinascimento." In *Les femmes écrivains en Italie au moyen âge et à la Renaissance*, 13–32.

Nohrnberg, James. *The Analogy of The Faerie Queene*. Princeton: Princeton University Press, 1976.

———. "Orlando's Opportunity: Chance, Luck, Fortune, Occasion, Boats, and Blows in Boiardo's *Orlando Innamorato*." In *Fortune and Romance*, ed. Cavallo and Ross, 31–75.

Novelli, Ettore. *Fetonte*. Imola: Galeati, 1879.

Noyes, Ella. *The Story of Ferrara*. London: Dent, 1904.

Nugent, George. "The Jaquet Motets and their Authors." Ph.D. diss., Princeton University, 1973.

———. "Anti-Protestant Music for Sixteenth-Century Ferrara." *Journal of the American Musicological Society* 43 (1990): 228–91.

Olini, Lucia. "Dalle direzioni di lettura alla revisione del testo: Tasso tra 'Allegoria del Poema' e *Giudizio*." *Rassegna della letteratura italiana* 7 (1985): 53–68.

Olivieri, Achille. "Alessandro Trissino e il movimento calvinista vicentino del Cinquecento." *Rivista di Storia della Chiesa* 21 (1967): 55–57.

Ong, Walter J. *Rhetoric, Romance, and Technology: Studies in the Interaction of Expression and Culture*. Ithaca: Cornell University Press, 1971.

———. *Orality and Literacy*. New York: Routledge, 1991.

Ossola, Carlo. "Dantismi metrici nel *Furioso*." In *Ludovico Ariosto: Lingua, Stile e Tradizione*, ed. Cesare Segre, 65–94. Milan: Feltrinelli, 1976.

Osthoff, Helmuth. *Josquin Desprez*. Tutzing: H. Schneider, 1962.

Owens, Jessie Ann. "Cipriano de Rore a Parma (1560–1565): Nuovi Documenti." *Rivista Italiana di Musicologia* 11 (1976): 5–26.

———. "Mode in the Madrigals of Cipriano de Rore." In *Essays on Italian Music in the Cinquecento*, ed. Richard Charteris, 1–15. Sydney, Australia: Frederick May Foundation for Italian Studies, 1990.

Pade, Marianne, Lene Waage Petersen, and Daniela Quarta, eds. *La corte di Ferrara e il suo mecenatismo 1441–1598 / The Court of Ferrara and its Patronage*. Modena: Panini, 1990.

Pampaloni, Leonzio. "La guerra nel *Furioso*." *Belfagor* 26 (1971): 627–52.

Papagno, G., and A. Quondam, eds. *La corte e lo spazio: Ferrara estense*. Rome: Bulzoni, 1982.

Pardi, Giuseppe. *Leonello d'Este: Marchese di Ferrara*. Bologna: Forni, 1904.

———. "Borso d'Este, Duca di Ferrara, Modena e Reggio." In *Studi Storici*, ed. Amedeo Crivellucci, 3–88, 134–204, 377–416. Pisa: Spoerri, 1906.

———. "Borso d'Este, Duca di Ferrara, Modena e Reggio." In *Studi Storici*, ed. Amedeo Crivellucci, 113–70. Pisa: Spoerri, 1907.

Park, Jacqueline. *The Secret Book of Grazia de Rossi*. New York: Simon and Schuster, 1997.

Parker, Patricia. *Inescapable Romance: Studies in the Poetics of a Mode*. Princeton: Princeton University Press, 1979.

Partner, Nancy F. "The New Cornificius: Medieval History and the Artifice of Words." In *Classical Rhetoric and Medieval Historiography*, ed. Breisach, 5–59.

Pauly, August Friedrich von, and Georg Wissowa, eds. *Paulys Real-Encyclopädie der Classischen Altertumswissenschaft, neue Bearbeitung*. 24 vols. Stuttgart: J. B. Metzler, 1894–1963.

Pavlock, Barbara. *Eros, Imitation, and the Epic Tradition*. Ithaca: Cornell University Press, 1990.

Pennington, Kenneth. *The Prince and the Law, 1200–1600*. Berkeley: University of California Press, 1993.

Peretti, Aurelio. *Dall'Eridano di Esiodo al Retrone Vicentino*. Pisa: Giardini, 1994.

Petrucci, F. "Caleffini, Ugo." In *Dizionario biografico degli italiani*, ed. Alberto M. Ghisalberti, 16:647–50. Rome: Istituto della enciclopedia italiana, 1973.

Picquet, Théa. "Profession: Courtisane." In *Les femmes écrivains en Italie au moyen âge et à la Renaissance*, 119–37.

Pine-Coffin, R. S. *Bibliography of British and American Travel in Italy to 1860*. Florence: Leo S. Olschki, 1974.

———. "Bibliography of British and American Travel in Italy to 1860: Additions and Corrections." *La Bibliofilia* 83 (1981): 237–61.

Piromalli, Alessandro. *La cultura a Ferrara al tempo di Ludovico Ariosto*. Florence: La Nuova Italia, 1953.

Pirrotta, Nino, and Elena Povoledo. *Li due Orfei*. Turin: Einaudi, 1975.

Pistofilo, Bonaventura. "Vita di Alfonso I d'Este, Duca di Ferrara," ed. Antonio Cappelli. In *Atti e memorie delle Reali Deputazioni di storia patria per le provincie modenesi e parmensi* III (1865): 490–554.

Pittorru, Fabio. *Torquato Tasso: l'uomo, il poeta, il cortigiano*. Milan: Bompiani, 1982.

Pizzagalli, Daniela. *La signora del Rinascimento. Vita e splendori di Isabella d'Este alla corte di Mantova*. Milan: Rizzoli, 2001.

Pocock, J. G. A. *The Machiavellian Moment: Florentine Political Thought and the Atlantic Republican Tradition*. Princeton: Princeton University Press, 1975.

Ponte, Giovanni. *La personalità e l'opera del Boiardo*. Genoa: Tilgher, 1972.

———. "Matteo Maria Boiardo dalla traduzione storiografica al romanzesco nella *Vita di Federico Barbarossa*." In *Il Boiardo e il mondo estense*, ed. Anceschi and Matarrese, 1:443–59.

Poppi, Antonino. "Il *De caelesti substantia* di Matteo Ferchi fra tradizione e innovazione." In *Galileo e la cultura padovana*, ed. Accademia Patavina G. Santinelli, 13–56. Padova: CEDAM Casa Editrice, 1992.

Portner, I. A. "A Non-Performance of *Il negromante*." *Italica* 59 (1982): 316–29.

Pozzi, Mario. "'Andrem di pari all'amorosa face': Appunti sulle lettere di Maria Savorgnan." In *Les femmes écrivains en Italie au moyen âge et à la Renaissance*, 87–101.

Praloran, Marco. "Matteo Maria Boiardo." In *Storia di Ferrara VII. Il Rinascimento. La letteratura*, ed. Moretti, 215–64.

Prandi, Stefano. *Il Cortegiano ferrarese: i Discorsi di Annibale Romei e la cultura nobiliare nel cinquecento*. Florence: Olschki, 1990.

Prizer, William F. "Isabella d'Este and Lorenzo da Pavia, 'Master Instrument-Maker'." *Early Music History* 2 (1982): 87–127.

———. "Isabella d'Este and Lucrezia Borgia as Patrons of Music: The Frottola at Mantua and Ferrara." *Journal of the American Musicological Society* 38 (1985): 1–33.

———. "Una 'Virtù Molto Conveniente a Madonne': Isabella d'Este as a Musician." *Journal of Musicology* 17 (1999): 10–49.

Prosperi, Adriano. "Le istituzioni ecclesiastiche nei domini estensi all' epoca dell' Ariosto." In *Il Rinascimento nelle corti padane: società e cultura*, ed. idem, 1–125.

———, ed. *Il Rinascimento. Situazioni e personaggi*. *Storia di Ferrara* 6. Ferrara: Corbo, 2000.

Pullan, Brian. *The Jews of Europe and the Inquisition of Venice, 1550–1670*. London: Blackwell, 1983.

Putnam, Robert D. *Making Democracy Work: Civic Traditions in Modern Italy*. Princeton: Princeton University Press, 1993.

Quint, David. "The Figure of Atlante: Ariosto and Boiardo's Poem." *Modern Language Notes* 94 (1979): 77–91.

———. *Origin and Originality in Renaissance Literature: Versions of the Source*. New Haven: Yale University Press, 1983.

———. "Political Allegory in the *Gerusalemme liberata*." *Renaissance Quarterly* 43 (1990): 1–29. Repr. in idem, *Epic and Empire*, 213–47.

———. *Epic and Empire: Politics and Generic Form From Virgil to Milton*. Princeton: Princeton University Press, 1993.

———. "Introduction." In *Cinque Canti / Five Cantos of Ludovico Ariosto*, 1–44. Berkeley: University of California Press, 1996.

———. "Narrative Interlace and Narrative Genres in *Don Quijote* and the *Orlando Furioso*." *Modern Language Quarterly* 58 (1997): 241–68.

Quondam, Amedeo, ed. *"Carte messaggiere": Retorica e modelli di communicazione epistolare. Per un indice di libri di lettere del Cinquecento*. Rome: Bulzoni, 1981.

Raffaele, Tamalio. *Federico Gonzaga alla corte di Francesco I*. Paris: Honoré Champion, 1994.

Rajna, Pio. *I Reali di Francia*, Vol. I: *Ricerche intorno ai reali di Francia*. Bologna: Gaetano Romagnoli, 1872.

———. "Ricordi di codici francesi posseduti dagli Estensi nel secolo XV." *Romania* 2 (1873): 5–59.

———. *Le fonti dell' "Orlando furioso"*. Florence: Sansoni, 1900; 2nd ed. Florence: Sansoni, 1975.

Ravid, Benjamin. "A Tale of Three Cities and their Raison d'État: Ancona, Venice, Livorno and the Competition for Jewish Merchants in the Sixteenth Century." *Mediterranean Historical Review* 6 (1991–1992): 138–62. Repr. in *Jews, Christians and Muslims in the Mediterranean World after 1492*, ed. Alisa Meyuhas Ginio, 138–62. London: Frank Cass, 1992.

Reichenbach, Giulio. *Matteo Maria Boiardo*. Bologna: Zanichelli, 1929.

Renucci, Paul. "La cultura." In *Storia d'Italia,* ed. Ruggiero Romano and Corrado Vivanti, vol. 2.2: *Dalla caduta dell'Impero romano al secolo xviii*, 1081–1466. Turin: Einaudi, 1988.

Répaci-Courtois, Gabriella. "Blaise de Vigenère et l'expérience des arts visuels." In *Blaise de Vigenère poète et mythographe au temps de Henri III*, ed. Centre V. L. Saulnier, 101–10. Paris: Ecole Normale Supérieure, 1994.

Residori, Matteo. "Colombo e il *volo* di Ulisse: una nota sul XV della *Liberata*." *Annali della Scuola Normale Superiore di Pisa, Classe di Lettere e Filosofia* 22 (1992): 931–42.

Rhu, Lawrence. "From Aristotle to Allegory: Young Tasso's Evolving Vision of the *Gerusalemme liberata*." *Italica* 65 (1988): 111–30.

———. *The Genesis of Tasso's Narrative Theory: English Translations of the Early Poetics and a Comparative Study of Their Significance*. Detroit: Wayne State University Press, 1993.

Rifkin, Joshua. "Ercole's Second-Hand Coronation Mass." In *Music in Renaissance Cities and Courts: Studies in Honor of Lewis Lockwood*, ed. Jessie Ann Owens and Anthony Cummings, 381–90. Warren, MI: Harmonie Park Press, 1996.

Rigolot, François. "A Literary Critic's Response to a Social Historian: The Gifts of Montaigne." *Journal of Medieval and Renaissance Studies* 17 (1987): 111–28.

Robertson, C. "Annibale Caro as Iconographer." *Journal of the Warburg and Courtauld Institutes* 45 (1982): 160–81.

———. "Paolo Giovio and the 'Invenzioni' for the Sala dei Cento Giorni." In *Atti del Convegno Paolo Giovio. Il Rinascimento e la memoria*, 225–37. Como: Società a Villa Gallia, 1985.

Rocke, Michael. "Gender and Sexual Culture in Renaissance Italy." In *Gender and Society in Renaissance Italy*, ed. Brown and Davis, 150–70.

Romano, Dennis. "Gender and the Urban Geography of Renaissance Venice." *Journal of Social History* 23 (1989): 339–53.

Rombaldi, Odoardo. "Lo stato estense e Matteo Maria Boiardo." In *Il Boiardo e il mondo estense*, ed. Anceschi and Matarrese, 1:549–606.

Rosand, David, ed. *Titian, His World and His Legacy*. New York: Columbia University Press, 1982.

Rosand, Ellen. *Opera in Seventeenth-Century Venice: The Creation of a Genre*. Berkeley: University of California Press, 1991.

Rosenberg, Charles M. "Notes on the Borsian Addition to the Palazzo Schifanoia." *Bollettino annuale dei Musei Ferraresi* 2 (1973): 32–42.

———. "The Erculean Addition to Ferrara: Contemporary Reactions and Pragmatic Considerations." *ACTA: The Fifteenth Century* 5 (1978): 49–67.

———. "Francesco del Cossa's Letter Reconsidered." *Bollettino annuale dei Musei Ferraresi* 5/6 (1978): 11–15.

———. "The Iconography of the Sala degli stucchi in the Palazzo Schifanoia in Ferrara." *Art Bulletin* 61 (1979): 377–83.

———. "Arte e politica alle corti di Lionello e Borso d'Este." In *Le Muse e il Principe. Arte di corte nel Rinascimento padano*, ed. Alessandra Mottola Molfino and Mauro Natale. Modena: Panini, 1991, 40–41.

———. *The Este Monuments and Urban Redevelopment in Renaissance Ferrara*. Cambridge: Cambridge University Press, 1997.

Rosenmeyer, Patricia A. *Ancient Epistolary Fictions: The Letter in Greek Literature*. Cambridge: Cambridge University Press, 2001.

Rosenthal, Margaret F. *The Honest Courtesan*. Chicago: University of Chicago Press, 1992.

Ross, Charles. "Introduction." In *Orlando Innamorato of Matteo Maria Boiardo*, ed. idem, 1–29. Berkeley: University of California Press, 1989.

———. "Damsel in Distress? Orrigille's Subjectivity." In *Fortune and Romance*, ed. Cavallo and idem, 175–90.

Rossi, Paolo, ed. *Il Rinascimento nelle corti padane: società e cultura*. Bari: De Donato, 1976.

Roth, Cecil. "The Marrano Press at Ferrara, 1552–1555." *Modern Language Review* 38 (1943): 307–17.

Roussiaud, Jacques. *La prostituzione nel Medioevo*. Rome-Bari: Laterza, 1995.

Rowe, Katherine. *Dead Hands: Fictions of Agency Renaissance to Modern*. Stanford: Stanford University Press, 1999.

Rubin, Patricia Lee. *Giorgio Vasari: Art and History*. New Haven: Yale University Press, 1995.

Ruffini, F. "Linee rette e intrichi: il Vitruvio di Cesariano e la Ferrara teatrale di Ercole I." In *La corte e lo spazio: Ferrara estense*, ed. Papagno and Quondam, 365–429.

Ruggiero, Guido. "Marriage, Love, Sex, and Renaissance Civic Morality." In *Sexuality and Gender in Early Modern Europe*, ed. James Grantham Turner, 10–30. Cambridge: Cambridge University Press, 1993.

Ruhmer, Eberhard. *Tura: Paintings and Drawings*. New York: Phaidon Publishers, 1958.

Sabatine, Barbara J. "The Church of Santa Caterina dei Funari and the Vergini Miserabili of Rome." Ph.D. diss., University of California, Los Angeles, 1992.

Sabbadini, Remigo. "Ancora l'Aurispa." *Giornale storico della letteratura italiana* 19 (1892): 357–66.

Saccone, Eduardo. "Cloridano e Medoro, con alcuni argomenti per una lettura del primo *Furioso*." In idem, *Il soggetto del "Furioso,"* 161–200.

———. *Il soggetto del "Furioso" e altri saggi tra Quattro e Cinquecento*. Naples: Liguori, 1974.

———. "Prospettive sull'ultimo Ariosto." *Modern Language Notes* 98 (1983): 55–69.

Salmons, J. "An Unpublished Account of the End of Este Rule in Ferrara: Niccolò Contarini's *Istorie Veneziane* and Events in Ferrara 1597–98." In *The Renaissance in Ferrara and its European Horizons*, ed. idem Salmons and Moretti, 127–30.

———, and J. Moretti, eds. *The Renaissance in Ferrara and its European Horizons*. Cardiff: University of Wales Press, 1984.

Salomon, Herman Prins, and Aron di Leone Leoni. "Mendes, Benveniste, De Luna, Micas, Nasci: The State of the Art (1532–1558)." *Jewish Quarterly Review* 88 (1998): 135–211.

San Juan, Rose Marie. "The Court Lady's Dilemma: Isabella d'Este and Art Collecting in the Renaissance." *Oxford Art Journal* 14 (1991): 67–78.

Sangirardi, Giuseppe. *Boiardismo ariostesco: presenza e trattamento dell' "Orlando innamorato" nel "Furioso"*. Lucca: Pacini Fazzi, 1993.

Santi, Venceslao. "La precedenza tra gli Estensi e i Medici e *l'Historia dei principi d'Este* di G. Battista Pigna." *Atti e memorie della Deputazione di storia patria ferrarese* 9 (1987): 37–122.

Santore, Cathy. "Julia Lombardo, 'Somtuosa Meretrize': A Portrait by Property." *Renaissance Quarterly* 41 (1988): 44–83.

Scaglione, Aldo. *Knights at Court*. Berkeley: University of California Press, 1991.

Scarsella, Alessandro. "Boiardo traduttore parodista ovvero la finzione di Turpino." In *Il Boiardo e il mondo estense*, ed. Anceschi and Matarrese, 1:387–98.

Schiffman, Zachary S. Review of Leonard Barkan, *Unearthing the Past*. *Sixteenth Century Journal* 31 (2000): 944–46.

Schmugge, Ludwig, ed. *Illegitimität im Spätmittelalter*. Munich: R. Oldenbourg Verlag, 1994.

Schreiner, Klaus. "'Defectus natalium' — Geburt aus einem unrechtmäßigen Schoß als Problem klösterlicher Gemeinschaftsbildung." In *Illegitimität im Spätmittelalter*, ed. Schmugge, 85–114.

Seem, Lauren Scancarelli. "The Limits of Chivalry: Tasso and the End of the *Aeneid*." *Comparative Literature* 42 (1990): 116–25.

Segal, Lester A. *Historical Consciousness and Religious Tradition in Azariah de' Rossi's Me'or 'Enayim*. Philadelphia-New York-Jerusalem: The Jewish Publication Society, 1989.

Segre, Cesare. "Un repertorio linguistico e stilistico dell'Ariosto: *La Commedia*." In idem, *Esperienze ariostesche,* 51–83. Pisa: Nistri-Lischi, 1966.

Sestan, E. "Gli Estensi e il loro stato al tempo dell'Ariosto." *Rassegna della letteratura italiana* 69 (1975): 19–31.

Seznec, Jean. *The Survival of the Pagan Gods: The Mythological Tradition and Its Place in Renaissance Humanism and Art*. Trans. Barbara F. Sessions. Princeton: Princeton University Press, 1972.

Shearman, John. "Alfonso d'Este's Camerino." In *"Il se rendit en Italie": Études offertes à André Chastel*, 209–29. Rome: Edizioni dell'elefante, 1987.

———. *Only Connect — : Art and the Spectator in the Italian Renaissance*. Princeton: Princeton University Press, 1992.

Sheehan, Michael M. "Illegitimacy in Late Medieval England: Laws, Dispensation and Practice." In *Illegitimität im Spätmittelalter*, ed. Schmugge, 115–21.

Shelley, Mary Wollstonecroft. *Rambles in Germany and Italy, in 1840, 1842, and 1843*. 2 vols. London: Edward Moxon, 1844.

Shemek, Deanna. *Ladies Errant: Wayward Women and Social Order in Early Modern Italy*. Durham, NC: Duke University Press, 1998.

———. "Aretino's *Marescalco*: Marriage Woes and the Duke of Mantua." *Renaissance Studies* 16 (2002): 366–80.

———. "The Collector's Cabinet: Lodovico Domenichi's Gallery of Women." In *Strong Voices, Weak History*, ed. Pamela Joseph Benson and Victoria Kirkham. Ann Arbor: University of Michigan Press, forthcoming.

Sherman, Claire Richter, ed. *Writing Hands: Memory and Knowledge in Early Modern Europe*. Seattle: University of Washington Press, 2000.

Sherr, Richard, ed. *The Josquin Companion*. Oxford: Oxford University Press, 2000.

Shinneman, D. "The Canon in Titian's *Andrians*: A Reinterpretation." *Studies in the History of Art* 6 (1974): 93–95.

Sitterson, Joseph. "Allusive and Elusive Meanings: Reading Ariosto's Vergilian Ending." *Renaissance Quarterly* 45 (1992): 1–19.

Slim, H. Colin. "Dosso Dossi's Allegory at Florence about Music." *Journal of the American Musicological Society* 43 (1990): 43–98.

Smith, Harold F. *American Travelers Abroad: A Bibliography of Accounts Published before 1900*. Carbondale: Southern Illinois University Library, 1969.

Soffientini, Anna. "Le *Vite* di Enrico IV ed Enrico V nell'*Istoria imperiale* di Matteo Maria Boiardo." In *Il Boiardo e il mondo estense*, ed. Anceschi and Matarrese, 1:461–79.

Solerti, A. *Ferrara e la Corte estense nella seconda metà del secolo decimosesto. I discorsi di Annibale Romei gentiluomo ferrarese*. Città del Castello: S. Lapi, 1900.

Spiegel, Gabrielle M. "Pseudo-Turpin, the Crisis of the Aristocracy, and the Beginnings of Vernacular Historiography in France." *Journal of Medieval History* 12 (1986): 207–23.

Starn, Randolph. "Reinventing Heroes in Renaissance Italy." In *Art and History: Images and their Meaning*, ed. Robert I. Rotberg and Theodore K. Rabb. Cambridge: Cambridge University Press, 1988, 67–84.

Stebbins, Theodore E. *The Lure of Italy: American Artists and the Italian Experience, 1760–1914*. Boston: Abrams, 1992.

Stedman, Wendy Sheard. "Antonio Lombardo's Reliefs for Alfonso d'Este's Studio di Marmi: Their Significance and Impact on Titian." In *Titian 500*, ed. Manca, 315–57.

Stefanini, Ruggero. "Formazione e dileguo del dittongo nei possessivi preposti del fiorentino." *Letteratura Italiana Antica* 1 (2000): 17–40.

Stephens, Walter. "Metaphor, Sacrament and the Problem of Allegory in *Gerusalemme Liberata*." *I Tatti Studies* 4 (1991): 217–47.

Stinger, Charles. *The Renaissance in Rome*. Bloomington: Indiana University Press, 1985.

Stowers, Stanley K. *Letter Writing in Greco-Roman Antiquity*. Philadelphia: Westminster Press, 1986.

Strano, Titina. *Isabella d'Este, Marchesa di Mantova*. Milan: Ceschina, 1938.

Straeten, Edmond Vander. *La Musique aux Pays-Bas*. Brussels: G.-A. van Trigt, 1867–1888.

Strocchia, Sharon. "Gender and the Rites of Honor in Italian Renaissance Cities." In *Gender and Society in Renaissance Italy*, ed. Brown and Davis, 39–60.

Summit, Jennifer. "Women and Authorship." In *The Cambridge Companion to Medieval Women's Writing*, ed. Dinshaw and Wallace, 91–108.

Suzuki, Mihoko. *Metamorphoses of Helen: Authority, Difference, and the Epic.* Ithaca: Cornell University Press, 1989.

Tabacco, Giovanni. *The Struggle for Power in Medieval Italy: Structures of Political Rule.* Trans. Rosalind Brown Jensen. Cambridge: Cambridge University Press, 1989.

Tamalio, Raffaele. *Ferrante Gonzaga alla corte spagnola di Carlo V.* Mantua: Arcari Gianluigi, 1991.

———. *Federico Gonzaga alla corte di Francesco I.* Paris: Honoré Champion, 1994.

Tedeschi, John, and James Lattis. *The Italian Reformation of the Sixteenth Century and the Diffusion of Renaissance Culture: A Bibliography of the Secondary Literature (ca. 1750–1994).* Modena: Panini, 2000.

Thompson, David. *Dante's Epic Journeys.* Baltimore: Johns Hopkins University Press, 1974.

Tiraboschi, Girolamo. *Dizionario topografico-storico degli stati estensi.* Modena: La Tipografia Camerale, 1824–1825; repr. 2 vols., Bologna: Forni, 2002.

———. *Storia della letteratura italiana.* Modena: Società Tipografica, 1771–1782.

Tissoni Benvenuti, Antonia. "Il mondo cavalleresco e la corte estense." In *I libri di* Orlando innamorato, ed. R. Bruscagli, 13–33. Modena: Panini, 1987.

———. "Note preliminari al commento dell'*Innamoramento d'Orlando.*" In *Il commento ai testi*, ed. O. Besomi and C. Caruso, 305–6. Basel-Boston-Berlin: Birkhauser Verlag, 1992.

———, and Maria Pia Mussini Sacchi, eds. *Le corti padane, Teatro del Quattrocento.* Turin: UTET, 1983.

Torelli, Pietro, ed. *L'Archivio Gonzaga di Mantova.* Vol. 1. Ostiglia: Mondadori, 1920.

Trachtenberg, Marvin, and Isabelle Hyman. *Architecture: From Prehistory to Post-Modernism.* Englewood Cliffs, NJ: Prentice Hall, 1986.

Treadwell, Nina. "'Simil combattimento fatto da Dame'. The Musico-theatrical Entertainments of Margherita Gonzaga's *Balletto delle donne* and the Female Warrior in Ferrarese Cultural History." In *Gender, Sexuality, and Early Music*, ed. Todd M. Borgerding, 27–40. London-New York: Routledge, 2002.

Trexler, Richard C. *Public Life in Renaissance Florence.* Ithaca: Cornell University Press, 1980.

Tristano, Richard. "Ferrara in the Fifteenth Century: Borso d'Este and the Development of a New Nobility." Ph.D. diss., New York University, 1983.

———. "Vassals, Fiefs, and Social Mobility During the Middle Ages and Renaissance." *Medievalia et Humanistica* 15 (1987): 43–64.

Tuohy, Thomas, *Herculean Ferrara: Ercole d'Este (1471–1505) and the Invention of a Ducal Capital*. Cambridge: Cambridge University Press, 1996.

Turnbull, Robert. *Olympia Morata: Her Life and Times*. Boston: Massachusetts Sabbath School Society, 1846.

Vecce, Carlo. "Vittoria Colonna: Il codice epistolare della poesia femminile." In *Les femmes écrivains en Italie au moyen âge et à la Renaissance*, 213–32.

Venturi, Adolfo. "I primordi del Rinascimento artistico a Ferrara." *Rivista storica italiana* 1 (1884): 591–631.

———. "L'arte a Ferrara nel periodo di Borso d'Este." *Rivista storica italiana* 2 (1885): 689–749.

———. "L'arte ferrarese nel periodo d'Ercole I d'Este." In *Atti e memorie della Deputazione di storia patria per le provincie di Romagna* (1888): 91–119, 350–422; (1889): 368–412.

Venturi, Gianni. "Scene e giardini a Ferrara." In *Il rinascimento nelle corti padane: Società e cultura*, ed. Rossi, 553–95.

———. *La scene dell'Eden: Teatro, arte, giardini nella letteratura italiana*. Ferrara: Bovolenta, 1979.

———, ed. *Torquato Tasso e la cultura estense*. 3 vols. Florence: Olschki, 1999.

Via, Claudia Cerri. "I Tarocchi cosidetti del 'Mantegna': Origine, significato, e fortuna di un ciclo di immagini." In *Le carte di corte. I Tarocchi. Gioco e magia alla corte degli Estensi*, ed. Giordano Berti and Andrea Vitali, 49–77. Bologna: Nuova Alfa, 1987.

Villoresi, M. *Da Guarino a Boiardo: La cultura teatrale a Ferrara nel Quattrocento*. Rome: Bulzoni, 1994.

Vinaver, Eugène. *The Rise of Romance*. Oxford: Clarendon Press, 1971.

Violante, A. "Il fiume Eridano: mito e storia." In *L'uomo e il fiume*, ed. R. H. Rainero et al., 22–24. Settimo Milanese: Marzorati, 1989.

Vivier, Robert. *Frères du ciel. Quelques aventures poétiques d'Icare et de Phaéton*. Paris: Nizet, 1962.

Wallace-Hadrill, Andrew. *House and Society in Pompeii and Herculaneum*. Princeton: Princeton University Press, 1994.

Walpole, Ronald. *The Old French Johannes Translation of the Pseudo-Turpin Chronicle*. Berkeley: University of California Press, 1976.

Ward, John O. "Some Principles of Rhetorical Historiography in the Twelfth Century." In *Classical Rhetoric and Medieval Historiography*, ed. Ernst Breisach, 104–11.

Warnke, Martin. *The Court Artist: On the Ancestry of the Modern Artist*. Cambridge-New York: Cambridge University Press, 1993.

Weaver, Elissa. "Lettura del intreccio dell'*Orlando furioso*: il caso delle tre pazzie d'amore." *Strumenti critici* 11 (1977): 384–406.

Webb, Ruth. "The Transmission of the *Eikones* of Philostratus and the Development of Ekphrasis from Late Antiquity to the Renaissance." Ph.D. diss., Warburg Institute, University of London, 1992.

Weddle, Saundra L. "Enclosing Le Murate: The Ideology of Enclosure and the Architecture of a Florentine Convent." Ph.D. diss., Cornell University, 1997.

Weinberg, Joanna. "Azariah dei Rossi: Towards a Reappraisal of the Last Years of His Life." *Annali della Scuola Normale di Pisa*, ser. 3. 8 (1978): 493–511.

———. "The *Me'or 'Enayim* of Azariah de' Rossi: A Critical Study and Selected Translations." Ph.D. Diss., University of London, 1982.

———. "Azariah de' Rossi and the Septuagint Traditions." *Italia: Studi e ricerche sulla storia, la cultura, e la letteratura degli ebrei d'Italia* 5 (1985): 7–35.

———. "The Quest for the Historical Philo in Sixteenth-Century Jewish Historiography." In *Jewish History: Essays in Honor of Chimen Abramsky*, ed. Ada Rapaport-Albert and Steven J. Zipperstein, 163–87. London: Peter Halban, 1988.

———. "'The Voice of God': Jewish and Christian Responses to the Ferrara Earthquake of November 1570." *Italian Studies* 46 (1991): 69– 81.

Weisinger, Herbert. "Ideas of History During the Renaissance." In *Renaissance Essays*, ed. Paul Oskar Kristeller and Phillip P. Weiner, 74–94. New York: Harper and Row, 1968.

Weiss, Roberto. *The Renaissance Discovery of Classical Antiquity*. Oxford: B. Blackwell, 1969.

Wethey, H. E. *The Paintings of Titian*. 3 vols. London: Phaidon, 1975.

Whalen, Molly. "The Public Currency of the Private Letter: Gender, Class, and Epistolarity in England, 1568–1671." Ph.D. diss., University of California, Santa Cruz, 1994.

White, Hayden V. "The Value of Narrativity in the Representation of Reality." In *The Content of the Form: Narrative Discourse and Historical Representation*, ed. idem, 1–25. Baltimore: Johns Hopkins University Press, 1987.

Wickham, Chris. *Early Medieval Italy*. 2nd ed. Ann Arbor: University of Michigan press, 1989.

Wickhoff, F. "Venezianische Bilder, I: Die Andrier des Philostrat von Tizian." *Jahrbuch der Königlichen Preussischen Kunstsammlungen* 23 (1902): 118–20.

Wiggins, Peter De Sa. *Figures in Ariosto's Tapestry: Character and Design in the "Orlando furioso"*. Baltimore: Johns Hopkins University Press, 1986.

Wilcox, Donald J. "The Sense of Time in Western Historical Narratives from Eusebius to Machiavelli." In *Classical Rhetoric and Medieval Historiography*, ed. Breisach, 167–237.

Williams, Robert. "The Facade of the *Palazzo dei Visacci*." *I Tatti Studies* 5 (1993): 209–44.

Williamson, E. *Bernardo Tasso*. Rome: Edizioni di Storia e Letteratura, 1951.

Wilson, Frank R. *The Hand: How Its Use Shapes the Brain, Language, and Human Culture*. New York: Vintage, 1998.

Yates, Frances. *Astraea: The Imperial Theme in the Sixteenth Century*. London-Boston: Routledge and Kegan Paul, 1975.

Yerushalmi, Yosef Hayim. *A Jewish Classic in the Portuguese Language*. Lisbo: Fundação Calouste Gulbenkian, 1989.

Zaccarini, Donato. "Il disegno di Ercole Grandi per il monumento di Ercole I d'Este." *L'arte* 20 (1917): 159–67.

Zaffanella, Chiara. "Isabella d'Este e la moda del suo tempo." In *Isabella d'Este. La primadonna del Rinascimento*, ed. Bini, 209–23.

Zamboni, Silla. *Ludovico Mazzolino*. Milan: Silvana, 1968.

———. *Pittori di Ercole I d'Este: Giovan Francesco Maineri, Lazzaro Grimaldi, Domenico Panetti, Michele Coltellini*. Milan: Silvana, 1975.

Zanella, Gabriele. "Cultura, scuola, e storiografia a Ferrara tra XIII e XIV secolo." In *Storia di Ferrara*, Vol. 5: *Il Basso Medioevo, XII–XIV*, ed. Augusto Vasina, 241–74. Ferrara: Corbo, 1987.

Zarri, Gabriella. "Pietà e profezia alle corti padane: le pie consigliere dei principi." In *Il Rinascimento nelle corti padane: società e cultura*, ed. Rossi, 201–37.

———, ed. *Per lettera. La scrittura epistolare femminile tra archivio e tipografia secoli XV–XVII*. Rome: Viella, 1999.

Zatti, Sergio. *L'uniforme cristiano e il multiforme pagano: Saggio sulla* Gerusalemme Liberata. Milan: il Saggiatore, 1983

———. *Il* Furioso *tra epos e romanzo*. Lucca: Pacini Fazzi, 1990.

———. "Il linguaggio della dissimulazione nella *Gerusalemme liberata*." In *Forma e parola: studi in memoria di Fredi Chiappelli*, ed. Dennis Dutschke et al., 423–47. Rome: Bulzoni, 1992.

———. *L'Ombra del Tasso: Epica e romanzo nel Cinquecento*. Milan: Bruno Mondadori, 1996.

Zevi, Bruno. *Biagio Rossetti, architetto ferrarese, il primo urbanista moderno europeo*. Turin: Einaudi, 1960, repr. 1971. Recast with some alterations as *Sapere vedere la città: Ferrara di Biagio Rossetti, "la prima città moderna europea"*. Turin: Einaudi, 1997.

Zimmermann, T. C. Price. *Paolo Giovio: The Historian and the Crisis of Sixteenth-Century Italy*. Princeton: Princeton University Press, 1995.

Zorzi, Ludovico. *Il teatro e la città: Saggi sulla scene italiana*. Turin: Einaudi, 1977.

Zucchini, M. *L'agricultura ferrarese attraverso i secoli*. Rome: Giovanni Volpe Editore, 1967.

Index